Protestation

In all that I shall say in this book I submit to what is taught by Our mother, the Holy Catholic Church; if there is anything in it contrary to this, it will be without my knowledge. Therefore, for the love of Our Lord, I beg the learned men who are to read it to look at it very carefully and to make known to me any faults of this nature which there may be in it and the many others that it will have of other kinds.

If there is anything good in it, let this be to the greater glory and honor of God in the service of His most sacred Mother, our Patroness and Lady, to whom I am, though all unworthy, bound and consecrated as a slave.[1]

Timothy Flanders

---

[1] Adapted from St. Teresa of Avila in *Way of Perfection*.

A 30,000 foot survey of Western Civilization through the lenses of Scripture, Augustine, Aquinas, Newman, Christopher Dawson, Dietrich Von Hildebrand and other Catholic saints and savants. A remarkable historical synthesis of six thousand years in one volume. Deep dogmatic and moral theological insights await discovery on every page.
-Edmund Mazza, Ph.D. Author, *The Scholastics and the Jews*

There are two ways of understanding history – as a random collection of ultimately pointless or at most cyclical dates, events, and players, or as something else. That something else is the working of the Divine Will in history, against a background of countless free and fallen wills – to the eternal benefit of the latter as individuals, if only they will allow it to be so. This is the Catholic view of history, as it must be that of any believer in Christ. Timothy Flanders expertly applies this understanding throughout this rollicking roller coaster ride through history. In this essential *precis*, he deftly weaves secular and religious history together in the light of the Faith, and shows the struggle between Good and Evil from the time of Christ to our own day. Especially good for homeschooler, it deserves a place in ever Catholic home, school, and library.
-Charles A. Coulombe, Author, *Vicars of Christ*, *Puritan's Empire*, *Everyman Today Call Rome*, *Star-Spangled Crown*, *Desire and Deception*, *The Pope's Legion* and *Blessed Charles of Austria: A Holy Emperor and His Legacy*

Not since Saint Augustine's *City of God*, has a book come along that so beautifully and inspiringly marries storytelling with philosophy to narrate the ongoing conflict that takes place within the visible and the invisible realms. Here, in *City of God versus City of Man*, Timothy S. Flanders not only brings us up to date in that metaphysical war but also offers a new framework by which we might more easily digest and engage that struggle through the Catholic understanding of Logos and through the insertion of insightful constructs on culture and society. The compelling manner and methods by which Timothy has arranged this work moves it from what might have been a just a mere work of reference to being a must read for every person of good will. Not only does the book offer many news things to learn, but many things we need to learn for the sake our culture and family.
Heretofore, Timothy S. Flanders has cemented himself as Master of

History and Storytelling within the body of those who came before him, which he exhaustively references.
-David L. Gray,
President and Publisher of Saint Dominic's Media, and author of *Catholic Catechism on Freemasonry*, and *The Divine Symphony: An Exordium on the Theology and History of the Catholic Mass*

City of God v. City of Man by T.S. Flanders is instantly recognizable as a modern classic. Not since Chesterton brought the realms of secular and ecclesiastical history into sharp focus with *The Everlasting Man* has such an intrepid undertaking been ventured. Featuring in depth research and plentiful citations, this work can appeal both to the layman and scholar alike. While Mr. Flanders certainly stands on the shoulders of giants, we all benefit from his courage in climbing the giants' backs in the first place. With joy I highly recommend this monograph to any who have a curiosity for where Christendom is today and how it got there.
-L.S. Predy
Co-Founder of TheByzantineLife.com and The Prayer League of The Holy Innocents and St. Stylianos.
Saskatoon, Saskatchewan

Timothy Flanders passionately offers a clarion call to all Catholics, urging us to stop focusing on the deficiencies of others, but rather, to concentrate on fulfilling our own vocations in life. He also presents a solution to the current crisis in the Catholic Church by going on a new crusade against sin, Satan and the things of this world, and by focusing on a restoration of the family, before entertaining a restoration of the Church.
– Michael Lofton
Founder and Host of Reason & Theology

Timothy Flanders has produced both an original and ambitious spiritual history of culture that will be of great help to the contemporary Catholic reader looking to understand the many roots of our current crisis and discern a navigable way forward. Throughout his thoughtful historical panorama, Flanders elucidates the meaning of historical events, figures and intellectual currents for Christians today, and does not flinch from judiciously and charitably assessing several

important, though contentious, topics. In this thematic account of Salvation History Flanders is alive to the complexity of the historical phenomena he examines, and yet does not neglect the quieter though significant stories of folk culture, art, familial piety, and, above all, men and women of heroic virtue and sanctity that leave the reader with revived hope for a truly Catholic restoration.
-Theo Howard
Columnist for Crisis Magazine, the European Conservative and Culture Wars Magazine
London, England

Upon reading *City of God v. City of Man*, the first phrase that comes to mind is *Magnum Opus*. This book will forever be a great literary accomplishment, and should be required reading. It is profound, systematic and eminently sourced. It challenges both Conservative and Traditional Catholics, and is a good step towards true unity of purpose amongst men of good will. Bravo to Mr. Flanders for such an incredible work.
-Kennedy Hall
Author of *Terror of Demons: Reclaiming Traditional Catholic Masculinity* and *Family Be Damned*

The current unraveling of our society is not about politics or the economy, and it did not start with any former president. If you believe, but still do not understand, here is the 2000-year spiritual combat between fallen angels and pious Catholics. Tolle, lege!
-Sergio Gonzalez
Santiago, Chile

Tim Flanders audaciously proposes an explanation of thousands of years of Western history in about 350 pages. This bold and sincere book employs a frame of reference developed from a study of a wide range of mostly contemporary Catholic writers and thinkers. Tim's work offers support for the proposition that the proper organization of society is crucial for the well-being of people and most importantly for the protection of a rightly ordered family. Too often emphasis is on the nuclear family and nothing more, but this approach only gets half the equation right. The other half of the equation is that the authority in society must fulfill its mission in accordance with either

the Natural Law, or as Catholicism emphasizes, the Divine Positive Law. You cannot protect the family without the right regime. That is because as I have said repeatedly, the higher controls the lower and the public informs the private.
-David Wemhoff
Author of *John Courtney Murray, Time/Life, and the American Proposition*

In this book, Timothy Flanders shows Christian history from a unique angle. He presents certain concepts that are bound to change the way we look at the history of our Church. Some of the conclusions he reaches are shocking
-Allan Ruhl
Catholic writer at allanruhl.com

Timothy Flanders' admirable book is a very well-informed and skillfully composed account addressing many important issues of Catholic belief. The presentation of this spiritual history is concise and informative and will be of significant benefit to both Catholic and non-Catholic alike.
-Felix Soden
Dublin, Ireland

Whether you are a cradle Catholic or new to the faith, or even if you are only curious about Catholicism—this well-sourced book is for you. From historical analyses to reasons to love the Faith, from facts that separate Truth from fiction to practical ideas you can integrate into your own life—you will learn that there is only One Faith and Christ is still King for all and forever, amen. Viva Christo Rey!
-Mark van Dijk
Groningen, The Netherlands

City of God v. City of Man is an essential read for any Catholic who is serious about taking up the duties implied in Confirmation.
-Francis Noel
Sohar, Oman.

Timothy's book is an eye-opening read on the cultural and socio-political factors influencing the rise and fall of Christendom. His

expose is a must-read for understanding the context of the current troubles in Catholicism in particular and Christianity generally.
-Colin Gordon
Houston, Texas

Timothy Flanders provides a lucid and insightful analyses of the major historical developments affecting the Catholic Church and the world over the past 2,000 years. For anyone looking for a well-researched, well-thought-out and concise rundown of the last 2,000 years from an orthodox Catholic perspective, this book is a must read!
-Terence Sequeira
Leicester, England

Flanders summarizes his *extensive* reading on the history of the Church to make it accessible to the rest of us. He provides a clear picture of the state of the Church and how we arrived here. This comprehensive work is a great addition to any library.
-Kevin Codd
Garner, North Carolina

This book fulfills its mission completely! Timothy Flanders provides the fairest view of the journey of catholic culture throughout history because he takes into account the most essential aspect of man's time here on earth: the spiritual battle. Instead of shying away from the more complex and often embarrassing moments of our history, he hits them head-on in order to open our eyes to the battle that rages on around humanity for our eternal souls. Our history is tumultuous and exciting, knowing it ties us more closely to the universal Church as we take up the battle for which our ancestors gave their lives and which we continue to fight for those who will come after us. Well sourced and thoroughly referenced, Timothy also gives us plenty of other areas to expand into should we wish to deepen our research and discover other authors.
-Liz
Lourdes, Hautes-Pyrénées, France

City of God vs. City of Man

Timothy S. Flanders

City of God
vs.
City of Man

The Battles of the Church from Antiquity to the Present

Timothy S. Flanders

© Our Lady of Victory Press, MMXXI

ISBN 978-0-578-31734-2

Our Lady of Victory Press is an imprint of The Meaning of Catholic, a lay apostolate dedicated to uniting Catholics against the enemies of Holy Church.

MeaningofCatholic.com

Design and layout by W. Flanders.

Cover art by Giorgio Vasari, The Battle of Lepanto 1572-73.

Our Lady of Victory, pray for us!

Please do not copy this book without permission, unless it be to save a soul in need of conversion.

All Scriptural citations from The Douay-Rheims Challoner translation (http://catholicbible.online) unless noted.

All Patristic citations from *Nicene and Post-Nicene Fathers*, Edited by Philip Schaff and Henry Wace (Buffalo, NY: Christian Literature Publishing Co., 1896) unless noted.

All citations from the Summa from https://www.newadvent.org/summa.

Dedication

*This book is dedicated to my parents
who raised me and taught me to call upon the Holy Name of Jesus.*

In gratias Septimis Papis ago—Piis, Johannibus, et Paulis—et omnibus sanctiis, patribus nostris, ex quibus precibus opus hoc factum est.

*For the triumph of Nuestra Señora de Guadalupe y Fatima—
"Mary of Ephesus"
—over the Artemis Ephesia in our time.*

Acknowledgements

I would like to thank the following individuals for their acuity and depth on the specific areas of their expertise without which this project would have not been possible: my wife and children, Kennedy Hall, Charles Coulombe, Theo Howard, Luis Medina, Erick Ybarra, Sergio Gonzalez, Michael Botiggi, Linden Predy and Mallory and the staff at Roots Brew Shop.

TABLE OF CONTENTS

Introduction 14

PART I
The Formation of Christendom 0-301

    1. Empire of Death 27

    2. Empire of Freedom 37

    3. The Kingdom of God 50

    4. The Conspiracy of Antichrist 65

    5. The Conquering Lion of Judah 71

    6. Mosaic Culture and the Rise of Christendom 76

    7. The Mustard Seed against Professional Armies 81

    8. Red Martyrs against Mob Bloodshed 90

    9. King of Kings 113

PART II
The Reign of Christendom 301-1773

    10. Nicaea and the Green Martyrs 125

    11. The Throne of Christ
    and the Crusade of the Holy Empress 134

    12. The Failed Crusade of the Earthly Empire (410-632) 141

    13. Abandon and Reason and Submit (632-964) 162

    14. Santiago and the Crusading Spirit (964-1274) 180

    15. The Wrath of God
    and the Second Pornocracy (1274-1517) 194

    16. Lust for Power and Certain Death (1517-1600) 208

    17. The Insidious Poison of Muhammad (1600-1773) 231

PART III
Mob Bloodshed or Modernity?
The Breaking of Christendom 1773-1965

    18. Anti-Culture Imposed on the Children 267

    19. The Pope Folds under Political Pressure 275

    20. The First American Civil War 284

    21. Break Every Vow, Every Oath, Every Bond 302

    22. Empires of Anti-Culture 310

    23. The Cross Conquers the Conquerer 320

    24. Pio Nono and the Ninth Crusade 329

    25. The False Spirit of Vatican I 346

    26. Pope St. Pius X the Great 359

    27. The Suicide of Europe 369

    28. The First Sexual Revolution 377

    29. A Mass Murderer and His Allies
    Against a Mass Murderer and His Axis 396

    30. The False Crusade of Earthly Empires 408

    31. The Medicine of Mercy for the Antichrist 419

PART IV
The Triumph of New Iconoclasm 1965-Present

    32. The Attempt to Suppress the Cultus 433

    33. Pope St. John Paul II the Great 452

    34. The Hermeneutic of Benedict XVI 467

    Epilogue: Uniting Against the Enemies of Holy Church 472

Glossary 482

Bibliography 487

Index 503

PREFACE

In the past few generations thousands of Catholics in Euro-America have lost their faith. Some have left the Church because they wanted to conform to the spirit of the world. Others, however, have painfully lost hope in the Holy Spirit to guide the Catholic Church, and have entered into schism as Eastern Orthodox, or heresy in one of the Protestant sects—all to their own eternal peril. The deep wounds of these souls from spiritual fatherlessness or other abuse have forced them into a place of hopelessness. The Church has entered another period of crisis.

Meanwhile, since grace enters the world through the Catholic Church, the peoples and societies of Euro-America have spiraled out of control into the darkness of intrinsic evils, broken families and demonic oppression.

There are various spiritual, cultural, and socio-economic factors for this situation. One of these which encompasses many issues is that Catholics have lost their history, and thus their identity. This is one of the issues that makes Catholics lose hope.

In place of their history, Catholics are fed an ideology made of half-truths which tempts Catholics to abandon their faith in the dogmas of the Catholic Church. This is perhaps no more true than with Eastern Orthodoxy, which utilizes old animosities to present a tempting veneer convincing many Catholics that the Orthodox churches are in fact the One True Church. But this is also true of new animosities, where Catholics have presently divided into party camps based on ignoring the complexities of modernity in favor of historical oversimplifications.

This work is intended to help in some way with this particular problem. It is an attempt to synthesize the two greatest historians into a one-volume, introductory history for the laity. To this end, it places before the reader the framework developed by the first historian: the cosmic war between the City of God and the city of man. This conflict

PREFACE

is the story of all history, as angels and men struggle on both sides to build, defend, and expand their cities. It is the great struggle between Logos and voluntarism.

And as the second historian has developed, it is the struggle between Christian culture and the numerous anti-Christian cultures which have been formed against the Church, united by the voluntarist principle of negation. As the enemies of Christ arise throughout history, the crusading spirit unites all the saints (our fathers) who laid down their lives as men of God and fought by the power of the cross.

It is hoped that when *cultus* and culture are understood as the soul of a people, we can more easily address the way society is shaped by spiritual and other forces. The unity of the Church plays a critical role, as the traditional alliance between moderate and strict parties produces the syntheses for renewal. All of these things contextualize the present crisis that the Church faces.

Since the beginning, God has worked in the saints to draw all souls to Himself, while reigning as King over time and history. *For the kingdom is the Lord's; and he shall have dominion over the nations* (Ps. xxi. 29). Through the merits and prayers of Our Lady of Victory and St. Joseph, Terror of Demons, may the King of Kings raise up new saints to triumph once again for the City of God.

Jesus is King!

T. S. F.

Feast of Our Lady of Victory
Anno Domini, MMXXI

INTRODUCTION

St. Augustine's greatest work, *City of God against the Pagans*, is a spiritual history of God's providential workings in time. In it he defines the City of God as the community of all the saints in God, beginning with the angels, the Old Testament remnant, and finally the Church of Christ, founded by the King of Kings. The City of God is built first in the hearts of men, and then as those men build altars to the Name of God within society, all of creation comes under the dominion of God. The vision of the City of God is consummated in the final chapters of Revelation, when the City is finalized by God Himself.

In the present work we will attempt to expand St. Augustine's work by means of one of his greatest disciples in the field of history, Christopher Dawson. In Dawson we find a penetrating analysis of culture, so that the true forces of history are discovered. Too often today historical writing is degraded by removing from consideration the spiritual forces affecting history and the religious impulse of man, reducing history to the tiny minority of kings and armies in battle and such material considerations. As a result, the materialism and atheism of today are reinforced by a history which is also materialistic. As an antidote to this type of history, one finds in Dawson's writings not only an impeccable historian even on material grounds, but a mind sensitive to the Providence of God in history, along the lines of Augustine's great history.

In our attempt to synthesize Augustine with Dawson in a spiritual history of culture, we will define a people as a body and soul. The body is the *society* of a people, which seeks the natural goods of this world. This society may be reduced to king (politics), coin (economy) and kitchen (the family). As Dawson notes again and again however, it is the culture which drives the impulse of a people. Therefore the *culture* is the soul of a people. We may summarize culture in four elements,

INTRODUCTION

following Dawson: the *cultus* (religious rite), tradition (that which is passed down), elders (the guardians of tradition) and piety (reverence for elders). These terms will be discussed and explained further in our text.

In Dawson's work we observe that this framework is the manner by which God builds the City of God by means of angels and men. This reveals the logos of the peoples and the generational transmission over time. The City of God is built to conform and worship the Logos of God, harmonizing with the logos He created.

In the Church as we will see, the transmission of Christian culture baptizes a society in order to make a Christian people. This is Christendom. We can further observe in the history of the Church that two parties form among the elders to create a new synthesis throughout history to convert souls and society. One party are the moderates, who seek to augment the tradition for the sake of His reign. The other party are the strict, who seek to maintain the tradition unchanged for the sake of His reign. In Church history we see these two parties sometimes in conflict, sometimes in harmony, and out of this holy rivalry comes the four great Greco-Roman renewals.

These renewals respond to the work of the city of man, which seeks not logos, but to impose its own will and maintain the status quo. It is made up of the various enemies of Christ who unite only to resist the transformation of all things in Christ. As Rao calls them, they are the "Grand Coalition of the Status Quo." We see that in the four periods we describe, in every case the City of God has triumphed, except in our own fourth epoch which is still ongoing. For the synthesis of moderate and strict has been broken in our own day, which has led to the dominance of the city of man. Yet all that is needed is the same renewal against the same enemy. This book attempts to interpret the present crisis within this framework, following Augustine and Dawson.

A Note on Terminology

Historical terms like "Middle Ages" and "Enlightenment," and others like "abortion," are words which obscure the reality of the things they represent, sometimes by design. Other words simply are inaccurate and anachronistic, like "Byzantine." This book proposes that Catholics should abandon words such as these and choose other terms which represent truth. To this end, this text has employed different terms, restored old terms and, where necessary, utilized new terminology. A glossary is provided at the end of the text for the assistance of the reader.

Using this Book as a Textbook

A secondary purpose of this book is its use as a textbook for Catholic high school students. This would serve for the subjects of Church history, cultural/world history, American history, economics, government, social studies, and theology. It can also serve the purpose of forming young boys into men of God by teaching them the history of the crusading spirit. It functions as a historical companion to Kennedy Hall's *Terror of Demons: Reclaiming Traditional Catholic Masculinity* (TAN, 2021).

This book intends to provide a foundation for the younger generation of Catholics to begin the work of restoring the Church.

However, it should be noted that some content in this book is not suitable for children under the age of sixteen, depending on their level of maturity. If there is any doubt about this, we recommend parents read the whole book before using it with your children, but in particular chapters 1, 2, 8, 12, 13, 14, 15, 16, 17, 20, 22, 28, 30, 31, 32, 33, 34.

INTRODUCTION

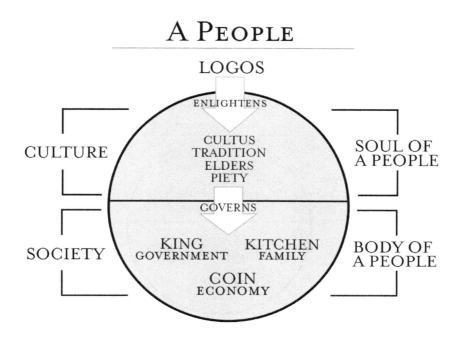

For downloadable color graphics, go to
www.meaningofcatholic.com/CityofGod

CITY OF GOD

LOGOS INCARNATE

ANGELS — REVEALS — SAINTS

CULTUS - TRADITION
ELDERS
MODERATE - STRICT
PIETY

BAPTIZES

KING
GOVERNMENT

KITCHEN
FAMILY

COIN
ECONOMY

CHRISTENDOM

TRANSFORMATION OF ALL THINGS IN CHRIST

INTRODUCTION

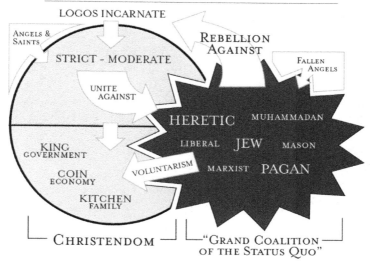

HOLY SPIRIT INCARNATES LOGOS	SPIRIT OF ANTICHRIST PROVOKES THE MOB
CONTEST OF HUMILITY	CONTEST OF POWER
LIBERATION OF LOGOS	IMPOSITION OF WILL (VOLUNTARISM)
UNITY OF TRUTH	UNITY OF NEGATION (ANYTHING BUT CHRIST)
BEAUTY OF LOGOS	UGLINESS OF CHAOS
APPEAL TO LOGOS (REASON)	MOB BLOODSHED
A PEOPLE	THE MASSES

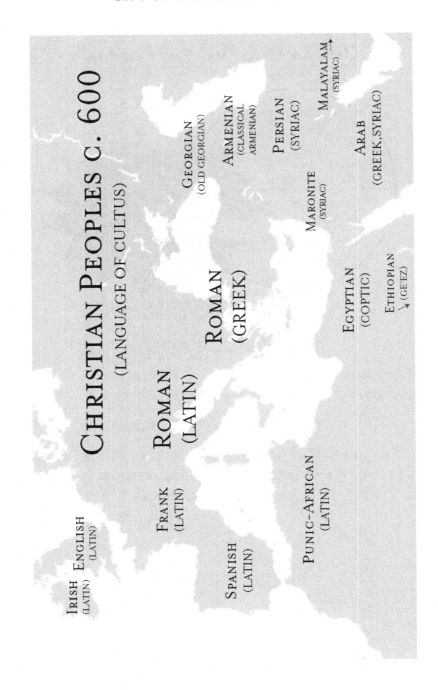

INTRODUCTION

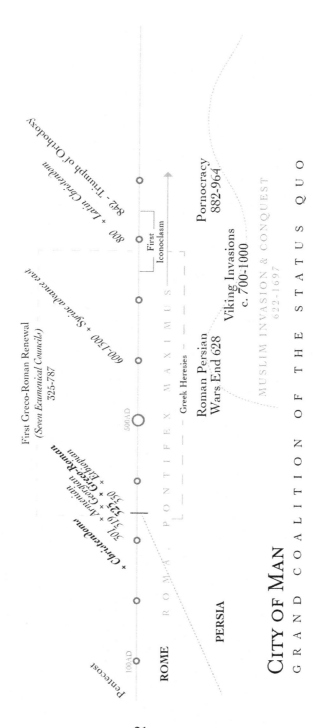

CITY OF GOD VS. CITY OF MAN

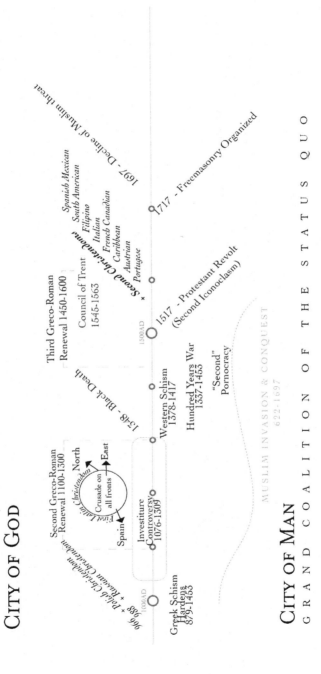

CITY OF GOD

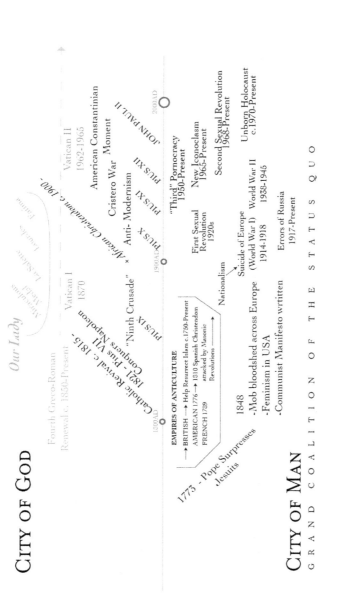

Our Lady

Fourth Greco-Roman Renewal c. 1850-Present

Miraculous Medal · La Sâlette · Lourdes · Fatima

Catholic Revival c. 1815-
1821 - Pius VII Conquers Napoleon

Vatican I 1870

"Ninth Crusade" · African Christendom c. 1900

Pius IX

Anti-Modernism

Pius X

Cristero War

Pius XI

"Third" Pornocracy 1950-Present

Vatican II 1962-1965

American Constantinian Moment

Pius XII

New Iconoclasm 1965-Present

JOHN PAUL II

Second Sexual Revolution 1968-Present

Unborn Holocaust c.1970-Present

1200AD — 1900AD — 2000AD

1773 - Pope Surpresses Jesuits

EMPIRES OF ANTICULTURE
BRITISH → Help Resurrect Islam c.1750-Present
AMERICAN 1776 → 1810 Spanish Christendom
FRENCH 1789 ← attacked by Masonic Revolutions

Nationalism

1848
- Mob bloodshed across Europe
- Feminism in USA
- Communist Manifesto wrtitten

First Sexual Revolution 1920s

Suicide of Europe (World War I) 1914-1918

World War II 1938-1945

Errors of Russia 1917-Present

CITY OF MAN
GRAND COALITION OF THE STATUS QUO

PART I

THE FORMATION OF CHRISTENDOM

AD 0-301

I

EMPIRE OF DEATH

In the year 27 BC, in the coastal city of Ariminum, Italy, the slaves heaved the last of the stone into place. After years of labor, the triumph arch was finally finished. It stood some sixty feet high into the air. It had a "strong religious character" that made it "sacred" as the gate to the city.[2] Crowds would henceforth pass under it and find a spiritual marvel.

Two columns reached up toward transcendence, holding the pediment that spread over the wide symmetry of the archway like Providence smiling down on the people with peace and security. Shepherds drove their herds through the wide, door-less gateway confidently proclaiming that no evil would penetrate the serenity of the city.[3] This monument, which was dedicated to the Emperor Augustus by the Roman Senate, was a symbol of

---

[1] Wikipedia Commons.
[2] *L'intera struttura è permeata da un forte carattere religioso che sottolinea l'aspetto sacrale di porta della città*. "Arco d'Augusto" *Commune di Rimini* <https://web.archive.org/web/20131225013955/http://www.comune.rimini.it/servizi/citta/monumenti/pagina12.html>. Accessed January 10, 2021.
[3] Ibid.

peace because of the phrase inscribed in the stone: the "son of god." It symbolized him, and he symbolized peace.

The Roman Senate proclaimed, "Providence has sent him as a savior."[4] His "epiphany" was "the beginning of his gospel for the world."[5] "I restored peace," he said, and "to me were sent supplications by kings...And in my principate many other peoples experienced the faith."[6] Looking up at the arch, his voice seemed to echo from the monument. It was a symbol of this "savior" whose "advent" brought logos to a world consumed in chaos.

What is logos? It is the rational order of the universe. The Greek word λόγος means order, word, reason, peace, logic, and collection and is related to binding, rest, and law. Logos has synonyms in the Sanskrit ऋत [*Ṛta*] and the Chinese 道 [*Tao*] all understood, Lewis notes, as "that great ritual or pattern of nature and supernature which is revealed alike in the cosmic order, the moral virtues, and the ceremonial of the temple."[7] Thus logos is also "known" as truth, "done" as moral goodness, and "created" as beauty. All of this was seen in the arch.

The logos was present in the beauty of the arch, which proclaimed that the "savior" had brought this logos, and the "ceremonial" made it manifest. This ceremony is the *cultus*. Every people has a *cultus*, a religious rite, which forms its soul.[8]

The people of Ariminum knew they were privileged to have not just any arch, but a triumphal arch used in the central *cultus* of the "savior": "the triumph."[9] This rite was "an elaborate ritual" which formed for this people one of the "most important institutions, a ritual at once religious and political, military and spectacular."[10] It was a symbolic enactment of the

---

[4] H S Versnel, *Triumphus: An Inquiry into the Origin, Development and Meaning of the Roman Triumph* (Leiden, 1970), 385.
[5] Craig A. Evans, "Mark's Incipit and the Priene Calendar Inscription: From Jewish Gospel to Greco-Roman Gospel" *Journal of Greco-Roman Christianity and Judaism*. 1: 67–81 (2000).
[6] Caesar Augustus, *Res Gestae,* trans. Thomas Bushnell (1998) <http://classics.mit.edu/Augustus/deeds.html>. Accessed January 10, 2021.
[7] C. S. Lewis, *The Abolition of Man* (MacMillan: 1947), 27, cf. 95-121. Bradley J. Birzer, *Sanctifying the World: The Augustinian Life and Mind of Christopher Dawson* (The University of Virginia: Christendom Press, 2007), 76-77.
[8] Christopher Dawson, *Religion and Culture* (New York: Meridian Books, 1960), 25-46, 47-64; T. S. Eliot, "Notes Towards the Definition of Culture," *Christianity and Culture* (New York: Harvest, 1976), 87.
[9] Dietrich von Hildebrand, *Aesthetics, vol. II* (The Hildebrand Project: 2018), 85.
[10] Popkin, *The Architecture of the Roman Triumph* (Cambridge: 2016), 2.

"savior" bringing logos to the world. "I triumphed twice with an ovation...three times I triumphed with a chariot."[11] He was the *pontifex maximus*, the high priest, celebrating the rite.

A long procession came through the arch: the "savior" rode high on a chariot with magnificent music and great pomp, torches, wreaths, epic paintings of battle scenes, decorative clothing, and fragrant incense spreading all over the crowds.[12] The prisoners—the representatives of evil and chaos—were led in front and then ceremonially executed as the act of triumph.[13] "In my triumphs nine kings or children of kings were led before my chariot."[14] The banquet was served and then the games began.

Every people has a body and soul, and the soul is *culture* that flows from *cultus*.[15] The triumph was the *cultus* that formed the soul of the Greco-Roman people. The arch of Caesar Augustus at Ariminum—which served both as the sacred site of the triumph *cultus* and its monumental commemoration—was a message for generations: Caesar is "lord," "savior," and "son of god." Logos comes by him as the high priest and emperor. This arch was raised four years after he had crushed the rival claimants to the title "son of god" with the help of "Apollo" at the Battle of Actium in 31 BC.[16] The arch was one of many others already still to come, carving scenes from the once-in-a-lifetime triumph rite for everyone who was not fortunate enough to see the event.

By this *cultus* Caesar and his supporters sought to form a unified culture and thus a people. The *cultus* and the arch made it possible for Caesar's military victories to be "transformed into political power."[17] From this rite of triumph and its monumental arch Caesar preached his "gospel," with his central slogan: "son of god." He minted his coins with the words *divi filius* (son of god) and an image of his face, and commanded his

---

[11] Augustus, *Res Gestae*, trans. D. Brendan Nagle, *The Roman World: Sources and Interpretation* (Pearson Education: 2005), 142.
[12] Versnel, 117.
[13] Scott Hahn and Curtis Mitch, eds. *The Ignatius Catholic Study Bible: New Testament* (Ignatius: 2010), 315.
[14] Augustus, *Res Gestae*, loc. cit.
[15] Christopher Dawson, *The Historic Reality of Christian Culture* (Routledge and Kegan Paul, 1960), 33-36.
[16] Mary Bowley, *Universal History on Scriptural Principles* (Samuel Bagster and Sons: 1850), 391.
[17] Tonio Hölscher, "The Transformation of Victory into Power: From Event to Structure," Ed. Dillon and Welch, *Representation of War in Ancient Rome* (Cambridge University Press: 2006), 27.

subjects to worship him, spreading his *cultus* everywhere.[18] Everyone had to pour libation to him like the rest of the gods and pay *cultus* to his spirit.[19] "The divinity of eternal Caesar presides over the eternal fire" wrote Ovid of Caesar's priesthood, and "the sacred rites" are performed by him "who is himself a god."[20] "No object escaped the emperor's stamp: utensils, textiles, ceilings, roof tiles, ash urns, jewelry, furniture, walls, clay facings, tombs."[21]

This was the "gospel" of the Roman peace. People were flocking to Rome because they believed in this "gospel" and the material wealth it afforded. Citizenship was a coveted privilege.[22]

The Logos of Greco-Roman Culture

But while the slaves were raising the arch to Augustus, Caesar found his best propaganda poet to memorialize his "victory of order over disorder...civilization over barbarism."[23] This was Virgil, who, says Eliot, "led Europe towards the Christian culture which he could never know."[24] Virgil summarized in *The Aeneid* how the Greeks were the ones who "hammer out bronze" and "draw living faces out of stone," with philosophy and science, but it is the Roman mind which is to "rule the world" and "establish peace."[25] Rome had succeeded where the Greeks had failed.[26]

Alexander the Great (d. 323 BC), who believed he was the son of the Greek god Zeus, had conquered the Persian Empire and spread the logos of Greek culture eastward.[27] He had taken for himself the coveted title

---

[18] The Latin is literally "son of the divine [Julius Caesar]." Nagle, 188; Valerie M. Warrior, ed., *Roman Religion: A Sourcebook* (Newburyport, MA: Focus Publishing, 2002), 136; Garth Jowett, Victoria O'Donnell, *Propaganda and Persuasion*, 4th ed., (Thousand Oaks, CA: Sage Publications, 2006), 55.
[19] Warrior, 118.
[20] Warrior, 135, 136.
[21] Floyd Schneider, *Mark Challenges the Aeneid* (Wipf & Stock Publishers, 2019), 36.
[22] Acts 22:28.
[23] James E. G. Zetzel, "Rome and its Traditions," Martindale et al., eds. *The Cambridge Companion to Virgil* (Cambridge University Press: 1997), 199.
[24] T. S. Eliot, *What is Classic?* (London: Faber & Faber, 1944), 32.
[25] Virgil, *Aeneid*, bk. VI, 1010-1015, trans. Stanley Lombardo (Indianapolis: Hackett, 2005), 159.
[26] Christopher Dawson, *The Formation of Christendom* (San Francisco: Ignatius Press, 2008), 111-125.
[27] Ian Worthington, *Alexander the Great* (Taylor & Francis: 2014), 113.

"king of kings" which the Persian emperor used.[28] This was the only rival the Greeks had for advanced civilization, and a certain bias against Persia still obtains in scholarship today, passed down from Roman times.[29]

The greatness of Greek culture was in its passion for truth, goodness and beauty, particularly in the *dialogos*—that act of humility whereby two or more parties penetrate and subordinate themselves to the truth—shown in the Greek literature as "love of wisdom" (*philosophia*).[30] The greatness of the Persian culture was its great acts of beauty and its scientific prowess and administrative ability, some of which the Romans adopted.[31] But Alexander had not been able to affect a melding of the Persian and Greek cultures, especially because Greeks could not unite amongst themselves, and it was their victims the Persians who had that talent of unity.

However, the effort to give order to the greatness of Greek culture fell to the Latin mind, as summarized by Virgil. After the Roman Empire took over Greece and the Hellenized realms of Alexander, a mutual help was effected between the two powers.[32] Instead of vying for dominance, the Latin mind accepted the superiority of Greek truth, goodness and beauty in its love of wisdom, art, architecture and literature. The Greek mind, in turn, accepted the superiority of Latin administration and order by transforming the chaos of Greek rivalries into the logos of a unified system. This hierarchy would form the body that the soul of Christian culture would vivify as Eliot observed.

Thus the logos in Greek language, art, architecture, literature, and especially the love of wisdom was universalized with the logos of Roman law and order. Latin was the language of law and administration. Greek

---

[28] For the sake of brevity, we will not distinguish in this work between the various dynasties of the Persian empire into Achaemenid, Parthian or Sasanian. All alike shared a common Persian culture since Cyrus and Darius, and all alike were feared by the Greco-Roman tradition.

[29] Zeev Rubin, "Persia and Sasanian Monarchy 224-651," *The Cambridge History of the Byzantine Empire C.500-1492* (India: Cambridge University Press, 2019), 130

[30] Humility means *conformity with the truth* (*Summa*, II-II q161) The Socratic Dialogues of Plato, particularly the *Republic* are undoubtedly the timeless example of this.

[31] Josef Wiesehöfer, "The Achaeminid Empire," *The Dynamics of Ancient Empires*, Morris and Scheidel, eds. (Oxford University Press, 2009), 90

[32] The term "hellenized" comes from *Hellas* (Greek for "Greece") and refers to peoples who learned the Greek language and Greek culture. On Latin and Greek mutual help, see Mikhail Emmanuelovich Posnov, *The History of the Christian Church Until the Great Schism of 1054*, trans. Thomas E. Herman (Bloomington, IN: Authorhouse, 2004), 210-211.

was the language for everything else. Greek culture was ruled by the logos of Latin, and the logos of Latin received its high culture from Greek. By the Second century AD, this mutual enrichment of culture was making the educated fluent in Greek and Latin and the term *Roman* meant both.[33] This cultural union will be fundamental to our tale.

All of this was seen in the arch and the triumph. The structure was held up by Greek columns (signifying the foundation of Roman culture in Greece), it had carved "living faces out of stone" and finally a hammered bronze statue of Augustus on top (now lost).[34] The rite of triumph then became the visual summation of Virgil's lines: by subduing the chaos of the evil Persians and rude barbarians, Greco-Roman civilization was the dawn of the new age of peace. And we can say without controversy that this civilization was indeed the greatest that man had ever built with his natural capacity for logos. This is why God chose it.

Voluntarism and Death

But there was a darkness hidden just below the surface. For the word for "rite of triumph" also meant "hymn to Dionysius," the Greek god whose rites included orgies, drunkenness, murder and debauchery.[35] This god was believed to be the first to perform the rite of triumph.[36] His was a *lust for power* both sexually and militarily.[37] He was also known as *Father Liber*— Father of Freedom.[38] But what kind of freedom was this?

The Dionysian spirit of fornication was itself a *rite of triumph*, says Ovid, which "whipped into line" its enemies—"conscience" and "modesty"—until a soul surrendered to "the raging beast, passion, out at

---

[33] Peter N. Stearns, ed., *The Encyclopedia of World History*, 6th ed. (Boston: Houghton Mifflin Co., 2001), 88.
[34] "Arco d'Augusto" *Commune di Rimini*.
[35] This etymology connecting *triumphus* and *thriambos* either "launched, legitimated, or followed" Dionysius' first triumph in his victory over the Indians which Alexander first copied. Mary Beard, *The Roman Triumph* (Belknap of Hardard: 2007), 315-318.
[36] Pliny the Elder, *The Natural History* 7.57, trans. John Bostock (London: George Bell, 1893)
[37] It was believed that Alexander the Great also did the rite of triumph in imitation to the original rite performed by Dionysius himself. A. B. Bosworth, *From Arrian to Alexander: NoteStudies in Historical Interpretation* (Clarendon Press: 1988), 67; Pliny the Elder, *The Natural History* 7.57.
[38] Literally "Free Father."

prowl in my breast."[39] The lust for power militarily, economically and carnally was all one spirit of the Dionysian demon. The body of the Greco-Roman people was indeed peace and order, but the soul was affected by this hidden, evil spirit.

And it was this lust for power, buried under a mountain of propaganda about peace, that animated the political entity that acted as an "empire." The Persian empire was enslaved to the same lust. The Persian emperor wanted to capture the title of "Caesar" and "son of god" while the Romans wanted the title "king of kings." As a result intermittent war between the two powers continued from Alexander (323 BC) to the Muhammadan invasions (632 AD). Just decades before Augustus erected his arch, the Romans had suffered a terrible loss at Carrhae that traumatized the Romans for centuries.[40]

Near the shifting borders between the two empires, an obscure Hebrew text, the Book of Daniel, spoke of four empires as four beasts: the Babylonians, the Medo-Persians, the Greeks and finally the last beast, Rome. All of these were in a contest of power with each other. The Persian "king of kings" had conquered Babylon, then Alexander the Great had conquered and become the "son of Zeus" and "king of kings." Finally Rome had conquered and become *a fourth beast, terrible and wonderful, and exceeding strong... treading down the rest with its feet* (Dan. vii. 7).

Burning with lust for power, Caesar had invaded and conquered from England to Spain to Egypt to Syria. He showed his empire yet more powerful and terrible than all the rest. Central to this military power was something unique—a professional standing army—only empires had such a force. Most kingdoms had no such thing, and were thus conquered (save Persia with their own standing army). One conquered king lamented that there was no escape "from the yet more terrible Romans," who "lust for dominion... To robbery, slaughter, plunder, they give the lying name of empire; they create a desolation and call it peace."[41]

Greco-Roman culture possessed logos, yet it expanded its borders by means of its bloodshed "always rolling, with dark fear and cruel lust," says St. Augustine, "in warlike slaughters and in blood."[42] For empires

---

[39] Ovid, *Erotic Poems* 1.2.19-52, trans. P. Green (Penguin Classics, 1982). In this poem Ovid equates the passion of carnal lust personified in Cupid with Dionysius' and Augustus' rite of triumph.

[40] Zeev *op. cit.*, 130.

[41] Tacitus, *Vita Agricolae*, in Charles W. Colby, ed., *Selections from the Sources of English History* (New York: Longmans, 1913), 7.

[42] St. Augustine, *City of God Against the Pagans*, bk. IV, ch. 3 in trans. Marcus Dods, *Nicene and Post-Nicene Fathers, First Series*, vol. II, Philip Schaff, ed. (Buffalo, NY: Christian Literature Publishing Co., 1887).

are merely "great robberies."[43] As the Christian Roman Emperor Manuel II Paleologus would write centuries later, "God is not pleased with blood, and not acting with logos is contrary to God's nature."[44]

This force of will and bloodshed is the antithesis of logos: voluntarism. It is "pure power, stripped of meaning." It is the idea that justice is not a matter of restoring the order of logos but merely the powerful exerting their will over the weak. It is "might makes right," and it is always the nature of empires, from the first beast to the fourth and beyond. Greek imperialists had articulated this when they said "justice...is only in question between equals in power, while the strong do what they can and the weak suffer what they must."[45]

Voluntarism is an ideology, and as Solzhenitsyn says, ideology is "what gives evildoing its long-sought justification and gives the evildoer the necessary steadfastness and determination."[46] Logos is order, and voluntarism is disorder. Logos is the order of the intellect knowing the truth, and the will following that truth to act with goodness. This then is what chiefly creates beauty.

Voluntarism means imposing one's will, regardless of right or wrong. Voluntarism is where the ends justify the means. As Jones puts it, "There are ultimately only two alternatives in the intellectual life: either one conforms desire to the truth or truth to desire."[47] Doing the latter ultimately ends in the ugliness of sin, but also the audible and visible as we will see.[48] Voluntarism is what happens when your emotions dictate truth and goodness.

The *cultus*, the very center of the Greco-Roman culture, despite the greatness of logos within its philosophy, literature, and the rest, was merely a celebration of voluntarism. Internally the Roman Empire had great order, but it conquered nations by means of the disorder of voluntarism: the strong over the weak. This was the means by which the empire of death extended and maintained its reign. This was the secret behind the rite of triumph and Dionysius. "The lust of rule," says St. Augustine, "existed among the Romans in more unmitigated intensity than among any other people," and

---

[43] Ibid., bk. IV, ch. 4.
[44] T. Khoury, "Manuel II Paléologue, Entretiens avec un Musulman. 7ᵉ Controverse", *Sources Chrétiennes* n. 115, Paris 1966), Controversy VII, 3 b–c: 144-145. Cited by Benedict XVI, "Regensburg Lecture" (Sept. 12, 2006).
[45] Thucydides, *Histories*, vol. II, bk. V.
[46] Aleksandr I. Solzhenitsyn, *The Gulag Archipelago*, trans. Thomas P. Whitney and Harry Willets., abbrev. ed., (New York: Harper Perennial, 1985), 77.
[47] E. Michael Jones, *Degenerate Moderns: Modernity as the Rationalization of Sexual Misbehavior* (Fidelity: 2012), 11.
[48] Cf. Von Hildebrand, *Aesthetics*, vol. I, 261-262.

"after it had taken possession of the more powerful few, subdued under its yoke the rest, worn and wearied."[49] The lust for rule actually enslaved those who possessed it, who then enslaved others.

The True Emperor of Death

Because they were enslaved by the lust for power, the Persian "king of kings" and the Roman "son of god" were merely slaves to a much more insidious master, which had infiltrated their own *cultus*. According to Augustine, it was "the seductions of evil-minded devils" who sought to "induce them to lead an abandoned life" by means of evil rites "reckoned devout in proportion to their lewdness"[50] The true emperor was Satan and his fallen angels. They enslaved Rome and Persia to voluntarist bloodlust, and then commanded all men to worship their own slavery to the same, installing themselves as "gods" to be worshipped. It was the "justification of an earthly order" of "divinized princes," says Rao, which required "willful divinity."[51] And thus the beauty of logos in their art, architecture, and coinage displayed "marked ambition to establish a line of communication" in order to "propagate a message"—the ideology of voluntarism, slavery to devils.[52]

This is why the carved "living faces out of stone" on the arch of Ariminum were four demons: Jupiter (the adulterous ruler of the gods), Apollo (also debauched, whom Augustus took for his father and patron), Neptune (against whom Augustus had triumphed), and finally the demonic personification of the empire: *Roma*.[53] This divinization of the earthly city was an assertion that it would last forever and never be destroyed. *Roma* was a cult and an ideology to justify the voluntarist empire of death.

But unlike the triumphal arches to Augustus elsewhere in Rome, Aosta, or Susa the arch at Ariminum did not have an inscription about

---

[49] Augustine, *op. cit.*, bk. I, ch. 30.
[50] Ibid., bk. I, ch. 33; bk II, ch 2, 27.
[51] John Rao, *Black Legends and the Light of the World: The War of Words with the Incarnate Word* (Forest Lake, MN: Remnant Press, 2011), 52.
[52] Anne-Marie Leander Touati, *The Great Trajanic Frieze* (Stockholm: 1987), 9.
[53] Neptune was claimed as father by Augustus' rival Pompey and Augustus boasted that he would triumph even over the will of Neptune. Paul Zanker and Alan Shapiro, *The Power of Imagers in the Age of Augustus* (University of Michigan Press, 1988), 39-40. Jeri Blair Debrohun, *Roman Propertius and the Reinvention of Elegy* (University of Michigan Press: 2003), 229.

imperial expansion.⁵⁴ It celebrated what this militarism enabled: roadbuilding. As Augustus himself had said: "I restored the Via Flaminia [road] from the city [of Rome] as far as Ariminum."⁵⁵ Roads meant traffic, and traffic meant economy. A man could walk on the Flaminian road from Rome over the Apennine mountains to the Adriatic coastal city of Ariminum and see the triumphal arch. The arch was the symbol of the Roman peace bought at the price of bloodshed.

The merchant who looked up and saw the faces carved in the stone knew that Augustus was merely imitating the voluntarism of their gods. That voluntarism gave freedom to the coin the merchant carried. It had its own "living face" chiseled into the metal, which was animated by the same spirit of Dionysius. The coin might even have a depiction of a triumph arch.⁵⁶

Augustus made Apollo his father, and then made Octavia (his sister) the daughter of Apollo's sister. That celebrity goddess, Artemis, known in Roman mythology as Diana, was worshipped *by all Asia and the whole world* (Acts xix. 27).⁵⁷ By 1 BC, this "gospel" of the "son of god" had been proclaimed throughout the empire for a generation. But the cult of this goddess was much older and universal. Here we will begin to uncover the true darkness behind the empire of death in the land where the Dionysian bloodlust was born.⁵⁸

---

[54] Paul Zanker and Alan Shapiro, *The Power of Imagers in the Age of Augustus* (University of Michigan Press, 1988), 81. Fred S. Fleiner, *A History of Roman Art* (Cengage Learning: 2016), 123.
[55] Caesar, *Res Gestae*, 20.
[56] Fred S. Kleiner, *The Arch of Nero in Rome* (Giorgio Bretschneider Editore: 1985), 30.
[57] ἦν ὅλη ἡ Ἀσία καὶ ἡ οἰκουμένη σέβεται. Rachel A. Diana "Sister of Apollo," *The Phases of Diana* <https://commons.mtholyoke.edu/arth310rdiana/sister-of-apollo/>. Accessed March 23, 2021.
[58] Versnel, 38 asserts it as "at least probable" that the rite of *thriamvos* originated in Asia Minor.

II

EMPIRE OF FREEDOM

Throughout the Roman Empire, magical incantations were chanted to the Greek goddess Artemis, seeking her protection. The Ephesian Letters were believed by all to invoke her magic power, especially through Damnameneus, the demon known as "the subdoer" who was believed to have great power.[1] People would hang silver amulets of the goddess around their necks in the hope of her protection. This goddess was a violent goddess of the hunt who could slay a man who offended her. Her arrows were the cause of death but she could ease a person's death if he appeased her wrath.[2]

Throughout the famous Greek Peloponnesian peninsula—where the Greeks had fought wars with each other, and where the great military city-state Sparta once offered human sacrifice to Diana in ancient times—young men now committed demonic orgies and bled themselves for her.[3] To its northeast, at Athens, where the great Socrates and Plato critiqued the voluntarism of the Athenian Empire, and where Aristotle founded his library in the Lyceum, seeking logos, the Athenians worshipped the goddess as "the best counselor," and sought to justify their voluntarism.[4]

On the nearby coast was the famous festival to the goddess at Brauron, which commemorated the human sacrifice she once demanded to appease

---

[1] James D. Rietveld, *Artemis of The Ephesians* (New York: Nicea Press, 2014), 67-86.
[2] When Odysseus meets his mother in *Odyssey*, bk. XI, he asks her if she has been slain by the arrows of Artemis.
[3] Carly Ionescu, "The Last Goddess: How Artemis Ephesia Lost Her Crown," *Bishops University Lecture* (Feb 26, 2018), <https://www.youtube.com/watch?v=9o_Y3yS-Ks4>. Accessed March 23, 2021.
[4] Jeffrey Smith, *Themistocles* (Pen and Sword Military, 288), 199.

her wrath.[5] Everywhere, her silver amulets were worn and sold and her Ephesian Letters incanted, with a number of demons in her wake.[6]

East of Greece and through the Aegean Sea was the center of worship for the goddess in all the Mediterranean: Ephesus, the fourth largest city in the whole Empire.[7] The Persian king of kings once captured the city and brought Persian elements into the rites, but Alexander had liberated the ancient site.[8] Here the virgin goddess had become a mother by melding with the ancient veneration to the demon Cybele, the Persian Anahita and the Egyptian Isis creating a sacred site.[9] The whole of Asia (modern Turkey) was dominated by sites founded by mythical woman warriors, the Amazons, and the power of the virgin mother had become a commercial center of demonic rites, with the silver amulets sold throughout the world. The proto-feminist nature is even seen in the deep custom of male priests castrating themselves and dressing like women.[10]

The city of Ephesus was filled with merchants and pilgrims, coming from all over the Empire to see the great temple of the goddess. The silver amulets were sold on every corner and the Ephesian Letters were heard everywhere. The goddess was no longer worshipped by a high priest, but only a priestess, whose priesthood was called "the demons of the air."[11]

Her great temple was one of the seven wonders of the ancient world. It was her—the pagan goddess, Artemis Ephesia, the great virgin mother of power and magic. There was a euphoria among the crowds and a latent violence beneath the surface just to see the greatness of the temple.

And behind her lay the Greek god Dionysius, for he was not only the inventor of the lust of triumph, but, says Pliny, "the first to establish the practice of buying and selling."[12] The commercialization of Artemis

---

[5] This is the story of Iphigenia, Agamemnon's daughter who was sacrificed to her mentioned in *Iliad*, ix, 145, 287 and appearing in Hyginus, Aeschylus and Euripides.
[6] Rietveld, 80-86.
[7] Michael Counsell, *The Canterbury Preacher's Companion* (Hymns Ancient and Modern, 2011), 206; Roland H. Worth, *The Seven Cities of the Apocalypse* (New York: Paulist Press, 1999), 9-30.
[8] Rietveld, 173.
[9] Ibid., 174; Samuel Augustus Mitchell, *Ancient Geography, Classical and Sacred* (Nabu Press, 2011), 25.
[10] Rietveld, 175.
[11] Ibid., 80-86, 172-194; James D. Rietveld Interview, *The Magician and the Fool* (Jul 15, 2019), <https://www.youtube.com/watch?v=YTJ-HR_gEwc >, accessed March 23, 2021.
[12] Pliny the Elder, *The Natural History* 7.57, trans. John Bostock (London: George Bell, 1893).

Ephesia shows us what the Dionysian lust for power in money meant: freedom to make money in whatever way you wanted. After the lust for power in bloodshed, this was the next means by which the fallen angels enslaved the human race.

The Cult of Freedom for the Coin

By the invocation of pagan gods and goddesses the empire of the "son of god" was understood to be an empire of freedom. The deified Julius Caesar was given the title "dictator for life" but also a temple to the goddess *Libertas* ("freedom").[13] Artemis promised freedom through magic, and "freedom" itself was a god to worship. Freedom and power were inextricably bound in the empire of death. Because of the bloodshed of the empire, the coin then had freedom to buy and sell anything. From the time of Augustus's military conquests, "the development of the plutocracy also proceeded more and more. Fabulous riches which were not the fruit of labor but of conquest streamed to Rome out of the Orient. This fostered a greed, a luxury," and "outrageous waste," and the Persians also used their coinage to consolidate their power as they fought over Armenia.[14]

Flowing from the *cultus* of lust for power in the rite of triumph, the coin was free from logos to be a means for voluntarism. This meant that after bloodshed conquered foreign nations, the coin could then make men yet more powerful. The coin was the means to instantiate voluntarism—to have power and impose power. The coin was stamped with an image of the emperor because the king must guarantee the legal use of money.[15]

At the same time, the freedom of commerce that was enabled by ancient banking and moneylending also helped citizens exchange goods and build the roads that would traffic better things than idols. Moneylending "made considerable sense in particular segments of these ancient economies, such as the maritime commercial trade" through the

---

[13] "Libertas," *Encyclopaedia Britannica*, <https://www.britannica.com/topic/Libertas-Roman-religion>, accessed March 23, 2021.
[14] Heinrich Pesch, *Liberalism, Socialism and Christian Social Order*, trans. Rupert J. Ederer (Lewiston: The Edwin Mellen Press, 2000), bk. II, 141; Michael Alram, "The Coinage of the Persian Empire," *Oxford Companion to Greek and Roman Coinage*, ed. William E. Metcalf (Oxford: 2012), 61-88; Zeev Rubin, "Persia and Sasanian Monarchy 224-651," *The Cambridge History of the Byzantine Empire C.500-1492* (India: Cambridge University Press, 2019), 130.
[15] Heinrich Pesch, *Teaching Guide to Economics*, trans. Rupert J. Ederer (Lewiston: The Edwin Mellen Press, 2004), vol. 5, 157.

Mediterranean, which the Romans called *mare nostrum* ("our sea").[16] This free market did help the poor because they had greater access to affordable food, shelter, communication and even education.

Nevertheless, because the *cultus* revolved around gods in a contest of power, the Romans could justify the same behavior in economics. In every transaction, the stronger party was tempted to take advantage of the weaker party.[17] Nearly every kind of sin was given freedom to make profit, and any sin that enslaved the weaker party was the most profitable.[18] Spiritual slavery has always been the most lucrative commodity.

The silver talismans of Artemis produced at her famous temple were trafficked throughout the world. As Scruton notes, "Idolatry is the paradigm profanation, since it admits into the realm of worship the idea of currency. You can trade in idols."[19] The lust for power, idols and debauchery was united in the lust of *avarice, which is idolatry* (Col. iii. 5). Thus voluntarism pervaded the economy, where men who worshipped voluntarism sought profit freely by any means necessary. The Dionysian spirit of freedom and bloodlust was the same spirit pervading the economy. Even in the late Roman republic debt was "the lifeblood of the system" for rich and poor alike.[20]

The freedom for power by means of the coin translated into the imposition of power over persons, and in ancient societies slavery "was everywhere present, nowhere disputed."[21] Half of the empire were slaves and another thirty percent were poor laborers enslaved by debt.[22] By means of usurious interest rates, wealth could be amassed exponentially, but even the Romans understood this threat of power and tried to curb this excess wealth with law and custom. The Romans limited the Greek usury (Athens famously charged 9,000% interest), but still allowed it with regulation.[23] Nevertheless the "Roman law of free enterprise allowed and made it

---

[16] Sam Gregg, *For God and Profit* (Crossroad, 2016), 25.

[17] Credit for this observation to E. Michael Jones.

[18] Paul Veyne, ed., *A History of Private Life* (Cambridge: Harvard University Press, 1987), vol I, 27.

[19] Roger Scruton, *Beauty: A Very Short Introduction* (Oxford University Press, 2011), 150.

[20] William V. Harris, "The Late Republic," Scheidel et. al., eds., *The Cambridge Economic History of the Greco-Roman World* (Cambridge, 2007) 521.

[21] Hilaire Belloc, *The Servile State* (London: T. N. Foulis, 1912), 30.

[22] Veyne, *op. cit.*, 133, 134; E. Cahill, S. J., *The Framework of a Christian State* (Fort Collins, CO: Roman Catholic Books, Reprint of 1932 Imprimatur), 5.

[23] Brian McCall, *The Church and the Usurers: Unprofitable Lending for the Modern Economy* (Ave Maria University, Sapientia Press, 2013), 45

possible for usurious wealth to deprive the old masters of estates of their possessions" squelching small businesses of the poor and middle class.[24]

While the imperial capital had "hundreds of thousands of hungry poor," "Roman economic attitudes were very aggressive" since they had a "penchant for profit." [25] "Roman notables were entrepreneurs who aimed to get rich. A wealthy Roman had the soul of a businessman and knew a great deal about making money."[26]

Like the voluntarism of imperial bloodshed, business exchanges were a means of gaining power over the weak. If the coin was free, why not take advantage of someone or deceive your neighbor? Plato could recognize that pressuring someone into a contract was evil, but if the *cultus* of society worshipped gods who did the same, why not get power by a forceful contract?[27] Thus the violent voluntarism of imperial expansion accorded with the peaceful voluntarism of the wealthy gaining power over the vulnerable.

Cicero illustrates the disparity when he says—with some hyperbole—that in Rome there were scarcely 2,000 individuals who owned property out of a population of 1.2 million—a percentage of .016—the rest were slaves or poor.[28] In theory, the philosophers told the Roman merchant to give back to the common good, but, in practice, why not give more glory to Artemis Ephesia through profit from idols?[29]

Manual labor was seen by the powerful to be the work of inferiors and slaves. These built the triumphal arches and the great temple of Artemis Ephesia. In public, a man was shunned for murdering his slave out of anger (which might disturb the Roman peace). But in private, he could legally put him to death.[30]

Greco-Roman culture had enough logos for men to know that they should free their slaves.[31] Even the pagan Seneca was able to discern that slaves were of the same nature as masters.[32] But the lust for power through money overcame their logos, provoking slave revolts and many slaves

---

[24] Pesch, *Liberalism, Socialism and Christian Social Order*, bk. II, 147.
[25] Cahill, 5; Veyne, 159.
[26] Veyne, 158-159.
[27] Cf. Plato, *The Laws*, Book 11, §23, Contracts.
[28] *De Officiis*, ii. 24 in Cahill, 6.
[29] The "sentiments of the philosophers" of "universal brotherhood...had little or no relation to real life" in ancient Rome (Cahill, 6 n3).
[30] Veyne, 67.
[31] Ibid., 51-69.
[32] Cf. Seneca, *Moral Epistles* 47.10-12.

killing their masters. A severe law was enacted that if any free man was found dead in his house, all of his slaves were immediately executed.[33]

Thus the empire of death bought at the price of bloodshed on the frontier was also built by the bloodshed of the whip. With the worship of avarice, freedom and Artemis Ephesia, the *traffic in human souls* (Apoc. xviii. 13) was necessary to satisfy the lust for power in the coin. After all, Aristotle himself had said that slaves were sub-human.[34] They forced the slaves to kill each other for entertainment at the gladiatorial games, also quite profitable.

The spirit of Dionysius wanted to use the logos present in Greco-Roman culture only to satisfy lust for power and make men into slaves. This is shown especially in its lust for power over beauty. Monuments like the temple of Artemis were truly a "matchless architectural structure" yet used for gain.[35]

The fact that pilgrims across the world and a whole economy had been formed around this beauty was testament to the logos present there, by which all human hearts were moved. By the same spirit of Dionysius, evil men sought to make beauty into currency for the sake of voluntarism, and hence the beauty of woman, too, was bought and sold. Ultimately the lust for power through bloodshed and money was deeply sexual.

Man's Freedom

The evil of voluntarism was corrupted still further in the *cultus* of demonic slave masters. Artemis was invoked over marriages for protection, but Venus was both the goddess of marriage and the goddess of prostitution—the empire of freedom worshipped both. The temple of Venus the Conqueror depicted nude Caesars subduing female nations—reflecting one demonic spirit animating bloodshed and lust. With voluntarism, "you are only as good as what you can do."[36] Plato and Aristotle could see that might does not make right, but still believed that a woman was sub-human since Greco-Roman culture "recognised nothing excellent in the human person apart from his goods or his power."[37] Therefore it was "formally admitted that the weaker members of society, such as women or slaves, were intended by nature for the utility of the

---

[33] Cahill, 6.
[34] Cf. Aristotle, *Politics*, bk. I.
[35] Dietrich von Hildebrand, *Aesthetics,* vol. II (The Hildebrand Project: 2018), 81.
[36] Credit for this summation to Julia.
[37] Cahill, 6.

strong."[38] Lust was a means to express dominion over another, male or female.[39]

Thus the *cultus* of various gods was celebrated with sins of the flesh, all shrouded in the shadows of Dionysius. He was "Father *Liber*" who was celebrated by parading a large phallus around the town or city, and young boys celebrated their becoming adult men in the festival *Libernalia*.[40] They donned the toga that represented their removal of innocent modesty (*pudor*) and their gaining the freedom (*libertas*) for sins of the flesh, which remained its own goddess, *Libertas*.[41]

A fully grown adult man indeed could worship freedom, which all the laws of Rome accorded to him. The Greco-Roman father was the *paterfamilias*, enjoying absolute power and freedom to abuse his wife in the empire of freedom. The beauty of a woman was an object of currency:

> Nothing could be more piteous than the wife, sunk so low as to be all but reckoned as a means for the gratification of passion, or for the production of offspring. Without any feeling of shame, marriageable girls were bought and sold, like so much merchandise, and power was sometimes given to the father and to the husband to inflict capital punishment on the wife.[42]

The Greco-Roman mind viewed woman in terms of how she could be used as a means to an end. "We have call girls for our pleasure, concubines for our daily needs, and wives to give us legitimate children and look after the housekeeping."[43] If a man was not rich and could not own and keep slaves, at least he could abuse women for his own pleasure, which, if the coin was free from logos, could be provided to him "for a small sum, without any risk."[44]

Corinth in Greece could boast that their streets "swarmed with brothel-girls and streetwalkers ready to serve sailors ashore."[45] The temple to

---

[38] Ibid.,, 4
[39] Stephen Garton, *Histories of Sexuality* (New York: Routledge, 2004), 32-36.
[40] Augustine, *City of God*, bk. VII, ch. 21.
[41] Michelle George, "The 'Dark Side' of the Toga," in *Roman Dress and the Fabrics of Roman Culture* (University of Toronto Press, 2008), 55.
[42] Leo XIII, *Arcanum* (1880), 7.
[43] Demostenes, *In Neastram*, 122 in Reay Tannahill, *Sex in History* (New York: Stein and Day, 1980), 100.
[44] Athenaeus II, 468 in Tannahill, 104.
[45] Ibid.

Venus at Corinth boasted one thousand "call girls" (*hetairai*) who worshipped the goddess and polluted the men.[46] At Ephesus, Artemis wrapped her protection over all this filth to make it sacred while Dionysius animated all things with his spirit of lust. St. Augustine remarked how one could see with the pagan cults "on this side a grand display of harlots, on the other the virgin goddess."[47]

But if this did not satisfy a Roman man, if he did not like his lawful wife, he could murder her and marry another.[48] If murder was too much of a bloody affair, he could simply cast her off by divorce, which was the most common means of abandonment.[49] Without a husband, the woman would be forced to look for shelter from another man, a family member, or turn over her body to be bought for sins of the flesh.

If this wasn't enough, the Roman empire not only appropriated the high Greek philosophy and literature, but also their practice of sodomy. Fathers kept pre-pubescent boys for their pleasure or practiced pederasty with young men, whom their wives were forced to tolerate.[50] They painted their wickedness on vases and pots as homosexual pornography.[51] Even Plato discussed pedophilia casually.[52]

This was also connected to the imperial cult, as male sodomy was practiced as a means of dominance and conquest, as it was in other ancient societies, where men even threatened each other with rape in the most obscene braggadocio.[53] These things were viewed as masculine, but in reality they were effeminate. The vice of effeminacy is the reluctance to suffer due to an attachment to pleasure.[54] The Greco-Roman cultural economy made men effeminate by endless addictions to pleasure causing them to use and abuse woman and other men.

---

[46] Ibid.
[47] Augustine, *City of God*, bk. II, ch. 26.
[48] Judy E. Gaughan, *Murder Was Not a Crime: Homicide and Power in the Roman Republic* (University of Texas Press, 2010).
[49] Veyne, 40.
[50] Ibid., 79.
[51] Tannahill, 91.
[52] Cf. Melissa J. Gillis and Andrew T. Jacobs, eds., "Plato and Same-Sex Sexuality," *Introduction to Women's and Gender Studies* (Oxford University Press, undated), <https://global.oup.com/us/companion.websites/9780199315468/student/ch5/wed/plato/>. Accessed March 23, 2021.
[53] See Eva Cantarella, *Bisexuality in the Ancient World*, (Yale University Press, 1992); Craig A. Williams, *Roman Homosexuality: Ideologies of Masculinity in Classical Antiquity* (Oxford University Press, 1999).
[54] *Summa*, II-II q138 a1.

Women too succumbed to the sins of the flesh with one another.[55] Meanwhile slaves were virtually forced to seek sexual relationships outside marriage, since they were forbidden by law to marry, if they were not raped by their masters who could do so lawfully.[56] Both sexes engaged in masturbation, and since the coin was free from logos, Miletus in Greece was the manufacturer of disgusting objects for this purpose.[57]

Under the aegis of Artemis Ephesia, the virgin mother goddess of protection, the spirit of Dionysius reigned in Ephesus in a special festival of rape and murder set to music:

> They carried around clubs and images of idols, disparaged with songs, and set upon free men and respectable women in an uncivilized fashion. They performed slaughters in no ordinary manner and poured out an abundance of blood on the distinguished places of the city... as if what they were doing was profitable for the soul.[58]

This was a ritual with elements of shamanic music, which we will discuss later in this book. Yet the Greco-Roman culture had enough logos to realize that the cult of Dionysius must be moderated. The problem was that the government, economy and family was imbued with the same spirit.

St. Paul would write to the Ephesians against this evil and the idolatry of avarice with these words:

> But fornication, and all uncleanness, or covetousness, let it not so much as be named among you, as becometh saints... For know you this and understand, that no fornicator, or unclean, or avaricious person (which is a serving of idols), hath inheritance in the kingdom of Christ and of God (Eph v. 3, 5).

---

[55] The term "Lesbian" comes from the homosexual poetry of Sappho (6th c. BC) on the ancient Greek Island of Lesbos.
[56] Veyne, 33.
[57] Tannahill, 98-100.
[58] *Acta Timothei*, xii, trans. Cavan W. Concannon in Brent Landau and Tony Burke, eds., *New Testament Apocrypha* (Eerdmans: 2016), 404.

Children

In the Roman Empire, marriage consent was *de facto* forced.[59] All classes of Roman society practiced contraception.[60] And the unborn child was murdered in the womb or killed after birth according to Roman law.[61]

> Immediately after the birth it was the father's prerogative to raise the child from the earth where the midwife had placed it, thus indicating that he recognized the infant as his own and declined to expose it [i.e. starve it to death]... A child whose father did not raise it up was exposed outside the house or in some public place.[62]

The wailing infant's tears could be heard through the streets. Anyone could come and take the child as his own slave, or let it starve and die in the empire of freedom. The Romans were astonished that the Egyptians, Germans and Jews did not expose their own children but raised them all.[63]

The Romans especially targeted any child who seemed to have a defect, which they exposed or drowned. The same Seneca who defended slaves also wrote of killing infants: "What is good must be set apart from what is good for nothing."[64] Even the great Aristotle taught that a woman was a misbegotten man, and thus female infants were more frequently starved to death.[65] If a child was accepted by his father and was able to grow, the father could always change his mind and legally murder him even as an adult.[66] As a result sons murdering their own fathers was a common fear, just like slaves.[67] The empire of freedom condemned patricide, but gave legal protection to murdering children.

With the power of life and death in the hands of the father, it made sense that women turned to Artemis Ephesia for power and protection through the help of magical incantations and amulets. Where else could they turn? A woman could simply buy an idol made out of silver to invoke the goddess for power. Artemis Ephesia, in the land of the woman warriors

---

[59] Veyne, 29.
[60] Ibid., 12.
[61] Ibid., 9; Brendan Nagle, *The Roman World: Sources and Interpretation* (Pearson Education: 2005), 242.
[62] Veyne, 9.
[63] Ibid.
[64] Ibid.
[65] Cf. Aristotle, *De Generatione Animalium*, II, iii 737a.
[66] Veyne, 27.
[67] Ibid., 29.

thus gave to feminine nature the hope of power. Since voluntarism made power the basis for human dignity, women sought power in kind, producing a contest of power in the family, in the economy and in the government. In this way the beauty of feminine nature was not honored, but made a means to power—whether used by men or used by women themselves. The logos of beauty was present in the temple and abused, but the greater beauty of feminine nature was also used for power.

The contest of power between man and woman was canonized by making her a goddess. This allowed the gods to be in endless wars with one another, reflecting the wars in the earthly households between man and wife. A natural instinct to love and honor motherhood was turned to Artemis Ephesia, and then twisted to rationalize the debasement of female dignity by means of Dionysius.

King, Coin, and Kitchen

Thus the empire of death was an empire of freedom for the powerful, producing the chaos of the contest of power, whether in Rome or Persia. These civilizations loved logos, yet sought freedom from logos by means of voluntarism. The lust for power flowed from the *cultus* to the people, whether through bloodshed in imperial expansion, domination of slaves and love of money, or the uncleanness in the family, causing a woman to seek the magic of goddess worship for escape. The Persians, for their part, had a far more "civilized" religion in the form of an ancient monotheism known as Zoroastrianism. Yet this too served a voluntarist empire, especially as their king also functioned as high priest.

We have said that the cultural purpose of *cultus* is to transmit logos to a people, which becomes the governing soul of the society. The *cultus* is the "principle of moral order," and the society can be broken down into these three: king, coin and kitchen.[68] In this work we will use the term "king" to denote any government and all ruling authorities. In the Roman and Persian Empires the government enjoyed absolute freedom to conquer more territory, spill blood and command worship for itself. They sought freedom for power and freedom from logos.

The "coin" is the economy: all transactions between families in any society. The Roman economy enjoyed freedom from moral law, to buy and sell *horses and chariots, and slaves, and souls of men* (Apoc. xviii. 13),

---

[68] Christopher Dawson, *The Historic Reality of Christian Culture* (Routledge and Kegan Paul, 1960), 68; *Progress and Religion* (Washington, DC: Catholic University of America Press, 2001), 82.

while the Persians also invoked spirits to seek riches.[69] The *cultus* governs the king, who governs the transaction between men. But since the king sought freedom from logos, the coin was free to buy and sell filth and idolatry.

The "kitchen" is the family, who must secure from the economy what is necessary for their lives. But the Roman father had freedom for himself and freedom from God. The *cultus* establishes the king who governs the coin, and through the coin governs the kitchen. In other words, in every society, the *cultus*, by communicating logos, becomes the moral principle for the way the government works, the way the economy runs, and the way the family functions. In all three cases the corruption of *cultus* meant freedom from logos to impose voluntarism.

In Rome the foundational freedom was religious freedom, for any man could worship as he chose within due limits—which meant to pay *cultus* to the civic religion of the "son of god." It was this fundamental *cultus* that gave freedom to every other *cultus* to exist, from the cult of Lady *Libertas* to the god of sexual freedom, *Liber*. As long as you paid your due to Caesar, he would give you the freedom you desired—freedom to create your own reality. This is what freedom of religion meant and what ultimately enabled voluntarism to dominate society.

But there was one type of religion that could not be tolerated, but represented a grave threat to the Roman "gospel," the "son of god", "lord" and "savior" and every empire of "freedom." This type of religion could never be given religious liberty. This type of religion could only be crushed with the full force of the empire of death. As Maecenas, one of the richest coin-carriers of the empire, wrote to Caesar Augustus:

> Worship the Divine Power everywhere and in every way in accordance with the traditions of our fathers, [and] compel all others to honor it. Those who attempt to distort our religion with strange rites you should abhor and punish... For such men... often encourage a great many to attempt revolutions.[70]

Notice here the virtue of piety toward "the traditions of our fathers." Despite its immorality, the Roman Empire was the greatest civilization that man could build by his own power: logos in philosophy, law, technology, art, architecture, and more. Its possession of beauty passed down proved it was a people with a real culture. Moreover, Virgil's prophecy would be

---

[69] Maneckji Nusservanji Dhalla, *Zoroastrian Civilization* (Oxford: 1922), 170.
[70] Dio Cassius, *Roman History*, bk. LII, ch. 36 in Nels Baikley, ed., *Readings in Ancient History* (Cengage Learning, 2011), 396.

proven true—but not in the way he expected. In Rome and in Persia, religion could be tolerated as long as it did not threaten freedom for the empire of death in king, coin, and kitchen. The real emperor of death and freedom was Satan who ruled through the voluntaristic spirit of Dionysius. The powerful were quite content with the status quo.

But at that moment, something was about to happen.

Suddenly, in the eastern extremities of the Roman Empire, the night sky is lit up by a bright star. Miles away in Bethlehem shepherds see a bright light:

> An angel of the Lord stood by them, and the brightness of God shone round about them; and they feared with a great fear. And the angel said to them: Fear not; for, behold, I bring you good tidings of great joy, that shall be to all the people: For, this day, is born to you a Saviour, who is Christ the Lord, in the city of David... And suddenly there was with the angel a multitude of the heavenly army, praising God, and saying: Glory to God in the highest; and on earth peace to men of good will (Lk. ii. 9-11, 13-14).

Suddenly the Roman "peace," the Roman "gospel," the Roman "freedom," the Roman "lord," "savior," and "son of god" and the Persian "king of kings" had a new rival.

> In the sixty-fifth week, according to the prophecy of Daniel... in the year seven hundred and fifty-two from the founding of the city of Rome; in the forty-second year of the empire of Octavian Augustus, when the whole earth was at peace, in the sixth age of the world, Jesus Christ, eternal God, and Son of the eternal Father... is born in Bethlehem of Juda, having become man of the Virgin Mary. The Nativity of Our Lord Jesus Christ according to the flesh.[71]

And the Logos was made flesh and made his tabernacle among us (Jn. i. 14).[72]

---

[71] Roman Martyrology, December 25.
[72] καὶ ὁ λόγος σὰρξ ἐγένετο καὶ ἐσκήνωσεν ἐν ἡμῖν. See below.

III

THE KINGDOM OF GOD

Where is he that is born king of the Jews?... And King Herod hearing this, was troubled, and all Jerusalem with him (Mt. ii. 1-3). They were troubled because they had built an earthly city in rebellion against the Kingdom of God. Their culture had been created by God and permeated with logos not only from the rational nature of man, but logos by direct revelation from God. This was for God's reign among men, but they had corrupted it with voluntarism. It is important to understand the history of Mosaic culture in order to grasp what happens next when the King comes for His throne. But first the framework for this cultural history must be broken down.

The Four Elements of Culture

In any people the logos is transmitted through *cultus* that is meant to govern society—the king, coin and kitchen. *Cultus* is the first element of culture. By transmitting logos to the people, the *cultus* manifests the metaphysical beauty of logos that is reflected in visible or audible beauty. This was in the triumph rite, what Von Hildebrand calls "quasi-sacramental beauty."[1]

But more than merely natural beauty, the *cultus* was believed to bestow divine power. If the *cultus* was celebrated properly the gods would bestow power to the people. In the corrupted rites of Persia and Rome, this was actual power, but coming from a preternatural source—Satan and the fallen angels—not God.

But *cultus* is tied closely with the second element of culture: tradition. The general sense of this term is "wisdom from the ancestors." Chesterton

---

[1] Dietrich von Hildebrand, *Aesthetics,* vol. I (The Hildebrand Project: 2018), 211; Christopher Dawson, *Religion and Culture* (New York: Meridian Books, 1960), 50.

called it "the democracy of the dead."² But besides wisdom in general, "tradition" is a word defined as "to pass down for safekeeping."³ While the *cultus* is concerned with the beauty of logos and divine power, the tradition explains from the *cultus* the truth—the logos of what man knows—and goodness—the logos of what man ought to do. This is "faith and morals" but it also encompasses *all things* passed down—laws and customs, cuisine, dance, music, and everything else. Thus tradition encompasses both wisdom from forefathers, explanations of the *cultus* and everything else that is passed down in written or oral form.⁴

This leads to our third element that is the office of elders, the "guardians of tradition.⁵ They pass down the tradition to the next generation and *interpret to them* the *cultus* (II Esd. viii. 13). This office is essential for a people, since the elders are the only living representatives of the ancient ancestors, and thus must prove faithful to the ancestors in passing down the whole tradition.

But the elders can only pass down the tradition if the fourth and final element of culture is present: piety. This is for the new generation "the first duty," whereby we give to our parents and elders the reverence due to them.⁶ This forms into a love of one's nation, which becomes the glue that binds men to their forefathers in one family. Until very recently, this virtue was not controversial in the slightest. In fact, piety of children to parents and nation is universal among all peoples.⁷ If the younger generation does not have piety, the passing down of the *cultus* and its meaning in tradition will stop after a single generation and a people will never form.

This is what is meant when Maecenas charged Caesar to act "in accordance with the traditions of our fathers." Every people forms around its soul: the *cultus* manifests the beauty of logos and the tradition explains its truth and goodness. The elders guard this tradition and *cultus*, and the next generation accepts it with piety. These four elements of culture are the soul of a people.

This soul of a people passed down through generations then develops laws and customs which transmit logos to the body of the people, which is

---

[2] G. K. Chesterton, *Orthodoxy* (London: John Lane, 1909), 83.
[3] In both Greek and Latin "tradition" is a verb and a noun.
[4] Contrary to modern historical prejudices, oral culture is an extremely accurate and universal form of cultural transmission. See David C. Rubin, *The Cognitive Psychology of Epic, Ballads, and Counting-out Rhymes* (Oxford University Press, 1997), 3; John Miles Foley, "What's in a sign," *Signs of Orality*, MacKay ed. (Brill, 1999), 1; Walter J. Ong, *The Presence of the Word: Some Prolegomena for Cultural and Religious History* (Yale University Press, 1967).
[5] Dawson, *op. cit.*, 51
[6] Janet, i. 9, in C. S. Lewis, *The Abolition of Man* (MacMillan: 1947), 104-105; *Summa*, II-II q101.
[7] Lewis, *loc. cit.*

society—king, coin, and kitchen. Thus the four elements of culture and the three elements of society together make up the soul and body of any people. The culture is the soul which directs the society, the body. This was true for Greco-Rome or Persia no less than Israel (see the first graphic contained on page 17).

The Sacred Order in Heaven and on Earth

God created all things through the Word, the eternal Logos (see Jn. i. 1, 3) resulting in a *sacred order* ("hierarchy").[8] This word hierarchy describes one aspect of the logos of the universe whereby the higher gives to the lower and the lower serves the higher. Hierarchy is the logos of interdependency and harmony. And so in Heaven there are nine choirs of angels divided into three orders. Hierarchy is the beauty which all points to the top—God as King.

The angel choirs sing in hierarchy in Heaven, and music itself gives us a picture of what hierarchy is (see Is. vi. 3). If you hear a song in four-part harmony, it is beautiful. This is the logos of sound—combining these pitches in a hierarchy creates great beauty. Now what would happen if one of the singers wanted to impose his own will on the song and sing at pitches that were not in harmony with the others? The result is excruciating because it is disordered. This is the sound of voluntarism.

Lucifer was the first voluntarist when he said of the divine order, *non serviam*, I will not serve. He rebelled with all his fallen angels, seeking to impose their will onto God's order. Satan and his angels fought but did not create an alternate order, only chaos.

In the natural creation God also placed the logos of his sacred order.[9] The six days of creation indicate an ordering to His creative acts, with the crown of these as man and woman. They were created in His own image, and who were charged with propagating God's rule—His image—by becoming fruitful and multiplying.[10] God created a hierarchy between man and woman so that they would serve each other and harmonize. These were predestined to inherit the thrones that the fallen angels lost in their rebellion, with God as King. Thus peace is the "tranquility of order."[11] This is the Kingdom of God. This is the City of God, whose King and founder

---

[8] Ἐν ἀρχῇ ἦν ὁ λόγος... πάντα δι' αὐτοῦ ἐγένετο, καὶ χωρὶς αὐτοῦ ἐγένετο οὐδὲ ἕν ὃ γέγονεν. Cf. Summa I q108.
[9] The following section is influenced by the explication contained in the forthcoming volume by Christopher Plance, *Kingdom by Creation*.
[10] The ancient mind an image was the symbol of kingship, such as Caesar put his image everywhere to express his sovereignty.
[11] Augustine, *City of God*, bk. XIX, ch. 13.

is the Lord Himself. As it is written, *God is our king before ages [of the east] he hath wrought salvation in the midst of the earth* (Ps. lxxiii. 12).[12]

Adam was given commandments as *cultus* from God to establish communion with Him. Then God created Eve. Thus Adam became the head by leading his wife to God in the *cultus* order God had established. This was the supernatural order that penetrated Eden. Yet it also included offering the creation to Him.

Adam's job as head of the home was to "till the ground" for the sake of Eve, while Eve's role—as heart of the home—was to be a "rescuing helper" for Adam.[13] He had to do the heavy lifting but he needed her to work as well. Both did manual labor, subordinating their bodies not only to each other but to God's order, building a home for their children and propagating the image of God. This was the original "law" (*nomos*) of the "home" (*oikos*), or *oikonomos*— economy.

Eve is called the *virago* in the Vulgate, as Hall observes:

> The root meaning of the word "submit" is to be "under the mission of" someone. Adam was created as the *Vir* to lead the *Virago* ["heroic maiden"] on a heroic mission of virtue and excellence.[14]

This mission was nothing less than to raise children to join the harmony of angels for eternity. But this meant union with the sacred order between man and woman and God, whereby a man's strength serves the woman, and the woman's femininity serves the man. Both find their excellence and dignity in God and His logos, not by imposing their own will for themselves. God filled them with divine grace, which was communion with Him. This is the Kingdom of God.

The Rebellion of the Earthly City

Yet the fallen angels, envious of man's predestination to inherit their thrones, subverted the ordering of man and woman. Satan induced them to imitate his voluntarism by imposing their will on the order of creation. As

---

[12] The Greek "before the ages" [πρὸ αἰῶνος] is a Hebraism meaning eternity. In this passage it translates the Masoretic text "of the east" [מִקֶּדֶם] which is the same word denoting the location of Eden in Gen. 2:8, which Jerome translates as *a principio* ("from the beginning") corresponding to *in principio erat Verbum*. "Wrought salvation" is *Jesusot*, the Hebrew verb form of Our Lord's Name in this passage, [יְשׁוּעוֹת]. Cf. Hab. iii. 18.

[13] The term for "helper" in the Masoretic is *ezer* corresponding to the rescuing help of God that is sought for in the Psalms.

[14] Kennedy Hall, *Terror of Demons: Reclaiming Traditional Catholic Masculinity* (Our Lady of Victory Press, 2020), 153-156.

a result he unleashed a contest of power between man and woman, so that each one sought their dignity by imposing their will on the other. By this sin, our first parents fell from the sacred order established by God.

Yet God still offered them the help of His grace, and provided for them by giving them offspring (Gen. iv. 1). But this wound of disorder then caused the transmission of culture to the next generation to be disordered. For the next generation, now cast out of paradise, was born without divine grace and thus in a state of Original Sin—their intellect was darkened, their will was weakened, and they were inclined to evil. Thus they were in desperate need of divine grace from God to not fall under the power of the fallen angels. The demons could enflame their passions at any moment to disorder their souls.

But God sent angels to protect them. They had not lost their nature created good, and ordered toward God. Our father Adam passed down the *cultus* of worshipping God to their sons, Cain and Abel. Abel cooperated with divine grace and piously offered the *cultus* to God. But Cain's *cultus* was not offered *well* in the manner that Abel did (Gen. iv. 7) and God warned him to have *dominion* over the *lust* of *sin* (ibid). This suggests that Abel offered worship to God according to the rite of Adam, but Cain wanted to impose his will on the *cultus*.

Cain gave into the dominion of the fallen angels, who induced him to rebel against the sacred order by means of bloodshed. Here is the first instance of voluntarist bloodshed. By this means, man became a slave to the fallen angels by imposing his will on the *cultus*.

Thus the fallen angels induced Cain to build a city and call it after the name of his son, Enoch. He was building his own earthly city in opposition to the Kingdom of God.[15] "This city is earthly both in its beginning and in its end—a city in which nothing more is hoped for than can be seen in this world."[16] The earthly city is the empire of death whereby men set up their own false kingdom as usurpers to God's throne. Voluntarism is the chain whereby men enslave themselves to Satan.

By building a city after the name of his own lineage, Cain and the wicked line rebel against the Kingdom of God and His sacred order, placing all hope in this earth. They make themselves kings and seize dominion apart from God, but in so doing they cut themselves off from divine grace, and, being weakened by Original Sin, are enslaved to the voluntarism of demons. Their *cultus*, therefore, will be some means to rationalize their own earthly power.

Meanwhile, Eve gives birth to Seth, and Seth's son is the righteous line who does not build to glorify his own name, but *this man began to call upon the name of the Lord* (Gen. iv. 26). The righteous line will not build

---

[15] Cf. *City of God*, bk. XV, ch. 8; Josephus, *Antiquities*, 1. 3. St. Gregory *Moral.* bk. XVI. ch. VI in Lapide, *Great Commentary* loc. Gen. 4:17.

[16] Augustine, *City of God*, bk. XV, ch. 17.

earthly cities to establish their own sovereignty but they will build to restore the order of God as King.

After the wicked line is destroyed in the Flood, Noah emerges from the Ark, not to build a city after his own name but he *built an altar unto the Lord* (Gen. ix. 20). He restores the order of the *cultus* passed down that glories in the Heavenly King. His three sons are Shem—the ancestor of the Israelites, Arabs, and Syriac peoples—Japheth—the ancestor of the Indo-Europeans—and Ham—the ancestor of all Africans.[17] These are our fathers.

But Ham, seeing his father's nakedness, causes his son, Canaan, to be cursed, which forms the basis for the conquest of the Canaanites as usurpers of the sons of Shem.[18] In Canaan's line especially the *cultus* is polluted with demonic rites, sacrificing to Moloch their own children (see Jer. xix). This event (and its misuse as ideology) will have devastating effects on world history as we will see.

The Book of Genesis is the story of two cultures and their buildings. St. Augustine sums up their nature: "Two cities have been formed by two loves: the earthly by the love of self, even to the contempt of God; the heavenly by the love of God, even to the contempt of self."[19] One is the men of the earthly city, which builds according to man (Gen. x. 11). This was the culture instigated by the fallen angels by means of bloodshed and voluntarism, overcoming man in his weakened state of Original Sin.

When men have all the same language, the wicked line uses it to build the earthly city in order to *make a name for ourselves* (Gen. xi. 4). The very logos of language, just like the beauty of the temple of Artemis, was used for the sake of voluntarism, and therefore God scattered the languages. "As the tongue is the instrument of domination, in it pride was punished; so that man, who would not understand God when He issued His commands, should be misunderstood when he himself gave orders."[20] Central to building the earthly city is the use of language for imperial domination.

This is the empire of freedom and death from Cain to Babel. This culture is still a true culture, retaining the four elements discussed above but corrupted by slavery to Satan and his fallen angels. The building of the

---

[17] There is some question as to who is the ancestor of the east Asian peoples, whether Japheth or Shem.
[18] Various interpretations have been offered by the Fathers regarding the nature of the sin, but the most plausible in the opinion of the author is that Ham saw his "father's nakedness" in the sense of Leviticus 18:8. meaning he committed incest with his mother in an attempt to usurp Noah's authority, as Reuben did (Gen. 35:22). Cf. Fr. Hezekias Carnazzo, "Genesis: In the Beginning," *Institute of Catholic Culture* <https://instituteofcatholicculture.org/talk/genesis/>.
[19] Augustine, *City of God*, bk. XIV, ch. 28.
[20] Ibid., bk. XVI, ch. 4.

empire of death would continue through the building of Augustus's arches and the temples to demons. Thus the voluntarist empire of Satan was in the heart of Cain as it was in the heart of the Four Beasts who build the earthly city and "presume in their own strength, and glory in themselves, not in the Lord."[21] They make themselves "son of god," and "king of kings." *They have called their lands by their names* (Ps. xlviii. 12).

But the angels are *sent to minister for them who shall receive the inheritance of salvation* (Heb. i. 14). And against the fallen angels and their city is raised up the line of just men who *build an altar* according to Heaven and *call upon the name of the Lord* (Gen. viii. 20; xii. 7; ii. 8; et al.).[22] Here we see another action of architecture and *cultus* that involves a logos of language that does not seek earthly power, but communion with the divine and His Kingdom. Language communicates the mystery of the divine, instead of dominion of the strong over the weak. This is the origin of every culture that sought to avoid the voluntarism of empire scattered across the world. Whatever good was in the peoples was an action of divine grace or a reflection of their nature preserving the good God created.

Every people passed down the *cultus* from Adam, but they were mixed with the worship of demons to a greater or lesser degree. Therefore the ancient monotheism shown in the historical record devolved into various degrees of polytheism and shamanism.[23] Shamanism in particular used disordered music to invoke evil spirits. All peoples fell into false worship and were held in bondage through the fear of death that empires used to impose their rule throughout the world. Greater attachment to the earthly city meant greater fear of death, and thus Satan and his fallen angels could keep man in slavery.

The Logos of Mosaic Culture

In order to liberate man from the rule of Satan, God created a people by the logos of the Mosaic Law, *being ordained by angels* (Gal. iii. 19, Acts vii. 53). God was restoring the order of His Kingdom by divinely instituting four elements of culture to form a people.

He first instituted the *cultus* with tradition (see Ex. xii. 43ff), then elders (see Ex. xviii), then more rites of *cultus* with moral tradition covering coin and kitchen (see Ex. xx-xxiii) and Moses ratified a covenant that God will be their King and no other (see Ex. xxiv. 7-8). Then God established an office of elder priests with angels (see Ex. xv. 18) and beauty in a tabernacle as God's throne on earth (see Ex. xxiv-xxxi). The *cultus* was then instituted to repair the disorder created by man's sin and make atonement for the whole people (see Lev. xvi. 30). God was establishing

---

[21] Ibid.
[22] Cf. Ibid., bks XV-XVI.
[23] E. Michael Jones, *Logos Rising* (South Bend, IN: Fidelity Press, 2020), 37-41.

Himself as King over the people and gradually restoring the sacred order of His rule. This was done slowly so that the generations would grow organically around His throne.

This beauty of the Tabernacle and the Aaronic *cultus* was the supernatural order compared to the natural disorder of the Augustan arch and the rite of triumph. They both possessed beauty—the logos of what God and man create. Yet the Mosaic beauty was supernaturally revealed, and thus higher than the natural logos of Rome, and the moral principles contained in the Mosaic Law were infinitely above what Greco-Rome could know merely by natural reason. Therefore idolatrous economy was condemned (see Ex. xx. 3), usury and slavery was mitigated (see Lev. xxv. 37), the exponential accumulation of wealth was not allowed (see Lev. xxv. 10-16), workers were protected by weekly rest (see Ex. xx. 8), and laws protected women and the purity of marriage (see Lev. xviii. 6-25; xix. 29; xx. 11-20).[24]

The most conspicuous mark of a people is that they possess beauty passed down. Besides the *cultus*, the beauty of Mosaic culture was in its sacred literature, "which excels all the writings of all nations by its divine authority."[25]

The Tabernacle is the Throne of the King

When St. John says that the Logos *made his tabernacle among us* (Jn. i. 14), he means the Kingdom of God. As Hahn and Mitch observe, the tabernacle is the central location of God's sovereign rule through the Holy Scriptures.[26] The Tabernacle is the throne of God on earth as it is in Heaven. The beauty of the Tabernacle made by Moses asserted that God was literally present when, after the construction of beauty reflecting logos, the glory of the Lord "overshadows" it and dwells there (see Ex. xl. 28-32).

God's appointed successor to Moses was named Jesus [Joshua], son of Nun, who led the people, with angel armies (see Jos. v. 13-16) against the usurping Canaanites.[27] Jesus son of Nun brought the Tabernacle throne of God to the Promised Land as a type of what would happen when Jesus

---

[24] Cf. Brian McCall, *The Church and the Usurers: Unprofitable Lending for the Modern Economy* (Ave Maria University, Sapientia Press, 2013), 47-50, Sam Gregg, *For God and Profit* (Crossroad, 2016), 28-30.
[25] Augustine, *City of God*, bk. XI, ch. 1.
[26] Scott Hahn and Curtis Mitch, "Kingdom Restoration," *Ignatius Catholic Study Bible: New Testament* (Ignatius, 2010), 233.
[27] For a discussion on why the Canaanites as sons of Ham were usurping the rights of the sons of Jacob, son of Shem in the Holy Land, see the study by Fr. Hezekias Carnazzo, "Genesis: In the Beginning," *Institute of Catholic Culture* < https://instituteofcatholicculture.org/talk/genesis/>.

the Christ arrived. In the Tabernacle of Jesus son of Nun, Heaven and earth united for *heaven is my throne* since God was King not only over Israel but over all nations (see Is. lxvi. 1-2; Ps. xxi. 29; Dan. iv. 31).

Instead of the rule of Satan and voluntarism through his puppet emperors like Caesar Augustus, God Himself was the King of Israel who ruled by Mosaic Law with divinely appointed judges and prophets (I Kngs. viii. 7).[28] The Tabernacle was commanded by God to be created as an *example and shadow of heavenly things* made *according to the type [typos]* God showed Moses on the mountain (see Ex. xxv. 40; Acts vii. 44; Heb. viii. 5).[29] The kingdom of earth had been built from the time of Cain in order to justify voluntarism. Building according to the *typos* of Heaven meant imitating the metaphysical beauty of logos, thereby creating a throne for God's Kingdom on earth. This logos would then be transmitted through law and custom to create a people according to logos, not voluntarism, *in the sight of nations* (Dt. iv. 6-8) as eventually the final prophet would arise as a lawgiver over all peoples (see Dt. xviii. 15-22; Ps. ix. 21).

Mosaic culture created twelve different tribes (plus one) and races that did not intermarry (see Num. xxxvi. 7) and spoke different dialects (see Judg. xii. 6) but were united in the one logos and one *cultus* of the Tabernacle.[30] Therefore each of the tribes had local customs and were developing different languages that distinguished them from the rest of the people, but were integrated by the universal Law of Moses. This harmony of local rule and universal sovereignty was the *typos* of the peoples of God that would be created when the building was finished. The disorder of Babel was being transformed into the sacred order of God's sovereignty. The sign of this covenant was in their strict loyalty to their culture as Israel, sealed by the blood of every male.[31]

Yet Israel did not destroy the usurpers nor pass down the culture to their children (see Jdgs. i.; ii. 10). They did not adhere to their culture, and the fallen angels induced them to reject God as king (see I Kngs. viii. 5).[32] They rejected the monarchy of logos for the tyranny of voluntarism.[33] The

---

[28] Haydock Commentary on I Kings.

[29] The term *typos* refers to the manner in which the Old Testament as a whole represents the architectural drawing of Christ and his Church. For more on this crucial teaching from the Fathers, see T. S. Flanders, *Introduction to the Holy Bible* (Our Lady of Victory Press: 2019), ch. XIV.

[30] The tribe of Joseph was split into two half tribes, typifying the addition of St. Paul into the college of the Apostles.

[31] Circumcision is the sign of not giving the daughters of Israel to be wives to foreigners. Conversely, foreign women can be grafted in to the nation, or foreign men can become circumcised.

[32] Haydock Commentary on I Kings.

[33] Later propagandists like Thomas Paine will use this passage to assert that monarchy itself is censured. However, the issue is not monarchy – God himself is

people wanted authority vested in themselves, not in God.[34] Thus God punished them with the tyranny of Saul who manifested his voluntarism when he refused the will of God (I Kngs. xxviii. 7).[35]

The Tabernacle of David

But the Tabernacle Kingdom of God is renewed by God in new promises made to David for his Kingdom to be established forever (see II Kngs. vii. 5-7; vii. 11-16; I Para. xvii. 14) by means of the Temple built by the king that *shall be to me a son* (II Kngs. vii. 10, 14; Heb. i. 5). Just as Jesus of Nun built the tabernacle throne of God the King in the Holy Land, Solomon continued this by building a Temple throne of God the King, which also had angels (see III Kngs. vi. 23) and was filled with glory (see II Para. vii. 1-3). By this means Solomon renewed the covenant with the people that God would be their King and the Temple would be His throne (see II Para. vi. 1-42).

Yet Solomon turned to voluntarism: oppressing his brethren (see Lev. xxv. 39-41; III Kngs. xii. 4) and worshipping the idolatry of 666 talents of gold (III Kngs. x. 14; xi. 1-7).[36] As a result the transmission of the *cultus* that had passed to Solomon was corrupted in his son Rehoboam, who then renounced piety for the elders and sought to impose more slavery on the tribes on the foolish advice of his young peers seeking power (III Kngs. xii. 1-16).

On the pretext of this real injustice, the ten northern tribes rebelled in their own name. This renewed the revolt of exalting the earthly nation against the heavenly kingdom, which broke upon linguistic and ethnic lines, building a rival *cultus* not according to Heaven, but the earth (III Kngs. xii. 49). Yet the Davidic kingdom also turned to idols, and the First Temple was destroyed and the three faithful tribes exiled (Judah, Benjamin and parts of Levi).

Nevertheless the Holy Spirit declared that the Kingdom of God would continue as planned: *I will resurrect the tabernacle of David, that is fallen...that they may possess all nations* (Am. ix. 11-12).[37] Moreover, the priesthood of Aaron would be supplanted by the priesthood of the King of

---

king – but legitimate authority ordained by God (building the tabernacle kingdom according to heaven) or illegitimate authority ordained by man (building the tower of babel according to earth).

[34] Haydock Commentary on I Kings.

[35] Ibid.

[36] H. C. Franco, "Slavery I, (In the Bible)," *New Catholic Encyclopedia*, 2nd Ed. (Catholic University of America: 2003), vol. 13, 207.

[37] LXX: ἐν τῇ ἡμέρᾳ ἐκείνῃ ἀναστήσω τὴν σκηνὴν Δαυὶδ τὴν πεπτωκυῖαν ... ὅπως ἐκζητήσωσιν οἱ κατάλοιποι τῶν ἀνθρώπων καὶ πάντα τὰ ἔθνη.

Justice, which would be a sacrifice *of bread and wine* (Gen. xiv. 18; Ps. cx; I Kngs. ii. 27-36).[38]

Jesus son of Jozadak then renewed the *cultus* at the city of David to restore the order of Mosaic culture (see I Es. iii. 2). After Jesus son of Nun, this new Jesus arose as leader of Israel, and this time as high priest, all foreshadowing the King. The Second Temple was built by the authority of the Holy Spirit (see I Es. v. 1) and the Aaronic eldership restored (see I Es. vi. 18). The remaining tribes of Israel wept because they believed the throne of God's rule was determined by the physical greatness of the Temple (see I Es. iii. 12). Moreover, no glory of the Lord came to overshadow this Second Temple.

And yet the Holy Spirit said that *great shall be the glory of this last house more than of the first*" (Agg. ii. 10) contrary to what their eyes observed, because the prophet said that *yet one little while, and I will move the heaven and the earth, and the sea, and the dry land. And I will move all nations: the desired of all nations shall come: and I will fill this house with glory saith the Lord of hosts* (Agg. ii. 7-8). God the King himself would come for his throne, destroy voluntarism and establish the direct reign of the Logos Incarnate. The Holy Spirit declared:

> The Lord, whom you seek, and the angel of the testament, whom you desire, shall come to his temple. Behold he cometh, saith the Lord of hosts. And who shall be able to think of the day of his coming? and who shall stand to see him? for he is like a refining fire...And he shall sit refining and cleansing the silver, and he shall purify the sons of Levi...and they shall offer sacrifices to the Lord in justice...And I will come to you in judgment, and will be a speedy witness against sorcerers, and adulterers, and false swearers, and them that oppress the hireling in his wages; the widows, and the fatherless: and oppress the stranger, and have not feared me, saith the Lord of hosts (Mal. iii. 1-5).

Notice the cultural implications of this prophecy taken from what the Holy Spirit says elsewhere about God establishing a *new covenant* not according to Moses (see Jer. xxxi. 30-31). The resurrection of the tabernacle of David would come when the true King—God Himself—truly filled His throne—the Temple kingdom—with His very presence. He would establish a new priesthood (*purify the sons of Levi*) in order to restore the full *cultus* to *offer sacrifices* that *please the Lord*. This is the Logos to be revealed against all the evil of voluntarism in society, whether king worshipping demons

---

[38] See Augustine's commentary on the passage from I Kings in *City of God*, bk. XVII, ch. 5.

(*sorcerers*), the coin free from logos (*wages, widows, fatherless, stranger*) and kitchen debauched with immorality (*adulterers*).

Voluntarism Under the Four Beasts

Yet as punishment God oppressed Israel under the four beasts aforementioned: Babylon, Medo-Persians, Greece and finally Rome. At first, the Judahites, Benjaminites and Levites prospered under the beasts with the help of the angels (see Dan. iii. 49; vi. 22) as holy Daniel under Babylon and Jesus of Jozadak, and Ezra under the Medo-Persians built the Second Temple. They would henceforth seek to adhere strictly to their culture (see I Es. x) and fulfill God's design by "their passionate loyalty to their own identity as Jews."[39] This loyalty to the nation is the glue that binds them to the covenant of God. Yet the lost tribes of Israel (the Samaritans) continued to oppose them and the true *cultus*. The *tabernacle of David* prophesied by Amos and the *greater glory* of the Second Temple seemed impossible.

The division deepened under the third beast, Greece, when many Israelites renounced the *cultus* and their Jewish identity (see I Mach. i. 14-16). This was the question of Hellenism that would divide the Jews into bitter parties—to what degree could Jews adopt the Hellenistic culture of Greece, and who had the authority to decide? The Holy Maccabees, seeking logos, fought against and defeated the Greeks (II Mach. xi. 8), re-established the *cultus* at the Second Temple and Jewish identity in loyalty to God. But they waited for a prophet to instruct them in regards to the Temple, knowing only one with the authority of Moses could do such a thing (see I Mach. iv. 46; xiv. 41).

But the successors to the first generation of Maccabees began to worship the beast through bloodshed, inviting Satan to enslave them like Rome. This was the Hasmonean dynasty. High priest John Hyrcanus I, son of Simon Maccabees, began to conquer the lost tribes in Samaria and the Edomites and enforce circumcision and the Law of Moses.[40] He even began to mint his own coins, which helped grow the economy, setting up the idols of avarice.[41] It was empire building like the Romans had done.

---

[39] Roy H. Schoeman, *Salvation is from the Jews* (San Francisco, CA: Ignatius Press, 2003), 353.
[40] Richard Gottheil and Meyer Kayserling, "John (Johanan) Hyrcanus I," *Jewish Encyclopedia* (1906), <https://jewishencyclopedia.com/articles/7972-hyrcanus-john-johanan-i>, accessed March 23, 2021.
[41] Ibid.

His son Judas Aristobulus seized power by starving his own mother to death and continued the empire building and forced conversions.[42] He then took for himself the name of "king" asserting that he was God's appointed vicar both in the priesthood and the kingship—never before had they been one man. Further successors continued the bloodshed and voluntarism as the Jewish kingdom descended into a contest of power.

This produced many rival factions among the Jews. The two dominant traditions both laid claim to authority over the Mosaic Law: the Sadducees and the Pharisees. They had one *cultus*: the Aaronic priesthood celebrating the tabernacle rite in the Second Temple. Yet without one tradition, the Mosaic culture was thrown into chaos instead of logos. The two parties vied for power with the Hasmonean priest-king both seeking to impose their will on the logos of Mosaic Law. New questions arose with king, coin and kitchen, but no authoritative prophet could adjudicate these questions. Another party arose—the Essenes—who withdrew from the high priest and rejected the Second Temple. Fundamentally, these parties were warring over Jewish identity, the meaning of the *cultus* and the proper moral order for their people and society. Loyalty to Jewish identity meant loyalty to God, but every party divided on what that meant.[43]

Meanwhile, the fourth and terrible beast of Rome was arising and conquering the Greek domains. When Judaea was becoming a Roman province, a man named Antipater arose from the descendants of the forcibly-converted Edomites. He was able to seize power from the high priest Hyrcanus II by placating the Romans in his favor.[44] After this Rome or Antipater began appointing the high priest.[45] After his rival poisoned him, Antipater's son, Herod "the Great," rose to power and Augustus made him King of Judaea, and Herod then proclaimed himself Messiah.[46] This was Herod "the Great" who, at the good news of Our Lord's birth, *was troubled, and all Jerusalem with him.*

---

[42] Richard Gottheil and Louis Ginzberg, "Aristobulus I," *Jewish Encyclopedia* (1906), <https://jewishencyclopedia.com/articles/1768-aristobulus-i>, accessed March 23, 2021.

[43] Cf. Schoeman, *op. cit.*, 64-72

[44] William Milwitzky, "Antipater," *Jewish Encyclopedia* (1906), <https://jewishencyclopedia.com/articles/1599-antipater>, accessed March 23, 2021.

[45] Joseph Jacobs and Isaac Broydé, "Herod I," *Jewish Encyclopedia* (1906), <https://jewishencyclopedia.com/articles/7598-herod-i>, accessed March 23, 2021.

[46] Lapide commentary on Mt. 22:15, citing "Jerome, Origen and others."

THE KINGDOM OF GOD

The Lord Comes for His Throne

All of the bloody contest of power whether in Greco-Roman culture or in Mosaic culture was seeking voluntarist power to build the earthly city against the Kingdom of God. Thus King Herod built onto the Second Temple seeking to make himself the Davidic King, but also built the coastal town of Caesarea and temples to Caesar to appease Rome.[47] The bitter rivalries between the Sadducees, Pharisees, and Herodians (with the Greco-Romans themselves) are suddenly frozen in suspense at the real threat to all of their lust for voluntarism—Logos Incarnate, leading the angel armies.

At the announcement of the angel Gabriel and Mary's glorious *fiat*, the glory that had never filled the Second Temple finally came and *overshadowed* the Virgin Mary *full of grace* (Lk. i. 28, 35).[48] She became the new tabernacle of beauty wherein the Logos is Incarnate, *and we saw his glory...full of grace and truth* (Jn. i. 14). It is she who gives flesh to the Logos, making the reign of God present and walking upon earth. By her Immaculate Conception, she proclaims the absolute need of divine grace—she is the throne of God. The Incarnation in Mary builds the Kingdom not according to the *type [typos] of truth* but according to the Truth Himself (Heb. ix. 24; Apoc. xxi. 3).[49] Here God made man could implant logos *in their bowels, and I will write it in their heart* (Jer. xxxi. 33) so that the Logos Incarnate would take for His throne the very soul of man in order to reign *on earth as it is in heaven* (see Jer. xxxi. 34).

Mary as Queen Regent brings the King to His throne. This is the Presentation in the Temple (see Lk. ii. 22-40) which the Church celebrates by chanting "O Sion, welcome Christ the King" and "Mary, the very gate of heaven" who bears "the glorious King of new light."[50] The remnant of Israel hail their King and prophesy the sword of division between Jewish identity in the earthly city and Jewish identity in their King: *this child is set for the fall and for the resurrection of many in Israel* and the sword shall pierce Mary's soul too (Lk. ii. 34-35). The Jews who identify Jewishness with the King of the Jews will be separated from those who identify Jewishness with the earthly city.

---

[47] Jacobs and Broydé, *op. cit.*

[48] Fr. Christiaan Kappes and William Albrecht, *The Definitive Guide to Solving Biblical Questions about Mary: Mary among the Evangelists* (Eagle Pass, TX: Patristic Pilllars Press, 2020), 97-109.

[49] οὐ γὰρ εἰς χειροποίητα εἰσῆλθεν ἅγια Χριστός, ἀντίτυπα τῶν ἀληθινῶν, ἀλλ' εἰς αὐτὸν τὸν οὐρανόν. Literally "For Christ did not enter into the holy things made with hands, which are *antitypes* of the true things, but into heaven itself" (Heb. ix. 24).

[50] 1st Antiphon for the Procession at the Purification of the Blessed Virgin Mary, *Missale Romanum 1962*.

Jesus, Anointed King

The Greek *christos* means "Anointed [King]." Daniel had prophesied that He would conquer the fourth beast and set up His own kingdom (see Dn. ii. 43-45). Jesus identified Himself as this *Son of Man* and proclaimed the true Gospel against the Roman propaganda: *The time is accomplished, and the Kingdom of God is at hand: repent, and believe the gospel* (Mk. i. 15).

Satan ruled in his puppet empires through voluntarism and bloodshed. *For this purpose, the Son of God appeared, that he might destroy the works of the devil* (I Jn. iii. 8). He would liberate man from slavery to Satan by breaking his power. In the face of Satan's voluntarism, Jesus Christ said He came *not to do my own will, but the will of him that sent me* (Jn. vi. 38) and the Logos Incarnate was present *healing all that were oppressed by the devil* (Acts x. 38). He was restoring the order of God's sovereign rule.

The Kingdom of God would not be of this earth, as the Temple would be the Logos Incarnate, *not made by hands* (Heb. ix. 24). The Kingdom of God would be Christian culture: the Logos of Greco-Roman and Mosaic cultures perfected by Logos Incarnate.[51] Yet he said also concerning the earthly city *I have not come to bring peace, but a sword* (Mt. x. 34).

Those in power were in bondage to Satan, and sought to keep their power over the hearts of men and society by voluntarism. Thus their power was threatened by the reign of the Logos. The Lord had finally come with His glory to fill His temple and claim His throne. *And who shall stand to see him? for he is like a refining fire*. As St. John the Baptist was sent to "prepare the way," he thus said of the King: *he shall baptize you in the Holy Spirit and fire... and he will thoroughly cleanse his floor and gather his wheat into the barn; but the chaff he will burn with unquenchable fire* (Mt. iii. 11-12).

I am come to cast fire on the earth: and what do I desire, but that it be kindled? (Lk. xii. 49).

---

[51] Christopher Dawson, *The Formation of Christendom* (San Francisco, CA: Ignatius Press, 2008), 157.

IV

THE CONSPIRACY OF ANTICHRIST

When the King came to His holy city, what did He find? The coin, free from logos, united with the same economy of Greco-Roman voluntarism. It was this coin that would be the manifestation of the uniting spirit that brought these two cultures together against the Logos Incarnate:

> In these streets and lanes everything might be purchased: the production of Palestine, or imported from foreign lands—nay, the rarest articles from the remotest parts. Exquisitely shaped, curiously designed and jeweled cups, rings, and other workmanship of precious metals; glass, silks, fine linen, woolen stuffs, purple, and costly hangings; essences, ointments, and perfumes, as precious as gold articles of food and drink from foreign lands—in short, what India, Persia, Arabia, Media, Egypt, Italy, Greece an even the far-offs lands of the Gentiles yielded, might be had in these bazaars.[1]

Thus the King found the Temple again defiled not by Canaanite or Greek idols, but a more insidious idolatry of avarice. "The priests were," says Lapide, "wholly bent on lucre...by usury and by other fraudulent arts and methods were wont to despoil foreigners and poor people."[2] The King had come for His throne, but the people were enslaved to the idols of

---

[1] According to Lapide and the Fathers, this was a different cleansing of the temple which "took place at the very beginning of His ministry." Lapide, commentary on John ii. 14.
[2] Lapide on Matt. xxi. 12.

avarice. Thus when the King saw the moneychangers in the Temple, "something fiery and starlike shot from his eyes," says St. Jerome.[3]

> And when he had made, as it were, a scourge of little cords, he drove them all out of the temple, the sheep also and the oxen, and the money of the changers he poured out, and the tables he overthrew.
>
> And to them that sold doves he said: Take these things hence, and make not the house of my Father a house of traffic (Jn. ii. 14-16).

The Second Temple was revealed as the *typos* of Heaven, and now the King of Heaven had claimed His throne. But all the parties of Israel would rather die than allow their Temple to be a *typos* of Heaven: they wanted it to be the throne of *earthly voluntarism*. They wanted to secure their power over the king, coin, and kitchen. The Herodians and the Greco-Romans wanted power over the coin, but the Sadducees and Pharisees wanted power to adjudicate the Mosaic Law concerning the coin, the idol of money corrupting all, and all other aspects of life under Roman rule. They both sought to impose their own, human will and did not wait for *a faithful prophet* as the Maccabees had done (see I Mach. xiv. 41).

It was the same rejection of God's Kingdom when Israel sought a king from Samuel against the Mosaic Law. It was the question of divine or human authority—logos or voluntarism. The glory of the Lord was meant to fill this Second Temple with the true temple of the Body of Christ the King himself. Would the Second Temple become the glorious Church of Jerusalem, the heart of Christendom? But the idols of avarice were usurping His throne. Thus he cleansed it, even with violence, preaching the Kingdom of God.

But *His citizens hated him* and they said *we will not have this man to reign over us* (Lk. xix. 14). "From the beginning of Jesus' public ministry, certain Pharisees and partisans of Herod together with priests and scribes agreed together to destroy him."[4] Suddenly all of the parties who had been frozen in suspense understood the threat to their voluntarist power over

---

[3] St. Jerome in Lapide, on Matt. xxi. 12. Lapide confirms the sense of the Fathers on this passage that the money changers were seeking to take advantage of the people by means of avarice. We can understand both cleansings of the temple in this same way.

[4] *Catechism of the Catholic Church*, 574.

society. Their good adherence to their Jewish identity had been twisted into a loyalty to the earthly city.⁵

The Spirit of Antichrist

Against all the warring parties of Israel and the nations, the judgement of the Anointed King was the "refining fire" that they could not abide. Seeking to liberate them from Satan's rule, He told them the truth about their master:

> You are of your father the devil, and the desires of your father you will do. He was a murderer from the beginning, and he stood not in the truth; because truth is not in him. When he speaketh a lie, he speaketh of his own: for he is a liar, and the father thereof. But if I say the truth, you believe me not. (Jn. viii. 42, 44-45)

As Augustine explains, "The Jews then were children of the devil by imitation, not by birth: *And the lusts of your father you will do*, our Lord says. You are his children then, because you have such lusts."⁶ This was the Greco-Roman lust for power and the empire of death—the power of the devil. The Pharisees and Sadducees rejected their King and instead chose allegiance to the devil, just as the Romans had, for the sake of voluntarism in their hearts and society. It was the same empire of death from days of the *blood of Abel the just* (Mt. xxiii. 35).

Thus began the conspiracy of the Antichrist, orchestrated by the fallen angels.

> As you have heard that Antichrist cometh, even now there are become many Antichrists...This is Antichrist, who denieth the Father, and the Son. Whosoever denieth the Son, the same hath not the Father. He that confesseth the Son, hath the Father also (I Jn. ii. 18, 22-23).

There is an end times figure known as the Antichrist or son of perdition (see II Thess. ii. 3), but there are also those who follow the same spirit. This is the spirit of Satan himself, stirred up by the fallen angels to unite

---

⁵ Roy H. Schoeman, *Salvation is from the Jews* (San Francisco, CA: Ignatius Press, 2003), 353-356.
⁶ *Catena Aurea* on John 8.

diverse parties against Christ. Haydock observes that an antichrist is "an adversary of Christ and the Christian religion."[7] Since the Jewish leaders sought voluntarism over logos, they rejected the Logos Incarnate.

Formerly enemies, the Pharisees and Herodians unite to present the King with the symbol of the spirit of voluntarism: the coin printed with Caesar's image (Mk. xii. 13). But the King proclaims that the image of God in Caesar must be given himself to God, even as the coin must be subject to logos.[8] As St. Augustine explains: "Let Caesar's image be rendered to Caesar, God's image to God."[9]

Rome Joins the Conspiracy

Now the Romans were following the spirit of the Antichrist because they held out to the world a false gospel about a false "son of god," seeking power in bloodshed and the coin. The Jewish leaders and Romans unite against Christ as signified by the words of the high priest to the Roman governor: *We have no king but Caesar* (Jn. xix. 15). Their opposition to Christ caused them to repudiate loyalty to the true Davidic Kingdom and choose an earthly city. They would rather unite with the Roman authority for the sake of voluntarism than have the Logos rule over them. The Romans would happily add Christ to their pantheon of gods, but not if He claimed to be the only-begotten Son of God and that their gods were false.

But while the Jewish leaders made a formal conspiracy, (see Mk. iii. 6; Jn. xi. 56), others followed, like the Romans, in an informal agreement. The Romans followed the same spirit of antichrist to reject Christ for the sake of preserving their power.

---

[7] Haydock Commentary on I John 2:22-23.
[8] Scott Hahn and Curtis Mitch, eds. *The Ignatius Catholic Study Bible: New Testament* (Ignatius: 2010), commentary on Mt. 22:21. Lapide makes mentions of Ambrose writing to Emperor Valentinian: "If you desire a long reign, be subject to God; for it is written, 'Give the things of God to God, the things of Cæsar to Cæsar.' To the emperor pertain palaces, but churches to the priest. You have authority over fortifications, not sacred buildings." And Hosius of Cordova said to the Arian emperor Constantius, "Do not intermeddle with matters ecclesiastical, neither give us orders with respect to such things, but rather learn them from us. To thee God has entrusted the imperial power, to us the things of the Church." And Theodosius the Younger said (*Epist. ad Conc. Ephesin.*), "It is wickedness for one who has not been enrolled in the catalogue of the holy bishops to thrust himself into ecclesiastical affairs and deliberations." S. Hilary says, "We are bound to render unto God the things of God, our body, soul, and will; for the coin of Cæsar is in gold, in which his image is engraven; but God's coin is man, in whom is the image of God. Give your money then to Cæsar, but keep for God the consciousness of your innocence."
[9] Augustine, *in Sententiis, Sent.* 15 in Lapide.

Judas Joins the Conspiracy

But just as the tribe of Dan was lost through idolatry (see Jdgs. xviii. 16-19; Apoc. vii. 4-8), so too Judas was lost from the twelve. Once again, like Solomon, his idol was money and he renounced his King for the sake of money, deceived by Satan. Judas became the archetype for the heretics that would arise within the Church to betray her for voluntarism.

Therefore at the Crucifixion we have a foreshadowing of all that will afflict the Church. The enemies of the Church, all seeking power for themselves will unite only to crush Christ the King. Judas leads soldiers from the priests and Pharisees (see Jn. xviii. 3), who then bring him to the High Priest and then the Roman who crucify Him. One spirit of the Antichrist animates them. Whereas one Spirit will animate the Church.

Rao characterizes their actions as:

> The emergence of a powerful but internally tense alliance dedicated to the maintenance of the existing order of things that I should like to call the *Grand Coalition of the Status Quo*. Although never a completely conscious union, either now or later, this force would eventually come to include in its ranks all men and women who, for immensely varied reasons, were contented with the old rules of "closure" and were repelled by boat-rocking rabble-rousers.[10]

The King was a "danger to the status quo."[11] The status quo was the earthly city. It was the reign of Satan. He gave men power to impose their will in their souls and society. This is why everyone was troubled at the birth of our Lord. In their blindness they wanted to maintain their power and voluntarism.

St. Augustine would later observe their alliance in saying that "Jews, heretics, and Heathens have made a unity against Unity."[12] These three parties were found in the Pharisees/Sadducees/Herodians, Judas, and the Roman soldiers/Pilate respectively.

---

[10] John Rao, *Black Legends and the Light of the World: The War of Words with the Incarnate Word* (Forest Lake, MN: Remnant Press, 2011), 50. Emphasis his.

[11] Roy Schoeman, *op. cit.*, 354.

[12] Augustine, *Sermon 12 on the New Testament*, trans. R.G. MacMullen, *Nicene and Post-Nicene Fathers, First Series*, Philip Schaff, ed., (Buffalo, NY: Christian Literature Publishing Co., 1888), ed. for New Advent by Kevin Knight, <http://www.newadvent.org/fathers/160312.htm>, accessed March 23, 2021.

Their uniting principle is one of negation: anything but Christ. They define dignity as power, and therefore it is not the logos which unites them—they reject reason itself in the person of Jesus Christ—but the power of will. This is the evil of voluntarism which causes them to exalt will over intellect. The spirit of antichrist unites them and the fallen angels motivate them. They are effeminate—addicted to the pleasure of their power and unwilling to suffer the loss of it.

Therefore as Rao says, their alliance is "internally tense" since it will instantly break out into civil war, based as it is on will and the contest of power. As Jones observes, "history is another word for the story of this alliance and its war against the Church."[13] Disparate parties will continue to unite under the one principle of "not Christ" as they did from the beginning of Christ's advent. But while there was a real conspiracy against the King in His lifetime, the enemies of Christ, as puppets of Satan, will henceforth be gathered together not by conspiracy, but by a general spirit of antichrist voluntarism against Logos Incarnate. This will be the Grand Coalition of the Status Quo.

The King enters the battle with his angel army (see Lk. xxii. 43) and the fallen angels attack. He is gradually surrounded until His hour comes: *this is your hour, and the power of darkness. And apprehending him, they led him to the high priest's house* (Lk. xxii. 53-54).

---

[13] E. Michael Jones, *The Catholic Church and the Cultural Revolution* (Fidelity Press: 2016), 143.

V

THE CONQUERING LION OF JUDAH

The King is now bound, rejected by many of His subjects and in the power of the Jewish leaders and the Romans. *We will not have this man to reign over us.* The Roman sought voluntarism in the power of the Augustan arch and the demonic coin at Ephesus. The Jewish leaders sought to maintain their earthly power over the supernatural Mosaic culture.[1] All sought their own power over their souls and society. They impose on the Logos Incarnate the power of voluntarism: death. No man has ever overcome death, this awesome power of Satan's empire!

In His Passion, Our King leads the angels and Our Lady into battle against the Dark Lord and all his minions. The world, the flesh and the devil are overcome at every point as the force of Truth advances against the deceptions, desolations and violence of voluntarism. Judas betrays Him and the Apostles flee in fear. The Jewish leaders whip up the mob and the pagans torture Him like demons but nothing overpowers Him as He dethrones the usurper: *My Kingdom is not of this world* (Jn. xviii. 36). Our King suffers manfully so that His soldiers will henceforth conquer by His own Passion. "Whoever has not partaken of His sufferings will not partake of His glory."[2]

At the Cross, the battle between the King and His enemies is consummated. They erect the Cross just as they have erected their earthly temples to themselves in arches and temples dedicated to voluntarism. They raise the wood of their empire to kill Christ. They seal the tomb and finally breathe a sigh of relief, and begin to make plans for the next attack

---

[1] Roy H. Schoeman, *Salvation is from the Jews* (San Francisco, CA: Ignatius Press, 2003), 354.
[2] Fr. Ignatius of the Side of Jesus, *The School of Jesus Crucified* (English translation London: 1866), day XXIII.

against each other in the contest of power. They think they can return to their ugly voluntarism. But the mustard seed was planted.

> In the grave with the body
> But in Hades with the soul
> In Paradise with the thief
> And on the Throne with the Father and Spirit
> Wast thou, O Christ, filling all things
> Thyself uncircumscribed.[3]

But the usurper could not withstand Him. *Now is the judgment of the world: now shall the prince of this world be cast out* (Jn. xii. 31). It was through death that Christ could *enter once into the heavenly tabernacle that, through death, he might destroy him who had the empire of death, that is to say, the devil. And might deliver them, who through the fear of death were all their lifetime subject to slavery* (Heb. ix. 11; ii. 14-15). Satan made slaves of men and ruled the earth through voluntarist bloodshed, and all his forces united to destroy the Logos Himself with this weapon, which contained all his power.

But the Logos Incarnate, *despoiling the principalities and powers, he hath exposed them confidently in open shew, triumphing over them in himself* (Col. ii. 15). Here St. Paul uses the word for the Roman rite of triumph (*thriambevsas*) to show how Christ triumphed over this Roman rite. He says *despoiling*, which means to strip an enemy's weapons from him after he has been defeated. In the Cross, all the power of Satanic bloodshed was destroyed, and the Cross becomes the banner of the new crusade against the fallen angels and their Conspiracy.

These are the principalities and powers, understood in the Latin as *principatus* and *potestates* respectively. The *principatus* was a word used for the period that began when Caesar Augustus became sole ruler and emperor (quoted as "principate" in Augustus' own words in chapter I), and *potestas* referred the legal authority conferred on Roman political offices. By disarming Satan, none of Satan's puppet empires could keep Him from His throne.

The early Greek hymn celebrates Christ as a conquering hero: "Christ is risen from the dead, trampling down death by death." The early Latin hymn too, praises Christ as conquering King:

---

[3] Liturgy of St. John Chrysostom, at the Great Entrance.

THE CONQUERING LION OF JUDAH

> Death and life contended
> in a spectacular battle:
> the Prince of life, who died,
> reigns alive...
>
> We know Christ is truly risen from the dead!
> On us, thou conqueror, King, have mercy![4]

St. John Chrysostom's triumphal homily at Easter was incorporated into the Easter liturgy in the Greek rite:

> The universal kingdom has been revealed... Let no one fear death, for the Savior's death has set us free. He that was held prisoner of it has annihilated it. By descending into Hell, He made Hell captive. He embittered it when it tasted of His flesh... It was embittered, for it was abolished. It was embittered, for it was mocked. It was embittered, for it was slain. It was embittered, for it was overthrown. It was embittered, for it was fettered in chains. It took a body, and met God face to face. It took earth, and encountered Heaven..
>
> O Death, where is your sting? O Hell, where is your victory? Christ is risen, and you are overthrown. Christ is risen, and the demons are fallen. Christ is risen, and the angels rejoice. Christ is risen, and life reigns. Christ is risen, and not one dead remains in the grave. For Christ, being risen from the dead, is become the first fruits of those who have fallen asleep. To Him be glory and dominion unto ages of ages. Amen.[5]

The Resurrection of Christ is the Resurrection of the tabernacle of David! It is the triumph of the City of God over the city of man. The whole power of Satan was in the freedom to sin and the power of death. The King, in absorbing in His own body all the power of death and conquering it, despoiled the enemy of His kingdom and set us free of its awful grip. Many in Israel thought that the Messiah would conquer Rome or Herod like the Hasmoneans, but God the King was not satisfied with a merely earthly kingdom.

---

[4] *Victimae paschali laudes*, Easter Sequence, Roman Rite.
[5] The Paschal Sermon of St. John Chrysostom, Greek Rite.

"For," says St. Fulgentius, "this King came, not to fight against and conquer earthly kings, but, by dying, marvelously to subdue them. Not, therefore, was He born to be thy successor, O Herod; but that the world might faithfully believe in Him."[6] "Christ seizes not thy royalty, [Herod]," says Pope St. Leo the Great, "nor would the Lord of the universe be contented with thy petty scepter. He, whom thou wishest not to be king in Judæa, reigns everywhere, and thyself wouldst reign more prosperously if thou wouldst be subject to His sway."[7] By destroying the power of the true emperor of death, Christ conquered all nations as the King of Kings. *Behold the lion of the tribe of Judah, the root of David, hath conquered* (Apoc. v. 5).[8]

Ascending His Throne

Therefore He spoke as the King who has now conquered and subdued the empire of death:

> All power is given to me in heaven and in earth. Going therefore, teach ye all nations; baptizing them in the name of the Father, and of the Son, and of the Holy Ghost. Teaching them to observe all things whatsoever I have commanded you (Mt. xxviii. 18-20).

And thus against the empire of death and freedom now crippled and powerless, the King promises to His new subjects the fire that He came to cast upon earth: *I send the promise of my Father upon you: but stay you in the city till you be endued with power from on high* (Lk. xxiv. 29; Acts i. 4-5). All power once held by Satan has now been given to the rightful heir to the throne—the Davidic ruler who is Justice Incarnate. The spirit of Antichrist united the forces of evil, but the Holy Spirit will unite Christendom with the angel armies against Satan and the enemies of Christ.

Conquer the nations, He says therefore, and extend my rightful authority over the whole earth. But not by conquest as the Romans and Persians did, nor by the bloodshed of the Hasmoneans' forced circumcisions, but by preaching *the Logos of God*.[9] Not through a force of will and power, but by the force of the Logos and the divine grace of the

---

[6] Sermon 1 on Epiphany in Lapide commentary on Matthew 2.
[7] Lapide on Matthew 2.
[8] ἰδοὺ ἐνίκησεν ὁ λέων ὁ ἐκ τῆς φυλῆς Ἰούδα, ἡ ῥίζα Δαυίδ.
[9] The subject of preaching in the book of Acts is "The Kingdom of God" and "the Logos [word] of God."

Holy Spirit. In this way the kings who formerly worshipped the false king would then worship the true King.

In the Ascension, the King ascends His throne (see Acts ii. 29-36) and commands His *ambassadors* (II Cor. v. 20) to announce His reign to His newly received subjects throughout the world. Give them the Good News, He says, that the reign of Satan is at an end. Give them the good news that their slave master has been driven out. I have broken the power of death, and therefore these false viceroys of Satan no longer have any power over you. Therefore claiming by right the title the Persians had usurped, He is called *King of Kings and Lord of Lords* (I Tim. vi. 15; Apoc. xix. 16).

The Apostles know that the kingdom is at hand, for they say: *Lord, wilt thou at this time restore again the kingdom to Israel?* (Acts i. 6). But "they had not any clear notion of the nature of that kingdom; for the Spirit had not yet instructed them."[10] For even as the King had spoken to them for forty days *of the Kingdom of God* (Acts i. 3), the Holy Spirit would complete this work.

Thus His kingdom is not merely earthly, but rather it is *not of this world* (Jn. xviii. 36). It is not merely a private matter, because *all peoples, tribes, and tongues shall serve him* (Dan. vii. 14). But it is also not merely spiritual: *For the kingdom is the Lord's; and he shall have dominion over the nations* (Ps. xxi. 29). When fire comes from Heaven, the kingdom is revealed.

---

[10] St. John Chrysostom, Homily II on Acts.

VI

MOSAIC CULTURE AND THE RISE OF CHRISTENDOM

The Book of the Acts of the Apostles begins: *The former treatise I made, O Theophilus, of all things which Jesus began to do and to teach* (Acts i. 1). For His Majesty had declared that His followers would continue His work: *Amen, amen I say to you, he that believeth in me, the works that I do, he also shall do; and greater than these shall he do, because I go to the Father* (Jn. xiv. 12). The Holy Ghost will continue the work of Christ on Earth in His Body the Church, "the kingdom of Christ on earth."[1]

It is in the Holy Ghost, Who is charity, that the very reign of Christ is made effective, beginning in Mary. But whereas the Kingdom of God revealed logos in Mosaic culture *to the cleansing of the flesh* (Heb. ix. 13) the Holy Ghost by supernatural grace could truly penetrate man with logos *in their bowels, and I will write it in their heart* (Jer. xxxi. 33).

An early Greek variant in the text of the Our Father in St. Luke replaces *thy kingdom come* with "thy Spirit come upon us and sanctify us."[2] And again the King says, *the Kingdom of God is within you* (Lk. xvii. 21), and *if I by the Spirit of God cast out devils, then is the Kingdom of God come upon you* (Mt. xxii. 28). The Holy Spirit is the Kingdom of God. He is the fire from Heaven that Christ came to kindle.

Since this Kingdom is founded on Charity Himself, not by the power of death, it is truly *within you*. It is when a person is clothed in Christ through baptism that the King drives out the devils from her, that He may reign by the Spirit of God. But His reign is not merely in our hearts.

The Kingdom of God is a fundamentally political reality. He is the King of Kings. The convert forsakes his former error, *we have no king but*

---

[1] Pius XI, *Quas Primas* (1925), 12.
[2] Nestle-Aland, *Novum Testamentum Graece et Latine* (Deutsche Bibelgesellschaft, 1986), 195.

Caesar, but *by the Holy Ghost says Jesus Christ is Lord* (I Cor. xii. 3). Therefore Caesar or the Persian king belongs to his true Lord, and he also must be made subject to His Majesty, *our great God and savior, Jesus Christ* (Tit. ii. 13). *We give thee thanks, O Lord God Almighty, who art, and who wast, and who art to come: because thou hast taken to thee thy great power, and thou hast reigned* (Apoc. xi. 17). *Not with an army, nor by might, but by my spirit, saith the Lord of hosts* (Zach. iv. 6). In the Holy Spirit, Christ may reign over souls and society. This was the true meaning of Mosaic culture all along, but since the days of Israel rejecting God as King until the giving of the Holy Spirit, *the mystery of the anointed king* (Eph. iii. 2-6; cf. Heb. i. 1-2) was not revealed in its fullness.[3] The Holy Spirit restores the Kingdom of Eden by the "unfathomable life-giving power of grace."[4] This alone can overcome Original Sin.

Christendom is Formed

The Apostles were united to Mary from the beginning: *persevering with one mind in prayer with the women, and Mary the mother of Jesus, and with his brethren* (Acts i. 14). She who is the spouse of the Holy Ghost becomes the center of the Kingdom of God when it is finally realized at Pentecost. This will be crucial, and as the Gospels are written, she becomes the source of information about Our Lord's hidden life, and the center of the beauty of holiness.[5]

They constitute Matthias as the twelfth Apostle to complete the recreation of Israel's twelfth "tribe" (Acts i. 26). Then on the feast of Pentecost, celebrating the giving of the Mosaic Law, the new rule of the Kingdom is revealed: *we have heard them speak in our own tongues the wonderful works of God* (Acts ii. 8-12). The Holy Ghost miraculously enabled the preaching of the Logos to all peoples.

The mark of the Holy Ghost is the speaking of other languages and the unity that results. This kingdom is not an earthly kingdom, where one culture or language is the norm, for many languages reflect the beauty of logos. God "sees the similarities and diversities which can contribute to the beauty of the whole."[6] For language was used by the empire of death for

---

[3] Eph. iii. 4: τῷ μυστηρίῳ τοῦ Χριστοῦ.

[4] Fr. Gregory Petrov, *Akathist of Thanksgiving*, <https://saintignatiuschurch.org/wp-content/uploads/akathistThanks.doc>, accessed March 23, 2021.

[5] On the role of our Lady in the Scriptures, the work of Albrecht and Kaapes is foundational: *The Definitive Guide to Solving Biblical Questions about Mary: Mary among the Evangelists* (Eagle Pass, TX: Patristic Pilllars Press, 2020.

[6] Augustine, *City of God*, bk. XVI, ch. 8.

power, but the Holy Ghost would use language to liberate men *out of darkness into his marvelous light* (I Pet. ii. 9).

> This heavenly city, then, while it sojourns on earth, calls citizens out of all nations, and gathers together a society of pilgrims of all languages, not scrupling about diversities in the manners, laws, and institutions...It therefore is so far from rescinding and abolishing these diversities, that it even preserves and adopts them, so long only as no hindrance to the worship of the one supreme and true God is thus introduced.[7]

Here the Holy Ghost forms Christendom, where a diversity of languages preaches one faith. At this stage, the fire of the Holy Ghost purifies the Church from an attachment to an earthly city, and logos is "incarnate" as it were, in every language.

The love of one's own nation is the virtue of piety and the glue which binds a people together. The Jews who rejected Christ thought, then as now, that accepting Him would sacrifice their loyalty to being Jews.[8] But the thirteen cultural tribes of Israel preserved their distinct families yet united in one *cultus* which governed king, coin and kitchen—this was true Jewish identity as Israelites of Mosaic culture. The Holy Spirit restores the order of God as King by preserving the nations and integrating them into the order of one *cultus—breaking bread*—governing their society.

> And all they that believed were together and had all things common. Their possessions and goods they sold and divided them to all, according as every one had need. And continuing daily with one accord in the temple and breaking bread from house to house (Acts ii. 45-46).

The New Cultus

The new citizenship of the Kingdom is not earthly like Roman citizenship, or hereditary, but the totality of being: physical, spiritual, and sacramental. Through Baptism we are all united into one Body, the Church: *Where there is neither Gentile nor Jew, circumcision nor uncircumcision, Barbarian nor Scythian, bond nor free. But Christ is all and in all* (Col. iii.

---

[7] Ibid., bk. XIX, ch. 17.
[8] Roy H. Schoeman, *Salvation is from the Jews* (San Francisco, CA: Ignatius Press, 2003), 354; David Klinghoffer, *Why the Jews Rejected Jesus* (Random House, 2005), 90-118.

11). This was communion not with an earthly temple, but the Body of Christ ascended into heaven, filled with the Holy Spirit.

The earliest extant Eucharistic liturgy prays this:

> Even as this broken bread was scattered over the hills, and was gathered together and became one, so let Thy Church be gathered together from the ends of the earth into Thy kingdom; for Thine is the glory and the power through Jesus Christ forever.[9]

Thus the new *cultus* of the Eucharistic sacrifice forms the *cultus* of the new and everlasting Kingdom, *for we, being many, are one bread, one body, all that partake of one bread* (I Cor. x. 16-17).

Throughout Acts we see the phrase breaking of the bread in reference to the sacrifice of the Mass (ii. 42, 46; xx. 11; xvii. 35). With the new Israel of the Twelve Apostles are the new priesthood fulfilling the Aaronic priesthood, and the new *cultus* for the eternal kingdom of Jesus Christ. Just as the old Israel had thirteen tribes, so also St. Paul is added to their number as the thirteenth Apostle. Against Caesar's triumphs with its fragrant incense, St. Paul says *now thanks be to God, who always maketh us to triumph [thriambevonti] in Christ Jesus, and manifesteth the odour of his knowledge by us in every place* (II Cor. ii. 14). Once again St. Paul uses the same Greek term for the pagan *cultus* to illustrate the triumph over the triumph rite of Rome. In this new *cultus*, there was not the evils of Dionysian bloodshed or even the animal sacrifice of the Mosaic Law.

This bond among the Apostles is the unity formed by the Holy Spirit for the Kingdom of God. The preaching of the Gospel is the announcement of His reign, and the effectiveness of His reign is called Christendom.

Cultus, Elders, and Oral Tradition

As we have seen, there existed already the *cultus* of the emperor of death, and the *cultus* of freedom. The Mosaic *cultus* was fought over by the Jewish factions who had their own oral traditions and conceptions of Jewish identity.

Our Lord revealed that the fundamental nature of Tradition is within the life of the divine Trinity: "the 'handing over' (*traditio*—tradition) of the Father's only-begotten Son" (Jn. iii. 16; i. 14).[10] In the place of the oral

---

[9] *Didache*, ch. 9.
[10] Rev. Antonio López, "Introduction to the English Critical Edition," in Karol Wojtyła, *Person and Act and Related Essays*, trans. Grzegorz Ignatik (CUA Press, 2021), xii.

tradition of the Pharisees, He gave the oral Tradition to the Apostles: *for forty days appearing to them, and speaking of the Kingdom of God* (Acts ii. 3). This oral Tradition formed the basis for the preaching of the Kingdom once the Power effected His rule.[11] Thus we see the formation of the Church taking place as the Apostles go about preaching the Gospel of Jesus Christ, with the help of the angel armies.[12] Their message was the Kingdom of God that liberated souls *from the power of Satan to God*.[13] The "gospel" of Rome now faced the true Gospel, Jesus Christ, the true Lord and Son of God.

In the apostolic succession, the Apostles entrusted the oral Tradition to their successors the bishops: *The things which thou hast heard of me by many witnesses, the same commend to faithful men, who shall be fit to teach others also* (I Tim. ii. 2). The succession of bishops from the Apostles formed the new elders to guard the *cultus* and the oral Tradition. All that was necessary was the final element of culture: piety, which is given with power by the Holy Spirit, preserving national identities in one *cultus* to be passed down from our fathers. But before this happened, the Kingdom would become a mustard seed so that *Out of the mouth of infants and of sucklings thou hast perfected praise, because of thy enemies, that thou mayst destroy the enemy and the avenger* (Ps. viii. 3).

---

[11] John Baptist Cardinal Franzelin, *On Divine Tradition*, trans. Ryan Grant (Sensus Traditionis, 2016), 317-332.
[12] Acts v. 19; viii. 26; x. 3; xii. 7, 23; xxvii. 23.
[13] Acts xxvi. 18. "Kingdom of God" Acts viii. 12; xiv. 21; xix. 8; xx. 25; xxviii. 23, 31.

VII

THE MUSTARD SEED AGAINST PROFESSIONAL ARMIES

The great Nebuchadnezzar had a vision of a great tree which was home for *the birds of the air* (Dan. iv. 9) which was torn down, signifying the humbling of the first beast, the Babylonian Empire. The King said that His Kingdom was *like a mustard seed* which would grow to be this greatest of trees to be home for *the birds of the air* (Mt. xiii. 32).

At the time of Pentecost, two of the greatest professional armies stood to eradicate the Church—those of Persia and Rome. In the face of the empires of death, Jesus Christ planted the mustard seed of the Christian family, which would grow over the generations.

Our Lord formed the Church from the Apostles, then turned to extend His reign within whole families, the most fundamental unit of society.[1] For the family is a miniature people, with its own culture governing its own society. Indeed, the "household" is likened by the saints to the Church (see I Tim. iii. 15, I Pet. iv. 17).

Just as the foundation of the earthly city was in Adam and Eve's fall and Cain's bloodshed, so too the Christian family would be the foundation of the Kingdom by restoring the logos of man, woman and child. The Gospel liberated the family from a contest of power into indissoluble marriage (the lifelong bond of security and provision for a woman and her children), monogamy (the perfected manifestation of man's and woman's equal dignity), and the rights and duties of man and wife to each other. Feminine nature once fallen in Eve is now restored to its regal throne in Mary.

---

[1] Jn. 4:53, Acts 8:33, 11:14, 16:15, 16:31, 16:35, 18:8, I Cor. 1:16, 16:15. Cf. Leo XIII, *Rerum Novarum* (1891), 12.

CITY OF GOD VS. CITY OF MAN

The Virgin Mary and the Truly Regal Throne

Voluntarism debased the beauty of woman into only a *means to end*—lust or children. In place of this, the Gospel raised up Mary as Queen: *a woman clothed with the sun with the moon under feet wearing a crown of twelve stars* (Apoc. xii. 1). This is the great gift of Semitic culture to the Greco-Roman world—its veneration for woman.[2] We see the glimpses of this veneration in the Scripture, and the documentary evidence begins to be found in the 200s.[3] But because of the Semitic love of the mother, it is reasonable to assume that such veneration was prominent, as St. Luke notes emphatically and St. John describes mystically.[4] The Immaculate Conception restored the New Eve, and the person of Mary radically altered the family.

Here the Christian man will look upon a woman's beauty not as object of use, but as a person to be revered. Thus he may raise his mind to the beauty of God's logos. Even Plato could see, "at the sight of beauty the soul grows wings."[5] Or as Hildebrand notes, "we become contemplative" for "beauty is a reflection of God, a reflection of His own infinite beauty" that "opens our hearts, inviting us to transcendence and leading us *in conspectu Dei* ('before the face of God')."[6] But Mary obliterates the pre-Christian conception of woman. As Cahill puts it:

> The doctrine of Aristotle, that the woman is a kind of inferior man is devoid of foundation, and is especially repulsive to the Catholic, who has been taught from childhood to honour the Mother of God next to God Himself.[7]

---

[2] This is shown in Proverbs 31 as well as the Muhammadan veneration of Mary, or anyone living in the Middle East. This may have something to do with the fundamental Semitic virtue in hospitality.

[3] The *Sub Tuum Praesidium* is found in Coptic, Syriac, Greek, Armenian and Latin and the earliest texts date to the 200s.

[4] Apoc. 12; cf. Christiaan Kappes and William Albrecht, *The Definitive Guide to Solving Biblical Questions about Mary: Mary among the Evangelists* (Eagle Pass, TX: Patristic Pilllars Press, 2020).

[5] *Phaedrus*, 249d in Dietrich von Hildebrand, *Aesthetics*, (The Hildebrand Project: 2018), vol. I, 5.

[6] Hildebrand, *op. cit.*, 5, 2, 7.

[7] E. Cahill, S.J., *The Framework of a Christian State* (Roman Catholic Books reprint 1932), 423.

The voluntarist pagan defined dignity by the power of the will, seeking earthly power alone. Christianity defined dignity by the nature of *logos*. Therefore woman possessed dignity not based on power, but based on nature. It is to this logos that Mary submits her will: *behold the handmaid of the Lord, be it done to me according to thy word* (Lk. i. 38).

Thus even anti-Catholic historians are forced to admit that Christianity raised dignity of woman, so that:

> No longer the slave or toy of man...woman rose in the person of the Virgin Mother into a new sphere, and became the object of a reverential homage of which antiquity had no conception.[8]

As Carrie Gress observes, Mary's beauty "is the outward expression of her complete perfection emanating from God's beauty."[9] It is "the splendor of a soul in grace," St. Thomas says, which "surpasses the beauty of all created things."[10] The Queenship of Mary testifies to the Kingship of Christ.

Since the woman's beauty is now an object of homage, the headship of the husband becomes a burden to provide for and protect that beauty, which creates security for the home. The man must imitate Christ and die for his wife: *husbands love your wives as Christ did the Church and gave up his life for her* (Eph. v. 25). Then can a woman love the sacred rule ("hierarchy"): *wives, submit to your husbands* (Eph. v. 22), and *the head of every woman is a man* (I Cor. xi. 3). This is because the husband adores feminine nature that was, as St. Irenaeus says, "the cause of salvation to the human race."[11] The union of the man with his wife is sacramentally elevated in spiritual joy to become "a solemn donation of himself to his partner once for all and for life," producing by God's grace, the ineffable fruit of children for the Kingdom of God.[12]

As Pope Pius XI would put it, "if the man is the head, the woman is the heart, and as he occupies the chief place in ruling, so she may and ought

---

[8] William Lecky, *Rationalism in Europe*, vol. I, ch. 3, 213 cited in Cahill, *op. cit.*, 431. Bonnie S. Anderson and Judith P. Zinsser, *A History of the their Own* (New York: Harper and Row, 1988), vol. I, 67-76.
[9] Carrie Gress, *The Anti-Mary Exposed: Rescuing the Culture from Toxic Femininity* (TAN, 2019), ch. 9.
[10] Ibid.
[11] St. Irenaeus, *Adv. Hacr.* III, 22, 4: PG 7, 9S9 A.
[12] Dietrich von Hildebrand, *In Defense of Purity* (The Hildebrand Project: 2007), 69.

to claim for herself the chief place in love."[13] He calls this "her truly regal throne."[14] The husband honors his queen, who adorns the sacred table of the family *cultus*. Catherine Doherty writes:

> The preparation of food... became exceedingly holy with the Coming of Christ. His mother sanctified it in a very special manner by transforming the fruits of the earth for the nourishment of His Human Body, which He assumed for our sake... The holiness of the kitchen is beyond the ability of human words to express.[15]

Thus we may call the family in society the "kitchen," for here the family's king and queen may provide for the fruit of their love: the child. Then in the family the next generation receives the liberation of the *cultus* in Baptism: but you evil spirit, begone, for the judgment of God has come.[16] Here then can the Christian man honor his wife and *let her works praise her* (Prov. xxxi. 31). The child's soul can be wed to Christ.

In her *cultus* the Church began to celebrate this beauty, at the heart of which is sacrifice, the subordination of the will to logos. As Scruton writes:

> Sacrifice is the core of virtue, the origin of meaning and the true theme of high art...When sacrifice is present and respected...it becomes an object of contemplation, something that 'bears looking at,' and which attracts our admiration and our love."[17]

With woman at the heart of the home, for whose beauty a man must sacrifice, thus flowed from Christian culture the creation of beauty. Rome had made beauty, retaining the best of logos that natural reason could know. The Mosaic Law revealed beauty in the heart of the *cultus*. But in Mary, the Church began to exult ever more in the beauty of feminine nature, raising her eyes to the contemplation of God's logos.

The ideal of Christ dying for the Church restores the masculine ideal of suffering for your bride, destroying the Greco-Roman effeminacy

---

[13] Pius XI, *Casti Connubii* (1930), 27.
[14] Ibid., 75.
[15] Catherine De Hueck Doherty, *Donkey Bells: Advent and Christmas* (Madonna House: 1994), 72.
[16] Rite of Baptism for children, Roman Rite, at the Final Exorcism, *Rituale Romanum 1964*.
[17] Roger Scruton, *Beauty: A Very Short Introduction* (Oxford University Press, 2011), 160-161.

addicted to pleasures. Our fathers embraced the Cross and died for their wives and children.

Cultural Momentum in the Private Order

With woman raised to her rightful throne in the home, the headship of man in Christ could direct the home toward God in truth, not by lust, while the woman obeyed her husband for the sake of Christ. This can only come about though the graces given to them by liberating them from Satan's kingdom in Baptism and the grace of the Sacrament of Matrimony. This hierarchy now transformed in Christ could end the contest of power between man and woman could then flow to make cultural momentum within the home for the children.

We will use this phrase "cultural momentum" to refer to the way a culture inclines a soul to act by law or custom. Cultural momentum describes what ought to be done. It develops over generations into instinctual expectations and cherished traditions. This cultural momentum begins during the earliest years of childhood before the age of reason, making it fundamental to piety. Cultural momentum is built first on a basic foundation of virtue, and through growth it grows toward virtuous understanding eternal Logos.

The most basic cultural momentum is that a child must learn that he cannot simply impose his will with superior force—whether physically or emotionally. In order for him to get his way, he has to "play by the rules." His will must be subordinated to logos.

The parents must punish the child if he fails to follow the rules and reward him when he does. This allows the child to habitually and instinctively associate certain behaviors with certain effects. It is simply the process of perceiving and acting upon cause and effect, the basic fundamentals of logos. Habituation of the will to this cause and effect is called virtue.

After this process has already begun, the child must learn to act with the next most fundamental logos—language.[18] Instead of using emotional noise or force to get what he wants, he must use language, the logos of audible truth and goodness. Animals communicate with noises and signals, but they do not have language. The most fundamental understanding about

---

[18] E. Michael Jones, *Logos Rising* (South Bend, IN: Fidelity Press, 2020), 108-113.

language is to connect the cause—a word—with an effect—a meaning of substance. The child learns through modeling and imitating.[19]

As the child grows toward the use of reason in the Christian family, the patriarchal hierarchy shows the child that power is not given for the sake of dignity—the father is not head because he has more power—but for the sake of hierarchy, the sacred order. By understanding that the father's physical superiority in the family is given to provide and protect the family, not impose his will, the child understands that the child's own power must be used according to a proper order. His will must be subordinated to logos.

All children are born at a biological distance from their fathers and this distance allows them to perceive transcendence from the smallest age. They fear their father's superior physical strength, and they instinctively know that he is at the top of the hierarchy. This image of the father allows them to perceive God Who is transcendent, which is why almost universally faith is dependent on the father whether for girls or boys.[20] This is the higher logos, understanding that I must do the will of God, not my own will, in order to have eternal life.

Most of all, this cultural momentum can only come about by the action of divine grace. Because further, the child sees that the father himself goes to the *cultus*, which transcends the father himself. This powerful sign shows the child that his own authority comes from above him, and through the rite God provides the grace to fill the private order with cultural momentum against Original Sin.[21]

Now since power was the basis for human dignity in Greco-Rome, a woman sought greater power as a source of her own dignity, as Eve did, creating a contest of power in the home. When the child perceives that the woman is using her emotions to impose her will on the father, he learns the same thing he would if the father was a violent abuser—I must impose my will by force. He will then throw fits to get his way. Children learn by following and imitating. If his parents are in a contest of power, the child

---

[19] Philip Mamalakis, *Parenting Toward the Kingdom: Orthodox Principles of Child-Rearing* (Cesterton, IN: Ancient Faith Publishing, 2016), 29-40.
[20] Meg Meeker, MD, *Strong Fathers, Strong Daughters* (New York: Ballantine Books, 2007), 177-198; *Boys Should Be Boys* (New York: Ballatine Books, 2008), 183-202; Harold M. Voth, MD, *Real Men Don't Abandon Their Responsibilities* (Huntington House, 1993), 25-40.
[21] Cf. Peter Kwasniewski, *Reclaiming Our Roman Catholic Birthright: The Genius and Timeliness of the Traditional Latin Mass*(Angelico Press, 2020), 17; Maria Montessori, *The Mass Explained to Children* (Kettering, OH: Angelico Press, 2015).

learns to impose his physical will on his smaller siblings and his emotional will on his larger siblings. This reinforces his Original Sin.

If the wife submits to her husband, she establishes the authority of the father in the child. Just as the Immaculate Conception establishes the throne of Christ by the absolute necessity of grace, so the submission wife exalts in humility, leading the children to their father as the ikon of the transcendent Father.

This leads us to cultural momentum in the private order by custom. These refer to all the traditions passed down in the family which ultimately connect back to virtue. Things like decorum—the logos of ordering externals according to person and place.[22] The innumerable acts of *eutrapelia*—right recreation—from games and music to feasts and dancing.[23] These are external things which bind the family together around culture also before the age of reason. Thus there is a momentum every week to attend the Lord's Day sacrifice. There's an emptiness if it doesn't happen. A feeling that something is missing.

Then could a child receive not the pressure from parents to perform or die, as the Romans, but the liberation of his own nature through the life-giving power of grace. Nor in the natural hierarchy of the children themselves, the older and stronger would not seek to imitate their parents in a contest of power by overcoming the weaker and imposing their will by force, but use greater strength for greater service to the younger. Just as Mary made the throne of Christ on earth, a woman's submission to her husband actualizes his authority for the children. Following St. Paul, Matrimony is the icon of the soul's union with Christ, and therefore the hierarchy of man and wife itself is a *cultus* for the children to know God and submit to him.[24]

Christian parents gave to their children momentum away from the fallen angels pressing upon them from the world. This was a movement of liberation from the kingdom of Satan. This was the conversion of the kitchen which first began to convert Greco-Roman culture. It was society of the private order, while the public order—the government and economy—was still under *Satan's throne* (Apoc. ii. 13). Because Our King violently cleansed the idols to establish His throne, the children could be safe from evil, public momentum to demons.

---

[22] Fr. Chad Ripperger, "Moral Virtues," (Sensus Traditonis, 2016), <http://www.sensustraditionis.org/Virtues.pdf>, accessed March 23, 2021.
[23] Ibid.
[24] Among the Fathers the soul is seen as feminine in relation to God, and thus sin is seen as adultery. See St. John Cassian, *Institutes* and *Conferences*.

The Christian family in marriage grew to the extended family so that the children could benefit from cultural momentum of grandparent, uncles, aunts and cousins. The Holy Spirit was growing the Christian people as families united in the Church.

And out of this mustard seed our fathers would arise and *conquer kingdoms* (Heb. xi. 33): St. Gregory the Illuminator in Armenia, St. Athanasius in the Empire, St. Nino Equal to the Apostles in Georgia, St. Frumentius in Ethiopia, St. Patrick in Ireland, besides the great Fathers St. Basil, St. Gregory Nazianzen, St. Gregory Nyssa, St. John Chrysostom, St. Ambrose, and St. Augustine. Christian families made the difference.[25]

But the young girls, once starved to death as infants because of their gender, would rise from Christian parents as daughters of Mary to trample upon the serpent. For in Mary they could become a *Bride of Christ*. As St. Ambrose relates concerning St. Agnes, a girl of twelve years old:

> What threats the executioner used to make her fear him, what allurements to persuade her, how many desired that she would come to them in marriage! But she answered: "It would be an injury to my spouse to look on any one as likely to please me...Why are you delaying, executioner? Let this body perish which can be loved by eyes which I would not."[26]

This glorious martyrdom won St. Agnes and the other virgin martyrs a place in the Roman Canon. Mary was revered, mothers were honored, virgins celebrated. And in every city where Christians abounded, noble women rose up as mothers of the community, patronesses of the poor, sick and stranger.[27] The spread of the Christian culture in the family would infiltrate the Greco-Roman culture and be "poised to assume more important social roles" when the facade of the imperial son of god was revealed.[28]

---

[25] St. Gregory the Illuminator was raised by foster parents and some of those listed only had one parent influencing them, often a Christian mother. St. Nino's origin is disputed in one tradition but firmly in her cult of the east and St. Frumentius almost certainly had Christian parents since he was brought to Ethiopia as a boy and spread Christianity.

[26] St. Ambrose, *De Virgin*. I, 9.

[27] Paul Veyne, ed., *A History of Private Life* (Cambridge: Harvard University Press, 1987), vol. I, 279.

[28] Peter N. Stearns, *The Encyclopedia of World History*, 6th ed. (Clarke and Co., 2001), 95.

THE MUSTARD SEED AGAINST PROFESSIONAL ARMIES

Just as Eden had the manual labor of man and woman for the economy as the law of the home, so also from Christian families would flow a new economy, restoring the coin to serve the family as the basic unit of society. Very early, then, we see the subordination of the coin for the sake of families (Acts ii. 43-47; iv. 32-37) and God strikes dead those who *lie to the Holy Spirit* concerning their economy (Acts v. 1-11). But when the love of money was threatened, the enemies of Christ reacted.

VIII

RED MARTYRS AGAINST MOB BLOODSHED

Just as from the beginning when the Jewish leaders conspired with Pilate against Our Lord, so also the Christians, says Eusebius, were "incessantly plotted against with a view to their destruction."[1] The enemies of Christ continued to whip up the mob against the preaching of the Logos.[2] The fallen angels henceforth would turn a people into the chaos of a mob so that they might become "an easy plaything in the hands of anyone who exploits their instincts and impressions."[3] This allows those in power to retain their power over the coin lest logos come *to reign over us* (Lk. xix. 14). The enemies of Christ build and then defend their earthly city.

But joining together, the Church prays against the mob:

> Why do the Gentiles rage, and the people meditate vain things? The kings of the earth stood up, and the princes assembled together against the Lord and his Christ.
>
> For of a truth there assembled together in this city against thy holy child Jesus, whom thou hast anointed, Herod, and Pontius Pilate, with the Gentiles and the people of Israel, to do what thy hand and thy counsel decreed to be done. And now, Lord, behold their threatenings, and grant unto thy servants, that with all boldness they may speak thy word [Logos], by stretching forth thy hand to

---

[1] Eusebius *Church History*, bk. III ch. 5.
[2] Acts vi. 12; vii. 54; ix. 23; xiii. 50; xiv. 2, 19; xvi. 22; xvii. 5, 13; xviii. 12; xix. 28; xxi. 27; xxii. 22.
[3] Pius XII, "Christmas Address" (1944), 24.

> cures, and signs, and wonders to be done by the name of thy holy child Jesus.
>
> And when they had prayed, the place was moved wherein they were assembled; and they were all filled with the Holy Ghost, and they spoke the Logos of God with boldness (Acts iv. 25-31).[4]

This prayer shows the history of the Church in which those who opposed her *assembled together... against his Christ*. They conspired by the force of will and mob violence; but the Apostles prayed for divine assistance to protect them.

The city of man seeks earthly goods and is thus "often divided against itself by litigations, wars, quarrels," because "each part of it that arms against another part of it seeks to triumph over the nations through itself in bondage to vice."[5] Insofar as they can unite to oppose Christ, they have unity. But insofar as they gain temporary power, they descend into lording it over one another and civil wars.[6] And thus a single comment makes them erupt into violence with one another (see Acts xxiii. 6-10) because their only unity is the negation of Christ.

The Birth of the Crusading Spirit

Therefore when St. Stephen rises up to proclaim the Logos Incarnate at the risk of his life, some among the Jews who opposed his preaching *with one accord ran violently upon him*, while he *falling on his knees, cried with a loud voice, saying: Lord, lay not this sin to their charge* (Acts vii. 56, 59). Christ said that He came into the world to *witness [martyreso] to the truth* (Jn. xviii. 37) and therefore he manifested charity *unto the end* (Jn. xiii. 1). St. Stephen's fight is "noble and sublime" far surpassing the greatest men of the earthly city.[7] He becomes a witness to the truth saying *Behold, I see the Son of man standing on the right hand of God* (Acts vii. 55). Proof of this truth is the love of enemies, which obliterates the power of Satan and henceforth all martyrs will be said to have obtained a "glorious crown [*stephanos*]."[8] Since the King has conquered death, so too can His

---

[4] Angel armies: Acts v. 19; viii. 26; x. 3; xii. 7, 23; xxvii. 23, translation my own.
[5] Augustine, *City of God*, bk. XV, ch. 4.
[6] John Rao, *Black Legends and the Light of the World: The War of Words with the Incarnate Word* (Forest Lake, MN: Remnant Press, 2011), 54-55.
[7] Dietrich von Hildebrand, *Ethics*, trans. (Hildebrand Project, 2020), 1.
[8] Cf. Gradual for a Martyr Bishop, Alleluia for a Martyr not a bishop, *Missale Romanum 1962*.

glorious martyrs. Since Satan's greatest weapon is the power of death, his false kingdom is overthrown by the martyrs conquering for the true King.

"The noble martyrs of Christ attained such towering strength of soul" because "suffering made them glorious."[9] This instantiates the masculine ideal of Christ suffering for His bride and even His enemies. Embracing the cross of Christ's suffering, the martyrs became the soldiers of Christ to join the angels in the spiritual battle against Satan, obtaining the true triumph against the false rite of Dionysius.

As St. Cyprian would later say, "If to soldiers of this world it is glorious to return in triumph to their country when the foe is vanquished, how much more excellent and greater is the glory, when the devil is overcome, to return in triumph to paradise."[10] With the cross the *true enemy* is identified in Satan and the fallen angels, so that Christians make war on him and seek to liberate their own persecutors from his power.[11]

This is the crusading spirit whose triumph in a victorious death—celebrated by Christians as a "birthday"—formed a central place in the Christian *cultus* from the beginning.[12] "It is difficult to exaggerate the importance of such an ideal... More than any other factor it secured the ultimate triumph of the Church."[13] Love of enemies and fearless witness to the truth proves the martyr stronger than the strongest voluntarism of the fallen angels. "The oftener we are mown down by you," says Tertullian, "the more in number we grow; the blood of Christians is seed."[14] In these they could conquer for their King by claiming citizenship in the eternal city.

The Mustard Seed Grows

The Holy Spirit continued to unite the Church around the Logos Incarnate in the *cultus* spreading His reign not by bloodshed, but by the preaching of the Logos and the miracles of the Holy Spirit. Christian culture spreads to the Samaritans (see Acts viii. 4-8), (previously conquered by the Hasmoneans), and to the Ethiopians (see Acts viii. 26-

---

[9] "Martyrdom of Holy Polycarp," in Eberhard Arnold ed., *The Early Christians In their Own Words* (Farmington, PA: The Plough Publishing House, 1997), 68; Secret for the Mass of St. Stephen, *Missale Romanum 1962*.

[10] St. Cyprian, *Exhortation to Martyrdom*, 13.

[11] Cf. Communion for Martyr not bishop, Magnificat for Martyr, *Missale Romanum 1962*.

[12] Clayton N. Jefford, *Reading the Apostolic Fathers* (Peabody, MA: Hendrickson Publishers, 1996), 93.

[13] Christopher Dawson, *The Making of Europe* (New York: Meridian Books, 1956), 45.

[14] Tertullian, *Apology*, 50.

39); Andrew goes north to the Scythians, Thaddeus east to the Kingdom of Edessa, while St. Thomas travels the silk road east through the Persian empire to India.[15] Every Apostle founds his church with the new *cultus* which then forms a people worshipping the same Logos in every tongue (see Apoc. vii. 9).

St. Peter receives the vision and baptizes the Gentile families on his own authority (see Acts x), showing the first example of papal authority. Yet this leads to a dissension over the adjudication of the Law of Moses. The Pharisees, Sadducees and Herodians all disagreed about the Mosaic Law, but they united against Christ and now the Church. Yet at this moment the Church shows herself animated by a different spirit.

St. Peter, showing the magnanimity which will be imitated by saintly popes, does not impose his will on the whole Church, but the Apostolic Council convenes with *much disputing* (Acts xv. 7) over his decision concerning the Mosaic Law. He rises up and proclaims that God has given him the authority and rebukes them for tempting the Lord, silencing the debate (xv. 7-12). This initiative unites the Council as Sts. Paul and Barnabas also confirm it, and finally St. James who convinces the Council to confirm the pope's decision as they understand that the *tabernacle of David* is the Kingdom of God over *all nations* (xv. 16-18). Thus against the forced circumcisions imposed by the Hasmoneans, the Church will spread and *preserve* the national character of every people. In this the icon of the twelve distinct tribes finds fulfillment.

Then our fathers make a binding decision, using Roman legal terms, and put forth *decreed dogmas for obedience* as apostolic *tradition* (Acts xvi. 4).[16] In contrast to the various sects of Judaism and the Judaizers, the Church shows herself to have the real authority of the King to act by *the Holy Spirit* (Acts xv. 28). The Spirit of God creates order out of chaos, and truth out of confusion. It is a new proclamation of the same *logos*.[17] Their opponents, by contrast, are incapable of uniting except under negation, and will immediately destroy themselves if they gain any power.

Unlike those who seek power by voluntarism, the Holy Spirit transforms the Church as it does marriage, into a contest of humility (Acts

---

[15] Eusebius, Bk. III ch. 1. On St. Thomas and Thaddeus, see Mar Bawai Soro, *The Church of the East: Apostolic and Orthodox* (San Jose, CA: Adiabene Publications, 2007), 41. Fr. Roberson says the apostolicity of the Thomas Christians has "considerable credibility" in ancient sources. *The Eastern Christian Churches: A Brief Survey* (7th Ed. Edizioni Orientalia Christiana: 2008), 17.

[16] Ὡς δὲ διεπορεύοντο τὰς πόλεις, παρεδίδοσαν αὐτοῖς φυλάσσειν τὰ δόγματα τὰ κεκριμένα ὑπὸ τῶν ἀποστόλων καὶ πρεσβυτέρων τῶν ἐν Ἱεροσολύμοις. For a discussion on these terms, see T. S. Flanders, *Introduction to the Holy Bible for Traditional Catholics* (Our Lady of Victory Press, 2019), 162-165.

[17] St. John Henry Newman, *An Essay on the Development of Doctrine* (Park Ridge: Word on Fire, 2017), 139-169.

xv. 28). The Holy Spirit implants the Logos within the soul so that each person submits himself to his brother in union with Christ *who humbled himself* (Philip. ii. 8). Then the Church unity is manifested in *the charity of brotherhood, outdoing one another in showing honor* (Rom. xii. 10).

To avoid chaos, those in power must be content with a mere "balance of power," or "equality" which results in the ugliness of monotone. Christian culture, by contrast, loves the humility of hierarchy joining the angelic choirs in harmony. Therefore, says the Apostle, *such as we think to be the less honourable members of the body, about these we put more abundant honour* so that

> There might be no schism in the body; but the members might be mutually careful one for another. And if one member suffer any thing, all the members suffer with it; or if one member glory, all the members rejoice with it (I Cor. xii. 22-26).

This contest of humility is thus not only manifested in Acts XV, but again in Galatians ii. 11 when St. Paul rebukes St. Peter on the basis of logos as decreed by the Council (Acts xvi. 4). St. Augustine observes that "Peter gave an example to superiors, that if at any time they should happen to stray from the straight path, they should not disdain to be reproved by their subjects."[18] Even within hierarchy, the two parties are *subject to each other out of reverence for Christ* (Eph. v. 21).

But in this fraternal relationship between the Apostles, we see the archetypes of the fundamental union within the eldership of Christian culture. For in order to achieve by God's grace a new proclamation of the same logos, two parties of elders must unite in order for this to come about. These parties existed among the Jews, but they could not unite. They are defined by their relation to tradition and its application now. It is these two parties which form the main narrative of our history behind the four great Greco-Roman renewals, as we will see.

One party are the strict elders, who seek to maintain the same logos and resist any kind of novelty against truth. Taken to an extreme, they would disallow any change whatsoever. While St. Peter initially led the way to baptize Cornelius and resolve the Gentile question, in Galatians he acts like an archetype of the strict, for he is resisting the change in the established tradition.

In St. Paul we may see the archetype of the other necessary party, the moderate elders. This party also has the same goal as the strict—the reign of Christ in souls and society. But the moderates assert that something

---

[18] *Summa*, II-II q33 a4.

within the Tradition—something not essential to the truth—must be changed for this goal to be accomplished. But if the moderate party is not fraternally united with the strict, some can fall into the temptation of heresy.

The heretical party, however, seeks to change something in the Tradition that is essential to the truth. They accept a heretical Christ so that he can be free to have his voluntarism and not the reign of the King. Against this depravity, the Church is formalized by a doctrine proclaimed by both the moderates and the strict, the new proclamation of the same logos. In every new crisis this process is the same as we will see, so that Satan never overcomes the Church, bound together in truth and charity.

> For all the enemies of the Church... exercise her patience if they receive the power to afflict her corporally; and if they only oppose her by wicked thought, they exercise her wisdom: but at the same time, if these enemies are loved, they exercise her benevolence, or even her beneficence, whether she deals with them by persuasive doctrine or by terrible discipline. And thus the devil, the prince of the impious city, when he stirs up his own vessels against the city of God that sojourns in this world, is permitted to do her no harm.[19]

The Soul is the Battleground Between Logos and Voluntarism

The Council of Jerusalem and the Pauline rebuke of St. Peter both show a crucial truth. Perhaps no one has said this point better than Solzhenitsyn:

> If only there were evil people somewhere insidiously committing evil deeds, and it were necessary only to separate them from the rest of us and destroy them. But the line dividing good and evil cuts through the heart of every human being. And who is willing to destroy a piece of his own heart?[20]

It is vital to take a sober look at the enemies of Christ and their machinations. At the same time, we also need to be honest about our own souls seeking to exonerate ourselves from sin. As St. Peter's rebuke from St. Paul illustrates, even the pope can fail to lead the Church as he should.

---

[19] Augustine, *City of God*, bk. XVIII, ch. 51.
[20] Aleksandr Solzhenitsyn, *The Gulag Archipelago*, trans. Whitney and Willets (Harper Modern Classics: 1985), 75.

Saints and sinners arise from all quarters and non-Christians sometimes surpass the moral failings of avowed Christians. What we speak of here most of all is *cultural momentum*. This story is one that illustrates the momentum of morals flowing from the logos-*cultus* in the heart of man into society. Baptism is not a guarantee of an eternal destiny, which is only decided at Judgment.

If we see an erring brother we must follow the wisdom of Bergamo: "We should ever learn lessons of humility from the faults of others: 'If I had found myself in like circumstances and had had the same temptation, perhaps I should have done worse.'"[21] We must always be on guard that we do not become like the Pharisee who *prays with himself* (Lk. xviii. 11) but offer the Gospel of life to convert those who do not have the light of Christ, even if they stir up the mob against us.

Mary Against the Mob at Ephesus

The Book of Acts is the first history of this war between the followers of Christ building the Kingdom against those who defend the earthly city. This conflict reaches a certain climax when St. Paul confronts the cult of Artemis Ephesia in chapter XIX, against which he preaches *so that all they who dwelt in Asia, heard the word [Logos] of the Lord, both Jews and Gentiles* (xix. 10). The demons are driven out even by third class relics of St. Paul (xix. 11-12) while the Ephesian magicians who once invoked Damnameneus were converted and burned their magic books which were worth *fifty thousand pieces of silver* (xix. 19).

But the worshippers of Artemis Ephesia understand that the Gospel is going to threaten their power over the coin and form a mob in an effort to fight for idolatry and greed (xix. 24-27) by means of exalting the greatness of Artemis Ephesia (xix. 28). The mob brings much confusion (xix. 29, 32) but unites to shout *Great is Artemis of the Ephesians* for two hours (xix. 34). But the logos of Greco-Roman culture prevails this time, for a Roman official succeeds in quieting the mob and asking the merchants to go to the courts against St. Paul (xix. 38). This foreshadowed the melding of Mosaic and Greco-Roman culture which would finally formalize the dethronement of the usurper as we will see.

It seems that the cult of Artemis Ephesia was so strong that St. John brought Our Lady herself to Ephesus.[22] It was fitting that the Mediterranean epicenter of Greek, Asian, Egyptian and Persian goddess worship should

---

[21] Fr. Cajetan Mary da Bergamo, *Humility of Heart*, trans. Herbert Cardinal Vaughan (TAN: 2006).
[22] Carla Ionescu, "The Enduring Goddess: Artemis and Mary, Mother of Jesus," PhD diss., (York University, 2016, 144-162.

be subdued by the Immaculate Conception, the greatness of woman was not in power but in divine grace.

The veneration of mother goddesses seems to be a demonic corruption of the ancient veneration of Eve, the *mother of all the living* (Gen. iii. 20). The demons had twisted the cult of the mother goddess so that women would seek power in magic for their contest of power, as they do in modern feminist Wiccan rites to Artemis. The demons had induced man to falsely divinize Eve into a goddess seeking blood sacrifice. The false worship of Artemis Ephesia was defeated by *cultus* of the Mother of God in the first instance of the Church cleansing the ancient cultures passed down from Adam from all demonic content.

Our Lady of Ephesus purified the demonic corruption of feminine nature, so that the *cultus* would instead venerate Mary. She is the New Eve, the Mother of all Christians who *have the testimony [martyrian] of Jesus Christ* (Apoc. xii. 17). By testifying that Christ has come in the flesh, Mary's life is the witness of the King upon earth. Thus the *cultus* of martyrs is united with the *cultus* of their Mother. The women conquer as brides of Christ as we have seen, and men conquer as soldiers of Christ.

St. Paul consecrates St. Timothy as bishop of Ephesus and writes to the Ephesians against the priestesses of Artemis and her winged demons *the prince of the power of the air* (Eph. ii. 2). These demons cause lust and bloodshed (see Eph iv. 19; I Tim. i. 9-10), disordered relations between men and women (see I Tim. ii. 8-15), and the idolatry of avarice (see Eph. iv. 28; I Tim. vi. 17; II Tim. iii. 2) because *the love of money is the root of all evil* (I Tim. vi. 10).

St. Thomas explains that "by riches man acquires the means of committing any sin whatever, and of sating his desire for any sin whatever, since money helps man to obtain all manner of temporal goods."[23] The lust for power is satisfied when a man obtains money, for money is simply the instantiation of power. Against the idolatrous economy of Ephesus, St. Paul proclaimed the true riches of Christ (see Eph. i. 7, 18; ii. 7, 10; iii. 8).

The Ephesians must seize upon their citizenship not in the earthly city but *the household of God* (Eph. ii. 19). All *deceitful lust* (Eph. iv. 22) of demons must be rooted out; men must rule as head yet die for their wives (Eph. v. 21-33) and women submit to their husbands and are queen of the household (I Tim. v. 14) while the rich must be *liberal and generous* (I Tim. vi. 18).[24] It is when writing to St. Timothy that the Apostle gives Our Lord the Persian title *King of Kings* (I Tim. vi. 15). Thus does St. Paul enunciate to the Ephesians the true crusading spirit:

---

[23] *Summa*, I-II q84 a1.
[24] I Tim. v. 14: βούλομαι οὖν νεωτέρας γαμεῖν, τεκνογονεῖν, οἰκοδεσποτεῖν.

> Finally, brethren, be strengthened in the Lord and in the might of his power. Put you on the armour of God, that you may be able to stand against the deceits of the devil. For our wrestling is not against flesh and blood; but against principalities and powers, against the rulers of the world of this darkness, against the spirits of wickedness in the high places (Eph. vi. 10-12).

The true crusading spirit uses the Cross to fight against the enemies of Christ, not *flesh and blood*—but those who are victims of these demons. This is why St. Stephen can forgive his enemies. From this point, as long as the true crusading spirit obtains, the Church is victorious against her enemies. As soon as her enemies succeed in calling the false crusade against flesh and blood, men think that other men are the true enemy, and Satan can quickly divide and conquer. This is the false masculinity that is in fact effeminate, addicted to pleasures.

Instead St. Paul exhorts the bishop of Ephesus to be a *man of God* (I Tim. vi. 11) and thus *take your share of suffering as a good soldier of Christ Jesus* (II Tim. ii. 3). The man of God loves the cross of suffering. Shortly after that tradition tells us that St. Timothy won a glorious crown facing the Dionysians himself.

> On the day of their abominable festival, he put himself forth...to exhort them saying, "Men of Ephesus, do not be mad for idols, but acknowledge the one who truly is God." The agents of the devil were angry at his teaching and, making use of the clubs and stones that they carried with them, they killed the just one.

> The holy and illustrious Timothy, apostle, patriarch, and martyr of Christ, completed his life... [when] Peregrinus was proconsul of Asia, but according to us when our Lord Jesus Christ was ruling, to whom be glory forever and ever, amen.[25]

The ancients counted years by the rulership of the earthly rulers. But by the blood of St. Timothy and the presence of the Queen of Heaven, Artemis

---

[25] *Acta Timothei*, 13-14, 16, trans. Cavan W. Concannon in Brent Landau and Tony Burke, eds., *New Testament Apocrypha* (Eerdmans: 2016), 404, 405.

Ephesia would be overthrown, Caesar subordinated to Christ. And the days would come when men would no longer count years by the rulers of the earthly city, but by the *Anno Domini*, the year of Our Lord.[26]

From the residence of Our Lady at Ephesus and the blood of St. Timothy, the idol economy of the demon declined, and the veneration of Our Lady increased.[27] In 167 and 251 God punished the pagans with a plague and in 259 the Goths set fire to the temple, with 262 bringing an earthquake and fires, making the roof collapse while famine and war did more damage.[28] These helped free the people from slavery to Artemis showing she was powerless against the growth of the mustard seed.

The Two Beasts of the Apocalypse

Sometime before or after the bishopric of St. Timothy at Ephesus, St. John received the final public revelation of Jesus Christ. The Church understands the Apocalypse as prophetically speaking to the early Church against those who persecuted her, and foretelling the whole of Church history and the end times as well.[29] It identifies the enemies of Christ who fight against the saints for the earthly city and predicts the triumph of the King and Kingdom, the heavenly New Jerusalem.[30]

Jesus appears as the almighty *prince of the kings of the earth* (i. 5), *who is, and who was, and who is to come* (i. 8). The King exhorts the Church to conquer (ii. 7, 11, 17, 26; iii. 5, 12, 21), condemns the heretics as those he *hates* (ii. 2, 6, 14, 15, 20) and the anti-Christian Jews as *the synagogue of Satan* (ii. 9; iii. 9). The imperial cult is *Satan's throne* (ii. 13) using the power of the devil (ii. 10, 13) for the sake of a society free from

---

[26] This contrast between the years of earthly rulers and the years of Christ the King is also seen in other Acts of greater antiquity in the manuscripts than *Acta Timothei*, such as *Acts of Polycarp*, "He was taken by Herod, Philip the Trallian being high priest, Statius Quadratus being proconsul, but Jesus Christ being King for ever, to whom be glory, honour, majesty, and an everlasting throne, from generation to generation. Amen" (21).

[27] James D. Rietveld, *Artemis of The Ephesians* (New York: Nicea Press, 2014), 327-331.

[28] Ibid., 332.

[29] Antonio Fuentes, *A Guide to the Bible* (Dublin: Four Courts Press, 1999), 235ff. Scott Hahn and Curtis Mitch, eds. *The Ignatius Catholic Study Bible: New Testament* (Ignatius: 2010), 489-492.

[30] The interpretation given here follows Hahn and Mitch, eds., *Ignatius Study Bible* in addition to the historical interpretation based on the Fathers in Taylor R. Marshall, *The Eternal City* (St. John Press, 2012), 151-167.

logos *worshipping demons, murders, sorceries, immorality* and *thefts* (ix. 21).[31]

God pours out his wrath on those who oppose the reign of Christ that they may repent (ix. 20). Some do but many perish, while the saints are martyred and proclaim His kingdom (chapters iv-xi): *The kingdom of this world has become our Lord's and his Christ's, and he shall reign for ever and ever. Amen* (xi. 15). These disasters from earthquakes and financial disaster to civil war can be seen in the history of the first seven emperors beginning with Julius Caesar. Then there is the great and beautiful vision of Our Lady enthroned as tabernacle also symbolizing the Church who gives birth to all the faithful, against whom Satan makes war (xi. 19-xii. 18). Then the ten-horned sea beast from Daniel reappears as Rome, specifically with Emperor Nero, who carried out the first sustained persecution of the Church for *two and forty months* (xiii. 5).[32]

After his war with the Persians over Armenia, Nero erected a triumph arch and a god-size statue of himself in the temple Mars Ultor.[33] It was in Nero that "all the vice, all the splendour, all the degradation of Pagan Rome seemed be gathered up."[34] Sulpitius Severus calls Nero "the basest of all men, and even of wild beasts,"[35] and Eusebius says "he gave himself up to unholy practices and took up arms against the God of the universe" becoming "a monster of depravity."[36] Satan as "dragon" is the source of his power:

> And all the earth was in admiration after the beast. And they adored the dragon, which gave power to the beast... And it was given unto him to make war with the saints, and to overcome them. And power was given him over every tribe, and people, and tongue, and nation (xiii. 3, 7).

The Roman beast then conquers the whole world and all worship his power, while he blasphemes God, God's Name, Mary (*his tabernacle*, xiii.

---

[31] Pergamum distinguished itself as the earliest and most enthusiastic center of emperor worship in the region. This and other forms of pagan religion made the seat of "Satan's Throne." Hahn and Mitch, *op. cit.*, 496.

[32] Marshall, *op. cit.*, 155-156.

[33] Fred S. Kleiner, *The Arch of Nero in Rome* (Giorgio Bretschneider Editore: 1985), 69.

[34] F. W. Farrar, *Early Days of Christianity* (Funk and Wagnalls, 1888), 10.

[35] Sulpitius Severus, *Sacred History*, bk. II, ch. 28.

[36] Eusebius, *The History of the Church*, bk II, ch. 25 in G. A. Williamson, trans. (Penguin, 1989). 62.

6) and the saints. Satan's attack on Mary will later become his most potent weapon.

But then the other beast comes from the land, signifying the place of God, i.e. Israel. The land beast is identified with the Synagogue and the Judaizing heretics, who ally with the Romans against the Church. The Jewish Encyclopedia confirms that Nero had strong Jewish influence, and evidence suggests the Synagogue instigated the Neronian persecution.[37] Thus this beast makes an alliance with Rome who looks like a lamb but speaks the lies of Satan: *And he caused the earth, and them that dwell therein, to adore the first beast... and that whosoever will not adore the image of the beast, should be slain* (xiii. 12, 15). Here we see the *synagogue of Satan* arise to not only ally with the beast of Rome but cause false worship to be offered to the beast, as Hahn and Mitch explain:

> Because Jews were the only ones in the Roman Empire legally exempt from worshiping the emperor and participation in the imperial cult, they could easily betray Christians to the Roman authorities for confession Jesus as Lord (instead of Caesar).[38]

Those who worship the beast worship power as the source of dignity, and thus money. Wherefore in the final passage the beast makes the faithful choose between the mark of apostasy to gain the earthly city of wealth or martyrdom for the Kingdom of God (xiii. 17). It names the cryptogram of Emperor Nero, 666, as his head and his triumph arch were minted on his coins, the same number of money by which Solomon apostatized.[39] Against this fury *the eternal gospel* is preached to the kings: *fear the Lord and give him honour, because the hour of his judgment is come* (xiv. 7).

The harlot of Babylon *with whom the kings of the earth have committed fornication* (xvii. 2) is *drunk with the blood of the saints* (xvii. 6) is *the earthly city*. It is the type of *every earthly kingdom* which exalts

---

[37] Kaufmann Kohler and Eduard Neumann, "Poppaea Sabina" *Jewish Encyclopedia* (1906) <https://jewishencyclopedia.com/articles/12274-poppaea-sabina>, accessed March 23, 2021; Joseph Holzner, *Paul of Tarsus* (Scepter Publishing, 2002), 517; Farrar, *op. cit.*, 36-37.

[38] Hahn and Mitch, *op. cit.*, 496; this is also seen in Acts v. 17; ix. 23; xii. 3; xiii. 45; xiv. 2; 19; xvii. 5-7; xviii. 12-13; xxiv. 9; xxv. 1-7, 24.

[39] Some manuscripts have 666 and others have 616, which are the cryptograms for Caesar Nero in Hebrew and Greek, respectively. Marshall, *op. cit.*, 154; Hahn and Mitch, *op. cit.*, 509; C. Van den Biesen, "Apocalypse," *The Catholic Encyclopedia* (New York: Robert Appleton Company, 1907), < http://www.newadvent.org/cathen/01594b.htm>, accessed March 23, 2021; Kleiner, *op. cit.*, 100.

itself against Christ the King.[40] At that time, the city was Jerusalem, but as we saw Ephesus was also being judged, as will Rome and the other cities of Antioch, Alexandria, Edessa and Ctesiphon in Persia.

Meanwhile, the book of Acts ends with St. Paul fulfilling his commission to *martyr-witness before the Gentiles, and kings* (Acts ix. 15) including the last of the Herodians, Agrippa II (xxvi. 1-32). The King had said to St. Paul that just *as thou hast testified [diemartyrota] of me in Jerusalem, so is it necessary to testify [martyresai] at Rome* (Acts xxi. 11). The earliest witness testifies that Sts. Peter and Paul "those who founded this church" were buried at Rome as "at the same time" becoming the mustard seed.[41] Again the Persian title appears in the Apocalypse: *King of kings* (xvii. 14; xix. 16) but now we see a vision of that authority.

By this martyrdom is Babylon given judgement (xviii. 20) and this is the history of every earthly city, family, or people which is built in opposition to the City of God. The time of building the earthly city has come to an end. All which is according to the earth will be destroyed by God's judgment without repentance.

At Babylon's fall, the powerful mourn that they can no longer fornicate with money and traffic in human souls, indicating the end of the slave trade as we will see (xviii. 11-19), yet still the enemies of Christ unite (xix. 19) but He defeats them (xix. 21) and completes the building of His kingdom on earth as it is in heaven (chs. xx-xxii).

Rome is conquered by the victorious apostles Sts. Peter and Paul. Linus is consecrated the successor of St. Peter and the Church rises victorious while her enemies disintegrate into war with themselves. The earthly city, says St. Augustine, "when it has conquered, it is inflated with pride, its victory is life-destroying."[42] Just as Nero was killing Sts. Peter and Paul, the Jews and Romans began the First Jewish-Roman War, seeking their own power, and Nero committed suicide like Judas.[43] From the time of this foundation, like Mary at Ephesus, the cult of eternal Rome, declines and the veneration of Christ the King increases.

In Christ, the vocation of Israel to the be the light of the world had been fulfilled. The Jews gave the world the throne of Christ in Mary, the King Himself, then established the Church with the Deposit of Faith as Christian culture. This is where every Jew is called to find his Jewish identity to be the light of the world.

---

[40] Hahn and Mitch, *op. cit.*, 515.
[41] Eusebius, *op. cit.*, 63; Marshall, *op. cit.*, 95-111.
[42] Augustine, *City of God*, bk. XV, ch. 41.
[43] Josephus claims the Jews revolted with the expectation of an imminent military Messiah. Heinrich Graetz, *The History of the Jews* (Philadelphia: The Jewish Publication Society of America, 1894), vol. II, 6 cited in E. Michael Jones, *The Jewish Revolutionary Spirit* (South Bend, IN: Fidelity Press, 2019), 41.

Then at Jerusalem according to Eusebius: "the judgment of God at length overtook those who had committed such outrages against Christ and his apostles, and totally destroyed that generation of impious men."[44] The Christians fled Jerusalem as the Romans laid siege to it, reducing the Jews to cannibalism even as mystical visions and prophets (as reported by Jewish historian Josephus) pronounce "woe to Jerusalem."[45] Then on the same calendar day the First Temple was destroyed by God's wrath, so too the Second Temple: *Tishba B'av*, in AD 70. This is why Hahn and Mitch note that the Apocalypse predicts the judgment *soon* (i. 1, 3; xxii. 6, 7, 10, 12), indicating that Jerusalem is the first "Babylon" to fall—the archetype of all cities which are built according to man. It was here that the power of the priesthood and the party of the Sadducees fell. They had rejected the warnings of Jesus Christ, and they were destroyed, even as their King had wept over their destruction (Lk. xix. 41).

Pharisaic Judaism

But soon after AD 70, Rabbi Yohanan ben Zakkai allied with the Romans in order to gain control over the other Jews.[46] Whether or not this was a naked seizure of power depended on his claim to divine authority. Unlike the Maccabees, who waited for a prophet with regard to the things of the Temple, Zakkai assumed to himself the authority to discontinue the sacrifice and the priesthood, thereby founding a new religion, Pharisaic ("Rabbinic") Judaism.[47] When the First Temple had been destroyed, Jesus son of Jozadak had immediately renewed the *cultus* before the Second Temple was built (I Esd. iii. 2). But now Rabbi Yohanan asserted that Hosea VI. 6 justified disobedience to Moses in Leviticus, so that the Rabbis could set aside the Mosaic *cultus*. But Samuel already rebuked Saul when he thought to make his own *cultus*:

> Doth the Lord desire holocausts and victims, and not rather that the voice of the Lord should be obeyed? For obedience is better than sacrifices: and to hearken rather than to offer the fat or rams. Because it is like the sin of witchcraft, to rebel: and like the crime of idolatry, to refuse to obey (I Kngs. xv. 22-23).

---

[44] Eusebius, *Church History*, bk. III, ch. 5.
[45] Josephus, *Histories*, bk. VI cited by Eusebius, *op. cit.*, bk. III, ch. 8.
[46] Jacob Neusner, *First-Century Judaism in Crisis: Yohanan ben Zakkai and the Renaissance of Torah* (Ktav Publishing House: 2006), 87, 91, 92. Ibid., *A Life of Rabban Yohanan ben Zakkai* (Brill: 1970), 167
[47] Solomon Schechter and Wilhelm Bacher, "Johanan b. Zakkai" *Jewish Encyclopedia* (1906) < https://jewishencyclopedia.com/articles/2893-ben-zakkai>, accessed March 23, 2021.

The rabbis asserted that they had the authority to set aside the Levitical Day of Atonement for the forgiveness of sins. As the Pharisees correctly said, *Who can forgive sins but God?* (Lk. v. 21). Therefore, by introducing a different rite than the Mosaic rite for the remission of sins, the Pharisees who invented Rabbinic Judaism placed their human authority over the authority of God to give the *cultus*. For if we grant that an oral Torah exists, nowhere did Moses stipulate that you can disobey the command to perform the Mosaic rite of Yom Kippur and invent a different rite for Yom Kippur for the remission of sins.

This new religion was eventually given a new Scripture, the Talmud. This new holy book codified changes to the Mosaic *cultus* in favor of the Rabbincal rite, saying that Jews must "be more careful in the observance of the words of the Scribes [Talmud] than in the words of the Torah [Law of Moses]."[48] The rabbis, by means of the Talmud and without "a faithful prophet" that the Maccabees had insisted on, assumed for themselves authority over the prophet Moses. This was simply imitating Saul imposing his will on the God-given *cultus*. As the Talmud confirms, the rabbis seem to have known that the Temple sacrifice was not acceptable to God since around the Crucifixion of Christ.[49] Without any claim to being divinely inspired prophets, judges, or lawgivers, they used remnants of the existing oral tradition (see II Esd. viii. 9, 13), as a pretext to suppress all other Jewish interpretations—Sadducees, Essenes, Herodians, Zealots, the followers of Philo—by imposing on the Jews the *Birkat Ha-Minim*, the curse on heretics, expelling all other Jews, and especially the Jews who accepted Our Lord as King.[50]

For His Majesty already identified at least some of the oral Torah of the Pharisees as *the traditions of man* (Mk. vii. 1-23). This is the origin of the *cultus* of man's voluntarism over *logos*. Pharisaic Judaism was the first "anti-culture" since it was a *cultus* not passed down from Adam but fabricated *in opposition to the King*. The Rabbinic rites preserved ancient traditions and blended them with new rites in order to create a *cultus* without the sacrifice of Leviticus or the sacrifice of Christ.

Schafer explains that the Talmud tells "a counternarrative to the New Testament's message" by showing Jesus Christ descending into hell to be

---

[48] *Erubin* 21b, *The Babylonian Talmud*, Rabbi Dr. Epstein, ed. (London: Soncino Press, 1935-38) in Roy H. Schoeman, *Salvation is from the Jews*, 111.
[49] *Rosh Hashanah* 31b, cited and explained by Schoeman, *op. cit.*, 129-132. Schoeman explains that a public miracle had shown the Jews when the sacrifice was acceptable. According to the Talmud, this public miracle had ceased about the time of the crucifixion.
[50] St. Justin Martyr, *Dialogue with Trypho the Jew,* ch. 16. Cf. Ruth Langer, *Cursing Christians? A History of the Birkat HaMinim* (Oxford: 2012), 3.

punished "with boiling excrement" for, says the Talmud, "whoever mocks the words of the Sages is punished with boiling excrement."[51] The Talmud teaches that Mary "played the harlot with carpenters" and Jesus was born of adultery between Mary and a man named Pandira, thus naming Jesus in the Talmud as "son of Pandira."[52] As Jewish scholars confirm, these attitudes toward Christ and the Blessed Mother, "reveal the predominant attitude among the most influential Jewish teachers."[53] According to Jewish sources, they are traced back to Zakkai's disciple Eliazar.[54] The disciple of Eliazar, Akiva (whom the Talmud calls "the great sage") was the chief supporter of the false messiah Symeon Bar Kokhba, who led a violent revolt for the earthly city which was crushed by the Romans (132-136 AD).

The leadership of Jewish identity was being solidified by the Talmud in the earthly city. This was Pharisaic Judaism, also known as Rabbinic Judaism. Nevertheless, it still imitated true culture since it retained the four elements: *cultus*, tradition, elders and piety. Thus their tradition was passed down in order to abrogate the Mosaic rite.

Three Parties of Jews

Since that time, the Jews have been internally divided. Some of the Jews (Rom. ii. 29) accepted their King, preached to the Gentiles, and innumerable Jews throughout history followed them.[55] These were *our fathers in the faith*. This was because they understood that the *tabernacle of David* was the *tabernacle of Japheth and Shem* (Gen. ix. 27). His Kingdom was all nations while preserving their distinct national character. These Jews who received Baptism "all saw it as their completion as Jews... the ultimate fullness of Judaism and of their identity as Jews."[56] They fulfilled their very *Jewishness* by receiving and spreading the reign of the King of the Jews. These Jews are truly Jews in every sense—blood, religion, and national character. This Jewish national character, as Schoeman discusses, is their loyalty to God and tribe.[57] The "fulfilled Jews" take this loyalty to be the light of the nations and fulfill it through Christ.

---

[51] Peter Schafer, *Jesus in the Talmud* (Princeton University Press, 2007), 82, 85.
[52] David Klinghoffer, *Why the Jews Rejected Jesus*, 141-142.
[53] Klinghoffer, *op. cit.*, 142. Klinghoffer comments that modern Rabbis have argued that this Jesus of the Talmud is not Jesus Christ, but "there is little room for doubt" that this assertion is in opposition to the traditional Jewish view for centuries, including Maimonides.
[54] Ibid., 141.
[55] St. Vincent Ferrer is said to have converted thousands of Jews.
[56] Schoeman, *op. cit.*, 346.
[57] Ibid., 317-356.

The second group took the logos present in Mosaic culture—most especially the Old Testament Scriptures themselves—and sought as best they could to be faithful to it, having a *zeal not according to knowledge* (Rom. x. 2) but laboring *in ignorance* (I Tim. i. 13). Just as Our Lord critiqued the Pharisees, the Talmud itself also says that most of the Pharisees were a "plague" of men who did not love God but quibbled over the minutiae for which Our Lord condemns them.[58] Therefore this second party represented the best of the Pharisaic tradition and not the negative aspects observed in the Gospels. This party would follow their greatest sage of logos, Rambam ("Maimonides," 1138-1204) and other such Jewish thinkers in a pious attempt to follow Moses. These would oppose Christ based on a *rational* zeal, imitating the spirit which animated St. Paul: *zealous for the traditions of my fathers* (Gal. i. 14). These Jews, despite their strong religious zeal against Christ, can be converted like St. Paul was, because they still believe in logos. In modern times this party would be known as "Orthodox Jews."

But the final party of Jews abandoned logos and, therefore, sought to destroy logos where it could be found. By their actions these Jews *profane the name of Jew*, which means to *praise God* (Gen. xxix. 35). These Jews in blood only, says St. Paul, *please not God, and are adversaries to all men* (I Thess. ii. 15). These are they who oppose Christ with *vincible* (i.e. culpable) ignorance, and it was because of these evil men that Jerusalem was destroyed as Our Lord said, *Because you did not know the time of your visitation* (Lk. xix. 44).[59] The Talmud itself again admits that the Temple was destroyed because "therein prevailed hatred without cause" which is the same Psalm which Our Lord quoted against them concerning Himself (Jn. xv. 25).[60]

These Jews take the piety of the fourth commandment and love of one's fathers, as St. Paul himself had for them (Rom. ix. 4) and take this to excess. In the Pharisaic rite this Jew is able to *pray with himself* (Lk. xviii. 11) and exalt his blood over other nations.[61] Like Babel, this voluntarism in the soul of man coalesced in the cultural effort to *make a name for ourselves*, in exalting the earthly city as superior to the Kingdom of God. While it is critical for Jews to keep their identity as their loyalty to God, this party has taken this idea to an excessive tribalism. St. John the Baptist

---

[58] *Șota* 22b.
[59] Vincible ignorance is that ignorance which is the fault of the soul who could have learned and known the truth, but chose against it. Dominic Prümmer, *Handbook of Moral Theology* (Roman Catholic Books reprint 1957), no. 14.
[60] *Yoma* 9b in Schoeman, *op. cit.*, 124-129.
[61] Compare "I give thee thanks that I am not as the rest of men" (Lk. xviii. 11) to the Talmud-required morning thanksgiving to God "who has not made me a gentile." Langer, *Cursing Christians? A History of the Birkat HaMinim*, 3.

had rebuked this attitude from the beginning (Mt. iii. 9) but some Jews were unconverted and believed blood alone was an acceptable sacrifice to God.

These voluntarist Jews, besides stirring up mobs and persecution against the Jews and Gentiles who accepted Christ, sent out from Jerusalem "chosen men" who spread "bitter and dark and unjust things" against the Christians.[62] Further, while they persecuted Christians, the occult Gnostic sects brought together voluntarist Jews, heretics and pagans to attack the Gospel and the Christian veneration of woman.[63]

These sects asserted that it was not Original Sin that was the problem with human nature, but *ignorance*, promoting fabricated mysticism to this end, against which parts of the New Testament (and the Fathers) were written.[64] From this point on, the fallen angels would whip up the mob of the Grand Coalition of the Status Quo against the Church in public attacks, while the secret movements would engage in covert warfare and sorcery, leading from the Gnostics to successive occult movements against the Church in the Paulicians, Bogomils, Cathars, Kabbalists, Rosicrucians, Freemasons, and the Thelema cult among others.[65] These Jewish-affiliated

---

[62] St. Justin Martyr, *Dialogue with Trypho the Jew*, ch. 17.

[63] Do not read any of these sources about the occult without permission from a priest. On the occult hatred of woman, see *Gospel of Thomas*, saying 114 <http://www.earlychristianwritings.com/thomas/ gospelthomas114. html>, accessed March 23, 2021; see comments and interpretation through the occult history in Richard A. Baer, Jr., *Philo's Use of the Categories Male and Female* (Brill, 1970), 35-53; Aleister Crowley, *Magick in Theory and Practice*, (Independent, 2019), 184, 196-225. On the Gnostics and the occult see Johannes Van Oort, *Gnostica, Judaica, Catholica: Collected Essays of Gilles Quispel* (Brill, 1990), 39-41, 113; Elaine Pagels, *The Gnostic Gospels* (Vintage, 1989), 36-38; Arthur Evans, *Witchcraft and the Gay Counterculture* (Fag Rag Books, 2014), 50-51.

[64] K. K. Yeo, *Rhetorical Interaction in 1 Corinthians 8 and 10* (Brill, 1997), 125-141, 142-155; Gerhard Kittel *Theological Dictionary of the New Testament*, vol. VII (Grand Rapids, MI: Eerdmans, 1971), 121-122, 135, 434, 498-514, 519-522; Martin Scott, *Sophia and the Johannine Jesus* (Sheffield Academic Press, 1992), 58-60; Albertus Frederik Johannes Klijn, *Seth: In Jewish, Christian and Gnostic Literature* (Brill, 1977), 74-86.

[65] Successive occult movements trace themselves back to the Jewish-Hellenic Gnosticism of this type period among other mixtures of pagan and heretical elements. Aleister Crowley, *Magick in Theory and Practice*, (Independent, 2019), 193, 274-278, 141-147, 156, 196-225, 343-344, 461-474, 494-515, 522-527, 539-547, 559-565, 654-656, 724-732; Albert Mackey, *Mackey's Revised Encyclopedia of Freemasonry*, vol. I (Masonic History Company, 1929), 51; vol. II, 772; Paul Foster Case, *The Tarot* (TarcherPerigee, 2006), 161-165; Eliphas Levi, *Transcendental Magic: Its Doctrine and Ritual* (Martino Fine, 2011), 194-195, 379, 398, 404-405.

sects will also be opposed by the rational Jewish party as well as the Church in the Inquisition, since they even attack the orthodox Jewish faith.[66]

Truth and Charity

Even though some of the Jewish leaders sought the crucifixion of Christ and others became voluntarist Jews and persecuted the nascent Church, it is important to remember that this was not the work all of the Jews at the time, and, certainly, the blame for these acts cannot be attributed to Jews today. As Christians, we must always act with charity for all Jews, as St. Paul said, who wanted to suffer hell if it would save their souls (Rom. ix. 1-15).

When we discuss the history of the Jews in their relation to the Church, we must avoid two extremes. On the one hand, an unchristian hatred of Jews has obtained in regions and time periods which has led to violence. These actions betray the Cross of Jesus Christ. It is also false to claim that all Jews are anti-Logos, since there is a rational Jewish party which opposed the voluntarist Jews from the beginning.

On the other hand, the opposite extreme seeks to avoid discussing any wrongdoing done by Jews against the Church at any time, then or now. This view has especially become prominent in the past few decades, where it is impossible to criticize the voluntarist Jews for their efforts to undermine Christendom in the past and present.

When addressing the actions of some of the Jewish leaders in history, we must speak the truth with charity, and, in doing so, we must be careful not impute guilt on Jews as a whole, especially those of later generations, who coalesce into the other two parties. The history of the Jews is complex, and even the three parties we have generalized here cannot describe in detail all the movements of Jews throughout history. But in regards to the Church, we must be aware of the different parties and the way they have affected Christendom. This balance with truth and charity must prevail in efforts to preach the Gospel and save souls.

Petrine Primacy

After the destruction of the Second Temple, the Church was led by the crusading spirit of the martyrs. The great St. Ignatius of Antioch (d. 108) condemned the spirit of the Antichrist with crusading zeal: "I am the wheat

---

[66] MacRae, George W. "The Jewish Background of the Gnostic Sophia Myth." *Novum Testamentum* 12, no. 2 (1970): 86-101. Accessed March 24, 2021. doi:10.2307/1560039; Gilles Quispel. "Valentinus and the Gnostikoi." *Vigiliae Christianae* 50, no. 1 (1996): 1-4. Accessed March 24, 2021.

of God, and let me be ground by the teeth of the wild beasts, that I may be found the pure bread of Christ."⁶⁷

Fundamental to this was that the Church as *the temple of the Holy Spirit* was not founded on the earthly city of Jerusalem, as the Apocalypse shows the true Jerusalem coming down from Heaven. Rather, the Church is *built upon the foundation of the Apostles and prophets, Jesus Christ himself being the chief corner stone* (Eph. ii. 20). St. Peter, universally recognized by the Fathers and the ancient liturgies as the "Prince of the Apostles," was understood to hold authority in every local bishop.⁶⁸ In other words, there was a Petrine authority of every bishop by the fact that he was a bishop. The celebration of the *cultus* with the local bishop (and his vicars the priests) was the *Catholic Church*.⁶⁹

But St. Ignatius was martyred in the city that "presides in charity"— Rome.⁷⁰ The Petrine authority also was passed down in the successors of St. Peter at Rome.⁷¹ Remarkably, the bishop of Rome did not claim primacy based on the fact that his city was the imperial capital—the earthly city— but rather on his *apostolic* origin. At the same time, the Apostolic authority of the other two major cities in the east—Antioch and Alexandria—also were understood to have a local primacy. The point here is to note that the Church's hierarchy was based not on the earthly city but the Apostles as vicars of a Kingdom *not of this world*. The Christians acknowledged the earthly authority of the emperor, but asserted that Jesus was the King of Kings.

Threats to the Powerful

The Christians therefore threatened the *cultus* of the king, coin and kitchen. Child murder was condemned explicitly along with magic, fornication and pederasty as well as "money-loving" in the earliest Christian document after the New Testament.⁷² The *slave-dealer* was ranked with the *fornicator* and *sodomite* (I Tim. i. 10).⁷³ While the *traffic*

---

⁶⁷ St. Ignatius, *Epistle to the Romans*, ch. 4; *Epistle to the Antiochians*, ch. 5.
⁶⁸ Laurent A. Cleenewerck, *His Broken Body* (Euclid University Press, 2013), 80-81; John D. Zizioulas, *Being as Communion* (St. Vladimir's Seminary Press, 1997).
⁶⁹ Clennewerck, *op. cit.*, 59-78; John D. Zizilouas, *Eucharist, Bishop, Church: The Unity of the Church in the Divine Eucharist and the Bishop During the First Three Centuries* (Holy Cross Orthodox Press, 2007).
⁷⁰ Epistle to the Romans, Salutation.
⁷¹ Adrian Fortescue, *The Early Papacy* (San Francisco, CA: Ignatius Press, 2008), chs. 4-7; Erick Ybarra, *The Papacy* (forthcoming).
⁷² *Didache*, 2, 3.
⁷³ πόρνοις, ἀρσενοκοίταις, ἀνδραποδισταῖς (I Tim. i. 10). The English renders ἀνδραποδισταῖς as "manstealer."

in human souls (Apoc. xviii. 13) was condemned, the Church converted families and their slaves and transformed this from within. Slave and master participated equally in the *cultus*, which obliterated any distinction of nature based on power, sex or nation (Gal. iii. 28) basing the dignity of man on *logos*, not power.

Then the hierarchy of master and slave was subordinated to *the Lord both of them and you...and there is no respect of persons with him* (Eph. vi. 5). This approach reconciled master and slave to each other as brothers (Philem. 6). St. Paul, who called himself the *slave of Christ* (Rom. i. 1) returns an escaped slave, Onesimus, and reconciles both parties within the slave hierarchy. Both became saints and Onesimus was consecrated bishop of Ephesus after Timothy. By this means the Church gradually abolished domestic slavery by a transformation of the economy through the *cultus*.[74] Moreover, the Christians more than anyone else cared for the poor and destitute, the widow and orphan. The pagan philosophers could recognize this virtue, yet they lacked the divine grace to overcome their Original Sin to make these ideals reality. The saints did.

Meanwhile the Kingdom was spreading east converting the Arab King Agbar VIII of Osrhoene in the third century AD, who may have been the first to mint crosses on his coins.[75] This is the origin of the Church of Edessa (modern southeast Turkey), the mother of St. Ephraim the Syrian.[76] To the south, under the Persian "King of Kings," Syriac Christians were martyred and venerated by the Roman Christians as well.

Continuing Pentecost, the New Testament was being translated into Latin, Syriac, Coptic, Old Nubian, Arabic and Ethiopic, and later Georgian and Armenian, with liturgical rites in many of these tongues.[77] At the same time we see traces in the historical record of the veneration of the Queen of Heaven in the early Coptic and Syriac witness to the prayer *Sub Tuum Praesidium*.

---

[74] Cahill, *Framework of a Christian State*, 11-12, 21-22; Belloc, *The Servile State*, 31-40.
[75] W.G. Sayles, *Roman Provincial Coins* (Krause Publications, 1998), 61.
[76] Dawson, *The Making of Europe*, 119; *The Formation of Christendom*, 123.
[77] Stephen Emmel, "Coptic Literature in the Byzantine and early Muhammadan World," *Egypt in the Byzantine World, 300-700*, (Cambridge, 2007), 83.

The Moderate and the Strict Concerning Hellenism

Meanwhile, the upper classes of Roman aristocracy were becoming fully fluent in Latin and Greek bringing an integrated Greco-Roman culture into their conversions to the Church.[78] As the faith was spreading, new questions were arising among our fathers regarding Mosaic Christian culture and its relation to the Greco-Roman peoples.[79]

A strict party held that *nothing* of Greco-Roman culture ("Hellenism") should be adopted by the Church. The prominent strict party was the Antiochian school, led by St. Theophilos (d. 185) with greater traditional Jewish influence.[80] They adhered to a more literal reading of the Holy Scripture, which was reflected in their theology thus focused on a greater practical, immediate philosophy. This led them to emphasize distinctions first to express ideas about theology.

The moderate party held that something of Greco-Roman culture could be used by the Church for the faith. This position was held notably St. Justin Martyr (d. 165) who found the logos of Greek philosophy to correspond to the Logos Incarnate.[81] The moderate school rose to prominence with Origen (d. 235) in Alexandria, with greater influence of Hellenized Jews following Philo (d. 50 AD). Their reading of Scripture was more mystical and Platonic, emphasizing the unity of ideas in expression. These two schools of Antioch and Alexandria will have a major role to play in what comes next as the Gospel is spread over all peoples.

The Persecution Continues

But in the Persian and Roman Empires:

> Ordinary men, always terrified by the potential consequences of thinking, and fearful lest satisfaction of their customary pointless or lewd appetites and entertainments by an exhortation to avoid sin and strive

---

[78] Stearn, *The Encyclopedia of World History*, 88.
[79] Dawson, *The Formation of Christendom*, 111-125.
[80] Veselin Kesich, *The Birth of the Church* (St. Vladimir's Seminary Press, 2007), 160; M. C. Steenberg, "The Two 'Schools' of Alexandria and Antioch: Categories, Classification, and Converging Christological Visions,"
<http: //www.monachos.net/patristics/christology/two_schools.shtml>. Accessed October 2nd, 2012. See also Kenneth F. Yossa, *Common Heritage, Divided Communion: The Decline and Advances of Inter-Orthodox Relations from Chalcedon to Chambésy* (Georgia Press: 2009), 23ff.
[81] Dawson, *op. cit.*, 118.

> for higher rewards, stormed the recruitment centers of
> the Grand Coalition of the Status Quo.[82]

These parties who fought each other—Jew, pagan, or heretic—all united into "frenzied mobs" and "anti-Christian riots," or else instigated official state persecutions against Christians under Nero (64-68), to Domition (81-96), Trajan (112-117), Marcus Aurelius (161-180), Septimus Severus (202-210), Decius (250-251), Valerian (257-259), Maximinus (235-238), Aurelian (270-275), Diocletian and Galerius (303-324) besides the Persian empire.[83]

Just as the bloodshed continued, the voluntarism of heresy sought to dethrone Christ. St. Newman notes how the voluntarist Jews united with the heretics in their "tendency to derogate from the honour due to Christ."[84] But our fathers fought against the rage of the earthly city, and "a great many soldiers of Christ's kingdom," says Eusebius, "without hesitation, instantly preferred the confession of him to the seeming glory and prosperity that they were enjoying."[85] They chose the Sign of the Cross over the mark of the beast.

But as time went on, it seemed to many that the hope of deliverance contained in the Book of Revelation was left unfulfilled. Many Christians were martyred, but many others apostatized. The cultural momentum in the public order inclined toward *Roma* and its gods, not Christ, making the little children always vulnerable to the allurements of money and idols. As the Church approached the fourth century, yet another a new and more terrible persecution was whipped up by the emperors. The Church lifted her weary head as her fighting spirit was exhausted to see the soldiers bearing down on her once more.

Yet "now indeed, when the hope of most of us was almost extinct... God, the defender of his own Church, exhibited his heavenly interposition in our behalf."[86] As the mustard seed had grown over several generations and Christian culture passed down in families, the time was now fulfilled for the Holy Cross to be exalted.

---

[82] Rao, *Black Legends*, 53-55.
[83] Marshall, *The Eternal City*, 171-172.
[84] St. John Henry Newman, *Arians of the Fourth Century*, (Longmans, Green and Co. 1908), 18.
[85] Eusebius, *Church History*, bk. VIII, ch. 4.
[86] Ibid., bk. VIII, ch. 7

IX

KING OF KINGS

In the year 297 AD, Rome was at war with Persia again. A Roman officer named Constantine was fighting in this struggle with the Persian "king of kings" over control of Armenia. At the same time another war was being fought over Armenia, this time by St. Gregory the Illuminator:

> When they had all been convinced to worship the only true God, Gregory and [King] Tiridates began traveling to other parts of the country to instruct the people and to destroy the altars of the false gods. In many of the provincial towns, demons in the form of armed soldiers fought against the evangelist's efforts. They were put to flight each time, and then Gregory would tell the people not to be afraid, but to drive out their own personal demons of false worship, and follow Christ. He performed miracles to show the people how loving and powerful God is. And the king gave testimony about his sinful acts, and the miracles and mercy of healing which God had shown him. So they traveled through the provinces and everywhere they spread the light of the Gospel and destroyed the dark pagan superstitions which had held the people captive.[1]

The time had come to overthrow the public thrones of the devils. *No man can enter into the house of a strong man and rob him of his goods, unless he first bind the strong man, and then shall he plunder his house*

---

[1] Agathangelos, *History of St. Gregory and the Conversion of Armenia*, bk. III, trans. anonymous <https://www.livius.org/sources/content/agathangelos/agathangelos-history-3/>, accessed March 23, 2021.

(Mk. iii. 27). The demonic power had been destroyed by the Resurrection of Christ, and the demons were usurpers over souls and society. The rightful King cannot take his throne unless he destroys the power of the usurper. This had happened before as seen in Scripture: *And all the people of the land went into the temple of Baal, and broke down his altars, and his images they broke in pieces thoroughly* (IV Kngs xi. 18). *He hath put down the mighty from their seat, and hath exalted the humble* (Lk. i. 52). This is why His Majesty used violence in the Temple—His throne had been polluted by the demonic idols of avarice. But with the proclamation of the Gospel to the peoples, the crusading spirit of St. Gregory now shows itself in a public act of violence to dethrone the demonic power. And this is the pattern followed by every saint.

This violence is necessary to show the people that the demons have no power, since the people feared the demons, being bound under the dominion of death. It is an act of cultural momentum to turn everyone to repentance and accept the Good News of liberation from malicious devils. When the saint fearlessly destroys the idols and the demons are powerless to kill him because of the Sign of the Cross, the people can breathe a sigh of relief and place their faith in the King of Kings, and no longer fear the demonic usurpers.

The saint then preaches the Logos and if necessary, works further miracles by the Holy Spirit in order to freely invite the souls of men to be baptized. Those who use their reason can recognize that the demons are powerless and these are miraculous proofs—they receive their King, accept Him and are baptized. Those who are attached to their voluntarist sin choose against reason and seek out their filthy lucre, resisting the Gospel.[2]

Notice the distinction however: in the public order—the king and the coin—where the demons are usurping the throne for all to see, the saint violently attacks them and destroys their false throne. But in the private order—the depths of the human heart and his family—there is no forced Baptism, since the Gospel must be accepted freely. Thus the public order is ruled by one of two forces: Christ the King or Satan the usurper. Therefore a purified, spiritual violence is necessary, detached from any earthly allurement. *The kingdom of heaven suffereth violence, and the violent bear it away* (Mt. xi. 12).

Once the public order is liberated from Satan, the human soul is freed from the fear of death so that they can be raised up from earthly attachments to the heavenly Kingdom. Thus they can be truly *free*—that is, free from Satan's coercion by means of the fear of death—to let go of the earthly city

---

[2] On the phrase "filthy lucre" see I Tim iii. 8; Titus i. 7, 11; I Pet. v. 2.

and accept the Kingdom of Heaven and be baptized for the hope of eternal life. This provides the cultural momentum in the public order to protect the little children and the faithful from the inclinations of Original Sin.

Baptism of the Society

The whole society and people is then baptized in the public order: some things are eradicated, some things stay the same, and some things are transformed. This is how Jesus King of Kings becomes "incarnate" in a people, as it is were. He unites the uncreated Logos with the created logos that the pre-Christian people has passed down from Adam.[3] The people's ancient culture passed down but corrupted is purified of all demonic customs—every token of the usurper which can still enslave the people—is pulled up from the roots. The saint has the spiritual knowledge to discern which things are from logos and which things are not.

Then the two swords are drawn over the public order to cut a covenant—the spiritual sword of the priest and the temporal sword of the king—both must sanction the public order. This is the fundamental inclination of natural law as the history of all peoples shows abundantly. *And Joiada [the priest] made a covenant between the Lord, and the king, and the people, that they should be the people of the Lord, and between the king and the people* (IV Kngs xi. 17).

This covenant is then ratified by the building of a church over the former idolatrous shrine. This is the thing that is chiefly transformed—the prior "sacred" site, which paid allegiance to the usurper, becomes the earthly throne of the King of Heaven, literally crushing the usurper's throne.

The *cultus* is celebrated publicly, which ratifies the covenant. Again we see this public covenant by *cultus* is seen in Scripture: *And he commanded all the people, saying: Keep the passover to the Lord your God, according as it is written in the book of this covenant* (IV Kngs xxiii. 21). Thus St. Gregory raised in Armenia what is said to be the oldest cathedral in the world: Etchmiadzin Cathedral. This is the new throne of Christ on earth. For at the altar, soul and sacrament become one, flowing to society.

In the case of Armenia and every kingdom converted since, the public order must be defined by the Logos Incarnate and not voluntarism. Only

---

[3] This is a spiritual analogy which applies the dogma of the Incarnation to the act of conversion. Jesus Christ was Incarnate of the Virgin Mary once and for all but *spiritually, not physically*, this act is repeated in every Christian people.

then can the king and coin come into order to truly serve the family and the salvation of souls.

Rome

While all this was happening in Armenia, the final attacks of Satan were poured out through Diocletian and his successors, who, says Eusebius, are punished by God with plague, famine and war.[4] Constantine was roused by God to punish the evildoers and received the vision *In Hoc Signo Vinces* "In This Sign Conquer." In this God showed a pagan emperor that the only power is in the Cross, not in force of arms. *Thou comest to me with a sword, and with a spear, and with a shield: but I come to thee in the name of the Lord of hosts, the God of the armies of Israel, which thou hast defied* (I Kngs. xvii. 45). With the banner of the Cross, Constantine's army rallied the crusading spirit to crush to usurpers.

In 313 the Edict of Milan ended Christian persecution in the Roman Empire.[5] Then the victorious Church already manifested in Armenia continued for Rome. With his mother St. Helena, Constantine rebuilt the great city of Jerusalem and "cast down the idols and the temples which were found there" so that "Jerusalem which had presented a horrible mass of ruins was then adorned with most numerous and magnificent churches."[6] By a miracle of healing, the True Cross was found and raised up as the new sign of power against the usurpers at the Church of the Holy Sepulcher in Jerusalem.

The public funding of churches is the manifestation of the King of Kings over the public order: the pagan Roman emperors had built the *royal stoa* ("basilica") for the glory of their names. Constantine built the basilicas of Old St. Peter's, St. Paul's Outside the Walls, and St. John Lateran for the glory of His Holy Name. "The splendor of political dominion over the world was united to the transfigured splendor of holy Rome."[7] Meanwhile, he built a new city on the Bosphorus as a Christian city, New Rome, and built the church of *Hagia Eirene* "Holy Peace." But coins were already being minted exalting the city in his name.[8]

---

[4] Eusebius, *Church History*, bk. IX, ch. 8.
[5] Socrates Scholasticus, *Church History*, bk. I, ch. 2; Sozomen, *Church History*, bk. II, ch. 3.
[6] Sulpitius Severus, *Sacred History*, bk. II, ch. 33.
[7] Dietrich von Hildebrand, *Aesthetics*, vol. II, 76.
[8] Richard Abdy "Tetrachy and the House of Constantine," William E. Metcalf ed. *The Oxford Handbook of Greek and Roman Coinage* (Oxford University Press: 2012) 595.

All Nations

And while Constantine and Tiridates were building churches to the King of Kings, St. Frumentius was converting King Ezana of Ethiopia. This kingdom too embraced the true King and converted the public order to His rule.[9] Together they ratified a Christian people with the building of St. Mary of Zion, trampling on the old throne of Satan.[10]

In neighboring Georgia, the devout woman St. Nino was taken captive by the Iberians (Georgians) around 327. Through the providence of God she healed the king's wife and they were miraculously converted and spread the Gospel. And "the king having ascertained from his prisoner the plan on which churches were constructed among the Romans, ordered a church to be built, and immediately provided all things necessary for its erection; and the edifice was accordingly commenced."[11] And, thus, the historic Svetitskhoveli Cathedral was built.

Within a few generations of this, a young boy from Roman Britain named Patricius became a victim of the Celtic slave raiders of Ireland. St. Patrick understood his captivity as a punishment from God for his own faithlessness.[12] Through God's intervention, he was converted and escaped back to Britain.[13] Here he received a vision from God to leave Roman Britain and bear "many persecutions, even chains, so that [he] could give up [his] freeborn state for the sake of others."[14]

Patrick lamented the slavery of the Irish to demons: "Never before did they know of God except to serve idols and unclean things."[15] They are "fellow-citizens of demons, because of their evil works. By their hostile ways they live in death."[16] They were under the dominion of shamans using music to commune with demons. But as Patrick returned to the island they prophesied "by their magical art," the coming of "a kingdom" that would

---

[9] Socrates, *Church History*, bk. I, ch. 19; Fr. John Meyendorff, *Imperial Unity and Christian Division* (St. Vladimir's Seminary Press, 2011), 118.
[10] "Sacred Sites of Ethiopia and the Arc of the Covenant," *World Pilgrimage Guide* https://sacredsites.com/africa/ethiopia/sacred_sites_ethiopia.html. Accessed February 3, 2021.
[11] Socrates, *op. cit.*, bk. I, ch. 20.
[12] St. Patrick, *Confessions*, 1, trans. McCarthy <https://www.confessio.ie/etexts/confessio_english#>, accessed March 23, 2021.
[13] Ibid., 17.
[14] Ibid., 23, 37.
[15] Ibid., 41.
[16] Ibid., *Letter to the Soldier of Coroticus*, 2, trans. McCarthy <https://www.confessio.ie/etexts/epistola_english#01>, accessed March 23, 2021.

"destroy all their gods, banish all the works of their craft, and reign for ever."[17] The pagan *cultus* (their "greatest feast day") coincided that year with the Easter celebration that forbade the lighting of fires in their superstition.[18]

When St. Patrick lit the Easter Fire in defiance of the usurping demons, the shaman druids cried out in fear to the pagan king that "the kingdom that has been brought upon by him will overpower us all and you, and will seduce all the people of your kingdom, and all kingdoms will yield to it, and it will spread over the whole country and will reign in all eternity."[19] The King then proceeded with his chariots and horseback to challenge Patrick, but he met them while uttering the verse *some trust in chariots and some in horses, but we will call upon the name of the Lord our God* (Ps. xix. 8). One of the druids blasphemed God openly to Patrick, against whom Patrick immediately pronounced a curse as St. Peter did and he died.[20]

At this the king roused his men to kill St. Patrick but he called upon God Who sent darkness and an earthquake while the pagans were thrown into chaos and started to kill one another. Then a showdown of miracles happened between the chief druid and Patrick. The druid, "through the invocation of demons," performed miracles of bringing snow and fog.[21] When Patrick commanded him to remove these, the druid could not.

> "You can do evil and cannot do good. Not so I." Then he blessed the plain all around, and in no time, without rain or mist or wind, the snow vanished, and the crowds cheered and were greatly astonished and touched in their hearts.[22]

The druid finally tested Patrick by an ordeal of fire, and the druid was killed. As the "wrath of God" began to fall upon the pagans, the king then converted with "many others" and "preached everywhere" working miracles.[23] He "destroyed the idol at Leitrim the idol, Crom Cruach," and continued on throughout the whole island:

---

[17] Muirchú, *Life of Holy Patrick the Confessor*, I.10, trans. L. Bieler <https://www.confessio.ie/more/muirchu_english#>, accessed March 23, 2021.
[18] Ibid., I.19, 1.
[19] Ibid., I.15, 6.
[20] Ibid., 1.17 5-6.
[21] Ibid., I.20.
[22] Ibid., I.20.
[23] Ibid., I. 21, 22.

Entering into a pagan territory he first preached to the chief men, knowing that when they were converted the people would follow. Wonderful indeed was his labour, and wonderful its results. He preached in almost every district in Ireland, confounded in argument the druids and won the people from their side; he built, it is said, 365 churches and consecrated an equal number of bishops, established schools and convents, and held synods; and when he died the whole machinery of a powerful Church was in operation, fully equal to the task of confirming in the faith those already converted and of bringing those yet in darkness into the Christian fold.[24]

He established a native clergy from the chieftains and by the 600s, paganism "had all but disappeared."[25] After learning Latin the Irish Church developed a written script for their native tongue in Gaelic and began to send missionaries to Europe. St. Patrick would be known in Irish as *Pádraig*.

Thus by the preaching of the Logos and the working of the Holy Spirit, Ireland was converted to the Faith and began to offer *cultus* to the true King. The public order would henceforth receive the cultural momentum not from the voluntarist demons, but from the Logos Incarnate. Thus from the eastern border kingdoms of the Roman Empire, Georgia and Armenia, to the southern extremities in Ethiopia, and the northwest in Ireland, the saints understood that the public *cultus* of demons must be overthrown, and the throne of the King of Kings raised in its place.

The Public *Cultus*

St. Thomas says of the *cultus* that "at all times and among all nations there has always been the offering of sacrifices... and consequently the offering of sacrifice is of the natural law."[26] Every people has offered *cultus* to the divine in a public act of the ruling government because this is the dictate of natural reason. The people received therefrom their principle of moral order.

Before the Gospel peoples offered *cultus* to false gods and fell into bondage to voluntarism, as the demons enslaved them to the "freedom" of

---

[24] E. D'Alton, "Ireland," *The Catholic Encyclopedia* (1910) <www.newadvent.org/cathen/08098b.htm>, accessed September 28, 2021.
[25] Ibid.
[26] *Summa*, II-II q85 a1.

their own will from logos. But the universal teaching of the saints was to transfer this public *cultus* from the false gods to the true God. This was due to the fundamental truth that human nature was wounded by Original Sin. Therefore divine grace was necessary for the public order, and hence the public *cultus*. Without this public supplication for divine grace, man, being ordered by natural reason to worship, would fall once again to the bondage to demons. The public *cultus* was the declaration of freedom from demonic occupation.

Just as it had been for the family in the private order, the public *cultus* would become the fundamental root of Christian culture everywhere, which began to form Christian peoples, the symbolic act of which was the king and bishop building a church on the ruins of pagan temples. This bond between bishop and king thus became the bond between soul and body of a people. The bishop publicly celebrated the *cultus*, from which came the soul of the people in the principle of moral order. The king, representing the body of the people, received direction from the *cultus* and then ordered the government, economy and families accordingly.

In the public order, the rights of God must be maintained and the king, coin and kitchen must be submitted to the King of Kings. In the private order, the rights of man must be maintained and no one should be forced to be baptized. The danger is that the rights of man could supplant the rights of God in the public order.

But while this conversion of faith was an event of Baptism, the conversion of morals would take centuries. For just as before, the powerful would not accept this new rule of logos without a fight. The enemies of the Church were ever at work seeking to undermine Christ's Kingdom ruled from the hearts of men. At this same time the Persian "king of kings," Shapur II (309-379) was provoked to "extreme cruelty," embarking on a campaign against every soul who said Christ was King of Kings.[27] Wigram suggests this was urged on by the enemies of Christ among the Jews, heretics and pagans, eventually killing, says Sozomen, 16,000 Christians and others "beyond enumeration."[28] Between 337-361 he would also make war on Rome from without. The Church's enemies sought to destroy the Kingdom in the Persian Empire with the old methods, but in the Roman Empire some new tactic had to be found. For "the devil, seeing the temples of the demons deserted, and the human race running to the name of the liberating Mediator...moved the heretics under the Christian name to resist

---

[27] Sozomen, *Church History*, bk. II, ch. 14.
[28] Ibid.; W. A. Wigram, *An Introduction to the History of the Assyrian Church* (London: Society for Promoting Christian Knowledge, 1911), 62.

the Christian doctrine."[29] This would necessitate a union between the moderate and strict parties to face a new danger.

---

[29] Augustine, *City of God*, bk. XVIII, ch 51.

PART II

THE REIGN OF CHRISTENDOM

AD 301-1773

X

NICAEA AND THE GREEN MARTYRS

In 315 AD, in the imperial capital of Rome, the slaves heaved the last of the stone into place. Constantine was hailed as "liberator" with the largest triumph arch known to Roman history, which was built next to the thirty-feet-tall statue of himself "as the new Jupiter" in the forum of Maxentius.[1] His minted medal included the Christian *chi-rho* as well as the goddess Victoria.[2]

For one of the "four living faces" on the Arch of Augustus at Ariminum was *Roma*, the divine personification of the Roman Empire. Constantine's arch used similar imagery, incorporating the work of at least three pagan emperors' previous work into his own arch. *Roma* divinized the empire, solidifying the emperor as the sacred high priest, *pontifex maximus*, continuing the religious veneration of the office into the Christian period.[3] Thus Constantine called himself a "bishop" and immediately began acting out his high priesthood by imposing his will regarding the schismatic Donatist controversy in the west.[4]

Meanwhile, the bishops were shifting the debate about Hellenism from *if* it could be used in the Church to *how*.[5] Our Lord "paid honor to the logos of history by waiting until the logos of metaphysics was in place because without that quintessentially Greek vocabulary no one could understand,

---

[1] Michael Siebler, *Roman Art* (Taschen, 2007), 88.
[2] Ibid., 86.
[3] Alan Cameron, "The Imperial Pontifex," *Harvard Studies in Classical Philology* 103 (2007): 341-84.
[4] Cameron, *op. cit.*, 351, 360
[5] Jaroslav Pelikan, *The Christian Tradition: A History of the Development of Doctrine*, (Chicago: University of Chicago Press, 1971), vol. I, 41-55.

much less explain, who He was."[6] But the strict school of Antioch still showed a marked difference to Alexandria.

The Antiochians' strict approach was reflecting Aristotle, while Alexandria continued to favor the mystical reading, reflecting Plato.[7] Antiochians highlighted the distinction between Logos and humanity in Christ as well as between the Persons of the Trinity, while Alexandria emphasized the unity of logos and flesh in Christ and the *one* united essence (*ousia*) of the Trinity. Their greatest exponent at this time would be St. Athanasius (d. 373).

These prominent schools could balance each other, for God "sees the similarities and diversities which can contribute to the beauty of the whole."[8] Therefore in His Providence, "just as God permits evil to bring about a greater good, He permits error to bring about a greater understanding of the truth."[9]

Dethroning the King of Kings

The fallen angels, while shedding the blood of martyrs in Persia, had to find some way to empty Christ of all authority over Roman society, so that the enemies of Christ could maintain their voluntarist power.[10]

> The fundamental truth and distinctive idea of Christianity is the perfect union of the divine and the human individually achieved in Christ, and finding its social realization in Christian humanity, in which the divine is represented by the Church, centered in the supreme pontiff, and the human by the State. This intimate relation between Church and State implies the primacy of the former, since the divine is previous in time and superior in being to the human.

---

[6] Jones, *Logos Rising*, 192.
[7] M. C. Steenberg, "The Two 'Schools' of Alexandria and Antioch: Categories, Classification, and Converging Christological Visions," <http://www.monachos.net/patristics/christology/two_schools.shtml>, accessed October 2nd, 2012. Kenneth F. Yossa, *Common Heritage, Divided Communion: The Decline and Advances of Inter-Orthodox Relations from Chalcedon to Chambésy* (Georgia Press: 2009), 23ff.
[8] Augustine, *City of God*, bk. XVI, ch. 8.
[9] Jones, *op. cit.*, 357.
[10] Rao, *Black Legends*, 56ff.

> Heresy attacked the perfect unity of the divine and the human in Jesus Christ precisely in order to undermine the living bond between Church and State, and to confer upon the latter an absolute independence. Hence it is clear why the emperors of the Second Rome [Constantinople], intent on maintaining within Christendom the absolutism of the pagan State, were so partial to all the heresies, which were but manifold variations on a single theme:
>
> Jesus Christ is not the true Son of God, consubstantial with the Father; God has not become incarnate; nature and mankind remain cut off from divinity, and are not united to it; and consequently the human State may rightly keep its independence and supremacy intact. Constantius and Valens had indeed good reason to support Arianism."[11]

Arianism was the means by which the authority of the King of Kings could be emptied so that the Roman Emperor could remain the *de facto* "son of god." If Christ was not fully divine, then the authority of the Church over the king, coin and kitchen were null and void. Arianism "allowed a continued space for other gods of nature, divinized secular customs, and sacred pagan kingship to flourish."[12] *Roma* could still divinize the empire and the emperor could retain his priesthood, rationalizing his pagan morals. Even Constantine was credibly accused of five different murders, including his wife and son.[13] Arius wrote his heresy to the tune of popular songs to "better disseminate his opinions among the illiterate."[14] Bewitching melodies created an emotional attachment to the music, even though one might not know what the words meant, therefore putting the will above the intellect—this was a form of shamanism which bewitched the masses and those in power spread the heresy to maintain their power.

---

[11] Soloviev, *Russia and the Universal Church*, 14-15.
[12] Rao, *op. cit.*, 70.
[13] Posnov, *The History of the Christian Church*, 206.
[14] Alvan Lamson, *The Church of the First Three Centuries* (London: British and Foreign Unitarian Association, 1875), 320.

The First Imperial Council

To his credit, Constantine did not support the heresy, but seemed to think he could maintain his priesthood without it. He organized the Council of Nicaea in 325 where the bishops adopted the Alexandrian term (*homoousion*) to express the unity of the Son with the Father.[15] They thought this would be sufficient to bind the Church as the Council of Jerusalem had done. St. Gregory the Illuminator's son, St. Aristacius was in attendance, including bishops from Arabia.[16] The Syriac Christians were cut off from communication and could not participate.[17]

This new "ecumenical council" was the melding of the Latin mind of administration with the Greek mind of truth. "Christianity appeared as the union and intimate reconciliation of the spiritual cultures of east and west."[18] It was extending the universal institution of Apostolic authority begun at the Council of Jerusalem.

But the strict Antiochians objected to the Alexandrian term *homoousion* while the Alexandrians supported it as moderates. At the same time, Constantine viewed the council as an exercise of his priesthood, threatening to depose St. Athanasius himself if he failed to implement it according to the imperial will.[19] This came into conflict with the Petrine primacy of the pope and bishops who insisted that their priesthood was the arbiter of the dispute. An uneasy peace continued until Constantine's death in 337, when he was not divinized but canonized with imagery from the imperial cult.[20]

There commenced "a long and bitter struggle" for the acceptance of Nicaea's Alexandrian terms.[21] Shapur II attacked Christian Rome from 337-361, while maintaining the persecution of Christians in Persia. At this

---

[15] Heinrich Denzinger, *Compendium of Creeds, Definitions, and Declarations on Matters of Faith and Morals*, edited by Robert Fastiggi, 43rd ed. (San Francisco, CA: Ignatius Press, 2010), no. 125-130.

[16] Syriac Ms. No. 14528 AD 501 and Codex Syriacus 38 contained in B. H. Cowper, ed., *Syriac Miscellanies* (Williams and Norgate: 1861), 8-13.

[17] Wigram, *An Introduction to the History of the Assyrian Church*, 58.

[18] Soloviev, *Veliki spor i khristianskaya politika* in Soloviev and Radlov, *Sobranie sochinenii*, IV, p. 172 cited in Aidan Nichols, *Sophiology Man: The Work of Vladimir Solov'ev* (Herefordshire, UK: Gracewing, 2020), 70.

[19] Athanasius, *Contra Arians*, C LIX *in* Posnov, *op. cit.*, 213.

[20] William Van Andringa, "Rhetoric and Divine Honours: On the 'Imperial Cult' in the Reigns of Augustus and Constantine," Maijastina Kahlos, ed., *Studies across Disciplines in the Humanities and Social Sciences 20* (Helsinki: Helsinki Collegium for Advanced Studies, undated), 18.

[21] J. M. Carmody, "Homoousios" *New Catholic Encyclopedia* (2003), vol. 7, 65.

time the chief Persian bishop, St. Simeon Barsabae, achieved the glorious crown. Meanwhile the Arian Emperor Constantius II fought for heresy in order to impose his will on reality.

The heretics divided into three main parties to use some other term to deny the Kingship of Christ—radical Anomoeans, Homoeousians, and the "devious Homoeans."[22] Each party was defined by its chosen term against *homoousion*. They showed "Satan's success in deceiving the human intellect by obscuring and perverting the meaning of words."[23] These all sought the imperial power to impose their view through violence, melding with the pagan elements of voluntarism.

Joining with the heretics, some Jewish leaders supported Arianism, says Newman, "evincing thereby, not indeed any definite interest in the subject of dispute, but a sort of spontaneous feeling, that the side of heresy was their natural position...that its spirit, and the character which it created, were congenial to their own."[24] Between the Jews, the various heretical parties and the pagan influences in Rome, they united with one principle of negation—anything but Christ the King.

On the other hand were the orthodox, surrounded on all sides within and without the Empire. But they were also divided into the Nicaea party, led by the Alexandrian St. Athanasius, and the orthodox Antiochian party. These were the men arising from Christian families to do battle with the world's empires. It would be up to them to unite against the enemies of Christ.

The pope sought to lead the Church to unity through the Petrine office, but almost the entire eastern episcopate followed the sacred priesthood of the emperor. All except St. Athanasius, however, who had a secret weapon: the green martyrs. They renounced the earthly city and claimed citizenship in the world to come. This new form of martyrdom anchored the Church in the City of God when the worldlines of *Roma* threatened to overwhelm her.

St. Athanasius wrote the first popular Christian book about St. Anthony who led an army of monks to join the angels in the desert against the demons. The story of his life vividly showed that this conflict was with angels and men, and the monks were on the front lines. Anthony was violently beaten by the demons nearly to death, but he returned to face them:

> And he could not stand up on account of the blows, but he prayed as he lay. And after he had prayed, he said with a shout, "Here am I, Anthony; I flee not from your

---

[22] Ibid.
[23] Don Felix Sarda y Salvany, *Liberalism is a Sin*, trans. Condé B. Pallen (Charlotte NC: TAN, 2012), 55.
[24] Newman, *Arians of the Fourth Century*, 23.

stripes, for even if you inflict more nothing shall separate me from the love of Christ." And then he sang, "though a camp be set against me, my heart shall not be afraid."[25]

The creation of green martyrdom continued the masculine ideal of martyrdom, renouncing the pleasures of this life and embracing the Cross. The fallen angels swarmed the empire seeking to empty Christ of His Kingship, but St. Anthony and the monks took the crusading spirit against them.

At first, the enemies of the Church had the upper hand as Shapur II was massacring Syriac Christians, and Constantius II managed to subdue the western resistance and depose all bishops in the east who confessed Nicaea. Every heretical party "held a council dominated by its leaders, and each had its hour of triumph."[26] Athanasius was deposed five times and spent seventeen years in exile.[27]

In 358, an Arian council was held near the arch of Augustus at Ariminum, and even Pope Liberius was ambiguous on orthodoxy and excommunicated Athanasius.[28] St. Jerome lamented: "The whole world groaned and found itself Arian."[29] Constantius was "the true founder of the state church in the eastern empire," and he imposed Arianism through his court bishops.[30] He built the first *Hagia Sophia* ("Holy Wisdom") as an Arian church at Constantinople as the new triumph arch—all would have known the reference to "wisdom," the favorite Arian prooftext from the Book of Proverbs.[31]

But "this apparent triumph caused the downfall of the anti-Nicene coalition: united in the battle against Athanasius and the faith of Nicaea, they fell out with each other when trying to impose a definitive substitute for the *Nicaenum*."[32] Since they were based on the negation of Christ and the contest of power, when they gained the upper hand, they erupted in civil war.

---

[25] Athanasius, *Life of St. Anthony*, 9.
[26] V. C. de Clercq, "Arianism" *New Catholic Encyclopedia*, (2003), vol. 1, 663.
[27] Posnov, *op. cit.*, 294.
[28] Charles Coulombe, *Vicars of Christ* (Arcadia: Tumblar House, 2014), 51-53.
[29] St. Jerome, *Dialogue Against the Luciferians*.
[30] Dawson, *Making of Europe*, 109.
[31] Prov. viii. 22-31. See Pelikan, *op. cit.* vol. I, 191-97. Barbara Newman, *God and the Goddesses*.
Vision, Poetry, and Belief in the Middle Ages (University of Pennsylvania Press, 2005), 195.
[32] De Clercq, *op. cit.*

NICAEA AND THE GREEN MARTYRS

The Mustard Seed Conquers

As the factionalism and bloodshed increased between the different parties, a new emperor came to power who would punish the Church for its failures. This was Julian the Apostate (361-363) who instigated a new persecution of Christians. He could not have done this had not the mass of Roman officials quickly switched their allegiance from Christ the King to Caesar as "son of god," showing the depth of their sincerity. Julian initiated himself into the occult and allied with the Jewish leaders to rebuild the Jewish Temple, but God sent fire to destroy the construction as even pagan authors admit.[33] Nevertheless the Jerusalem Talmud was codified at this time, attempting to respond to the challenge of Christianity.[34]

Julian, thinking like the enemies of Christ, "invited to his palace the leaders of the hostile sects, that he might enjoy the agreeable spectacle of their furious encounters."[35] "But," says Newman, "in indulging such anticipations of overthrowing Christianity, he but displayed his own ignorance of the foundation on which it was built."[36] St. Hilary saw that there were many orthodox who used the wrong terms without knowing it.[37] St. Cyril of Jerusalem did not use *homoousion* due to its association with Sabellian heresy, which denied the separate Persons of the Trinity.[38]

Seizing the opportunity, Athanasius was able to hold a council in 362 with all orthodox critics of Nicaea's Alexandrian terms.[39] "We discuss the matter with them as brothers with brothers, who mean what we mean, and dispute only about the word"[40] In this way he won over all orthodox parties to the formula of Nicaea, unifying the moderate and strict by means of the Petrine primacy of bishops, not the emperor.[41] "They desired peace," says Newman "as soon as the interests of truth were secured; and their magnanimous decision was forthwith adopted by Councils at Rome, in Spain, Gaul and Achaia."[42] This was nothing less than the work of the Holy

---

[33] Ammianus Marcellus, cited in Stanley L. Jaki, *To Rebuild or Not to Try?* (Royal Oak, MI: Real View Books, 1999), 8; cf. E. Michael Jones, *The Jewish Revolutionary Spirit* (South Bend, IN: Fidelity Press, 2015), 73-76.
[34] Jacob Neusner, *Introduction to Rabbinic Literature* (New York: Doubleday, 1994), xxii.
[35] Newman quoting Gibbon, *Arians of the Fourth Century*, 354.
[36] Ibid., 354.
[37] Ibid., 358.
[38] Athanasius, *De Syn.* 41 cited in Carmody, *op. cit.*
[39] Newman, 359.
[40] St. Athanasius, *De Synodis*, 41.
[41] Newman, *op. cit.*, 369, 372. Pelikan, *op. cit.*, 210.
[42] Newman, 359-360.

Spirit. It was the best of Greek culture—the *dialogos* of subordinating parties to the truth—with the Latin mind of order and administration.

In Athanasius, by truth and charity we see personified the synthesis of moderate and strict, which formed the basis for the first Greco-Roman renewal which was just beginning. The Antiochian school, as the strict party, naturally resisted imposing Greek philosophical terminology from Nicaea onto the mystery of the Trinity. And this was a good instinct, since an excessive speculation about God would destroy faith in the mystery.

But Athanasius from the moderate Alexandrian school was able to win them over through the true *dialogos*, which was ratified with the Latin mind of universal order. The terms of Nicaea were understood as necessary to safeguard the mystery of orthodoxy. Von Hildebrand describes the importance of these rivalries:

> There exists an antithesis that also implies a certain hostile character, an investible struggle of the one against the other, but in a fertile, complementary manner; it is the antithesis that tends to prepare for a high synthesis. This fertile polarity displays itself in history, especially in the history of thought, in the realm of culture, and in the relations between nations.[43]

In Athanasius bringing together these separate parties we see this synthesis beginning, so that the mystery of Christian doctrine is forged in the fires of a fraternal struggle for truth. By means of charity, this was being brought about so that the Logos would shine through the chaos of that period. Thus there was the Logos of truth, but there existed also a logos of charity by which churchmen could struggle with each other to ratify that truth. The schools of strict Antioch and moderate Alexandria were coming together against heresy. This inchoate synthesis was the beginning of the first Greco-Roman renewal, which would occur over the next few centuries.

The opponents of orthodoxy attempted a counterattack of Arianism under Valens (364-378), but the unity of the Church was too much for them. It was a unity in truth, not the hollow slogans of voluntarism from the heretics. The unity for Nicaea formed through the working of charity between the moderates and the strict: St. Hilary worked with St. Basil and Gregory Nyssa and Nazianzus, the latter of whom helped convert Constantinople back to the Faith, and St. Meletius and St. Cyril both

---

[43] Von Hildebrand, *Ethics*, 149.

reconciled to St. Athanasius, supported by pope St. Damasus, and our holy fathers conquered Satan and his allies.[44]

The final destruction of Arianism in the east came under the Spaniard Theodosius I (379-395) At first, he tried to impose the authority of Rome and Alexandria to finish off Arianism, but a new council became necessary to win over all parties.[45] This council finally brought the order of the Latin mind to a universal rule of orthodoxy. It was here that the opponents of orthodoxy were forced to hatch a new plan based on *Roma* and the *pontifex maximus*, ideas which still dominated the emperor.[46] Even he was guilty of excessive brutality in massacring the inhabitants of Thessalonica.

But at the rebuke of St. Ambrose, the emperor "did penance in such a way that the sight of his imperial loftiness prostrated made the people who were interceding for him weep."[47] This event showed that the divine grace of the *cultus* forming the morals of the emperor, causing St. Augustine to describe him as "a true Christian."[48] He enriched the empire with "just and merciful laws," consulted the saints in times of war and forgave his enemies.[49] Along with saints like Ambrose, he opposed the public altars to idols and *Hagia Sophia* was reconstituted to worship Christ as God.

While all this was happening, God had sent more earthquakes to destroy the shrine of Artemis Ephesia in 358 and 368, eroding the power of Satan over men's minds, and increasing the devotion to Our Lady.[50] Now that God had been confirmed as King, His throne had to be adorned.

---

[44] On the Petrine primacy in this period, see Erick Ybarra, *The Papacy* (forthcoming).
[45] Codex Theodosianus, XVI 1, 2 cited in Dawson, *Making of Europe,* 109-110; W. Barry, "Arianism" *The Catholic Encyclopedia* (1907) <https://www.newadvent.org/cathen/01707c.htm>, accessed March 25, 2021.
[46] Posnov, *op. cit.*, 215.
[47] Augustine, *City of God*, bk. V, ch. 26.
[48] Ibid.
[49] Ibid.
[50] Rietveld, *Artemis of the Ephesians*, 333.

XI

THE THRONE OF CHRIST AND THE CRUSADE OF THE HOLY EMPRESS

When Theodosius died in 395, his son Arcadius married Eudoxia, and from that point on, the effeminate Arcadius was dominated by his ambitious wife, who embodied the disordered ideal of Artemis. For his wife's "impetuous caprice was Arcadius's only law" as she was "intoxicated" with a "vain and passionate existence."[1] In 400 AD, she was named Augusta.

But God raised up a mighty crusader in St. John Chrysostom, an Antiochian, who codified the Greek *cultus* that still bears his name.[2] At Ephesus he destroyed the remnants of the temple of Artemis, then turned to face the evil empress.[3] As bishop of the capital, he was the defender of the widow and the orphan and a fearless preacher of the Gospel, condemning the idol of money that Eudoxia worshipped.

She formed a conspiracy against him with his Alexandrian rival bishop Theophilos and the wealthy who hated his sermons, and they deposed and exiled him. But being punished by God immediately, Eudoxia hesitated and brought him back. He was piously greeted by "a vast multitude, with veneration and honor."[4]

---

[1] Ada B. Teetgen, *The Life and Times of Empress Pulcheria* (London: Swan Sonnenschein, 1907), 14.
[2] The Greek rite of St. John Chrysostom is celebrated by all Greek Catholic Churches.
[3] Posnov, *The History of the Christian Church*, 209.
[4] Socrates, *Church History*, bk. VI, ch. 16.

But Eudoxia's domination of her husband was not satisfied even after he named the city of Eudoxioupolis after her, so she had a silver statue of herself erected outside the Hagia Sophia.[5] The mob then gave themselves to "loud and licentious revelry" of pagan morals defying the throne of Christ.[6]

St. John Chrysostom thundered against Eudoxia as "Herodias" and her statue he denounced as "an insult offered to the church."[7] This time they got him deposed again provoking a riot, and a fire burned down the Hagia Sophia.[8] Resisting the wrath of God, they marched the old man into exile. But the forced march brought on a sudden illness and the man of God died with the words, "Glory to God for all things."[9] Chrysostom's glorious crown was the beginning of the crusade for Our Lady's throne. Shortly thereafter Eudoxia died.

Pulcheria's Crusade

A great mass of the pious followed St. John Chrysostom, and one of those women was Eudoxia's own daughter, St. Pulcheria (398-453).[10] Unlike her mother, St. Pulcheria, "patterned her life from a very early age on the model of the Virgin Mary."[11] By the blood of St. Timothy and the prayers of Our Lady of Ephesus, she would be the one to continue the crusade for the Christ's throne. In 408, Arcadius died, and the seven-year-old Theodosius II, St. Pulcheria's brother, was proclaimed emperor. She took leadership over the family until her brother could be the man of God.[12]

But in 410, when St. Pulcheria was eleven, terrifying news reached Constantinople: God had delivered the city of Rome into the hands of Alaric the Goth, who raped the women and pillaged through the streets under the triumphal arch of Constantine the Great, mocking the hubris of "eternal Rome."[13] To protect themselves against the invaders,

---

[5] Teetgen, *op. cit.*, 31; Socrates, *Church History*, bk. VI, ch. 18.
[6] Socrates, *Church History*, bk. VI, ch. 18.
[7] Socrates, *op. cit.*, bk. VI, ch. 18.
[8] Ibid., bk. 6, ch. 18.
[9] Palladius, *Dialogue*, trans. Herbert Moore (1921) <http://www.tertullian.org/fathers/palladius_dialogus_02_text.htm#C11>, accessed March 25, 2021.
[10] Teetgen, *op. cit.*, 39.
[11] Vasilikli Limeris, Divine Heiress: The Virgin Mary and the Creation of Christian Constantinople (London: Routledge, 1994), 55.
[12] Sozomen, *Church History*, bk. IX, ch. 1.
[13] Augustine, *City of God*, bk. I, ch. 5, 16ff.

Constantinople began to fortify the defensive walls which was completed in 413. The next year, at fifteen, St. Pulcheria, looking to the Mother of God, made a vow of virginity with her sisters. This consecrated her zeal for the heavenly city.

She did not seek opulence in fine clothes, jewelry or physical beauty (see I Pt. iii. 4). Instead she turned the imperial palace into a monastery with twice weekly fasting, chanting and reciting Scripture, an act "unprecedented" for an Empress.[14] She founded hospitals and services for the poor.[15] Pope St. Leo praised her devotion as she moved public piety "from the Hippodrome to the Church" and starting in 415, the Hagia Sophia was rebuilt.[16] At her inspiration pious festivals praised Mary and "the glory of the female sex."[17] She knew Greek and Latin, embodying the Greco-Roman ideal in piety, intellect and leadership.[18]

Meanwhile around 420, the Syriac Christians destroyed a Zoroastrian fire altar, and the king renewed the persecution with St. Abdas of Susa winning the crown of martyrdom. Persian refugees fled to Constantinople, where they found the pious court of Theodosius (now nineteen) not fighting for the earthly city, but "ready to do anything for the sake of Christianity."[19] This led to what Holum calls "Pulcheria's Crusade," where the Romans went to war against the Persian "king of kings" for the sake of the true King and His Cross.[20] This ended the persecution of Syriac Christians, which a monument credited to the vows of St. Pulcheria and her sisters. Because St. Pulcheria embodied Mary, a new Christian masculine ideal was being born which sought to fight for the heavenly city. This was the military application of Christendom.

The Throne of Christ

In 428, Nestorius, now presiding over the rebuilt *Hagia Sophia*, attacked St. Pulcheria's influence by calumniating her purity and denying

---

[14] Sozomen, *op. cit.*, bk. IX, ch. 1.
[15] Ibid., bk. IX, ch. 1; Limeris, *op. cit.*, 59.
[16] The Hippodrome was the site of chariot racing. Limeris, 43.
[17] Sermon of Proclus at the Virginity Festival c. 429, PG 65.680-681 in Limeris, 55.
[18] Sozomen, bk. IX, ch. 1.
[19] Socrates, *Church History*, 7, 18.7; Kenneth G. Holum, *Theodosian Empresses: Women and Imperial Dominion in Late Antiquity* (University of California Press, 1989), 102.
[20] Kenneth G. Holum, "Pulcheria's Crusade AD 421-422," *Greek Roman, and Byzantine Studies* (1977, no. 18), 153-172.

Our Lady the honor of the title *Theotokos*.[21] By papal authority, St. Pulcheria and St. Cyril confronted Christendom at the Council of Ephesus where the bishops enshrined the dogma of *Theotokos* at the city of Artemis Ephesia, crushing the demon and building the throne of Christ over the ruins.[22]

This dogma was an attack against "those 'spirits,'" says Newman:

> Which denied that "Jesus Christ had appeared in the flesh," and which "dissolved" Him by denying either His human nature or His divine. And the confession that Mary is *Deipara* [*Theotokos*], or the Mother of God, is that safeguard wherewith we seal up and secure the doctrine of the Apostle from all evasion, and that test whereby we detect all the pretences of those bad spirits of "Antichrist which have gone out into the world."[23]

The Immaculate Conception is the throne of Christ the King. If Mary is not present, Satan can abstract Christ's Kingship into the netherworld of Platonic forms, leaving the powerful to unite and defend the status quo of the earthly city. Thus the dethroning of Artemis and the exaltation of the *Theotokos* at Ephesus signals the end of the traffic in idols and the subjection of the society to the Logos Incarnate.

Logos and the Coin

Our fathers took the Cross to strengthen their families, and women were afforded dignity based on logos, which was "a positive factor for the peasant economy and society in general."[24] The silver amulets of Artemis Ephesia were melted down, and St. Pulcheria built three churches to honor

---

[21] "Theotokos" means "Birthgiver of God." Limeris, 54.
[22] Denzinger, 250-268. On Petrine authority in this council, see Erick Ybarra, *The Papacy* (forthcoming) and ibid., "Pope St. Celestine (422-432) and Immediate Universal Jurisdiction," *Erickybarra.org* (May 24th, 2019) < https://erickybarra.org/2019/05/24/pope-st-celestine-i-422-432-and-immediate-universal-jurisdiction/>, accessed March 25, 2021.
[23] John Henry Newman, "Discourse 17: The Glories of Mary for the Sake of Her Son," *Newman Reader* (National Institute for Newman Studies, 2007), <http://newmanreader.org/works/discourses/discourse17.html>, accessed March 25, 2021.
[24] Angeliki E. Laiou and Cécile Morrisson, *The Byzantine Economy* (Cambridge University Press: 2007), 18.

the *Theotokos* at the capital, which housed the shroud, cincture, and icon of Our Lady written by St. Luke.[25] The *cultus* reflected in sight and sound the beauty of the Logos Incarnate in Mary. Little children could experience everywhere the public throne of Christ as they received divine grace.

By 439, Theodosius promulgated a revision of Roman Law in which the "absolute supremacy of the state and the unchecked despotism of its ruler were no longer acknowledged."[26] There was acknowledged an eternal law of the Logos that was Himself the King of all creation. No longer did the Roman father have the freedom to kill his slave or children in the Theodosian Code.[27] Constantine added the *chi-rho* to the coin and his face looking up in prayer, and by the time of Pulcheria's Crusade the cross was even more prominent on the coin.[28] The *cultus* now sought to order the coin so that it would no longer buy and sell free from logos.

The Dionysian bloodlust of the gladiatorial games had been abolished in 313, but not until the fifth century did the Romans force this out of the economy, by the Holy Spirit in martyr St. Telemachus.[29] Following St. Pulcheria, public funds not only built churches but hospitals, orphanages, and houses for widows and strangers.[30]

The most conspicuous change for daily life with the Romans was the observance of the Third Commandment: from now on, commerce would cease on the Lord's Day.[31] This represented the union of Mosaic culture with the Greco-Roman, and tempered the greed and avarice that was worshipped knowing that "the love of money is the root of all evil." Before this, masters were able to grind workers into long hours seven days per week with little rest.

Meanwhile, St. Patrick was doing the same thing outside the borders of the Roman empire saying that "avarice is a deadly crime," and

---

[25] Limeris, *op. cit.*, 57.
[26] Cahill, *Framework of a Christian State*, 6.
[27] Ibid., 8.
[28] Eusebius, *Vita Constantini IV, 15* in Richard Abdy "Tetrachy and the House of Constantine," William E. Metcalf ed. *The Oxford Handbook of Greek and Roman Coinage* (Oxford University Press: 2012) 593.
[29] Theodoret, *Church History*, bk. V, ch. 26.
[30] Cahill, *op. cit.*, 9.
[31] Thomas Slater, "Sunday," *The Catholic Encyclopedia* (1912), <http://www.newadvent.org/cathen/14335a.htm>, accessed March 25, 2021; *Codex Theodosianus*, C.Th. XI.vii.13; cf. *Codex Justinianus*, lib. 3, tit. 12, 3.

instructing the Irish to keep the Third Commandment and cease work on Sundays, working miracles to prevent their work.[32]

Since Constantine, the Church had been able to preach that the coin had to be subordinated to logos. Nicaea condemned those who were "following covetousness and lust of gain" and deposed all those who "receive usury" for "filthy lucre's sake."[33] Following Mosaic culture, the exponential accumulation of wealth was condemned. Excess wealth belonged to the poor. "It is the hungry man's bread that you withhold," says St. Basil, "the naked man's cloak that you have stored away, the shoe of the barefoot that you have left to rot, the money of the needy that you have buried underground: and so you injure as many as you might help."[34]

Slavery

Constantine had immediately curbed the trade of slaves and protected their families, and recognized the slave as a person, which was followed by his successors.[35] "The disappearance of slavery among the European nations was a result of Christian principles."[36] No one exemplified this better than St. Patrick, himself a former slave who sought to become "slave of a foreign people" to end slavery to demons and condemn the Celtic slave trade.[37]

"Christianity brought down the contempt with which the master regarded his slaves and planted among the slaves themselves a principle of moral regeneration which expanded in no other sphere with equal perfection. Its action in procuring the freedom of slaves was unceasing."[38] In this way the Church abolished the slave economy by the work of divine grace through successive generations.[39] Furthermore the heroic green

---

[32] St. Patrick, *Letter to the Soldier of Coroticus*, 9; Muirchú, *Life of Holy Patrick the Confessor*, I.25.
[33] Nicaea, Canon 17.
[34] Hom. super Luc. xii, 18 in *Summa*, II-II, q32 a5.
[35] Pesch, *Liberalism, Socialism and Christian Social Order*, vol. II, 153.
[36] Ibid., 11
[37] St. Patrick, *Letter to the Soldier of Coroticus*, 10, 15.
[38] Lecky, History of European Morals, vol. II, p. 69 (1913), cited in Cahill, 12.
[39] The reason this was possible is because the master-slave relationship is not *per se* intrinsically evil, but is a result of sin and tends to evil. In other words, domestic slavery—the situation that many Christians found themselves in—could be tolerated and transformed by grace to eventually abolish the condition, since it was ultimately created by sin when it first started by the slave trade. The slave trade, as opposed to domestic slavery, is *per se* intrinsically evil, because it

martyrs did manual labor, dignifying the servile work the pagans had despised and the *cultus* made no distinction between slave and free, and all received the same sacraments and burial, and former slaves even became bishops of Rome.

The Christian Family

When Theodosius died in 450, St. Pulcheria was at the height of her power.[40] But "to maintain the imperial tradition that only males could rule," she submitted to a husband, Emperor Marcian, who promised to respect her vow of chastity.[41] Thus she completed the ideal of the Virgin Mary as a submissive wife. By respecting her vow, Marcian transformed pagan effeminacy into Christian masculinity. A man now venerated the *Theotokos*, and thus honored his wife. The gradual conversion of the upper classes to Christian morals was accomplished "not by force or persuasion, but by the patronage and example of the imperial family."[42]

Once again St. Pulcheria solidified the Petrine authority of the pope by presiding with Marcian over the Council of Chalcedon, which enshrined the orthodoxy of Nicaea.[43] Marcian and St. Pulcheria were hailed as the new Constantine and Helena. When she died in 453, she stipulated that any remaining wealth should be given to the poor. Hers was the life of divine grace flowing from the private order into the public order, stamping out the Dionysian bloodlust. Christian law and custom were governing souls and society as the *Theotokos* was enshrined as throne of Christ. These things helped especially the souls of women and children, the poor and the slave by providing the *cultus* at the heart of society.

But all this was the work of the Holy Spirit in the souls of the saints. While this was happening, the fallen angels were hard at work.

---

involves violence against the family. See J. Fox, "Ethical Aspect of Slavery," *Catholic Encyclopedia* (1912).

[40] W. H. C. Frend, *The Rise of Christianity* (Fortress Press, 1984), 769.

[41] Limeris, *op. cit.*, 57.

[42] Peter N. Stearns, *The Encyclopedia of World History*, 6th ed. (Clarke and Co., 2001), 99.

[43] Denzinger, 300-303. On Petrine authority and the Council of Chalcedon, see Soloviev, *Russia and the Universal Church*, 125-146; Ybarra's examination is here: <https://erickybarra.org/?s=chalcedon&submit=Search>, accessed March 25, 2021.

XII

THE FAILED CRUSADE OF THE EARTHLY EMPIRE

In 537, in the imperial capital of New Rome (Constantinople), after five brutal years of exhausting and hurried labor, the slaves finally heaved the last of the stones into place. When the dome was raised, it sparkled with a beautiful mosaic of the sacred emperor Justinian with a halo and the glory of New Rome and the empire and also Christ. It was the greatest church in all Christendom for a thousand years. Justinian set up his throne in the church and proclaimed proudly his gospel: *Solomon—I have surpassed thee!*[1]

Since the enemies of Christ had failed to destroy the King of Kings with Arianism, and His throne was being established in the *Theotokos*, they latched on to the one thing left to break the orthodoxy of Nicaea: *Roma*. This was the ideology that the Roman empire was eternal or had some divine attributes. If the demons could reincarnate *Roma* so that men placed loyalty to their earthly city above the heavenly, they could initiate a false

---

[1] The quotation about Solomon is a later tradition which illustrates how the church was memorialized in the Greek mind. The existing Mosaic of the emperor is likely a recreation from this period, much of which is lost due to Iconoclasm. It is reasonable to assume, however, that the mosaics of Justinian's Hagia Sophia mirrored those made at the same time in San Vitale in Ravenna. Tom Devonshire Jones, ed., *The Oxford Dictionary of Christian Art and Architecture* (Oxford University Press, 2014), 571; William Richard Lethaby, *Architecture, Mysticism and Myth* (New York: MacMillan, 1892), 205; Rousseau, Philip. "Procopius's 'Buildings' and Justinian's Pride," *Byzantion* 68, no. 1 (1998): 121-30. Accessed March 15, 2021. http://www.jstor.org/stable/44172475; Eugene Russell Hendrix, *If I had not Come; Things Taught by Christ Alone* (1916), 89.

crusade. "Christianity now had to be attacked as itself actually being anti-Christian."[2]

We have seen how Athanasius unified the Church around Nicaea out of a patient, rational *dialogos* among "brothers" over the language used for the *cultus*. In this he focused on the *substance* of the language, understanding that some who opposed the *homoousion* did so on the basis of terminology, not substance.

Their challenge now was to translate that Greek formula into Latin in the west, and Syriac in the east. From 410-632 AD, the devil would use partisanship over language to induce men to exalt their earthly city more than the Kingdom of God, leading to civil war. But there were a number of reasons why this tactic worked in the east and not in the west at this stage.

The Latin mind easily incorporated other languages, including Greek and Syriac, and many Greeks and Syrians were Roman popes during this period.[3] Rome had been sacked and *Roma* repudiated by St. Augustine's political theology in *City of God Against the Pagans*: "The heavenly city outshines Rome, beyond comparison. There, instead of victory, is truth; instead of high rank, holiness."[4] The pope, moreover, had asserted for centuries his primacy based on the Apostolic foundation of Jesus Christ in St. Peter, *not the earthly city*. This made eldership in Christian culture divorced from worldly politics. These factors did not exist in the east to the same degree.

In the east there were two highly civilized empires, the Roman and the Persian, which influenced each other in political ideology no less than art.[5] While the open paganism had been suppressed in the Roman Empire, the hidden idols of avarice and *Roma* remained, the latter of which identified the Kingdom of God with the Roman Empire.[6] The Persians continued their

---

[2] Rao, *Black Legends*, 107.
[3] Andrew Ekonomou, *Byzantine Rome and the Greek Popes* (Lexington Books, 2007); Rao, 91ff.
[4] Augustine, *City of God*, Bk. II, ch. 29. Dawson's essay on *City of God* is found in Christopher Dawson, *Dynamics of World History* (La Salle, IL: Sherwood Sugden, 1978).
[5] Dawson, *Making of Europe*, 114.
[6] "[B]y the appointment of the Cæsars, [Constantine] fulfills the predictions of the holy prophets, according to what they uttered ages before: And the saints of the Most High shall take the kingdom. And thus the Almighty Sovereign himself accords an increase both of years and of children to our most pious emperor, and renders his sway over the nations of the world still fresh and flourishing... And thus our emperor, like the radiant sun, illuminates the most distant subjects of his empire through the presence of the Cæsars, as with the far piercing rays of his own brightness." Eusebius, *Oration in Praise of Constantine*, 3.2-4.

intermittent Christian persecution with their own version of a divinized empire, while the two empires continued in their contest of power. These idols ended up influencing the ecclesiastical organization of both the Persian and Roman churches.

Theodosius I still thought of himself as high priest, and even at Chalcedon Marcian and Theodosius II were called priests.[7] Even St. Pulcheria had a mosaic of herself in the *Hagia Sophia*, albeit "to instruct the faithful," and did not repudiate the role of *pontifex maximus*.[8] Thus from 381, the bishop of Constantinople was elevated above the Apostolic sees of Antioch and Alexandria "because it is the imperial capital," making the bishop of the capital "an imperial bureaucrat."[9] Henceforth the priest-emperor would depose and appoint new bishops of Constantinople to serve his own ends, whether for the City of God or man. Thus the eldership of Christian culture was asserted not based on apostolicity but the greatness of an earthly city. When this happened in 381, St. Gregory Nazianzus mocked this hubris of exalting the earthly city:

> It is right, they said, that in the Church things should follow the course of the sun, and that they should have their origin in the same part of the world where God Himself deigned to be revealed in human form.[10]

The Romans of the capital themselves knew this was a shaky foundation, and in the fourth century some began to promote the myth of an Apostolic founding from St. Andrew. "But who really believed this tradition and on what was it founded except the desire to have an Apostle found the Church of Constantinople?"[11] Henceforth, the priest-emperor, through his appointed bishop of the capital would seek to dominate the apostolic sees of Antioch and Alexandria, and eventually Rome itself.

From 381 we see the emergence of the schismatic party and their ambitions. This party, says Soloviev, "preferred to be Greeks rather than Christians" and as long as they retained their power, they were indifferent to Christ.[12]

---

[7] Cameron, "The Imperial Pontifex," 365.
[8] Limeris, *Divine Heiress*, 50, 55.
[9] Posnov, *The History of the Christian Church*, 455. Denzinger, 150-151.
[10] *Carmen de Vita Sua*, 1690-1693 cited in Dawson, *Making of Europe*, 161.
[11] Posnov, 455; Francis Dvornik, *Byzantium and the Roman Primacy* (Fordham University Press, 1966).
[12] Soloviev, *Russia and the Universal Church*, 17.

After the sack of Rome in 410, refugees streamed into Constantinople, and, with its advanced aqueduct and defense technology, it was easy to believe in some form of *Roma*. While the pope did not believe this greatness should determine eldership in Christian culture, the schools of Antioch and Alexandria were different. Both "looked hungrily at Constantinople" to promote their "favorite sons," "enhance their own cities' reputations," and impose their "distinctive brand of theology."[13] When Eudoxia condemned the Antiochian St. John Chrysostom, the Alexandrian St. Cyril was also present at the show trial.

Following this model of conforming Church authority to the earthly city, the Persian capital city at Seleucia-Ctesiphon was elevated above his other bishops in 410 "based on purely political grounds.[14]" This of course won the approval of the Zoroastrian king, who was given the right to approve this bishop in exchange for ending persecution.[15]

Nicaea was translated into Syriac according to their existing creeds, which added a "Filioque clause" and particular canons for the Persians.[16] The same thing happened for the Latins, conforming to their local *cultus* and existing creeds that included the Filioque.[17] At the same time, St. Mesrop Maštoc' was applying his Greek learning to developing the Armenian, Georgian and Caucasian-Albanian alphabets for the churches north of both empires.[18]

---

[13] Roger E. Olson, *The Story of Christian Theology* (InterVarsity: 2009), 202.
[14] Wilhelm Baum and Dietmar W. Winkler, *The Church of the East: A Concise History*, trans. Miranda G. Henry (London: Routledge, 2003), 15, 17.
[15] Aubrey R. Vine, *The Nestorian Churches* (London: Independent Press, 1937), 47.
[16] The Filioque clause is the phrase "The Holy Spirit Who proceeds from the Fathers *and the Son* [Filioque]." Baum and Winkler provide the Filioque version of the Syriac Nicene creed (p. 16) but the eastern Syriac version conforms more closely to the Greek. Scholars are divided as to which was the original but this underscores the fact that like the west, the Greek creed played a less prominent role in the *cultus* than in the Greek rite of Constantinople. Daniel H. Williams, "The evolution of pro-Nicene theology in the Church of the East," Dietmar W. Winkler and Li Tang, eds., *From the Oxus River to the Chinese shores: Studies on East Syriac Christianity in China and Central Asia* (Zurich: Lit, 2013), 390.
[17] T. S. Flanders, "The Three Interpolations in the Latin Nicene Creed," *Meaning of Catholic* (2019), < https://www.meaningofcatholic.com/2019/07/05/the-three-interpolations-in-the-latin-nicene-creed/>, accessed March 25, 2021.
[18] Robert Thomson, "The Formation of the Armenian Literary Tradition," Garsoian, Matthews, and Thomson, eds., *East of Byzantium: Syria and Armenia in the Formative Period* (Dumbarton Oaks: 1982), 140; G.W. Bowersock and Peter Brown, eds., *Late antiquity: a guide to the postclassical world*, 2nd ed., (Cambridge, MA: Belknap Press of Harvard University Press, 1999), 289.

But the zeal of Syriac Christians for Christ destroyed a Zoroastrian throne as we said, leading to Pulcheria's Crusade. Mar Dadisho, bishop of Seleucia-Ctesiphon, was "slandered as a Roman sympathizer" and imprisoned.[19] After peace was restored, Dadisho elevated his see with "Petrine" authority and proclaimed it independent of all bishops outside the Persian empire.[20] The Syriac bishops began fighting over dominance and betraying each other to the Persian king. The Zoroastrians considered marriage a religious duty, and so in 486 the Syriac Church disastrously abolished celibacy so that even their bishops were married and green martyrdom disappeared.[21]

St. Athanasius was the model bishop for the orthodoxy of Nicaea who skillfully navigated the machinations of enemies by three means. First, the Petrine authority of the pope and bishops against *Roma* and the *pontifex maximus*; second, the green martyrdom of monks to renounce completely the earthly city; and finally the *dialogos* among brothers to distinguish between words and their meaning and unite the moderate and strict parties. In the Councils of Ephesus and Chalcedon God brought good out of evil.

Orthodox Unity Fails on the Eastern Front

Nestorius bitterly opposed St. Pulcheria, but he also opposed pornography, so that evil men took the side of orthodoxy for pagan motives.[22] St. Cyril bribed the officials, and his monks imposed the truth by voluntarism—violence, sedition and murder.[23] Mary is the Destroyer of All Heresies specifically because no member of the Church militant could have brought orthodoxy out of that chaos.

But Cyril was a saint because by divine grace he completed *dialogos* with his Antiochian rival St. John Chrysostom confirming *Theotokos* as Christ's throne.[24] This union of the moderate and strict parties led to Chalcedon's confirmation of Pope St. Leo's decree, which wove together Latin, Greek, and Syriac traditions to confirm Nicaea. Thus came the doctrine of our holy fathers: born of Mary the Virgin *Theotokos* in

---

[19] Baum and Winkler, 19.
[20] Ibid.,, 20.
[21] Ibid., 32. Dhalla, *Zoroastrian Civilization*, 77-81.
[22] Soro, *The Church of the East*, 226ff.
[23] Kallistos Ware, *The Orthodox Church*, (Penguin, 1993), 34; Meyendorff, *Imperial Unity and Christian Division*, 165.
[24] Denzinger, 271-273.

manhood, one and the same Christ, Son, Lord, unique: acknowledged in two natures [*duo physesin*]...one person, one substance [*mia hypostasis*].[25]

But the extreme parties present in Alexandria, Antioch and Persia divided according to loyalty to the earthly city. The Antiochians rejected the terminology as too Alexandrian, insisting on δύο ὑπόστασεις [*duo hypostaseis*], according to their theologian Theodore Mopsuestia. The extreme Antiochians instigated a civil war including bloodshed at Antioch.[26]

The Alexandrians rejected the terms because they did not use μία φύσις [*mia physis*], the phrase of their theologian St. Cyril. The extreme Alexandrians instigated a civil war in Alexandria.

The Persians further distinguished these terms in Syriac and stood firm on Antiochian grounds and their king made war on the Romans. The Roman Emperor sought to impose unity by means of bloodshed and ambiguous compromises.

At the same time, the error of *pontifex maximus* was at war with the Petrine primacy. The schismatic Greeks exalted their imperial see of Constantinople with new decrees, but Pope St. Leo proclaimed that "by the authority of the blessed Apostle Peter we annul them completely by a general decree."[27]

As Newman notes, all heresies had sought from the beginning the principle of negation:

> In one point alone the heresies seem universally to have agreed—in hatred toward the Church. This might at that time be considered one of her surest and most obvious Notes. She was the body of which all sects, however divided among themselves, spoke ill... The Meletians of African united with the Arians against St. Athanasius; the Semi-Arians of the Council of Sardica corresponded with the Donatists of Africa; Nestorius received and protected the Pelagians; Aspar, the Arian minister of Leo the Emperor, favoured the Monophysites of Egypt; the Jacobites of Egypt sided with the Moslems, who are charged with holding the Nestorian doctrine. It had been so from the beginning: "They huddle up a peace with all everywhere," says Tertullian, "For it maketh no matter

---

[25] Pelikan, *The Christian Tradition*, vol. 1, 263.
[26] Posnov, *op. cit.*, 339ff.
[27] St. Leo, *Works* (ed. Minge, Paris 1846) I.1000 cited in Soloviev, *op. cit.*, 130.

> to them, although they hold different doctrines, so long
> as they conspire together in their siege against the one
> thing, Truth."[28]

The principle of negation united the Grand Coalition of the Status Quo of heretics, Jews and pagans. Yet the enemies of Christ were hidden alongside the orthodox partisans of mere terminology like tares among wheat. The situation desperately needed the *dialogos* of St. Athanasius, but "instead, there was, on one side, Christological ambiguity and imperial power-politics, and on the other, blind conservatism, brutal demagoguery and, later, the defense of ethnic particularism against imperial centralization."[29]

At stake was nothing less than the identity of the Logos Incarnate and the *cultus* of His reign in the soul of man for eternal life. It was right and just that good men should fight with zeal for this cause. But by exalting the earthly city, the fallen angels made the civil war into a crusade for the city of man.[30]

The enemies sought to impose voluntarism on souls and society at any cost, including truth, "typical of the sophist word merchant on the hunt for a gimmick to support the 'business as usual' concerns of the powerful."[31] In the face of "brutal demagoguery" by monks and the populace, the priest-emperors relied on "brute strength and sophistry alone" in their successive ambiguities decreed by the emperor. They deposed their own bishops and the pope, even resorting to the "despicable" anathematizing of long dead theologians who could not defend themselves.[32]

As the war raged on, the development of distinct Christian languages was twisted by those in power to exalt the earthly city against the Kingdom. Meanwhile, Pope St. Leo was boldly preaching the gospel to Atilla the Hun, and the barbarian "was so impressed by the presence of the high priest" that he ceased raping and decided to "give up warfare."[33]

---

[28] Newman, *An Essay on the Development of Doctrine*, 208-209.
[29] Meyendorff, 193. It should be noted that Meyendorff, as an Eastern Orthodox scholar, minimizes the importance of the Holy See in this event.
[30] Thomas Fitzgerald, "Toward the Reestablishment of Full Communion," *The Greek Orthodox Theological Review*, vol. 36, no. 2 (1991), 176ff.
[31] Rao, *Black Legends*, 109.
[32] Ibid., 75, 113.
[33] As recorded by Prosper three years after the event. James Harvey Robinson, *Readings in European History* (Ginn and Co., 1904), vol. 1, 49-50.

Two Swords Crusade for the City of God

The first prolonged schism between east and west happened when the Emperor Zeno attempted to impose a compromise with truth, the *henotikon*, which attempted to reconcile the supporters of Chalcedon with its opponents. For this, the pope excommunicated all who held this doctrine. This was the Acacian schism (484-519).

Pope Gelasius wrote to the emperor saying that the demons had inspired the pagan emperors to assume the title *pontifex maximus*.[34] He enunciated the foundation of the covenant for Christian peoples:

> There are two swords, august Emperor, by which this world is chiefly ruled, namely, the sacred authority of the priests and the royal power. Of these that of the priests is the more weighty, since they have to render an account for even the kings of men in the divine judgment. You are also aware, dear son, that while you are permitted honorably to rule over human kind, yet in things divine bow your head humbly before the leaders of the clergy and await from their hands the means of your salvation. In the reception and proper disposition of the heavenly mysteries you recognize that you should be subordinate rather than superior to the religious order, and that in these matters you depend on their judgment rather than wish to force them to follow your will.[35]

The two swords were meant to work together, each in its own proper sphere, to baptize all of society and make a Christian people.

This is what the saints, our fathers had instinctively followed in Armenia, Georgia, Ethiopia, Ireland and at this time, France, where king Clovis was baptized during this schism. The king must rule according to the *cultus* as determined by the elders of Christian culture. Yet between king and bishop there exists an organic mutual aid. Just as body and soul are united in one person, so the two swords are united in one body politic. This was the proper ordering of Christian culture and peoples. In theory, the east agreed, but in practice, the Roman emperor was *pontifex maximus*,

---

[34] Cameron, "The Imperial Pontifex," 362.
[35] Robinson, *op. cit.*, 72-73.

deposing bishops at will, rearranging the *cultus* to serve his ends.[36] This was in imitation of Cain and the rabbis who imposed their will on *cultus*.

Because of this, over the course of 464 years from Constantine (323) to the Seventh Ecumenical Council (787), the eastern bishops would hold heretical doctrines and be out of communion with Rome for at least 203 years.[37] These were the schismatic Greeks, while the orthodox Greeks chose to suffer or flee to the west.

The emperor did not listen to the pope in the Acacian schism, and in 516, he continued to style himself *pontifex*.[38] The central question was this: who is the *pontifex maximus*, the high priest: the emperor or the pope? It was true that the Roman emperor held a relationship with the bishops that was sacred, but in what sense could he be said to have a priesthood?

Justinian's Crusade for the Earthly City

The Acacian schism was ended in 519 when a new dynasty conceded the Petrine primacy of "Roman doctrinal prestige" and imposed this on all the eastern bishops.[39] Justinian came to the imperial throne in 527 with his wife, the powerful Theodora, who grew up from prostitution to become the Christian *Augusta*. Would she be an Artemesian Eudoxia or a Marian Pulcheria?

Dawson says Theodora "fascinated and subdued" Justinian who, according to his contemporary critic Procopius, "overturned the social order" by failing in masculinity and letting his wife dominate.[40] Indeed he himself codified the Two Swords doctrine yet in a way that left open the question of whether he remained in some sense the *pontifex maximus*.[41]

A sympathetic reading sees his whole reign as an attempt at "the deliberate restoration of the ancient Roman empire" now Christianized.[42]

---

[36] Alan Ryan, *On Politics* (New York: Liveright, 2012), vol. I, 215ff; Posnov, *op. cit.*, 217.

[37] Monsignor L. Duchesne, *The Churches Separated from Rome* (Kegan Paul, 1907), 109.

[38] Cameron, *op. cit.*, 363.

[39] Meyendorff (*Imperial Unity*, 212-216) admits this yet attempts to obviate the significance of the event.

[40] Dawson, *The Making of Europe*, 117; Leslie Brubaker, "The Age of Justinian: Gender and Society," Michael Maas, ed., *Cambridge Companion to the Age of Justinian* (Cambridge, 2005), 433-436.

[41] Posnov, 215-217; Robert Browning, *Justinian and Theodora*, rev. ed., (London, Thames and Hudson: 1987) 61.

[42] Louth, "Justinian and His Legacy," *Cambridge History of the Byzantine Empire*, 107.

That meant conquest and monuments. Justinian did not lead his army in battle but sent his generals to fight wars with Persia (527-532, 540-562). The Christians under Persia were not only recovering from an internal schism over the sons of Syriac bishops but also, under St. Aba the Great, spreading the Gospel east of the Persian empire and south to modern Yemen and Socotra.[43]

But while the Syriacs were conquering with the Gospel, Justinian was conquering the west with a brutal twenty-year campaign in north Africa and Italy (535-554). This restored most of the borders of Caesar's empire, allowing his top general Belasarius to celebrate a Christianized rite of triumph in 553.[44]

In his decrees, Justinian celebrated that by his conquests the Persians were made "quiet," the barbarian Vandals and Moors were made "obedient," the western Romans "have recovered their former freedom" and "the Tzani [barbarians] have, for the first time, been subjected to Roman domination (which is something that God had not permitted to take place up to this time and until Our reign)."[45] A new Virgil composed a Latin epic poem about the conquests.[46] Meanwhile, the local Roman populace of Italia suffered with the loss of land and souls under the decades of bloodshed.

Justinian imposed punishing taxes on the populace that allowed him to build great building like the hippodrome. But his strict rule, taxes and corrupt bureaucracy, exacerbated the economic and religious tensions. This led to the brutal Nika riots, which burned down much of Constantinople, destroying the Theodosian *Hagia Sophia*. Justinian was considering running away when Theodora told him in the presence of the Roman senate, "may I never be separated from this [royal] purple, and may I not live that day on which those who meet me shall not address me as mistress" proclaiming that she would rather die in her royal garments than flee.[47] He then killed 30,000 civilians and put down the riots.[48]

Immediately he began to rebuild *Hagia Sophia* greater and more excellent than ever before. This seems to have become the Christianized

---

[43] Baum and Winkler, *op. cit.*, 33-34.
[44] Mary Beard, *The Roman Triumph* (Harvard University Press, 2009), 318-319.
[45] *Novella I*, preface, trans. S. P. Scott, *The Civil Law*, XVI, (Cincinnati, 1932) <https://droitromain.univ-grenoble-alpes.fr/Anglica/N1_Scott.htm>, accessed March 25, 2021.
[46] *Johannis* and *De Bellis Libycis* by Flavius Cresconius Corippus.
[47] Procopius, *Wars* 1.24, trans. H. B. Dewing (London: William Heinemann, 1914).
[48] Ibid.

triumph arch to cement himself as *pontifex maximus* presiding over the holy city of *New Rome* and the sacred empire. Theodora also received a halo in the mosaics of the time. Like Caesar Augustus, Justinian's propaganda made it seem like "the hidden influence of God" was made "to support the self-assured brilliance of the emperor."[49]

While this was being built, in 535 Justinian named the city *Justiniana Prima* after himself and attempted to exalt its bishop's authority.[50] Missionary activity was closely linked to forming diplomatic alliances to the earthly city.[51]

While Justinian's wife may not have understood the terminology, she "was emotionally deeply committed to the [Alexandrian] cause."[52] Even though in theory Justinian believed in the Petrine primacy of pope and bishops, he proved he still saw himself as *pontifex* by devising a doctrinal compromise between the Antiochian and Alexandrian factions.

For a time he sponsored true *dialogos* between the parties, but he soon took matters into his own hands.[53] His plan was to suppress some of the terms of the Fathers and then condemn Theodore Mopsuestia to appease the Alexandrians and his wife.[54] The problem was the Petrine authority. Therefore, Meyendorff admits that Theodora "groomed" Vigilius to be pope and extracted a promise to follow the Imperial program of compromise once "elected."[55] Theodora worked with the wife of the general Belasarius and got him to depose Pope St. Silverius, who died in exile from harsh treatment, and appoint Vigilius instead.[56]

At the same time, Theodora also appointed a parallel hierarchy for the Alexandrians known as the "Jacobites." This hierarchy elected a new bishop of Alexandria, Theodosius I, whom Justinian himself later deposed.[57] Before this, most faithful simply communed with the local bishop. But the actions of Theodora "led to a permanent schism."[58]

---

[49] Rousseau, *op. cit.*, 123-124.
[50] Posnov, *op. cit.*, 245.
[51] Browning, *op. cit.*, 62.
[52] Ibid.
[53] Meyendorff, *op. cit.*, 222, 233-234, 236ff.
[54] Browning, 63.
[55] Meyendorff, *op. cit.*, 227.
[56] J. P. Kirsch, "Pope St. Silverius," *Catholic Encyclopedia* (1912) <https://www.newadvent.org/cathen/13793a.htm>, accessed March 26, 2021.
[57] Meyendorff, 256.
[58] Ibid., 228-230.

Then in 543 God sent a severe plague that afflicted, according to one contemporary "the whole world" and left cities "altogether depopulated."[59] Modern estimates range from 15-100 million dead.[60] It is still called the "Plague of Justinian" to this day. Procopius said this wrath was for Justinian's brutal taxes and persecution, while Alexandrian John of Ephesus said it was "not only a sign of threat and of wrath, but also a sign of grace and a call to repentance."[61] In fact, the emperor himself was struck with this plague. In 548, Theodora went to her eternal reward. The Alexandrian Oriental Orthodox venerate her as a saint.

The plague and the death of Theodora seem to have only galvanized his zeal to impose his doctrine as *pontifex maximus*, seemingly to appease God's wrath. He called on Pope Vigilius, therefore to keep up his bargain and support the imperial doctrine. But the grace of office proved to give Vigilius back his crusading spirit, and Justinian had to resort to violent coercion to force the pope to sign the "conciliar unanimity" of the Fifth Ecumenical Council, provoking another schism with the west.[62]

Shortly thereafter an earthquake rocked the east, and even parts of *Hagia Sophia* collapsed. Justinian instituted a service of supplication every year to commemorate the earthquake, and told the city that the immorality of the citizens had caused God's wrath.[63] He then "employed drastic measures" of coercion to enforce the council. But after Theodora's parallel hierarchy was set up, he now faced "the resistance of the masses led by 'underground' leaders, proud of their martyrdom and gradually beginning

---

[59] Evagrius, *Church History*, bk IV, ch. 24. XXIX, trans. E. Walford (1846) <http://www.tertullian.org/fathers/evagrius_4_book4.htm>, accessed March 25, 2021.
[60] Lee Mordecha et. al., "The Justinianic Plague: An inconsequential pandemic?" Elsa M. Redmond, ed., Proceedings of the National Academy of Sciences Dec 2019, 116 (51) 25546-25554; Thomas Maugh, "An Empire's Epidemic," *Los Angeles Times* (May 6, 2002), *University of California Los Angeles School of Public Health* <https://www.ph.ucla.edu/epi/bioter/anempiresepidemic.html>, accessed March 25, 2021; William Rosen, *Justinian's Flea: Plague, Empire, and the Birth of Europe* (New York City: Viking Adult, 2007), 3.
[61] In Rosen, *Justinian's Flea* excerpt, <http://www.justiniansflea.com/bio.htm>, accessed March 25, 2021.
[62] On the story of this schism, see Erick Ybarra, "Vigilius," <https://erickybarra.org/?s=vigilius&submit=Search> and his forthcoming volume, *The Papacy*.
[63] Brian Croke, "Justinian's Constantinople," in Michael Maas, ed., *The Cambridge Companion to the Age of Justinian*, 71.

to identify their religious cause with cultural non-Greek and non-Roman identity of Syrians, Armenians, Arabs and Copts."[64]

In 563, Justinian went on pilgrimage to the shrine of St. Michael in Germania seeking healing from the plague.[65] He then suddenly began imposing yet another new doctrine—*aphthartodocetism*, which proclaimed that Christ's body was divine—and deposed his bishop of Constantinople for opposing it.

He died without establishing a lasting earthly city, nor a lasting peace for the heavenly, and his religious policy is seen by Meyendorff as a "failure."[66] To the Imperial Greek Christians, he is officially "the great and glorious...holy emperor" yet there seems to be very little devotion to him.[67] The Copts condemn Justinian but praise Theodora, while the Roman martyrology does not commemorate either.[68] His successors attempted the same mixture of *dialogos* and violence with the same result. Then in 572, while the plague still raged, war broke out with Persia again. No doubt every pious soul cried out to the King of Kings for mercy.

The First Greco-Roman Renewal

Because Justinian had made the greatest monument yet—the great *Hagia Sophia*—it was easy for Greek Christians to believe in a Christianized *Roma* with its sacred emperors adorned with halos. Who else but a saint could have built such a great church? Justinian firmly cemented in the minds of Greeks the Christianized ideology of *Roma*, which still persists to this day. Just as *Roma* was worshipped as the divinization of the Roman Empire, so too in the Christian Roman Empire of the East, a certain veneration of a divine empire still exerted an immense influence.

At the same time, there was a "watershed" moment: the Roman Empire in the east lost the Roman language, Latin.[69] St. Pulcheria had known Greek and Latin, but from this point the Greeks of the Eastern Roman empire increasingly viewed Latin as a "barbarian" language. The same hatred would be felt for the Syriac Christians, who could "hardly be

---

[64] Meyendorff, 230.
[65] Peter Brown, *The Rise of Western Christendom*, 181.
[66] For a further sympathetic overview of his legacy, see Meyendorff, 245-250
[67] Prologue of Ohrid, November 14th,
http://www.westsrbdio.org/prolog/my.html?month=November&day=14&Go.x=1 5&Go.y=7
[68] Ethiopian Synaxarion, St. Severus of Antioch, February 21(Yekatit 14).
[69] Louth, "Justinian and His Legacy" *Cambridge History of the Byzantine Empire*, 108.

considered Christians."[70] And they disdained also the Armenians, and one of the Greek rubrics would describe them as, "the thrice accursed Armenians" who practice a "blasphemous fast...but we eat cheese and eggs in order to refute their heresy."[71] Thus with the loss of the Latin language, the schismatic Greek party was able to gain more influence until "Greek patriotism had become synonymous with Orthodoxy," completing the crusade for the earthly city[72]

Nevertheless with Justinian the Greek *cultus* acquired the most heightened fusion of heavenly and imperial elements yet, redounding to great beauty.[73] His last Latin decrees confirmed the observance of the Lord's Day and improved the lives of slaves but still retained certain pagan exploitation of the weak.[74]

But while the east was splitting along ethnic lines, Rome was becoming the center of the first Greco-Roman renewal.[75] Latins, Greeks, and Syriacs worked together defending orthodoxy and the Petrine primacy against the emperor, and solidifying the role of green martyrdom in monasticism.

In 590, the monk Gregory (540-604) was elected pope and he immediately led the faithful in penance.

> The plague was still ravaging Rome, and Gregory ordered the procession to continue to make the circuit of the city, the marchers chanting the litanies. An image of Blessed Mary ever Virgin was carried in the procession … We are also told that the voices of angels were heard around the image, singing:

---

[70] Baum and Winkler, 60.
[71] The old editions of the Triodion contain this rubric on the Zacheus Sunday, N. Nilles, *Kalendarium Utriusque Ecclesiae*, II, 8 cited in Dawson, *The Making of Europe*, "Byzantine Renaissance," n5, 254.
[72] Henry Chadwick, *East and West: The Making of a Rift in the Church* (Oxford University Press, 2005), 248.
[73] Robert Taft, S. J., *The Byzantine Rite: A Short History* (Collegeville, MN: The Liturgical Press, 1992), 28-41; Hugh Wybrew, *The Orthodox Liturgy* (Crestwood, NY: St. Vladimir's Seminary Press, 2003), 67-102.
[74] Herbert H. Cave and Roy C. Coulson, *Source book of Medieval Economic History* (New York: Biblio and Tannen, 1965).
[75] Cf. Meyendorff, 161. Rao, 76-82.

THE FAILED CRUSADE OF THE EARTHLY EMPIRE

Regina coeli laetare, alleluia,
Quia quem meruisti portare, alleluia,
Resurrexit sicut dixit, alleluia![76]

In 591, the war with Persia ended, and peace was restored, while the plague continued elsewhere but eventually receded. The Syriac Catholicos Ishoyahb I was judged orthodox by the Romans at Constantinople and they shared communion.[77] This divine grace allowed the Syriac Christians to restore monasticism to their church.[78]

The pope sent St. Augustine of Canterbury to England to convert their peoples. The unity of Greeks, Syrians, and Latins of Rome, having been cleansed of *Roma* by St. Augustine's *City of God*, did not view these conversions as extending the Roman Empire but *the Kingdom of God*. Thus St. Gregory had no problem appointing a Greek monk as the Archbishop of Canterbury.[79] The covenant that had created so many other Christian peoples at that point coalesced also for the English people. Notice the Two Swords doctrine latent in the words from St. Gregory to King Ethelbert:

> Almighty God advances all good men to the government of nations, that He may by their means bestow the gifts of his mercy on those over whom they are placed... Therefore, my illustrious son... hasten to promote the Christian faith, which you have embraced, among the people under your subjection; multiply the zeal of your uprightness in their conversion; suppress the worship of idols; overthrow the structures of the temples; edify the manners of your subjects by much cleanness of life, exhorting, terrifying, soothing, correcting, and giving examples of good works, that you may find Him your

---

[76] "Rejoice, O Queen of heaven, alleluia / for he whom so meetly thou barest alleluia / hath arisen as he promised alleluia." Jacobus de Varagine, *The Golden Legend*, trans. William Granger Ryan (Princeton: Princeton University Press, 2012), 174.

[77] This judgment of orthodoxy was made by Patriarch John the Faster (venerated as a saint by the Eastern Orthodox) and Gregory of Antioch. Baum and Winkler, 36.

[78] Ibid.

[79] Andrew Louth, *Greek East and Latin West* (St. Valdimir's Seminary Press, 2007), 16.

rewarder in heaven, whose name and knowledge you shall spread abroad upon earth.[80]

St. Gregory exhorts him to freely convert his people not by violence but persuasion while in the public order the thrones of demons are destroyed. Yet no king has the authority to change the *cultus*, like Justinian had done. Gregory himself codified the Roman rite and helped establish this rite in England, which then grew organically. In the Roman rite, the custom arose to proclaim the Gospel to the north, in the direction of the barbarians.

The Christian People and the Jews

But the Greco-Roman renewal on Petrine authority led to the establishment of fundamental principles of rights and duties regarding the Jews. Since Constantine relations with the Jews had been codified by law and decree, riotous bloodshed was sometimes committed by both parties.[81] Yet Justinian was the first to begin forced baptisms of Jews and to prohibit their worship.[82]

In the covenant of Christian peoples, the public order must respect the rights of God, and thus the public *cultus* destroys false worship. Yet in the private order, the rights of man prevent forced Baptism. In 598, the bishop of Naples was faced with Jews who wanted to continue their religious practices, but were threatened by mobs attacking them. He appealed to Pope Gregory.

The holy Pontiff issued the ruling *Sicut Judaeis*, "a sort of papal charter of protection" for the Jews.[83] The Christian ruler had the duty to protect the Jews from the unjust violence against their persons, property, or even their religion. This is the origin of the "Jewish ghetto." It was meant to be a place where the Jews could live and worship freely without disturbance.

On the other hand, this charter also placed the Jews under obligation to the Christian ruler who protected them. The Jews were obliged to respect the public order devoted to Christ the King. Though they did not

---

[80] Venerable Bede, *Ecclesiastical History of the English People*, trans. L. C. Jane (1903), bk. I, ch. 32.
[81] Richard Gottheil and Samuel Krauss, "Byzantine Empire" *Jewish Encyclopedia* (1906) <https://jewishencyclopedia.com/articles/3877-byzantine-expire>, accessed March 25, 2021.
[82] Ibid.
[83] H. Thurston, "History of Toleration," *Catholic Encyclopedia* (1912) <http://www.newadvent.org/cathen/14761a.htm>, accessed March 25, 2021.

acknowledge His rule in their private order, they had to follow the law of the land in their public morals and economic interactions with Christians. Most importantly, this meant respecting the Christian laws against usury.

Gregory's precedent would last until the 1800s. When pious Jews and Christians followed this charter, peace was maintained. But when they undermined the public order by committing the sin of usury, violence often erupted and Jews were expelled from various cities.[84]

While Justinian, acting as *pontifex maximus*, imposed his will on the *cultus*, forcibly baptizing the Jews, Gregory, with Petrine authority, prevented this excess, safeguarding the proper celebration of the *cultus*, so that many Jews accepted Baptism freely. The Greco-Roman renewal required Greek and Latin, but the doctrine of the Two Swords was necessary to cleanse *Roma* from the public and private order.

The Year of Our Lord

Because the pope did not face a rival Roman empire in the west, the barbarians understood the superiority of Roman civilization and *wanted to be Romans*. This allowed the priesthood to form culture and plant the mustard of seed of Christendom with the first renewal.

A significant sign of this cultural momentum is seen in the shift in dating. The eastern Roman empire was still dating their documents by the years of the emperor or the year of the world. But at this time arose the practice of dating documents by *Anno Domini* ("The Year of Our Lord"). As noted above, the early Church already had this consciousness, but our fathers began codifying it in official records.

We see this in the English Church with the Church History of St. Bede (672-735), who records the adjudication of the *cultus* among the Irish and English peoples by invoking not the earthly city but "the most blessed prince of the apostles... Peter."[85] St. Gregory did not live to see this but joined the chorus of angels in 604. At that time, a false crusade was overcoming the east.

---

[84] On the subject of Jews in Christendom, find an introduction to this topic in Edmund Mazza, *The Scholastics and the Jews: Coexistence, Conversion, and the Medieval Origins of Tolerance* (Angelico Press, 2017).
[85] Bede's Ecclesiastical History, Bk. III, Ch 25

The Crusade of Herakleios

In 605, disaster struck the Roman empire as the Persians penetrated into Roman territory, taking Jerusalem, Antioch and Alexandria, which some Christians saw as liberation, and others as punishment.[86] Many of the Jews joined the Persians in expressing their "long repressed parochial wrath" and some murdered unarmed Christians.[87] The Persian general Shahrbaraz took the True Cross from Jerusalem and brought it to the Syriac Christians at Seleucia-Ctesiphon.[88] Suddenly the enemies had triumphed.

Roman Emperor Herakleios, himself barely pious, had forced his clergy to perform the rite for his incestuous marriage to his niece Martina. But even he was shocked into action and suddenly the "deep crusading spirit" seized him.[89] He put icons of the King of Kings and the *Theotokos* on the banners of his army and launched a "holy war" against all odds.[90] Unlike Justinian, he marched out from the walls of the capital and led our fathers into battle.[91]

But with the army away from Constantinople, a conspiracy of Persians, Avars and Slavs besieged the capital. The patriarch led the procession in beseeching the Mother of God to save them. It was the application of the Immaculate Conception—their absolute dependency upon the grace of the Holy Spirit. When all hope was lost, God sent a sudden hurricane that dispersed the enemy fleet.[92] All the people understood the divine intervention and filled St. Pulcheria's church of the *Theotokos* and sang all night without sitting, hence the term "Akathist," meaning "not sitting." The military role of the *Theotokos* was first hailed as *strategos* ("general") with this crusading hymn:

> To thee, the Champion Leader [*strategos*]
> we thy servants dedicate a feast of victory
> and of thanksgiving as ones rescued out of sufferings, O
> *Theotokos*;

---

[86] Abba Andronikos, *Ethiopian Synaxiaron*, Tir 08 (Jan 16), 269; Meyendorff, 341.
[87] Rao, 70; Gottheil and Krauss, *op. cit.*
[88] Theophanes, *Chronicle*, trans. Henry Turtledove (University of Pennsylvania Press, 1982), 29; Peter Brown, The Rise of Western Christendom, 2nd ed., (Malden, MA: Blackwell, 2003), 284.
[89] Rao, *Black Legends*, 90-91.
[90] Andrew Louth, "Byzantium Transforming (600-700)," *Cambridge History of the Byzantine Empire*, 227.
[91] Rao, *op. cit.*, 90-91.
[92] Louth, *loc. cit.*

> but as thou art one with might which is invincible,
> from all dangers that can be do thou deliver us, that we
> may cry to thee:
> Rejoice, thou Bride Unwedded

Only the *Theotokos* provides the throne of Christ in the hearts of men to overcome the effeminacy of the false, earthly crusade. By the unfathomable life-giving power of grace, Almighty God had resurrected the Church in the east out of nowhere by His salutary punishment. It was the moment that God gave to all eastern Christians and the Persians—to be humbled under the power of the Cross. What did the Syriac Christians think when they saw the battle lines with the Romans showing the banners of their own King? Did they not feel a grave loyalty to fight no longer for earthly cities?

Because Herakleios fought in the Name of the true King of Kings against the Persian who had usurped that title, God gave him a miraculous victory. As he charged fearlessly against them, suddenly a palace coup unseated the Persian king and all the territory was restored to the Roman Empire. God showed that the Cross was stronger than the weapons of the earthly city. The Persian general Shahrbaraz is said to have converted.[93]

When the Roman Emperor grasped the True Cross at Seleucia-Ctesiphon, they commenced the true rite of triumph for the King of Kings. What grace must have filled our fathers as they solemnly marched in procession!

> Heraclius came to Jerusalem and bore it with solemn pomp unto the Mount whereunto the Saviour had borne it. This event was marked by a famous miracle. Heraclius, who was adorned with gold and jewels, stayed perforce at the gateway which leadeth unto Mount Calvary, and the harder he strove to go forward, the harder he seemed to be held back, whereat both himself and all they that stood by were sore amazed. Then spake Zacharias, Patriarch of Jerusalem, saying: See, O Emperor, that it be not that in carrying the Cross attired in the guise of a Conqueror thou showest too little of the poverty and lowliness of Jesus Christ. Then Heraclius cast away his princely raiment and took off his shoes from his feet, and in the garb of a countryman easily finished his journey, and set up the Cross once more in

---

[93] Shepard, ed., *The Cambridge History of the Byzantine Empire*, 136.

the same place upon Calvary whence the Persians had carried it away. That the Cross had been put by Heraclius in the same place wherein it had first been planted by the Saviour caused the yearly Feast of the Exaltation of the Holy Cross to become the more famous thenceforward.[94]

Thus was added the crusader chant for the feast:

O Lord, save Thy people and bless Thine inheritance,
granting to Thy people, victory over all their enemies.
And by the power of Thy cross, preserve Thine estate.

It was only in the power of the Cross that the City of God could be established, sustained, and protected, for "everything must crumble that is not grounded on the one corner stone which is Christ Jesus."[95]

Under the standard of the Cross, the Syriac bishops were continuing the *dialogos* with the Romans, now that green martyrdom had been restored among the Syriacs. During the war, God had raised up the Syriac monk Babai the Great to put to writing the Syriac inheritance since St. Ephraim and Theodore Mopsuestia.

He had clarified the Christology of the Syriac term *qnoma* or "instantiation" [ܩܢܘܡܐ] as providing the distinction between *hypostasis* ("person" ὑπόστασις) and *prosopon* ("face" πρόσωπον).[96] This was the moment when the great Syriac tradition could be synthesized with the Greco-Roman theology passed from the fathers and the Semitic soul could reinvigorate the Orthodoxy of Nicaea. As Pelikan observes, "Syriac was a richer and more complex language than Greek or Arabic, and it allowed for more precise distinction."[97]

This chance now depended on one thing most of all—the eradication of *Roma* and the pagan *pontifex maximus*. God had humbled Herakleios by working a miracle, and now He had given over to him the dominion to work, by His grace, this renewal of Greco-Syriac Christendom.

But when his heart was lifted up, his spirit hardened unto pride (Dan. v. 20). Herakleios refused to repent of his incestuous fornication with Martina, but preserved her as *Augusta*, once refusing the Marian legacy of

---

[94] *Breviarium Romanum 1960*, Matins of the Feast of the Exaltation of the Holy Cross.
[95] Pius XI, *Divini Redemptoris* (1937), 38.
[96] For a critical view of Babai, see Pelikan, vol. 2, 39-48; for a sympathetic view, see Baum and Winkler, 36-39.
[97] Pelikan, vol. 2, 44.

St. Pulcheria. He renewed his role as *pontifex maximus* by imposing on the Church his own doctrines so that the synthesis of Greco-Syriac Christendom would be founded on a compromise with truth and not the Petrine primacy.

And finally, he fulfilled the dream of many Roman emperors before him and took the title "king of kings," as Alexander the Great had done, exalting himself as conqueror in his monuments. This title belonged to Christ alone, and the New Testament had rebuked this usurpation. Now the Roman emperor had taken this crown for himself. He was even rumored to have been ordained a priest.[98] Hail son of god! Hail *Roma*! Hail *Pontifex Maximus*! *And finding out a device he made two golden calves, and said to them: Go ye up no more to Jerusalem: Behold thy gods, O Israel, who brought thee out of the land of Egypt* (III Kng. xii. 28).

Therefore is the wrath of the Lord kindled against his people... And he will lift up a sign to the nations afar off, and will whistle to them from the ends of the earth: and behold they shall come with speed swiftly (Is. v. 25-26).

---

[98] *Corpus Scriptorum Chrsitianorum Orientalium*, Scriptores Syri III, 4, *Chronica minora*, ed. I. Guidi, I, 24 in Gilbert Dagron and Jean Birrell, *Emperor and priest: The Imperial Office in Byzantium* (Cambridge University Press, 2003), 3.

XIII

ABANDON REASON AND SUBMIT

In 610, on the outskirts of Mecca, an Arab man from the tribe of Quraysh retreated to a cave to pray. He later recounted what happened next:

> [The angel] came to me while I was sleeping in a manner with a silk garment and a book. He said "Read!" I said, "What shall I read?" Then he choked me until I thought that I would die. Then he released me and said "Read!" I said, "What shall I read?" Then he choked me until I thought I would die. Then he released me and said "Read!" I said 'How shall I read?'[1]

It was an encounter with a fallen angel, whom he thought was the archangel Gabriel. At first, Muhammad was "afraid that he had gone insane."[2] But his elder wife consoled him, and through some form of sexual persuasion, convinced him he was a prophet."[3]

Over the next twenty-two years Muhammad claimed to receive visions from an angel that helped him to lead an army in bloodshed and impose his sexual will on multiple women and slaves.[4] He told his

---

[1] *Ibn Hishaam* (Brünnow and Fischer (eds.), *Arabische Chrestomathie* (Leipzig: Veb Verlag Enyzklopädie, 1966), 41-43. Translation my own.
[2] Muhammad ibn Jarir al-Tabari, *History of Prophet and Kings*, 1150 trans. Ehsan Yar-Shater, ed., *The History of al-Ṭabarī* (Albany: State University of New York Press) in Bill Warner, *The Life of Mohammed: The Sira* (CSPI, 2010), 18.
[3] While he had the vision of the angel, she had him "sit in her lap" and then "she took off her clothes," and said, "Rejoice, he is an angel, not a devil." Ibn. Ishaq, *The Life of Muhammad*, trans. A. Guillaume, 154 in ibid.
[4] His favorite wife was Aisha, whom he married at six years old and consummated the marriage when she was nine. Muhammad said "Allah's

followers to kill for him and take sex slaves, and if they died in conquest they would be able to fornicate with heavenly prostitutes for eternity.[5] His teachings and life would be recorded in the Qur'an and the Sunna. This was the founding of Muhammadanism, a religion of the earthly city that would threaten the very existence of Christendom for centuries.[6]

The Wrath of God

Muhammad, in just a few decades, brutally subdued all of Arabia, assassinated his opponents and boasted of taking Constantinople.[7] Muhammad taught that violent conquest was a pious deed, and died with the words, "I have been victorious with terror."[8] The califs who succeeded him continued the bloodshed, swallowing up the Persian empire and reducing the Roman empire to Asia Minor (modern Turkey).[9]

Jews and Christians both wondered what this sea change meant. One Jew named Jacob asked a wise, older Jew for advice:

---

revelations do not come to me when I am not in her bed." Muhammadan ibn al-Hajjaj, *Sahih Muslim*, bk. 8, 3309; Muhammad al-Bukhari, *Sahih al-Bukari*, vol. 3, bk. 47, 755ff in Warner, *The Life of Muahmmad*, 60.

[5] "Allah says to the Muhammadans in paradise: go to your slave-girls and concubines in the garden of Paradise." Hadith 101 Ibn Arabi, *Mishkat* in Warner, *The Doctrine of Slavery: An Islamic Institution*, 29. Cf. Sura 2:217, 4:71-104, 5:51, 8:24-65, 9:123, 36:55, 37:48, 38:52, 44:54, 47:4, 52:20, 55:56, 56:8, 78:31-33. The Qur'an is a demonic book. Do not read it without permission from a priest.

[6] The terms "Muslim" or "Islam" seem to have not been used by Christians until the 20th century, and in this work we employ the traditional terms used by our fathers, "Muhammadan" or "Saracens." The reason is because the term "Islam" means "submission" and "peace" bringing out the full meaning according to their beliefs as *submission to God for peace*. Thus the term "Islam" is not accurate for their heresy, just as we do not call Lutherans "Christians of the Gospel" as they called themselves ("evangelicals"), but rather "Lutherans," since this expresses the truth of what they are—followers of Luther more than Christ.

[7] Surah 33:50-52; Ibn Ishaq, *The Life of Muhammad* (A. Guillame, 693) in Bill Warner, *The Doctrine of Slavery: An Islamic Institution* (CSPI: 2010), 23-41. Sahih Muslim, *The Book of Tribulations and the Portents of the Last Hour*, ch. 54, sec. 9, Hadith 2897 <https://sunnah.com/Muslim/54/44>. Accessed January 26, 2021. Robert Spencer, *The History of Jihad: From Muhammad to ISIS* (New York: Bombardier, 2019), 15-46.

[8] Warner, *loc. cit.*; Spencer, 15, n3.

[9] Fortunately, the vast majority of the world's one billion Muhammadans do not follow these deeds of Muhammad. Spencer, 47-76; Andrew Bieszad, *Lions of the Faith* (Lux Orbis Press, 2013), 5-7.

"What can you say to me concerning the prophet who appeared with the Saracens?" The [sage] groaned greatly and said to me "He is false. For do prophets come armed with swords? Indeed the things being set in motion today are the works of chaos, and I fear that the one who came first, whom the Christians worship, is the Christ. He is the one who was sent by God and instead of him we accepted Hermolaos [the Antichrist]."[10]

Meanwhile, the Christians understood that it was the wrath of God. "These people came, at God's command, and took over as it were both kingdoms," wrote Syriac Yohannan bar Penkaye (c. 680), "God having called them from the ends of the earth so as to destroy by them 'a sinful kingdom' [the Roman Empire] and to bring low through them the proud spirit of the Persians."[11] St. Sophronios lamented: "The godless Saracens entered the holy city of Christ our Lord, Jerusalem, with the permission of God and in punishment for our negligence, which is considerable... We are ourselves, in truth, responsible for all these things and no word will be found for our defense."[12]

Dawson asserts that "the coming of Islam seems to be nothing less than a divine judgement on the Byzantine [Eastern Roman] world for its failure to fulfill its mission."[13] This was why St. Ephraim the Syrian had "reproached the Greeks in the fourth century—the unbridled lust for theological controversy, which made the most sacred dogma of the faith slogans of party warfare, sacrificed charity and unity to party spirit."[14]

This party spirit was the exaltation of the earthly city, whether ethnic rebellion, *pontifex maximus*, or Syriac sycophancy with Persia. If the crusading spirit had not been swallowed by the earthly city, they could have faced the Muhammadan onslaught.

But the eastern Christians had "thought it lawful and laudable to confine Christianity to the temple while they abandoned the market-place

---

[10] *Doctrina Iacobi*, 2060-2963, trans. J. Hatter and Timothy S. Flanders in Gilbert Dagron et Vincent Déroche, *Travaux et mémoires / Juifs et Chrétiens dans l'Orient du VIIe siècle*, volume 11 (1991), 17-273.
[11] John bar Penkaye, 141-42 (tr. Brock, 57-58) in Robert Hoyland, *Seeing Islam How Others Saw It* (Gorgias Press, 2019), 524.
[12] John Moschus (Georgian tr.), *Patrum spirituale*, 100-103 (tr. Garitte, 414-16) in Hoyland, 63; Sophronius, *Holy Baptism*, 166-7 in Hoyland, 73
[13] Dawson, *The Formation of Christendom*, 165.
[14] Ibid.

to the principles of paganism."[15] The great beginning made by St. Pulcheria was decimated by mobs and bloodshed fighting for Christian faith with pagan morals.[16]

But the crusade of Herakleios was too little, too late. He exalted himself and thought he could continue *Roma* with himself as the newly exalted *pontifex maximus*. The Roman Empire of the Greeks would never again be restored.

The Spirit of the Antichrist Finds a New Incarnation

In a similar manner to Arianism, which attacked the Person of Jesus Christ, the Logos Incarnate, Muhammadanism preached a radical transcendence that denied the Incarnation because they believed that *Allahu Akhbar* "God is greater [than that]."[17] For Muhammadans, it was an unforgivable sin to conceive of God as a Trinity since the Muhammadan creed held that "there is no God but God."[18] In other words, theirs was a God "in *one* person." The Qur'an is filled with disputations where Muhammad tells how the Christians are wrong about God and Christ, making these common phrases, in context, into attacks on the central dogmas of Christianity. Thus like Pharisaic Judaism, their religion, by denying Christ, codified the spirit of Antichrist.

St. John Damascene said Muhammadanism was "a forerunner of the Antichrist" and that Muhammad "devised his own heresy."[19] Since

---

[15] Soloviev, *Russia and the Universal Church*, 27.

[16] Ibid. The Catholic teaching is that when man lifts himself up with pride and sins, God's wrath is poured forth *by removing the protection of His grace*. After this, the demons are able to take control of souls and society. All of this is within the Providence and Power of God and as the Scriptures show (particularly in the book of Judges), as soon as men repent of their evil, by means of His grace, God forgives the soul and welcomes the soul back into Sanctifying grace. The same is true for societies when the public order is so disturbed that the little children are threatened—then God calls men to repent by means of salutary punishment. *If my people had heard me: if Israel had walked in my ways: I should soon have humbled their enemies, and laid my hand on them that troubled them* (Ps. lxxx. 14-15).

[17] This phrase is falsely translated by the media as "God is great." That would be *Allah Kabir*. *Akbar* is a superlative in Arabic meaning "God is greater" or "God is the greatest." In the context of the Qur'an, which is filled with disputes with Christians, it is clearly a critique of Christianity.

[18] Surah 4:47-52.

[19] St. John of Damascus, *Fount of Knowledge*, translated by Rev. G. N. Warwick (Patristics Society), 40.

Muhammadanism professed belief in the one Abrahamic God and condemned polytheism, St. John considered it yet another Christian heresy.[20] But Muhammadanism was pervaded with the same voluntarism of pagan Rome—bloodshed and the objectification of woman. "Muhammad, says St. Thomas, "seduced the people by promises of carnal pleasure to which the concupiscence of the flesh urges us[.]...Mohammed said that he was sent in the power of his arms—which are signs not lacking even to robbers and tyrants."[21]

The voluntarist power of Muhammadanism offered to the conquered Christians a real culture: it had *cultus*, tradition, elders and piety, capable of transforming the nascent Christian culture into peoples who denied Christ. It even created its own beauty in literature, music, art and architecture. Above all the political subjugation of the faithful shows how the *cultus* of the ruler creates cultural momentum.[22] The followers of Muhammad called their new religion "Islam," meaning "submission." But in reality it was "abandon reason and submit to power," just as Muhammad did to a fallen angel during his first "revelation." Muhammad offered no rational reason for his prophethood by performing miracles, but only the power of his sword.[23] His only gospel, then and now, is *abandon reason and submit*. The Muhammadan voluntarism helped to justify a renewed Dionysian spirit which objectified woman for lust or procreation, so that the folk practice of female genital mutilation was not abolished by Muhammadanism, but reinforced theologically.[24]

It was an awful spiritual weight pressing down on the Christian spirit, and one by one, the vast majority of our Greek and Syriac fathers succumbed and renounced the King of Kings for the false promises of

---

<https://gotiskakyrkan.weebly.com/uploads/1/2/9/5/12957650/thefountofknowledge.pdf>, accessed July 11, 2020.

[20] Cf. *Lumen Gentium*, 16; *Nostra Aetate*, 3.

[21] St. Thomas, *Summa Contra Gentiles*, bk. I, ch. 16, a4.

[22] Dawson, *Religion and Culture*, 53.

[23] "In order that the submission of our faith should be in accordance with reason, it was God's will that there should be linked to the internal assistance of the Holy Spirit external indications of His Revelation, that is to say divine acts, and first and foremost miracles and prophecies, which clearly demonstrating as they do the Omnipotence and Infinite Knowledge of God, are the most certain signs of revelation and are suited to the understanding of all" Vatican I, Dogmatic Constitution on the Catholic Faith: Chapter 3, On Faith.

[24] A woman was an object to be used for lust or procreating children, and thus it was an offense to this voluntarism that a woman should have sexual pleasure within intercourse. This is the voluntarism of Muhammadanism which has entrenched female genital mutilation to this day among Muhammadans.

Muhammadanism.[25] A strong minority of Greek, Syriac and especially Coptic resistance formed, with the national resistance in Ethiopia, Armenia and Georgia.[26]

But under Muhammadan societies, Christian faithful would now grow up hearing an attack on the Blessed Trinity called by the *muezzin* five times per day (the "call to prayer"). This false cultural momentum weighs on vulnerable souls, especially children. This is why historians today say Christians converted to Muhammad freely over centuries. Invading a kingdom and imposing generational oppression is not a free will conversion but a slow manipulation of the faithful to renounce their Baptism for power. The whole of the Middle East and North Africa (outside Arabia and Iran)—once wholly Christian—was now almost wholly Muhammadan.

The Muhammadans saw the divisions among Christians and exploited them to their advantage—this would be their tactic for centuries. Christendom was broken as each party sought an alliance with the Muhammadans against their own Christian brethren. Coptic Abba Benjamin of Egypt handed over Alexandria to the Muhammadans so that the Arab would depose his Greek Christian rival, and to this day the Ethiopian *cultus* celebrates the Patriarch blessing the Muhammadans for his war against the other Christians![27] Christians sought out divorces from the Muhammadan authority, and power over their brethren, which the voluntarist religion of "abandon reason and submit" afforded them.[28] Or if they renounced Jesus Christ, they could legitimate their adultery with "polygamy." The party spirit already at work in the Syriac church continued as the Muhammadans gained great power over the appointment of the Catholics.[29] Despite all this, the Kingdom of Christ advanced east, but we will return to this below.

---

[25] It seems that, to a great degree, the origins of Sufism as a mass movement lie in Christian converts to Muhammad attempting to Christianize the Qur'an. For an introduction to Sufism, see the works of Arberry, Burckhardt, Nicholson, Schimmel, Sells, and Trimingham or see Frederick Denny, *An Introduction to Islam* (Upper Saddle River, NJ: Pearson, 2006), 211-262.
[26] Bieszad, *op. cit.*, 49.
[27] *Chronicle of Dionysius of Tellmahre* in Hoyland, *op. cit.*, 133; Abba Benjamin, *Ethiopian Synaxiaron*, Tir 08 (Jan 16), 271ff.
[28] Hoyland, 135, 150, 171, 177, 193, 194.
[29] Baum and Winkler, *The Church of the East*, 43.

The Petty Earthly City

What would the usurping "king of kings" Herakleios do against this new invasion? *And awaking from sleep, he said in his mind: I will go out as I did before, not knowing that the Lord was departed from him* (Jdg. xvi. 20). He confidently came forth from New Rome to face the Muhammadans with a superior army, but he had lost the unity of the crusading spirit and his army divided into a contest of power and was decisively defeated by a numerically inferior Muhammadan force.[30] No pious Christian could fail to see that God was punishing His people.

Even after this, like Justinian and all his predecessors, Herakleios and his successor Constans II did not submit themselves to the bishops, much less the pope, and imposed on the Church his own doctrine, Monothelitism (that Christ had only one will), provoking more schism with the west. Constans deposed and exiled pope St. Martin and the Greek confessor Maximos. But the next emperor, Constantine IV, made his imperial Greeks yield to the Syro-Greco-Latin efforts headed by the Greek Pope St. Agatho. Agatho reasserted once again that eldership was not based on an earthly kingdom but on St. Peter, "the Prince of all the Apostles."[31]

Then persisting in the poison of *Roma*, we see a new shift in strategy for the schismatic Greeks at this time: moving from imposing heresy to condemning Roman customs. The Greek St. Maximos had defended the Filioque (the Latin interpolation in the Nicene creed), since he was fluent in Latin.[32] But the schismatic Greeks had rejected the Latin language as a barbarian language. In 692 they met at the Quinisext Council and condemned Latin customs such as Saturday fasting, shaving beards, unleavened bread, and the representation of Christ as Lamb. This heralded the loss of Latin in the east and its increasing exaltation of Greek patriotism against the City of God since the worship of the Lamb is contained within the very Word of God (see Apoc. v. 12).

---

[30] Walter E. Kaegi, *Byzantium and the Early Islamic Conquests* (Cambridge University Press, 1995), 112-146.

[31] Ekonomou, *Byzantine Rome and the Greek Popes*, 199. Letter of Agatho to Constantine IV.

[32] An objective Orthodox scholar, Kallistos Ware, admits that the Orthodox themselves are divided about the Filioque (*The Orthodox Church*, new ed., 213). For an Orthodox defense of the Filioque, see Peter Gilbert, who defends the union of Lyons and translates the work of John Bekkos (Cf. "St. Maximus on the filioque," <https://bekkos.wordpress.com/2008/01/21/st-maximus-on-the-filioque/>, accessed March 25, 2021). For a critical reading of Maximos and the Filioque from an Orthodox source, see A. Edward Siecienski, *The Filioque*.

In response, the Syrian pope Sergius I added the chanting of the *Agnus Dei* to the Roman Rite and enriched the front atrium of St. Peter's depicting the worship of the Lamb as seen in Scripture.[33] This was an example of organic development of the liturgy in order to safeguard the Tradition itself.

The emperor sent troops to impose his will on Sergius, but remembering the treatment of Justinian, Herakleios and Constans, local troops defended the pope and forced them to retreat.[34] The pope personified the doctrine of Two Swords by rejecting the authority of the emperor over the *cultus* without rejecting his temporal authority. Yet this was the first moment of successful western military resistance to the voluntarist bloodshed of the Roman emperor of the east. The blood of so many popes and bishops at the hands of the *pontifex maximus* had finally merited the seed that would grow into Christendom. Meanwhile, the Greco-Roman-Syriac renewal brought the feast of the Holy Cross into the Roman Rite.

Meanwhile, St. Boniface was chopping down Donar's Oak in Germany while the saintly Arab monk Mar Shubhalisho was doing the same in modern Iran where the doctrine of the enemy "was made a mockery, and...the fire-temples and the fire-altars of his cakes were pulled down."[35] Despite a separation of hundreds of miles and no contact whatsoever, our fathers understood that the public order must be claimed for Christ the King.

Further east, the Gospel began to flourish in China during this time (618-907), and the Chinese noticed that the Christians "keep no slaves, and accumulate no wealth" and "make no distinction between rich and poor in worship,"[36] Monuments found in China date from this period that praise the "beauty and the eternal truth of the luminous religion."[37] Syriac Christians were translating Aristotle into Arabic, which would provide an opportunity for the Muhammadans to receive the Gospel.

The Muhammadans swept across Christian North Africa and began to penetrate south against the Christian Kingdom of Ethiopia. At this time,

---

[33] H. Henry, "Agnus Dei (in Liturgy)," *The Catholic Encyclopedia* (1907) <http://www.newadvent.org/cathen/01221a.htm>, accessed March 25, 2021. Ekonomou, *op. cit.*, 210, 223.
[34] Ekonomou, 224.
[35] Thomas of Marga, *The Book of the Governors*, trans. E. A. Wallis Budge (London, 1893), 484; Brown, *Rise of Western Christendom*, 41.
[36] Michael Keevak, *The Story of a Stele: China's Nestorian Monument and Its Reception in the West 1625-1916* (Hong Kong University Press: 2008), 9; Li Tang, *East Syriac Christianity in Mongol-Yuan China*, (Harrassowitz Verlag, 2011), 15.
[37] Keevak, *loc. cit.*

the Jews were "active in the slave trade" east and west, while the Christians were abandoning the wicked trade.[38] The Muhammadans renewed this practice and began a centuries-long trans-Saharan slave trade allied with African emperors.[39] This brutal reinvigoration of the slave trade would ultimately devastate the Christian kingdoms.

A New Birthday for the Crusading Spirit

The Christian Spaniard Juan of Ceuta betrayed Spain to the Muhammadan Moors, who invaded seeking money and "a large number of ravishingly beautiful Greek maidens."[40] They swept over Spain as far as the northern kingdom of Asturias, where King Pelayo alone refused to submit. The Moors brought an army of 187,000 and sent Bishop Oppas to find Pelayo, who was hidden in the mountain at Covadonga. Pious legend relates how the bishop tried to convince Pelayo to surrender:

> If when the entire army of the Goths [Spaniards] was assembled it was unable to sustain the attack of the Ishmaelites, how much better will you be able to defend yourself on this mountain top?...heed my warnings and recall your soul from this decision, so that you may take advantage of many good things and enjoy the partnership of the Chaldeans.
>
> To this Pelayo responded: "Have you not read in the divine scriptures that the Church of God is compared to a mustard seed and that it will be raised up again through divine mercy?"
>
> The bishop responded, "It is indeed written thus."
>
> Pelayo said, "Christ is our hope that through this little mountain, which you see, the well-being of Spain and of

---

[38] J. A. S. Evans, *The Age of Justinian* (Routledge, 2000), 242.
[39] Tidiane N'Diaye, *Le genocide voilé* (Continents Noirs: 2008), 43-63, 95-116; Warner, *The Doctrine of Slavery*, 42-48.
[40] "Al Maggari: Tarik's Address to His Soldiers, 711 AD" Charles F. Horne, ed., *The Sacred Books and Early Literature of the East* (New York: Parke, Austin, & Lipscomb, 1917), vol. 6, 241-242 in Spencer, *op. cit.*, 80. <https://sourcebooks.fordham.edu/source/711Tarik1.asp>, accessed May 15, 2021.

the army of the Gothic people will be restored[.]...As for the battle with which you threaten us, we have for ourselves an advocate in the presence of the Father, that is, the Lord Jesus Christ, who is capable of liberating us from these few."[41]

Henceforth this story would animate the struggle of the mustard seed of the Kingdom of God against the earthly city of Muhammad. Pelayo led his men against the Moors and triumphed miraculously, crediting the victory to the intercession of Our Lady of Covadonga, who began to unite the Spanish and the French against the Moors in Spain. This was the beginning of the *Reconquista*.[42]

But the Moors made it around the Pyrenees mountains and into central France, stopped only at Tours by Charles Martel, of the Merovingian dynasty of Clovis, allied to his rival, Odo the Great.[43] This marked the beginning of the crusade in southern France and eventually the eastern crusade.

Meanwhile, the Syrian Pope Gregory III appealed to Charles Martel against the Lombards, with no reply.[44] During this time the Greek clergy of Rome outnumbered Latins by three and half to one.[45] By the authority of the Greek Pope Zacharias, Pepin was crowned king of the Franks by St. Boniface. This established that the authority for Christian rulership came from Christ the King mediated by the Church, establishing a Christian people based on the Two Swords.[46]

First Iconoclasm

Meanwhile, the Roman emperor at Constantinople was imposing his new doctrine on his bishops and the pope in order to restrict once again the

---

[41] *The Chronicle of Alfonso III*, 9 in Barbara H. Rosenwein, ed. *Reading the Middle Ages*, vol. 1 (University of Toronto Press: 2018), 134. Modern scholarship doubts the details of the legend, but the story accurately portrays the constant faith of the *Reconquista*.
[42] Bieszad, *op. cit.*, 15. The best sources on the *Reconquista* come from Claudio Sánchez-Albornoz, Guillermo Pérez-Galicia, José Javier Esparza, Dario Fernandez-Morera, and Fr. Javier Olivera Ravasi.
[43] Ibid., 30.
[44] Ekonomou, *op. cit.*, 245, 300.
[45] Ibid., 245.
[46] Roy Strong, *Coronation* (Harper Perennial: 2005), 12.

reign of the Logos.⁴⁷ This was the horror of Iconoclasm—all images but the Holy Cross would be torn down and whitewashed. Innumerable icons and Christian monuments would be destroyed and lost to history. This movement imposed on tradition the hubris of false *pontifex maximus* who boasted "I am priest and emperor."⁴⁸ This was the First Iconoclasm (726-842). Some say it produced more martyrs than the Roman persecution as the pious Greeks resisted unto blood or fled to Rome to join the Christians there. Because of the military alliance already formed with the Franks, the emperors of the east were unable to force this on the pope, although they seized the Balkan territory, imposing their heretical bishops there.

An alliance was formed between the Greek monks, the pope and the Latin bishops against the Roman emperor and his army of soldiers and appointed bishops.⁴⁹ Once again the Petrine authority, not the *pontifex maximus* was vindicated, and Christian culture was safeguarded by this decree from the Seventh Ecumenical Council: "If anyone rejects any written or unwritten tradition of the church, let him be anathema."⁵⁰ This was the fundamental difference between the moderate and strict parties against the heretics. Christendom sought to preserve tradition, but the heretics wanted compromise for power.

Invasion from the North

But the barbarian hordes continued to threaten the papacy in the west. Even worse, a new threat appeared on the northern borders—the Northmen, ruthless savages out of Scandanavia who attacked without warning and burned villages, stole property and raped women. They carried off men to be worked to death as slave "thralls," young girls for sex slaves, and children for either purpose.⁵¹ Churches and monasteries were plundered, priests and monks were killed and nuns ripped from their convents for debauchery.

---

⁴⁷ Rao, *Black Legends*, 86-90.
⁴⁸ Dagron and Birrell, *op. cit.*, 3. An eastern forgery appeared where the pope conceded the title of priesthood to the emperor. Cameron, "Imperial Pontifex," 367.
⁴⁹ Dawson, *The Making of Europe*, 155.
⁵⁰ Seventh Ecumenical Council, "Anathema Concerning Holy Images," <https://www.papalencyclicals.net/councils/ecum07.htm>, accessed March 25, 2021.
⁵¹ "Viking Sex Slaves, Behind the Founding of Iceland," eds. *Archaeology World Magazine* (July 16, 2019) <https://archaeology-world.com/viking-sex-slaves-behind-the-founding-of-iceland/>, accessed March 25, 2021.

The Northmen's *cultus* was corrupted to worship great demon warriors, which fed their zeal for bloodshed. These incursions shattered the Christian peoples of western Europe and destroyed whole towns and cities. The people started to cry to God and a new petition was added to the Litany: *A furore Normannorum libera nos, Domine* ("from the fury of the Northmen, deliver us O Lord!). The Celts were formerly slave raiders like the Northmen, but they had been converted by St. Patrick. Europe was besieged by slave raiding armies even while the Roman empire of the east had fallen to the Arabs.

But in the year 800, God heard their cry.

The Holy Roman Emperor

After decades of bloody struggle between the Christian culture and the temporal authority in the empire, Pope Leo III crowned Pepin's son, Charlemagne, as the Emperor of the Romans. Some of the sacred character of the *pontifex maximus* was retained (in that the Holy Roman Emperor had a sacred duty regarding the Church) but the office was further cleansed of its pagan character, since it was established on the basis of the Two Swords under the pope, not inherited from Caesar Augustus. In other words, the emperor was not a priest.

Charlemagne was charged with the duty of protecting the Church, especially the papacy, from the hordes of barbarians, Muhammadans and Northmen. It was Charlemagne and his successors, the Carolingians, who stopped the Northmen and Muhammadan advance. This Carolingian Empire stretched from the borders of modern Spain at the Pyrenees, north to modern Denmark and south to Rome. The Greco-Roman-Syriac union had now integrated not only the Christian peoples of England, Ireland, Spain and Germany but now a new Christendom was being born with the Franks. The pope was given a sovereign domain to protect the Church from dominion by temporal rulers—the Papal States.[52] This allowed the pope to govern the Church unhindered by temporal authority as he had been by the Roman Emperor at New Rome.

---

[52] Near this time the infamous forgeries of the Donation of Constantine and the Isidorian Decretals began to be spread. Someone in Rome forged these to bolster the claims to these lands, but as Erick Ybarra shows, these forgeries are unnecessary since the papal claims are fully documented in numerous and sound passages from the Fathers. Nevertheless, Orthodox and Protestant critics still allege the papal claims are based primarily on forgeries.

In theory, this was simply a revival of the western Roman empire since there had been co-emperors since the days of Diocletian. The first Greco-Roman renewal of Rome had produced the momentum that caused this to come about. His pious biographers say Charlemagne did not want to offend the Greeks as a rival "Roman Emperor," but from this point the schismatic Greek party viewed the Latins as "odious political enemies" and the bishops of New Rome "began their own fantastic program of self-elevation" against the pope.[53]

Roma was so deeply ingrained in the minds of the schismatic Greek party that they could not distinguish between the earthly city and the heavenly city, and this emotional disdain still promotes the risible myth that Charlemagne was a Frankish-Latin conspiracy.[54] Yet Charlemagne himself seems to have been a promiscuous adulterer and he forcibly baptized the Anglo-Saxons.[55] As his Carolingian empire advanced east, the heretical seizure of the Balkans by the Iconoclasts renewed the conflict over Petrine authority. The conflict arose in the new Christian mission territory of Bulgaria, which the Franks and Greeks both sought to add to their own domains. This was the moment when the false earthly city would be broken.

The Carolingian Renaissance

For at that moment, God was instantiating the Greco-Roman-Syriac synthesis that had obtained on the level of theology in Rome. Now with Charlemagne under the tutelage of the Petrine authority, the ideology of *Roma* could be eradicated and the Christian culture truly convert society with divine grace. The Carolingian Renaissance "created a new social unity in which the Germanic and Latin elements were combined organically

---

[53] Notker the Stammerer, *The Deeds of Charlemagne*, Bk. I in David Ganz, trans. *Two Lives of Charlemagne* (Penguin: 2008), 77.

[54] Ekonomou is an excellent example of this. Although his scholarship is professional, his tone paints the Greek and Syrian popes as pious subjects of the sacred *pontifex maximus* who would never dare betray this sacred emperor, even if he was a heretic. Another obvious example comes when you look at Orthodox scholarship on the tragedy of the Fourth Crusade. The Greek massacres of Latin women and children are left out, as well as the Greek dynastic involvement in the sack of 1204, and the Franks are not brothers in Christ committing sin, but sub-human barbarians, while the pope's only concern is more power. This is ideology, not historical scholarship. Aristeides Papdakis, *The Christian East and the Rise of the Papacy 1071-1453 AD* (SVS Press: 1994), 199-238.

[55] E. Macpherson and T. Shahan, "Charlemagne," *Catholic Encyclopedia* (1908) < https://www.newadvent.org/cathen/03610c.htm>, accessed March 25, 2021.

instead of coexisting as two independent traditions."[56] Like all Christian kings before him, he built a cathedral at Aachen as a public throne of the true King.

The central factor in this was the *cultus* that was beautified organically through the successive generations in sharing the old Frankish rite with the Roman.[57] Through the celebration of the Holy Sacrifice, divine grace was merited to convert souls and society.

As this was happening, in 813, a bright star led shepherds to the site of the relics of St. James in Spain. This miraculous discovery added further power from Heaven for the western crusade against the Muhammadans. Now Santiago Matamoros ("St. James the Moorslayer") would join Our Lady of Covadonga against the Moorish captivity of Hispania. A pilgrimage route was established as *El Camino de Santiago* ("The Way of St. James") Santiago de Compostela became the greatest pilgrimage site in Europe outside Rome and Jerusalem. The Muhammadan occupiers could never counter the force of millions of poor Christian pilgrims and their prayers. This was the mustard seed of Pelayo.

Meanwhile the Carolingian Renaissance was in full swing in the Frankish empire. The Latin tongue was being taught to Christian families through the empire, the Gospel was preached and thrones to Christ the King were erected all over, penetrating souls and society with divine grace.

Thus the king and the coin were converted as well. In the Carolingian era "actual slavery was overcome in principle and in practice."[58] The slave economy was slowly transformed, protecting families by avoiding bloodshed and the *cultus* informing the legal development of the coin.[59] What emerged was an economic system of hierarchy and interdependency between priests, nobles and laborers.

The priests and religious ("those who pray") had the duty to offer the *cultus* to merit the divine grace necessary for souls and society. Most importantly for the sake of the *cultus*, Benedictine monasticism was promoted by Aachen and green martyrdom spread over the lands of western Europe, keeping a strong alliance with the angel armies against the demons. These efforts provided pilgrims for *El Camino*.

---

[56] Christopher Dawson, *Medieval Essays* (Image Books, 1959), 63.
[57] Alcuin Reid, *The Organic Development of the Liturgy* (San Francisco, CA: Ignatius Press, 2005), 21-27.
[58] Pesch, *Liberalism, Socialism, and Christian Social Order*, vol. II, 163-241.
[59] Cave and Coulson, eds., *A Source Book for Medieval Economic History*, 270-279.

The nobles ("those who fight") had the duty to fight and protect their people from the Northmen, Muhammadans and anyone else, and give their lives if necessary. The Christian ideal of nobility overcame the old pagan, false masculinity which was addicted to pleasures. On the contrary, as Plinio Corrêa de Oliveira summarizes, "there cannot be nobility without suffering."[60] The masculine ideal was the cross, where Our Lord laid down His life for His friends. The nobles had the duty to obtain wisdom from the priests and be perfected by them in faith and morals in order to govern their peoples with justice. They were obliged to use their wealth to provide for the poor, the widow and the orphan.

The laborers ("those who work") had the duty to stay at the village and work to produce the food necessary to sustain the community. The parish church was the center of these Christian villages and the liturgy imbued the people as public processions and festivals continued to provide the cultural momentum for children as the Faith was passed down in this Benedictine period, falsely called "the Dark Ages."[61]

The Frankish emperors, meanwhile, had a fraction of the power possessed by the Roman Emperors at New Rome as the whole realm was governed by the local lords who swore an oath to fight for the emperor if necessary. Charlemagne had all his court read St. Augustine's *City of God*, and continued to spread the saint's repudiation of *Roma*, while the dating system of *Anno Domini* gained dominance during this time.[62] The writings of Augustine were disseminated as the most widely available theological manuscripts at that time. This Augustinianism would be the foundation for the first Western Christendom.

Revenge of the Earthly City

The last Iconoclast emperor went to his eternal reward in 842. Five years later, the office of *pontifex maximus* had barely finished imposing heresy when the holy monk St. Ignatios was raised to the patriarchal throne of Constantinople. He refused communion to the regent Bardas, who was

---

[60] Plinio Corrêa de Oliveira, "Address to the Marian Congregation of São Paulo," 23 April 1964 in Roberto De Mattei, *Plinio Corrêa de Oliveira: Prophet of the Reign of Mary* (Preserving Christian Publications, 2019), 136.
[61] The term "Benedictine period" seems to have been coined by St. Newman, *Mission of St. Benedict*, reprint, 76 in Cuthbert Butler, *Benedictine Monasticism* (Speculum Historiale, 1924), 335.
[62] Dawson, "St. Augustine and the City of God," *Dynamics of World History*, 294; De Mattei, *op. cit.*, 155-161.

committing adultery with his daughter-in-law.[63] Thus Ignatios was deposed to a monastery in 858, and Bardas raised the layman Photios (810-893) in five days to the patriarchate. Photios was brilliant and completely orthodox, but like most Greeks, ignorant of the Roman tongue.[64]

Pope St. Nicholas I condemned Photios' elevation "on the basis of canonical norms unknown in the east."[65] Photios wrote back to Rome saying he was willing to accept Latin customs like Saturday fasting, shaving and celibacy that the Quinisext Council had condemned, saying that as long as "the faith remains inviolate... a sensible man respects practices and laws of others."[66]

The schismatic Greek party and the newly converted Carolingian empire both viewed each other as rivals, and began to fight over Bulgaria for their earthly cities. When the Franks began to condemn Greek practices, Photios, admits Meyendorff, "resorted to purely disciplinary and liturgical accusations against the Latins."[67] In 867, Photios condemned those who fasted on Saturdays, practice priestly celibacy, Latin Confirmation rites or the Latin Creed.[68] Photios then excommunicated the pope. St. Athanasius' method of *dialogos* was abandoned.

The central dispute for Christian culture was the Petrine office against the latest incarnation of *pontifex maximus*, which made Photios "an Imperial bureaucrat."[69] His erudition gave new theological justification for the schismatic Greek party to exalt their Greek patriotism as synonymous with the City of God. This gave new force to what Kolbaba calls "inventing Latin heretics."[70]

But our holy fathers among the orthodox Greeks, led by Sts. Cyril and Methodius, did not recognize the authority of Photios and went to the pope for approval of their Slavic liturgical rites in the Balkans. The Franks,

---

[63] Ignatios also refused to obey Bardas and tonsure Empress Theodora against her will. Posnov calls Bardas "a debauched man" (458).

[64] Dawson, *The Making of Europe*, 161.

[65] John Meyendorff, *Living Tradition* (St. Vladimir's Seminary Press, 2011), 24

[66] EP. 2, PG 102, cols. 604-605D in Ibid., *loc. cit.*

[67] Ibid.

[68] He called them "forerunners of apostasy, common pests and servants of the enemy, we, by divine and synodal decree, condemn them as impostors and enemies of God." Photios, *Encyclical to the Eastern Patriarchs, 867*, translation posted by Stephen J. Shoemaker Professor of Religious Studies, University of Oregon <https://pages.uoregon.edu/sshoemak/324/texts/photius_encyclical.htm>. Accessed March 16, 2021.

[69] Posvnov, *op. cit.*, 455.

[70] Tia M. Kolbaba, *Inventing Latin Heretics: Byzantines and the Filioque in the Ninth Century* (Medieval Institute Publications, 2008).

ignorant of the many languages in which the *cultus* was already celebrated in the east, sought to impose the error of "trilingualism," that Greek, Latin or Hebrew were the only licit languages for the *cultus*. But manifesting the legacy of the Greco-Roman-Syriac League, Pope Adrian II approved the Slavic liturgy and the efforts of the Greek saints.

And once again, the Photian schism, like every schism before, was resolved when the Petrine authority of Rome was vindicated against *pontifex maximus* in the Ecumenical Councils of 869 and 879.[71] The haughty condemnation of Roman customs and terminology by Photios was rescinded. The fallen angels, however used the love of money to induce the wealthy Romans to strike back against the papacy itself. The Roman priests were directed to poison Pope John VIII and then club him to death. This was beginning of the First Pornocracy, which we will return to below.

For the Greeks, a new incarnation for *Roma* was found. For when the pope had sought to restore the Balkan jurisdiction stolen by the Greek iconoclasts the schismatic Greek replied: "It is completely inappropriate that you, who have rejected the Greek Empire and united yourself in union with the Franks, should preserve any right of jurisdiction in our empire."[72] Thus the affairs of the Church should be subordinated to the earthly city.

Fortunately during this period (800-1100) the work of divine grace from the Greek *cultus* still created saints like Cyril, Methodius and Symeon the New Theologian (949-1022), and the mass of the Greek faithful was not concerned with these earthly rivalries. Meanwhile, the great beauty contained in the Greek *cultus* converted St. Vladimir (980-1015) who destroyed the demonic thrones among his people and built the churches of St. Basil and the Dormition of the Virgin. This brought to fruition the mustard seed of Cyril and Methodius and our fathers began Slavic Christendom.[73] But while the Greek liturgical books still confirmed the priesthood for the emperor, the schismatic Greek clergy attempted to impose anti-Roman ideology them.[74] Bulgaria tried to restore *Roma* for themselves in 913 and Serbia in 1346. Meanwhile, the occult movement of the old Greco-Jewish Gnosticism was turning into new occultism against Christendom. This was shown in the Paulicians and Bogomils in the

---

[71] Posnov, 458-464; For a sympathetic reading of Photios see Francis Dvornik, *The Photian Schism*. Dvornik's work was groundbreaking for the period but has been disputed among scholars ever since its publication.
[72] Vignol, *Liber Pontificalis* B, III, 250 in Posnov, 455.
[73] A. Shipman, "St. Vladimir the Great," *The Catholic Encyclopedia* (1912) <http://www.newadvent.org/cathen/15497a.htm>, accessed March 26, 2021.
[74] Ibid.; Cameron "Imperial Pontifex," 369; Soloviev, 45-46.

Balkans, which spread to Southern France as proto-Cathars.[75] This would bring the occultism into open revolt against Christendom in a few generations.

As this was happening, the Carolingian empire fractured into a contest of power, splitting between the French kings while the Germans were Roman emperors. This allowed the kings to turn and dominate the Latin priesthood, turning their bishops into bureaucrats, and to oppose the impulse of divine grace converting society.

The First Pornocracy

Lamentably, the love of money dominated the papacy during this perod, swallowing much of the clergy in a cesspool of Dionysian bloodlust and fornication. This found its nadir in Pope John XII (937-964), whom St. Robert Bellarmine calls "practically the worst of all pontiffs."[76] "According to an unanimous description of the sources," writes de Mattei, "the young Pope was a dissolute pontiff, who didn't interrupt his life of reckless abandon in unbridled pleasures, even with his election to the Papal Throne."[77] His crimes were well known to the inhabitants of Rome: "simony, sacrilege, blasphemy, adultery, incest, abstention from the sacraments, use of weapons and trafficking with the devil."[78] The enemies of Christ hoped to drown the Petrine primacy in debauchery so they could celebrate the Year of Our Lord 1000 as the Year of Lucifer, 5000.

But at that crucial moment, a messenger was dispatched to the Holy Roman Emperor, Otto I.

---

[75] Malcolm Barber, *The Cathars, Dualist Heretics in Languedoc in the High Middle Ages* (Routledge, 2000), 6-33; Evans, *Witchcraft and the Gay Counterculture*, 52-53.
[76] De Romano Pontifice, l. II, cap. XIX, in *De controversiis christianae fidei, Apud Societatem Minimam, Venetii* 1599, 689 cited by Roberto de Mattei, "Who Was the Worst Pope in the History of the Church?" *Corrispondenza Romana* (December 4th, 2019) trans. Francesca Romana <https://rorate-caeli.blogspot.com/2019/12/de-mattei-who-was-worst-pope-in-history.html>, accessed March 16, 2021.
[77] Ibid.
[78] Paolo Chiesa, *De Iohanne papa et Ottone imperatore*, (Edizioni del Galluzzo, Firenze 2018), 15 in Ibid.

XIV

SANTIAGO AND THE CRUSADING SPIRIT

The Emperor Otto, who was known as a man of God, took his men and marched over the alps. He came to Rome and convoked a council which condemned Pope John XII, who fled the charges. "We strongly entreat thee, father," he wrote to the pope "do not refuse a return to Rome to defend thyself against all these accusations."[1] The pope was obstinate, so the emperor's synod deposed him and elected Leo VIII as pope. A struggle ensued between them but God gave the judgement when Pope John XII was murdered by the husband of his mistress. Eventually Pope Leo VIII was established as pope. The demons shrieked with rage while the angels rejoiced.

In his favor, Pope John XII had, "despite himself," confirmed the charter of the Cluny monastery.[2] When the emperor broke the first Pornocracy, God gave the papacy over to the Cluniac monks and the angels streamed in against the foe.

The Green Crusade and Chivalry

The mustard seed of Benedictine monasticism now flowered into a new spiritual crusade against the western kings' domination of the *cultus* and priesthood. Our fathers initiated the "revolutionary change" of restoring the order of the Two Swords among Christian peoples.[3] This was known as the Investiture Controversy (1000-1300) that fought for the "freedom of the Church" from control by temporal authority. It was a new form of the struggle between the Petrine primacy and the *pontifex maximus*

---

[1] Ibid.
[2] Coulombe, *Vicars of Christ*, 132.
[3] Dawson, *The Formation of Christendom*, 215-219.

transferred to the west. This struggle produced, at best, a mutual help between the Two Swords which allowed a greater baptism of souls and societies. The lay ruler was a coworker with the bishops, but had no priesthood. With no parallel in the east, Greek and Slavic Christendom was dominated by *Roma* suppressing their monks' influence on society. At worst, this led to a cultural ossification and haughty patriotism among their clergy (despite the vast majority of eastern faithful having little interest in these earthly ambitions). This would also happen later in the west.

But for the monks in the west, the priesthood must be free to destroy the idols in the public order, set up the throne of Christ, preach to all men of Christ's authority over king, coin and kitchen. This spiritual crusade of the monks fought against the world, the flesh and the devil seeking to use temporal power for the love of money. The important figure in this regard is St. Thomas Becket (1119-1170), the bishop who opposed the control of the English king over the priesthood.

Out of this internal crusade grew the perfection of the Christian masculine ideal: the Christian knight. Many barbarian warlords were no better than street gangs, but the chivalrous ideal turned them literally into knights in shining armor. This was one of the greatest social miracles of divine grace in the history of the Church.

This cultural momentum was first seen in the Peace of God and the Truce of God. These decrees excommunicated those who fought on Sundays, Feast Days, Lent, or attacked women or pilgrims.[4] This threatened the tyrants, who wanted their soldiers to fight for the earthly city. But if the priesthood was given freedom in the culture, the feast of Christmas could truly join the angel armies singing *in terra pax hominibus bonae voluntatis*. Christian knights would only pick up their swords for the true King. This summarizes the Code of Chivalry:

> 1. Thou shalt believe all that the Church teaches, and shalt observe all its directions.
> 2. Thou shalt defend the Church [priests and religious, Church property].
> 3. Thou shalt respect all weaknesses [women, children, pilgrims, Jews, slaves and the poor], and shalt constitute thyself the defender of them.
> 4. Thou shalt love the country in the which thou wast born.
> 5. Thou shalt not recoil before thine enemy.

---

[4] Cf. Cologne Episcopal Decree c. 1075, "The Truce of God," in Norman F. Cantor, ed., *The Medieval Reader* (HarperCollins, 1994), 89-90.

6. Thou shalt make war against the Infidel without cessation, and without mercy.
7. Thou shalt perform scrupulously thy feudal duties, if they be not contrary to the laws of God.
8. Thou shalt never lie, and shall remain faithful to thy pledged word.
9. Thou shalt be generous, and give largess to everyone.
10. Thou shalt be everywhere and always the champion of the Right and the Good against Injustice and Evil.[5]

The ideal of chivalry imposed an obligation on the nobility to partake of the cross of suffering, and raised Christian masculinity to the imitation of Christ.

The Western Crusade

Since Pelayo, Santiago de Compostela had led the faithful to gradually liberate Hispania from the Moors through grueling generations of the *Reconquista*, supported by the streams of pilgrim prayers and red martyrs who refused to renounce Christ and won the crown, like saints Adolphus and John, Perfectus, Sancho and countless others.[6] But from 1062-1269, the Moors led a counterattack into Spain through a new surge of Muhammadan resolve.[7]

But our fathers sounded the battle cry: "*Santiago!*" and the western crusade was renewed. Our Lady worked innumerable miraculous cures at Santiago de Compostella for pilgrims, the Christian slaves were rescued, and the devotion of the Rosary was beginning to spread at this time. The tide began to turn back the Muhammadan invasions at the miraculous battle of Las Navas de Tolosa in 1212.

Eastern Crusade

The Turks amassed on the eastern front, and subdued Armenia, Syria, Palestine and began massacring pilgrims like the 12,000 Germans killed on

---

[5] Leon Gautier, *Chivalry: The Everyday Life of a Medieval Knight* (Tumblar House, 2015).
[6] Biezsad, 49, 51-62 Spencer, 129-130,
[7] Spencer, 126-130, 171-175.

Good Friday, 1065.⁸ The Greeks asked for help from the west, and Cluniac monk Pope Urban II called on the Franks to "manly achievements" "for your eastern brethren are in urgent need of your help."⁹ The crusaders were seized with zeal and all shouted the battle cry *Deus Vult!* [God wills it!] and, leaving their families and wealth, "took up the cross." The crusader marched east against the horde to *lay down his life for his friends* (Jn. xv. 13). Thus arose the new crusader chant:

> He bore the Holy Cross,
> who broke the power of hell;
> He was girded with power
> He rose again the third day.
> Alleluia.
>
> The stone which the builders rejected as become the headstone of the corner, alleluia.

Pope Urban instituted the morning and evening Angelus for the crusaders to fight under the banner of the *Theotokos*, calling on the Holy Spirit to make the eastern crusade detached from the earthly city.

The Muhammadan threat that Christians faced was a daily consideration in many places, where at any moment the Muhammadan soldiers could attack. Cities had walls against these invaders for a reason. Some Christian orders bound themselves by oath to give their lives to free their brethren from Muhammadan slavery, as did the Mercedarians founded by St. Peter Nolasco (1189-1256). This is why the Christian knight was charged to fight against the Saracen "without mercy," knowing from experience that they did not believe in the sinfulness of lying, but preached their doctrine of "sacred deceit" (*taqiyya*).¹⁰ Nevertheless, saints attempted to preach the Gospel to the Muhammadans, often winning the crown of martyrdom.

---

⁸ Jonathan Sumption, *Age of Pilgrimage—The Medieval Journey to God* (Mahwah, NJ: HiddenSpring Books, 2003), 257-258 in Steve Weidenkopf, *The Glory of the Crusades* (Catholic Answers Press, 2014) 257, n69; Spencer, *op. cit.*, 136-143.
⁹ Spencer, 145-153.
¹⁰ Sura 16:106; Ibn Ishaq, 224, 771 cf. Bill Warner, "The Doctrine of Deceit," *Center for the Study of Political Islam* (2008) <https://www.politicalislam.com/the-doctrine-of-deceit/>, accessed March 26, 2021.

Crusade on All Fronts

Meanwhile, the occult had stirred the Cathars in Southern France, taking over cities, preaching fornication, hatred of woman, sodomy and the righteousness of child murder.[11] The Cathar doctrine attacked the Old Testament yet many of the Jews who followed occult practices allied with them in their common principle of negation—not *Christendom*.[12] These Jews also attacked the rational Jews and tried to burn works of Rambam ("Maimonides," 1138-1204).

After generations of preaching including the great St. Anthony of Padua (1195-1231) working miracles, the Church called a crusade to defend the children. The chaplet of Mary, which would eventually become the Rosary, was revealed against the Cathars, converting souls. According to Fr. Calloway, Feast of the Holy Name of Mary, September twelfth, 1213, saw the Rosary overcome at Battle of Muret.[13]

At its best, the Inquisition attempted to save the innocent from unjust punishment by giving a fair trial to all.[14] It is crucial to note that the Inquisition and the rational Jews were on the same side opposing the Kabbalah Jews who were helping the Cathar cause. On the other hand, men who profaned the name of Christ also broke out in violent anger against the Jews in general. This was against the long tradition of *Sicut Judaeis*,

---

[11] Barber, *The Cathars*, 22, 25-26, 28, 73, 80-81, 94-95, 98-99, 101-103, 109, 187-189, 198, ; John M. Riddle, *Contraception and Child murder from the Ancient World to the Renaissance* (Harvard University Press, 1994), 113; John Abert, *From the Brink of the Apocalypse* (Routledge, 2009), 133-134; Donald Kagan et al., *The Western Heritage*, 10th ed., (London: Prentice Hall, 2009), combined volume, 214; Evans, *Witchcraft and the Gay Counterculture*, 54-61, 88-89.

[12] Jewish and other historians confirm the connection between the Cathars and the Kabbalah Jewish party. Lewis Browne *Stranger Than Fiction* (Macmillan, 1932), 222; Israel Abrahams, *Jewish Life in the Middle Ages* (Philadelphia: The Jewish Publication Society of America, 1930), 402; Norman A. Cantor, *The Sacred Chain: The History of the Jews* (New York: HarperCollins, 1994), 178; Heinrich Graetz, *History of the Jews* (Philadelphia: The Jewish Publication Society of America, 1894), vol. III, 501. Jones provides an overview of the anti-Christian Jews in this period with these sources in *Jewish Revolutionary Spirit*, 103-113.

[13] Donald H. Calloway, MIC, *Champions of the Rosary: The History and Heroes of a Spiritual Weapon* (Marian Press, 2016), 41.

[14] On an accurate understanding of this, see H. J. A. Sire, *Phoenix from the Ashes* (Angelico Press, 2015), 32-47; Steve Weidenkopf, *The Real Story of Catholic History: Answering Twenty Centuries of Anti-Catholic Myths* (Catholic Answers Press, 2017), 111-136; Henry Kamen, *The Spanish Inquisition: A Historical Revision* (Yale University Press, 2014), 86-91.

necessitating a renewal of the charter under Calixtus II in 1120, and again by at least eighteen popes through Nicholas V in 1447. We will discuss this further in the next chapter.

To the North, the Gospel was continuing to the reach the hearts of the Northmen in Scandinavia and Iceland toward "acceptance of a higher spiritual ideal."[15] This was the end of the slave trade through the northern waters, but the latent pagan aggression necessitated the calling of the Northern Crusades that were seen "as a just war fought primarily to defend Christian missionaries and converts from harassment at the hands of the pagan Wends and to create a political context conducive to the peaceful expansion of Christendom through missionary work."[16] This helped our fathers convert the Scandinavian culture to Christ by the sixteenth century.

Meanwhile, against the betrayal of Coptic Abba Benjamin, *Sam'ān al-Kharrāz* galvanized the Coptic Christians by miraculously moving a mountain when challenged by the Muhammadans. To this day, the Coptic Church is the strongest Church under the Muhammadan yoke.

Further east, God's Providence was raising up a new empire in the far east: the Mongols, who were subduing Asia from modern Korea to the Ukraine. At this time the Syriac Christians were finding "mass converts" among the Turkic-speaking peoples of inner Asia: the Uighur, Kerait, Naiman, Merkit and the Ongut.[17] The Mongols were curious about Christianity and as the Syriac script was used to write Uighur and Ongut, the Mongols adopted Syriac script before the Kublai Khan period (1260-1294).[18] Ambassadors from the Syriacs and Mongols would soon reach Rome.

Freedom from Tyranny

Within Europe, the first Western Christendom was created by the Crusades as the "living parable of the doctrine of the spiritual sword."[19] It

---

[15] Dawson, *The Making of Europe*, 216
[16] Andrew Latham, "Medieval Geopolitics: What were the Northern Crusades?" (Medievalists.net, undated) < https://www.medievalists.net/2019/02/what-were-the-northern-crusades/>; Accessed March 16, 2021. Marek Tamm "How to justify a crusade? The conquest of Livonia and new crusade rhetoric in the early thirteenth century," *Journal of Medieval History*, 2013 Vol. 39, No. 4, 431–455; Eric Christiansen, *The Northern Crusades* (Penguin, 1998).
[17] Li Tang, *East Syriac Christianity in Mongol-Yuan China*, 15.
[18] Ibid., 16
[19] E. G. Passant, *Cambridge Mediaeval History*, vol. V, 322 cited in Dawson, *The Formation of Christendom*, 220.

was this movement, "more than any other single factor" which restored the order of the Two Swords.[20] This was exemplified most of all in the great king St. Louis IX in whose life "the leaven of paganism is entirely purged away," says Dawson, while the characteristic heroic idealism of the northern warrior remains."[21]

It was the fusion of the masculine ideals of green martyrdom and Christian knighthood that repudiated the effeminacy of tyranny, that the Christian sovereign "obeys the law and rules the people by its dictates, accounting himself as but their servant."[22] This is only possible because the *cultus* is free to infuse society with divine grace. In England the pilgrims streamed to the tomb of St. Thomas Becket and his popular movement of freedom for the Church is found in the first oath of the Magna Carta:

> First, we have granted to God, and by this our present
> Charter have confirmed, for Us and our Heirs for ever,
> that the Church of England shall be free, and shall have
> all her whole Rights and Liberties inviolable.[23]

Magna Carta was a charter of rights drawn up by the Catholic Church which attempted to harmonize the interdependence of hierarchy in Catholic England between the king and the nobles. It was a "Bill of Rights" wherein the king promised to protect the rights of Englishmen. The first right had to be that the Church was totally free to baptize society.

If the priesthood was not free from any form of *pontifex maximus*, the *cultus* would become a department of the state, so that tyrants could take the law into their own hands and make the Christian knights fight for filthy lucre instead of the Cross. The fundamental logos that bound king, coin and kitchen to the *cultus* was the oath. The oath involved three parties—two men with God as witness. This repudiated the voluntarism of the strong over the weak, subjecting all to the King of Kings. The fundamental oaths were Baptism and Marriage, which redounded to the public oaths of *Sicut Judaeis*, the Magna Carta and economic contracts.

---

[20] Dawson, *loc. cit.*
[21] Dawson, *op. cit.*, 221.
[22] John of Salisbury, *The Nature of a True Prince* in James Bruce Ross and Mary Martin McLaughlin, eds., *The Portable Medieval Reader* (New York: Viking, 1961), 251.
[23] "Magna Carta (1297)," *Legislation of the United Kingdom*, <https://www.legislation.gov.uk/aep/Edw1cc1929/25/9/section/I>, accessed March 26, 2021.

The freedom of the Church, therefore, was vital to the freedom from tyranny, making the sovereign into "the temporal organ of a spiritual society."[24] In this way he was viewed as a lay member of the Church. The distinction was not between "Church and state" but between "clergy and laity." Thus the Two Swords doctrine was "represented by the canon law as a whole."[25] Canonist Stephen of Tournai (1128-1203) summarizes this:

> In the same city, and under the same King, there are two peoples and two authorities. The city is the Church, the King is Christ, the two peoples are the clergy and the laity... and the two authorities are the priesthood and the monarchy.[26]

Vincent of Beauvais writes that "the whole Church is made up of two orders, clergy and laity, as if two sides of one body."[27] Thus first Western Christendom saw the blossoming of Christian culture in that the soul in Christian culture and the body in temporal society are working together. Here the body and soul of the people were in union by what Pope Clement IV called "mutual help" so that each could convert souls and society.[28] The principle of this union was the divine grace of the Holy Spirit, flowing from the *cultus* freely celebrated by the bishop, attended by the king and the people. This was liberation from being "subject to unclean demons" to restoring the order of Christ's Throne.[29] Moreover, even the opposing viewpoint that saw the emperor as the head of the spiritual power, is still "the same unitary conception of Christian society."[30] Furthermore, God's Providence showed in emperor Otto that in some grave circumstances such actions of the temporal power may be necessary.

---

[24] Dawson, *op. cit.*, 216.
[25] R. W. Carlyle, A History of Mediaeval Political Theory (New York: Barnes and Noble, 1915), vol. II, 198.
[26] Carlyle, *loc. cit.* in Dawson, *The Formation of Christendom*, 216.
[27] Vincent of Beauvais, *The Moral Instruction of a Prince*, 3 cited by Andrew Willard Jones, *Before Church and State: A Study of Social Order in the Sacramental Kingdom of St. Louis IX* (Emmaus Academic: 2017), 247.
[28] Pope Clement IV to St. Louis IX, *Layettes du Trésor des chartes*, 4:5404 cited by Jones, *op. cit.*, 450.
[29] Augustine, *City of God*, bk. XIX, ch. 23-24.
[30] Dawson, *op. cit.*, 217.

Cultus Over King and Coin

When the covenant of the Christian people was confirmed, the *cultus* could merit divine grace for souls and society without hindrance. The tripartite feudal society of our fathers discussed in the last chapter was more than ever imbued with divine grace unhindered by *Roma* ambitions of temporal rulers. Dom Ursmer Berliere observes,

> The Benedictine abbey was a little state which could serve as model to the new Christian society which was arising from the fusion of conquered and conquering races, a state which had religion for its foundation, work resorted to honour as its support, and an new intellectual and artistic culture as its crown.[31]

Already by 1000, the Church's influence had abolished the old slavery without bloodshed, making it into an interdependent hierarchy of rights and duties. As the generations progressed, the peasant had a right to partial ownership of his land and product, allowing him to invest in his own welfare. The public order also obeyed the Third Commandment so that "there was besides Sundays an average of more than one holyday of obligation every week."[32] Thus a workman worked four or five days a week, with a great deal of rest in the winter with more work during agricultural season. He enjoyed security, "life insurance" (his widow and children were provided for upon his death), and most of all, he enjoyed the true wealth of Christendom: the true, the good and the beautiful.

But he also had a duty to provide food for the nobles who fought to protect him and were bound to provide for a man's family if he died. This was the feudal system, which did not have police or homelessness, nor centralized taxes, but whole communities bound themselves by oath to keep the peace.[33] A peasant paid his food to his lord, who himself governed the village or city. In cities, a merchant class and guild communities arose, who sought to make excellent products for the greater glory of God. The divine grace of the *cultus* permeated the economic relationship between master and apprentice as this guild document of the period shows:

---

[31] U. Berliere, *L'Ordre Monastique*, 41 in Dawson, *Medieval Essays*, 64.
[32] Brown, *Synod of Maynooth* (Dublin: 1927), 16 in Cahill, *The Framework of a Christian State*, 401.
[33] Christopher Dawson, *Religion and the Rise of Western Culture* (Garden City, New York: Image Books, 1958), 164.

> No trade or profession can succeed honourably unless the apprentice is early taught to fear God and be obedient to his master, as if he were his father. He must morning and evening and during the week beg God for help and protection, for without God he can do nothing...Every Sunday and holy day he must hear Mass and a sermon and read good books. He must be industrious and seek not his own glory but God. The honour of his master and of his trade he must also seek, for this is holy, and he may one day be a master himself, if God wills and he is worthy of it...When the apprentice fails in obedience and the fear of God, he shall be punished, so that through the pain of the body, the soul may benefit.[34]

The mind of Western Christendom understood that "Power corrupts, and absolute power corrupts absolutely."[35] Thus the power of the kings was minimal, but most of all, the power of money was viewed with great caution as a possible temptation, since money only instantiated power. Avarice was understood as the "vice that most seriously foments disorder in the soul and thus encourages us to embrace false gods."[36] Thus in economics the voluntarism of strong over weak was mitigated by the morality that God must be the third party to every contract. In this way the saints guarded against the idol of money. Women were an integral part of this economy as the law of the home, as mothers and girls managed the household and did field work together with the fathers and sons.

The *cultus* was penetrating the peoples with divine grace. Even Protestant authors confirm that:

> Real faith and piety were common; most people lived and died believing that they were trying to follow God's will. Most clergy genuinely felt called to the cure of souls and sought to minister faithfully. We hear more about the exceptions—immoral and lazy clergy—

---

[34] Jansenn, *History of the German People at the Close of the Middle Ages*, trans. Mitchell, bk. III, ch. 2, p. 20 in Cahill, 76.
[35] Acton to Archbishop Mandell Creighton, Apr. 5, 1887.
[36] Scott Hahn and Brandon McGinley, *It is Right and Just* (Steubenville, OH: Emmaus Road, 2020), 108.

because, then as now, bad news was news, but good news was not.[37]

Historians typically call this period falsely by the term "Middle Ages." But this term indicates that this period was a "middle" between antiquity and the so-called "Enlightenment" when western Europe lost the faith. In order to promote this, history typically focuses on the tiny minority of people — petty kings paying soldiers to fight small land battles. These men were a fraction of the population, while the mass of people were imbued with faith and it showed in their society.

Another non-Catholic scholar praises the period as an "age of faith" in which "the clergy was more numerous and influential in politics, economics philosophy and other intellectual pursuits than it has ever been since," and "any conception of the world from which the supernatural was excluded was profoundly alien to the minds of that age."[38] Instead of the pejorative "Middle Ages," Christians should adopt terms like "Age of Faith," or "First Western Christendom."

The Monuments of Our Fathers

In the year 1220, the whole community of nobles, priests, craftsmen, and laborers finally put the last of the stones into place. The Cathedral of Chartres had taken generations to build but our fathers had lived and died trying to fulfill a spiritual ideal for generations, as was done in the building of Santiago de Compostela, Canterbury, Amiens, Reims, London, and later Strasburg, Paris, Seville, and Florence and more. These great works were a cooperative effort of an entire city of people raising great monuments without a profit motive. The cathedrals took hundreds of years to build at great expense. Their beauty is still admired to this day by people around the world.

To think that barbarian hordes of knights and peasants could all work together and communicate over dozens of languages and erect the most awesome monuments to God is astounding. Such things are only possible with divine grace. Artisans carved beauty into the very tops of the roofs, offering them to God alone. In this is beauty seen as "the extension of the

---

[37] Paul R. Spickard and Kevin M. Cragg, *A Global History of Christians* (Grand Rapids: Baker Academic, 1994), 68.
[38] Pelikan, quoting with approval Lopez and Bloch, *The Christian Tradition* (Chicago: The University of Chicago Press, 1978), vol. 3, 3.

artistic act that is begun in nature."[39] Beauty was created by imitating the logos present in creation, now empowered by the grace of the *cultus*.

Numerous cathedrals were dedicated to the honor of Our Lady, pointing to the depth of the transformation in the Christian family.

The *Cultus* and the Kitchen

As Mary was exalted as throne of Christ, the order of humility in the Christian family provided the due honor to the Christian wife and mother. Marian devotion spread with the Rosary at this time and the chivalrous ideal raised up woman to a place of honor in the home and in the community. This finds its full literary expression in Dante (1265-1321) whose praise of woman is unsurpassed as he is cleansed from his sins by the Marian perfection of Beatrice in the *Paradiso*. In England, the miracle of Our Lady of Walsingham beautified the English love of liberty with the Annunciation of Mary.[40]

The Christian family could live in a community free from strong government control. The life of the village centered around the parish church and numerous annual festivals celebrated everything from the harvest to the Holy Cross. The Feast of Christmas was kept with great pageantry, and not even a robber would dare to shed blood during Christmastide. This was the cultural momentum of the freedom of the Church.

Music at this time continued to develop in beauty as the Gregorian chant developed with composers such as St. Hildegard of Bingen (1098-1179) who raised their voices to join the chorus of angels at the Holy Sacrifice. A form of harmony later began with more voices in a proto-polyphony which would flower during the Renaissance.

We must also comment on *volk* music from the German meaning "of the people."[41] The vernacular hymns and songs were being passed down in an oral tradition celebrating the great joys of human life, love and hardship. These *volk* songs are fundamental to "build up community" in strong traditions from the instrumental merriment of the Irish to the Parisian and Viennese charm to countless Christmas carols, and folk dancing music everywhere. These *volk* songs helped replace the old Shamanic sounds of the pagan past of the Huns, Celts, Northmen and other barbarians, which were designed to induce trances and invoke evil spirits.

---

[39] Vladimir Soloviev, "The Universal Meaning of Art," in Vladimir Wozniuk, trans., *The Heart of Reality* (University of Notre Dame, 2003), 68
[40] This insight from Englishman Theo Howard.
[41] Von Hildebrand, *Aesthetics*, vol. 2, 439-450.

Children were taught by public art, architecture and ritual that inclined them away from Original Sin and toward divine grace. They were baptized as infants, and raised with a cultural momentum of truth, goodness, and beauty in the Age of Faith. They had security, a job to do whether laboring or craftsman or fighting or praying. They had rights and duties that everyone understood. Virtue was publicly praised and vice was publicly shunned.

An unbiased historical view suggests that the man of western Christendom in 1200 arguably worked less and had more—especially ownership of his own productive property—than the modern man in 2021.[42] The greatest threat to an adult was invasion or disease while the fallen angels had to fly against the strong current of Christian cultural momentum. Adults could expect to live into their sixties or seventies.[43] But strong pagan morals and brutality could still be seen among the powerful. Nevertheless all that is great in modern civilization would surely have developed out of Christendom yet in an economic order subordinated to the family.

The greatest challenge that children faced was the primitive medical technology. Many infants or children died due to sickness or other difficulties. But even these children were baptized, giving them the sure hope of eternal life. Thus their infant saints merited the grace in Heaven for the glories of our fathers crusading on all fronts, but especially in the soul. Thus innumerable saints arose in this period, such as St. Francis (1181-1226) and St. Dominic (1170-1221), bringing about the next renewal.

The Second Greco-Roman Renewal

The first renewal was the Greco-Roman-Syriac orthodoxy of Nicaea against the *Roma* of the eastern *pontifex maximus* that culminated in the Carolingian Renaissance. Now that *Roma* was thoroughly crippled in the west, the second Greco-Roman renewal could come about. The Syriac Christians translated Aristotle into Arabic, and the Muhammadans briefly

---

[42] Recommended works in this regard is the work of Cahill, *Framework of a Christian State*, and Pesch, *Liberalism, Socialism, and Christian Social Order* as well as Belloc, *The Servile State*.

[43] H. O. Lancaster, *Expectation of Life* (New York: Springer Science, 1990), 8. Amanda Ruggeri, "Do we really live longer than our ancestors?" (*BBC*, 2nd October 2018 <https://www.bbc.com/future/article/20181002-how-long-did-ancient-people-live-life-span-versus-longevity>, accessed March 17, 2021.

passed this down for a few generations before it was crushed by al-Ghazali (1058-1111).

But through Greeks, Muhammadans and Jews, the western Europeans gained Aristotle for the first time in centuries. The old debate was renewed: the strict party wished to have nothing to do with the new Greek philosophy, and the moderate party wanted to adopt the same.

The greatest of the strict party was St. Bonaventure (1221-1274), who sought to maintain the Augustinian inheritance from the first renewal, especially his Platonic method.[44] The greatest moderate was St. Thomas Aquinas (1225-1274) who sought to integrate Aristotle into a new synthesis. Filled with the Holy Spirit, this was not a balance of power but a contest of humility, shown especially when Pope Urban IV asked both to compose hymns for the office of Corpus Christi to beautify the *cultus*. When St. Bonaventure heard the beauty of St. Thomas' words about the Real Presence, he was overcome by "its depth and sweetness" and decided to destroy his own composition as unworthy.[45] Thus in *Paradiso* Dante has both saints praise each other for "the labors of the two were toward one goal."[46]

The vast philosophy of St. Thomas achieved a synthesis of "the union of material and spiritual worlds" drawing upon Aristotle.[47] Yet St. Bonaventure "integrated the distinctively Greek spirituality" with the "emerging Franciscan devotion to the humanity and passion of Christ."[48] Thus from different sides of the moderate and the strict, the second Greco-Roman renewal formed the philosophical, theological and spiritual foundations of the first Western Christendom. This philosophical foundation was "the foundation of European science" that found its nascent form in St. Albert the Great (1200-1280), the tutor of St. Thomas.[49]

With so many souls dying with the sacraments, the fallen angels seethed with envy as little children inherited their former thrones. Christians would no longer be fooled with the idols of stone, wood, or fire. The fallen angels were burning to renew their attack somehow. They noticed what was accumulating in the vaults of the kings.

---

[44] Dawson, *Medieval Essays*, 132.
[45] Dom Jerome Vaughn, *The Life and Labours of Saint Thomas of Aquin* (Abridged 2nd Ed., London: Burns and Oates, 1980), 485
[46] Dante, *Paradiso* Canto XI, 42 (trans. Mandelbaum, Bantam: 1984).
[47] Christopher Dawson, *Religion and Progress* (Washington, DC: Catholic University of America Press, 2001), 138.
[48] Ewert Cousins, "Introduction" in *Bonaventure* (Mahwah, New Jersey: Paulist Press, 1978), 1.
[49] Sire, *Phoenix from the Ashes*, 28-30; Jones, *Logos Rising*, 333-366; Dawson, *Progress and Religion*, 136.

XV

THE WRATH OF GOD AND THE SECOND PORNOCRACY

In 1497, in the kingdom of Naples, the slaves finally heaved the last of the stone into place. They had created the first triumph arch since the days of the pagan *pontifex maximus* and his evil ideology *Roma*. From this point the momentum was shifting away from building for the glory of the King of Kings and His City. Finally, the true Gospel of the true king had arrived whose name would last forever! Hail, son of god! Above the arch the inscription read: Alfonsus, King of Spain, Sicily and Italy, Kind, Merciful—Unconquered. But how many remember him now?

> But now his flock has become so greedy.
> ...[they] have now turned back...
> And soon we are to see, at harvest time
> The poor grain gathered, when the tares will be
> Denied a place within the barn—and weep.[1]

While the glory of Western Christendom was making saints, the "mutual antipathy of Greeks and Franks" had been strengthened by the love of money as they began to fight over power. Excesses on both sides led to impious soldiers raping and murdering, sparking hatreds and allowing the schismatic Greek party to gain strength.

The Greek patriarch Michael III (1110?-1178) publicly argued that the yoke of Muhammadanism was better than submitting to the pope.[2] The "errors of the Latins" multiplied in various "lists" condemning every

---

[1] Dante, *Paradiso*, Canto, XI, 124.
[2] Dawson, *The Formation of Christendom*, 275.

western custom from adding salt to water to wearing different hats.³ The Latins were vilified as "Azymites" because they used unleavened bread for the Eucharist.⁴ The usurper Andronikos "won power by appealing to the anti-Latin sentiment of the mob" that massacred the Venetian and other Italian men, women and children, and sold the rest for slaves to the Muhammadans.⁵

Thus the Venetians allied with the Greek usurper Alexios IV to wickedly divert the Fourth Crusade to conquer Constantinople. But the Latin domination of New Rome (1204-1274) raped and murdered, furthering the mutual hatred between Christian peoples. Meanwhile, the French pope Urban IV not only approved the Feast of Corpus Christi but created a "French party" among the cardinals and started an intrigue with Charles of Anjou (1226-1285) for the earthly city.⁶

Meanwhile, the "rabbinical and capitalist elite in the Jewish communities... abandon[ed] the Aristotelian rationalism of Maimonides, and instead embrace[d] an esoteric theosophy called Kabbalah" which they introduced to the Christian "mercantile and banking elite."⁷ This melded the Jewish leaders with the impious Christians worshipping money and gradually decreasing their support for the eastern Crusade.⁸

The Mongol Crusade

Meanwhile the truth, goodness, and beauty of Christendom reached its climax during the pontificate of Bl. Gregory X (1271-1276). Following the Latin Patriarchate of Constantinople, the orthodox Greeks led by John Bekkos gained enough influence to achieve the union of Lyons II (1274) led by saints Bonaventure and Albert. This formalized the second Greco-Roman renewal and was the basis for yet greater things for Christendom. For at this council an envoy from the Mongol Khan Abaka was baptized, and new communication had been opened to the far east.⁹ Pope Gregory

---

³ Tia Kolbaba, *The Byzantine Lists: Errors of the Latins* (Illinois Medieval Studies, 2000), 189-202.
⁴ Dawson, 273.
⁵ Ibid., 275.
⁶ Coulombe, *Vicars of Christ*, 197.
⁷ Norman F. Cantor, *In the Wake of the Plague*, Reissue ed. (Simon and Schuster, 2015), 151. Cf. Jones, *Jewish Revolutionary Spirit*, 103-113.
⁸ Weidenjopf, *Glories of the Crusade*, 180-184.
⁹ Dawson, *The Formation of Christendom*, 277; Dawson, *Mission to Asia* (University of Toronto Press, 1980), xxxiv.

was winning over the kings to a new crusade, and the Greek emperor also took up the Cross and looked toward the rising sun.

Contacts had been made with the Syriac Christians during the crusades, and letters came from the Church in China to have union with Rome.[10] During the Mongol-Yuan Dynasty (1271-1368) there was a "second heyday of Christianity in China" with Christians at court, and 1318 would see the height of Syriac Christianity in the east with thirty metropolitan bishops and 700 dioceses.[11] Meanwhile Giovanni da Pian del Carpine, Benedict the Pole, William of Rubruck, John of Monte Corvino, Brother Peregrine, Andrew of Perugia were penetrating into the far east converting souls and restoring contact with the Syriac Church.[12]

This was the moment for the Mongol Crusade, supported by Popes Gregory X and Nicholas III, when the second Greco-Roman renewal was about to reunite with the Syriacs to liberate forever mankind from the sword of Muhammadanism. Indeed, says Dawson, "if there had been more men of similar courage and faith to carry on this work in the same spirit, the whole history of the world, and especially of the relations between Europe and the Far East, might have been changed."[13]

The banner of this Mongol Crusade had to be the Immaculate Conception, which the great "Subtle Doctor," Franciscan Bl. Duns Scotus (1265-1308) was at that time crucially expounding.[14] For this doctrine solidified the absolute dependency of man upon the divine grace of God to overcome Original Sin. Mary alone was saved from this wound by the merits of Christ, and through her the Christian peoples were brought to the priesthood for the healing of the soul.

Filthy Lucre

But when Pope Nicholas III died in 1281, Charles of Anjou brought his army into Viterbo and threw the leading Italian cardinals into prison, demanding a pope who would support his ambitions.[15] The cardinals

---

[10] R. Rabban, eds. "Chaldean Catholic Church (Eastern Catholic)," *New Catholic Encyclopedia* (2003), vol. 3, 366.

[11] Tang, *East Syriac Christianity in Mongol-Yuan China* 16; John Binns, *An Introduction to the Christian Orthodox Churches* (Cambridge University Press, 2002), 29; Philip Jenkins, *The Lost History of Christianity* (HarperOne, 2008), 71-96.

[12] Dawson, *Mission to Asia*.

[13] Ibid., xxxv.

[14] Richard Cross, *Duns Scotus* (Oxford University Press, 1999), 5.

[15] Coulombe, *Vicars of Christ*, 201.

showed they had lost all manly courage when they elected Simon de Brie as Pope Martin IV who "allowed himself to become a tool" of the earthly city. Charles induced him to excommunicate the Greeks so that he could "crusade" against Constantinople.[16] God protected the city from this wicked pride and punished Charles with a revolt in Sicily, but Pope Martin IV did not repent and called a new "crusade" against Christians in 1291. It was Charles of Anjou who began the dynasty that eventually led to the triumph arch of Naples.

At the very same moment, the thinning support for the eastern crusades had reached the breaking point as the knights of Palestine were fighting "overwhelming odds" against the Muhammadan horde.[17] The women and children were sent to escape ships while the knights made their last stand when Turks streamed into the castle.[18] The knights of the Templar tower were surrounded and negotiated a surrender, but when the Muhammadans tried to rape the women the knights fought back. In the end, 30,000 Christians had been killed and their cities razed. The love of money had caught up to Christendom.

Forsaking the crusade for the City of God, France looked for greater power and managed to get French popes to stay in Avignon (modern France) instead of Rome from (1309-1376).[19] But the papacy had overextended its power into politics, and the moral leadership of the pope was waning in the popular mind.[20] A new national consciousness was arising at this time that was natural with the development of vernacular culture: the Spanish and Portuguese fighting spirit with the German knighthood, the nobility of the Italians and Austrians with the French chivalry, the English innocence, the Irish merriment and the Polish strength.[21] But the powerful wanted to twist this good into an exaltation of the earthly city.

The powerful of France and England ignored the Church's restrictions on violence and usury so that they could commit fratricide in the Hundred Years War (1337-1453). In Germany and Italy, nationalist movements were arising with Marsilius of Padua (1275-1342) and Wilhelm of Ochkam

---

[16] Dawson, *The Formation of Christendom*, 278.
[17] Ibid.
[18] Weidenkopf, *Glories of the Crusades*, 203-205.
[19] Christopher Dawson, *The Dividing of Christendom* (San Francisco, CA: Ignatius Press, 2008), 39.
[20] Ibid., 40.
[21] Plinio Corrêa de Oliveira, "Vocations of the European Peoples," <https://www.traditioninaction.org/OrganicSociety/A_006_Vocations_PCO.htm>. Accessed March 17, 2021.

(1287-1347). Englishman Ockham introduced the plague of Nominalism into Christian philosophy.[22] This was the idea that there existed no logos in God, but only "pure power, stripped of meaning."[23] God was a voluntarist god. It was the Muhammadan error that God could change His mind and alter His own divine law like the Ten Commandments. St. Thomas had already refuted this when he said that "to say that justice depends simply upon the will of God, is to say that the divine will does not act according to wisdom, and this is blasphemy."[24] But if kings could have power stripped of meaning, they could rationalize voluntarism, and gain false power from the world, the flesh and the devil.

In order to finance their wars with each other to impose voluntarism, the Christian kings practiced usury with Jewish money lenders or Catholic bankers like the Medici (who gained prominence especially later in the Renaissance). These were doing experiments in magic seeking power from demons.[25]

This led to the reaction of the populace in expelling the Jews from France in the twelfth through the fourteenth centuries, as well as Naples (1288), England (1290), Hungary (1360), Switzerland (1392) and more. The popes then were trying to renew *Sicut Judaeis* to protect the Jews from violence. While some Jews were greedy for gain, other Jews, who opposed them, suffered for it. Jews were also not the only ones practicing usury, but they served as a scapegoat for angry and exploited populations. Greed was so rampant that the Fifteenth Ecumenical Council (1311) was forced to declare, "If indeed someone has fallen into the error of presuming to affirm pertinaciously that the practice of usury is not sinful, we decree that he is to be punished as a heretic."[26]

Finally, says St. Louis de Montfort, "God punished the whole of Europe and sent the most terrible plague that had ever been known."[27] This was Black Death (1347-1350), which killed a full third of Europe and most

---

[22] Jones, *Logos Rising*, 353-359; John Wild, *Introduction to Realistic Philosophy* (New York: Harper and Row, 1948), 27-29.

[23] The phrase is from John Darnielle.

[24] Copleston, *History of Medieval Philosophy*, 160 in Jones, *Logos Rising*, 355.

[25] Woodhouse, *George Gemistos Plethon: The Last of the Hellenes* (Oxford: Clarendon Press, 1986), *passim.*; Gutkind, *Cosimo De' Medici: Pater Patriae* (Oxford: Clarendon Press, 1938) in E. Michael Jones, *Barren Metal* (South Bend, IN: Fidelity Press, 2014), 71-78, 123-142.

[26] Ecumenical Council of Vienne 29, <https://web.archive.org/web/20060402233228/http://piar.hu/councils/ecum15.htm>, accessed March 26, 2021.

[27] St. Louis de Montfort, *The Secret of the Rosary* (TAN Books: 1987), 24.

of the clergy.²⁸ God preached penance to the powerful through St. Bridget of Sweden and St. Catherine of Siena.

At the same time, says Dawson, among the common people "it was not an irreligious age" with multiple saints across Europe in Johannes Tauler and Bl. Henry Suso in Germany, Bl. John van Ruysbroeck and Gerard Groote in The Netherlands, Bl. John Colombini (1300-1367) in Italy.²⁹ The cathedrals were still being raised to the glory of God and pilgrims still streamed to Santiago de Compostela. The Avignon Papacy approved the miraculous discovery of Our Lady of Guadalupe in Extremadura leading in 1340 to the victory of Rio Salado. The Spanish Inquisition attempted to protect the faithful from false Jewish and Muhammadan converts.³⁰ And the public *cultus* was still center of life for the common man.

But the powerful did not repent of their evils, and the contest of power raged on until the love of money created three rival popes and the nations chose sides between them in the Great Western Schism (1378-1417). God raised up one of his greatest saints in Vincent Ferrer (1350-1419) who raised the dead, preached in tongues and converted thousands of Christians, Jews, and Muhammadans. It was St. Vincent who authorized withdrawing obedience to the man he believed was the true pope (Benedict XIII) so that Christendom could be reunited at Constance under one pope, Pope Martin V.³¹

Meanwhile, God raised up another great saint in Joan of Arc (1412-1431) who turned French identity toward the heavenly city to end the Hundred Years War, dying as a martyr for Christendom. By the 1400s, *The Cloud of Unknowing* was being copied and *The Imitation of Christ* was spread by Thomas à Kempis (1380-1471) becoming one of the greatest bestsellers in history.³²

---

[28] Dawson, *The Dividing of Christendom*, 43.
[29] Ibid., 44.
[30] Steve Weidenkopf, *The Real Story of Catholic History: Answering Twenty Centuries of Anti-Catholic Myths* (Catholic Answers Press, 2017), 111-136; Henry Kamen, *The Spanish Inquisition: A Historical Revision* (Yale University Press, 2014), 86-91.
[31] John Salza and Robert Siscoe, "St. Vincent Ferrer was never a Sedevacantist: The True Story of St. Vincent and Benedict XIII" (*True or False Pope: Refuting Sedevacantism and Other Modern Errors*, undated). < http://www.trueorfalsepope.com/p/st-vincent-ferrer-sedevacantist.html>. Accessed March 16, 2021.
[32] Dawson, *The Dividing of Christendom*, 44.

But to the east, the divisions among Christians had been exploited by the Muhammadans as the Eastern Roman emperor John VI Kantakouzenos married his daughter to a Muhammadan and sought his help to fight other Christians. In 1365, the city of Constantinople was the only thing left of the Eastern Roman Empire. It was besieged by the Muhammadan armies in 1376, 1411, and 1422 with a blockade attempt in 1390 and 1402. Further east, the brutal Timur massacred millions in his campaigns, undoing any hope of the Mongol Crusade.[33] The emperor found enough support to try to renew Christian unity at the Council of Florence (1431-1449).

The Third Greco-Roman Renewal

By the time the Greeks and Latins met at Florence the world had changed since Lyons one hundred fifty-seven years prior. While the common man remained faithful, the momentum among the powerful had continued to grow toward idols. The love of money had polluted many Italians combined with pride in their earthly cities. The pious effort to return the papacy to Rome was also supported by Italians who hated the French, like Petrarch (1304-1374) who dubbed the Avignon papacy as "the Babylonian Captivity of the Church."[34] He exalted the pagan Romans over the Christian heroes like Charlemagne and became fascinated with the ancient rhetoric of Cicero and Varro. His linguistic skill allowed him to rely on the beauty of words alone so that his words "do not aim at the representation of some objective reality, but at the creation of a reality by the sheer power of speech."[35]

At Florence this fascination with words led to a fascination with *magic* words in discovering ancient occult texts of the Greeks spread by Gemistos Plethon (1355-1454). The Medici bankers sponsored him to found a new Platonic academy in Florence, which helped Giovanni Mirandola spread Kabbalah magic and "the dignity of man." The bewitching words would soon be applied to the Catholic people, while the Kabbalah melded with the merchants for centuries promoting magic and occultism for power.[36]

---

[33] Dawson, *Mission to Asia*, xxxiv.
[34] Albert Russell Ascoli, "Epistolary Petrarch," and David Marsh, "Petrarch's adversaries: the *Invectives*," in Albert Russell Ascoli, ed., *The Cambridge Companion to Petrarch* (Cambridge University Press, 2015), 1, 4, 113-116, 173-176.
[35] Giuseppe Mazzotta, "Petrarch's confrontation with modernity," Ibid., 237.
[36] Daniel Jütte, *The Age of Secrecy: Jews, Christians, and the Economy of Secrets, 1400–1800* (Yale University Press, 2015).

Another devotee of this movement, Marsilio Ficino, wrote that "Man is a great miracle... for he knows the genus of the daemons [*sic*] as if he were related to them, and he transforms himself into God as if he were God himself."[37] This statement was really the repudiation of the Immaculate Conception, which said only one person was ever saved from Original Sin.

But as the pride of man in his own power was growing, the ugliness of the love of money was revealed. During the council, news reached Pope Eugene that Christians had succumbed to the temptation of the Muhammadan slave trade and invaded the Canary Islands to enslave the Africans there. The pope immediately saw that not only did this destroy the Black families, but also profaned the name of Christ among the pagans "putting their souls in danger."[38] He demanded that the Christian slave traders immediately free the slaves and restore their property or incur excommunication. This was the beginning of the poison of Muhammad infecting Christendom, but we will return to that below.

At the same time, the Renaissance was nothing less than the third Greco-Roman renewal. For not only were new Latin texts discovered, but the study of the Greek language was revived in the west for the first time since the first renewal. This time, grammars were being published and even the Semitic language was being renewed with Hebrew studies.

Florence succeeded in formalizing a new alliance particularly with the help of the Greek-friendly Franciscans.[39] It followed the *dialogos* method of St. Athanasius. This council would become the basis of almost all Eastern Catholic Churches.[40]

But in order to turn the tide against the Turks, the Church needed funds for a new crusade. Between the new slavery and the new magic, kings and princes were seeking ways to tax their subjects and were uninterested in the taking up the Cross in a new crusade. The clergy of Rome were also

---

[37] Marsilio Ficino, *The Soul of Man* c. 1474, in James Bruce Ross and Mary Martin McLaughlin, eds., *The Portable Renaissance Reader* (New York: Viking, 1969), 390.

[38] Eugene IV, *Sicut Dudum* (1435) <https://www.papalencyclicals.net/eugene04/eugene04sicut.htm>, accessed March 26, 2021.

[39] On the Franciscans' involvement see Christiaan Kappes, "A Latin Defense of Mark of Ephesus at the Council of Ferrara-Florence (1438-1439)," *Greek Orthodox Theological Review* 59 (2014), 161-230. See also T. S. Flanders, "The Council of Florene: No Scholarly Consensus?" *Meaning of Catholic* <https://www.meaningofcatholic.com/2019/05/28/council-florence-scholar-consensus/>.

[40] Aidan Nichols, *Rome and the Eastern Churches*, 2nd ed. (San Francisco, CA: Ignatius Press, 2010), 323-350.

succumbing to the love of money and magic. The Crusade of Varna raised against the Turks was defeated in 1444.

Meanwhile the Greek Catholics led by Emperor Constantine XI were finding stiff resistance among the schismatic Greeks led by Mark of Ephesus. As the Turks were at the gates of the city, the Greek commander of the Navy said, "I would rather see a Turkish turban in the midst of the City than the Latin mitre" and a mob of Greeks cried "Death to the Azymites!"[41] At this moment the schismatic Greek party gained the upper hand against the Greek Catholics.

The love of money won when Hungarian Orbán sold his cannon technology to Sultan Mehmed II, which helped overcome the defenses of Constantinople. They breached the walls in May of 1453 and the Turkish army streamed in. The Catholic Emperor tore off his imperial purple robe and plunged into the melee "to die fighting as a common soldier against the triumphant infidel... His body was never recovered."[42]

Mehmet II entered the Church of Hagia Sophia to see a mass of civilians taking refuge. He declared the church to be a mosque and the victorious Turks raped women, while 30,000 Christians were enslaved.[43] The schismatic Greeks allied with him and their leader Gennadios II was installed as the new patriarch, by the Sultan who called himself *Kayser-i Rum* ("Caesar of the Romans"). Thus was created the Greek Vatican ("Phanar"), giving Gennadios absolute power over all Christians under the Turkish yoke. Thus as one Orthodox source argues, the Turks most of all nullified Florence and imposed the Greek schism.[44] The Antiochians accepted Florence in 1457 and 1460, and Kievan Ruthenians in 1458, but the Turk-appointed Phanar sought to suppress them.[45]

Meanwhile, the schismatic Slavic party being born at this time saw the opportunity to seize *Roma* for themselves and rejected the Catholic Isidore of Kiev, seeking to impose on the Russian people a new *Roma*. Yet through the efforts of Paul II and the Greek Catholic Cardinal Bessarion, Grand Prince Ivan III married the Greek daughter of Constantine XI. This act could help cleanse Slavic Christendom and renew the crusade against the Turks. But Ivan consolidated his power and by 1498 had himself

---

[41] Dawson, *The Formation of Christendom*, 275.
[42] Carroll, *The Glory of Christendom* cited in Weidenkopf, *The Glory of the Crusades*, 280 n596
[43] Weidenkopf, *op. cit.*, 212.
[44] Lina Murr Nehme, *1453: Muhammad II Imposes the Orthodox Schism*, trans. Alfred Murr and Michel Nehme (Beirut: Aleph et Taw, 2001), 175-209.
[45] Nichols, *loc. cit.*

proclaimed as Caesar ("Czar"), re-establishing the *pontifex maximus*.[46] At this time, Hopko admits, "all the elements were essentially in place for the ideology of Moscow as the 'Third Rome.'"[47] From this point, Eastern Orthodoxy was dominated by a debate among the Greek and Russian clergy over how to be *Roma* without the *Roman Primacy*, as it exists to this day.

But after Mehmet conquered New Rome he continued onward, while all of Christendom shuddered in fear. Pope Calixtus attempted to meet the threat bearing down on them from the east, instituting the noon Angelus for all of Christendom.[48] God raised up St. John Capistrano who roused 8,000 on crusade that saved Belgrade and Hungary in 1456.

The Greek schismatics of Athens gave over the city to the Turks, and the Genoese sought to aid the Turks against the Venetians for the love of money. Pope Pius II attempted to rouse the lethargy of Christian men to arms but gathered only a meagre force. He turned his old heart to battle and himself left Rome to face the foe himself, dying on the way to battle.

The Venetians chose the love of money and made a treaty with the Turks in 1479, allowing the Saracens to land in Italy in 1480. They took control of the town of Otranto, where they seized 813 who faced execution if they did not submit to Muhammadanism. But a tailor named St. Antonio Primaldo raised his voice and said he would die a thousand deaths for Christ.[49] The martyrs of Otranto won the glorious crown and their courage converted one of their executioners who chose to die with them.

Finally Pope Sixtus IV roused a crusade from Naples and Hungary to meet the foe. Then God heard the prayers of all the faithful and Mehmet died on the Feast of the Cross in the month of Mary, 1481.

Within a generation too, in the west, Our Lady had finally cleansed Spain from the Moors, and the Angelus bell rang in Granada, signaling the end of the *Reconquista*. Christendom was saved once more by God in His angels and in His saints. But just as this external threat was beaten back a new and more terrible foe would come from the love of money.

---

[46] Thomas Hopko, *Orthodox Church History*,
<https://www.oca.org/orthodoxy/the-orthodox-faith/church-history/fifteenth-century/russia2>. Accessed March 17, 2021; Nehme, *op. cit.*, 219-221.
[47] Hopko, *loc. cit.*
[48] Roberto de Mattei, "The Angelus: A Militant Christian Prayer," trans. Giuseppe Pellegrino, *The Remnant* (March 6 2020)
<https://remnantnewspaper.com/web/index.php/articles/item/4796-the-angelus-a-militant-christian-prayer>, accessed March 26, 2021.
[49] Steve Weidenkopf, *Timeless: A History of the Catholic Church* (Huntington, IN: Our Sunday Visitor, 2018), 456.

The Second Pornocracy

By 1500, the printing press had been printing the Holy Scriptures and all sorts of Renaissance texts for two generations. But the third renewal was turning into social chaos. While the good men of Christendom were crusading for their wives and children, the love of money was growing a corrupt, effeminate class of men in the Vatican. This we might call a "Second Pornocracy," since it imitated the first period of the 10th century. The Dionysian bloodlust was forcing its way back into the papacy, finding its nadir in Alexander VI (1492-1503). He fathered nine children, seven while a cardinal with two different women, and when he was pope, in his sixties, he convinced nineteen-year-old Giulia Farnese to become his concubine.[50]

The horror of the Second Pornocracy was made worse by the pope's own army, as Erasmus lamented:

> Though that apostle tells our Saviour in the gospel, in the name of all the other disciples, we have left all, and followed you, yet they [our popes] challenge as his inheritance, fields, towns, treasures, and large dominions; for the defending whereof, inflamed with a holy zeal, they fight with fire and sword, to the great loss and effusion of Christian blood, thinking they are apostolical maintainers of Christ's spouse, the church, when they have murdered all such as they call her enemies; though indeed the church has no enemies more bloody and tyrannical than such impious popes, who give dispensations for the not preaching of Christ; evacuate the main effect and design of our redemption by their pecuniary bribes and sales; adulterate the gospel by their forced interpretations, and undermining traditions; and lastly, by their lusts and wickedness grieve the Holy Spirit, and make their Saviour's wounds to bleed anew.[51]

---

[50] Weidenkopf, *The Real Story of Catholic History*, 213. It should be noted however that some scholars question the common, negative view of Alexander VI as another anti-Spanish black legend. See Lorenzo Pigniotti, *La Legenda Nera Di Papa Borgia* (Fede & Cultura; 2° edizione, 2016); GJ Meyer *The Borgias the Hidden History* (Bantam, 2014).

[51] Erasmus, *In Praise of* Folly, trans. Anonymous (London: 1876). Pt. 3.

THE WRATH OF GOD AND THE SECOND PORNOCRACY

The Vatican obsession with magic words and paganism began to invade the *cultus* itself. This got to the point where the "most famous orator of the Pontifical Court," on Good Friday in the presence of the pope, preached about the greatness of the human sacrifice to Artemis in Greek mythology.[52]

These Renaissance men planned to change the sacred *cultus* by introducing their great Renaissance learning and concoct an amazing Breviary with bewitching words that everyone would love, an idea that originated with the corrupt Renaissance pope, Leo X (1513-1521).

This breviary would strip all the beauty from the fathers passed down from ancient times and leave only what they thought was "eloquent" according to their contemporary world.[53] With the blessing of the pope, they tried to impose their ideas not only on the priests, but even on the people.

Meanwhile, the increased state power and state wars throughout Christendom led to higher taxes and revolts of peasants throughout Europe. The common faithful were working out their salvation in revival movements like the Brethren of the Common Life following the *Imitation of Christ*. But the unfaithful of the city of man burned with hatred against the clergy for their licentiousness and open concubinage. The black death had killed much of the faithful clergy, who had sacrificed their lives giving the sacraments to plague victims. It had also destroyed the labor force, killing the economy. The corruption of the second Pornocracy had spread across the clergy of Europe, and meanwhile, rumors were spreading that the Turks had regrouped and were advancing again on Europe.

The situation was reaching a breaking point, when an Ecumenical Council was called to try to reform the situation and defend against the advancing Turks. Erasmus wrote to Pope Leo X begging him make "war on vice."[54] But while the Lateran Council V was closing in early 1517, news was spreading that the Turks had taken Egypt. The threat was growing closer and closer. The eastern Christians were already under the Muhammadan yoke.

---

[52] P. de Nolhac, *Erasme en Italie* (Paris, 1888), 76; J. Burckhardt, *La civilization en Italie au temps de la Renaissance*, French ed. (Paris, 1885), t. I., 277, 311-317 in Pierre Batiffol, *History of the Roman Breviary*, trans. Atwell M. Y. Baylay (London: Longmans, 1898), 177.
[53] Batiffol, *op. cit.*, 177ff; Reid, *Organic Development of the Liturgy*, 34ff.
[54] Erasmus to Leo X, 1515 in W. T. H. Jackson, ed., *The Essential Works of Erasmus* (Bantam, 1965), 258.

> Towards the close of the council (1517) the noble and highly cultured layman, Gianfrancesco Pico della Mirandola, delivered a remarkable speech on the necessity of a reform of morals; his account of the moral condition of the clergy is saddening, and reveals the many and great difficulties that stood in the way of a genuine reform. He concluded with the warning that if Leo X left such offences longer unpunished and refused to apply healing remedies to these wounds of the Church, it was to be feared that God Himself would cut off the rotten limbs and destroy them with fire and sword. That very year this prophetic warning was verified.
>
> The salutary reforms of the Lateran Council found no practical acceptance... Leo himself did not scruple to set aside repeatedly the decrees of the council. The Roman Curia, then much despised and against which so many inveighed with violence, remained as worldly as ever. The pope was either unwilling or not in a position to regulate the unworthy and immoral conduct of many of the Roman courtiers. The political situation absorbed his attention and was largely responsible for the premature close of the council.[55]

Christendom had suffered from the Hundred Years War, the Black Death and terrible famine, and now the second Pornocracy. *And the rest of the men, who were not slain by these plagues, did not do penance from the works of their hands, that they should not adore devils, and idols of gold, and silver* (Apoc. ix. 20). For men, enraptured in the truly exquisite beauty of Renaissance opulence mixed with the love of money, chose to be seduced by the lies of the fallen angels: *Let us eat and drink, for tomorrow we shall die* (I Cor. xv. 32).

Therefore Almighty God was forced to remove the protecting hand of His divine grace from Christendom.

> I destroyed some of you, as Sodom and Gomorrha, and you were as a firebrand plucked out of the burning: yet you returned not to me, saith the Lord. Therefore I will do these things to thee, O Israel: and after I shall have

---

[55] K. Löffler, "Pope Leo X," *The Catholic Encyclopedia* (1910), <http://www.newadvent.org/cathen/09162a.htm>, accessed March 26, 2021.

done these things to thee, be prepared to meet thy God, O Israel (Amos iv. 11-12).

XVI

LUST FOR POWER AND CERTAIN DEATH

In the year 40 AD, St. James the Apostle was finding a great resistance among the Roman Spaniards to the Gospel. The man of God was overcome by discouragement when the Mother of God appeared to him and told him that that Spain would one day spread the Gospel around the world and raised a pillar to dedicate a church for this event. Our Lady of the Pillar has been celebrated on October twelfth ever since.[1]

In 1456 when Calixtus instituted the midday Angelus against the advancing Turks, he encouraged pilgrimages to her shrine. In 1492, the holy monarchs Ferdinand and Isabella paid for the flag ship *La Santa María de la Inmaculada Concepción* ("Holy Mary of the Immaculate Conception") for Columbus to sail to the Indies in August.

By October, Columbus's provisions were running low and his men were ready for mutiny. He promised them that if land was not sighted by the feast of Our Lady of the Pillar, he would turn back. Then when the feast day came, October 12 the cry rang out: *"Land!"* Our Lady of the Immaculate Conception arrived at the island named San Salvador (Holy Savior), in modern Bahamas. On Christmas the *Santa María* was wrecked and made into Fort Navidad, so that the second Western Christendom would be built upon the Immaculate Conception and divine grace of Christ.

But a struggle immediately began between the Gospel and the love of money. By October twelfth, 1517, this struggle was twenty-five years old and a Catholic priest named Martin Luther was about to turn thirty-four.

Martin Luther was a truly brilliant man tormented by his scrupulous conscience and deeply burdened by a childhood with an overly strict father.

---

[1] J.M. March, "Nuestra Señora Del Pilar," *The Catholic Encyclopedia* (1911) <http://www.newadvent.org/cathen/12083b.htm>, accessed June 5, 2021.

He was an Augustinian monk whose great intellect won him a professorship, and whose zeal would win him a following. What is more, like every soul at that time—even the most profligate—the *cultus* had deeply imbedded faith in Christ into his bones and an unshakable faith in the Real Presence.[2] In many ways his life was a summation of all that was best and worst of the souls of men at that dark hour. His father confessor, Johann von Staupitz, understood that he needed the most tender fatherly care for his agonizing soul. Unfortunately, he had never been trained in St. Thomas or even Duns Scotus, nor even the most basic textbook of the Fathers—the *Sentences of Peter Lombard*—but only the voluntarist Ockham who denied piety and Tradition in his doctrine and method.[3]

When Martin Luther went to Rome, like the King, he immediately went to the temple. But unlike Decameron's Jew who found faith out of darkness, Luther was enflamed with Christian zeal against the idols of the money changers. But because Luther lacked all restraint on his tongue, he allowed his disgust to turn his true crusading zeal "against flesh and blood." He would soon begin his writing career that consisted of an encyclopedic tirade of insults. He had the mind of a professor, and like all heretics, he was a genius.

Initially some Catholic clergy reacted to Luther with ridicule, as one translated his works into German in order to show just how irrational he was, filled with mudslinging and straw men. But instead of viewing Luther with logos, the weary sheep erupted in mob bloodshed. This shows how much even the good shepherds had lost touch with their flock at that time. Almost immediately Luther was forced to write a work entitled "Against the Murderous, Thieving Hordes of Peasants."

At the same time, Martin Luther, having already been examined by the erudite Cajetan and found to be penetrated with the errors and contradictions of Ockham, persisted with the Holy Father for more *dialogos*. "In every good work the just man sins."[4] Luther's errors were obvious enough, since most educated men could see it.[5] But they were not

---

[2] Luther's doctrine of consubstantiation was an attempt to reject scholasticism (and Catholic dogma) while maintaining the same dogma of the Real Presence.
[3] His chief study was Gabriel Biel who was prominent interpreter of Ockham. See William Marshner's brilliant lectures on the theological origins of the Lutheran heresy. "The Protestant Revolution," *Institute of Catholic Culture*, <https://archive.org/details/WilliamMarshnerTheProtestantRevolution>.
[4] Leo X, *Exsurge Domine* (1520), proposition 31.
[5] "We are dealing with this: would a stable mind depart from the opinion handed down by so many men famous for holiness and miracles, depart from the decisions of the Church, and commit our souls to the faith of someone like you

obvious enough to all erudite men and certainly not to the mob who knew the clergy all the way to the See of Peter were polluted with the love of money.

Thus when the opulent and corrupt Renaissance pope Leo X condemned Luther's errors, it may as well have been Balaam's ass speaking truth. As will be the case in the nineteenth century, powerful men, who took the side of the Church in faith, also took the side of the enemy in morals. As a result very few saw the truth. Luther publicly burned the bull condemning his errors as well as the *Corpus Christianum*, which was "comparable to burning the United States Constitution."[6] It was literally a declaration of war.

But just as this was happening Hernán Cortés had discovered the brutal Aztec empire of death in modern Mexico that sacrificed 20,000 people each year to their cruel gods.[7] After peaceful negotiations failed, Cortés allied with other Indians and sounded the battle cry: "Santiago!" And God overthrew their empire and gave over the Aztecs to Spanish rule. This liberated the Indians from an empire of death.

Every Tribe, Tongue and Nation

But the reason Martin Luther could burn the legal document of Christendom as an act of revolt was because his movement, like all heresies, contained a half truth. It was an effort to complete the formation of Christian peoples into the distinct nations by means of vernacular culture. This had occurred long ago for the Irish. The barbarian tribes were Christianized enough to be largely civilized with vernacular cultures, yet barbarian enough to use this national identity to lead a revolt of the earthly city against the heavenly, in the same way as the Greek schisms in the first millennium. Dawson elucidates the cultural dynamics at play:

> Just as... the religious revolt of Syria and Egypt [410-632 AD] against the Imperial Church represents a national reaction of the oriental element against the dominance of

---

who has sprung up just now with a few followers, although the leading men of your flock do not agree either with you or among themselves" Erasmus, *Hyperaspistes I* in Peter Macardle and Clarence H. Miller, trans. *Collected Works of Erasmus, Controversies: De Libero Arbitrio / Hyperaspistes I* (University of Toronto Press, 1999), 76, 203.

[6] Carter Linberg, *The European Reformation* (Blackwell, 1996), 88.

[7] Victor Davis Hanson, *Carnage and Culture: Landmark Battles in the Rise of Western Power* (New York: Anchor Books, 2001), 195 in Weidenkopf, *Timeless: A History of the Catholic Church*, 400-403.

the Hellenistic-Roman culture, so, in the Reformation, we may see a Nordic revolt against the Latin traditions of the mediaeval culture. The syncretism of Roman and Germanic elements which had been achieved by the Carolingian age, was terminated by a violent explosion which separated the mediaeval culture complex into its component elements.

Hence it is no mere coincidence that the line of religious division after the Reformation follows so closely that of the old [Roman] imperial frontier. On the one hand the Teutonic lands outside the Empire—Scandinavia and Northern Germany—form a solid bloc of Lutheran territory. On the other, the Latin world as a whole remained faithful to Rome, and so also to a great extent did the Germanic provinces within the frontiers of the Empire, such as Flanders, Bavaria and the Austrian provinces.

Finally Calvinism, which is the form of Protestantism that appeals most strongly to the Latin mind, has an irregular distribution along the frontier line itself. It appears in Scotland [north of the Roman British frontier] and in the Netherlands, in Switzerland and along the Rhine, as well as on the lower Danube in Hungary and Transylvania. It is also well represented in the two western kingdoms—England and France. The former was mainly Calvinist with considerable Catholic and Catholicizing elements. The latter was Catholic with a strong Calvinist minority and a Calvinizing influence represented by the Jansenists. But in each case the dominant religion is strongly national. In England the Church is Protestant, but above all Anglican; in France it is Catholic, but also Gallican [French].[8]

Meanwhile, the two great exceptions to this—the peoples of Catholic Ireland and Poland—"found in Catholicism an invaluable ally against the forces that threatened their own national identities" and so remained in the bosom of the Church.[9]

---

[8] Dawson, *Progress and Religion*, 141-2.
[9] Ibid., 142 n1.

Thus the fallen angels took the natural law inclination of piety toward one's fathers and fatherland and poisoned it with the lust for power using religious controversy as a pretext, exactly as they had done when they gained the east exalting the earthly city. The fundamental need of a nation is for motherhood to provide the foundation. Then, Our Lady of Ephesus had solved this problem by destroying the dominion of Artemis Ephesia and becoming the true mother of the Mediterranean peoples. But the Greeks, Copts and Syrians had refused to repent and chosen bloodshed, provoking God's wrath.

As this was happening, the national identity of the native peoples in the Americas was cast into doubt. They had been freed from the worship of false gods, but did not know who they were anymore.

The Birth of Tyranny

The nobles, having forsaken their *oblige* and been consumed with the love of money, almost simultaneously understood that this was their moment to give *freedom* to their lust for power. The technology of the printing press could mass produce not only words, but pictures, and it was able to turn Martin Luther into an instant celebrity in a way completely unprecedented in the history of the world.

The powerful were given the most advanced technology to prevail by means of mob bloodshed and emotional manipulation. Burning with the lust for power, those in power pushed their princes to join Protestantism in order to seize the wealth of the poor. Heretics and Jews together began printing Protestant Bibles with Hebrew Old Testaments.[10]

Meanwhile across the channel, English King Henry VIII was seeking power. Having no male heir, it seemed to him the only thing to do it was to declare his marriage to Queen Catherine null and void and then marry his mistress, Anne Boleyn. But the pope would not break the law of God and grant a declaration of nullity to a valid marriage. Bishop St. John Fisher said he was ready to die for this marriage like St. John the Baptist.

In order to break his vow of marriage, King Henry had to break his oath to the Magna Carta. Those in power wanted more power so they joined with him and created the Act of Supremacy, which created a tyrannical theocracy, giving Henry and Parliament absolute spiritual authority over English souls. All of Henry's bishops, emptied of every manly strength, fell on their knees to keep their earthly glory instead of a glorious crown.

---

[10] Jones, *The Jewish Revolutionary Spirit*, 264.

The martyrs John Fisher and Thomas More stood up against the heretical powers and trampled down the serpentine regime slowly strangling Our Lady's Dowry.[11]

St. Thomas condemned the Act because it violated Magna Carta and the vow to protect the Church that "every other Christian prince always" made "at their coronations."[12] This point is absolutely crucial. Magna Carta guaranteed the freedom of the Church in its first article. The breaking of the Magna Carta came when the king became an *absolute monarch* and the Parliament became an absolute parliament over culture. They united over the principle of negation—*not Rome*. By means of absolute state power, they were able to impose the Act of Supremacy by sheer force of will—the very definition of voluntarism. This was the true beginning of tyranny because if the Church is not free to convert king, coin and kitchen, the powerful will impose their tyranny. After this Englishmen will talk of "liberty" but only if the freedom of the Church is restored will any true liberty be found. Everything else will be a mirage of slogans.

Tyranny had existed in England before, but no king had created an ideology which broke the Magna Carta itself by creating a rationalized alternative. This was nothing but another Iconoclasm. Henry and Parliament were rejecting the Two Swords and creating the absolute, divine right of the secular state.

The accusers of St. Thomas pointed out that all of England had approved of this tyranny, but St. Thomas countered that they were rejecting the tradition of all the fathers and saints in Heaven.[13] He fought with the crusading spirit and he preached the Cross:

> More have I not to say (my Lords) but like as the blessed Apostle St. Paul... consented to the death of St. Stephen... and yet be they now both twain holy saints in heaven, and shall continue there friends for ever, so I verily trust and shall therefore right heartily pray, that though your Lordships have now in earth been judges to my condemnation, we may yet hereafter in heaven merrily all meet together to our everlasting salvation.[14]

Thus his son-in-law and first biographer wrote the motto on his panegyric for this great saint: "In this sign, you will conquer." And thus all the

---

[11] Dawson, *The Dividing of Christendom*, 118ff.
[12] William Roper, *The Life of Thomas More* (1626), pt. IV.
[13] Ibid.
[14] Ibid.

glorious martyrs of Catholic England and Ireland, one and all knights of St. George and sons of *Pádraig*, trampled on the Serpent and merited the grace for the miracles that would swiftly come in God's Providence.

Meanwhile, the powerful convinced Henry to break the Seventh Commandment as well and seize all the wealth and power that the Church held for the poor. In those days, land was like a trust fund. Henry greedily grabbed up the food of the poor peasants and gave it to his allies. Like every revolution that was to come, it was the "will of a determined minority against a confused majority."[15] We must note here, however, that this action was not without some just cause. For at this time every human heart was filled with good and evil, and heresies cannot be promoted without half-truths. For even in the time of St. Thomas Becket, King Henry II had just cause to oppose the wicked clergy of his day and seize lands that corrupt clergy were abusing to commit sin.[16] And, indeed, the clergy of England in the sixteenth century were even worse. But Henry understood that in order to destroy the people's will to have Christ as King, he thoroughly destroyed their ancestral pilgrimage shrine to St. Thomas Becket, the shrines of Our Lady of Walsingham, and suppressed holy days so that the peasants would work more for the lusts of filthy lucre.[17]

Across the British Isles the Catholic people rallied to the Sign of the Cross. Peasants brought pitchforks, machetes, whatever they could find, ready to die for their King. But no greater valor was found on the battlefield than among the fearless sons of *Pádraig*. These violent movements were the same spiritual acts of violence that had first cleansed them from the dominion of Satan—they were just wars in defense of their baptismal vows. They were the true revolts against tyranny as the kings resurrected the old role of *pontifex maximus* and the ugliness of *Roma* to prop up their earthly cities.

The Catholic people, the *cultus* having imbedded Christ the King in their souls for generations, instinctively understood that the king was imposing idols on them. Every king and prince who usurped the spiritual sword of the priesthood in all of Europe intended to impose the idol of filthy lucre onto the Christian people. It was as if, instead of the Blessed Sacrament of the King elevated by the priest, the prince proclaimed himself priest and now lifted high for all to see the coin with his face on it. Henry

---

[15] Rao, *Black Legends*, 378.
[16] Dan Hitches, "Becket and His Critics," *First Things* (January 2021) <https://www.firstthings.com/article/2021/01/becket-and-his-critics>, accessed March 26, 2021.
[17] Richard Rex, *Henry VIII and the English Reformation* (Macmillan International Higher Education: 2006), ch. 3.

committed tyranny by the judicial divorce of two of his six wives and the murder of two more, foreshadowing all horrors to come.

By the time the tyrant went to his eternal reward, those in power understood they could never convince the pious English masses to be "liberated" with merely the change in eldership. So they convinced Henry's son Edward VI to follow Luther and attack the *cultus*—the root of Christendom—even though the Protestants all disagreed among themselves:

> The Reformers themselves were bitterly divided concerning the doctrine of the Lord's Supper, but they were united in a common detestation of the sacrificial interpretation which had always been taught by the Church.[18]

This was the same spirit which animated the Pharisees to concoct their own rite to disobey the Mosaic rite of Atonement—the authority of man's will over God's *cultus*. All that was necessary was to fabricate an elaborate lie within the *cultus*. Understanding the great power of beauty, symbols, and *Logos*, Cramner and his successors suppressed nearly every beautiful thing in the *cultus* passed down by our fathers to safeguard the faith in the Real Presence. These were made to undermine the dogma of the Eucharist:

1. Everything said audibly
2. Altar turned into a table facing the people
3. Tabernacle removed and forbidden
4. Prayers at the foot of the altar removed
5. Offertory Prayers removed
6. Incense removed
7. Roman Canon removed
8. Communion in the Hand, standing[19]

---

[18] Michael Davies, *Liturgical Revolution*, rev. ed., (Kansas City, MO: Angelus Press, 2015), vol. 1, 55.

[19] Davies, *Liturgical Revolution, vol. 1: Cramner's Godly Order*, 143-193, 193-222. For a comparison of Cramner's mass changes, see *Whispers of Restoration*, "Charting Liturgical Change," <https://docs.wixstatic.com/ugd/c3b8e6_6a3859c8bc344686a8b2891a5e2412f5.pdf>, accessed June 7th, 2021.

This corrupted *cultus* thus mixed the true rites of our fathers with the ideology of power. Even if all their heresies were true, the idea that they could fabricate the *cultus* of a people and impose it on them would attack culture since it denied that the *cultus* was guarded and passed down through piety. The elders of a culture were the guardians of the *cultus*, and only made changes to safeguard the beauty of logos already present in the tradition—like Pope Sergius against the Eastern Roman attack on Latin customs. This was the "organic development of the liturgy."[20] The greatest note of this organic development is that it changes as fast as children grow up and generations pass away, thereby always keeping the bond of piety for generations within a people, since the rite is the bond that unites them all to logos.

But for the English heretics, their only desire was to manipulate the Catholic populace so they could keep their power. Above all, this was an iconoclastic attack on innumerable English, Welsh, Scottish and Irish children, whose faith in the Real Presence was formed by the signs and symbols of the rite and the customs of cultural momentum.

This is the moment when the nobles of England lost all chivalry and abused their position for power and greed. They were reluctant to suffer due to their attachment to pleasure. And since "there cannot be nobility without suffering," this was the end of nobility. While the empire of death in Mexico was in ruins, a new empire of death was being created in England. These were the great grandfathers of Freemasonry.

After Queen Mary restored the order of the faith, those who had gained power under Henry VIII were determined to destroy her. The division between the moderates and the strict among the Catholic bishops helped Pope Paul IV alienate the English Cardinal Pole and reject Queen Elizabeth, influencing her to reject the pope in turn.[21]

When Elizabeth ascended the throne in 1558, Catholics formed a majority in England. She allied herself with the Muhammadans and used the power of the state to hunt down and eradicate every Catholic *cultus* celebrated throughout the realm.[22] Meanwhile, similar tactics were being used on the Scottish by the John Knox, who loved the theocratic state that Calvin had created, thinking that by the act of man the Kingdom of Heaven could be created on earth—denying the divine grace in the sacrament to alone make the Kingdom in the lives of the saints who are foreigners in this world.

---

[20] Reid, *passim*.
[21] Coulombe, *Vicars of Christ*, 264.
[22] Jerry Brotton, *The Sultan and the Queen: The Untold Story of Elizabeth and Islam* (Penguin, 2017).

The powerful in England set to work for four decades with the most sophisticated tools of a corrupted *cultus* and endless propaganda—the faithful were viciously attacked and brainwashed by this evil. It was "the creation of a reality by the sheer power of speech." They made Elizabeth a propaganda against Mary by calling her a "Virgin Queen," while hunting down anyone who did not attend their churches. With men such as Richard Hooker, a façade of Catholicism was able to be concocted, winning over Catholics to the tyranny of the new *pontifex maximus*.[23] While Hooker was brilliantly discussing "the consent of the people," the Elizabethan state was imposing engineered consent in the most massive propaganda operation since Imperial Caesar.[24] In 1570, the pope excommunicated Queen Elizabeth.

She gave power and influence to occultism with John Dee and others, and created a massive spy network fueled by the love of money.[25] A new generation received the lies, and by the time of her death in 1603—England was a nation of Anglicans with a tiny minority of faithful Catholics. Thus through state propaganda, they destroyed the faith so that the wealthy could have power. This was the fruit of breaking the Magna Carta.

Matricide

Luther and his monk friends began a sex trade in "convincing" nuns to be "liberated," and his teaching of *sola Scriptura* led some, such as Muentzer, to reinstate polygamous "marriages."[26] Luther himself could not find a basis for disallowing polygamy in principle and removed the sacramental dignity of marriage itself.[27] Additionally, Luther told Philip of Hesse that he could not forbid his adulterous bigamy based on Holy Scripture. Thus a sexual revolution helped motivate Catholic priests to join

---

[23] Dawson, *The Dividing of Christendom*, 124-125.
[24] For a sympathetic reading of Hooker, see Robert Reilly, *America On Trial: A Defense of the Founding* (San Francisco, CA: Ignatius Press, 2020), 158-171.
[25] Jason Louv, *John Dee and the Empire of Angels, Enochian Magick and the Occult Roots of Empire* (Inner Traditions, 2018); Jones, *Jewish Revolutionary Spirit*, 321-402.
[26] Ibid., 253-288.
[27] "I confess that I cannot forbid a person to marry several wives, for it does not contradict the Scripture. If a man wishes to marry more than one wife he should be asked whether he is satisfied in his conscience that he may do so in accordance with the word of God." Martin Luther, De Wette II, 459, in Hartmann Grisar, *Luther* (1916), Vol. 5. 329–330. Luther did, however, discourage the practice while allowing it in principle.

the "Reformation" as Luther's group helped to bring the nuns out of the convent to get priests to break their vows with them.

> Trafficking in nuns had become one of the chief ecclesial transactions of the Reformed party in Germany, and throughout the 1520s [Luther's] Wittenberg became one of their favorite meeting places... Libido culminating in broken vows was the engine that pulled the Reformation train. It was a uniquely effective way of organizing ex-clergy in opposition to the Church.[28]

One contemporary witness remarked that "Luther's counsels had been carried out to such a degree that there is absolutely more chastity and honor in the married state in Turkey than among evangelical [Protestants] in Germany."[29]

When men commit such acts of unclean wickedness, they must run and hide from their mothers. In order to rationalize their sins against the Sixth commandment, the Protestants forced themselves to hate their own mother, for they knew she would destroy all of their "Athenian word-webs" with a single glance.[30]

Thus came one of the most devastating features of Protestantism: the assault on the Mother of God. To this day, nothing shows the diabolical character in the Protestant heresy more than their attitude toward their own Mother, the All-Pure Virgin. "The evil spirits," says Newman:

> When they came up again from the realms of darkness, and plotted the utter overthrow of Christian faith in the sixteenth century, then they could find no more certain expedient for their hateful purpose than that of reviling and blaspheming the prerogatives of Mary, for they knew full well that, if they could once get the world to dishonour the Mother, the dishonour of the Son would follow close.[31]

---

[28] Jones, *Degenerate Moderns*, 220-227.
[29] Heinirch Denifle, *Luther and Lutherdom* (Somerset, Ohio: Torch Press, 1917), 298n in Jones, *loc. cit.*
[30] Akathist Hymn to the Theotokos
[31] Newman, "Discourse 17: The Glories of Mary for the Sake of Her Son."

By removing the veneration of Mary, Protestants turned Christ the King merely into "a poetical expression" and a "mystical economy," which can be controlled at will by the powerful.[32] Without Mary, there is no incarnation. Without the incarnation, God is in the skies and man is down on earth and able to impose his will. Thus as Cahill writes, the "prestige of the woman suffered an incalculable disaster by the abolition under Protestantism of the veneration and cult of the Mother of God."[33]

The Other Solas: *Liber* and *Libertas*

The Greco-Roman world sought to make woman into an instrument to be *used*: "We have call girls for our pleasure, concubines for our daily needs, and wives to give us legitimate children and look after the housekeeping."[34] For the Christian, with Mary in his heart, Christ in his bones and logos in his mind, there exists an instinct planted there by Our Lady to respect woman, (hence modern "feminism"). This instinct was so strong that even Ockham couldn't remove logos from the bones of European men. Thus, having removed the *cultus* of the *Theotokos*, the Protestants used the third Greco-Roman renewal to reincarnate *Liber* and *Libertas*.

Liber was the name for Dionysius who suddenly flashed out and overcame you, just as lust darkens the rational mind. Its conspicuous element is *drunkenness*—i.e. complete loss of rationality. *Liber* was the spirit of Muentzer who reintroduced the practice of polygamy. It was the heresy that the conjugal act—and indeed all good things in life—was meant for pleasure alone. This specific proposition would be condemned by the Holy See in 1679.[35] If pleasure is everything, then reason can be dispensed with, and hence "folly is the daughter of lust."[36] *Liber* makes woman into an object to be used for pleasure alone.

But the *cultus* of the Virgin Mary was embedded too deeply in the heart of European man that such a spirit against logos could never attack

---

[32] Ibid.
[33] Cahill, 432
[34] Demostenes, *In Neastram*, 122 in Reay Tannahill, *Sex in History*, 100.
[35] Condemned as "at least scandalous and pernicious in practice": "the act of marriage [sexual intercourse] exercised for pleasure only is entirely free of all fault and venial defect" and the same is condemned for eating and drinking. Heinrich Denzinger, *Compendium of Creeds, Definitions, and Declarations on Matters of Faith and Morals*, ed. Peter Hünermann, 43rd ed. (San Francisco, CA: Ignatius Press, 2012), 2108-2109.
[36] *Summa*, II-II q46 a3.

Christendom directly. The acts of Muentzer were viewed as extreme even by Luther. Instead, having torn down the throne of the *Theotokos* he resurrected *Libertas*. The spirit of *Libertas*, being rational (unlike *Liber*), is the Puritan spirit which uses woman only "to give us legitimate children and look after the housekeeping." Woman is reduced from her royal throne of beauty as the *queen of the home* (I Tim. v. 14) to a mere servant girl used for "legitimate children."[37] The Puritans were a heretical sect which sought to impose morality by Calvin's police state, and suppress all lawful pleasure.

But because the Puritans had lost the grace of Sacramental Marriage, they burned with lasciviousness to use their wives to fulfill all of their lusts while vehemently rejecting the Catholic doctrine that celibacy is objectively superior and supernatural.[38] The Puritan spirit sought to satisfy their desires but rationalize it into the Christian marriage bed. The idea was that if you are simply monogamous, then you can have your way with her. This error was far more deceptive than the first, and thus more wicked.

Thus *Libertas* was merely *Liber* in disguise, which would burst out into adultery and bloodshed, only to quickly rationalize everything. No one shows these better than the spirit of John Milton's rationalization of divorce to legitimize his adultery.[39]

Thus the Dionysian *Liber* and the Puritan *Libertas* are merely one spirit denying Sacramental Marriage for the sake of using a woman to satisfy the lust for power.[40] It is seeking to make the sacramental nature of Marriage into the earthly city. The love of money will unite these evil spirits into the total commoditization of women.

---

[37] οἰκοδεσποτεῖν. The verbal term is used here by St. Paul.
[38] On this important teaching, see the excellent work here: <https://religious-vocation.com/index.html>.
[39] Jones, *Jewish Revolutionary Spirit*, 416-421. Thus Milton selectively quotes the New Testament to boast against Catholic Sacramental Marriage and celibate clergy, making the "marriage bed undefiled" into the "Perpetual Fountain of Domestic sweets," where Love "Reigns here and revels" (*Paradise Lost*, bk. IV). He seems to be rationalizing his own adultery by attempting to moralize marriage into a legitimate way for spouses to use each other for lust, as long as they are married.
[40] This insight comes from St. John Paul II, *Love and Responsibility* (San Francisco, CA: Ignatius Press, 1981), 57-72.

LUST FOR POWER AND CERTAIN DEATH

Mary, Destroyer of All Heresies

Now at first, the second Pornocracy was still fast asleep, drunk with the old wine of pagan Rome. In 1527, news spread that Hungary had fallen to the Muhammadans as they advanced deeper into Catholic Europe. Rome was sacked that year and its churches looted by iconoclastic Protestants. With the "mother of all the churches" now in danger, the nobles of Christendom were finally set aflame with the zeal to take up the Cross once more. It is "the fierce anger of Heaven," wrote Bishop Sadoleto, "let us seek in God the true glory of sacerdotal dignity."[41]

But the King of France was plotting with the Muhammadans even while they were besieging Vienna, the last outpost of Christendom on the frontier, while Germany was in flames. Evil seemed to permeate the very air in every land and every man of good will felt helpless. *Who shall rise up for me against the evildoers? or who shall stand with me against the workers of iniquity?* (Ps. xciii. 16).

Thousands of miles across the ocean, the Indians of Mexico were still in despair over disease and displacement. A Chichimeca peasant named St. Juan Diego embodied all the fear and despair in that hour on Tepeyac Hill. Our Lady responded to him in his native tongue of Nahuatl: "Am I not here? I who am your Mother?"

The miraculous image of Our Lady of Guadalupe—itself a union of Our Lady of Guadalupe in Extremadura with Spanish flowers—was the spiritual banner for the new crusade. She was and is the new "Mary of Ephesus" against the wicked Artemis Ephesia of that time—the lust for power. For she perfectly turned the Indians from their cruel gods: as a pure Mestiza—mixed blood Spanish and Aztec—the ethnic identity of every soul was safe in Christendom. Matrimony is a sacrament instituted by Christ, and the Spaniards and Indians intermarried and created the peoples of second Christendom in the Americas (and Asia), and by her prayers as Empress of the Americas, she formed innumerable new peoples in the Catholic Americas: the mestizos, métis, the free people of color, the Afro-Hispanic-Indian tribe of the Seminoles in Florida, the Filipinos, and more.

Just as Europe was erupting in religious warfare, Our Lady All Pure and Immaculate united all the many tribes and petty empires of the Americas (and parts of Asia) into Christian culture for Christ the King. She is called the Destroyer of All Heresies and she came just at the right moment.

---

[41] Quoted in Batiffol, *History of the Roman Breviary*, 181.

However, these new Christians of the Americas were defenseless especially against the slavers succumbing to the temptation of the Muhammadan slave trade. Second Christendom needed an army. But many bishops and priests were corrupt. The faithful cried out: "Who shall rise up for me against the evildoers?"

The New Crusaders

For at the same moment as Our Lady appeared to bring the Americas to the King, the Spaniard St. Ignatius of Loyola was completing his studies to become a priest. The central moment of his life was a conversion from the false crusade against flesh and blood to the true crusade against the demons. He had been a worldly soldier shedding Christian blood for the sake of the earthly city.

It was only Spain's *Reconquista*, by the prayers of Our Lady of Covadonga and Guadalupe with all of Europe streaming to Compostela, that could purify the crusading spirit from earthly attachments. Ignatius was converted from voluntarism to the Kingdom of God. This purity of true detachment from earthly things can only be accomplished by a man's zeal for Our Lady, Mary Immaculate, and the Bride of Christ. The Society of Jesus, the "Jesuits" were formed to not only save their brethren from heresy, but convert all nations to Christ the King. They would become a great spiritual army at the service of Our Lord.

In 1534, three years after Guadalupe, the Jesuits were founded, and they were approved in 1540. The challenge was to redirect the third Great Greco-Roman renewal from the heresies to the faith. To do that, God worked yet another miracle.

The Council of Trent

It was not an easy task to unite the chaos of that day into an Ecumenical Council. The fundamental cultural conflict of nations in revolt had to be subordinated to the eldership of Christian culture in the see of St. Peter, which had been challenged for centuries since before Ockham.

Besides this, the increased nationalism was thwarting the third Greco-Roman renewal into a battle for the earthly cities. France was in a state of rebellion, and refused to cooperate, while the lesser Catholic powers sent as many good men as they could but it was nothing without the cooperation of Carlos I ("Charles V"), King of Spain and Holy Roman Emperor. Knowing the corruption of the papacy at that time, Carlos did not trust the papacy, who had only recently been allied against him and whose own troops had sacked and pillaged Rome just a few years prior. Carlos, meanwhile, was succumbing to the temptation of a voluntarist empire with the worldwide empire that God had given into his hand.

Besides this, there was a strong division among the priests and bishops over the third renewal. On the one hand, a strict party was deeply critical of the new learning and distrusted their chief hero, Erasmus, who haughtily mocked the lack of learning of the clergy.[42] But taken to an extreme, this party would reject the Greek New Testament of Erasmus and any linguistic knowledge obtained by the renewal. On the other side, the moderate party that followed Erasmus wanted to use the new learning for the sake of the Faith. But taken to an extreme, the moderate party could be tempted to leave the Church to become Protestants.

God overcame all of these insurmountable obstacles and more to produce the miracle that was the Council of Trent. It was dominated by Spanish, German and Italian bishops, with one French bishop, Charles de Lorraine. God raised up our holy fathers to help with true reform before and after Trent: St. Cajetan, St. Charles Borromeo, St. Philip Neri, St. Peter Canisius, St. John of the Cross, St. Francis de Sales.

Fundamentally, the fathers of this great council did not merely repeat St. Thomas, they imitated St. Thomas, thus continuing his great synthesis. The council bound together the strict Scholastic party with the moderate Renaissance party into a concise synthesis addressing every major heresy of the day. They employed "pastoral language" with Scripture in order to speak to the contemporary world. This was the new language of Trent. Most importantly, it bound the whole Church with the charitable anathema and produced the *Roman Catechism*, the sword of the spirit upon which the Church's armies would burst forth to liberate those in darkness from the principalities and powers.

Baroque Civilization

From the cultural perspective, the most important thing Trent did was safeguard the *cultus* without succumbing to the voluntarism of the Protestants. For even as the Jesuits were being founded, the truncated breviary was officially published by Paul III for use by the clergy in 1535. The final version had removed innumerable traditions of the fathers and

---

[42] Erasmus died a Catholic, but he was not a saint. His works helped provoke the Protestant revolt, but also helped expose the corruption of the day and cause the third renewal of Greco-Roman culture by his publishing the first Greek New Testament in many centuries in the west.

replaced them with "contemporary" arrangements based on Renaissance humanism. This was exposed to the common people in Zaragoza, causing an "uproar" among the pious Spanish peasants.[43]

This new breviary was vigorously opposed by St. Francis Xavier and the great men of the age, even though some good Catholics did appreciate it.[44] The opposition was vigorously expressed at the Council of Trent based on the "rights" of Tradition, and this led to St. Pius V completely revoking the approval of the new breviary.[45] It became "the preeminent demonstration in liturgical history of the priority organic development of the Liturgy enjoys over approbation by competent authority."[46] The Church easily rejected the heretical *cultus* of the Protestants, fashioned to destroy the faith of children, but she also rejected an invention of Catholics of good will. Its principles, method, and execution did not come from deep and pious meditation on the Logos and the tradition but rather the quick patchwork of geniuses with too much knowledge and not enough wisdom.

Instead, Trent produced an organic development of the liturgy and combatted abuses by promulgating a new Roman Missal. By means of the charitable anathema, it dogmatized the most exquisite and exalted metaphysical beauty of Logos Incarnate that has burned in every Christian heart to make them ready to die for their Lord: *My soul longeth and fainteth for the courts of the Lord. My heart and my flesh have rejoiced in the living God... Thy altars, O Lord of hosts, my king and my God* (Ps. lxxxiii. 3-4).

> If any one denieth, that, in the sacrament of the most holy Eucharist, are contained truly, really, and substantially, the body and blood together with the soul and divinity of our Lord Jesus Christ, and consequently the whole Christ; but saith that He is only therein as in a sign, or in figure, or virtue; let him be anathema.[47]

This truth is the metaphysical beauty of Logos Incarnate which fulfills the words of our Savior.[48] *He that eateth my flesh, and drinketh my blood, abideth in me, and I in him* (Jn. vi. 57). This doctrine is the instantiation of

---

[43] Reid, *Organic Development of the Liturgy*, 37.
[44] Many Jesuits in fact accepted this Breviary, probably because its abbreviated nature gave more opportunity for their active apostolate. Ibid., 36.
[45] Ibid.
[46] Ibid., 38.
[47] Council of Trent, Session 13, Canon 1.
[48] Von Hildebrand, *Aesthetics*, vol. I, 75-101, 203-214.

the truth that *God is charity* since it renews at the altar the ineffable love of God for man which is the highest beauty, inspiring the greatest love in man:

> The beautiful calls us to apprehend it, to be happy in it, to take delight in it. This is why beauty plays such a fundamental role in love. Love responds to the overall beauty of the person who is loved. The highest love, the love for Christ, responds to the divine holy beauty of Jesus. It is not for nothing that one of the last invocations in the Litany of the Sacred Heart of Jesus says... "Heart of Jesus, delight of all the saints."[49]

The Protestant doctrines obscured the truth. Therefore the *cultus* that they invented to reflect those errors could never reflect the "splendor of truth."[50] Nothing they created could ever compare to the beauty that Christ Himself created in His Incarnation by giving Himself in the Real Presence. Visible and audible beauty flows from the metaphysical beauty of truth.

Therefore, from this moment on, nothing that the Protestants created *qua* Protestants would ever compare to the beauty which flows from this fundamental *Catholic* dogma of the faith. None of the Protestant rites which deviated significantly from the Catholic Mass—i.e. anything *not* High Anglican or High Lutheran—would ever compare to the innumerable works of beautiful art, architecture and music produced for the Catholic rite.[51] And this is all because of the ineffable life-giving power of grace. This will cause the fundamental problem for the fallen spirits, since their uglified rite will fail to keep the souls of children away from Christ, and necessitate the founding of a new religion.

Therefore the reform of the Roman Missal by the Council of Trent intended and accomplished a recovery of "the beauty of the Roman liturgy" from Renaissance captivity.[52] By uniting the moderate and strict parties, God's grace created through Trent the beauty of Baroque Civilization, the

---

[49] Ibid., 85-86.
[50] St. John Paul II, *Veritatis Splendor* (1993), Blessing.
[51] For example, the greatest Protestant composer, Johann Sebastian Bach (1685-1750), had a Lutheran liturgy with a great deal of Latin which looked very similar to the Roman Catholic Mass. Other Protestant composers such as Anglicans produced great beauty in art, architecture and music, but as soon as the Protestants began to make something that no longer looked and sounded like Catholicism in order to be more Protestant, its beauty was greatly diminished. Protestants were never able to build up an alternative to Catholic civilization and beauty.
[52] Reid, *op. cit.*, 41.

soul of second Christendom. Baroque was the Christianized Renaissance of our fathers.

Trent had dogmatized the metaphysical beauty of the Real Presence. Baroque visible and audible beauty would be "the pedestal on which this beauty mysteriously appears."[53] For the metaphysical beauty of the sacraments is immaterial, whereas the audible and visible beauty of Baroque is "quasi-sacramental."[54] Thus by diminishing or even removing the sacraments, the Protestants removed the *cultic* origin of material beauty in the audible and visual realms.

The concurrent flowering of this was the musical form known as polyphony, which was approved at the council. Since music is "the most spiritual of all arts," the music in particular for the Holy Sacrifice needed to be very carefully guarded.[55] There is no greater example of Trent than this sublime beauty. Having developed for many centuries since the days of St. Hildegard, the Renaissance produced the full flowering of this exquisite art reflecting the beauty of the Real Presence.

But this music was substantially different from Gregorian chant, utilizing multiple voices, timbres, harmony, blending and a depth nowhere present in traditional chant. The extreme of the strict party would have a suppression of this art, while the extreme of the moderate party would be a capitulation to the extravagance of Renaissance opulence. But the legacy of Trent brought forth the purity of this art by integrating the work of Palestrina (1525-1594) into the Roman Rite.[56] Many talents were raised to build beauty for the greater glory of God, leading to the rich heritage of polyphony that our fathers have passed down to us. The mark of this true beauty is that men will still pay great wealth to hear this exquisite beauty after many centuries.

Then God in His mercy provided the Church with a Holy Father imbued with the true spirit of the Cross. Antonio Ghislieri was born of a poor but noble family and as a Dominican he had learned to love suffering and despise the empty praises of men by enforcing discipline and, as bishop, opposing the nepotism of Pope Pius IV. Ghislieri ascended the throne of St. Peter in 1566 as Pope Pius V, imbuing the Church with the

---

[53] Von Hildebrand, 209-211. In this section Von Hildebrand is not specifically asserting the point about Baroque culture, but he is saying that natural beauty has a "quasi-Sacramental" beauty which is analogous and related to the Sacraments, but having no actual supernatural quality.

[54] Ibid.

[55] Ibid., vol. II, 366.

[56] Notable works include *Sicut Cervus*, *O Bone Jesu*, and *Missa Papae Marcelli*.

true crusading spirit, which would work yet another miracle against the enemies of Christ. He promulgated a reformed Roman Breviary in 1568 with the reformed Roman Missal following in 1570.

Then arose the second Angelic Doctor, St. Robert Bellarmine (1542-1621). In his vast corpus of writings, he expertly refuted the errors of every heresy and achieved the heights of sanctity for the heavenly city.[57] Of the tens of thousands of Protestant sects, none of them can constitute a council to dogmatize unity, but they can all agree in their rejection of Rome and the Mother of God. Thus their method is voluntarism under the principle of negation—anything but Rome. And thus they were no match for the army of Jesus, and innumerable Protestants were converted and by the early 1600s, the Protestant advance had been isolated to Holland and Sweden alone, and by 1630 the "Catholic culture was unmistakably in the ascendant."[58] Meanwhile, the Society of Jesus was helping to take the Gospel to the world.

Sacramental Marriage

After the central *cultus* of the sacrifice was dogmatized and promulgated, we must note the incalculable importance for Christian culture: the dogma of the sacramental and indissoluble character of Holy Matrimony. Those who impinged on Mary as throne of Christ were anathematized, safeguarding the glory of Heart of the Home, lifting every woman of God above the mire of abuse from wicked men. Polygamy was anathematized, and Sacramental Marriage defended. The sacred character of Matrimony was nothing less than the icon which manifested the metaphysical beauty of Christ the Bridegroom and the Bride of Christ, and more deeply, the soul of every person with his God in the Real Presence. This then safeguarded the deep and ineffable beauty of the consecrated Virgin Bride of Christ, which had of old trampled upon the serpents of Rome. Above all, the great St. Teresa of Ávila (1515-1582) rose in this time to reform the Carmelite Order, and she would become known as one of the great mystics of contemplative prayer.

The purity of the virgin ideal only made the mothers of Christian families shine with greater luster against those who had forsaken the Virgin Mary. For Our Lady of Guadalupe rose against the Aztec gods and made every woman of God burn with the zeal of a mother to zealously guard her children.

---

[57] This was Second Scholasticism. Read his works in English translation by R. Grant at Mediatrix Press.
[58] Sire, *Phoenix from the Ashes*, 70, 76.

The sacraments dogmatized at Trent, especially the Holy Sacrifice and Matrimony were the cultural foundation upon which the Tridentine Church was built, from the glory of Philip II's Spain to the Cathedral of Our Lady of Guadalupe in Tepeyac, Mexico, to the Immaculate Conception Cathedral of Manila in the Philippines. But in these great works the *cultus* of the Sacrament of Matrimony was celebrated. Because of Our Lady of Guadalupe appearing as a mestiza speaking Nahuatl, the natives were no longer afraid to marry the Spanish, and the marriages between these two peoples created the peoples of Southwestern United States, Central and South America to this day. The first Christian marriage recorded in the area of the modern United States was between the full-blooded African Luisa de Abrego and the full-blooded "white" Spaniard Miguel Rodríguez in 1565 in Spanish Florida.

The *cultus* now dogmatized safeguarded against the excesses of nationalism that was being created in this time owing to the movement of natural law, exploited by the fallen spirits. Instead, the same Christendom that had produced the timeless beauty of St. Thomas Aquinas, Notre Dame de Paris and Dante would be extended over the Americas and begin to expand to Asia. St. Francis Xavier reconnected with the ancient foundations of Christianity in China and India and made numerous converts while the Philippines became a Catholic people.

Moreover, the lost eastern peoples were beginning to be integrated back into the Church.[59] Since the Council of Florence some number of every eastern Christian people had been reconciled to the Church.[60] The Syriac Christians became the Chaldean Catholic Church in 1553 for which their Patriarch Sulaqa suffered martyrdom at the hands of the Syriac anti-union party.[61] Ukrainians ("Ruthenians") were reconciled in 1596, the Syriacs of India in 1599, and later the Romanians 1698, the Armenians Copts in 1713 and a part of all others.[62] Many Antiochians were Catholic, but they were not able to elect their own Catholic Patriarch until 1724, provoking the Phanar.[63] Each of these Christian peoples has retained their

---

[59] Nichols, *Rome and the Eastern Churches*, 323-350.
[60] This excludes the Maronites and Italo-Albanians who predate Florence.
[61] R. Rabban, "Chaldean Catholic Church (Eastern Catholic)," *New Catholic Encyclopedia* (2003), vol. 3, 367.
[62] For a survey of these movements, see Ronald Roberson, *The Eastern Christian Churches: A Brief Survey* (7th Ed., (Roma, Italy: Edizioni Orientlia Christiana, 2008).
[63] The Phanar reacted by imposing their own Greek bishop and canonizing Mark of Ephesus.

cultus and their ethnic identity, despite these excesses of those who sought to impose Latinizations against the will of the Holy See.

But while the English king exalted himself, Slavic Christendom was suffering under their own tyrant, Caesar ("Czar") Basil III, who used a *Roma* ideology to justify his adultery and impose his will on the Russian Church.[64] He promoted a new ideology of *Roma* by making Moscow the "Third Rome" identifying the earthly city with the City of God. This allowed him to divorce his wife and force his clergy to perform an adulterous marriage ceremony, suppressing the good Russian monks who opposed him and forcing the Czar *pontifex maximus* onto the Russian people by means of Church councils. Henceforth Slavic Christendom would suffer under this tyranny yet were not deprived of divine grace, as had been the English.

But in May, 1565, the Turkish "Caesar of the Romans" landed at Malta, and our fathers gripped their swords and their Rosaries.[65]

Confronting the Turks

Since 1517, the Turks had sought to submit Europe to Muhammadanism. As the powerful fought over power "one party might win the support of other Christian powers, the other might seek the help of Istanbul."[66] There existed "a certain collusion of Protestants with Muhammadanism, and it was largely the Catholic forces that resisted the Muhammadan advance."[67] And thus "Lutheranism in Germany by 1555 should be attributed to Ottoman imperialism more than to any other single factor."[68] Lamentably, however, some French and Hungarians sought an alliance with the Turks.

But as the Saracens advanced, a new army was gathered to face them. Mary shined out more than ever in claiming victory over the Turks. On the eve of the Holy Name of Mary, September 11th, 1565, the Turks gave up their siege of Malta. In 1568, the parish of Fatima, Portugal was founded, named after a Christian woman who had been liberated from Muhammadanism.

---

[64] Hopko, *Church History* <https://www.oca.org/orthodoxy/the-orthodox-faith/church-history/sixteenth-century/russia3>.
[65] Weidenkopf, *Timeless: A History of the Catholic Church*, 458.
[66] Jack Goody, *Islam in Europe* (John Wiley and Sons, 2013), 45.
[67] Ibid.
[68] Fischer and Galati (1959), 117 in Goody, 45.

Meanwhile, the Turks amassed a navy of 100,000 men in 300 ships manned by Christian slaves.[69] The men of Christendom rose to meet them at Lepanto led by Don Juan at 24 years old: 26,000 men in 208 ships. But Don Juan gave all his men a rosary and raised the crucifix: "You have come to fight the battle of the Cross!" A third class relic image of Our Lady of Guadalupe was placed in the flagship of Admiral Doria, and Pope Pius V called on Christendom to pray the Rosary against all odds.

Don Juan formed his ships into the shape of the cross, while the Muhammadans shaped in a crescent. *Thou comest to me with a sword, and with a spear, and with a shield: but I come to thee in the name of the Lord of hosts, the God of the armies of Israel, which thou hast defied.*

Far away in Rome, Pope Pius V suddenly rose and said "make haste to thank God, because our fleet this moment has won a victory over the Turk." God gave the Turks into their hands, and the Christian forces won a mighty victory, crippling the Turkish navy and stopping their advance. Wounded at Lepanto, Cervantes said it was "the greatest day's work seen for centuries." However, he said, "those Christians who died there were even happier than those who remained alive and victorious."[70]

Yet the love of money again caused the Venetians to form an alliance with the Saracens, allowing them to regroup for the next attack.

---

[69] Weidenkopf, *op. cit.*, 461-465.
[70] Jack Beeching, *The Galleys at Lepanto* (New York: Charles Scribner's Sons, 1982), 216; Victor Davis Hanson, *Carnage and Culture* (New York: Anchor Books, 2001), 253; in Weidenkopf, *op. cit.*, 462 n84.

XVII

THE INSIDIOUS POISON OF MUHAMMAD

In the year of Our Lord 750, God punished the Arab Muhammadans by overthrowing the Umayyad dynasty and allowing the Abbasid Caliphate to take over. These Muhammadans destroyed the city of Seleucia-Ctesiphon, the Holy See of the Syriac Christians, and built their new capital city of Baghdad, declaring themselves the new caliphate, the center of the Muhammadan world.[1] When the Abbasid Caliph understood that the Eastern Romans hated the Syriac Christians, he gave the Catholicos, Timotheos I (d. 823) a great deal of freedom.[2] Timotheos was able to re-establish the missionary activity east to India, China, Turkestan, and, as we mentioned above, he sent the Arab monk Mar Shubhalisho who destroyed idols and baptized many in the cities around the Caspian sea in modern Iran.

In the Providence of God, the Syriac Christians began to preach the Gospel to the Muhammadans. It was this activity which sowed the seeds of the overthrow of Muhammadanism. The Abbasid Caliph al-Ma'mun (d. 833) understood the cultural superiority of the Greek philosophy that the Syriac Christians were translating into Arabic, and a Syriac Christian named Al-Kindy fearlessly disputed with the Muhammadans around 830 in a *dialogos* that is still extant.[3] Lamentably, the Muhammadans resisted

---

[1] To Muhammadans, the Caliph is analogous to the Pope and Roman Emperor combined into one person. The term means "Successor to the Prophet" and is believed to be a holy office. The majority Sunni Muhammadans believe there to have been four main caliphates, of which the Abbasids are the third. Whereas other Sunnis and the particularly the Shia dispute this claim.
[2] Baum and Winkler, *The Church of the East*, 60-63.
[3] William Muir, *The Apology of Al-Kindy in Defense of Christianity Against Islam* (Smith, Elder & Co: 1882)

this valiant effort, but through the efforts of Christians such as this, they were introduced to logos in their disputes instead of brute force and charm.[4]

A new movement was born among the Muhammadans, *al-Mu'tazilah*.[5] This movement attempted to apply logos to their religion submission. The most basic application was the principle of non-contradiction. The Qur'an itself contains contradictions without a problem, since the Meccan *Suras* are contradicted by the Medinan *Suras* by abrogation.[6]

But *al-Mu'tazilah* was confronted with an even larger problem: their creed was that *there is no God but God*. But the Muhammadans also believed that the Qur'an itself was *eternal:* that all the words of the Qur'an, in Arabic, existed in Heaven and then were brought down to earth in the form of the Qur'an by Muhammad. In a word, as Sebastian Maisel told this author, "God speaks Arabic."[7]

The Mutazilites, however, applying logos to their own religion understood that there was a contradiction between the doctrine that the Qur'an is eternal and the *shahada* attack on the Trinity. If the Qur'an is eternal, is not the Qur'an itself another god?[8]

But at that time, the Muhammadans rejected not only the Gospel, but Greek philosophy itself. For if logos could be brought to bear on Muhammadans, it would disintegrate. Moreover, logos would prevent the Muhammadans from practicing polygamy, as well as allowing mistresses, sex slaves and *houri* girls in paradise, and lose all the infinite wealth that could be gained by *jihad*.

---

[4] The chief proof that Muhammadans often give for the Qur'an's divine origin is that it is so beautiful that only God could have composed it, revealing how little their whole religion is based on rational arguments. By that standard, Shakespeare is divinely inspired. More insidiously, it reveals how demonic the Qur'an actually is.

[5] Frederick Mathewson Denny, *An Introduction to Islam*, 3rd ed. (Upper Saaddle River, NJ: Pearson, 2006), 174; Ira M. Lapidus, *A History of Islamic Societies*, 2nd ed., (Cambridge University Press, 2002), 87-90.

[6] Abrogation is the theology in Muhammadanism where God literally commanded one thing, and then "changed his mind" to command something contradictory. But for Muhammadans who believe in voluntarism, this is not a problem.

[7] Discussion at Grand Valley State University, 2009. Maisel is the co-author of *Modern Standard Arabic: Integrating main Arabic dialects* (Edition Hamouda (September 12, 2013) and other academic texts in Arabic and English.

[8] This belief is what God left in Muhammadanism so that they could be converted to the faith, since this concept is the seed for accepting the co-eternal Logos Himself. As such, it is the philosophical open door to the baptism of the whole Muhammadan world through the intercession of Our Lady of Fatima.

Therefore the Mutazilites and their heirs, the great Ibn Sina ("Avicenna" d. 1037) and Ibn Rushd ("Averroes" d. 1198) were all suppressed by the Muhammadans and no philosophical tradition developed among them.[9] Through the work of al-Ghazali (d. 1111), "the greatest Muhammadan since Muhammad," logos was crushed out of existence in Sunni civilization, so that Ghazali could preach *jihad*.[10] The Shia alone received and passed down logos, testifying to the persistence of man's rational nature.[11] But it was in part due to this movement that St. Thomas learned of Aristotle, a philosophy that sowed the seeds of the destruction of Muhammadanism. In contrast to the Muhammadans, the Jewish sage Rambam ("Maimonides") integrated Greek philosophy into Rabbinic Judaism and became the "greatest Rabbi since Moses," yet provoking the Kabbalah Jews against his own Jewish followers.[12]

But the work of Rambam, Ibn Rushd and Ibn Sina, the logos of Aristotle was transmitted to St. Thomas, who then took what was good from these thinkers and refuted what was bad. Lamentably, the Muhammadan voluntarism was too tantalizing for our fathers to resist, and Ockham preached it to justify his wickedness as we have seen.

Arabism, the Curse of Ham, and the Racial Slave Trade

But Muhammadans believe that "God speaks Arabic," and that the Arabic Qur'an is co-eternal with God. This is why Muhammadans have the custom of calling a printed version of the Qur'an a "copy of the Qur'an" since the *real* Qur'an exists in Heaven for all eternity. It is also a common custom across the Muhammadan world of one billion (millions of whom do not understand Arabic) to fully memorize the entire *Qur'an* by the age of puberty. That's the entire Qur'an—which is about the length of the New Testament—entirely in an unintelligible language. The Muhammadans imitated the beauty of Greek and Coptic chant and now they chant their Qur'an with this beauty, bewitching the masses.

But consider: if God speaks Arabic only, and my native tongue is not Arabic, then my language is inferior to Arabic. If God speaks Arabic, then

---

[9] Jones, *Logos Rising*, 295-332.
[10] The designation comes from William Montgomery Watt.
[11] Jones, *op. cit.*, 308.
[12] This is on his tombstone and how Orthodox Jews revere him. He is analogous to St. Thomas Aquinas or St. Robert Bellarmine in his command of multiple languages written in an encyclopedic corpus. Indeed, St. Thomas himself respected him, but in the Providence of God, Rambam died in 1204 shortly before Thomas was born in 1225.

the Arabs are more like God than any other people. Therefore an Arab is superior to other peoples. Hence the Hadith: "Muhammad said: 'Love the Arabs for three reasons: Because I am an Arab, The Qur'an is in Arabic and the language of paradise is Arabic.'"[13] Thus some Muhammadans assert that it is a dogma of their faith to love Arabs as the best people. We may call this "Arabism," which is ultimately theological racism.

Now this is in contrast to Christianity, in which Logos—language itself, not any one language—is God is manifested in every tongue. Thus no form of racism could find a basis in Christianity. *Where there is neither Gentile nor Jew, circumcision nor uncircumcision, Barbarian nor Scythian, bond nor free. But Christ is all and in all* (Col. iii. 11).

Now the Church tolerated *domestic*, non-racial slavery yet Catholics gradually abolished it. And the Church fought against the non-racial *slave trade* as being intrinsically evil, *contrary to sound doctrine*. Slave trading was an attack against marriage and the family: breaking a man, assaulting a woman, and separating children from parents.

It was nothing less than the antithesis of every social good that the Gospel brought to a people, in particular, its great moral good in healing and sanctifying the souls of the family. Slave trading was the physical equivalent of demonic possession in the spiritual order—destroying the very heart of the family in order to fornicate with filthy lucre.

The godless Saracens, already inclined against non-Arabs theologically, found further ideology in "the curse of Ham." As we mentioned in chapter three, Canaan was cursed, but the other descendants of Ham were *not cursed*. The most conspicuous descendant is of course Egypt which has a much closer relationship with Israel than the Edomites or the Moabites, sons of Shem. Moreover the Holy Spirit declares, prophesying the glory of the Coptic Church, *blessed be Egypt my people* (Is. xix. 25). Thus any man reading the Scripture cannot find a teaching that *Ham* is cursed, but rather only one of his sons, Canaan alone, and not Egypt nor any other of his African descendants.

But this clear understanding from Holy Scripture was darkened by filthy lucre. As we mentioned above in chapter eight, Pharisaic Judaism already had a strong racial ideology based on exalting the race above others. According to some Talmudic myths, Canaan's curse included black

---

[13] Mustadrak Hakim, vol. 4, 87; Al Mu'jamul Kabir, Hadith: 11441; Shu'abul Iman, Hadith: 1364. For a discussion on the strength of this Hadith, see Moulana Suhail Motala, "Love the Arabs," <https://hadithanswers.com/love-the-arabs/>, accessed February 23, 2021.

THE INSIDIOUS POISON OF MUHAMMAD

skin.[14] The Muhammadans who conquered the Jewish communities of Mesopotamia and spread into Egypt were the first ones to pick up on this and find a justification for their evil.[15] Thus was born the racist, trans-Saharan slave trade. This was the poison of Muhammad and its ideological root was the curse of Ham and Arabism. This error justified the sacrifice of human souls to the wicked idol of money.

The Arab Muhammadans made alliances with the powerful black African Empires and together they destroyed untold millions of black African families. Just as Muhammadan voluntarism used and objectified woman for lust or procreation, so also their slave trade objectified whole families, to the point of genital mutilation which was sterilizing and eradicating African populations.[16] The force of Arabism and the curse of Ham created the first slave trade based on racial ideology.

The Poison Infects Second Christendom

Catholics founded religious orders to stop the slave trade, like the Trinitarian Order and the Mercedarians. But the evil men who profane the name of Christian, after the Gospel had raised them out of their barbarism, could not resist the temptation to join in the lucrative slave trade. The inhabitants of the Canary Islands became the first victims, which was condemned immediately by Pope Eugene IV (*Sicut Dudum*, 1435). This condemnation was repeated numerous times by the papacy over the next three centuries in 1537, 1591, 1639, 1676, 1741, 1839, 1888 and 1890. Like the treatment of the Jews, these papal condemnations were ignored as the freedom of the Church over society was suppressed by tyrants.

Yet the love of money also polluted the Vatican. During the second Pornocracy in 1498, Annius of Viterbo produced an elaborate forgery for Alexander VI "as part of a Vatican campaign to legitimize and bolster papal claims to parts of Italy" allowing the pope's armies to invade.[17] This forgery included the heresy of the curse of Ham and the book became one of "the most famous publications of the entire sixteenth century."[18] Despite papal condemnations of the slave trade, the papacy succumbed to the love

---

[14] It is unclear to what degree this was contained in the Talmud or in commentaries of the same. The Christians also tried to use this to oppress peasants and serfs by saying they were descendants of Ham. David M. Whitford, *The Curse of Ham in the Early Modern Era* (AshGate, 2009), 22-27, 118-120.
[15] N'Diaye, *Le genocide voilé*, 238.
[16] Ibid., 187-205.
[17] Whitford, *op. cit.*, 44.
[18] Ibid.

of money in promoting this racist traffic in human souls, which polluted the efforts of Christendom, leading to disaster.[19]

The Portuguese mission to the Africans, begun in 1491, was extremely successful in kingdoms of Benin and Lower Congo. Within a generation in 1518, they consecrated as bishop the Congolese nobleman Henry, the son of Pedro III, the King of the Congo. But due to the love of money working against the Gospel to destroy African families by means of the slave trade, by the 1800s "there was no trace of their work."[20]

When the Spanish arrived in the Americas, many succumbed to the temptation for money and started enslaving the Indians, leading the Dominican Bartolomé de las Casas (1484-1566) to defend them to King Carlos. But the labor force had been destroyed by disease and the king's money, needed to pay soldiers against internal heretical violence and the Turkish advance, was evaporating through usury.[21] De las Casas then, at first, supported joining the Muhammadan slave trade and Carlos succumbed in 1518, polluting the second Christendom with slavery that destroyed black families for filthy lucre. De las Casas later regretted this.

De las Casas continued to defend the natives, writing *Destruction of the Indies* in 1542, leading King Carlos to enact new laws in 1544 to defend them. But many Spanish in the Americas fought to keep slavery, leading to bitter struggle within the second Christendom which would last for centuries.

But when De las Casas defended the natives, he greatly exaggerated the brutality of the Spanish and his account contained many errors and inaccuracies, which were corrected by his contemporaries.[22] But the English regime exaggerated it still further. Since the English kings had

---

[19] For a defense of the papacy in its treatment of the slave trade, see Joel Panzer, *The Popes and Slavery* (Alba House, 1996). For a critique of the papacy on the same subject, see Pius Onyemechi Adiele, *The Popes, the Catholic Church and the Transatlantic Enslavement of Black Africans 1418-1839* (Georg Olms Verlag, 2017). For an introduction to the history of the Catholic teaching on slavery, see John Francis Maxwell, *The History of Catholic Teaching Concerning the Moral Legitimacy of the Institution of Slavery* (Barry Rose, 1975).
[20] Bernard Tissier de Mallerais, *The Biography of Marcel Lefebvre* (Kansas City, MO: The Angelus Press, 2004), 96 n96.
[21] Jones, *Barren Metal*, 265-276, 396-396.
[22] Fr. Toribio Motolinia and Fr. Francisco de Vitoria, in a recent edition *Relecciones Sobre Los Indios y El Derecho de Guerra* (Madrid: Espasa-Calpe, 1975); see also Pedro Insua Rodríguez, *1492: España contra sus fantasmas* (Ariel, 2018), 191ff.; Iván Vélez, *Sobre la leyenda Negra* (Ediciones Encuentro, S.A, 2014), 103-115; Marion A. Habig, "The Franciscan Provinces of Spanish North America," *The Americas* 1.3 (January 1945), 330-344.

rejected the Magna Carta, they had to resort again to "the creation of a reality by the sheer power of speech." Thus they also spread the curse of Ham ideology through writers like George Best (1555-1584) and turned it against the Spanish, arguing that they were "tainted" with Jewish and African blood.[23] Milton later repeated the "heavy curse of Ham" on the "vicious race" in *Paradise Lost*.[24] They also spread the calumny of Casiodoro de Reina (1520-1594) that the Spanish Inquisition was a tool of oppression.

Building Second Christendom

As this was happening, the conquistador Francisco Pizarro was liberating Peru from the Incan Empire. This allowed Jesuits like Alonso Barzana to produce dictionaries and prayer books in five Indian dialects and set up the San Pablo University.[25] Meanwhile in Brazil, the Portuguese Empire funded Jesuits like Manuel da Nóbrega and José de Anchieta who liberated the pagans from darkness and created grammars for their Tupi language creating Christian hymns out of native songs.[26] The Society of Jesus (the Jesuits), Dominicans, Franciscans and other orders and Christian families were building a new Christendom across the world.

Nearby in Spanish Paraguay the Society of Jesus was preserving the language and culture of the ancient Guarani peoples and creating the integrally Catholic economies of the Reductions to protect them from the slave traders.[27] By 1600 more than a hundred Jesuits were working in the Philippines creating catechisms in their languages like Tagalog and protected Filipinos from Japanese slave traders.[28] At the same time, the Society of Jesus in India were preaching the Gospel in the Tamil

---

[23] Whitford, *op. cit.*, 105-122; Margaret R. Greer et al., eds., *Rereading the Black Legend: The Discourses of Religious and Racial Difference in the Renaissance Empires* (University of Chicago Press, 2008), 1-24, 76-82, 88-98; Philip Wayne Powell, *Tree of Hate: Propaganda and Prejudices Affecting United States Relations with the Hispanic World* (University of New Mexico Press, 2008), 14-18, 39-59.

[24] John Milton, *Paradise Lost*, bk. XII.

[25] John W. O'Malley, S.J. *The Jesuits: A History from Ignatius to the Present* (Lanham: Sheed and Ward, 2014), 47.

[26] Ibid., 23.

[27] Jones, *Barren Metal*, 623-648.

[28] O'Malley, 52.

language.[29] But tragically, the mission to the ancient empires of China and Japan ended in disaster.

St. Francis Xavier received permission from the *daimyo* Ōuchi Yoshitaka and preached the Gospel to the Japanese who quickly converted, making 300,000 lay converts and two Japanese priests by the early 1600s. But the Japanese Empire noticed the growing power of the Spanish and Portuguese, and believed the Jesuits were seeking to overthrow his earthly empire.[30] This led to a vicious persecution, crucifying Christians and torturing them. But the Japanese Catholics around Nagasaki survived for two hundred years without priests and with baptism as their only sacrament, testifying to the power of the Christian *cultus* giving grace to Japanese piety. They would keep the faith until they could restore the hierarchy in Japan and build the greatest cathedral in Asia.

The Jesuit Matteo Ricci preached the Logos in Chinese according to Chinese philosophical categories and gained "many thousands" of Chinese converts by his death in 1610.[31] The ancient culture of China was difficult to baptize, and the Protestants who hardly understood Chinese culture began to slander the Jesuits' efforts.[32] At the same time, some Jesuits were disobeying the liturgical rubrics for the sake of inculturation, causing a crisis of the mission. The Dominicans also sought to prove that the Jesuits had allowed pagan rites into their liturgies. What was needed was a union between moderate Jesuits and strict Dominicans in this case to bring the Gospel to the noble Chinese civilization. Lamentably, this led to a condemnation by Rome in a way that was a pastoral disaster, leading Emperor Kangxi to immediately stop the advance of the Gospel by the 1700s.[33]

But if the Chinese Jesuits did indeed fall into syncretism, other Jesuits among the Venetians and Portuguese fell into Latinizations, when they imposed Latin rites on the eastern Catholics' ancient Apostolic rites approved by the Holy See.[34] It was one thing to freely share devotions like the Sacred Heart, but Latinizations were a voluntarist abuse of empire. The pope condemned this multiple times, but impious Catholics disobeyed, leading to division among Eastern Catholics to this day.

---

[29] Ibid.
[30] Rao, *Black Legends*, 314-315.
[31] Ibid., 51.
[32] Ibid., 64-68; Jones, *Logos Rising*, 336-341.
[33] On the Chinese Controversy, see OMalley, Rao, and E. Michael Jones
[34] R. Rabban, eds., "Chaldean Catholic Church (Eastern Catholic)," *New Catholic Encyclopedia* (2003), vol. 3, 366.

THE INSIDIOUS POISON OF MUHAMMAD

The Tyranny of the Goddess *Libertas*

When Pope St. Pius V had absolved all oaths of Catholics to Queen Elizabeth it was because she had "monstrously usurped the place of supreme head of the Church in all England to gather with the chief authority and jurisdiction belonging to it...[and] abolished the sacrifice of the mass."[35] By breaking the first stipulation of the Magna Carta, the English Crown became a tyrant, breaking the oath to the covenant of Christian peoples.

Oaths and vows were the fundamental fabric of Christendom. Therefore, if a man broke his oath, it could only be done under the strictest and gravest conditions, the most obvious being the dictum of the Holy Apostles: *we must obey God over man* (Acts v. 29). Thus if a king commanded his knight to commit sin the knight was bound to disobey him in Name of Jesus Christ who held authority over the king.

Thus Pope Pius V absolved oaths to Elizabeth because she was commanding her subjects to break the covenant with Jesus the King and Mary the Queen, mediated by the Petrine authority of popes and bishops.

Now a certain set of circumstances led to the growth of the heresy of *Libertas* with the iconoclasm in France and the Netherlands. In the 1560s, certain powerful Frenchman, known as "Huguenots," began attacking the Blessed Virgin Mary and all the saints by viciously destroying the beautiful monuments of our fathers. France firmly resisted this mob violence, but in the Netherlands the heretics could have more power to provoke the mob. In the *Beeldenstorm* of 1566, they became frenzied in smashing and destroying the beauty that raised the hearts of little children to Jesus Christ and gave hope to the souls of widows and orphans.[36]

But the excess of their wickedness provoked excess in reaction, and Catholic kings and peoples rose against them in defense of the social order of Christ the King in France and the Spanish Netherlands. God allowed the Netherlands to be torn from the domains of Spain. When the son of Carlos, Felipe II, could not pay his troops in the Netherlands. They, showing their own faithfulness to their oaths, rebelled and began raping and pillaging the Dutch themselves in the "Spanish Fury." Meanwhile, the French were violently suppressing the mobs themselves.

This then provoked further excess in reaction by which the Protestants produced the political heresy of *Libertas*. It transferred the existing

---

[35] Pius V, *Regnans in Excelsis* (1570).
[36] G. Kurth, "The Netherlands," *The Catholic Encyclopedia* (1911) <http://www.newadvent.org/cathen/10759a.htm>, accessed June 5, 2021.

Libertas in sexual morals to the political realm. The influential propaganda appeared in France in 1579 with a pamphlet entitled "The Vindication of *Libertas* Against Tyranny."[37] Like all heresies, this propaganda was half true. As Pope Pius V had just unequivocally demonstrated, if a sovereign breaks the covenant he becomes a tyrant to be overthrown. And yet *Libertas* chose to change the definition of the covenant, since they invented their own *cultus*. In short, they judged the covenant based on their own will to power. Thus *Libertas* as a heresy defined as subjecting oaths to voluntarism against logos. The definition is vague because oaths and contracts are complex and the terms and conditions cannot be universally defined, even though we can identify the spiritual forces behind them. The covenant is being defined no longer by logos but by mere consent. By using heresy as a pretext, the consent of the governed could change the terms of the covenant and impose the will of the powerful on society.

While the Hugenots had suffered injustice, this did not give them the right to impose heresy on the people. Restoring the old pagan mythos of *Libertas* against the tyrant Tarquin the Proud gave them the rationalized pretext to break the covenant with their king. The king and people had made a covenant. The powerful who wanted more power then chose to change the terms of the covenant, allowing them to accuse the king of breaking the covenant. The Huguenots could then revolt, smugly celebrating their "just cause" of *Libertas* against the king.

This culminated in the 1581 Act of Abjuration, which claimed to be a "defense of liberty" against the "tyrannical" acts of King Felipe. They made use of the popular propaganda against the Spanish by slandering the king about his "tyrannical pleasure" in the Indies and the "rigorous inquisition." Felipe was a tyrant, they said, because he wanted the Dutch "to obey and follow the decrees and ordinances of the Council of Trent, which in many articles are destructive of the privileges of the country."[38] The Dutch then absolved all their neighbors of oaths to this alleged tyrant and threatened everyone that if they did not swear a new oath to them, they would be "punishing the offenders impartially and without delay." Voluntarism always requires more power to sustain itself.

---

[37] Anonymous, *Vindiciae contra tyrannos* (1579).
[38] *Ende d'ordonnantie van het concilie van Trenten (die in vele poincten contrarieerden de privilegien van de voorsz. landen) t'achtervolgen*. Oliver J. Thatcher, ed., *The Library of Original Sources* (Milwaukee: University Research Extension Co., 1907), vol. V: 9th to 16th Centuries, 189-197 <https://web.archive.org/web/20070406040703/http://www.h4.dion.ne.jp/~room4me/docs/abj_dut.htm>, accessed March 17, 2021.

Thus *Libertas* was an elaborate rationalization and propaganda for them to seize power and impose stricter oaths on the common people.[39] The Dutch founded their oligarchy on *Libertas* and relegated the *cultus* to the private order, setting fire to the civil war known as the Eighty Years' War (1568-1648) that pitted the Dutch supported by England, Scotland and France against the Army of Flanders consisting of Dutch, Spanish, Germans and others fighting for the Spanish King.

This hubris of *Libertas* was immediately rebuked when God worked the miracle of the Battle of Empel in December, 1585. The Army of Flanders was surrounded by enemies on the island of Bommel, enduring long hours of siege and facing certain death. Two hundred enemy ships barraged the island with cannons, breaking the dikes and flooding the island, forcing a retreat to the hill of Empel. On the Vigil of the Immaculate Conception, the soldiers were desperately fortifying their defense by digging ditches and one is said to have uttered "this is more likely to be my grave than a trench."[40] Suddenly he discovered a beautiful icon of the Immaculate Conception. "The colors were magnificently preserved as if it had just been painted."[41] Perhaps it had been buried to guard it from the Iconoclasts. The army processed the image and sang the Salve Regina, and the soldiers renewed the crusading spirit. That night a freeze came over the river which froze the ships and, on the feast of the Immaculate Conception,

---

[39] Cf. K.W. Swart. "The Black Legend during the Eighty Years War," in J.S. Browley and E.H. Kossman, eds., *Britain and the Netherlands. Some Political Mythologies* (The Hague: Martius Nijhoff, 1975), 36-57; Geoffrey Parker. *Dutch Revolt* (Penguins, 2002), 61-62; Gustaaf Janssens, "La guerra en los Países Bajos. Guerra civil, conflicto religioso y consecuencias políticas, 1564-1648,"," in Alain Barsacq and Bernardo J. García García, eds. *Hazañas bélicas y leyenda negra. Argumentos escénicos entre España y los Países Bajos* (Madrid: Fundación Carlos de Amberes, 2004), 12; Peter J. Arnade, *Beggars, Iconoclasts, and Civic Patriots. The Political Culture of the Dutch Revolt* (Ithaca: Cornell U.P., 2008); P.A.M. Geurts, *De Nederlands Opstand in de Pamfletten, 1566-1584* (Nimega-Utrecht, 1956) in Powell: *Tree of Hate*, 86.

[40] "The Feast Day Of The Immaculate Conception" (Madrid News, December 7th, 2020) <https://www.madridmetropolitan.com/the-feast-day-of-the-immaculate-conception/>, accessed March 17, 2021. C.M. Schutten, "Een episode uit de Tachtig jarige Oorlog" (*Army Museum of the Netherlands*, undated) <https://web.archive.org/web/20110724161238/http://www.collectie.legermuseum.nl/sites/strategion/contents/i004546/arma12%20een%20episode%20uit%20de%20tachtig%20jarige%20oorlog.pdf>. Accessed March 17, 2021.

[41] Rex Teodosio, "The Marvelous Miracle of Empel Shows the Power of the Immaculate Conception" (*The American TFP*, December 15, 2020) <https://www.tfp.org/the-marvelous-miracle-of-empel-shows-the-power-of-the-immaculate-conception/>, accessed March 27, 2021.

the Army of Flanders charged over the ice, and the enemies were delivered into their hand. This is commemorated in the modern work *El milagro de Empel*, by Augusto Ferrer-Dalmau (2015) which emphasizes the great piety of the people and the cross and Our Lady as centerpiece of a spiritual struggle. Henceforth the Immaculate Conception was the patroness of the Army of Flanders fighting against *Libertas*.

Second Christendom against *Libertas*

But the Protestant alliance pushed forward and created the United Provinces of the Netherlands. Jews and Protestants worked together to form a public order based on the principle of economics, instead of the *cultus*.[42] This helped create the great national banks of the Netherlands, managing the Dutch Empire of slaves by founding the Dutch East India Company in 1604. It was the Dutch "Golden Age," but art, while retaining the logos of beauty in its form and style, lost all interest in spiritual themes due to the Iconoclasts and the emphasis on money, which is seen in Rembrandt's focus on secular life. This art could be mass produced because of the growing economy and innovation, but the hearts of men were not lifted to God by this beauty, but merely to man. The architecture too, showed a focus on reviving the pagan glory of *Libertas*. The cultural momentum influencing children, then, pointed them to the coin and the triumph of the will.

This was the beginning of the bourgeois civilization in contrast to the Baroque second Christendom. The Baroque placed the public *cultus* as the "moral principle" of society. The bourgeois placed the coin as the principle of society. It was "dominated by the money power," moving to the city of machines effecting "the divorce of man from nature and from the life of the earth."[43] This was the beginning of transforming the economy from the "law of the home" into the "law of profits." It subordinated king, coin, and kitchen to the voluntarism of individuals.

The Dutch to the south in Spanish Netherlands, offers a marked contrast. For keeping the faith, the *cultus* was the central principle of society. The society sought the harmony of hierarchy, not the balance of power. The art and architecture shows the beauty of logos, such as a great

---

[42] Aaron L. Katchen, *Christian Hebraists and Dutch Rabbis* (Harvard University Center for Jewish Studies, 1984), 16ff.
[43] Christopher Dawson, "Catholicism and the Bourgeois Mind," *Dynamics of World History* (La Salle, IL: Sheed & Ward, 1958) 200-212
<https://www.crisismagazine.com/2011/catholicism-and-the-bourgeois-mind>.

Baroque masterpieces of Peter Paul Rubens (1577-1640). The guild houses of Ghent and Bruges show a Christianized merchant class, subordinating the coin to moral principles.[44] This Baroque culture of the second Christendom grew and flowered in Spain, Portugal, Italy, Catholic Germany, and the Christendom of the Americas and the Philippines and Austria, where it was still seen late into the 1700s.[45]

A "telling example" of the Baroque in visual art is *The Surrender of Breda* by Velasquez (1625), which celebrates a victory of the Army of Flanders over the Dutch rebels at the battle of Breda.

> Almost in the background we see the victorious general Spinola, in sober black armour. He is almost dwarfed not only by the upright Spanish lances behind him, but even the dejected Dutch solders on the left. His effacement is increased by the human gestures by which he stoops to embrace his Dutch opponent—a true incident—to soften his humiliation as the keys of the city are surrendered. If the picture is a celebration of victory it is of the humility and decency of victory.[46]

Jan Morris calls this painting "one of the most Spanish of all pictures," which indicates how much the Spanish soul became identified with second Christendom.[47]

This culture is heard in the music of the Baroque era, which flows from the dogmas of Trent, taking the exuberance of the Renaissance and elevating it with the divine grace of the sacraments. What one hears in Baroque music is a searching of Christ into the human heart, from the sorrows of Pergolesi's *Stabat Mater* and the joy of Vivaldi's *Gloria* and *Laetatus Sum*. The most common piece heard today is Pachelbel's *Canon* which is commonly played at weddings in America, testifying to the endurance of the Baroque spiritualization of the heart.

But we also see a great spiritualization existing among Protestants while their *cultus* still imitates the Holy Mass, most notably in Handel's *Messiah* and the immense beauty of Bach shown in his *Prelude in C*, *Air on a G String*, *Cello Suite No. 1*, and *Mass in B Minor*. At this time the Lutheran liturgy still contained Latin and the Anglican rite, especially under Archbishop Laud, attempted to imitate the exquisite beauty flowing

---

[44] This observation given to the author by Theo Howard.
[45] Sire, *Phoenix from the Ashes*, 115-118.
[46] Ibid., 103.
[47] James Morris, *Spain* (London: Faber & Faber, 1964), 29.

from the Catholic Mass. But as these liturgies slowly eroded from any semblance of Catholic worship in the Roman rite, a corresponding degradation in beauty was shown in subjecting beauty to the cultural dominance of money. Sire comments,

> Wealth and comfort of modern life became the bribe by which man was brought to ignore the riches of the spirit. That was the bid by which Satan offered limitless power in this world to a humanity that had been shown the vision of the next: "All these will I give thee, if falling down thou wilt adore me."[48]

This is why non-Catholic art historians admit, "All in all, Reformation and Counter Reformation did not lead even temporarily to the creation of two separate cultures. This was one world rather than two. Nevertheless...the great majority of these [artistic] influences flower in one direction: from Catholic into Protestant Europe."[49] This is *not* to say that Catholics are "better" than Protestants. Indeed, during this era far too many Catholics, crusading against flesh and blood, alienated and pushed Protestants out of the Church. Rather, this observation is simply to say that the *cultus* of Logos Incarnate produces greater beauty than the *cultus* of Protestants or *Libertas*. Beauty is the audible and visible presence of Logos in any culture. Since Christendom has the *cultus* of Logos Incarnate, it produces the greatest beauty. Catholicism does this because it possesses the fullness of truth. Every subtraction of truth from this fullness produces a corresponding subtraction in audible and visual beauty.

Spain was the great example of integrating the Council of Trent into the souls and society of the many peoples within the Spanish Empire, funding innumerable missions to save souls and keeping the *cultus* at the center of life. We see this especially in comparing the Spanish court to the French court. The Spanish had the *cultus* celebrated at the architectural center in the basilica, making grace the very soul of their whole empire. In contrast, the French put the chapel on the side, showing the pagan element of indifference to Christ to keep up royal opulence.

Nevertheless, the French still funded numerous missions to New France, particularly in Canada. Remarkably, even though France and Spain were at war with each other during this, the fundamental *cultus* created the same second Christendom in the Americas:

---

[48] Sire, 157
[49] A. G. Dickens, *The Counter Reformation* (Norton & Company: 1979), 188.

Under both powers, there was the same emphasis on correct and impartial administration; education, particularly higher, and the arts; and on public and private works of charity. Similarly, there was the same concern for the spiritual and temporal welfare of Indians and Blacks, to a degree simply unheard of in the English colonies.[50]

Yet a strong form of *Libertas* could be found in two important Catholic realms: France and Venice. The French crown induced the French bishops to impose Gallicanism on the people—proclaiming the independence of the French Church against Rome and refusing to obey Trent.

The Venetian system included a sophisticated rationalization of *Libertas* to rebel against Trent and keep the coin flowing with the Turk. This enlightened and noble republican government alone, they said, was the voice of God governing society, and any dissenters would be justly and viciously punished, as Rao observes.[51] The Venetian Friar Paolo Sarpi (1552-1623) helped articulate this vision in a vigorous polemic against the Council of Trent. A copy of this book was in fact "cherished" by the Puritans who sailed on the Mayflower and promoted the "City on a Hill mentality" in New England years later.[52]

Absolute Tyrannies

Meanwhile, the kings and powerful of England had to find some way to rationalize their desire for tyranny against the Magna Carta. Recall that Magna Carta's first stipulation was the freedom of the Church—only if the Church was free to Christianize society could there be freedom from tyranny. Under Henry and Elizabeth, the voluntarist absolutism of Parliament and Monarchy had agreed on the principle of negation—not Rome. But James I of England (1566-1625) was the one who first articulated the divine right of kings, which was immediately contested by the Parliament, who sought equal absolute power.

But both were brilliantly refuted by St. Robert Bellarmine and Suárez. "Thinking that a king could exercise any spiritual function was wrong,"

---

[50] Charles Coulombe, *Puritan's Empire: a Catholic Perspective on American History* (Tumblar House, 2008), 48.
[51] Rao, *Black Legends*, 361.
[52] Ibid., 358. See W. Bousma, *Venice and the Defense of Republican Liberty. Renaissance Values in the Age of the Counter-Reformation* (California, 1968).

argued Bellarmine, "because spiritual authority was superior to temporal authority."[53] By taking power over the public *cultus*, the English king became a tyrant wielding both of the Two Swords against the faithful. The Council of Trent had had this subject on its agenda and did not complete a definition on the Two Swords, allowing an ambiguity. If it had defined it, perhaps a great deal of the problems after Trent and in our own era could have been resolved. It was left to churchmen to attempt a definition using the Catholic principles of Christendom.

The problem was that these Catholic principles were quickly used by English Parliamentarians against James I since Bellarmine and Suárez acknowledged that the king's authority did not come directly from God but through the people in the Christian covenant mediated by the Church.[54] But the Parliamentarians did not want the Catholic Church to be free in England either, so they wanted a tyranny of the Parliament. The Parliamentarians could look to the Dutch for an example, while the Royalists could look to the French. All of these forces began fighting each other in a contest of power, and thus *Libertas* was gaining strength among these parties.

Scientism

But the English were developing something new: scientism. Starting with St. Albert the Great, Catholics had used the scientific method to study the logos of God's natural world in order to reverently use it for the service of God. This was an act of logos by knowing the truth, using it for the good, and standing in awe of its beauty, created by God.

Yet the English empire wanted to find some way to gain power over the second Christendom. The pivotal figure in this regard was Francis Bacon (1561-1626) who "rejected classical arguments seeking to conform human nature to the natural order—[and] instead urged human dominion over nature."[55] In *New Atlantis* (1626) he believed that if men could simply unlock the mysteries of the universe, they could impose their will and create a new perfect world.[56]

This was beginning of science as an ideology, instead of a method to investigate the truth. This is scientism. It is the use of empirical observation to make philosophical conclusions. It is a "superstition," says Sire, that

---

[53] Stefania Tutino, *Empire of Souls* (Oxford: 2010), 125, paraphrasing Bellarmine.
[54] Reilly, *America On Trial*, 196-224.
[55] Patrick J. Deneen, *Why Liberalism Failed* (New Haven: Yale University Press, 2018), 14.
[56] Jones, *Jewish Revolutionary Spirit*, 345-363, 467-511.

contradicts the "fundamental principles" of science by claiming to be a "general philosophy."[57]

Like the cult of *Libertas*, the concern of scientism is *power*. It was heavily imbued with mysticism and magic, chiefly alchemy, the magic art of making money out of non-valuable metals. Money was their god, not logos. Bacon, and others helped spread the occult movements, leading to the Royal Society and Rosicrucianism, a proto-Masonic sect associated with the Italian occult movement.[58]

Shortly thereafter another pivotal figure in this regard, René Descartes, wrote *Discourse on Method* (1637). He introduced doubt into the reality of the universe itself, in order, he said, "to find a practical philosophy" which would "render ourselves as *masters and possessors* of nature."[59] Descartes helped to undermine the philosophy of logos, based on Plato and Aristotle, and create modern, irrational philosophy in its place.

Meanwhile, Catholics were leading the discipline with actual science—"Scheiner in optics, Cabeo in magnetism, Grassi in astronomy, and Arriaga in physics"—pushing discoveries and innovation into new territory fundamentally integrating faith and reason, which secular publications confirm.[60] Their science was an act of logos. From this point on both true science and scientism would develop together as if they were one system of thought and method, but in fact were diametrically opposed to one another. From this moment on "the scientific community" as the modern phrase puts it—meaning the whole of all "scientists" from every field—would be divided between those who were using science for truth, goodness and beauty, and those were only seeking power. Many had a little of both in them. One such man was the occultist and astrologer Giordano Bruno (1548-1600).[61]

---

[57] Sire, *op. cit.*, 113.
[58] Jones, 468-474.
[59] Cited by Peter Kwasniewski, "Listening with an Attentive Ear to God's Poetry," in Thomas Storck, ed., *The Glory of the Cosmos: the Catholic Approach to the Natural World* (Arouca Press: 2020), 143.
[60] Sire, *Phoenix from the Ashes*, 99; Modechai Feingold, ed., *Jesuit Science and the Republic of Letters* (Cambridge, MA: MIT Press, 2003); Paula Findlen, *Athanasius Kircher: The Last Man Who Knew Everything* (London: Routledge, 2004); Marcus Helyer, *Catholic Physics: Jesuit Natural Philosophy in Early Modern Germany* (University of Notre Dame Press, 2005); William Wallace, *Galileo and His Sources: The Heritage of the Collegio Romano in Galileo's Science* (Princeton University Press, 1984).
[61] Ronald L. Numbers, *Galileo Goes to Jail And Other Myths About Science and Religion* (Harvard University Press, 2010), 59-67; Guido del Giudice, "Giordano Bruno and the Rosicrucians. A mystery unveiled, among magic, alchemy and

Galileo Galilei (1564-1642) also practiced Bruno's occultism and agreed with his critique of the old Greek system of the planetary movements. But he also had more scientific reasons for this critique based on actual experimentation. Thus Galileo could show in his model of the solar system a convincing reasoning for accepting a different conception of the universe. However, his theories had scientific and theological problems, causing St. Robert to urge caution in order to practice true science in harmony with logos.[62]

Nevertheless, Galileo haughtily mocked all his intellectual opponents as no better than idiots, showing that his real concern was power, not truth. Tycho Brahe (1546-1601) proposed a different system which solved the issues, but Galileo insisted that his system alone was correct. Nevertheless, the matter needed to be thoroughly investigated through *dialogos* and scientific debate.

But after the death of St. Robert there arose an opulent, worldly pope worthy of the Second Pornocracy. His name was Pope Urban VIII (1568-1644), who promoted mutilation of young boys, sorcery, militarizing the Papacy and the bewitching opulence of the worst of the Renaissance.[63] He himself felt slighted by Galileo because Galileo had promised him to avoid controversy. The scientific colleagues of Galileo also complained to Urban about Galileo's ridiculous *ad hominem* attacks which poisoned true scientific debate.[64] Thus as "a personal act of revenge," Pope Urban VIII condemned Galileo in 1633.[65]

Sungenis argues vigorously that the Church was right to condemn Galileo even on scientific grounds, asserting that the Michelson–Morley experiment of 1887 and modern probes like the Wilkinson Microwave Anisotropy Probe of 2001 prove the Brahe model.[66] Moreover, Einstein

---

philosophy,"
<https://www.academia.edu/5128141/Giordano_Bruno_and_the_Rosicrucians_A_mistery_unveiled_among_magic_alchemy_and_philosophy>, accessed March 27, 2021.

[62] Bellarmine's letter of 12 April 1615 to Foscarini, in Finocchiaro, Maurice A., ed., *The Galileo Affair: a Documentary History* (Berkeley: University of California Press, 1989), 67–8.

[63] He employed castrated boys for the papal choirs and Fr. Tommaso Campanelli did séances for him in the Vatican. Sire, *Phoenix from the Ashes*, 88-89.

[64] Coulombe, *Vicars of Christ*, 276.

[65] Sire, 99.

[66] Robert A. Sungenis and Robert J. Bennett, *Galileo was Wrong and the Church was Right*, 2nd ed. (Catholic Apologetics International Publishing, 2008), vol. 1: 61-98, 194-224.

himself (with most modern physicists) admit that the Tycho Brahe system is entirely in accord with observable science.[67]

However, Galileo's theories were at least rational and should have been thoroughly investigated and debated among the scientists instead of swiftly condemned out of hand as a means of personal vengeance. Instead, by silencing the debate before a thorough investigation, Pope Urban gave fuel to the fire of English propaganda that the Church was opposed to science. The propaganda surrounding Galileo would serve to silence the Church's critique of scientism as it does to this day.

The War of the Three Kingdoms

Meanwhile the absolute tyrannies of king and Parliament could not hold. Since they both united with pure power stripped of meaning, they were bound to destroy each other. Now James's son King Charles I (r. 1625-1649) had come to the throne. Various parties were at play—the High Anglican element wanted to compete with the Catholic by creating beauty like them, knowing its spiritual power and fearing the Catholic logos to bring the people back to Rome. The Puritan element wanted to destroy all beauty and joy as opulent in the worst spirit of *Libertas* flowing from their conception of marriage. In addition, the Presbyterians of the Scottish north dissented from the Anglican established church based on their own errors. Meanwhile, other Puritans sailed away on the Mayflower inspired by the Venetian republic in 1620. Meanwhile, the wealthy wanted to keep the property they had stolen from the poor, while king Charles I had the allegiance of the lower classes.[68] All of these groups and more agreed on one thing—not Rome.

Meanwhile, the stalwart sons of *Pádraig*, with the Sign of the Cross across their breast and their merry fighting spirit, stood like an immovable wall, united with their bishops against the wickedness flowing from London.[69] The power of the Sacrament alone was their lifeblood, uniting them forever as Catholics,. Yet the Irish nobles, forced off their land and burning for the love of God and their people, were nearing exhaustion.

In 1639, the Scots rebelled against the English. In 1641, the Irish nobles came together and, with the bishops' blessing for a just war, charged against the enemies of Christ. Meanwhile, the king and Parliament erupted in violence. The Royalists fought for King Charles I, and the

---

[67] Ibid., vol. 1: 306-347, 348-380.
[68] Coulombe, *Puritan's Empire*, 53.
[69] Cahill, 649.

Parliamentarians, led by Puritan Oliver Cromwell, began mobilizing a new professional army to defeat the king. The New England colonies supported parliament.[70]

The Irish succeeded in establishing their own country, *Comhdháil Chaitliceach na hÉireann* (The Irish Catholic Confederation) in 1642 and, with full support from the papacy, set about to restore the stolen lands and re-establish the Christian order of Catholicism throughout society.[71] However, the crusading spirit did not fill all Irish, and in the chaos some burned for revenge against those who stole their land. This led to atrocities committed by the Irish in killing even women and children. Thus, the purity of the crusading spirit among the Irish was polluted by this evil, but it would soon be exploited to the full by English propaganda.

Meanwhile, the Puritans under Cromwell defeated King Charles and then perfected their voluntarism: they put him to death in a "judicial murder" in 1649, shocking the whole of Christendom. The Puritan republicans set about trying to rationalize their seizure of power by drawing upon the superior arguments of St. Robert Bellarmine, Francisco Suárez or Robert Persons. Among these was Algernon Sidney, who waffled on the question of the judicial murder. His writings would become a fundamental source for the American Founders.[72] Meanwhile the king's son Charles II fled from the Puritan horror and ended up in a priest's hole, and, by God's Providence, found there a Jesuit who instructed him in the true faith.

But the Puritans, like their supporters in New England, set out creating a republic known as the Protectorate (1653-1659). But since voluntarism always requires more power to sustain itself, they created a Puritan state that hunted down everyone who celebrated Christmas or baked hot cross buns. This was the rigor of the Puritans whom Chesteron would call "the English Moslems."[73] Cromwell then turned to the Irish and unleashed the fury of his new army.

But as his brutal repression continued, he could find no way to eradicate the Faith from the sons of *Pádraig*. He reportedly complained to the Puritans in London:

---

[70] Coulombe, 64.
[71] E. D'Alton, "Ireland," *The Catholic Encyclopedia* (1910) <http://www.newadvent.org/cathen/08098b.htm>, accessed June 5th, 2021.
[72] Timothy Gordon, *Catholic Republic* (Sophia Institute Press, 2019), 68-72.
[73] G. K. Chesterton, "Column for September 11, 1909," *Illustrated London News* <https://www.chesterton.org/puritanism/> Accessed March 17, 2021.,

> All is not well with Ireland yet. You gave us the money, you gave us the guns. But let me tell you that every house in Ireland is a house of prayer, and when I bring these fanatical Irish before the muzzles of my guns, they hold up in their hands a string of beads, and they never surrender.[74]

The Irish still prayed a prayer with the Rosary for God to "crush the serpent" and to "not permit the enemy to penetrate into these places where the Rosary is recited."[75] But the Puritans sought every means to impose the triumph of their will.

To their great credit, something of English Catholicism was not lost after nearly hundred years of propaganda, and the English rejected the Puritan grotesquery and brought back the king to rule them and restore order: Charles II (r. 1660-1685). Under him Algernon Sidney was executed, whose final testament defined what tyranny meant to him:

> I had from my youth endeavored to uphold the common rights of mankind, the laws of this land, and the true Protestant religion, against corrupt principles, arbitrary power, and Popery, and I do now willingly lay down my life for the same.[76]

Note here the identification of "arbitrary power" with "popery," which will be crucial to the development of *Libertas*. The problem was that without the divine grace from the *cultus*, the only "arbitrary power" was the contest of power between an absolute monarch and an absolute parliament. Forebodingly, the voluntarist rationalization of Milton's adultery began to bear ugly fruit as divorce was being forced on women by 1670.[77]

---

[74] Donald H. Calloway, *Champions of the Rosary* (Stockbridge, MA: Marian Press, 2016), 94.
[75] Ibid.
[76] "Sidney, Algernon (1623-1683)," *Libertarianism.org* (Aug 15, 2008) <https://www.libertarianism.org/topics/sidney-algernon-1623-1683>, accessed March 27, 2021.
[77] The vast majority of divorces were initiated by men. "A History of Men's Divorce," *Cordell Cordell Family Law Solicitors* (undated) <https://cordellcordell.co.uk/news/a-history-of-mens-divorce/>, accessed March 27, 2021.

The Betrayal of Pope Urban VIII

While all this was happening, the enemies of Christ knew that the voluntarist rationalizations of their inspired word merchants could never compete with the encyclopedic logos of St. Robert Bellarmine. As a result, they roused up the Protestants in Bohemia to revolt against Catholic order in 1618. At first the new violence was beaten back by the League of Catholic powers manifesting the crusading spirit with Mary and the angels working victory at White Mountain commemorated in the painting by Anton Stevens.[78]

But at the same time in France, the spirit of voluntarism was growing, led by Cardinal Richelieu who cared nothing for Christ but only for the glory of France. St. Vincent de Paul was attempting to convince Louis XIII to dismiss Richelieu. But the king chose the petty glory of the earthly city in the "Day of the Dupes" in 1630.

At the same moment the Swedish Protestant Gustavus Adolphus forced his citizens into his army and invaded the continent.[79] This forced conscription, like Cromwell's army, was a new increase in militarism. Henceforth the military would increasingly transform from the masculine ideal of a fighting nobility based on chivalry to the effeminate ideal of paying armies or whipping up mobs for the love of money. Once again, voluntarism required more power.

Lamentably Pope Urban VIII, with burning concern for the earthly city, induced Richelieu to join the alliance with Sweden against Christendom. This led to end of the war as a stalemate in 1648, with all territory divided into its own national religion leaving the east vulnerable to the renewed Muhammadan advance. Other Catholic powers followed a public charter like *Sicut Judaeis* for their Protestant subjects, permitting them toleration but keeping the public order for the King of Kings. This vicious war had cost untold lives, and the failure of France and Pope Urban to support Catholicism had helped Protestantism survive.[80]

---

[78] Sire, 77-79. Roberto de Mattei, "Victory of White Mountain: An Anniversary to Remember," *The Remnant* (October 15, 2020), vol. 53, no. 17.
[79] Ibid., 81.
[80] The Christians of Rome cried "Gustavus Aldophus has more zeal for Lutheranism than our pope for Catholicism!" the Curia wondered rhetorically, "Is His Holiness by chance a Catholic?" Ibid., 91.

Another Attempt Against the *Cultus*

In accordance with his Renaissance opulence, the pope sought to revise the Divine Office. The Humanist fascination with the greatness of the Classical Latin of Cicero, and the rhetoricians of ancient Rome caused a fad in Rome under the decadence of Pope Urban. Imposing the contemporary principles on the inheritance of the fathers was the underlying principle of his action—completely contrary to the fundamental responsibility of the eldership of Christian culture.

Fortescue sums up the universal judgement of all scholars on this point: "No one who knows anything about the subject now doubts that the revision of Pope Urban VIII was a ghastly mistake, for which there is not one single word of any kind to be said."[81]

The power and influence of Catholic Spain, meanwhile, greatly diminished, leaving room for the secularizing force of France, the Netherlands and England to fill the gap. However, due to the deeply imbedded Catholic *cultus* in both New Spain, New France, and Portuguese South America, the mass conversions to the faith and the deepening of Christian culture in the second Christendom across the world would continue.

Meanwhile, Capuchin John Baptist of St. Aignan was helping to reconcile more Syriac Christians to the faith, and for this they suffered persecution for the truth, especially bishop Joseph of Diarbekir, in modern east Turkey, and Joseph III in Mosul, modern Iraq.[82]

The Ugly Revolution

Back in England, however, Charles II was showing that he was taught by a soldier of Christ. Meanwhile, his wife and mother were both Catholic, allowing the *cultus* of the King of Kings to procure divine graces for all the people and setting everything in motion for England to receive the *Theotokos*. He even attempted to introduce toleration for Catholics.

The power structure was becoming more and more disturbed, and attempted every legal means to prevent more logos from threatening the chaos of voluntarism. Suddenly it became clear that the King's nephew, the Catholic James II would become king. So they began trying everything

---

[81] Fortescue, "Concerning Hyms," Alan G. McDougall, ed., *Pange Linguia: Breviary Hymns of Old Use* (London: Burns and Oates, 1916), xxxvii in Reid, *Organic Development of the Liturgy*, 47.
[82] R. Rabban, "Chaldean Catholic Church (Eastern Catholic)," *New Catholic Encyclopedia* (2003), vol. 3, 368.

to prevent this including mass hysterical propaganda, lies, witch hunts and mass executions of innocent Catholics, an assassination attempt—all to no avail. Clearly the advance of the Gospel was unstoppable now the divine grace was flowing down on England. Charles II, near death, called for a priest and died a Catholic in 1685.

James II now ascended the throne. He removed the oaths against Rome in the Anglican rite of coronation and the pope, with great sagacity, approved this rite to accommodate the advance of the Gospel. He received the papal nuncio at court, gave positions of influence to Catholics, and tried to use absolute monarchy to impose toleration of Catholics, restoring something of the Magna Carta. But he acted too quickly, too soon. When Queen Mary gave birth to a son, the powerful "knew that James must be deposed if they were to keep power."[83] The Whigs and Tories then divided over the best way to depose him, but they were united in the principle of not Rome.

Finally: William of Orange was brought from the Netherlands and usurped the throne, forcing James II to flee. Henceforth the enemies of Christ called this the "Glorious Revolution" but Catholics should call this the "Ugly Revolution." It was nothing less than "the greatest victory that Protestantism had won since the independence of the Netherlands themselves," says Dawson,

> [Since] it united Puritans and Episcopalians in defense of their common Protestantism[.]...Never has the influence of class interests and selfish greed been more nakedly revealed in political action.[84]

The Dutch love of money was melded with the British Empire when William gave absolute power to the wealthy, leading to:

> The golden age of the great landlords and the squires, and the man of property enjoyed a freedom and a social prestige such as he had never known in the world before. But it was an age of ruin and decay for the peasants and the yeoman and the free craftsman: it was the age of the enclosures of the commons and the destruction of the guilds; it was an age which abandoned the traditional Christian attitude to the poor and substituted a harsher

---

[83] Coulombe, *Puritan's Empire*, 54.
[84] Christopher Dawson, *Gods of Revolution* (New York University Press, 1972), 16-18.

doctrine which regarded poverty as the result of sloth and improvidence and charity as a form of self-indulgence. It made self-interest a law of nature which was providentially designed to service the good of the whole so that the love of money was transformed from the root of all evil to the mainspring of social life.[85]

A New Birth of *Libertas*

John Locke summed up the concern of the wealthy for their stolen property when he said that "the papists" hold "dangerous opinions which are absolutely destruction to all governments but the pope's."[86] Thus he set to work to "establish the throne of our great restorer, our present King William."[87] He explained that their usurpation of the papist king was an action of "the people" against the "arbitrary power" of "popery."

He rationalized the usurpation by saying that "if [the people] see several experiments made of arbitrary power, and that religion underhand favoured [Catholicism]... which is readiest to introduce it" and "a long train of actions shew the councils all tending that way" a man would seek to "how to save himself."[88] And thus "if a long train of abuses, prevarications and artifices, all tending the same way, make the design visible to the people," they should "rouze themselves, and endeavour to put the rule into such hands which may secure to them the ends for which government was at first erected" instead of the "ancient names, and specious forms [which]... are much worse, than the state of nature."[89]

Locke followed the cult of *Libertas*, but not the *Liber* he found in the secret societies of the Netherlands. His fundamental error was the denial of Original Sin that Trent had dogmatized. He based his ideas on the ahistorical belief in a "state of nature," in which men were in a contest of power and thus decided to organize themselves into government for the sake of order. This was half true of course, as this is part of history of

---

[85] Ibid.
[86] John Locke, *Essay Concerning Toleration*, in *Locke: Political Essays*, ed. Mark Goldie (Cambridge: Cambridge University Press, 1997), 150 cited by Christopher Ferrara, *Liberty: the God that Failed* (Angelico Press, 2012), 48.
[87] John Locke, *Second Treatise on Government*, preface (London, 1688) < https://www.gutenberg.org/cache/epub/7370/pg7370.txt>, accessed March 17, 2021.
[88] Ibid., ch. 18, sec. 210.
[89] Ibid., ch. 19, sec. 225.

western Europe when the chaos of that period developed into the feudal system of order.

But the piece that was missing from his history was *culture*. The historical record in fact shows universally that men of every age, people and land have inherited an ancient culture passed down from God that was then polluted with idols.[90] The *cultus* of the people was relied upon to appease the gods or receive divine grace so that society could have order. In the context of uniting Protestant sects to remove the Catholic Mass and Catholic king from the land, it was impossible that any *cultus* could unite the Protestants.

Therefore Locke proposed his system of *Libertas* without any *cultus*. In his system, man did not need to rely on any ancient rite to receive supernatural power to achieve order. Man could simply do this himself without such things. Note here the scientism of Francis Bacon: he thinks Catholicism is tyranny, and elects instead a "state of nature" that has no need for the divine grace of the sacraments ("specious forms"). This was a rebirth of the ancient heresy of Pelagianism, which said that Jesus Christ was a virtuous man to be imitated, and therefore if one simply worked hard enough, one could achieve salvation.[91] This heresy had already been thoroughly repudiated by St. Augustine, but in Locke the heresy was reborn in a complex political argument.

But he made yet another fundamental error which would cause immense damage. "The original cell-unit of human society is the family." [92] Locke was asserting that the original cell-unit was the individual. But no human being exists without the family and none can become "an individual" without many years of development within this structure. Locke's concern was property rights for the wealthy, but his philosophy was removing the field of economics from the "law of the home." Thus Locke was constructing a philosophical and political system that by its fundamental principles was an attack on children by reducing them to individuals without parents. The stage was set in Locke's system for the growth of the government to interact with its people now against the family and culture, while denying the absolute necessity of divine grace.

The most crucial thing Locke wrote, however, is rarely discussed. That is his work on pedagogy.[93] For it is certainly one thing to rationalize a

---

[90] Jones, *Logos Rising*, 38-41.
[91] Ludwig Ott, *Fundamentals of Catholic Dogma* (Baronius: 2005), 240.
[92] Heinrich Pesch, *Ethics and the National Economy*, trans. Rupert Ederer (Norfolk, VA: IHS Press, 2004), 43.
[93] *An Essay Concerning Human Understanding* (1690) and *Some Thoughts Concerning Education* (1693).

usurpation—that in itself had been going on for centuries, even though it took a new form after the Dutch *Libertas*, which Locke built upon. His pedagogical work, however, argued against the study of Greek and Latin and the classical texts of antiquity and argued instead that the mind was a blank slate and simply needed to be programmed. Thus not only is divine grace removed as a necessity for all of life, but even the ancient wisdom passed down by our fathers.

These ideas by Locke were fundamentally anti-culture. Consider the four elements of culture. In *cultus*, Locke denied that divine grace was necessary through the *cultus* not only for the state, but also for the child. In tradition, Locke denied the need for the ancient wisdom of the past. In piety, Locke denied that the fundamental cell-unit is the family, and thus reduced everyone to an individual. Finally, the only role of eldership was to simply program the child to be virtuous. But if this was the case, then the government could simply dispense with the family altogether and program children to be virtuous. Thus, having removed Mary from the hearts of men, Christ could finally be dethroned. But there was something else to this process that would be fundamental.

The Cosmic Energy of the Universe

Locke was an alchemist, and he worked on magic with his friend, Isaac Newton, another believer in scientism. Newton discovered the mathematical properties of motion and published them in 1687. This is the masterpiece of scientism because it perfectly blends true science with scientism. On the one hand, Newton made the scientific observation that the rate of motion was always constant with the inverse square law.

But what caused this order of motion? Without any evidence, this was a philosophical question, not empirical. True science would answer that this was simply the *logos* of motion. God made it that way, and the angels move the stars and planets according to this logos, and other causes could be admitted only by empirical or philosophical proof.

But Newton was not even a Christian.[94] Therefore he said that the planets were not moved by God somehow, but by the cosmic energy of the universe. He called this cosmic energy "gravity." He admitted that "I have not as yet been able to discover the reason for these properties of gravity"

---

[94] Newton denied the Nicene Creed.

but it could be "based on occult qualities."[95] Thus his critics immediately accused him of smuggling magic into his science.[96]

It is crucial to seize upon what is happening here. "Gravity" is not something that is observable in empirical science. What is observed is the rate of motion and how things in motion interact. The existence of a cosmic energy called gravity is a metaphysical assertion.

But because of Newton, the holes in Galileo's system were answered and explained and true Catholic scientists generally accepted Newton's physics, but not his philosophy.[97] It would not be until modern quantum physics that scientists would discover the holes in Newtonian physics.

But the Newtonian universe of cosmic energy fit perfectly with Locke's denial of Original Sin. If the universal was governed by cosmic energy, it need not call upon God for divine grace to be healed from the wounds of sin. The universe did not need God, but only a good programmer to erect the glorious earthly city imagined by Bacon. The English set to work to do just that.

Meanwhile, the only hope was in restoring Catholic James II to the throne. Thus was born the Jacobite cause to restore the true king to the throne and throw off the usurper. This became a strongly Catholic movement, but others joined in as well. Jacobite uprisings occurred in 1708, 1715, and 1719. Thus a constant threat to the voluntarism of the powerful was the restoration of the Catholic order.

During this century, the Slavs were suffering from a "Time of Troubles"—a famine in 1601, and widespread epidemic, a "campaign of terror" in which Czar Boris was struck dead in 1605, which was followed by civil war and an invasion by the Poles. Under the new Romanov dynasty (1613-1917), the *pontifex maximus* imposed on the Russian people a form of the Greek *cultus* against the ancient Slavic *cultus* passed down from their fathers. The dispute devolved into an ethnic dispute between two voluntarist parties of the Greeks and Russians, both asserting their authority based on *Roma*, just as the English Parliament and king had fought. Another element, however, wanted to imitate the great beauty of the second Western Christendom, and eventually imposed a form of Russian polyphony.

---

[95] Isaac Newton, *Philosophiae Naturalis Principia Mathematica*, General Scholium, 3rd ed. (1726), in I. Bernard Cohen and Anne Whitmans, trans. (University of California Press, 1999), 943.
[96] Christiaan Huygens and Gottfried Wilhelm von Leibniz. Jones, *Barren Metal*, 449, cf. 445-468.
[97] Sire, 99-100.

But while they were fighting about how to impose their voluntarism on the Russian people, the common peasants revolted. Hopko admits this was "up to one-third of all Russian Orthodox Christians—many of them among the most pious, most dedicated Christians in the land."[98] They possessed, says Soloviev, "a spark of the divine fire," for they understood instinctively the pretense of *Roma*:

> This Church "established" by the Tsar, though totally subservient to the secular power and destitute of all inner vitality, none the less makes use of the hierarchical idea to assume over the people an absolute authority which by right belongs only to the independent Universal Church founded by Christ.[99]

They were anathematized as heretics in 1666 and viciously persecuted by the Czar *pontifex maximus*. Having no contact with Petrine authority, they divided into various sects but they held to doctrine of the Immaculate Conception.[100] The Czar abolished the Moscow Patriarchate and commenced direct rule of the Russian Church, condemned by all Russian bishops but approved by the Greek patriarchs.

Also by 1666, Shabbethai Zebi, who practiced Dionysian orgies and breaking the Ten Commandments convinced many of the Jews to follow him as a messiah.[101] He was the embodiment of the earthly city and all its voluntarism. But Zebi folded under pressure and converted to Muhammadanism. This movement, says the Jewish Encyclopedia, was "of the gravest consequences for the whole of Jewry," because, says another Jewish writer, it allowed the Magic-Kabbalah Jews to henceforth gain the upper hand against the rational Jewish party of Rambam.[102]

---

[98] Hopko, *Church History* <https://www.oca.org/orthodoxy/the-orthodox-faith/church-history/seventeenth-century/russia4>, accessed March 27, 2021.
[99] Soloviev, *Russia and the Universal Church*, 49, 50.
[100] According to Vitalis Varaioun, a former Old Believer now Catholic, the Immaculate Conception "was accepted almost by everyone." See his sources here: "Thou hast rauished my heart, with one of thine eyes, with one chaine of thy necke," *Russia and the Universal Church* (April 24, 2019) < https://rutheniacatholica.blogspot.com/2019/04/thou-hast-rauished-my-heart-with-one-of.html>, accessed March 27, 2021.
[101] Jones, *Jewish Revolutionary Spirit*, 436-462.
[102] Kaufmann Kohler and Henry Malter, "Shabbethai Zebi B. Mordecai," *Jewish Encyclopedia 1906* <https://jewishencyclopedia.com/articles/1604-anti-shabbethians>. See Rabbi Marvin S. Antelman, *To Eliminate the Opiate* (2 vols.) and the writings of Gershom Scholem. The Jewish writer Charles Moscowitz first

Sobieski and the Crusading Spirit

During all this, a new threat had arisen. After a hundred years since Our Lady of Victory crushed the Muhammadan threat at Lepanto, the Muhammadans had finally regrouped their forces with help from the Venetian merchants. The Protestants had weakened Austria in the Thirty Years War, and now their eastern front was vulnerable to Muhammadan invasion. The Turk marched on the eastern outpost of a beleaguered Christendom: Vienna. It was the year of Our Lord, 1682.

The pope called Christendom to arms. Fortuitously, the pope of the day, Innocent XI, had just brokered an alliance between the Holy Roman Empire and the Kingdom of Poland, which was also menaced by the Muhammadans. When it became known that a massive army of Turks were advancing on Vienna, Pope Innocent ordered that Rosaries be recited in the religious houses and churches of Rome. The same prayers of supplication were offered throughout the empire. The imperial court fled Vienna for Passau and took refuge there. In the meantime, there were special devotions at the Capuchin Church in Vienna to Our Lady Help of Christians, whose famous picture hangs there.

As if out of nothing, the men of God arose. The Hapsburg Roman Emperors arose, joined by the Catholic princes of Bavaria, Bohemia, Franconia, Saxony, Swabia, with the Hungarians and Lithuanians. Even the Republic of Venice saw their error and joined the new Holy League against the Muhammadan invaders. The Turks reached Vienna in July, 1683 and began the siege. As many as 300,000 Turks now surrounded 13,000 defending the city.[103] The defenders fought valiantly but the Turks were able to cut off all food supplies. All the Turks needed was time.

To the north in Poland, King John Sobieski rode to the shrine of Our Lady of Częstochowa to dedicate his battle to Our Lady on the Feast of the Assumption, 1683. His confessor St. Stanislaus Papczyński had already prophesied "by the name of the Virgin Mary, you will conquer."[104] The king set out with a force of 27,000 including his heavy cavalry, the winged hussars.

---

asserted this to the author in an interview with *Meaning of Catholic* (Jan 27, 2021) <https://www.meaningofcatholic.com/podcast/observance-of-mosaic-law-with-charles-moscowitz/>, accessed March 27, 2021.
[103] Weidenkopf, *Timeless: A History of the Catholic Church*, 465-468.
[104] Aleksandra Polewska, "Cud Pod Wiedniem, 1683" <https://opoka.org.pl/biblioteka/Z/ZF/ZFS/rafael_2013_bron_03.html>, accessed September 6, 2021.

But by September, the defenders of Vienna were dying of disease and exhausted from lack of food. Troops had dwindled to 5,000. The Turks had found a way to blow up parts of the walls defenses. The defenders prayed for help and prepared to fight the Turk inside the city.

But on September 11, Sobieski appeared with reinforcements of 80,000 against hundreds of thousands of Turks. Trusting in God, he led decisive the cavalry charge of 18,000—the largest such charge in history—and broke the power of the Turkish army. The Feast of the Holy Name of Mary, September 12, 1683 was instituted to commemorate the miracle. Sobieski said, "I came. I saw. God conquered."

By 1689 "for the first time the European powers had pushed back the frontiers of the Ottoman empire."[105] On September 11, 1697, at the Battle of Zenta, the Holy League, now joined by Russia beat back the foe and Christendom continued taking back Muhammadan territory. The Muhammadans who had rejected logos and thus true scientific innovation, "were forced to recognize their military inferiority" and succumbed to the cultural dominance of the second Christendom in art, architecture, theatre, opera, dress and taste.[106] This was the triumph of logos over Muhammadan voluntarism.

But as Russia had joined the Holy League, the 1700s saw an increasing influence of the Jesuits on the country. A true Greco-Roman renewal began to take shape in the eighteenth century that had not been seen in the east since the Roman empire lost the Roman language in the sixth century. The enduring influence of the Society of Jesus in Russia would have a lasting influence and bear fruit in the nineteenth century.

The Eldest Daughter of the Church Plays the Harlot

Meanwhile in France, God had inspired two figures to make her repent of her crimes against the Christendom—St. Louis de Montfort (d. 1716) and St. Margeret Alocoque (d. 1690). St. Louis spread the devotion to Our Lady and the Rosary and brilliantly called all to repent and turn to the true Queen.

With the contest of power unleashed by the voluntarism of Richelieu, French society was divided between the crown and his allies (including Gallican bishops in rebellion against Rome), secularizing forces who wanted to imitate English ideas, and the Jansenists who were promoting a Puritan rigorism against the opulence of the crown. The Jansenists were

---

[105] Lapidus, *A History of Islamic Societies*, 281.
[106] Ibid., cf. 275-282.

nothing less than a Protestant infiltration of the Church.[107] They had a great influence on Catholicism for many years to come, even after they were condemned as heretics beginning in 1653.[108] All of these forces were tearing French society apart in their efforts to impose their will against the Church whether by mimicking Catholicism (as in the Gallicans or Jansenists) or by attack it (the secularists and *philisophes*).

God in His great mercy intervened in France. Jesus Christ appeared to St. Margaret Mary Alacoque to instruct her in a new devotion to His Sacred Heart.[109] This devotion had the power to unite the French people once again against all of the evil forces and their opulent king. St. Margaret sent to Louis XIV the command from Our Lord to consecrate France to the Sacred Heart. This would renew the covenant and provide the divine grace needed to restore the order of His Reign in souls and society, finally implementing Trent, with the help of the angels and saints.

But Louis XIV refused. He chose the opulence of his court and the ascendency of British power as his model, exalting the earthly city. Instead of joining the Holy League against the Turk, he defeated the British in 1690 and gloried in his earthly city, following in particular the divine right monarchy of the French Protestant King, Henry IV.[110] This is when the deep piety of Spanish and Baroque culture passed into what Sire calls the "prancing pomposity" of crushing absolutism and French secularization.[111]

Out of this would come the Classical period of music exemplified in Haydn, Schubert, early Beethoven and above all, Mozart, which emphasized this new scientific, mechanization of the world. The *cultus* still played a major role, as in the Masses of Mozart, and the Classical still has a rich beauty. But in listening to this music, it is evident that the same spiritual force is beginning to be lost as the human heart is subsumed into the emptiness of the earthly city. In Mozart's *Eine Kleine Nachtmusik* of 1787 one hears the development of the Classical in the excitement of secularization in the soul. This secularization began to invade the Holy Mass as more and more, even in Rome, sacred music turned to the secular tunes of the classical operas and theatres. Despite this, because this music retained great beauty, it could still transcend the earthly city, as the masses of Mozart were sung for centuries and lifted many hearts to God.

---

[107] This was in many ways a result of the failure to resolve the *De Auxiliis* controversy against the Jesuits.

[108] *Cum Occasione*, cf. St. Alphonsus, *History of Heresies*, trans. John T. Mullock (Dublin: James Duffy, 1847), XIII, art. III.

[109] Msgr. Bougaud, *Life of Margaret Mary Alacoque*, trans. anonymous (New York: Benzinger Brothers, 1890), 236-237, 267-271.

[110] Sire, *op. cit.*, 103.

[111] Ibid.

THE INSIDIOUS POISON OF MUHAMMAD

But after 1688, the voluntarism only created more contest of power, as England under the usurper believed they could achieve the vision of Heaven on earth by Francis Bacon. They would create a new empire. They began to build up their navy. In 1694, the Bank of England was created to practice usury and finance the new empire. In 1707 Scotland and England were united in one kingdom—the first glimmer of the growth of empire.

The Frenchmen Paul de Rapin wrote a history of England, concocting, like the Venetians, a mythological history of the slow advance of *Libertas* shown in English history. Now the blessings that God had given to their earthly city was not about increasing the reign of Christ, but increasing the reign of *Libertas*. This was beginning of "Whig history."

When Charlemagne spread the political theory of the *City of God* and the dating system of *Anno Domini*, he proclaimed that time itself was ruled by Jesus Christ. He was the King and Lord of history, not man. Newton asserted that God was not the Lord of motion who orchestrated the logos of planets and the universe. Rather, the cosmic energy of the universe ("gravity") made everything move and God was not involved in the affairs of the universe. De Rapin went further. Christ was not the Lord of history, *Libertas* was. "Whig history" was the idea that *Libertas* was the real force that drove progress in history so that more and more societies were "freed" from Christendom and embraced the English anti-Catholic disorder of Henry VIII. The time had come for the Empire of Freedom to be resurrected.

Meanwhile, a mysterious temple was being constructed across the Irish sea. A hidden army of shadow agents who would confect a new religion for the masses. It was this movement that would finally break the fighting spirit of the stalwart sons of *Pádraig* and shatter Christendom to its core. In the Year of Our Lord, 1725, in Dublin, Ireland, it is said that a hand wrote these words: *In the year of Masonry, 5725*.

Part III

Mob Bloodshed or Modernity? The Breaking of Christendom

AD 1773-1965

XVIII

ANTI-CULTURE IMPOSED ON THE CHILDREN

The "bad spirits of Antichrist" says Newman,

> knew full well that, if they could once get the world to dishonour the Mother, the dishonour of the Son would follow close. The Church and Satan agreed together in this, that Son and Mother went together; and the experience of three centuries has confirmed their testimony, for Catholics who have honoured the Mother, still worship the Son, while Protestants, who now have ceased to confess the Son, began then by scoffing at the Mother."[1]

By attacking Mary as Christ's throne on earth, the fallen angels were able to use Protestantism to make the King's sovereignty into a "poetical expression, or a devotional exaggeration, or a mystical economy, or a mythical representation."[2] The *cultus* of the Protestants (with few exceptions) denied the Real Presence of Christ, and thus their worship lacked the physical reality of Christ's rule. Removing the divinely-appointed human authority of the Mother, the fundamental hinge of Christian culture in piety of the Fourth Commandment received a devastating wound.

The fundamentals of a wounded culture remained among the Protestants: they all had *cultus*, tradition, elders and piety. And so, especially in England, despite the vast chaos of the regime of

---

[1] Newman, "Discourse 17: The Glories of Mary for the Sake of Her Son."
[2] Ibid.

Anglicanism—religious revivals were common over the centuries, and this is true for the American colonies as well.[3] These were Christians who had a true love of Christ and a zeal without knowledge. This shows that the Christian culture remained there and at any moment could be converted back to the divine grace of the sacraments.

But in 1700, the errors of *Libertas* that rationalized the lust for power, were still restricted to the wealthy dabbling in the occult during the "Age of False Reason" or "Endarkenment" falsely called the "Enlightenment" (c. 1700-1800).[4] The common man was Christian. He still passed down Christian law and custom and his children respected his elders. So the enemies of Christ had to find a new way, which they could do if the throne of Mary was removed.

> If the liberal ideas of the Enlightenment were to penetrate beyond the limited world of the privileged classes and change the thought and the life of the people, they had to make an appeal to psychological forces that lay beneath the surface of rational consciousness. They had to be transformed from a philosophy into a religion: to cease to be mere ideas and to become articles of faith. This reinterpretation of liberalism in religious terms was the work of Jean-Jacques Rousseau, who thus became the founder and prophet of a new faith—the religion of democracy.[5]

His new religion was based on a different diagnosis of the problem: "He saw that all the ills of man and all the evils of society were due not to man's own sin and ignorance but to social injustice and the corruptions of an artificial civilization."[6]

Thus the first tenet of this new religion following Locke is not the prescription of "democracy" as such, but rather its diagnosis of the problem of human nature. By removing Mary as throne of Christ, it was the denial of Original Sin and the corresponding belief in infinite progress, or Neo-Pelagianism, first seen in Whig history. "The history of modern revolutionary movement has been a continuous one," says Dawson, "so

---

[3] Dawson, *The Dividing of Christendom*, 217-233.
[4] The phrase "Age of False Reason" is Henry Sire's.
[5] Dawson, *Gods of Revolution*, 35.
[6] Ibid.

that democracy, nationalism, socialism and communism are all of them successive or simultaneous aspects of the same process."[7]

If there is no Original Sin, then the need for divine grace can be replaced with a blind faith in human progress based on so-called "reason." But "its appeal to Reason was in itself an act of faith which admitted of no criticism."[8]

This new faith was only more voluntarism—a means to justify the status quo of breaking the Fourth, Fifth, Sixth, Seventh and Eighth Commandments by finally eradicating the *cultus* from the public order and breaking the First, Second and Third. The influence of scientism was fundamental to this new religion because men were so bewitched by the technology that humbled the Turk that they believed this was due to their own learning and power instead of the logos of the human mind enlightened by divine grace.

Anti-Culture

Thus came the hideous concoction of our modern epoch: anti-culture. This above all must be the term used to describe all the movements of modernity, from Masonry, Liberalism, Feminism, Communism, Nazism, Nihilism, neo-Occultism, neo-Paganism, and the rest. All have the same dogma: there is no Original Sin and infinite progress will solve human nature, and therefore the public worship of the supernatural is not needed. Therefore the earthly city is the only allegiance necessary—yet another instantiation of *Roma*.

They are all united on one negating principle: not Christ. But this was different than the cultures of the Jews, Muhammadans, and the Protestants, for at least they had a public *cultus*. But the essence of anti-culture is that it not only sets up a culture against Christ, it also attacks the four elements of culture themselves. This is why Von Hildebrand would write decades later that "it would be a great error to characterize this perversion of the modern man as paganism."

> Classic paganism is nobler than the modern stance... the pagan Greek or Roman approached life *de facto* as a creature, conscious of his very dependence upon factors

---

[7] Christopher Dawson, *The Movement of World Revolution* (New York: Sheed and Ward, 1959), 62.
[8] Dawson, *Progress and Religion*, 151.

> which he could not control. He even lived thoroughly in the attitude of *religio* [strict observance of the *cultus*].⁹

Von Hildebrand then observes the fundamental voluntarism of the modern epoch:

> The pagan man shared neither in the superstition of an unlimited automatic progress nor in the ideal of discarding all bonds, of determining everything by his arbitrary will. He was reverent, and conscious of his dependence on something above himself.¹⁰

Here Von Hildebrand explicates perfectly why the classics were so fundamental to Christian education for centuries, and also why the anti-culture figures from Locke, Rousseau, and later Noah Webster, all disdained this ancient wisdom as being too filled with logos.

Anti-culture denies Original Sin and thus the need for a *cultus*, loves breaking tradition and disdaining piety, making the ruling government the only thing left. Eldership is the only cultural element included in anti-culture. This allows the modern anti-culture empires to exalt their power more than any other governments before them. They will become tyrannical regimes subsuming all cultures, smelting them down into obedient citizens mesmerized by opulent luxury and addicted to endless pleasures. The fuel of the modern age is the economy of effeminacy.

Anti-culture will enable individuals to break all bonds of souls and society, then limitlessly impose their own will on reality. This would allow the powerful to easily control the masses and have their way while being themselves slavish puppets of Satan.

It is fundamental to note that while the ancient pagan did have a true culture with a piety for "the gods," the problem was not that they failed to worship something above them, it was that these "gods" were false. Pagan man knew he could not impose his will without the gods, so he worshipped the gods for power in the public *cultus* and was corrupted for it. Still, because the four elements of culture were still present, passed down from Adam, he could be converted to the true Christian culture and liberated from the bondage to Satan. He had a public throne to the supernatural to

---

⁹ Dietrich von Hildebrand, *The New Tower of Babel* (Manchester, NH: Sophia Institute Press, 1994), 43.
¹⁰ Ibid.

legitimize his own government, therefore the public throne could be restored to its true King.

The modern epoch uses worship differently. Since man, by natural reason, must set up a *cultus* to something in the public order, he is oriented to worship something.[11] What we will see presently is the gradual altering of life by means of this new religion of anti-culture in order to impose, by shadows and slogans, the idol of money, what Dawson calls "the reign of Mammon."[12] In this way we can understand the word of Our Lord: *you cannot be a slave to both God and mammon* (Mt. vi. 24).[13] This is why slavery to God is one of St. Paul's titles, announcing himself as the "slave of our Lord Jesus Christ."[14] The inclination of natural reason to have a public order subordinated to a public *cultus* means that man will be a slave to something above him in the public order, one way or another. This is especially true of children, who imitate their parents before they have natural reason. This is why all Christian peoples have been converted by means of the king proclaiming the public *cultus* and the covenant of a Christian people.

Thus by removing the *cultus*, anti-culture will shift the cultural momentum away from the divine and toward something else. Since this something is defined with vague slogans like *Libertas* or *Equality*, a hidden idol remains. Men will now remove the public *cultus* so that, as Pope Leo XIII will observe, "the efficient cause of the unity of civil society is not to be sought in any principle external to man, or superior to him, but simply in the free will of individuals."[15] This allows voluntarism to triumph in the soul of every man and make him once again a slave to Satan:

> For, once is ascribed to human reason the only authority to decide what is true and what is good, and the real distinction between good and evil is destroyed; honor and dishonor differ not in their nature, but in the opinion and judgment of each one; pleasure is the measure of what is lawful; and, given a code of morality which can have little or no power to restrain or quiet the unruly propensities of man, a way is naturally opened to

---

[11] *Summa*, II-II q85 a1.
[12] Christopher Dawson, *Christianity and the New Age* (Angelico Press, 2021), 9; Hahn and McGinley, *It is Right and Just*, 89-100.
[13] οὐ δύνασθε θεῷ δουλεύειν καὶ μαμωνᾷ.
[14] Παῦλος δοῦλος Χριστοῦ Ἰησοῦ Rom. 1:1, Philipp. 1:1, Tit 1:1.
[15] Leo XIII, *Libertas* (1888), 15.

> universal corruption. With reference also to public affairs: authority is severed from the true and natural principle whence it derives all its efficacy for the common good; and the law determining what it is right to do and avoid doing is at the mercy of a majority. Now, this is simply a road leading straight to tyranny.[16]

Thus will Cahill observe in 1932,

> Seeing that the powerful frequently are able to secure in their own favor the decision of the majority, through the operation of finance and of the press, personal rights have in practice little more security in the Liberal [Secular] State than under the old pagan regime. Thus arise the exploitation of the poor and the tyranny of the monied interest.[17]

The idol of Liberty hides the reality of tyranny. The real tyranny was breaking the Magna Carta to subvert the freedom of the Church over society. This allowed nobles to become powerful and manipulate the majority. No one will be free as long as the *cultus* is not free to govern the public order. The most important tyranny to face is the tyranny of Satan who enslaves us by means of our fallen nature. Thus it is fundamentally necessary for the public *cultus* to provide divine grace to the whole of the common good. The Holy Spirit is the Kingdom of God that liberates man from Satanic slavery.[18]

Not only this, but the *cultus* is the "efficient cause of unity of civil society" because it proclaims that the Logos Incarnate is the principle of all oaths and vows in souls and society. Anti-culture will proclaim that the will to power is the principle of all things in the society. Thus the will governs the intellect, and a voluntarist contest of power is the result, as man's natural inclination to worship is turned to the idol of power.

From the first movements of anti-culture it will be proclaimed that human dignity is based in power. You are only as good as what you can do. Thus Original Sin can be denied as undignified, and the superstition of progress can be relentlessly pursued by breaking all bonds and imposing

---

[16] Ibid., 16.
[17] Cahill, *Framework of a Christian State*, 454.
[18] T. S. Flanders, "The Holy Spirit of Pentecost and Christ the King," *One Peter Five* (June 3, 2020) <https://onepeterfive.com/pentecost-christ-king/>, accessed July 8th, 2021.

will and power. Hierarchy thus becomes an attack on this fundamental dignity in power. After the attack on Mary during the Protestant period, this epoch will turn to an all-out war on feminine nature, and, thus, attack what they fear most—motherhood.

Imposing Anti-Culture by False Education

Above all, people must be guided by the divine grace of the sacraments and the logos of truth, goodness, and beauty in the private and public orders.

But an anti-culture will replace culture and tradition with the worship of the government, slogans of the media and finally the slavery to luxury and entertainment, all of which will replace the family as educator of children. Therefore the public works of art and architecture and public spectacle will be devoted to the idols of the state and the triumph of the will.

All things in the public order will tend not toward the King, but the will to power. What this does is shift the public cultural momentum away from Christ and toward the lust for power.

But more insidious than this—for patriotism can be virtuous—is a false education imposed by those in power, which follows the ideas of Locke, Rousseau and Webster, not to "pass down the logos and teach the classics" as every culture has defined education. Rather, with the advent of *anti-culture*, those in power sought to program the citizen to obey the state and worship the idols it sets up. Perhaps more than ever however, it will be the economic changes to come which will enable all of these things to be possible. The superstition of unlimited progress will be transferred here as well.

Thus in these ways as we will see, the regime of *anti-culture* will be born across the world. It is fundamentally not a culture because it lacks three of the four elements. By this means the earthly city can be built. This will be the iconoclasm that gradually breaks all the monuments of our fathers and attempts to erect a new, mechanized earthly city to solve the problem of human nature without grace. It would be an all-out assault on fatherhood, and motherhood. This will be what finally breaks Christendom.

There was one force above all which controlled so many educational institutions in society and was on the forefront of maintaining and advancing second Christendom. Therefore, the enemies of Christ united around another principle of negation:

Stirred by their passions, the arguments of their rhetoricians, and the encouragement of so many fellow travelers of the [Grand Coalition of the Status Quo] from inside the Protestant and Catholic camps themselves, the eighteenth century Grand Coalition was ready to go on the march. It was to do so across the entire globe, in Asia and Latin America as well as Europe. In the process, it would employ every tool useful for imposing the impassioned will of a determined minority upon a confused majority. All of the destructive consequences would be justified as the satisfaction of either the rational wishes of "nature" or the fulfillment of the democratic wishes of the population and the dictates of the outraged consciences of individuals. It began its demolition derby with a simple, easily defined, and readily demonized enemy: the Society of Jesus.[19]

---

[19] Rao, *Black Legends*, 378.

XIX

THE POPE FOLDS UNDER POLITICAL PRESSURE

In the fall of 1745, when George Washington was thirteen years old, living as a member of a powerful colonial family in Virginia, foreboding news spread of an uprising in Britain. The Catholic King Charles III, the grandson of Catholic James II, was leading a movement to reclaim his throne. It was "widely asserted" by Englishmen that an international conspiracy of "papists" directed by the pope were trying to take over the established disorder of English dominance.[1]

But the enemies of the Church had formed a new "advance guard" to challenge the Society of Jesus.[2] Knowing they could never defeat them in open battle—through public debate and logos—they had to resort to deception, secrecy and above all, *mob violence*. "If they were not doing evil," wrote Pope Clement XII in 1738, "they would not have such a great hatred for the light."[3]

Masonry would promote the magic of scientism, the superstition of infinite progress, and the emotional manipulation of propaganda. Since the *Propaganda Fide* was founded in Rome in 1622, it was the propagation of the Gospel against the propaganda of slogans. By 1700, the pamphlet was in decline and the newspaper was gaining popularity. Increasing technology had only given the enemies more word power to whip up the mob bloodshed.

---

[1] Geoffrey Plank, *Rebellion and Savagery: The Jacobite Rising of 1745 and the British Empire* (Philadelphia: University of Pennsylvania, 2006), 78 quoted in *Barren Metal*, 673.
[2] Cahill calls Masons "the advance guard of Liberalism," *The Framework of a Christian State*, 221.
[3] Clement XII, *In Eminenti Apostolatus Specula* (1738), 1.

What made Masonry different was that it was a *true culture*. It had a rite and tradition concocted from a fabricated history of ancient Egyptian Gnosticism and Talmudic Kabbalah. It also had elders and piety (swearing oaths to the "brotherhood").[4] They began dating their documents *Anno Lucis* ("The Year of Light"), inventing a new "Year of Masonry." Freemasonry was a culture of the private order that promoted the religion of anti-culture for the public order. As such, it was able to unite the messianic hopes of the Jewish Kabbalah, Bacon's scientism, and Locke's triumph of *Libertas* for one goal which was, says Pope Leo XIII, the "utter overthrow of the whole religious order of the world which Christian teaching has produced."[5]

But the Masons were merely the "advanced guard" of a greater movement. Masonry was not uniform, nor all coordinated. Many enemies of Christ were not Masons. Some Masons were actually good Catholics, like Joseph de Maistre or Dónall Ó Conaill. The real coordination was in gathering forces from all corners to be enslaved to voluntarism for the sake of dethroning Christ the King.

Yet Masonry provided the central incarnation of the spirit of Antichrist. Before Masonry, the enemies of Christ could not come together for one *cultus* of Antichrist, even though this spirit united them. With Masonry, they finally could.

But this occultism sought to convert men not to Masonry, but the religion of progress and anti-culture. Therefore it melded with the spiritual force of all others in one mass religion of anti-culture. For the triumph of the religion of progress, writes Dawson, "it was necessary that the new believers should organize themselves in a new church whether it called itself a school of philosophers or a secret society of *illuminati* or freemasons or a political party."[6] All alike would believe in anti-culture and promote the idols of progress, power and above all, money.

The Love of Money in England

It is here above all that the wickedness of slavery was about to destroy everything in a punishing act of Almighty God. For if men could rationalize the destruction of the Black family for love of money, there would be no limit to their rationalizations to destroy human life for their ends. The fallen

---

[4] David L. Gray, *The Catholic Catechism on Freemasonry* (Belleville, IL: Saint Dominic's Media, 2020), 39-50.
[5] Leo XIII, *Humanum Genus* (1884), 10.
[6] Dawson, "The Christian View of History," *Dynamics of World History*, 247.

angels stoked the flames of avarice in the minds of men and under everything was a burning lust for filthy lucre.

Thus its goal in Britain was the promotion of *Libertas* to rationalize the established anti-Catholic disorder that allowed the wealthy to keep their stolen Church property meant for the poor and impose slavery in the world (rivaled at this time only, perhaps, by the Dutch). Moreover, the banking practices of London sought more and more to justify unlimited usury and acquisition of wealth—economic factors that the Church threatened to challenge.

In 1741, the Papacy again condemned the evil of the slave trade. Pope Benedict XIV then issued *Vix Pervenit*, the most authoritative Magisterial teaching on usury to date. It set forth the Catholic principles governing usury, confirming its sinful nature and articulating the principles of a just title and an unjust title in economics. All usury is unjust interest on a loan, but not all interest is itself usury. The English status quo for Britain and the American colonies of unlimited acquisition of wealth at any cost to human life or justice was thus deeply threatened by the Catholic Church. Then in 1751, Masonry was condemned by the papacy again.

But the English, now firmly established in their anti-Catholicism, used the government to seize yet more land from the poor and make them work in factories, a movement known as the "Enclosures." It also allowed them to gain greater control over the Irish, leaving them extremely vulnerable to the false education program.[7]

This was the beginning of the first Industrial Revolution (1760-1840). It has been described as "one of the most significant transformations that has ever taken place, not only in the most intimate aspects of human life, but also in the nature of social organization."[8] From this point more and more parents left their extended families in rural villages and created the nuclear family in urban environments. The nuclear family itself is a corruption of culture since it isolates the parents and children away from their extended families and the cultural momentum of their Christian community. The superstition of progress was fundamental to justifying this new seizure and its mechanization of families, and men have debated it ever since.

Flood asserts that mechanization, urbanization and the seizure of land was "an increase in the productivity of the soil" using new farming

---

[7] Cahill, 651-655.
[8] Lawrence Stone, *The Family, Sex, and Marriage in England 1500-1800* (New York: Harper and Row, 1977), 687 in David Popenoe, *Families without Fathers*, new ed., (New Brunswick: Transaction Publishers, 2009), 81.

technologies which addressed the rapid population growth.[9] In and of itself, this kind of innovation certainly helps the poor, since it produces more food in a more cost-effective way. Yet do the ends justify the means? The powerful used the government to force the theft of common land, and so Médaille is still able to critique that "history shows, beyond any reasonable doubt, that the growth of capitalism and the growth of government go hand in hand."[10] According to the superstition of unlimited progress, theft could be justified by use of force.

Just as the Protestant kings had created economic disorder by seizing lands in the first place, their solution to seize more lands for profit did not solve the underlying injustice. A growing belief melded Newtonian scientism and Whig history so that the basic goods of Free Market Capitalism was expanded into a theological belief that "rather than despising the market order, Christian should see it as a way that God providentially governs the actions of billions of free agents in a fallen world."[11]

On the one hand, there is a sense in which this is true. If men are free to create economic relationships without a strong government bureaucracy, they can work out the best ways to innovate and serve the needs of the people, including their own families. We may call this free market economy in the sense that it has subsidiarity and is free from undue control from higher authority. This was achieved in Christendom because the central government had very little power.

But because of Original Sin, in every economic transaction the stronger party is tempted to take advantage of the weaker party. Thus the Church has always said that there must be three parties in every contract—two parties conforming their arrangement to God's justice. Moreover, the public *cultus* must provide the divine grace to souls and society, so that they can overcome their inclination to evil in economics.

But there was a growing belief based on Newton and the superstition of unlimited progress that Original Sin was either nonexistent, or easily overcome, even without the grace of the Holy Spirit. Its proponents believed that just as the cosmic force of the universe governed motion, Providence would govern markets too. And if Providence governed markets, there was no need to conform contracts and transactions to the Third Party, God, nor govern the economy with *cultus*. Furthermore, Providence was calling them to seize this land so that the wretched poor

---

[9] Anthony Flood, *Christ, Capital and Liberty* (2019), 144-146, 150.
[10] John C. Médaille, *Toward a Truly Free Market* (Intercollegiate Studies Institute, 2011), 15.
[11] Jay Richards, *Money Greed and God*, rev. ed. (HarperOne, 2019), 244.

did not starve. It was their duty to provide for them when they could not provide for themselves. Indeed, this would only improve their lives, and lead to a greater progress of liberty.

Thus we may distinguish this thinking from free market economy by calling it "providential capitalism." This is the theological assertion that God governs and overcomes Original Sin affecting the moral actions in economic transactions by means of Providence without the divine grace of the *cultus* governing society with its tradition informing economic morality. At this stage we can see providential capitalism at work in rationalizing yet another theft in the name of progress and the assertion that ends justify the means because it was as increase in the productivity of the soil.

But we may first distinguish providential capitalism in general from "crony capitalism" in particular. This use of the government to steal land would be termed "crony" by men like Flood today.[12] This means the use of government by big business to achieve an unfair advantage in the market. However, even when providential capitalism does not justify theft, it does still assert that economy works better without the integration of the *cultus* as is maintained in Christendom. In their mind, if everyone is just left alone to be free to do economics with minimal interference even from Christianity, the whole system is governed by Providence to work out for the best for everyone.

But this assertion was impossible to prove empirically then and even now is deeply disputed by economists of every stripe, not the least of which are the erudite Catholic economists like Von Kettler and Pesche with moderns like Rupert Ederer and John Mueller.[13] Therefore it was not an assertion of fact, but a proposition of faith. In short, the economic justification for the government-sponsored theft of the land of the poor (again) was dubious at best, and its moral justification rested on the theological assertion of providential capitalism. Henceforth economic growth would be a mixture of free market and providential capitalism. The Church had long accepted the former, but the latter was viewed at best with

---

[12] Cf. Samuel Gregg, "Crony Capitalism: Inefficient, Unjust, and Corrupting," *Public Discourse* (March 7th, 2016)
<https://www.thepublicdiscourse.com/2016/03/16439/>, accessed July 7th, 2021.
[13] Wilhelm von Ketteler, *Die Arbeiterfrage und das Christenthum* (Mainz, 1890); Jones, *Barren Metal*, 1195-1106, 1122-1123, 1215-1216; Heinrich Pesch, *Liberalism, Socialism and Christian Social Order,* trans. Rupert J. Ederer. (Edwin Mellen Press, 2000); Heinrich Pesch, *Ethics and the National Economy*, trans. Ederer (IHS Press, 2004); Rupert Ederer, *Economics as if God Mattered* (Scarecrow, 2011); John Mueller, *Redeeming Economics* (ISI, 2014).

suspicion based on the corrupting influence of the love of money as the instantiation of power.

Thus in the face of the Jacobite Catholic efforts to restore order, the English promoted, says Dawson, a "conservative attitude in defense of the *status quo*."[14] It was the conservative anti-Catholicism of *Libertas*. They needed only to present the veneer of "established order" to justify their ill-gotten gains.

The Idol of Money in Catholic Kingdoms

In France, the economy could never sustain the regime of opulence, but the powerful were "the chief obstacle to financial reform."[15] They turned the royal court into a brothel of orgies and demonic rites, including child murder.[16] This spread across Europe, as we see divorce was growing in England as well, which was almost entirely initiated by men.[17] This caused St. Alphonsus (1696-1787) to write, "I do not hesitate to assert that everyone who has been damned was damned on account of this one vice of sexual impurity (or at least not without it)."[18] The most prominent of these in France was the king's concubine, Madame de Pompadour, who practiced occultism for power and hated the Jesuits for refusing to absolve her sin without repentance.

Against this spirit of *Liber* was the Puritan infiltration of the Church by Jansenists whom St. Alphonsus describes as "hardened" heretics using "subterfuge" to promote rebellion against the Church authority.[19] In the face of the opulence of *Liber* they held the veneer of piety, but they wanted to impose on the Sacrament of Matrimony the Puritan rigorism against Trent. They opposed the Sacred Heart and frequent Communion and

---

[14] Dawson, *Gods of Revolution*, 22.
[15] Ibid., 53.
[16] Anne Somerset, *The Affair of the Poisons: Murder, Infanticide, and Satanism at the Court of Louis XIV* (St. Martin's Press, 2004).
[17] Amanda Foreman, "The Heartbreaking History of Divorce," *Smithsonian Magazine* (Feb 2014) <https://www.smithsonianmag.com/history/heartbreaking-history-of-divorce-180949439/>, accessed March 27, 2021; Sybil Wolfram, "Divorce in England 1700-1857," *Oxford Journal of Legal Studies* 5, no. 2 (1985): 155-86.
[18] The saint is making a pastoral observation in his manual of moral theology, not making a theological assertion that damnation only happens with this sin. St. Alphonsus, *Moral Theology*, bk. IV, Treatise IV, ch. II, in Ryan Grant, trans. (Mediatrix Press, 2018), vol. II, 465.
[19] Alphonsus, *History of Heresies*, XIII, art. III.

viewed the Jesuits as morally lax. Their arguments relied on half-truths of exposing real issues and using them for revolution.

At the same time, their movement was mixed with the seeds of a fourth Greco-Roman renewal, seeking to restore the works of Church Fathers and Scripture study.[20] But because they had such a strong mixture of good and bad elements, they were the most dangerous group. Their infiltration would have a lasting effect on the Church and their movement spread across Europe.

Finally, another group known as the *philosophes* wanted to rebel against the Church—these were men like Rousseau and Voltaire who envisioned a brave new world of freedom like the English, if only the outdated traditions of the Church could be overthrown. But because the established order in France was Catholic in name and form, they promoted a *liberal anti-Catholicism*.

Thus a conspiracy formed in France from the opulent wealthy, the Jansenists and the *philosophes* with the same goal. This "strange group of bedfellows coalesced" against the monarchy, the pope, and the Jesuits.[21]

But the Jesuits were educating children to be Catholic in North and South America, Asia, and all over Europe. Their pupils numbered in the "hundreds of thousands: lawyers, professors, state officials, officers of the army, priests and bishops," building institutions across the world.[22] Their educational edifice stood in the way of all the progress of the religion of anti-culture. Other Catholic orders as well, like the Franciscans and Dominicans were also leading this advance of second Christendom. Yet the Jesuits were targeted because of their immense influence and numbers.

Meanwhile in the American domains of Spain, France and Portugal, the Jesuits checked the love of money. They protected the natives from slavery and even armed them against slave raiders. By 1767 the Jesuits were administrating Indian villages of 110,000 in South America alone, building economies fully integrated with the *cultus* and Catholic morals.[23] They baptized the blacks and catechized them as St. Peter Claver had done for up to 300,000 souls. They learned the native languages and printed grammars for them: Nahuatl in Mexico, Quechua and Guaraní in South

---

[20] Shaun Blanchard, *The Synod of Pistoia and Vatican II: Jansenism and the Struggle for Catholic Reform* (Oxford University Press, 2020), 79-83.
[21] Ulrich L. Lehner, *The Catholic Enlightenment* (Oxford University Press, 2018), 51.
[22] Robert Schwickerath, *Jesuit Education: its history and principles viewed in the light of modern educational problems* (St. Louis, Mo., B. Herder, 1903), 173.
[23] O'Malley, *The Jesuits*, 73.

America, and in North America Huron, Chippewa, Mi'kmaq, Innu, Inuktitut, Cree and many others.

During all this time the wealthy had been fighting against the Jesuits for the love of money. They wanted to enslave the blacks and Indians, destroy their languages and cultures, and use slavery to impose a rigid caste system. The French of Haiti had been most successful with these aims, but in New Orleans they were forced by the Church to allow the slaves to rest on Sundays and Holy Days and give freedom to slave children, creating a whole community of *gens de couleur libres* ("free people of color"). Meanwhile, the Jesuits and other orders were freely preaching the Gospel everywhere, frustrating the desire for the unlimited acquisition of wealth.

Catholic Powers Succumb

Thus the strategy in France, unlike the "conservative" anti-Catholicism in Britain, was *Liber*—to set free the Dionysian orgy—it was a "liberal" anti-Catholicism. Some Jewish leaders would later join in France but be countered directly by a miraculous act of the Virgin Mary. Thus this point cannot be stressed enough: both the English established disorder of 1688 that Locke rationalized and the later order established in France are of the same spirit and follow the same principles—*not Rome*. The unity was the lust for power and avarice. The spirit of *Liber* desired to destroy the Jesuits in order to achieve unlimited power and wealth. They succeeded in getting King Louis XV to suppress them in 1764.

The strategy in the Catholic kingdoms of Spain and Portugal was different. Not all Jesuits had lived up to the crusading ideal and excess is always fodder for propaganda. Thus like the Venetian rebellion against Trent, the Masons here were concocting brilliantly *Catholic* reasons why the Jesuits should be suppressed that were "rational, nuanced, and understandable grievances," which were but a pretext for dismantling the work of the Holy Spirit through the Gospel.[24]

What was really at stake was nothing less than the Gospel against the love of money. It was the Baroque culture of the second Christendom, led by the Jesuits that stood in the way of anti-culture.[25] The Masons succeeded in Portugal in 1759 and in Spain in 1767, allowing the government to take over seminary education.[26] It was professed Catholics themselves who were attacking the Jesuits at that time, attempting to deprive the pope of

---

[24] Rao, *Black Legends*, 378-389.
[25] Ibid., 379
[26] Henry Chadwick, *The Popes and the European Revolution* (Oxford University Press, 1981), 120.

THE POPE FOLDS UNDER POLITICAL PRESSURE

this great spiritual army. If they could only force the pope to sanction their actions, then they could rationalize their voluntarism.

By the time of the conclave of 1769, they united to force the conclave to elect a pope who would officially suppress the Jesuit order. They found him in Pope Clement XIV. He hesitated for four years. The Catholic powers threatened him with schism, and in the end, he chose to "keep unity, even at the expense of truth."[27] He was more willing to suppress the Jesuits than suffer.

On February 15th, 1769, Pope Clement XIV suppressed the whole Jesuit order. Then came the "systematic and officially sanctioned looting," and the Masons began to dismantle everything that had been built from the second Christendom.[28] They destroyed libraries, stole funds, locked up Jesuits and seized paintings.

This act of the Vicar of Christ was a complete capitulation to the spirit of the world, and the spirit of the earthly city, and he failed countless men who had given their lives to crusade for the King of Kings. Above all, this was a suppression of fatherhood in Catholic culture. And at that moment, the English were erupting in another civil war.

---

[27] Dietrich von Hildebrand, *The Charitable Anathema*, (Roman Catholic Books, 1993), 3, 30.
[28] O'Malley, *The Jesuits*, 80.

XX

THE FIRST AMERICAN CIVIL WAR

In "the Year of Masonry 5793," as the newspapers put it, the procession of lodge masters finally reached the sacred site.[1] George Washington laid the silver plate with the Masonic inscriptions under the cornerstone, and the worshipful masters "consecrated" the ground with corn, wine and oil. Prayers and chants were offered and then the games began. This public Masonic *cultus* would later receive a triumphal arch — the bronze Senate door sculpted in bronze within a few generations by Thomas Crawford.[2]

Present was, no doubt, Catholic Daniel Carroll, for his name was listed as a "Commissioner" on the Masonic silver plate. He had signed the new Constitution of the United States of America just a few years prior. His brother was bishop John Carroll who, in the same year as this public Masonic *cultus*, dedicated the United States to the Immaculate Conception. It was the year of Our Lord 1793, and by that time, blood had already been spilled for a vague slogan on two continents and one Caribbean Island. This vague slogan was "Liberty" and the movement would be known as "Liberalism." It was the idea that man had "progressed" and should now violently kill their forefathers, destroy their monarchies and set up new systems of republican government because of the progress of *Libertas*. It was the first movement of anti-culture.

---

[1] The contemporary account is given by the Columbia Mirror and Alexandria Gazette, September 25th, 1793, and is reproduced on the Capitol website to this day: <https://www.aoc.gov/explore-capitol-campus/buildings-grounds/capitol-building/first-cornerstone>, accessed March 8, 2021.

[2] "Senate Bronze Doors," *Architect of the Capital*, <https://www.aoc.gov/explore-capitol-campus/art/senate-bronze-doors>, Accessed March 8, 2021.

Causes for Blood

The founders of the United States were great men, but they cannot compare to the least of the saints. That is why this history is complex. The American Revolution had Masonic elements, but this was just one of many factors. It was in fact a civil war because it was a dispute that degenerated into bloodshed between the English colonists.[3] King George and the Loyalist colonists fought King Louis XVI and the Patriot colonists, with Blacks and Native Americans joining both sides according to their local interests. A great many colonists, meanwhile, simply refused to shed the blood of their neighbors and did not fight. Scholars debate if Loyalists equaled or outnumbered Patriots, or if the neutral party was the largest.[4]

However, the Catholic Church also divided on this point, bringing the civil war into the Mystical Body of Christ, which is the origin of the fracturing Christendom.

Let us consider the heretical cultures built in the thirteen English colonies. These were separate republics or oligarchies that were characterized by a strong religious and economic interest. The colonies had immense economic opportunities in land acquisition yet threatened by natives and famine.[5] Even in colonies with an established church, a strong effort to tolerate all sects mitigated the influence of any one *cultus* on the public order. These conditions made the political unity of the colonists unite for common defense and economics, and relegate religion to the private sphere, allowing the idol of money to dictate the public order, as in Britain and the Dutch provinces. This meant slavery or factory work, which may or may not be governed by any religious principles.

As Coloumbe notes "none of the colonies were what we call democratic" and most of the colonists who paid taxes to the powerful in government "could not vote for them, and so were unrepresented."[6] The leadership of each colony was created by royal decree or other allowance, and the colonies essentially created their own governments and leaders held power according to their particular situation. The point here is that they governed themselves and made money for the wealthy in England so the situation was an extension of the Whig anti-Catholic status quo.

The threats to the established order came from Catholic France in Canada, New Orleans and Haiti, Catholic Spain in Florida, Mexico, Cuba and the Caribbean, and the Jacobite internal threat in England.

---

[3] Coulombe, *Puritan's Empire*, 94-101.
[4] Ibid., 101.
[5] Dawson, *Gods of Revolution*, 38-41.
[6] Coulombe, *op. cit.*, 93.

The English businessmen in America had Whig history and the Puritans had the Venetian "City on a Hill" history—both melded into one spirit of "Manifest Destiny" against the existing Catholic civilizations in the Americas. This was just another theory of unlimited progress: Christ is not the Lord of history, American Liberty is. "Manifest Destiny" was the idea that God had chosen America's earthy city to become the new City of God on earth. Like the Anglican establishment and the English enclosures, the American colonists sought to get land where it could be found, with government help if necessary, providential capitalism working with the unlimited progress, mixed with sincere Christian piety. With Manifest Destiny, as with Whig history, the progress of *Libertas* made the ends justify the means. This allowed men to rationalize their evil actions as part of a greater good for the progress of *Libertas*.

When George Washington was twenty-two years old in 1754, he led a force of English militia to ambush a French Canadian force in modern Pennsylvania over a land dispute. This event became the pretext for the Seven Years War between France and Britain, which was joined by Spain, Portugal, Russia, and Prussia in the first world war over economic interests. Gone now were the old Christian limitations on warfare, and the increased barbarous militarism already glimpsed with Cromwell and Adolphus. During this war Thomas Jefferson was in college studying the scientism of unlimited progress taught by Bacon, Newton, and Locke. While Washington was learning manliness on the field of battle, Jefferson was filled with idealism far from battle.

In 1763, the British and French signed a treaty that ceded great amounts of land to Britain. This led Britain to make concessions to two groups of people that the English colonists hated, imposing taxes to pay for war debts. Like the usury controversies during first Christendom, more militarism always cost more money.

But these taxes hurt the business interests of the English merchants. Adam Smith wrote his book on providential capitalism because these policies hurt his business.[7] The New Englanders like Samuel Adams went beyond writing or politics and started to harass Boston with mob violence, burning ships and destroying property.

Even though the colonial leaders taxed their own people without representation, they used the Catholic principles against divine right monarchy to argue their case against the taxes. King George III was asserting his power more than his predecessors. The Patriots did have a good argument for their cause in seeking to maintain the colonies' long-

---

[7] Arthur Herman, *How the Scots Invented the Modern World* (New York: Three Rivers Press, 2001), 217.

established self-government, which followed more along the lines of subsidiarity than what Parliament wanted to do.

But like the War of Three Kingdoms, there was a certain voluntarism on both sides. They attempted to use some Catholic principles to justify themselves, without accepting the whole of Catholic teaching. The Patriots used the Catholic principle of popular sovereignty to seek to impose what they thought was right, and the Loyalists used the Catholic principle of oaths and hierarchy to impose what they thought was right. Both had some justification. Neither wanted to restore the Magna Carta's stipulation about the Catholic Church.

But the Declaration of Independence would say "all men are created equal" and be immediately understood in two ways. On the one hand, this phrase is merely establishing the principle of popular sovereignty, that the rule of the government is in some sense by the consent and for the sake of the people, and Reilly notes this goes back to Hooker.[8] Since all men are equal, rulership is established in some way by consent, such as when the peasant families established relationships with feudal lords for protection. Bellarmine had argued this point against heretical divine right monarchy since this was the "common world of discourse" at that time, but he had in mind the freedom of the Church like the Magna Carta.[9]

Yet at the same time, this phrase was also taken immediately to repudiate hierarchy in general and monarchy in particular. The Declaration was promulgated in the context of Thomas Paine's *Common Sense*; the most popular interpretation was that monarchy was *per se* tyranny.[10] Because all are equal, the hierarchy of monarchy was an affront to human dignity. Thus this amounted to the idea that human dignity is based on power, which is voluntarism.

The Declaration of Independence did not intend to restore the Magna Carta and the freedom of the Catholic Church. It sought to justify the cause of the colonists shedding the blood of other colonists. It was an argument that their war was just. But the phrase is a half-truth, which is true in one sense and false in another. On the one hand, all men are equal in dignity. But did that mean that all men should therefore be equal in power? Is hierarchy inherently unjust? "All men are created equal" must be balanced with the other truth that "all men are bound in a hierarchy of rights and duties beginning with the family." The Patriot faction contained men who accepted hierarchy and men who did not.

---

[8] Reilly, *America On Trial*, 158-171.
[9] Ibid., 214.
[10] Ferrara, *Liberty: The God that Failed*, 140-143.

There were noble men among the Patriots, like Washington, who would show great magnanimity toward the Catholics, but heretics on both sides of 1776 were using half-truths to support one principle of negation — *not Rome*. It was two groups of powerful men both trying to find popular support so that ordinary men would shed blood to support their power. Since Henry VIII had already broken the Magna Carta by creating his own church, the debate was not about whether the Magna Carta would be broken, but how. Each side asserted their claim based on "the ancient Constitution of England." But without the divine grace of the sacraments, both sides could be manipulated for the same end of *not Rome*.

Recall again that the first principles of Christian chivalry are defense of the Church. The English elites had lost their nobility because they had plundered the Bride of Christ, imposed their regime upon the faithful, and tenaciously defended their stolen, filthy lucre. Now their sons were fighting over who would possess that stolen property and create a better alternative to Catholicism. And yet, the Patriots would give greater freedom to Catholics than they had previously.

The Indians and French

But besides taxes, the other important factors for colonist bloodshed came from the king's efforts to win over his new subjects in Canada and the Great Lakes region. But these were subjects that the Patriot colonists hated.[11]

The first hated group were the Indians, many of whom were Catholic and métis, mixed race French with Algonquian, Ojibwe or Cree tribes. The king tried to protect them from the Patriot colonists by issuing the Proclamation of 1763 that restricted the land seizures of the colonists west of the Appalachian Mountains. This provoked the patriots who wanted that land for their business interests, and they were willing to break their oaths to the king to do it.

In a letter on the seventeenth of September 1767, Washington began writing to his friend William Crawford, a soldier fighting the Indian tribes and others on the frontiers of the colonies. Washington shared a plan to circumvent the king's proclamation by surveying the Indian land "under the pretense of hunting" since he viewed the proclamation as merely a

---

[11] Coulombe, *Puritan's Empire*, 81-82, 94.

"temporary expedien[t] to quiet the minds of the Indians & must fall of course in a few years."[12]

Through the pressure of violence from the colonists, the natives had already been ceding the land the king had promised them, and so Washington says "Indians are consenting to our Occupying the Land." And thus he urges Crawford to spy out the land and "keep this whole matter a profound Secret" because "I might be censured for the opinion I have given in respect to the King's Proclamation" and it might alert others to the scheme "putting them upon a Plan of the same nature (before we could lay a proper foundation for success ourselves)."

This began Washington's partnership with Crawford to gain land from the Native Americans against the king that lasted until Crawford's death in 1782.[13] This was representative of many colonists' efforts to unite against the tribes in order to gain their land or land near them.[14] Thus the king's efforts to stop this land expansion would be condemned in the Declaration of Independence as "raising the conditions of new Appropriations of Lands."

To make matters even more provocative, the British Parliament decided to allow the French Catholics of Quebec to continue to openly practice Catholicism, and leave them alone to continue the second Christendom with the Quebec Act of 1774. This act in some way was beginning to restore the Magna Carta because it gave freedom to the Catholic Church in the public *cultus* for the first time since James II.

But this threatened the conservative anti-Catholic status quo in the colonies. Thus the Continental Congress in 1774 condemned the Parliament "establishing the Roman Catholic religion in the Province of Quebec, abolishing the equitable system of English laws, and erecting a tyranny there."[15] This grievance made it into the Declaration of Independence as:

> Abolishing the free System of English Laws in a neighboring Province, establishing therein an Arbitrary

---

[12] George Washington to William Crawford, 17th of September, 1767 <https://founders.archives.gov/documents/Washington/02-08-02-0020>, accessed March 27, 2021.

[13] Edward Redmond, "Washington as Land Speculator," *Library of Congress* (undated) <https://www.loc.gov/collections/george-washington-papers/articles-and-essays/george-washington-survey-and-mapmaker/washington-as-land-speculator/>, accessed March 27, 2021.

[14] Dawson, *Gods of Revolution*, 40.

[15] *Declaration and Resolves of the First Continental Congress*, 1774.

government, and enlarging its Boundaries so as to render it at once an example and fit instrument for introducing the same absolute rule into these Colonies.

This evoked the popular conspiracy theory that Catholicism would be imposed on the colonies.[16] As Sidney and Locke had done, the "free" laws of Protestant Englishmen are contrasted with the "Arbitrary government" and "absolute rule" of Catholicism. Thus in the minds of many leaders of the Patriot faction, "freedom" meant "freedom from the Church."[17] This was the lie that the Magna Carta's freedoms could be secured without the freedom of the Church. If the Church is not free to destroy public idols by means of the public *cultus*, fallen man will set up his own idols to worship, and continue his slavery to the world, the flesh and the devil.

The Ugly Revolution of 1688 was meant to stop a Catholic king James II, who had freed Catholicism, from creating a Catholic dynasty and restoring something of the Magna Carta. In this proposition against the Quebec Act, the Declaration of Independence was doing the same thing in 1776 that the English had done against Catholicism in 1688. But Gordon admits that "the American Revolution of 1776 largely *mimicked* the principles of the Glorious Revolution waged by the Whigs in England in 1688."[18] The Bill of Rights of 1689 said that "it hath been found by experience that it is inconsistent with the safety and welfare of this Protestant kingdom to be governed by a papist prince."[19] The Bill of Rights of the United States in 1789 would take that further and make the Federal government free from any public *cultus* whatsoever.

Further, the rhetoric of "all men are created equal" originally included a vigorous denunciation of the king for the slave trade which would condemn Jefferson, Washington and Carroll themselves, committing them to forsaking their economic power by freeing their slaves.[20] Yet instead the

---

[16] Ferrara, *Liberty the God that Failed*, 138-140.
[17] The same fear of "Popery" is seen in the *Suffolk Resolves* of Boston and Hamilton's *Full Vindication of the Measures of Congress*. Coulombe, Puritan's Empire, 107.
[18] Emphasis his. Gordon, *Catholic Republic*, 64, n64.
[19] *Bill of Rights*, 1689.
[20] "He has waged cruel war against human nature itself, violating its most sacred rights of life and liberty in the persons of a distant people who never offended him, captivating & carrying them into slavery in another hemisphere, or to incur miserable death in their transportation thither. This piratical warfare, the opprobium of INFIDEL Powers, is the warfare of the CHRISTIAN king of Great Britain. Determined to keep open a market where MEN should be bought & sold,

delegates were more willing to unite against "tyranny"—and gain more power for themselves—than forsake their own tyranny of destroying black families for filthy lucre. Thus this grievance was removed from the Declaration, whereas the grievance against the Catholic "arbitrary government" in Quebec remained. No one refused to sign that, not even Carroll, the only Catholic on the document.

It is also important to note at this time the methods used by the Patriots to promote their cause, described by Dawson as "mob law and mass terrorism."[21] They whipped up crowds to violence and bloodshed using emotional rhetoric to convince men to commit sedition, which is stirring up "tumults tending to fight" that are against "the unity and peace of a people."[22]

At the same time, if tyranny was indeed present, such acts were not seditious since "it is the tyrant rather that is guilty of sedition."[23] Was the taxing of businesses an act of tyranny that could justify breaking oaths and bloodshed? The Dutch and English had already rationalized their rejection of Catholicism in a similar context, and Whig history had begun to promote the superstition of unlimited progress. Were the American Patriots now picking up the sacred mantle of unlimited progress without the grace of the sacraments, or were they restoring the ancient Catholic principles of constitutional government? In truth, it was a mixture of both and more.

In order to understand the backstory of what Catholics faced in 1776, we need to look at England under Queen Elizabeth.

The Origins of the Breaking of Christendom

George Calvert, ("Lord Baltimore") was the son of a wealthy Catholic who had been forced to compromise his faith under Elizabeth's engineered consent and subject his children to a Protestant education. Calvert took the

---

he has prostituted his negative for suppressing every legislative attempt to prohibit or to restrain this execrable commerce. And that this assemblage of horrors might want no fact of distinguished die, he is now exciting those very people to rise in arms among us, and to purchase that liberty of which he has deprived them, by murdering the people on whom he also obtruded them: thus paying off former crimes committed against the LIBERTIES of one people, with crimes which he urges them to commit against the LIVES of another." Jefferson's "Rough Draft," 1776, <http://founding.com/founders-library/government-documents/federal-government-documents/jeffersons-rough-draft-of-the-declaration-of-independence-1776/>, accessed March 27, 2021.
[21] Dawson, *Gods of Revolution*, 43.
[22] *Summa*, II-II q42 a1.
[23] Ibid., II-II q42 a2 ad3.

oaths against Catholicism and gained political power under James I (r. 1603-1624). To his great credit, he later returned to the Faith of his Baptism and publicly professed his Catholicism, resigning his career under Charles I. Using his existing favor with the monarchy, he endeavored to create a prosperous colony in the New World in which Protestants and Catholics would both be free to worship. This eventually resulted in the founding of the colony of Maryland by his son Cecil in 1634.

Cecil ("The 2nd Lord Baltimore") was the Catholic proprietor of Maryland and his brother Leonard was the governor over both Catholics and Protestants, including three Jesuits who had resisted the English regime. Knowing that the Protestants could at any time complain of their Catholicism to Virginia or London and shut down the colony, Cecil ordered that:

> All Acts of Roman Catholic Religion to be done as privately as may be, and that they instruct all the Roman Catholics to be silent upon all occasions of discourse concerning matters of Religion; and that the said Governor & Commissioners treat the Protestants with as much mildness and favor as Justice will permit.[24]

Despite this, when their ship arrived in New England, Jesuit father Andrew White erected a large cross on a Maryland island (later named St. Clement's after the pope and patron saint of mariners) and sung high Mass on the Annunciation, 1634 writing "this had never been done before in this part of the world."[25]

Fr. White went on to evangelize the Anacostans, Patuxent, Potomac, and Piscataway tribes, and became the first Englishman to compose Indian language grammars.[26] In contrast to other English colonies, Fr. White facilitated good relations with the Indians and even baptized the Emperor of the Piscataway tribe by 1640.[27] He established a chapel as St. Ignatius

---

[24] Lord Baltimore, "Instructions from Lord Baltimore to Leonard," 13th of November, 1633
<http://nationalhumanitiescenter.org/pds/amerbegin/settlement/text4/BaltimoreInstructions.pdf>. Accessed February 24, 2021., ch. I

[25] *Relatio Itineris in Marylandiam* cited in A. Knott, "Maryland," *The Catholic Encyclopedia* (1910) <http://www.newadvent.org/cathen/09755b.htm>., accessed February 24, 2021. Coulombe, *Puritan's Empire*, 57-58.

[26] E. Devitt, "Andrew White," *The Catholic Encyclopedia* (1912)
<https://www.newadvent.org/cathen/15610b.htm>, accessed March 27, 2021.

[27] Ibid.

church in 1641, which served as the seat of the Jesuit mission to the tribes. Nevertheless, the stipulations of Cecil became the norm for Catholics in Maryland. He would not make Mary the public throne of Christ over the public order in Maryland, but attempt to establish religion as a private matter for the sake of peaceful coexistence.[28]

The Moderate and the Strict in Colonial America

The most sympathetic reading of this endeavor, however, makes Cecil into a pious Catholic who is simply filled with gratitude at being able to have the Holy Sacrifice at all, without being hunted down by the English regime, after what his grandfather and father had suffered. This gratitude of the immigrant to find in America freedom from the persecutions and poverty of the mother country is at the heart of every truly patriotic American immigrant ever since.

Further, we justify Calvert's suppression of public Catholicism as an act of prudence to help the colony survive in the hostile environment of Puritan New England. If he was pious, he probably wanted to establish economic ties with Virginia in order to have an amicable relationship of peaceful trade, allowing Catholics to have churches and the Holy Mass without restrictions.

The difficulty was that the cultural momentum of New England was thoroughly anti-Catholic and secular. The reason is that the public *cultus* of Maryland was nothing but the coin, since economic relationships were the only thing ceremonially tying the colonists of Maryland together.

But we may consider the legacy of Lord Baltimore to be the moderate policy of Catholics in the United States and other anti-Catholic regimes. If this were an act of prudence, it could be justified for the sake of public order as an exception for an extraordinary situation. It was similar to the charter of *Sicut Judaeis*, as a means to protect the peace of society.

Taken to an extreme, the moderate impulse will succumb to the cultural momentum of the American *cultus* of coin and nation, and especially the superstition of "Manifest Destiny." But most frequently, mixed marriages weakened the faith of this party, since the children will not only suffer cultural momentum from the public order, but also from one of the parents as well. In order to avoid this extreme, they needed unity with the strict party.

---

[28] Lord Baltimore, "Instructions," ch. IV. In ch. VIII he does instruct a church to be built at the governor's place and that the intention of the founding is "the honor of God by endeavoring the conversion of the savages to Christianity" (VI), but trade and commerce are the main concerns.

The strict party is represented by Fr. White and his zeal to publicly celebrate the Holy Sacrifice, erect the Holy Cross as the symbols of Christ's rule over souls and society, and bring the Gospel to the heretics and pagans. It is important to note at this stage that as we have attempted to trace in this brief history, Fr. White's strict approach regarding the public *cultus* is the norm for Catholics throughout history.

Taking the moderate approach of Lord Baltimore in terms of evangelization and the public order is only reserved for extraordinary circumstances. Maryland was certainly such a situation, so we can at least understand Baltimore's actions here. The problem is that the moderate, extraordinary approach will become the norm for Catholics in the United States because of the strong cultural momentum and deep public *cultus* toward Manifest Destiny.

Nevertheless we may also note an extreme tendency among the strict, which was seen during the Catholic response to early Protestantism—an excessive zeal against opponents of the Church can quickly lead to bloodshed and disorder, or at least words and deeds against charity which alienate non-Catholics from the Faith. Cecil wanted Catholics to "treat the Protestants with as much mildness and favor as justice will permit." As St. Francis de Sales put it, "a spoon full of honey gets more flies than a barrel full of vinegar." And this saint converted all of Geneva back to the Faith. The strict party needed the moderate to temper their zeal for truth with charity.

But, as we will see, this division among the American Catholics was the origin of Catholic division in our own time. The question was this: should these new orders in society be welcomed as "modernity" or be resisted as "mob bloodshed?" From this point especially, Catholics will divide over this question more and more until it will become not only a matter of prudential decisions, but even doctrine.

The Carroll Family

The Calvert sons continued this policy of freedom of religion and were supported by Charles Carroll the settler, a wealthy Irish Catholic attorney who arrived later in the seventeenth century. But after the Ugly Revolution of 1688 the Protestants seized power over Maryland and mimicked the English Bill of Rights by excluding Catholics like Calvert and Carroll from political power. The Calvert sons finally compromised their Faith and became Protestants but the Carrolls, to their credit, kept the Faith. Unfortunately, they engaged heavily in slavery and achieved great wealth, but were thus able to build their own chapels on their private land to provide for the Catholic populace.

By 1763, the Carroll family was one of the wealthiest slaveowners in the colonies, but they were still barred from political power because of their Faith. When war broke out, the Carroll family had an opportunity to regain the political power it had lost generations ago by the hands of Protestants. It could also re-establish the legacy of Baltimore by making the public order free from religion. This would allow Catholics to again build churches and worship freely. The Patriot cause thus was an opportunity for Catholics to regain a great deal of freedom that they had lost, restoring something of the Magna Carta.

The Carrolls and their clergy supported the Patriot faction, while the established Anglican clergy in Maryland were Loyalists.[29] The Carrolls were joined by the other most wealthy Catholics John Barry of Pennsylvania, Stephen Moylan and Thomas Fitzsimmons.[30] This moderate party seems to have lost any unity with the strict at this point and adopted the ideas of the Patriots mixed with their Catholic Faith. Some Patriots were willing to tolerate Catholics, so the Catholic Patriots looked past the anti-Catholic rhetoric for this goal of freedom.

Meanwhile, most of the Catholics on the Loyalist side were of lesser means, including Major Clinton and Fr. John McKenna, and the whole of the Catholics further north. These no doubt heard the anti-Catholic rhetoric and did not trust the Patriot movement.

At this stage it is not clear where the moderates and the strict lie. On the one hand, the strict Jacobites would certainly support a revolt against the usurping heretic king to restore the order, yet the Carrolls and other Catholic Patriots seem to be of the moderate legacy of Lord Baltimore. We could see strict among the Loyalists in putting down sedition, as well as with the French Catholics of Quebec maintaining their order of Christendom. On the other hand, the French Catholics under Louis XVI were supporting the Patriots to weaken the British empire. On Catholic just war principles, it is difficult to justify the bloodshed, since the grievances of the Patriots over taxes were relatively minor.

The Patriot Faction Seizes Power

After the British Parliament tried to punish the colonies for their acts of mob violence, the Patriot faction assembled in 1774 at the First Continental Congress and attempted to seize power over the colonies. It is

---

[29] A. Knott, "Maryland," *loc. cit.*
[30] Coulombe, *Puritan's Empire*, 101.

important to note here that the body that became the Federal government did not have any precedent before this time, and these men were literally attempting to convince all the other colonists to accept their rule. It was a seizure of power by force.

On the other hand, these men were leaders in their own colonies and men who "believed it was their right under the British constitution."[31] And to be fair, a seizure of power would not be as much of a problem for noblemen taking control of the community in a crisis to defend their people against an unjust aggressor. But their cause would also use the anti-hierarchy ideas that would undermine claims to nobility and the anti-Catholicism rhetoric in order to convince mobs of the common men to shed blood.

Unfortunately this self-appointed government seems to have showed itself willing to resort to base deception to win over the colonists and impose their will, and the principle of the conspiracy of anything but Rome. This is seen in the two letters that were sent from this congress concerning Catholicism in the Quebec Act. They sent one letter to the people of England denouncing Catholicism as having "dispersed impiety, bigotry, persecution, murder and rebellion through every part of the world."[32] They sent another to Quebec seeking military support by praising the "liberality of sentiment distinguishing your nation" and that "difference of religion" should not prevent "a hearty amity with us."[33]

Charles Carroll had a cousin who was a Jesuit, Fr. John Carroll. Benjamin Franklin went with him to Quebec to try to win over the French to the Patriot cause. But Bishop Briand of Quebec had received both of the letters of congress and excommunicated Fr. Carroll and forbade his priests to associate with him. So the Catholics of French Canada sided with the Loyalist cause, and the Canadian Catholicism was later denounced by the Declaration of Independence as we have seen. Thus the principle was established by the Patriot faction: as long as Catholics did not seek to establish Christendom and kept their religion private, they could be tolerated (which was a step better than their condition in England but worse than Quebec). While the Jesuits had been suppressed in Catholic countries, the Catholics of North America were divided against each other on this question. Eight years of bloodshed began in 1775.

---

[31] Thomas Woods, *The Politically Incorrect Guide to American History* (Regnery Publishing, 2004), 14.
[32] Coulombe, *op. cit.*, 106.
[33] Ibid.

Barbarism of the Civil War

During the fighting we see the erosion of Christian culture and the return to barbarism in two acts. What is commemorated about Christmas of 1776 is not Washington reading to his men the Nativity story of the Christ child and the angels armies proclaiming "Peace on earth" against the tyranny of Satan. Instead, according to various reports, he read the latest propaganda from Thomas Paine, *The American Crisis*. "Tyranny, like hell, is not easily conquered" and "the harder the conflict, the more glorious the triumph."[34] The Patriot cause was imagined as a holy crusade, thereby elevating their earthly conflict to something supernatural. Yet the Patriots were not fighting in the name of Christianity, but nevertheless claimed some divine sanction. This was helping to create the new religion of unlimited progress and anti-culture.

Washington then took advantage of the Christian culture of his enemy by attacking them at dawn on the feast of St. Stephen, December 26th. The Lutheran Germans fighting for the Loyalist side were still recovering from celebrating the Nativity and were easily subdued. This event is commemorated with the paintings by Leutze and Bingham ("The Crossing of the Delaware") illustrating how Christmas was transformed into American mythology.[35] In Christendom such bloodshed associated with the feast of Christmas would have merited excommunication, but this attack by Washington is still celebrated by Americans.

Another instance of this barbarism is the Sullivan Campaign, in which the atrocities on both sides climaxed in the extremes of targeting civilians. Washington ordered total war against the Indians and the Loyalists, which devastated forty Indian villages with their crops, while the women and children fled as refugees to Canada.[36] This disregard for civilian casualties would only increase as the unlimited progress of anti-culture began to take hold. Nevertheless, Washington still showed himself to have great virtue and noble character in refusing political parties and his willingness to

---

[34] Thomas Paine, *The American Crisis*, no. 1, 1776.

[35] For a critical review of the documentary evidence, see Jett Conner, "The American Crisis Before Crossing the Delaware," *Journal of the American Revolution* (Feb 25, 2015), <https://allthingsliberty.com/2015/02/american-crisis-before-crossing-the-delaware/>, accessed March 27, 2021.

[36] Colin G. Calloway, *The American Revolution in Indian Country: Crisis and Diversity in Native American Communities* (Cambridge University Press, 1995); Max M. Mintz, *Seeds of Empire: The American Revolutionary Conquest of the Iroquois* (New York: New York University Press, 1999).

tolerate the Catholics, thus Pope Leo XIII would justly call him "the great Washington."[37]

Meanwhile, Catholics were still bringing the civil war into the Church. The erosion of Catholic unity at this point was different than France betraying the Church in the Thirty Years War. For at that time, and even up to 1773, culture itself remained intact in France and England. Now, an entirely new order was being born, as Thomas Paine exuded with enthusiasm that the blood that had been spilled had "contributed more to enlighten the world and diffuse a spirit of freedom and liberality among mankind than any human event (if this may be called one) that ever preceded it."[38] From this point all regimes of anti-culture would justify their killing by means of unlimited progress in an unrelenting rebellion against all fatherhood and hierarchy. Prior conflicts were between cultures, but this new conflict was between culture and anti-culture seen as a religious crusade for progress deeply mixed, especially in America, with a strong and sincere Christian piety.

Triumph of the Patriots

The Patriots did not have their own *cultus*, since their cause was united under a strong principle of negation—unity against taxes, or against Popery, or against Indian land rights or against tyranny or against something else. Thus there was a strong current of voluntarism among them. They were fighting for freedom from something, but after the war, there was no clear vision of what specifically they had been fighting for.

At first, it seemed the colonies could simply go back to the self-government they had before. But since voluntarism always requires more power to sustain itself, the Patriots soon moved to persecute their fellow colonists who had sided with the king and began hunting down dissenters and imposing stricter oaths.[39] Jefferson wanted to punish these colonists and create an "empire."[40] As a result, the number of refugees from the Patriot regime was ten times greater than in the French revolution, leading Rothbard to admit that "a myth has been promulgated by neoconservative historians that the American Revolution was a uniquely mild revolution."[41]

---

[37] Leo XIII, *Longinqua* (1895), 4.
[38] Thomas Paine, *The American Crisis*, No. 13, 1783.
[39] Ferrara, *op. cit.*, 154-175.
[40] Timothy Pitkin, *A Political and Civil History of the United States of America*, (New Haven, CT: Hezekiah House, 1828), vol. 2, 246.
[41] Murray Rothbard, *Conceived in Liberty*, online ed. (Auburn, AL: Von Mises Institute, 1999), vol. IV, 423 in Ferrara, 168.

Most Loyalists fled to Canada or back to Britain, although others managed to adjust to the new regime, like the family of St. Elizabeth Ann Seton.

Although he had previously conceded public acts of religion, Jefferson then vigorously campaigned against a public *cultus* in Virginia. Nevertheless, most colonies were able to continue their publicly funded church. Meanwhile, the new empire had gained the Great Lakes region that Washington had worked to have, as well as the Indian Reserve land west of the Appalachians.

The thirteen colonies formed the United States of America by a unanimous ratification of the Articles of Confederation by 1781, which, after Loyalist opposition was suppressed, mostly restored the former self-government of the colonies. The federal government only received the same powers that had formerly been held by the British government.

But just as Parliament had had debts to pay for their war, so the new United States raised taxes just the same, encountering violent resistance, including an armed rebellion led by American Revolution veteran Daniel Shays ("Shays' Rebellion").

The rebellion was put down, but the Patriots split in two. One faction—the Federalists—sought to increase the power of the government even beyond what Britain had had in order to collect taxes and regulate all the states.[42] They were opposed by the Anti-Federalists who saw this as a seizure of power no better than King George and maybe worse.[43]

But the Federalists were able to win over enough people to their cause and thus was born the United States Constitution, in which the rulers gained more power over the states than the British government had previously had over the colonists.[44] Voluntarism always needs more power to sustain itself.

This included a Bill of Rights like the British Bill of Rights, but unlike the British laws, the American did not include any restrictions against Catholics building churches and having the Mass, or even holding political office. In these areas the life of American Catholics was very much improved by the war.

At the same time when compared to Quebec, the Catholics in the United States were restricted from converting the public order by the Constitution, whose first amendment repudiated the very notion of a public *cultus*. In this the American was far worse than the English. For the English preserved the public *cultus*, albeit heretical, which preserved the four elements of culture. But by repudiating the public *cultus* altogether, the United States ratified anti-culture in their very constitution.

---

[42] Coulombe, *Puritain's Empire*, 146-152, 155-159.
[43] Ferrera, *Liberty: the God that Failed*, 187-192.
[44] Ibid., 170-194.

Worse, this implied that divine grace was not necessary. Instead, a general Christianity was promoted in public with a quasi-official status, which De Toqueville would note in 1835, which was melded with Manifest Destiny.[45]

James Madison, "the Father of the Constitution," reasoned that if all of the Protestant sects could be divided against each other, they would not have enough power to influence society too much.[46] The founders wanted morality, but Gordon admits that they created a "large commercial republic that would bear, by design, lots and lots of faction (meaning popular diversity and vice)."[47] The purpose of religion was to make people live virtuously, not govern society.

Thus the Constitution proclaimed the supremacy of its own *cultus*, as it were, which honored not God but "we the people" and its commercial ends. It sought to mitigate the influence of religious "factions," above all, Catholicism. This *cultus* would amount to, at best, sheltering innumerable immigrants from tyranny in the mother country, and at worst, more unlimited progress in service to filthy lucre. This cultural momentum from the highest realm of government would eventually cause the state churches to also remove the public *cultus*, creating a powerful anti-culture by the time of the second Civil War.

Thus just as the Dutch did, a voluntarist *Libertas* threw off order, required always more power to impose itself and its "order" on the old customs and laws of the people. The Patriot faction began the powerful new Constitution with "we the people" asserting that their oligarchy was in fact not an imposition of a powerful minority but an act of the people's general will. This allowed the government to impose more taxes and enforce them.

But then another war veteran, Major James McFarlane, led another popular revolt against taxes. This time George Washington was able to use

---

[45] Cf. Coulombe, *op. cit.*, 105-108.

[46] "In a free government the security for civil rights must be the same as that for religious rights. It consists in the one case in the multiplicity of interests, and in the other in the multiplicity of sects. The degree of security in both cases will depend on the number of interests and sects; and this may be presumed to depend on the extent of country and number of people comprehended under the same government... In the extended republic of the United States, and among the great variety of interests, parties, and sects which it embraces, a coalition of a majority of the whole society could seldom take place on any other principles than those of justice and the general good." James Madison, *Federalist 51* (1788) <https://guides.loc.gov/federalist-papers/text-51-60>, accessed March 27, 2021.

[47] Gordon, *op. cit.*, 115.

the new power to force citizens into the army and met McFarlane with a massive force of 13,000 men, which frightened the revolutionaries away. The next major revolt would not come until the second Civil War, but would be fought on the same principles. Thus when compared to life in the English colonies before the war, the Patriot Federalist faction, after convincing citizens to shed blood for "freedom," had by 1796 decreased the freedom of American citizens and greatly *increased* the power of the central government.

By that year, the Patriots further divided against each other and "most of those men could not stand each other."[48] Since there was no *cultus*, the politics must have a balance of power, not a harmony of hierarchy like in Catholic order. Just as the English king and Parliament had agreed on absolute voluntarism against Rome in 1534 which erupted in civil war in 1642, so also the absolute voluntarism of 1776 would erupt in civil war in 1861. But "all men are created equal" would become the slogan to identify dignity with power and impose anti-culture everywhere.

Meanwhile, the unity among Catholics would continue to erode as Catholics brought the civil war over anti-culture into the Church.

---

[48] "Only Jefferson and Madison still got along." Larry Schweikart and Michael Allen, *Patriot's History of the United States*, rev. ed. (Sentinel, 2014), 138.

XXI

BREAK EVERY VOW, EVERY OATH, EVERY BOND

French Civil War

Just as an alliance formed among Puritans, Anglicans, Masons and Catholics to defend the established anti-Catholic regime in America, so also they united the powerful, Jansenists, and *philosophes* against the Church of Christ in France. The rhetoric and mythos surrounding 1776 was beginning to inspire bloodshed elsewhere. Dawson observes that:

> The myth of the American Revolution acquired definite shape in France long before the United States themselves had acquired political form, and exerted a far stronger influence than the latter on public opinion and the development of democratic ideals in France.[1]

Turgot, Mably and Reynal, as well as Brissot, Condorcet and Lafayette were inspired by this myth and "forgot the mob law" of the Patriots, their "ruthless proscription of minorities," and that the wealth of Jefferson and Washington was "only rendered possible by the existence of Negro slavery."[2]

In 1789, shortly after the American Constitution was imposed, the *Dionysian* spirit of *Liber* was unleashed onto the French people. The mob

---
[1] Dawson, *Gods of Revolution*, 46.
[2] Ibid.

burst forth in blood thirsty rage, murdering priests, nuns, and many of the faithful. They freed Marquis de Sade and the economic freedom allowed him to mass produce pornography for the first time in Christendom.[3]

Just like in the Americas, Catholics were divided. Moderate Catholics had for some time advocated some reforms that the revolutionaries were now implementing.[4] When the revolutionaries imposed the oath to renounce the Church, half of the clergy signed, representing the moderate party moving into heresy. Meanwhile, the strict party would rise up among the Vendée Catholics who rose up in a desperation to defend the order of Christ the King.[5] Their motto was *Dieu, le Roi!* (God, the King!) knowing instinctively that Christ was being dethroned from society and a usurper was being set up. Their villages were massacred—men, women, and children—in the name of Liberty, Equality, and Freedom. By 1797, 115,000 people had been slaughtered by another Empire of Liberty and their "first modern genocide."[6]

For the most part, the American Founders were disgusted with this excess, showing their English spirit of *Libertas*, which hadn't murdered that much since the 1640s. It would be a few generations until the English porn novel *Fanny Hill* was printed freely in Britain and America. Nevertheless Jefferson justified killing the innocent as the movement of progress: "The liberty of the whole earth was depending on the issue of the contest, and was ever such a prize won with so little innocent blood?"[7] Indeed, Jefferson urged, yet more killing may be necessary, and this was the opinion, he said, of virtually all Americans:

> I would have seen half the earth desolated. Were there but an Adam and an Eve left in every country, and left free, it would be better than as it now is. I have expressed to you my sentiments, because they are really those of 99 in a hundred of our citizens. The universal feasts, and rejoicings which have lately been had on account of the

---

[3] E. Michael Jones, *Libido Dominandi: Sexual Liberation and Political Control* (South Bend, IN: Fidelity Press, 2000), 30.
[4] Lehner, *The Catholic Enlightenment, passim*.
[5] Reynald Secher, *The Vendée: A French Genocide* (University of Notre Dame Press, 2013).
[6] Mark Levene, *The Coming of the West and the Coming of Genocide*, 103-161 in Lehner, 209.
[7] Thomas Jefferson to William Short, January 3rd, 1793 <https://founders.archives.gov/documents/Jefferson/01-25-02-0016>, accessed February 26, 2021.

successes of the French shewed the genuine effusions of their hearts.[8]

Just as the love of money had been willing to destroy innumerable Black families, so the love of "freedom" would not count the cost to impose one's will on souls and society. One spirit of voluntarism was flamed to desolate half the earth indeed.

Meanwhile in November of 1789, Pope Pius VI asked Benjamin Franklin who should be appointed bishop in the United States, and he suggested John Carroll. It was Bishop Carroll who dedicated the United States to the Immaculate Conception in 1793, just as Washington was performing public Masonic rites for the capital.

The Anti-Culture Assault on the Fourth Commandment

The hinge of culture is piety, which obliges the next generation to revere what their fathers' wisdom passed down. It is at this root that anti-culture will from this moment erode all bonds in souls and society. Considering the French civil war, Edmund Burke (1729-1797), to his great credit, understood that "If men are discharged of the reverence for ancient usage, they will treat this world...as if it were their private property, to be consumed for their sensual gratification."[9]

Piety, wrote Burke, is "one of the first and most leading principles on which the commonwealth and the laws are consecrated" and "whole original fabric of their society."[10] Throwing off piety, he said, was "teaching these successors [i.e. the next generation] as little to respect their contrivances, as they had themselves respected the institutions of their forefathers."[11] This prediction would in short order be proved true as Soloviev would write later that the "parricidal children, becoming fathers, cannot but beget a new generation of parricides, and so on to infinity."[12] Or as St. Thomas had already summarized that "the order of justice requires that subjects obey their superiors, else the stability of human affairs would cease."[13]

---

[8] Ibid.
[9] Russell Kirk, *The Conservative Mind* (Chicago: H. Regnery Co, 1953), 51.
[10] Edmund Burke, *Reflections on the Revolution in France* (1790).
[11] Ibid.
[12] Soloviev, *Russia and the Universal Church*, 198.
[13] *Summa*, II-II q104 a6.

But the belief in unlimited progress could not be moved. Paine responded to Burke with a thorough exposition of anti-culture by a firm rejection of piety and fatherhood.

> Every generation is, and must be, competent to all the purposes which its occasions require. It is the living, and not the dead, who are to be accommodated... Those who have quitted the world [died], and those who are not yet arrived in it, are as remote from each other, as the utmost stretch of moral imagination can conceive. What possible obligation, then, can exist between them; what rule or principle can be laid down, that two nonentities, the one out of existence, and the other not in, and who never can meet in this world, that the one should control the other to the end of time?[14]

Thus Chesterton's "democracy of the dead," could not be countenanced.

However, Burke's own censure of the French was the very censure that St. Thomas More had leveled against the whole Anglican Church of Henry VIII of which Burke himself was a member. But Burke did not have piety for the rest of Christendom. Like Luther condemning the peasants, the anti-Catholic *status quo* of England wanted just enough voluntarism, but not to follow these principles to their conclusion. They forgot that souls and society are governed by the graces of the Holy Spirit, the principle of universal fatherhood.

Women and Children

After the powerful began rebelling against each other on the basis of voluntarism, the sacred order of the family began to be attacked. If, following voluntarism, power was the basis for dignity, why did woman have to be subject to man? Indeed, voluntarism called for every sacred order to be abolished. But after some ten generations of attacking the Virgin Mary, the dignity of feminine nature could not be safeguarded in the *cultus* and a contest of power was unleashed in the heart of the family.

Already in March of 1776 when the Continental Congress was seizing power, Mrs. Abigail Adams threatened her husband John Adams that if "particular care and attention is not paid to the ladies, we are determined to foment a rebellion, and will not hold ourselves bound by any laws in which

---

[14] Thomas Paine, *Rights of Man* (1791).

we have no voice or representation."[15] Women had suffered under the regime of Anti-Mary for nearly three hundred years. Feminism was and is a revolt against effeminate men and the regime of Anti-Mary.[16] It is understandable that the women would reject this. When they do, they are merely rejecting a disordered tyranny of fallen man deprived of grace.

But with 1773, the revolution against fatherhood was instigated by men. If by 1776 they were killing based on the dignity of power, they silenced themselves against the errors of feminism. Even worse, men would allow their children to receive this disorder, rather than giving up their claim to rebel against fatherhood and culture. The anti-culture of 1776 was the ideological root of feminism, continued after the French joined the killing in 1789 with Mary Wollstonecraft writing *Vindication of the Rights of Women* in 1792.

But this identification of dignity with power was the "debasing of the womanly character and the dignity of motherhood."[17] From this point on, as women were slowly seduced by power, children became more vulnerable, since feminism caused the children to lose motherhood—the "ever watchful guardian of the whole family."[18]

False Education

Rousseau had argued that the state needed to take over the education of children from their parents, so that "the state remains, and the family dissolves."[19] This principle would be a fundamental axiom of the regimes of anti-culture.

A crucial figure in this regard was American Noah Webster who sought to remove piety in education to the classics like Locke and Rousseau had argued. He decried the "defect in our schools" that paid reverence to "foreign and ancient nations" and "dead language."[20] He called on all Americans to bring the revolt against Fatherhood into education:

---

[15] Abigail Adams to John Adams, March 31, 1776 in Miriam Schneir, ed., *Feminism: The Essential Historical Writings* (New York: Vintage Books, 1972), 3.
[16] Carrie Gress, *The Anti-Mary Exposed: Rescuing the Culture from Toxic Femininity* (TAN, 2019).
[17] Pius XI, *Casti Connubii* (1931), 75.
[18] Ibid.
[19] Jean-Jacques Rousseau, "Political Economy," Gendzier, ed., *Encyclopedia*, 195 in Gertrude Himmelfarb, *Roads to Modernity* (New York: Alfred A. Knopf, 2004), 175.
[20] Noah Webster, *A Grammatical Institute of the English Language* (1783), pt. I.

> Americans, unshackle your minds, and act like independent beings. You have been children long enough, subject to the control, and subservient to the interest of a haughty parent. You have now an interest of your own to augment and defend. You have an empire to raise and support by your exertions, and a national character to establish and extend by your wisdom and virtues. To effect these great objects, it is necessary to frame a liberal plan of policy and build it on a broad system of education. Before this system can be formed and embraced, the Americans must believe — and act from the belief — that it is dishonorable to waste life in mimicking the follies of other nations and basking in the sunshine of foreign glory.[21]

As Coulombe notes, with the republican empires, "education ought not be the expansion of the mind so as to assist both in life and salvation, but at base, ideological indoctrination" and "nation-worship."[22] This would be the goal of education in the empires of the anti-culture. But luckily, it would take a few generations for these efforts to take hold.[23] Nevertheless this was the beginning of the identity crisis of American culture, whereby a group of Englishmen (the American Founders) imposed a fabricated culture onto their own English culture, and asserted that they were no longer Englishmen, but "Americans." But power cannot simply impose a different ethnic identity on a people, yet the American Empire has tried to do this in vain ever since, leading to sorrows for Indians and Blacks. Without a public *cultus* or Sacramental Marriage, these peoples would never been integrated into one with the Anglo-Americans as they were with the French, Spanish and Portuguese in the second Christendom. Even today, there is still little mixed culture of Anglo-Indian-African — nothing like the mestizo, métis or creole.

The Haitian Civil War

But because the French were promoting the anti-hierarchy of Jefferson's phrase about "created equal," the way was open for a worldwide revolt on all hierarchy. In March of 1791 Pope Pius VI condemned these ideas as contrary to logos. "This equality and this

---

[21] Ibid.
[22] Coulombe, *Puritan's Empire*, 137.
[23] Christopher Dawson, *The Crisis in Western Education* (Steubenville, OH: Franciscan University Press, 1989), 59.

unbridled liberty," he said, "will snuff out reason."[24] The next month he declared those who had taken the oath were schismatics, exhorting the Frenchmen loyal to the Sacred Heart to fight for the King of Kings for He is the "the faith of your fathers," the "one and the true religion, which bestows eternal life and protects citizens, even societies, and makes them prosperous."[25] He condemned the seizure of the land from the poor.

Meanwhile, the Haitian slave revolt began in August of 1791. Once again, Catholics were on both sides of this conflict as well. The Catholic free people of color allied with the slaves against the slave owners.

This revolt gave to the new religion of anti-culture further strength as a faith, since more than any other grievance yet claimed by the revolutionaries, the slave revolt was a rebellion against *real* tyranny. Because so many Catholics had refused to obey the pope regarding slavery, they only gave fuel to the fires of revolution, since the errors of *Libertas* could be mixed with a just cause against slavery. The Church sought to reconcile slave and master and nullify the institution, but the bloodshed of 1776 had now spread back across the Atlantic.

The Haitian Revolution forced many among the American and French empires to implicitly admit what they really meant by "freedom"—power for the wealthy against their enemies. As Charles Carroll would write regarding his own slaves: "It is admitted by all to be a great evil."[26] The French Empire quickly moved to uphold the economic *status quo* while their imprisoned King Louis XVI, finally consecrated France to the Sacred Heart in early 1792.[27] But in response to Haiti, in 1793 the black codes "entrenched" slavery in the United States.[28] That was the "Year of Masonry 5793." Like the English before them, the French murdered their father the king. The pope hailed him a martyr.

Tensions were building between those gaining power in France and the papacy, and something else had happened while the chaos was exploding. Following the suppression of the Jesuits, the Jansenists had gained power over the diocese of Pistoia in Tuscany, and promulgated Jansenist decrees that "sent shockwaves through Catholic Europe."[29] For

---

[24] Pius VI, *Quod Aliquantum* (1791).

[25] Pius VI, *Charitas* (1791).

[26] Charles Carroll to Robert Goodloe Harper (Feb 17, 1820) in Kate Mason Rowland, *The Life of Charles Carroll of Carrollton 1737-1832* (The University of Virginia, 1898), 320.

[27] Charles Coulombe, "The Politics of the Sacred Heart," *Catholicism.org* (Jun 21, 2013), <https://catholicism.org/the-politics-of-the-sacred-heart.html>, accessed March 27, 2021.

[28] Schweikart and Allen, *Patriot's History of the United States*, 167.

[29] Dale van Kley, "Civic Humanism in Clerical Garb: Gallican Memories of the Early Church and the Project of Primitivist Reform 1719-1791," *Past and Present* 200 (2008): 78 in Blanchard, *The Synod of Pistoia and Vatican II*, 5.

this council injected the revolt against fatherhood deeply inside the Church, with its strong mixture of true and false notions of reform.

Most importantly, this synod placed the nascent fourth Greco-Roman renewal in opposition to Christendom by capitulating to the empire of anti-culture. Mixing with good efforts of restoring patristic and scriptural foundations, the synod attacked the tradition and the *cultus* and sought to subordinate the Church to the secular ruler. When Pope Pius VI condemned it in 1794, he witnessed to the deepening division among Catholics over the matter of the fourth renewal, in a time of killing and chaos. This would foreshadow how the unity of the Church would be broken in a few generations.

But two years later, the French under Emperor Napoléon entered into Italy and captured the papal states. Nearby in Imola, not far from Pistoia, bishop Barnaba Chiaramonti sparked controversy when he preached submission to the French authorities "as there is no opposition between a democratic form of government and the constitution of the Catholic Church."[30] But the next year Pope Pius VI himself was taken prisoner and carried from Rome in 1798, powerless to stop the progress of the revolutionaries. The French Empire was strewn with the dead bodies of whole Catholic families.

In the same year, another Catholic country, Ireland, supported by France, launched more anti-culture violence. This revolution helped spread the ideas of anti-culture through the Catholic island. Some Catholics joined the rebellion in the spirit of the just war of 1641, but knowing the Masonic principles of their cause, the bishops condemned the bloodshed as unjust. This was the fruit of the Masonic lodge from 1725. The British Empire successfully put down the revolt.

As Napoléon's forces continued to make war on Europe, Pope Pius VI was moved through the northern Italian states until he finally arrived in southeastern France. Six weeks after he arrived at his new prison, he died in August, 1799.

That winter, the body of the pope, the head of the Catholic Church, the Vicar of Christ, lay unburied in the empire of France. The emperor boasted that he was "Pius the Last."[31] As the cold darkness of winter closed in, Catholics around the world celebrated Christmas without a pope, and many in France without a priest. The blood of priests, nuns, men, women, and children had been spilled for the progress of *Libertas*. Widows and orphans sought refuge from the bloodshed, food and shelter. The enemies of Christ were about to celebrate the Year of Lucifer, 5800.

---

[30] N. Weber, "Pope Pius VII," *The Catholic Encyclopedia* (1911) < http://www.newadvent.org/cathen/12132a.htm>, accessed March 18, 2021; Coulombe, *Vicars of Christ*, 299.

[31] Weidenkopf, *Timeless: A History of the Catholic Church*, 489.

XXII

EMPIRES OF ANTI-CULTURE

Alexander Hamilton was pleased with the factories because of "the employment of persons who would otherwise be idle (and in many cases a burthen on the community)."

> Women and Children are rendered more useful and the latter more early useful by manufacturing establishments, than they would otherwise be. Of the number of persons employed in the Cotton Manufactories of Great Britain, it is computed that 4/7 nearly are women and children; of whom the greatest proportion are children and many of them of a very tender age.[1]

The year was 1791. Hamilton was the visionary for the new American Empire, now rival to its parent, the British Empire. Now that Hamilton's Federalist faction had won out and imposed their Constitution on the other states, he could build the empire with enough military and economic power to "confront the British, French and Spanish" in the Americas.[2] The factories were the backbone of this empire. In this we can see the whole breakdown of the family.

---

[1] Alexander Hamilton, "Final Version of the Report on the Subject of Manufactures," (December 5, 1791) Original Reports of the Secretary of the Treasury, 1791–1792, National Archives <https://founders.archives.gov/documents/Hamilton/01-10-02-0001-0007>, III, accessed February 25, 2021.
[2] Donald Lee Walker, *Alexander Hamilton's American empire: The intellectual foundations of federalist foreign policy* (University of Nebraska Lincoln, 2005) <https://digitalcommons.unl.edu/dissertations/AAI3186887>, accessed March 27, 2021.

First, the removal of the extended family of grandparents, uncles and cousins uprooted the family out of its context of kin and culture, disrupting the flow of culture from generations. This was the creation of the nuclear family, which was a corruption of the family, since it isolated parents and children far away from their extended family.

Next, by separating men, women and children in the new economy, "the marital union in this new family form was based on intimacy and companionship rather than joint economic function" as it had been in the rural villages.[3] Before, the man, wife and children were all working out of the household as part of the law of the home. Industrialization separated the man from the family and gave him money away from his home, leading, without culture, to alcohol abuse, debauchery and abandonment. Meanwhile, the woman and children were either without work or isolated themselves in factories.

Economics was beginning now to be no longer the "law of the home," where the family was the basic unit of society, but now individuals became the basic unit of society. It became not the family working together for theirs and the community's good, but individuals were paid according to their individual contribution, with or without concern for their families.

This new economy violated the rights of women. For women had the right to be a mother to their children, and not be forced down from their thrones as queen of the household into the drudgery and dreariness of factory life. They had a right to be with their children and be provided for by their husband, but this was squandered for the sake of "usefulness."

Yet even worse, it violated the rights of the child. For a child has the right to be protected by his father and to have his mother to shelter and care for him from birth to whenever he is ready to be more independent. He has the right to be educated by his parents and live and work with his parents in the law of the home. The new economy separated children from their parents and placed them at the mercy of factory owners, the tyranny of stronger children, and the mechanization of profits over people.

Further we see the commoditization of women and children for profit. By uprooting the family's basis in culture, then putting women and children in a value system of profit, the family and generations were vulnerable to the effects of anti-culture.

On the other hand, as Woods asserts, the scarcity suffered by the poor at that time was ameliorated by the factories that increased the amount of goods available and put more people to work.[4] Poor children "are prevented from contracting bad Habits," wrote Hamilton, "and are introduced thereby to a Habit of Industry, by which we may hope to see them become useful

---

[3] Popenoe, *Families without Fathers*, 81.
[4] Thomas Woods, *The Church and the Market*, rev. ed. (Lexington Books, 2015), 59-67.

Members of Society."[5] Some pious Methodist and Quaker businessmen did help their workers and their families, but ultimately these ethics were not as profitable as taking advantage of employees.

The Industrial Revolution from this point on would be a mixture of amelioration for the poor and a breakdown of family and culture based on a new morality. The problem was that it was not the "law of the home" which was the principle of this economy, but the law of consensual contracts—agreements between employer and employee based *solely on consent*, however forced by necessity. Contracts at this point were being subordinated totally to voluntarism. Now man and man made a contract, and more and more excluded Him Who is the third party to every agreement among men.

Providential Capitalism

Adam Smith published his *Wealth of Nations* in 1776. At a time when Scotland's economy was being hurt by Parliament's economic sanctions of American business interests, Smith devised a way to remove the economy from the control of culture. He would motivate the wealthy not by morality and *noblesse oblige*, but by their own lust for money. As Woods admits, "the whole system is driven by the profit motive."[6] The businessman running a factory, wrote Smith:

> Intends only his own gain; and he is in this, as in many other cases, led by an invisible hand to promote an end which was no part of his intention. Nor is it always the worse for the society that it was no part of it. By pursuing his own interest, he frequently promotes that of the society more effectually than when he really intends to promote it.[7]

If we incentivize greed, Smith reasoned, the rich are motivated to give jobs to the starving masses, and thus:

> They are led by an invisible hand to make nearly the same distribution of the necessaries of life, which would have been made, had the earth been divided into equal

---

[5] Alexander Hamilton, "Report of a Committee Appointed to Obtain Information on Manufacturing in Providence" (October 10, 1791) Hamilton Papers, Library of Congress. < https://founders.archives.gov/documents/Hamilton/01-09-02-0316-0003>. Accessed February 25, 2021.
[6] Woods, 61.
[7] Adam Smith, *Wealth of Nations* (1776), bk. IV, ch. II.

portions among all its inhabitants, and thus without intending it, without knowing it, advance the interest of the society, and afford means to the multiplication of the species."[8]

The cosmic energy of the universe has now become an "invisible hand" of Providence. This is what Mueller calls "a strong and empirically questionable claim," and economists have debated it ever since.[9]

But this is the basic assertion of providential capitalism, which says that the economy does not need the divine grace of the sacraments and the traditional morality of the Church, since God directs it by His "invisible hand." This providence is so strong that the idolatry of money can be overcome without the *cultus* governing the coin and providing the grace to overcome Original Sin's inclination to take advantage of the weak in economic transactions. Instead, we quoted above from Richards, "rather than despising the market order, Christians should see it as a way that God providentially governs the actions of billions of free agents in a fallen world."[10]

Henry VIII had stolen the lands of the poor and turned chivalrous nobility into effeminate elitism. He turned the law of the home into the law of power. Adam Smith created a scientism like Newton to transfer economy from the law of the home into the law of profits and numbers guided by "providence" without sacramental grace. The Christian economy was truly the law of the home, since it developed and alleviated poverty and slavery at a speed subordinated to the needs of the family, especially the children. The slow development of Christian economy since Roman times was due in large part to the Christian's distrust of the corrupting influence of power in money, as well as subordinating all social life to the needs of the family. The relationship between master and slave or worker was gradually changed over generations so that the family was not threatened.

Smith was removing economics from the domain of morality and placing it into the field of physics.[11] In this he created a "moral

---

[8] Adam Smith, Theory of Moral Sentiments (1759), pt. IV, ch. I.
[9] John D. Mueller, *Redeeming Economics* (Intercollegiate Studies Institute, 2014), 53.
[10] Richards, *Money Greed and God*, 244.
[11] This summation by E. Michael Jones, but the Newtonian influence on Smith is conceded by partisans of Smith's economics such as Woods: "If economic law exists, then it no more makes sense to say that economic law should be subordinate to moral law than it does to say that physical laws should be subordinate to moral law... Economic law... is purely descriptive and necessarily

Newtonianism," where the moral choices of individuals in the economy act like gravity and inertia: the rich are greedy and the poor are envious, but these vices actually produce the greatest social goods in business.[12] By his avarice, the businessman is motivated to innovate to produce more profit for himself, which provides low-cost goods for the poor and employment. Put in a positive light, Sirico asserts, "it provides incentives to serve others."[13] This was the moderate approach, which sought to emphasize the need for free market economic activity in order to help the poor.

This is what Gregg calls "an economy of Liberty"—enough freedom and law in the economy to help immigrant entrepreneurs provide for their families and the poor.[14] This allowed Catholics to invest and create the beautiful Catholic cathedrals raised to the glory of God amid the ugliness of the earthly city. One such immigrant was the Haitian Ven. Pierre Toussaint whose relics would be enshrined at the cathedral of St. Patrick's in New York City. For many immigrants seeking refuge and provisions for their families, the "American dream" could become a reality, producing the gratitude and patriotism that fueled the moderate American Catholics.

But the strict pointed to the worst aspects of this, as Dawson asserts, "the love of money was transformed from the root of all evil to the mainspring of social life."[15] The problem is that the idol of avarice and the love of the common good became inextricably bound and indistinguishable in the breakdown of anti-culture and relentless political and economic revolution, which amounted to "mob bloodshed."

The moderates, however, would hail this as "modernity." They would highlight all of the positive aspects of industrialization—more affordable goods for the poor, medical innovation, transportation and communication—while the strict would emphasize its negative results— the breakdown of the family and culture with the rise in avarice, breaking the Lord's Day, and eventually Communism. The moderate Catholics began to be more loyal to non-Catholics like themselves and the strict did the same with secular monarchists. The changing economics would continue to erode the unity of the Church as Catholics divided on this question as well.

Further, the new economic theory fit perfectly with unlimited progress. The poor had been robbed of their lands and livelihood, and now the wealthy could make them more productive employees and rationalize

---

amoral, having nothing to do with morality one way or another" (Woods, *Church and the Market*, 29-30).

[12] Mueller, 53.
[13] Robert Sirico, *Defending the Free Market* (Regnery Publishing, 2012), 51.
[14] Samuel Gregg, *Tea Party Catholic* (New York: Crossroad, 2013), 57-96.
[15] Dawson, *Gods of Revolution*, 16-18.

the process as "progress." But this required using the power of the government against culture once again.

The most conspicuous change in the public order was that, after rationalizing the breaking of the Fifth through Eighth Commandments, the partisans of progress proceeded to work their employees even on Sundays, which of course was more profitable. Not even the slaves of New Orleans were forced to break the Third Commandment and work on Sundays and Holy Days.[16] Thus the economy was now violating the rights of God in the public order and threatening the family in the private order.

At the same time, the economic changes allowed the business interests to finally justify freeing the Blacks from slavery, since machines were starting to make slavery no longer profitable. This change would continue to gain momentum, but the poison of slavery would be used against the Church, even though the pope had been calling for its abolition since 1435.

Empires of Freedom

While this economic revolution was changing everything for the family, the French and American empires were militarizing ordinary citizens. The American Revolutionary War had promoted ordinary citizens to shed blood and forced conscriptions under Washington, and the French had done the same. Both empires went on the march.

Napoléon imposed a Masonic king on Spain, provoking the spirit of Santiago. He destroyed the Catholic infrastructure across Europe reducing 25,000 monasteries with 350,000 members to "barely a handful" by 1813.[17] This provoked even the secularized kingdoms of Europe to unite against him. The French Empire advanced east and even took Egypt.

Nearby, pious Muhammadans were revolting against the westernized Ottoman Empire, following a new movement begun by Muhammad ibn Abdul Wahhab and his ally, Ibn Saud.[18] Wahhab gained "great admiration" when he personally stoned a woman to death for accused adultery, and preached that "Jihad will always be valid," fearlessly imitating Muhammad by conquering much of Arabia.[19] This was the beginning of Saudi Arabia. To the west, the Usman dan Fodio was declaring *jihad* against sub-Saharan Africa, leading to the creation of Muhammadan states in Central and West Africa.[20]

---

[16] Gilbert C. Din and John E. Harkins, *The New Orleans Cabildo* (Louisiana State University Press, 1996), 12.
[17] John O'Malley, *Vatican I: the Council and the Making of the Ultramontane Church* (Belknap Harvard University Press, 2018), 59.
[18] Spencer, *History of Jihad*, 253-259.
[19] Ibid.
[20] Spencer, 259.

Meanwhile, the United States was looking west. As *Patriot's History* admits, the idea of Manifest Destiny was what Americans "believed to be their destiny—to occupy all North American lands east and west of the Mississippi and Missouri river valley."[21] But this vision was challenged by the second Christendom already built in the Americas in nearby Quebec, Florida, and New Orleans filled with Catholic French, Spanish, Africans, mestizos, Métis and Catholic Indian tribes. These Christian peoples united under the public *cultus* to the King of Kings that governed their economies by divine grace.

But the Americans were confident the United States would overcome them. John Adams would write how he was glad that Catholicism had received a "mortal wound" so that "the monster must finally die."[22] Jefferson concurred by saying that his "blessed country... has surrendered its creed and conscience to neither Kings nor priests" so that every American will die a non-Christian Unitarian.[23] Again *Patriot's History* admits, Jefferson "always envisioned a nation with steadily expanding borders...bringing under its wings natives who could be civilized and acculturated to the Empire of Liberty." [24] "Civilized" meant, at best, abandoning their sacramental culture (and in many cases their language and customs) and adopting the latest sect of eighteenth century European Protestantism. To be fair, many pious Protestants did baptize Native Americans, but they did not create a native Christian culture integrated into the American Empire.

For a Catholic, "civilized" meant preserving their culture passed down from Adam, cleansing it from demons by Baptism, and elevating it by the divine grace of the Holy Spirit. This then integrated it into a Christian civilization especially by means of Sacramental Marriage with Africans and Europeans. The whole of Mexico had already been miraculously created like this by Our Lady of Guadalupe, Empress of the Americas. The founders of the United States mocked this as outdated and proudly proclaimed the Catholic age was over.

As the pope's body lay unburied in France, Jefferson was hoping to gain Catholic Florida and New Orleans, and soon started negotiations with Napoléon.[25] As Schweikart and Allen admit, Jefferson did not wait for approval from the Senate but sent a "military expedition" into the French Louisiana territory "secretly" wherein he "dreamed" of "an expanded agrarian American Republic."[26] He succeeded in purchasing the lucrative

---

[21] Schweikart and Allen, *Patriot's History of the United States*, 249.
[22] Adams to Jefferson (July 16, 1814) in Coulombe, *Puritan's Empire*, 136.
[23] Jefferson to Waterhouse (June 26, 1822) in Coulombe, 135.
[24] Schweikart and Allen, *loc. cit.*
[25] Coulombe, 161.
[26] Schweikart and Allen, 176.

port of Catholic New Orleans from France and a large swath of land, doubling the American Empire, which was quickly approaching the size of the Roman Empire at its greatest extent.[27]

Jefferson "had little but contempt" for the civilized Creole, African, Indian and French Catholics of New Orleans, and imposed restrictions on their political power.[28] This was the beginning of the economic empire using the great Catholic culture of New Orleans for profit, which would become fundamental to the history of the twentieth century. Meanwhile, he encouraged a revolt in Spanish Florida so that the American military could seize it as an act of "restoring order," and moved to expel the native tribes, which included an unknown number of Catholic Choctaw and the nascent Apache mission.[29] Meanwhile, with Marbury v. Madison in 1803, the United States Supreme Court seized greater power over the Federal Government, continuing the voluntarist contest of power.[30]

The Invasion of Canada

Patriot's History admits that the "frontier warfare fueled expansionist desires to invade Canada, and perhaps Spanish Florida as well. Southern and western farmers openly coveted the rich North American agricultural lands held by Britain and Spain" although some Federalists also opposed it.[31] Canada also contained two hated enemies of the Americans: French Catholics and Loyalists who fled the Patriots' persecution. The invasion of Canada finally commenced in 1812. The Americans burned York, the Capital of Canada, and the British burned the American Capital with Masonic foundations.

The war was a stalemate, but it greatly enflamed the confidence of Americans in the Manifest Destiny of their empire. The wars had broken the power of many Indians in the west as well, leading to the wars against or removals of most of the Creek, Cherokee, Choctaw, Seminole and

---

[27] The greatest extent of the Roman Empire was approximately 1.9 million square miles under Trajan in 117 AD. After the Louisiana purchase the American Empire grew to approximately 1.6 million square miles. Coulombe, 163. Nick Routley, "Mapped: The Territorial Evolution of the U.S." (*Visual Capitalist*, June 22, 2019) <https://www.visualcapitalist.com/us-territorial-expansion/>, accessed March 18, 2021.
[28] Coulombe, 163.
[29] W. Fanning, "Apaches," *The Catholic Encyclopedia* (1907) <http://www.newadvent.org/cathen/01592a.htm>; J. Mooney, "Choctaw Indians," *The Catholic Encyclopedia* (1908) <http://www.newadvent.org/cathen/03692a.htm>, accessed March 18, 2021. Coulombe, 163.
[30] Schweikart and Allen, 172.
[31] Ibid., 183-188.

Chickasaw tribes.[32] Thus had commenced the "Indian Wars" (1811-1924) wherein the United States advanced west and fought some fifty-three wars against Indian tribes, many of which were Catholic.[33]

Obviously the savagery, rape and pillage was on both sides of this conflict. The myth of the peaceful "noble savage" Indian is a risible invention of anti-Christian historians. Indian tribes were innumerable peoples scattered across the Americas with distinct cultures and languages. They ranged from the murderous Aztecs and the demonic possession of shamanism practiced everywhere to the Catholic Jumano tribe converted miraculously by Ven. Mary Agreda bilocating from Spain.[34] The sadistic Iroquois tortured and ate parts of the bodies of the North American martyrs in the north, but in the south, the mixed race Indian, Spanish and African Catholics of the Seminole tribe in Florida were growing the second Christendom.[35]

Concurrently with the Indian Wars, the United States promoted an assimilation campaign to make the Native Americans not only Protestant, but Anglo-American. The program created the so-called "Five Civilized Tribes" of Anglicized Protestant Indians. Tragically, this ended in disaster when Andrew Jackson defied the Supreme Court and forced all of them west with the "Trail of Tears." The American military force marched the Cherokee men, women and children west, killing thousands from the march. Like the Catholic powers suppressing the Jesuits, the Protestants also succumbed to the love of money. Nevertheless, because Jackson helped poor Anglo-Americans, he was well loved.[36]

Now this regime was in marked contrast to the settling of the west in Canada. Sacramental Marriage produced the mixed race Métis people with

---

[32] Ibid., 188.
[33] Tecumseh's War (1811-1813); Creek War (1813-1814); Peoria War (1813); First Seminole War (1817-1818); Winnebago War (1827); Black Hawk War (1832); Creek War (1836); Florida-Georgia Border War (1836); Second Seminole War (1835-1842); Arikara War (1823); Osage War (1837); Texas-Indian Wars (1836-1877); Cayuse War (1847-1855); Apache Wars (1849-1924); Navajo Wars (1849-1866); Yuma Wars (1850-1853); Ute Wars (1850-1923); Sioux Wars (1854-1891); Rogue River Wars (1855-1856); Yakima War (1855-1858); Mohave War (1858-1859); Paiute War (1860); Yavapai Wars (1861-1875); Snake War (1864-1869); Hualapai War (1865-1870); Modoc War (1872-1873); Nez Perce War (1877); Bannock War (1878); Crow War (1887); Bannock Uprising (1895); Yaqui Uprising (1896); Battle of Sugar Point (1898); Crazy Snake Rebellion (1909); Battle of Kelley Creek (1911); Last Massacre (1911).
[34] Coulombe, *Puritan's Empire*, 35.
[35] Ibid., 35, 73-74; Lillian M. Fisher, *The North American Martyrs* (Pauline Books and Media, 1996), 110.
[36] Allen Sinclair Will, *Life of Cardinal Gibbons* (New York: E. P. Dutton and Co., 1922), 10.

their own distinct Indian-French Catholic culture, who helped found the province of "Almighty God" (*Manitoba*). Canada also struggled with the love of money, but with less superstition about progress, Catholic missionaries spread the Gospel and wrote grammars and catechisms for the Algonquin, Potawatomi, Kalispel, Huron, Chippewa, Mi'kmaq, Innu, Inuktitut, Cree and other tribes. As a result by 1900 close to half all Indian peoples in Canada were Catholic.[37] This was the continued expansion of the second Christendom, thanks to the Quebec Act condemned by the Declaration of Independence. This may not have been a reality if the United States would have conquered Canada in the invasion of 1812.

But while the empires of freedom raged, the enemies of Christ fixed their eyes on the millions of Catholic mestizos in Spanish Mexico and they burned with hatred for Our Lady of Guadalupe. Since they could never hope to turn the pious natives against Our Lady and the Church, they used the Masons to concoct an elaborate deception that exalted the Aztec empire of death that had enslaved and sacrificed their ancestors to the sun god. They exalted their ethnic identity that had been rescued by the Gospel and turned Our Lady into a symbol of this Masonic movement. This was the Mexican War of Independence (1808-1821), which amounted to "the complete destruction of all anterior forms of government, as well as the whole social structure... demanded by a handful of people out of millions."[38] Thus began the war of *Libertas* against Mexican Christendom, whose history Kelley summarizes as "Blood-Drenched Altars." This engineered, mob bloodshed would be multiplied through Spanish and Portuguese Christendom, aided by the United States.

But there was one force which could stop all this.

---

[37] A. Morice, "Catholic Indian Missions of Canada," *The Catholic Encyclopedia* (1911) <http://www.newadvent.org/cathen/10378a.htm>, accessed March 27, 2021.
[38] Francis Clement Kelley, *Blood-Drenched Altars: A Catholic Commentary on the History of Mexico* (Milwaukee, WI: Bruce Publishing Company, 1935), 132.

XXIII

THE CROSS CONQUERS THE CONQUERER

On January 1st in the Year of Masonry 5800, the Vicar of Jesus Christ lay dead in a French prison unburied. Rome was occupied by the French Empire while it continued to conquer east. Wars raged and widows and orphans fled. Against all odds, the Catholic cardinals managed to make it out of Rome and escape to Venice. There they started a papal conclave.[1]

The Holy Roman Emperor of Austria, still recognizing his ancient role as protector of the pope, paid for the conclave to proceed. They faced a grave difficulty: who could face the leaders of anti-culture? Pope Pius VI had condemned the French vehemently, the Synod of Pistoia, and suffered abduction and death. Should the conclave elect a strict to stand fast against the revolution, or a moderate who would be willing to work with the French Empire?

After several months of struggle, they finally elected a moderate, the Bishop of Imola, Barnaba Chiaramonti who had spoken positively about democracy after the French invaded. Thus the strict feared he would be too soft against the French. There was no papal tiara, so the Venetian women created a paper mache tiara and adorned it with their own jewels. But on the fourteenth of March, in the Year of Our Lord 1800, the new pope received the tiara and immediately defied Napoléon's boast of "Pius the Last" by taking that name.

Servant of God Pope Pius VII

A few short months after the papal election in March of 1800, Napoléon unexpectedly changed his policy toward the Catholics in France. During the Revolution they were massacred. Now Napoléon told Pius VII

---

[1] Coulombe, *Vicars of Christ*, 299-302.

he wished to restore the pope's jurisdiction to France. The Papal States were returned to the pope's rule.[2]

It appears that Napoléon recognized the futility of the revolution to suppress Catholicism in the mass of the population, and thought it best to unify the country under his rule by using Catholicism. In order to do that, he needed the pope's support.

Pope Pius VII the moderate signed a concordat with Napoléon in 1801, and his predecessor Pope Pius VI was finally brought to Rome and given a full Catholic burial in 1802. Pope Pius VII believed that a gentle approach would win over Napoléon, and he even traveled to Paris to celebrate Holy Mass at Napoléon's coronation in 1804 (where Napoléon snatched the crown and placed it on his own head).

But Napoléon's ambition was manifested when he immediately disobeyed the concordat and sought complete control of the Catholic Church. He again began to conquer Europe in 1806. A Triumph Arch started construction in this year depicting nude Frenchmen subduing Germans.

Napoléon naively believed the pope who crowned him would support him. Pope Pius VII refused, infuriating Bonaparte. With full knowledge of the emperor's military might, the pope wrote to him and boldly proclaimed he would never support wars for the earthly city: "We shall endure with resignation, faithful to the gospel and accept every kind of calamity as coming from God."[3] Napoléon responded in kind and marched on Rome, annexed the Papal States, and imposed the regime of Liberty on the Italians again.

Pope Pius VII was a moderate because he was willing to work with the French Republic. But at this moment he showed his holiness and excommunicated Napoléon and all who helped annex the Papal States. The time of moderation and dialogue had now ended. Enraged, Napoléon seized the pope and locked him away at Savona, north of Rome. Pope Pius VII was then in prison with little food and few to support him for another five years. But for the holy Benedictine monk, it was like returning to the peace of his cell. He steadfastly refused Napoléon's efforts to dominate the Church.

However, back in France, Christendom was eroding rapidly. By signing the concordat the pope had reconciled all schismatic priests without asking for penance. This allowed the heretical clergy to promote their ideas in the French Church, dividing the French into monarchists and republicans. The American Revolution and the new economics were

---

[2] N. Weber, "Pope Pius VII," *The Catholic Encyclopedia* (1911) <http://www.newadvent.org/cathen/12132a.htm>, accessed June 7th, 2021.
[3] Matthew Bunson, "The Pope Who Outlasted a Tyrant," *This Rock* (Catholic Answers, Inc., El Cajon, CA, April 2008), 38-40.

eroding Christendom, and now the French Church even more. The orthodox moderates were finding common cause with the Church's enemies to promote republicanism, while the orthodox strict were finding alliance with secular monarchs.[4] It was the central question which divided Catholics at this time and in our present period: is our epoch "modernity" or it is merely "mob bloodshed?"

The Holy Alliance

Meanwhile, as Napoléon continued to make war on Europe, the combined forces of England, Russia, Prussia, Austria and others began to unite in opposing him, forming the Holy Alliance. Napoléon began to lose his battles, retreating from Russia in 1812 and defeated at Leipzig in 1813. During all this time, Servant of God Pope Pius VII resisted Napoléon, and the emperor was finally forced to give him up to the Austrians as his enemies closed in.

Pope Pius VII triumphantly returned to Rome in 1814, while all of Europe hailed him as a hero who stood up to Europe's tyrant.[5] That year, he reversed the decision of Clement XIV and restored the Jesuit Order. Nearly a generation of suppression had already done immense damage to souls and society, but the Jesuits quickly grabbed their spiritual swords and joined the melee. From this point they would slowly grow. Providentially, God had saved the Jesuits in Russia, keeping the Greco-Roman renewal alive in Slavic Christendom. This created a climate which produced Timofey Granovsky and the great Sergey Soloviev, whose son Vladimir would lay the foundation for the Russian Catholic Church in the twentieth century.

At the same time, the enemies of Christendom were forming their shadow army with networks across Europe and the world. New occult sects were arising in Italy, like the Carbonari.[6] Some sects would later claim they were focused on "winning" "a pope according to our own heart" who would facilitate a republican revolution and "the complete annihilation of

---

[4] John Rao, *Removing the Blindfold: 19th-Century Catholics and the Myth of Modern Freedom* (Kansas City, MO: Angelus Press, 2014), 7-9.

[5] Lehner, *The Catholic Enlightenment*, 215.

[6] It is unclear to what extent the Carbonari were Masons or what association the Alta Vendita lodge had to other lodges. Jacques Crétineau-Joly, *L'Eglise romaine en face de la Révolution* (Paris: Henri Plon, 1859), vol. II, 101-102; R. John Rath, "The Carbonari: Their Origins, Initiation Rites, and Aims," *The American Historical Review* 69, no. 2 (1964): 353-70; J.P. Kirsch, "Carbonari," *The Catholic Encyclopedia* (1908) <http://www.newadvent.org/cathen/03330c.htm>, accessed March 19, 2021.

THE CROSS CONQUERS THE CONQUERER

Catholicism."[7] These were condemned by the popes along with Freemasonry.

The next year, the Holy Alliance dealt the final blow to Napoléon at Waterloo in 1815. He was exiled from Europe to the island of St. Helena, off the southwest coast of Africa (due west from Modern Angola), where he was a prisoner of the English.

Napoléon showed signs of repentance, and Pope Pius VII petitioned England to send a Catholic priest to the remote island. Napoléon said concerning Servant of God Pope Pius VII "Alexander the great declared himself the son of Jupiter. And in my time I find a priest who is more powerful than I am."[8] They say he admitted defeat with these words:

> I know men, and I tell you, Jesus is not a man. He commands us to believe, and gives no other reason than his awful word, I am God...He speaks with authority. His religion is a mystery; but it subsists by its own force. He seeks and absolutely requires the love of men, the most difficult thing in the world to obtain. Alexander, Caesar, Hannibal conquered the world, but had no friends. I myself am perhaps the only person of my day who loves Alexander, Caesar, Hannibal. Alexander, Caesar, Charlemagne and myself founded empires; but upon what? Force. Jesus founded his empire on Love; and at this hour millions would die for him.
>
> I myself have inspired multitudes with such affection that they would die for me. But my presence was necessary. Now that I am in St. Helena, where are my friends? I am forgotten, son to return to the earth, and become food for worms. What an abyss between my misery and the eternal kingdom of Christ, who is proclaimed, loved, and adored, and which is extending over all the earth. Is this death? I tell you, the death of Christ is the death of a God. I tell you, Jesus Christ is God.[9]

---

[7] Gray, *The Catholic Catechism on Freemasonry*, 96-98.
[8] Bunson, *op. cit.*
[9] These words may be apocryphal, reported by General H. G. Bertrand, yet even if they are, they testify to the immense confidence of the faithful in Christ over earthly empires in their revival that was just beginning.

Napoléon made his confession, received Holy Communion and Extreme Unction and died reconciled to the Church in 1821.[10] The emperor surrendered to the King of Kings. The Cross had conquered the conqueror.

American Empire

Meanwhile the Holy Alliance represented a real threat to the United States, and was showing signs of restoring a Catholic unity after being shocked into action by Napoléon. This could defend and restore the second Christendom not only in Europe but in the Americas. It was weak, however, because it was also filled with secular monarchists who sought not Christendom, but merely to retain their voluntarist power. Nevertheless it was the only option available to defend against the onslaught of anti-culture. It was supported by all the great Catholics of the era—Von Baader, De Maistre, Chateaubriand, De Bonald, Adam Müller, and Karl von Haller.

But Masonic revolutionaries all condemned this alliance, and so did the leading men of the United States. "Conservatives" like John Quincy Adams said the "republican spirit of our country" is working "against the relapse of Europe into the opposite principle of monkery and despotism" while Henry Clay urged that a new coalition should be formed against the Holy Alliance "for freemen and for freedom."[11] Jefferson wrote to Monroe about the issue of Spanish Christendom in the Americas:

> We have, first, to ask ourselves a question. Do we wish to acquire to our confederacy any one or more of the Spanish provinces? I candidly confess that I have ever looked on Cuba as the most interesting addition which could ever be made to our system of states. The control which, with Florida point, this island would give us over the Gulf of Mexico... would fill up the measure of our political well-being.[12]

As a result the Monroe Doctrine was proclaimed. It was a declaration of immediate war if any European power threatened the control of the United States over North and South America. The kings of England, Spain and Portugal thus had to risk war with the Empire of Liberty to protect their people in the Americas. The Doctrine "basically declared to the world that

---

[10] Coulombe, *Vicars of Christ*, 302.
[11] *Writings of John Quincy Adams*, vol. VI, 274 and *Papers of Henry Clay*, vol. III, 80 in Coulombe, *Puritan's Empire*, 171, 172.
[12] H. A. Washington, ed., *The Writings of Thomas Jefferson*, vol. VII, 317 in Ibid., 176.

the Americas were henceforth open only to United States exploitation."[13] This was the declaration of war against Christendom in the Americas. From this point, utilizing the English anti-Spanish propaganda tradition, the United States would seek to dominate Central and South America by means of military invasion, engineered revolutions and economic dominance from 1823-1914.[14] Together with the Indian Wars, this will be the second phase of the American Empire.

Restoring the Throne of Christ

Meanwhile, having sent His salutary wrath to the Church, God gave the grace of penance, and a massive Catholic revival rose out of the ashes of the Napoleonic wars. The fundamental lie of neo-Pelagian progress was repudiated by the dogma of the Immaculate Conception. This proclaimed that Our Lady alone was born without Original Sin not because progress or she herself had done it, but because of the divine grace of Christ.[15] Just as she had led the Army of Flanders against the Dutch Provinces and Columbus in discovering America, so Our Lady of the Immaculate Conception would be the doctrinal rallying point to attack heresy as well as liberate woman from her slavery to *Libertas* as we will see.

She appeared in 1830 to St. Catherine Labouré and told her to promote the Miraculous Medal and her Immaculate Conception. The writings of St. Louis de Montfort were miraculously rediscovered and Marian devotion was being spread everywhere.[16] Our Lord appeared to Servant of God Marie of St Peter in 1844 to reveal the Holy Face Devotion, which Our Lord said was "against the Communists."[17]

God was also providing with His grace souls ripe for conversion. The hubris of scientism's unlimited progress and the mechanization of the Industrial Revolution caused an aesthetic reaction known as Romanticism. This sought to express the longings of the human heart and the emotions of love, seeking to reclaim something of the past against the "Liberty" of Napoléon. This was the music of late Beethoven and Chopin, and later Wagner, with the literary works of Victor Hugo and great beauty and longing in art and architecture.

In Beethoven's *9th Symphony* the human heart rises out of the hubris of the classical ascending the spiritual mountain of holy desire. This is seen

---

[13] Ibid., 176.
[14] Powell, *Tree of Hate*, 113-130, 145-158; Kelley, *Blood-Drenched Altars*, 13-14, 184; Antonio Caponnetto, *The Black Legends and Catholic Hispanic Culture* (Central Bureau of the Catholic Central Verein of America, 1991), 124-125.
[15] Roberto de Mattei, *Blessed Pius IX*, 93-108.
[16] Fr. Frederick William Faber, "About True Devotion to Mary," in St. Louis de Montfort, *True Devotion to Mary* (TAN, 1985), xii.
[17] Sr. Marie of St. Peter, *The Golden Arrow* (TAN, 2010).

in that although Beethoven wrote his own secular lyrics the tune itself was transferred into a hymn to Christ by Henry van Dyke ("Joyful Joyful We Adore Thee," 1907). Thus the Romantic quickly melded with the Catholic revival as men, women, and children began to use the modern technology like railroads to go on pilgrimages.

Louis Veuillot would write *L'Universe* and Cardinal Manning wrote *The Dublin Review*. The soldiers of Christ were taking logos to the front lines. Gregory XVI condemned the lies of *Libertas* in 1836 and once again the slave trade in 1830. The Catholic bishops in America, however, were embarrassed. But the Frenchman Jean-Rémy Bessieux was soon learning and writing a grammar of the Myene language in West Africa in order to restore the African mission for the sake of souls.

Yet at the same time, the mob violence was provoking what would become the commercialized popular shamanism—songs that mocked the priesthood and Catholicism were "on everyone's lips" who attended a hall, a dance, or any common public gathering.[18] Like the songs of Arius, these would be an effective tool of Satan by means of emotional manipulation. In Arabia, the *jihad* of the Wahhab Saudis continued as they took Mecca in 1806, forcing the Ottomans to attempt to suppress their Muhammadan piety.[19]

The Jews and Society

Napoléon had destroyed the public charter of *Sicut Judaeis* because he did not believe the public *cultus* must worship Christ. From this period, the struggle of Jews for their own ethnic identity and culture would have a massive effect on Christian society. Dawson would note in 1931 that the Jews create "almost the only original element in the thought of the new age" with men like Einstein, Freud and Marx exerting an influence "that far transcends the limits of his particular subject."[20] Yet this would break upon three party lines.

Having achieved dominance over the Jewish population since 1666, the liberal party was able to lead this effort to influence society, forming the modern movement Reform Judaism, which sought to conform to the spirit of the anti-culture, or even lead it. Jews, as Chadwick observes, "were naturally among the radical leaders of Europe."[21]

---

[18] John Rao, "Interview: The Catholic revival of the 19th Century confronts the Revolution," *Vendee Radio* (Sep 20, 2018).
[19] Spencer, *History of Jihad*, 258.
[20] Dawson, *Christianity and the New Age*, 15.
[21] Owen Chadwick, *The Secularization of the European Mind in the 19th Century* (Cambridge University Press: 1975), 49.

By 2010 the dying Christopher Hitchens would reflect proudly on his own Jewish heritage and observe that "the most post-religious group in the history of humanity so far, the most self-emancipated from religion are the Jews... The most significant scientific, philosophical and ideological underminers of the mad idea that we are a special creation... are all Jews."[22] This would be the work of the Liberal Jews who would seek to undermine Christendom and Christian influence on society up to the present, including leading the promotion of pornography, child murder and atheism.[23]

Meanwhile, the rational Jews, holding to the logos still present in Rabbinic Judaism's possession of the Old Testament, pushed back and became known as Orthodox Jews. They, however, have been in the minority of Jewish influence on the world in the modern world. Some of these rational Jews became bearers of logos to the world, like Victor Frankl and Erik Erikson, or the philosopher Mortimer Alder, who died a Catholic.

But just as this "Jewish question" was arising in society, God intervened. In 1842, Our Lady appeared to the Liberal Jew Alphonse Ratisbonne who was immediately converted. He joined his brother, also a converted Jew, in becoming priests and forming the Congregation of the Sion for the conversion of Jews. He would be joined shortly by the Lehmann brothers and other prominent Jews in the twentieth century, and inspire the Polish crusader we will meet in a few chapters. These Jews finally found peace in their ethnic identity as Jews accepting the King of Kings, Yeshua Ha-Meshiach (Jesus Christ) to be the light of the world.

The Law of Profits

The mob violence, however, continued in France and elsewhere as Catholics fought with all their might against the plots and propaganda of the enemies. The new technology of the newspaper was everywhere, making all opinions "more potent in action... expressed more loudly and felt more forcibly" as this cacophony of noise reflected the bloodshed in the streets.[24] The newspaper formed minds, morals, and military action, while the money fueled the profits of each in turn.

Even as Catholics revived and did penance and spread devotion, the economics remained one of the most insurmountable barriers. Thousands of families had been driven out of the countryside, and into the cities. The

---

[22] Christopher Hitchens, interview with *The Atlantic*, 2010.
[23] See E. Michael Jones, *The Jewish Revolutionary Spirit*, 2nd edition (Fidelity Press, 2021), volumes 2 and 3. Jones' text, however, mostly ignores the Orthodox Jewish party which opposes the Liberal Jews. See for example, Roy Schoeman's contrast between traditional Jewish reactions to the Holocaust and that of Jewish writer Ellie Wiesel, who promotes Atheism (*Salvation is from the Jews*, 135-178).
[24] Chadwick, *op. cit.*, 39.

Church had difficulty building enough churches to accommodate the migration, much less feed the starving poor with bread and mercy.[25] This situation was already producing a crisis of fatherhood in the 1840s and more fathers, displaced from cultures, were deserting their families for alcohol.[26] Factories were increasingly working men on Sundays against the Third Commandment, and the Second Commandment was widely broken.

In response, Our Lady appeared to two children in 1846, in La Salette, France.

> If my people will not submit, I shall be forced to let fall the arm of my Son. It is so strong, so heavy, that I can no longer withhold it... "Six days I have given you to labor, the seventh I had kept for myself; and they will not give it to me." It is this which makes the arm of my Son so heavy. Those who drive the carts cannot swear without introducing the name of my Son. These are the two things which makes the arm of my Son so heavy.[27]

In that same year, Giovanni Ferretti was elected Pope Pius IX. He was a moderate, and wanted to be gentle with the mobs. Perhaps they could be won over with the medicine of mercy.

---

[25] Ibid., 97.
[26] Popenoe, *Families without Fathers*, 81.
[27] La Salette Missionaries, "The Message of La Salette," <https://www.lasalette.org/about-la-salette/apparition/the-story/705-the-message-of-la-salette.html>, accessed March 27, 2021.

XXIV

PIO NONO AND THE NINTH CRUSADE

In 1818, in May, Henrietta Pressburg gave birth to the son of Heinrich Marx. Heinrich came from a long line of rabbis, but seeking career advancement he was baptized in the Prussian Lutheran Church. He named his son Karl.

Heinrich managed to have some financial success and agitated with mob violence against the monarchy of Prussia. The family was wealthy enough to send Karl to get an excellent education in 1830.

By that time, with the Jesuits rising from the ruins of *Libertas*, the enemies of Christ desired to spread the religion of the *anti-culture* further into the society. They would use the same tactics as *Libertas*: rationalize bloodshed against real injustice, promote the superstition of unlimited progress, then impose an anti-culture on society.

Satan found in Marx the perfect man to impose these plans. Around 1837, Marx made contact with the evil spirits. He wrote "with Satan I have struck my deal" saying his soul "is chosen for hell."[1] He witnessed the condition of the poor under the unlimited progress of industry and realized he could provoke mob violence more effectively by using the poor to gain power. His ideas would take anti-culture to its next fatal step in destroying society.[2]

---

[1] Karl Marx, "The Pale Maiden," and "The Fiddler," in *Early Works of Karl Marx: Book of Verse*, Marxists Internet Archive <www.marxists.org/archive/marx/works/1837-pre/verse/verse24.htm>. Accessed August 28, 2019, cited in The Epoch Times, *How the Specter of Communism is Ruling Our World* (Epoch Times, 2020), vol. 1, 38-41; Paul Kengor, *The Devil and Karl Marx*, (TAN, 2020), 33-94
[2] Chadwick, *The Secularization of the European Mind in the Nineteenth Century*, 48-87.

The Irish Fighting Spirit

At this same time, Ireland was uniting. Although the Masonic rebellion of 1798 had failed, the Dublin Lodge continued to churn out the propaganda to confuse the good Irish. The lodge even succeeded in preventing the Irish bishops from publishing the papal bulls against Masonry in Ireland.[3] As a result, a good Irish man named Dónall Ó Conaill (Daniel O'Connell, 1775-1847) joined the Lodge unwittingly in 1790.

In 1800, the British Empire was able to seize the Irish Parliament by creating the United Kingdom with more direct rule over the Irish. Ó Conaill arose and fought for his people against this, and for Catholic emancipation in England, inspiring many other Catholics to join the fight.[4] London was forced to reckon with the logos burning from Ó Conaill, and in 1829, the United Kingdom removed legal restrictions on Catholics. This gave greater freedom to the *cultus* to call down the grace of the Holy Spirit on the Irish, English, Scots and the Welsh people. While the Irish were beating the war drums of *Comhdháil Chaitliceach na hÉireann* (Irish Catholic Confederation of 1642), graces were flowing into the soul of an Anglican priest named John Henry Newman.[5]

But Ó Conaill fought on to secure independence for Ireland. Ó Conaill was a great man who fought with the Irish fighting spirit. Once he realized that Masonry was in fact outlawed by the Church, he renounced the evil. But like all great men, he made mistakes, the worst of which seems to be that he advocated the abandonment of the Irish language.[6] The language was the glue that bound all Irish to Éire and Éire to the faith of *Pádraig*.

This abandonment of Irish played straight into the hands of the enemies of Christ as now, using English, they could "educate" the Irish. According to Cahill (writing in 1932), the economic oppression and this propaganda (falsely called today "public education") is what finally broke the Irish fighting spirit.[7] A young James Gibbons was growing up in Ireland

---

[3] R. D. Edwards, "Daniel O'Connell," *New Catholic Encyclopedia* (2003), vol. 10.

[4] Thomas P. Neill, *They Lived the Faith* (Mediatrix Press, 2020), 17-24.

[5] Especially after 1829, Newman's turn toward Rome continued in the Oxford movement. Frank M. Turner, *John Henry Newman* (Yale University Press, 2002), 135ff. The Passionist Order established by St. Paul of the Cross (who had prayed for decades for the conversion of England) was established in England after 1829 and helped convert Newman.

[6] Gearóid Ó Tuathaigh, "Gaelic Ireland, Popular Politics and Daniel O'Connell," *Journal of the Galway Archaeological and Historical Society* (1975), 34: 21–34; Éilís Ní Anluain, "Daniel O'Connell's Irish legacy," *The Irish Times* (26 August 2019), retrieved 2 August 2020.

[7] Cahill, *Framework of Christian State*, 650-653.

at this time, and the widespread loss of Gaelic would be devastating for American Catholicism.[8]

But suddenly the wrath of God fell upon them. It was *An Drochshaol*, the Irish Potato Famine (1845-1851) that killed one million Irish and spread throughout Europe. The English economic system of landlords and breaking of the Second and Third Commandments had finally run its course. This was the moment for both Irish and English to repent and turn to God. The London government believed in Providential Capitalism, and hesitated to help the Irish, which killed thousands.[9] To their credit, many Protestants in Britain were roused from their slumber to help the Irish. But soon the landlords began mass evictions and the Irish fled in the millions to the American Empire. The French meanwhile, led especially by St. John Vianney, one of the greatest saints of this period, with the "unceasing war that he waged against the desecration of the Lord's day," repented in large numbers.[10] Like St. Patrick, the Cure d'Ars also worked miracles to convince people to stop work on Sunday.[11]

As this was happening, many Americans immigrated to Texas, then part of Mexico, making oaths to be Catholic and to free their slaves. They soon revolted and proclaimed the independence of Texas, denouncing "the eternal enemies of civil liberty" namely, "the priesthood."[12] Within a few years, the United States took Texas and moved to invade Mexico claiming "our manifest destiny to overspread the continent alloted by Providence for the free development of our yearly multiplying millions."[13] As the Irish arrived in New York City, the United States forcibly recruited them to the Mexican border to help conquer Mexican Christendom.[14] Nearly half of the American army was made up of European immigrants without citzenship.[15]

But the Irish fighting spirit, seeing the Mexican priests blessing their cannons before the fight, suddenly realized that they were supporting the

---

[8] Will, *Life of Cardinal Gibbons*, 14.

[9] Jones, *Barren Metal*, 975-1016.

[10] *Life of St. John Vianney*, (New York: Joseph Schaefer, 1911).

[11] "One Sunday in July there was a full harvest, the wheat bending to the earth. During the High Mass a violent wind arose and threatening clouds gathered; a destructive tempest was apparently about to break. The holy priest entered the pulpit, forbade his people to touch their crops that day, and promised them a continuation of good weather sufficient for the gathering in of the harvest. His prediction was verified; the storm passed over and no rain fell for twelve days." Ibid.

[12] Texas Declaration of Independence, 1836; Schweikart and Allen, *Patriot's History of the United States*, 249-252.

[13] Bailyn et al., *The Great Republic*, 398 in Schweikart and Allen, *Patriot's History of the United States*, 250.

[14] Coulombe, *Puritan's Empire*, 204-209.

[15] Ferrara, 269.

imperialism of the regime of *Libertas*.[16] They fled the ranks of the US Army and joined the Mexicans, forming the *Batallón de San Patricio*, hoisting the cross to fight with the true crusading spirit.

However, the Mexicans were defeated by the American army and fifty of the *Batallón de San Patricio* were executed by the American military — the largest mass execution in American history.[17] The United States now gained the northern half of Mexico—New Mexico, Arizona, Utah, Nevada and California, filled with Catholics and with cities named after saints. The American Empire now surpassed the Roman Empire in land area. The Americans moved to destroy the Mexican Christendom of the mestizos and Catholic Indian tribes like the Pueblo, Papago, and Pima, continuing the process already begun by the Mexican Masonic regime.[18] The United States government then pushed to support the Masonic revolts across South American Christendom.

The Ninth Crusade

But at that moment, Pope Pius IX was trying to appease the mob violence by the medicine of mercy from 1846-1848. Bl. Pope Pius IX, popularly known as Pio Nono, gave amnesty to the rioters, freedom of press, and even began republican reforms in his domains causing Chadwick to call this period that of "A Liberal Pope."[19] But as one observer said, this put the Papal States "at the mercy of a flagrant revolution."[20] For the Alta Vendita already said they planned to use this mercy as a "popular weapon."[21] The mobs were quickly roused using the media and their shadowy sects, trying to create the illusion of a "Liberal Pope" and all of Europe began agitating with bloodshed. The unit of Christendom had been severely strained as the moderates sided with non-Catholic republicans and the strict sided with non-Catholic monarchists.[22]

By February, 1848, as the violence began to explode, the *Communist Manifesto* was published which rationalized the worst killing the world had yet seen on the basis of anti-culture and progress. But the impact of this

---

[16] Ibid., 267-277.
[17] James M. McCaffery, *Army of Manifest Destiny: The American Soldier in the Mexican War, 1846–1848* (New York University Press, 1994), 196; John S. D. Eisenhower, *Agent of Destiny: The Life and Times of General Winfield Scott* (University of Oklahoma Press, 1999), 297.
[18] Coulombe, 210-218.
[19] Owen Chadwick, *A History of the Popes 1830-1914* (Oxford University Press, 1999), 61-94; Roberto de Mattei, *Blessed Pius IX*, trans. John Laughland (Herefordshire: Gracewing, 2004), 12-27.
[20] Metternich, VII, 417 in de Mattei, 21.
[21] Crétineau-Joly, II, 139, cf. Delassus, I, 606 in de Mattei, 12.
[22] Rao, *Black Legends*, 429-430.

treatise was not yet felt. That summer, it was still the revolutionary mob bloodshed that was tearing apart France, Germany, Austria, Hungary, Denmark, Moldavia, and Poland. By November, in the Papal States, the mob surrounded the papal minister of justice, Pellegrino Rossi and slit his throat.[23] The pope fled Rome.

Pope Pius IX assembled troops from Catholic Austria, and restored order to Rome. It was a call to arms—what would be called "the Ninth Crusade." Although not a formal crusade, this nickname would be given to the temporal struggle, as on the spiritual level Blessed Pius began fighting vehemently. By turning pastorally from the gentle father to the disciplinarian, as it were, against the mobs, he unsheathed his spiritual sword against the enemy. He helped form the Jesuit newspaper *La Civiltà Cattolica* to give "a systematic presentation of the Catholic position," inspiring Catholic newspapers to use the media against the enemies of Christ.[24]

Meanwhile, the Holy Roman Emperor of Austria unsheathed his temporal sword, and men of God from across the world came to the Papal States to defend the Church. The crusaders fought against the advance of the Italian Empire from 1848-1870, not the least of which were numerous sons of *Pádraig* with their merry fighting spirit.[25]

The Next Phase of Anti-Culture

But at that moment in the United states, the contest of power was unleashed inside the family:

> We hold these truths to be self-evident: that all men and women are created equal... but when a long train of abuses and usurpations, pursuing invariably the same object, evinces a design to reduce them under absolute despotism, it is their duty to throw off such government, and to provide new guards for their future security. Such has been the patient sufferance of the women under this government, and such is now the necessity which

---

[23] De Mattei, 30.
[24] Rao, *Removing the Blindfold*, 20-27.
[25] On the Ninth Crusade of the temporal order, see Rao, *Black Legends*, 429-495; Roberto de Mattei, "The "Ninth Crusade" of the Papal Zouaves," *Remnant Newspaper* (April 1, 2020) <https://remnantnewspaper.com/web/index.php/headline-news-around-the-world/item/4833-the-ninth-crusade-of-the-papal-zouaves>, accessed March 28, 2021.

constrains them to demand the equal station to which they are entitled.[26]

Because the men had promoted the ideology that dignity is power, the women, having suffered under the regime of Anti-Mary, now revolted, claiming dignity on the basis of power.[27] The author of this document was Elizabeth Cady Stanton, the non-Christian abolitionist, who was able to mix the just cause against racial slavery (the poison of Muhammad) into a twisted revolt inside Holy Matrimony.[28] Above all in feminism we see the deceptive rationalization to poison the family, all to the detriment of children, already vulnerable under the regime of the factory. The men, having justified their lusts by destroying Mary and their own bloodshed based on power as dignity, were effeminate, and would gradually capitulate to this quasi-just revolt from the women, which would be urged on by the United States and Communist Russia.[29]

At the same time, another movement of Scientism arose in two areas: history and biology. Charles Darwin promoted an idea of the evolution of species, which justified every voluntarism yet in society by providing a scientism of racism. Like Newton, some of his work was science, and some was scientism.[30] Now Darwin could promote eugenics in which "the

---

[26] *Declaration of Sentiments* (1848).

[27] "Our laws and constitutions, our creeds and codes, and the customs of social life are all of masculine origin." Elizabeth Cady Stanton, Address to International Council of Women, 1888 in Schneir, ed., *Feminism: The Essential Historical Writings*, dedication.

[28] Stanton was a Quaker, even though she was baptized.

[29] Lenin in 1920, when women's suffrage was passed in the United States: "We must by all means set up a powerful international women's movement on a clear-cut theoretical basis." Clara Zetkin, "My Recollections of Lenin: An Interview on the Woman Question," in Miriam Schneir, ed., *Feminism: The Essential Historical Writings*, 336.

[30] Darwin's observation of microevolution seems to have helped the development of the field of genetics. However, his theories concerning macroevolution have been strongly challenged by scientists, even though this is considered a dogma by the majority Atheist "scientific community." For example the movement "Dissent from Darwinism," now has over 1000 signatures from Ph.Ds in various fields. <dissentfromdarwin.org>. For an introduction into the scientism of Darwinian macroevolution see Christopher Ferrara, *Against Evolution: A Theory Not Worthy of Catholic Credulity* (Latin Mass Magazine, Fall 2015) <http://www.latinmassmagazine.com/pdfs/Ferrara-Evolution-TLM-2015-Fall.pdf>, accessed November 23, 2019. Ferrara reviews the evolutionists who admit the lack of evidence as well as their strange speculations about life's origin, including extraterrestrials. See also Michael Behe in *Darwin's Black Box: The Biochemical Challenge to Evolution* (Free Press, 2006) and *Darwin Devolves* (HarperOne, 2019) as well as Jones, *Logos Rising*, 11-100.

civilized races," as he put it, could "exterminate" the "savage races."³¹ Marx quickly wrote to Engels that Darwin was the "foundation of our viewpoint."³²

At the same time, massive historical discoveries in manuscripts and archaeology were completely unprecedented. Suddenly men had access to more sources of knowledge than ever before, leading to more hubris. In historical studies, a movement of scientism arose through the works of Ludwig Feuerbach and later Julius Wellhausen that asserted that man now had enough knowledge to recreate minute details of history.

It haughtily denied all oral tradition as unreliable, even though it is the "single most dominant communicative technology of our species."³³ This led to the pride of academics, thinking they could disdain the ancient traditional memory of all peoples passed down through oral culture. This worked well to present a veneer of historical reliability, leading quickly to dismantle all faith in the reliability of the Holy Scriptures.³⁴ This would have a massive impact on the *cultus*.

These things worked perfectly for the plans of the new national powers working as *pontifex maximus* to center the religion of anti-culture on worshipping the government's power. The false education, what Dawson calls "an immense machinery of organization and control," were finally able to achieve the dreams of Locke, Rousseau and Webster in the later nineteenth century, controlling the education in the public sphere.³⁵ The new revolutions were destroying culture, asserted Louis Veuillot, creating only "men without history, without cradles and without tombs."³⁶ By dismantling historical studies and controlling education, the state power was gaining absolute control over persons.

---

[31] Darwin, *Descent of Man* (Princeton, NJ: Princeton University Press, 1981), pt. I, ch. 6, 201 in Donald de Marco and Benjamin Wiker, *Architects of the Culture of Death* (San Francisco, CA: Ignatius Press, 2004), 82.
[32] Epoch Times, *How the Specter of Communism is Ruling Our World*, vol. 1, 42; de Marco and Wiker, *Architects of the Culture of Death*, 121-134.
[33] John Miles Foley, "What's in a sign," *Signs of Orality*, MacKay ed. (Brill, 1999), 1. See also Walter J. Ong, *The Presence of the Word: Some Prolegomena for Cultural and Religious History* (Yale University Press, 1967).
David C. Rubin, *The Cognitive Psychology of Epic, Ballads, and Counting-out Rhymes* (Oxford University Press, 1997).
[34] T. S. Flanders, *Introduction to the Holy Bible for Traditional Catholics* (Our Lady of Victory Press, 2019), 169-191.
[35] Dawson, *The Crisis of Western Education*, 102, cf. 101-118.
[36] L. Veuillot, Mélanges (Oeuvres complete, iii series, 1933), xi, 333 in John Rao "Louis Veuillot and the Catholic 'Intransigence': a Re-evaluation," *Faith and Reason* (Winter, 1983), 282-306.

CITY OF GOD VS. CITY OF MAN

The Fourth Greco-Roman Renewal and Threats to Church Unity

But with the immense historical discoveries, the fourth Greco-Roman renewal was now in full swing. The most important development in this regard was the publication of a massive collection of the Church Fathers. This was no small task indeed. It involved sifting through innumerable manuscripts, removing spurious additions and collecting them all and organizing them. The Latin Fathers were published in 221 volumes (1841-1855), Greek Fathers in 161 volumes from (1857-66), and the Eastern Fathers **Syriac, Coptic, Armenian, Ethiopic, Georgian, Old Church Slavonic** and Arabic) would begin in 1897 and continue to the present day.

This fourth Greco-Roman renewal could now become the greatest renewal of the Church hitherto seen. Never before had churchmen had access to so many edited manuscripts.

The problem was that with the chaos of limitless free press fueled by the love of money, this great knowledge was also fuel for a far more insidious fire than the mobs. For like the Synod of Pistoia, the Church's enemies intended to use this vast knowledge to promote heresy within the Church.

The fourth renewal, like the three that preceded it, required nothing less than saints who could navigate the chaos with *dialogos* and create the synthesis necessary form a new Christendom. But as the Ninth Crusade fought valiantly with both swords, this war was faster than any that had been seen before. The whole world was exploding in violence turning wives against husbands, children against parents, and bloodshed and fire in new places with each passing month. In such hurried, chaotic warfare, it was inevitable that excesses would be committed by those supporting the Church, since war always produces this. Some soldier fighting for a just cause, suddenly succumbs to a moment of temptation.

And much more damaging than excesses with the earthly sword were the excesses with the spiritual sword. The spiritual side was the movement known as Ultramontanism. This was the effort to defend Christendom on the foundation of papal authority.

The victory achieved by the Masons in 1773 was in enabling the regimes of anti-culture to destroy all elements but eldership of a tyrannical bureaucracy. Ultramontanism sought to restore the place of the *cultus* in society by means of exalting the eldership of the pope, which would culturally solidify all elders everywhere.

Ultramontanism sought to restore logos as the principle of truth, solidifying the whole tradition approved by the popes as infallible, and the current pope as the infallible guarantee of the logos contained therein.

This required an immense synthesis of the infallibility of Scripture and Tradition and the whole Church, balancing the Petrine primacy of the pope with the bishops, and the infallibility of the consensus of the Fathers, scholastics and all the faithful.³⁷ The orthodox strict put all their focus on the infallibility of the pope above all else in Ultramontanism, but the orthodox moderates, drawing upon the patristic renewal, wanted to balance this with all the other sources of infallibility. The synthesis would require the Church to respond to the new world of anti-culture.

But as we have attempted to trace, the unity between the moderate and strict parties had already been eroding in America and France, and now Catholics everywhere were dividing over the economic, social and political questions, which flowed straight into these theological questions, leading to excesses and attacks between them. As the English Catholic politician, historian, and writer, Lord Acton, observed by 1863, "the distance between the two parties was such as to justify a doubt as to the agreement in the same faith or in the same morality."³⁸ Acton, especially in his legacy, remains among the great moderates of this period.

But Acton, whom Dawson praises as a historian, was also prone to excess, being heavily influenced by Whig history and his mentor Ignaz von Döllinger, who would die a heretic.³⁹ Acton's superstition of unlimited progress in particular is called by the *New Catholic Encyclopedia* "hysteria," leading Kirk to admit that "Acton, over and over again, expressed his confidence that the universal growth of conscience would end in perfect, or nearly perfect, universal liberty. This is to ignore the Christian dogma of Original Sin."⁴⁰ This insidious superstition caused Acton to use his immense historical knowledge to assert that "it is certain" that King Charles I was murdered "unjustly" but that the "progress toward a more perfect freedom" made it so that he "must be condemned."⁴¹ This then justified the right of the Americans to "cover the country in a lake of blood" to advance the "principle of subversion" wherein "we have the broken chain, the rejected past, sons wiser than their fathers, ideas rooted

---

³⁷ Fr. Chad Ripperger, *The Binding Force of Tradition* (Sensus Traditionis, 2013); *Magisterial Authority* (Sensus Traditionis, 2014).
³⁸ Lord Acton, "Ultramontanism," in *Essays on Church and State* (Thomas Y. Cromwell Company: 1968), 64.
³⁹ Dawson wrote in 1959 that Acton's "vast knowledge and powers of research have never been surpassed." *Movement of World Revolution*, 27.
⁴⁰ H. A. MacDougall, "John Emerich Edward Dalberg Acton," *New Catholic Encyclopedia* (Washington DC: Catholic University Press, 2003), vol. I, 85; Russell Kirk, "Lord Acton on Revolution," Samuel Gregg, ed., *Lord Acton: Historian and Moralist* (Grand Rapids, MI: Acton Institute, 2017), 132.
⁴¹ Acton, *Lectures on Modern History* John Neville Figgis et. al, eds., (London: Macmillian, 1907), 202-203, *Selected Writings of Lord Acton* ed. J. Rufus Fears (Indianapolis: Liberty Fund, 1985-88), vol. I 95 in Kirk, 133.

in the future.⁴² This went to the point of saying against the Papal States: "I pray to God that I may live to see the whole of this Fabric destroyed, and the Tiber glow with the blood of the massacred Priests."⁴³ In a century of bloodshed, Acton never actually saw combat, allowing him to hold on to this risible and dangerous superstition.

Although Acton was a great man, the saint among the moderates was St. John Henry Newman, who, by the grace of the Holy Spirit had come into the Church in 1845, becoming the patron of the rebirth of the Catholic Church after centuries of persecution. His most excellent treatise, representing the foundational principle as we will see, is his *Essay on the Development of Christian Doctrine*.

Among the strict, one of the most prominent figures was Louis Veuillot (1813-1883). He condemned the endless revolutions as "elevating the world to commercial and industrial civilization" fueled by a mob which "only knows how to cry for money."⁴⁴ The state was teaching children to "ridicule orthodoxies of all kinds, whether they be religious, political, or literary."⁴⁵ Yet it seems Veuillot also was prone at times to excess, with careless words which seemed to divinize the pope as God Himself, producing prayers to the pope and praising him as the begetter of the Holy Spirit.⁴⁶

Another important figure among the strict was Dom Prosper Guéranger, the Benedictine Abbot who launched the modern liturgical movement by his fifteen volume *The Liturgical Year*, seeking to use historical knowledge to bring the faithful to appreciate the riches of the liturgy. At that time most Masses were either low Masses or celebrated with extravagant secular music, even in Rome: theatrical, operatic or orchestral. Thus Guéranger "resurrected the Gregorian chant almost from oblivion."⁴⁷ But there was also a moderate side of the liturgical movement which sought to change parts of the liturgy for the sake of the faithful. As a fruit of the liturgical movement there began to proliferate hand missals. It is very crucial to understand that the use of hand missals was something new in the liturgical life of the Church.

---

⁴² Acton, review of *The American Commonwealth*, in *Selected Writings of Lord Acton* ed. J. Rufus Fears (Indianapolis: Liberty Fund, 1985-88), vol. I, 404l; quoted in Kirk, 131-132.
⁴³ Letters of Odo Russell, 12 March 1867, Public Records Office, F. O. 912/84, 66, crown copyright, in Chadwick, *Secularization of the European Mind in the Nineteenth Century*, 112.
⁴⁴ Rao "Louis Veuillot and the Catholic 'Intransigence': a Re-evaluation."
⁴⁵ The phrase is Rao's paraphrase.
⁴⁶ Klaus Schatz, *Vaticanum I*, vol. I, 266 in O'Malley, *Vatican I*, 87.
⁴⁷ O'Malley, *Vatican I*, 76-77.

But the greatest among the strict was another saint, Blessed Pope Pius IX himself. The doctrine of the Immaculate Conception, he said, will "confute those who deny that human nature was corrupted by the first sin and who amplify the powers of human reason in order to deny or diminish the benefits of revelation."[48] The exaltation of Mary in the modern epoch would be a refuge from the regime of Anti-Mary.

On December 8, 1854, he dogmatized the teaching with papal authority, raising the banner of the *Theotokos* for Christendom. In the same year God gave rest to the Japanese Catholics after two hundred years without priests. They would soon erect the Cathedral to Our Lady of the Immaculate Conception as the throne of Christ in their ancient region of Nagasaki, which would become the greatest church in Asia. God confirmed the doctrine with the miraculous apparition of Our Lady of Lourdes in 1858 when she said to St. Bernadette in Occitan: "Que soy era immaculada concepciou [I am the Immaculate Conception]."[49] On December 8, 1864, he fiercely condemned anti-culture in *Quanta Cura* and its attached *Syllabus of Errors*. Yet this severe action would only prelude the trouble that was brewing.

The Second American Civil War

Like the War of the Three Kingdoms in the British Isles, the balance between two voluntarisms could never last, since both were pure power stripped of meaning, and the United States erupted into bloodshed in another civil war (1861-1865).[50] Like most modern wars, it was a conflict between two powers over economic dominance. But in this conflict was foreshadowed all the horrors of the violence that were to come.

The North, in a general sense political descendants of the Federalists, wanted to use the western lands of the United States for their economic gains, and sought to limit their rivals and their agrarian slave labor force.[51] But abolitionists used propaganda to urge bloodshed, saying this was a war to end the crime of slavery. Hence the song, "Battle Hymn of the

---

[48] Pio IX, Allocution *Singulari quadam* at the Consistory of 9 December 1854 in De Mattei, *Blessed Pius IX*, 104 n25.
[49] "I am the Immaculate Conception" in Occitan.
[50] Ferrara, 248-301, 302-440
[51] In a general sense the North's argument was similar to the Federalists' argument during the Constitutional ratification controversy. However, Whigs, later Republicans, and Democrats were all present in the North. The observation here is simply that similar forces of voluntarism were at work in both instances, just as the same thing happened in English history before their civil war of the seventeenth century.

Republic." Lincoln was not an abolitionist, but he freed the slaves as a means to keep the union and win the war.[52]

Lincoln's *Gettysburg Address* decreed that killing and dying for the government was a "sacrament" that "consecrated" the land of the United States, which, paraphrasing the Nicene creed, "shall not perish from the earth." With this phrase, the United States replaced the Kingdom of God with the American Empire. This propaganda convinced nearly hundreds of thousands of Northern men to shed blood and created a multitude of widows and orphans.

The Southern slaveowners, generally political descendants of the Anti-Federalists, were wanting to extend slavery into the western lands for their own profit. Thus their Vice President A. H. Stephens sought to canonize slavery by saying that the Black man "by nature, or by the curse against Canaan, is fitted for that condition that he occupies in our system... slavery — subordination to the superior race."[53] Moreover, he was confident that just like "Galileo," "science" would soon vindicate slavery. And indeed, the scientism of Darwin's eugenics was already doing just that. Thus the Southern leaders wrote their Constitution beginning with the lie of "we the people," so that slavery should be "recognized and protected" in the Confederacy.[54]

But only the wealthy had slaves, with only about five to twenty percent of the population of the Southern states owning slaves, since most were too poor to buy and feed them.[55] Thus the powerful resorted to the propaganda that the southern men should fight to defend their wives and children from the "Northern Aggression" of the Yankee businessmen. Lamentably for American families throughout the union, this propaganda was unfortunately true. The South was now facing an army of hundreds of thousands to invade their towns and cities. This propaganda convinced

---

[52] Lincoln: "I am not, nor ever have been, in favor of bringing about in any way the social and political equality of the white and black races which I believe will forever forbid the two races living together on terms of social and political equality." Lincoln supported deportation of Blacks to Liberia. Coulombe, *Puritan's Empire*, 233.

[53] A. H. Stephens, "Cornerstone Speech" (March 21, 1861), <https://www.owleyes.org/text/the-cornerstone-speech/read/text-of-stephenss-speech>, accessed March 28, 2021.

[54] *Constitution of the Confederate States* (March 11 1861).

[55] The percentage of slaveowners is still hotly debated in American scholarship, yet even partisans against the South admit that the number was 5.67 percent of the whole Confederacy considering the father of the family only, and 30.8 percent if you count the whole family. Ann Brown, "Fact Check: What Percentage Of White Southerners Owned Slaves?" *The Moguldom Nation* (Aug 10, 2020) <https://moguldom.com/296030/fact-check-what-percentage-of-white-southerners-owned-slaves/>, accessed March 28, 2021.

hundreds of thousands of Southern men to shed blood and create widows and orphans.

The militarism foreshadowed all the horrors to come—hypnotizing propaganda, increased technology, tyrannous conscriptions, martial law, total war destroying civilian homes and towns, 50,000 old men, women and children dead and thousands more widowed or orphaned.

In April, 1861 the Catholic bishops held a council which took a neutral stand on the war, preaching peace.[56] This has been the wisdom in the modern warfare, now that men were shedding so much blood for the idol of petty kingdoms. Lamentably, the American Empire began forcing even Catholic seminarians into the army, causing them to flee to Canada.[57]

But interestingly, two men who disagreed vehemently on politics agreed to support the South in some way—Lord Acton and Pius IX. What was at stake in the war was nothing less than the local rule of subsidiarity against the unlimited power of the central government. On this point, the South was correct, despite using this truth to rationalize their wicked slave regime by means of "state's rights."

With the loss of the South, the central government and the godless anti-culture of Feminism and unlimited industrial revolution, now moralized as crusaders against slavery, gained the upper hand in the American Empire, and the world. These godless forces would use and abuse Africans and the African culture to destroy the family in the twentieth century as we will see. Meanwhile, without a public *cultus* and Sacramental Marriage, the Indians continued to be warred against and the former slaves faced one hundred years of Jim Crow and lynching. The Empire of Freedom, having disdained the "tyranny" of priests, only tyrannized the Indians and Africans with anti-culture.

At the same moment, the British empire decided to start funding the Saudi-Wahhab movement against the Ottomans, which "ended up aiding global jihad."[58] This will resurrect the sword of Muhammad within a few generations.

---

[56] Ven. Frederic Baraga was a missionary bishop in Michigan who traveled on foot with snowshoes across the wintery Upper Peninsula to minister to a flock of Catholic Indians and Immigrants, preaching on most Sundays in Chippewa, English, German and/or French, writing also an Ottawa-Algonquian language catechism and grammar. Ven. Frederic Baraga, *Diary*, trans. Joseph Gregorich and Paul Prud'homme (Detroit: Wayne State University Press, 1990), 229, n64.
[57] Ibid., 244 m102.
[58] Spencer, *History of Jihad*, 259.

The Monarchy of the Church

At the same time, the Italian Empire was gaining ground against the combined forces formed from the ranks of twenty-five different countries especially Ireland and Austria, but also Poland, England, Switzerland, Germany, Holland, Canada, and even the United States.[59] Since Napoléon and especially from that time, one by one the ancient Italian city states and kingdoms had been succumbing to the unlimited progress of the Empire of anti-culture: Venice, Sardinia, Tuscany, Genoa, Sicily, Parma, Florence.[60] Just like the United States, the subsidiarity of local rule could no longer endure.

Our Lady spoke **Nahuatl** to St. Juan Diego and Occitan to St. Bernadette. As with public education, "the tongue" became **an** "instrument of domination."[61] The language of the powerful would be imposed on all local communities and local languages suppressed. Excluding other languages would be an important factor for the empires of anti-culture to impose their excessive nationalism on the people.

As the Italian Empire slowly advanced toward Rome, Pio Nono called the Ecumenical Council of the Vatican. Now all bishops from around the world came—Italians, French, Austrians, Germans, with the English, Irish, Polish and bishops from the Americas, the Middle East and East Asia. Yet because of the machinations of so many temporal rulers, Bl. Pius IX did not invite the Catholic kings and nobles, breaking with centuries of tradition. French prime minister Émile Ollivier said that by this act the pope proclaimed the separation of Church and state, which he had formerly condemned.[62] The pope's act was understandable, as he did not know who he could trust, but it ended up alienating further the organic bond between the spiritual and temporal swords of Christendom. This contributed greatly to a false understanding of the Church as only clerics, and not lay people.[63] Nevertheless on the Feast of the Immaculate Conception, 1869 the Vatican Council opened.

In their zeal for the truth, like St. Cyril, the strict immediately seized control of the Council in what O'Malley calls "orchestrated" and a "coup" already speaking of the moderates as "heretics.[64] This voluntarism shocked

---

[59] De Mattei, "The 'Ninth Crusade of the Papal Zouaves."
[60] Cf. Spencer M. di Scala, *Italy: From Revolution to Republic 1700-Present* (Boulder: Westview Press, 1995).
[61] Augustine, *City of God*, bk. XVI, ch. 4.
[62] Sir Rowland Blennerhassett, "The Hohenlohe Memoirs," *The Eclectic Magazine*, vol. 148 (University of Iowa, 1907), 236.
[63] *Acta et decretal sacrorum conciliorum recentiorum: Collectio lacensis*, (Freiburg, Germany: Herder: 1870-1890), 7:1221 in O'Malley, *Vatican I*, 114.
[64] Ibid., 152-156.

the other Council Fathers who were justly indignant. The strict rationalized their voluntarism by thinking that their ends justified the means, and the council moved forward according to the will of the strict.[65]

The first act of the Council was to anathematize the evolution of dogma:

> If anyone shall assert it to be possible that sometimes, according to the progress of knowledge, a sense is to be given to doctrines propounded by the Church different from that which the Church has understood and understands; let him be anathema.[66]

This principle would be the fundamental axiom against the anti-culture, since in this sentence is restated the anathema: "If anyone rejects any written or unwritten tradition of the church, let him be anathema." The integrity of Christian culture was safeguarded by this anathema which is the fundamental principle of Christendom.

If the strict went to the extreme, they would say that *no sense* could ever be given to a doctrine that was different in any way—no change was possible, ever. If the moderates went to the extreme, they would say that every change was possible, which was the heretical evolution of dogma. Instead, the Holy Spirit acted in this anathema to define precisely the limits of doctrinal change, as Newman had done, by restricting change to the "same sense and understanding." This phrase would soon become dogmatized in the Oath Against Modernism.

But the Italian Empire continued to advance on Rome. The strict formed the majority who wanted to dogmatize papal infallibility. The moderates like Newman and eastern bishops like Chaldean Joseph VI Audo believed in the dogma but opposed the definition on pastoral grounds, warning that it would create a false spirit of absolute power for the pope.[67] A third party did not believe the dogma at all, and some ended up dying as heretics. Meanwhile, Acton and Döllinger who opposed the definition began manipulating the press to undermine the council, which even O'Malley confirms was filled with lies.[68] They were aided by Dr. Georg Ratzinger, the great uncle of Joseph Ratzinger.[69] Their actions were simply more voluntarism in response to voluntarism.

---

[65] Sire, 205.
[66] *Dei Filius* (1870).
[67] R. Rabban, "Chaldean Catholic Church (Eastern Catholic)," *New Catholic Encyclopedia* (2003), vol. 3, 369.
[68] O'Malley is a Liberal historian, *Vatican I*, 149.
[69] Peter Seewald, *Benedict XVI: A Life*, trans. Dinah Livingstone (Bloomsbury, 2020), vol 1, 374.

As the Italian armies closed in, the strict imposed on the Council their will—papal infallibility would be defined next, skipping any other aspect of infallibility and thus isolating this from the necessary nuance desired by the moderates.[70] In July the German-French war broke out, and the French troops were forced to leave the Vatican vulnerable to the Italian Empire.[71]

While the Germans began marching toward Paris, the papal definition finally came in July, which, despite everything, carefully distinguished the concerns of the strict and moderate parties, stating clearly the same principle of culture contained in the aforementioned anathema:

> For the Holy Spirit was promised to the successors of Peter not so that they might, by his revelation, make *known some new doctrine*, but that, by his assistance, they might *religiously guard and faithfully expound* the revelation or deposit of faith transmitted by the apostles.[72]

The eldership of Christian culture guarded the *cultus* and tradition. When a pope promulgated something new, it was always in the same sense as what came before, just as a child who grows into an adult is the same person as they were before, as Newman had brilliantly elucidated already.[73]

The two saints at the council agreed—Pope Pius IX promulgated it and Newman signed. But in August, Newman privately lamented that it was bringing about a false spirit by the "tyrant majority":

> I have various things to say about the Definition... To me the serious thing is this, that, whereas it has not been usual to pass definition except in case of urgent and definite necessity, this definition, while it gives the Pope power, creates for him, in the very act of doing so, a precedent and a suggestion to use his power without necessity, when ever he will, when not called on to do so. I am telling people who write to me to have confidence—but I don't know what I shall say to them, if the Pope did so act. And I am afraid moreover, that the tyrant majority is still aiming at enlarging the *province* of Infallibility. I can only say if all this takes

---

[70] Ibid., 184-185.

[71] At this time it was actually Prussia, since Germany as a country was not created until after 1870. This is said to bring out the significance of what happens in 1918.

[72] *Pastor Aeternus* (1870), 6. Emphasis mine.

[73] Newman, *Essay on the Development of Doctrine*, 139-170.

place, we shall in matter of fact be under a new dispensation. But we must hope, for one is obliged to hope it, that the Pope will be driven from Rome, and will not continue the Council, or that there will be another Pope. It is sad he should force us to such wishes.[74]

St. Newman knew by faith that the Church would not define any error—and the Church did not then, nor ever will define error. But he was concerned about how the words of Vatican I would be misinterpreted by the general populace. The Holy Spirit was acting through the Council to speak, as He does in every Council, even when there was confusion and great difficulty. As with many Councils of the Church and the machinations of sinful men, God always brings good out of any evil present within or without the Church's hierarchy.

But the council was not able to continue to clarify anything. In September, the Italian Empire was reaching Rome, and the Ninth Crusaders were faced with "a preponderance of enemy forces."[75] Pope Pius IX sought to avoid more bloodshed and surrendered. The Italian army invaded Rome and the council was stopped. Acton paid a group of bandits to break into the archives to steal records of pope Honorius to undermine the council. The plot was discovered and Acton was thrown into prison.[76] The popes henceforth condemned the invasion and declared themselves "Prisoners of the Vatican."

---

[74] Newman to Ambrose St. John (August 21, 1870), Charles Stephen Dessain and Thomas Gornall, eds., *The Letters and Diaries of John Henry Newman* (Oxford University Press, 1973), vol. 25 cited by Peter Kwasniewski, "My Journey from Ultramontanism to Catholicism," *Catholic Family News* (Nov. 2020-Jan. 2021) < https://catholicfamilynews.com/blog/2021/02/04/my-journey-from-ultramontanism-to-catholicism/>, accessed March 28, 2021.
[75] De Mattei, *op. cit.*
[76] This is mentioned by Russel Kirk in the audio for his lecture cited in Gregg, *Acton: Historian and Moralist* published by the Acton Institute (April 11, 2017) <https://blog.acton.org/archives/93067-kirk-on-acton-on-revolution.html>, accessed March 28, 2021.

XXV

THE FALSE SPIRIT OF VATICAN I

On January 18th 1871, France was defeated by the Germans, who proclaimed William I emperor. In March, the first Communist revolution took over Paris, executing Archbishop Darboy by firing squad. Marx gushed it was "Paris, all truth," and the old order, "all lie."[1]

But the Church had preserved her divine monarchy in the person of Peter. While they had lost the Papal States, there was a much greater success on the spiritual level, which was much more important. More than ever before the Catholic world was united because of one thing: *the charitable anathema*. God had already worked everything necessary for the Church to continue—all that was necessary was that men respond to the divine graces He provided and repent.

The evil that Acton had done at the council was indeed terrible because it showed what power the media had in undermining the sacred office of the bishop. By manipulating the press with Döllinger, he had helped create the false spirit of Vatican I. To be fair, the council was not able to dogmatize the infallibility of Ecumenical Councils, the *sensus fidelium*, the consensus of the Church Fathers, nor the consensus of the Scholastics.[2] Döllinger turned heretic and died excommunicated, but Acton and Georg Ratzinger stayed moderate and died in the Church.

Unfortunately, some falsely believed that the pope was above the authority of *cultus* and tradition, despite the best efforts of men such as

---

[1] Marx, *The Civil War in France* (English Edition of 1871 Zodiac & Brian Baggins), ch. 5.
[2] Once again the reader is recommended to these crucial works: Fr. Chad Ripperger, *The Binding Force of Tradition* (Sensus Traditionis, 2013); *Magisterial Authority* (Sensus Traditionis, 2014).

Franzelin, a *peritus* at the Council.³ The German bishops clarified that "the opinion according to which the Pope is 'an absolute sovereign because of his infallibility' is based on a completely false understanding of the dogma of Papal Infallibility" and that the pope "is restricted to the contents of Holy Scripture and Tradition and also to the dogmas previously defined by the teaching authority of the Church."⁴ Pope Pius IX called this "the true meaning of the Vatican decrees" and approved the same for the Swiss bishops.⁵

But this imbalance began to change the center of Christian culture from the *cultus* and the tradition to the person of the pope. This alienation is implied in the famous dictum of Acton "power corrupts, absolute power corrupts absolutely," which was written after the council in a letter defending the justice of the Protestant revolt against a tyrannical papacy.⁶

Following the council, as if in reaction, the revolutionary forces in Europe continued gaining strength through nationalism. In addition, military buildup began a long crescendo amid rising tensions. Small conflicts erupted over nationalism and territory, but they were localized

---

³ John Cardinal Baptist Franzelin, *De Divina Tradione*, 1875. In English translated by Ryan Grant (Mediatrix Press, 2016). See also Russell Hittinger, "The Spirit of Vatican I," *First Things* (October 2018).
⁴ Gerhard Ludwig Müller, "By What Authority: On the Teaching Office of the Pope," *First Things*, Jan. 16, 2018, <https://www.firstthings.com/web-exclusives/2018/01/by-what-authority>, accessed March 28, 2021. See also Ludwig Müller, "Statement on the Limits of Papal Authority," in *Roman Encounters: The Unity of the Faith and the Holy See's Responsibility for the Universal Church*, translated by Susan Johnson (Irondale, AL: EWTN Publishing, Inc., 2019), 230-31.
⁵ Olivier Rousseau, "Le vraie valeur de l'épiscopat dans l'Église d'après d'importants documents de 1875," *Irénikon*, 29 (1956): 131-150, in Patrick Granfield, *The Limits of the Papacy* (Crossroad, 1987), 116, n21. Granfield references Denzinger 3112-17 which also has Pius IX's letter to the German bishops. Cf. Yves Congar, *My Journal of the Council*, trans. Mary John Ronayne and Mary Cecily Boulding, Denis Minns, eds. (Collegeville, MN: Liturgical Press, 2012), 97, n3. The Swiss bishops said that dogma "in no way depends upon the caprice of the Pope or upon his good pleasure, to make such and such a doctrine the object of a dogmatic definition: he is tied up and limited to the divine revelation, and to the truths which that revelation contains; he is tied up and limited by the Creeds already in existence, and by the preceding definitions of the Church; he is tied up and limited by the divine law and by the constitution of the Church." The pope "wrote to the Swiss Bishops that nothing could be more opportune or more worthy of praise, or cause the truth to stand out more clearly." Dom. Cuthbert Butler, *The Vatican Council (1869-1870): Based on Bishop Ullathorne's Letters*, ed. Christopher Butler, Abbot of Downside (Westminster, MD: The Newman Press, 1962), 464-465.
⁶ Acton to Archbishop Mandell Creighton, (Apr. 5, 1887).

and did not spread (Franco-Prussian War, Morocco crisis, Balkan wars). The German Imperial Navy began in 1871 to build up power to challenge the British Empire on the seas, alarming the British. In 1879, the German confederacy and the Austria-Hungary Empire signed an alliance at Vienna in opposition to any attacks from Russia. Italy would later join this alliance as well.

Is Christ King over America?

A false understanding of Papal Infallibility gave governments the pretext to persecute Catholics. Otto von Bismarck united the German principalities and suppressed Catholics, considering them enemies of the state serving a foreign monarch. Everywhere the increased nationalism was attempting to control the Church. The German Catholics had had a Catholic civilization in Germany since the days of St. Boniface chopping down Donar's Oak. They fought against this usurpation of Christ the King, but many fled to the United States.

In the United States, a group of Protestants, showing how much Christian culture they still retained, were convinced that the Civil War was God's punishment for disregarding Him as King in the Constitution of the United States. They formed the National Reform Association to amend the Constitution:

> "We the people" would acknowledge "Almighty God as the source of all authority and power in civil government, the Lord Jesus Christ as the Ruler among nations, His revealed will as the supreme law of the land, in order to constitute a Christian government..."

At the very least, this change would formally remove the principle of voluntarism and introduce the Logos Incarnate as the fundamental principle of law for the United States. At this point the whole of politics, economy, and family was rapidly being subordinated to voluntarism— every oath, vow, contract and bond of any kind had only two parties whose wills were the only thing that mattered, not God. If a majority could consent, therefore, they could create reality itself.

As the National Reform Association was lobbying for this amendment, the influx of German Catholics into the United States set up a conflict with the ascending Irish bishops. The Germans were fresh from Germanic Christendom speaking their mother tongue, and naturally wanted to convert the United States to Christ similar to what the National Reform

Association was advocating. In 1867 they founded the German Catholic Newspaper *Der Wanderer* in St. Paul, Minnesota (later *The Wanderer* and *The Remnant* of today). They represented the strict party originally shown by Fr. White.[7]

The Irish Catholics were the moderate party, led by Bishop James Gibbons, who, by contrast, had lived under the English regime suffering for centuries just to have the Mass. While James Gibbons was growing up in Ireland, Ó Conaill had inspired the whole Catholic world and won emancipation from London, while advocating the use of English.[8] The Irish had just recently escaped a deadly famine and their families back in Ireland were now facing another famine of 1879, which was leading many Irish to violence in the Land Wars.

Thus we can understand the gratitude to America that must have flowed from the Irish like James Gibbons, being free to have the Mass and make enough money to feed their families. They wanted to abandon Gaelic and adopt English, and moreover, like Catholics in other countries following Vatican I, were under extreme pressure from the American leaders to not threaten the status quo with orders from a "foreign Monarch" in Rome.

Thus Gibbons wrote a defense of Catholicism in 1876 called *The Faith of Our Fathers,* which became quite popular among American Catholics (it went through over ninety editions by 1917). In this work, he brilliantly defended papal infallibility. But instead of joining the National Reform Associaton in calling for an amendment acknowledging Christ the King, he drew upon the legacy of Lord Baltimore and the Carrolls by claiming that the Church was the true originator of the religious liberty proclaimed in the United States Constitution.[9] This created an extremely convincing argument that the American concept of religious liberty was actually Catholic and did not need amendment.

It was true, as Gibbons wrote, that "the Church has ever resisted the tyranny of kings" as St. Thomas More did when Henry VIII broke the Magna Carta.[10] Gibbons also rightly condemned the contemporary seizure of Church power that was happening in Europe at that time. Yet he did not elucidate the true legacy of "freedom of conscience" contained in the Catholic tradition. He mentioned how *Sicut Judaeis* protected the Jews

---

[7] Paul Likoudis, "Joseph Matt and Americanism," *The Wanderer Press*, St. Paul, MN, Orig. 1950-51; January - August 2012.
[8] Thomas Neill, *They Lived the Faith*, 25-26.
[9] James Gibbons, *Faith of Our Fathers*, 93rd ed. (Baltimore, MD: John Murphy Co., 1917), ch. 17.
[10] Ibid.

from coercion, but did not mention that this was on the condition that the public order be subordinated to Christ. He did not attempt to balance this with the Syllabus of Errors, nor discuss the National Reform Association's effort to amend the Constitution

Rather, he implied that Catholics should never try to amend this part of the Constitution when he said that "if Catholics should gain the majority in a community where freedom of conscience is already secured by law, their very religion obliges them to respect the rights thus acquired by their fellow-citizens."[11] This was only half true, since the Church had condemned at this time an absolute freedom of religion notwithstanding its legacy of toleration. Gibbons could have known this since the popes had been elucidating this point since he was a boy in Ireland.

In 1879, thanks to the countless hours of sacrifice from pious immigrants, the massive Cathedral of St. Patrick was completed in New York City, which outshined the monuments to money surrounding it. This burning love of Jesus and Mary would continue to combine with the zealous love for the freedom of America to have the Mass and enough wealth to feed your children. Our fathers sacrificed immensely to build these monuments because they loved God and country—and this spirit was truly great.

But Gibbons' vision seemed to coalesce with that of Lincoln that the American Empire "shall not pass from the earth," and Gibbon's first biographer called Jefferson's condemnation of French Canadian Christendom, "the immortal Declaration" of Independence.[12] This deep and abiding gratitude for what America gave the immigrant needed to be balanced with the strict party of the Germans, so that it did not get swallowed up by Manifest Destiny.

Economic Revolution

As this was happening on a theological level, young men grew up during the Civil War and others came back from the war, both confronted with up to twice the population of women in their local towns, many lonely who had lost brothers or husbands. Recovering from the war, the veterans turned to alcohol, and no one could be surprised about what happened next. Fornication and adultery became rampant.[13] As a result the divorce laws in

---

[11] Ibid.
[12] "He was Charles Carroll, and the hand that turned the heavy brass door knob had signed the immortal Declaration." Will, *Life of Cardinal Gibbons*, 9.
[13] Popenoe, *Families without Fathers*, 109ff.

United States and elsewhere began to be challenged.[14] In 1880, the pope wrote the first encyclical on Marriage, *Arcanum*.

Even though John Milton had rationalized divorce, to their credit most Protestants still abhorred divorce because they believed in the Holy Scriptures. But the movements of rationalism at this time gave them the pretext to doubt the Scripture and promote divorce.

To make matters still worse, a new economic revolution was assaulting the family: the second Industrial Revolution. More factory and mining work proliferated, and the power of the machine began to grow immensely. The rights of women to be mothers to their children were continually threatened by the law of profits as it continued its march against the law of the home. The rights of the children were constantly ignored, with no concern for how these changes affected them and their need for their parents in general and their mother in particular.

The superstition for unlimited progress motivated business owners to force their people into more and more mechanization, in order to prove the Catholic Church's council wrong—the earthly city could indeed be built, and we will raise it to heaven to make a name for ourselves.

The German Imperial Navy was continuing to be a massive threat to British power. By 1891, the British were trying to find a way to check Germany's rise to power. Germany meanwhile, was doing the same thing.[15] It was a widespread belief that war was good for nations, so the powerful were trying to find ways to provoke the war. The military industrial complex continued in all nations.

Meanwhile in Africa in 1876, Jean-Rémy Bessieux died, having evangelized the Agekaza-Quaben and Pongoues with the Holy Ghost Fathers and established the new foundation of African Christendom.

On February seventh, 1878, Pope Pius IX joined the chorus of angels. Because of the violence of the Masonic mob, his body was secretly guarded and when it was moved to its final rest, men of God had to defend it against rioters trying to throw it into the Tiber.[16] His body was later found to be incorrupt.[17]

---

[14] Ibid., 116.
[15] Carroll Quigley, *The Anglo-American Establishment* (New York: Books In Focus, 1981), 3 in James Corbett, "The WWI Conspiracy" <https://www.corbettreport.com/wwi/> accessed March 28, 2021. See also Gerry Docherty, *Hidden History: The Secret Origins of the First World War* (Mainstream Publishing, 2014).
[16] Charles Murr, *The Godmother* (2017), 78.
[17] The testimony of Madre Pascalina in seeing the body is recorded in Ibid., 82.

CITY OF GOD VS. CITY OF MAN

The Lion Roars

In 1878 God began to bring great good out of the loss of the Papal States. The moderate Pope Leo XIII was elected to the pontificate. His name meant "Lion," harkening back to St. Leo I who fearlessly beat back Atilla the Hun with the spiritual sword. Pope Leo XIII unsheathed this same sword and wielded it by the Holy Spirit. In more encyclicals than any pope before him, he brilliantly dismantled the lies of anti-culture one by one, establishing the principles of the Catholic restoration.

The first Greco-Roman renewal had overcome the pride of the eastern emperor and synthesized the Antiochian and Alexandrian schools of thought with Syriac help. The second renewal had synthesized Aristotle and St. Augustine to create Thomism and Scotism. The third Greco-Roman renewal had synthesized the Renaissance Humanism with Scholasticism to bring about the second Christendom. Now Pope Leo XIII sought to bring about the fourth renewal by means of Thomism.

St. Thomas was the model because it was he, more than anyone in history, who had taken something so controversial as Aristotle and, surgically removing its impurities, placed it at the service of the Gospel.[18] If men followed the method of St. Thomas, they could synthesize the unprecedented Patristic texts now available with the existing Scholastic Tradition and respond to the modern philosophies. This was the moment that another renewal was possible, just like Trent.

But this could only come about with the union of moderate and strict. Even though their alliance had been greatly strained by the voluntarism at the Vatican Council, it had still given the Church the fundamental dogmas to start the renewal.

Unwittingly, Pope Leo XIII's innumerable encyclicals were helping to reinforce the false spirit of Vatican I, as the office of the papacy for the first time in its history had become under him a universal teaching office.[19] This great pope—indeed a saint—was doing what any father would do. But the false spirit of Vatican I was changing Christian culture to slowly subordinate the *cultus* and the tradition to the office of eldership in the person of the pope. It is crucial to understand this shift that seems to happen under Pope Leo XIII's twenty-five year pontificate—men everywhere began to think that Christian culture revolved around the pope, when it fact Christian culture flowed from the *cultus*, informed by the Tradition, and guarded by the eldership. Thus eldership is third in importance for culture, whereas now it was beginning to become first in importance.

---

[18] Leo XIII, *Aeterni Patris* (1879), 17-24.
[19] O'Malley, *What Happened at Vatican II*, 56.

To make matters worse, Pope Leo XIII himself sought to extend his authority over the temporal sword in France. While Pius IX had formed an ecumenical council without lay involvement, Leo XIII pushed French monarchists to accept the secular Third French Republic in his program of *ralliement*. When French Catholics opposed Pope Leo, knowing it was beyond his authority to dictate politics of the temporal sword, and moreover following the anti-Liberal principles of Pius IX, Cardinal Lavigerie opposed them with this principle: "The only rule of salvation and life in the Church is to be with the pope, with the living pope. Whoever he may be."[20] Pope Leo XIII reinforced this by saying in a public letter in *Osservatore Romano* not that Two Swords govern the Church, but that "two distinct orders have been established most clearly: the teaching Church [the Magisterium] and the taught Church."[21] This helped to establish the false spirit of Vatican I, removing the temporal sword from the Church even in matters of politics. It seems this otherwise great pope had a moment of imprudence after the loss of the papal states.

Meanwhile the greatest philosopher in Russian history, Vladimir Soloviev, was promoting a restoration of Holy Russia with the Petrine authority. This was the great fruit of the Greco-Roman renewal that they had worked out of the evil of Czarist *Roma* devastating the Russian people since 1498. Leonid Feodorov was at that time growing up and would soon discern his vocation to the Russian Orthodox priesthood. But his contact with Soloviev would change everything.

Modernism and Americanism

Realizing that the fourth renewal would devastate all of their propagandized mob violence for anti-culture, the enemies of the Church used the new historical discoveries and manuscripts and tried to turn them against the Holy Scriptures themselves. This they did with Frenchman Alfred Loisy, who boasted that his great erudition had shown him that the breath of the Holy Spirit had erred in Holy Scriptures. This was vehemently condemned by Pope Leo XIII in 1893, and Loisy was eventually excommunicated.[22]

---

[20] Roberto de Mattei, *Le ralliement de Léon XIII – L'échec d'un projet pastoral* (CERF, 2016), 95. See José Antonio Ureta, "Leo XIII: First Liberal Pope Who Went Beyond His Authority," *OnePeterFive* (October 19, 2021) <https://onepeterfive.com/leo-xiii-first-liberal-porpe-who-went-beyond-his-authority/>, accessed October 21, 2021.

[21] Léon XIII, lettre « Epistola Tua », 17 Juin 1885.

[22] Leo XIII, *Providentissimus Deus* (1893).

Then—and far more devastatingly—a son of Ireland became puffed up as well. George Tyrell grew up Protestant in Dublin. However, he could not escape the historicity of the Catholic Faith and became Catholic in the first year of Pope Leo's pontificate, taking his final vows as a Jesuit in 1891.

Meanwhile, the German and Irish Catholics in America were coming to blows over the assimilation promoted by the Irish bishops. The St. Raphael Society, led by the Germans, observed that as the immigrants had moved to the United States, they had sustained losses of more than ten million of their children who fell away from their Faith due to a lack of priests who spoke their language.[23] Language was the glue that tied a man to his ethnicity and culture, and thus to God. The society sought to remedy this by recruiting priests who spoke the language of the people.

But Gibbons vehemently opposed this, and was under pressure from President Harrison and other government leaders to make the Catholic immigrants abandon their mother tongue.[24] At the same time, he rightly understood that if Catholics refused to speak English at all, then conversion of Protestants would be difficult. One solution of course, was bilingualism. But the pope ruled against the Germans and sided with Gibbons. The immigrants would not be given priests who spoke their language.

Pope Leo XIII probably was looking at the American situation like Europe. If one European Catholic migrated to another European country, this was not as spiritually difficult. Europe had Catholicism in its bones. Everywhere there were the monuments of our fathers to Christ and Our Lady, and in many rural places the faith and custom was still strong. Assimilating to a different language and culture in Europe—especially rural—had little effect on the cultural momentum which influences children.

In United States, the public order was devoted to the gods of *Libertas*, nation and money. If the children of immigrants lost their language, they would be susceptible to the cultural momentum to worship false gods. Gibbons also promoted a full assimilation including sending Catholic children to public schools. Fortunately for American Catholicism, the Catholic school system would endure.

But Leo addressed the American situation in two encyclicals. In 1895 he rightly praised the nobility of Washington, and saw the Providential Hand of God in forming the close bond between him and the Catholics

---

[23] David A. Wemhoff, *John Courtney Murray, Time/Life, and the American Proposition: How the CIA's Doctrinal Warfare Program Changed the Catholic Church* (South Bend, IN: Fidelity Press, 2015), 84.
[24] Wemhoff, 85.

when Carroll offered America to the Immaculate Conception. Yet against Gibbons's assertions, but in accord with his predecessors, he concluded that "it would be very erroneous to draw the conclusion that in America is to be sought the type of the most desirable status of the Church, or that it would be universally lawful or expedient for state and Church to be, as in America, dissevered and divorced."[25]

Finally, having recently been informed by St. Katherine Drexel that the Blacks and Indians were languishing in the poverty of spirit and body, Pope Leo XIII urged them to help them with the Gospel. By God's hand, St. Katherine was to fill the void the American bishops had avoided for fear of the Protestant leaders. The bishops, meanwhile, wanted to assimilate the Catholic Faith itself to the United States.

The Jewish Question

In 1888, Pope Leo XIII beatified St. Louis de Montfort and promoted the Rosary. This helped the work of Fr. Ratisbonne whose Congregation of Our Lady of Sion was laboring for the conversion of Jews. Ratisbonne, a French Jew, went to his eternal reward as a Catholic in 1884.

Pope Leo's work to support the French Republic inspired Marc Sangnier to found *Le Sillon* for promoting Catholicism in a republican context. The French were still divided however, as many French supported a restoration of the monarchy even against the pope. The Dreyfus Affair would soon further divide them in regard to the treatment of Jews in society.[26]

At the same time, German Catholic priest Franz Brentano made what Ripperger calls "a good start" in founding the field of Psychology on the basis of the logos contained in Aristotle.[27] He taught two Jews who took his ideas and had a massive effect on the twentieth century—Sigmund Freud and Edmund Husserl. Freud was from the liberal Jewish party and would turn and make the most destructive scientism hitherto known, which we will return to below.

---

[25] Leo XIII, *Longiqua Oceani* (1895), 6.
[26] The Dreyfus Affair was a public scandal over the conviction for treason of French Jew Alfred Dreyfus which involved falsified evidence and government cover-up. This event pushed the division in French society further into extremes and embittered Frenchmen against each other.
[27] Fr. Chad Ripperger, *Introduction to the Science of Mental Health* (Sensus Traditionis, 2013), xvi.

Husserl was a rational Jew who would be baptized and found the school of Phenomenology as a means to restore logos to philosophy with an Augustinian, Platonic method.[28] This philosophical school would become the basis for the moderate Catholics in the twentieth century. It would help convert Dietrich von Hildebrand and St. Teresa Benedicta of the Cross.[29] Karol Wojtyła (who would become Pope St. John Paul II) would also utilize this philosophy from a Thomistic foundation. (It should be noted, however, that later in his life Husserl began to advocate an erroneous philosophy. It is for this reason that some today still criticize phenomenology, since Husserl's later works are indeed anti-logos.[30])

At the same time, Reform Judaism was provoking intense hatred from men who profaned the name of Christian. Men who had lost all charity began to blame every social evil on the powerful Jews promoting unlimited usury and other evils as leaders in the Grand Coalition of the Status Quo. Europe was becoming obsessed with "the Jewish question" about how to "deal with" the Jews after *Sicut Judaeis* was abolished everywhere.

In 1890, the Jesuits at *La Civiltà Cattolica* lamented that Europe was "in the grips of a very sad question," which "in the twentieth century, there will possibly be... calamitous consequences."[31] In a strong critique, the Jesuits articulated the "Jewish problem" and attempted to provide a solution to the economic and social problem.[32] In 1891, Pope Leo condemned "rapacious usury" in *Rerum Novarum*, and began to synthesize the Catholic moral teaching about economics, seeking to restore economics as truly the law of the home instead of the law of profits.[33] In a few short years Soloviev would deliver his last message before death, warning of a

---

[28] Von Hildebrand, *What is Philosophy?* (Hildebrand Project, 2021), 205-208; St. Teresa Benedicta of the Cross (Edith Stein), *Knowledge and Faith*, trans. Walter Redmond, (Washington, DC: ICS, 2000), 1-64; Ibid., *Potency and Act*, trans. Walter Redmond (Washington, DC: ICS, 2009), viii

[29] Von Hildebrand was converted by Catholic Max Scheler, who was a phenomenologist following Husserl. Alice von Hildebrand, *Soul of a Lion: Biography of Dietrich von Hildebrand* (San Francisco, CA: Ignatius Press, 2000), 65-150.

[30] Thus Husserl's students and followers, such as Von Hildebrand and St. Teresa, abandoned him when he promoted anti-logos philosophy after 1913 with his work *Ideas* and subsequent works.

[31] La Civiltà Cattolica, *The Jewish Question in Europe* (1890), trans. anonymous (South Bend, IN: Fidelity Press, 2020), 13.

[32] The critique censures the liberal Jews but ultimately fails to distinguish between them and the rational Jewish parties as Von Hildebrand would later do in his defense of Jews against the Nazis.

[33] Leo XIII, *Rerum Novarum* (1891), 3, 12-14.

"'final solution'—a globalist utopia organized without reference to the incarnate God" which will be seen by "our immediate descendants."[34]

But at that very moment, Our Lady was building the throne of Christ in Moscow—the Cathedral of the Immaculate Conception (Собор Непорочного Зачатия Пресвятой Девы Марии) for the conversion of Russia. Across the Russian empire, through China and in the ancient Japanese civilization, another throne for Christ was being built at the same time in the ancient Catholic area in Nagasaki, Our Lady of the Immaculate Conception (無原罪の聖母司教座聖堂). Asia was being claimed for the King in the twentieth century. At that time Nagasaki's cathedral was the largest in Asia.[35]

Empire of Liberty

On April 20, 1898, the Empire of Liberty began to fulfill Jefferson's dream to take Cuba and began a war with Spain. At this point the United States had used bloodshed, lies and covert operations to dismantle the second Christendom in the Americas for more than a century. Many Catholics had been seized with the superstition of Manifest Destiny. During the war, Fr. O'Connell wrote to Bishop John Ireland:

> It is the question of all that is old and vile and mean and rotten and cruel and false in Europe against all that is free and noble and open and true and humane in America. When Spain is swept off the seas much of the meanness and narrowness of old Europe goes with it to be replaced by the freedom and openness of America. This is God's way of developing the world.[36]

Soon the Americans had conquered not only Cuba but Puerto Rico, Guam and Asian Catholicism in the Philippines. They began immediately dismantling Christendom by legalizing divorce, restricting the public *cultus*, expelling priests, and imposing state education upon the children.[37]

---

[34] Nichols, *Sophiology Man*, ix.
[35] Soichi Iijima, "The Effects of the Atomic Bombs – Hiroshima and Nagasaki," Joseph Rotblat and Michiji Konuma, eds., *Proceedings of the Forty-Fifth Pugwash Conference on Science and World Affairs* (Singapore: World Scientific, 1997), 199.
[36] Gary Potter, *In Reaction*, 84 in Coulombe, *Puritan's Empire*, 314.
[37] Ibid., 312.

CITY OF GOD VS. CITY OF MAN

In January, 1899, Pope Leo XIII addressed the United States and condemned "Americanism," the idea that "in order to more easily attract those who differ from her, the Church should shape her teachings more in accord with the spirit of the age."[38] His encyclical did not mention America's war with Spain.

Two months later in Corning, New York, Margaret Higgins was a fornicator at nineteen, watching her mother die as a devout Catholic. Her mother had raised eleven children, and Higgins was convinced that large families were afflicted with "poverty, toil, unemployment, drunkenness, cruelty, fighting, jails."[39] She soon married socialist William Sanger and become a crusader for liberty, leading to the proliferation of birth control in the United States, and eventually the unborn holocaust.

Nearby in New York City, the massive idol of the Roman goddess *Libertas* was already thirteen years old. Her title explained the gospel of the American empire: *Liberty enlightening the world.*

---

[38] Leo XIII, *Testem Benevolentiae Nostrae* (1899).
[39] Marco and Wiker, *Architects of the Culture of Death*, 287-289.

XXVI

POPE ST. PIUS X THE GREAT

On January 1st, 1900, the whole of Europe vastly secular.[1] Mass attendance had plummeted everywhere, men were uprooted, and in the city many were facing extreme poverty. With the loss of family structure and rooted culture, many were tempted to fornication, adultery and drunkenness, while there was a growing belief that dignity was based on power. The economic changes were quickly creating a situation where adolescents would be neglected. The businessmen had not planned their brave new world to consider the long term consequences to the family.

For millennia, every culture had distinguished between two types of people—children and adults. "Adolescents" were merely children who were now in the process of becoming adults, whose culture taught them the values and duties that were to be incumbent upon them for the sake of the family and the common good. Men were initiated at fifteen years old in most cultures, where they were expected to marry, beget children and die in defense of the village.[2] Hence the canonical age for marriage in the Church is the age we currently think of as "teenager."[3] This is actually the age of adulthood. These young families would be supported not only by parents but extended families and an entire cultural support to protect their children.

As the family continued to erode on the economic and moral level, the adolescents were abandoned by their parents—some unwillingly, having

---

[1] Chadwick, *The Secularization of the European Mind in the 19th Century*, passim.
[2] Fr. Richard Rohr's historical research on Male Initiation is important in this regard, but unfortunately like Brentano, Rohr seems to have drifted into heresy in his theology.
[3] P.M.J. Rock, "Canonical Age," *The Catholic Encyclopedia* (1907) <http://www.newadvent.org/cathen/01206c.htm>, accessed March 29, 2021.

to work twelve hour days, others due to their own moral failings. Popular movements were arising at this time to restore the order of the Third Commandment and force businesses to respect culture and family.[4] But this effort was too little, too late. These abandoned adolescent children would be easy prey in just a few short years. Already by 1910 good priests were alarmed at the breakdown in the family and courtship customs, leading to increased immorality among the young.[5] This was the creation of the "teenager."[6] Before this time teenagers, as we know them today, did not exist.

The extended family had largely been eliminated by urbanization, creating the corruption of the nuclear family with less cultural rootedness. The Catholic economic principles that excluded contracts based solely on voluntarism, removing any distinction between usury and interest, the just wage and price, unlimited acquisition of wealth and above all, the subordination of the coin to the logos contained in the *cultus*—these had all been thoroughly removed in favor of the gods of *Libertas*, nation, utopian progress and the love of money.

This century would show how true were the words of the Holy Spirit:

> Give me neither beggary, nor riches: give me only the necessaries of life: Lest perhaps being filled, I should be tempted to deny, and say: Who is the Lord? or being compelled by poverty, I should steal, and forswear the name of my God (Prov. xxx. 7-8).

Because power corrupts and money is the most common form of power, the Church always understood that money was merely a means to an end—the family. But nations were rapidly industrializing not for the sake of the family, but for the glory of the nation and the wealth of men.

In 1903, Pope Leo XIII went to his eternal reward at ninety-three. The conclave first elected Rampolla, but this was vetoed by the representatives from the Holy Roman Emperor (now Austrian Emperor), exercising the ancient right of cooperation between lay rulers and priests. His veto may reflect the rising tension between the empire and France, and Rampolla had favored France.

---

[4] These produced the so-called "Blue Laws" which forced businesses to close on Sunday.
[5] F. X. Lasance, *The Young Man's Guide* (Benziger Brothers, 1910), 475-482.
[6] John Savage, *Teenage: The Prehistory of Youth Culture: 1875-1945* (Penguin, 2008).

Rampolla was alleged to be a member of the occult sect, *Ordo Templi Orientis* although the evidence is not conclusive.[7] Whatever the case, he had guided the moderate policies of Pope Leo XIII and his episcopal descendants would all follow a moderate approach—Benedict XV, who would suppress the *Sodalitium Pianum*, Pius XII who would turn the Church toward America, John XXIII who would open Vatican II, and finally, Pope Francis.[8]

Meanwhile Englishman Aleister Crowley would be a public member of the *Ordo Templi Orientis*, and at the time of the conclave he was surrendering to a demon named Aiwass and creating his Satanic Bible, *The Book of the Law*. This evil book canonized voluntarism into its own religion with one commandment: "'Do what thou wilt' shall be the whole of the Law." This occultism was simply making *Libertas* public in what the fallen angels had worked to erect in the New York City harbor and permeate the hearts of every man, woman and child. Rock musicians like the Beatles would soon praise Crowley and his occultic voluntarism.[9]

So instead of Rampolla, the conclave elected an Italian peasant, Giuseppe Sarto, who took the name Pius X. He immediately revoked the right of veto, further alienating the temporal sword from Christendom as Bl. Pius IX had done. Yet following the encyclopedic scholarship of Pope Leo XIII, God chose this peasant to humble the pride of *knowledge falsely so called* (I Tim. vi. 20). Only a saint could prevent disaster now. Pope Pius viewed the looming militarization with a sober concern and made it his motto "to restore all things in Christ."[10]

Renewal of the *Cultus*

The distinguishing mark of his pontificate was his fatherly love of children. This would motivate all his actions as pope. He showed great care and tenderness in lowering the age to First Holy Communion but also zeal in his strong defense of his children against the wolves. He was known for

---

[7] The accusation is listed as "alleged" by OTO archivist Peter-Robert Koenig (Das OTO-Phaenomen, Germany 1994) who cites Georges Virebeau: *Prelats et Franc-Maçons*, Paris 1978.

[8] Randy Engel, *The Rite of Sodomy* (New Engel Publishing, 2012), vol. V, 1090-1093; *From Rome*, "'Team Bergoglio' and the Legacy of Cardinal Mariano Rampolla del Tindaro," (Jan 10, 2015) https://fromrome.info/2015/01/10/team-bergoglio-and-the-legacy-of-cardinal-mariano-rampolla-del-tindaro/>, accessed March 29, 2021.

[9] Aleister Crowley is on the cover of the Beatles' *Sgt. Pepper's Lonely Hearts' Club Band* (1967).

[10] Coulombe, *Vicars of Christ*, 314.

his great love of children, always carrying sweets for the little ones in the streets and gathering them to teach catechism and smile and laugh with gentleness and fatherly affection. He brought the children together at papal audiences and worked especially for their souls in his reforms. He was a true father. Pope Pius X would be an incorrupt saint.

His most conspicuous acts as pope regarded the *cultus*. He helped to eradicate the poison of Jansenist infiltration by promoting the frequent reception of Holy Communion. He continued the Gregorian chant revival to cleanse the celebration from secular music. But his greatest influence on the *cultus* was in coining the term "active participation."

As we said there existed a moderate and strict view regarding the liturgical movement pioneered by Guéranger. More than anything, it was fundamental that these two parties unite for the sake of the *cultus*. Pope Pius was strict but also very moderate by promoting frequent and worthy Communion, the most important participation in divine grace itself, but which was a significant change in custom.

Regarding active participation, the strict believed that participation was achieved by educating the faithful and elevating them to the liturgy while changing nothing of liturgical law and custom. The moderates believed in keeping the liturgy yet making minor changes to law and custom in order to achieve the fruitful effects of divine grace. The heretics, meanwhile, wanted Americanism—to conform the liturgy to the spirit of the world—as Pius VI had already noted and condemned in *Auctorem Fidei* against Pistoia in 1794.

But the phrase "active participation" could quickly be subsumed into anti-culture. Since dignity was power and everything was based on consent, it was very easy to define participation based on the laity singing more or doing other things in the liturgy.

Or, even if it was not a vocal participation, the use of the hand missal was promoted by the liturgical movement. The strict party deeply felt the liturgy and its rites but participated above all through *beauty*—visible and audible. The sacred rites of the Apostles passed down from tradition all came from *oral cultures* that communicated the metaphysical beauty of logos by visual and audible means, *not* through reading.

Most importantly for us to seize upon here is this aspect of the *cultus* because it is the aspect most important for children who cannot read. They can only see and hear. They learn language by hearing it. They learn behavior by seeing it. They know logos by means of beauty. This beauty is what converted St. Vladimir.

The liturgical movement was cleansing the audible beauty from secular music and restoring Gregorian chant and polyphony. With hand missals, it unlocked the riches of the sacred prayers passed down reverently by the elders of Christian culture. But there was also a danger in an excessive emphasis on reading and intellectual understanding of the liturgy by means of the hand missals. A growing attitude began to proliferate that those who participated silently without a hand missal were "spectators" and were not actually participating. It is easy for those who love the sacred rites to desire to open their riches to the faithful. But for an old, pious widow who does not read well but prays the Rosary at Mass, how will you do that? Or for all the children who cannot read, how will they appreciate the sublime poetry of *Lauda Sion*?

At the same time, with the increased secularization, many faithful indeed were completely ignorant of the liturgy or the feast days and what they meant. They were indeed silent spectators. The liturgical movement was attempting to raise them to true devotion at the Holy Sacrifice.

With these considerations, we need to also understand the centuries-old customs and cherished devotions of the faithful. These include traditional prayers inside and outside the liturgy—from the ocular communion, veneration, pious recitations, and meditations to passion plays, vigils, processions, pilgrimages and "the liturgy of the streets." This was no more apparent than in Holy Week, when the liturgy was fully integrated with the pious devotions of the faithful, creating the cherished days of Our Lord's Passion for every pious heart.

These devotions were fundamental to the spiritual culture of every Christendom throughout the world and had been for centuries. A very common custom was simply meditating on the reality of the Holy Mass by means of the Holy Rosary. Pope Pius X therefore revered this custom as well, saying that the Rosary during Mass was truly profitable, even though he also promoted a participation of the faithful that revolved around the words of the rite.[11]

But as the liturgical movement continued, more and more scholars began to discourage these pious devotions during the liturgy. At best, they lamented the loss that the faithful experienced in not knowing the immense riches of the sacred liturgy. At worst, they considered the faithful's prayers as inferior to their own ideas, lacking any pastoral love of souls and polluted with the errors of anti-culture. However, real renewal comes from preaching the Gospel, penance and divine grace.

Lamentably, even in the Vatican of the peasant saint there existed those who prevailed upon Pope Pius X to revise the divine office, where

---

[11] *Catechism of Pius X*, Question 490

they successfully imposed ideas that "radically altered the ancient arrangement of the Roman psalter" with the "summary abolition" of pious tradition.[12] "That a pope could discard ancient liturgical tradition by sole virtue of his own authority," writes Reid, "is found nowhere in liturgical history before Saint Pius X."[13]

This significantly changed the prayers of priests and all religious. As we noted, Popes Leo X and Urban VIII had tried similar ideas but their efforts had been rejected. When Pope Pius X did the same, the false spirit of Vatican I prevented any significant opposition, leading to a crucial precedent. "Lamentably, in a period where the prevalent ultramontanism led to the assumption that even the prudential judgements of popes were unquestionably correct, Saint Pius X contravened that part of the principle of liturgical reform that obliges even popes to respect objective liturgical Tradition and to develop it organically."[14] Fortunately, his change only effected the clergy and religious, and few of the faithful felt it. The liturgical movement, however, needed a synthesis between the moderates and the strict in order to avoid the dangers that lay ahead. Despite this minor difficulty regarding the breviary, the holy pontiff embodied the necessary synthesis on the whole.

The Earthly City

During this time Pope Pius X received and approved the organization of the pious Catholic Marc Sangnier at the Vatican.[15] His movement, *Le Sillon* was working to Christianize the Third French Republic in accordance with the directives of Pope Leo XIII. But the mask was soon torn off when the republic moved to attack the Christian culture and the clergy, provoking Pope Pius X's breaking off diplomat relations. What was worse, some of the members of *Le Sillon* began to promote the superstition of unlimited progress building the earthly city. As a result Pope Pius X was forced to suppress the movement. His words summed up the Two Swords building the City of God:

> The City cannot be built otherwise than as God has built it; society cannot be setup unless the Church lays the foundations and supervises the work; no, civilization is not something yet to be found, nor is the New City to be

---

[12] Reid, *Organic Development of the Liturgy*, 74-78.
[13] Ibid., 78
[14] Ibid.
[15] J. Caron, "Marc Sangnier," *New Catholic Encyclopedia* (2003), vol 12, 667.

built on hazy notions; it has been in existence and still is: it is Christian civilization, it is the Catholic City. It has only to be set up and restored continually against the unremitting attacks of insane dreamers, rebels and miscreants. *Omnia instaurare in Christo* [restore all things in Christ].[16]

It was one thing to promote Christian values in a republican system as Pope Leo XIII had advocated. It was an entirely different thing to accept wholesale the lies of anti-culture and the superstition of progress. Pope Pius saw the growth of extreme nationalism and "progress" and did everything he could to help the nations restore order.

Immediately proving his piety, Sangnier, who had spent his own fortune on the movement, immediately suppressed it, and Pope Pius X was deeply moved.[17] Many French Catholics opposed him in a monarchist organization called *Action Française*. One prominent member would be the French Dominican Reginald Garrigou-Lagrange who, in 1904, was attempting to create a Thomistic synthesis for the modern world. One of his first texts in this regard was *Le sens commun* ("Thomistic Common Sense") which addressed the development of doctrine.[18]

Meanwhile, the Russian Czar was granting new freedoms to his subjects to convert to Catholicism, and 250,000 Russian Orthodox left their schism to be reunited with Rome and another 200,000 Ukrainians.[19] In 1911, with the personal blessing of Pope Pius X, Leonid Feodorov, now reconciled to Rome with the help of Soloviev, was ordained the first Russian rite Catholic priest in five hundred years.[20] Missionaries were talking about the "conversion of Russia."[21] Meanwhile, the wealthy Jew

---

[16] Pius X, *Notre Charge Apostolique* (1910).
[17] "Sangnier's loyalty to the Church had never faltered, but in order to win over his anticlerical adversaries he had at times been conciliatory to the point of imprudence. He and his disciples submitted immediately to the Holy See and the pope was deeply moved by this proof of their loyalty." J. Caron, *op. cit.* Von Hildebrand, who knew Sangnier personally and worked with him for peace after the Great War, called him "an exemplary, orthodox Catholic, highly esteemed by Pius X" *The Charitable Anathema* (Roman Catholic Books: 1993), 29.
[18] In English as *Thomistic Common Sense: The Philosophy of Being and the Development of Doctrine*, trans. Matthew Minerd (Emmaus Academic, 2021).
[19] Robert Royal, *The Catholic Martyrs of the Twentieth Century* (New York: Crossroad Publishing, 2000), 45, 68.
[20] Paul Mailleux, S.J., *Blessed Leonid Feodorov* (Fitzwilliam, NH: Loreto Publications, 2017), 43.
[21] Ibid., 83; Jozef de Vocht, *Eternal Memory! Father Achiel Delaere* (Gravelbooks, 2005), 167-168.

Leon Trotsky and peasant Vladimir Lenin were organizing Marxism in Russia. To counter Marxism, Pope Pius X promoted labor unions to help the poor under the regime of the factory.

By that time France signed an alliance with Great Britain and Russia, forming the Allied Powers against the Central Powers (Germany, Austria, Italy). The alliances were built on the foundation of voluntarism and money. France was still seething from the siege of Paris by the Germans. The powerful were trying to find a way to start a war.

The Synthesis of All Heresies

The war of the spiritual sword—the conflict which will define our current crisis—began at this time. Europe had become significantly secularized, but the problem was that the people still had Christian custom and law. Divorce was still illegal. Adultery abhorrent. Fornication shameful. Even the Third Commandment was being enforced in some places and businesses had to shut down on Sunday. Even the cult of nation had a certain piety to it. The bones of Christian culture remained, waiting to be resurrected.

The scientism of Newton and now Darwin combined with the false historical criticism had put enormous pressure on Catholics in societies where Jews and Protestants had great influence—France, Germany, Belgium, The Netherlands and England. This was combined with the real work of the fourth renewal that was trying to synthesize hundreds of volumes of Patristics and other authors. This combination of truth and error helped the ideas of Loisy and Tyrell spread—they asserted the evolution of dogma, otherwise known as "Modernism." Dogma could evolve and change as it had from the beginning. Tyrell said correctly that the Church was not Thomistic per se, but then used this a pretext to invent his own doctrine.

Against this error, Pope Pius X unleashed the full force of his paternal love—the charitable anathema. He came down like a hammer on the heretical poison spreading in the Mystical Body of Christ.

Two things made the difference against Loisy and Tyrell—they were excommunicated and the Oath Against Modernism was enforced. The oath simply elaborated on the fundamental anathema from Vatican I against evolution of dogma. This action was the only effective means to stop the spread of Modernism in its tracks.

In order to do this, the saint was unafraid to be hated by a world gone mad. Those with an inferiority complex were embarrassed by this action, but those with faith to see the fundamental danger understood that his action was just. The Church had shown that the Greco-Roman renewal could only proceed while maintaining the same sense and the same understanding.

Tyrell went to France to teach and a young man named Teilhard de Chardin was there. Teilhard was in formation as a Jesuit from 1899-1911, just as Tyrell's prominence among the Jesuits was at its height.[22]

Teilhard was very familiar with the controversy, but distanced himself from Tyrell's movement and identified himself with "integrism" against "Modernism," even though his ambiguities with Original Sin would have the same results.[23] The strong superstition of progress was soon consuming Teilhard.

Pope Pius X funded a group called *Pianum Solidatum* to oppose the Modernists and suppress them. The difficulty with Modernism was that it harnessed all the important aspects of the fourth renewal. The Church was in full support of this renewal, but it had to proceed very gradually and organically, using the method of St. Thomas.

Pope Pius X defended the faith, but not everyone who fought in this just cause was a saint like him. According to his critics, Umberto Benigni, the head of the *Pianum Solidatum*, was prone to excess. Pope Pius X, admits Sire, ended up "imposing on the Church's middle ground a strict form of integrism."[24] O'Malley says it was because Benigni promoted not only orthodoxy, but monarchism, and if a man was an orthodox republican like Sangnier he also might be condemned as a "semi-Modernist."[25] For the destruction of Modernism and the fourth renewal, everything depended on implementation and execution. Tyrell died excommunicated but Loisy was still at large. A delicate balance was needed to promote the renewal and also suppress all Modernism.

But in the 1910s, the world was quickly disintegrating. Everyone was made to worship their nation and believe that they were headed for infinite progress in a utopia of the earthly city. Pope Pius X felt the opposite, and

---

[22] E. L. Boné, "Pierre Teilhard de Chardin," *New Catholic Encyclopedia* (2003), vol. 13, 788.
[23] Henri de Lubac asserts the claims about Teilhard being anti-Modernist in *The Faith of Teilhard de Chardin* trans. René Hague, (London: Burns and Oates, 1965), 179.
[24] "Integrism" was generally the term used for the strict party at this time. Sire, *Phoenix from the Ashes*, 139.
[25] See Umberto Benigni, *New Catholic Encyclopedia*, John O'Malley, *What Happened at Vatican II* (Belknap Harvard University Press, 2008), 68-71.

pleaded with all nations to restore order. He feared "a great conflict, and Armageddon."[26] He believed that the Antichrist was already on earth.[27]

In 1913, Pius X was seventy-eight and suffered a heart attack. In April 1914, on Holy Saturday, Dietrich Von Hildebrand and his family were baptized. The following June, Austrian archduke Franz Ferdinand, knowing he would be murdered, was piously completing the First Friday devotion to the Sacred Heart.[28] On the twenty-eighth he was shot and went to his eternal reward, allowing the world's leaders to rapidly mobilize their armies to execute their plans for war. On August second the Holy Father pleaded for peace. The next day, Germany declared war on France and invaded Belgium. The next day, Britain declared war on Germany. On August 12, Austria was invading Serbia and on the seventeenth, Russia invaded the German Empire. A few days later on the twentieth of August, Pope Pius X died.

The war of the spiritual sword was just beginning. The war of the temporal sword was next.

---

[26] Coulombe, *Vicars of Christ*, 314.
[27] Ibid.
[28] This according to Charles Coulombe in an interview with Taylor Marshall, *The Taylor Marshall Show* (Oct 20, 2020) <https://taylormarshall.com/2020/10/542-blessed-charles-austria-emperor-father-saint-charles-coulombe-podcast.html>, accessed March 28, 2021. See Charles Coulombe, *Blessed Charles of Austria* (TAN, 2020).

XXVII

THE SUICIDE OF EUROPE

By Christmas, 1914, World War I had gone on for just a few short months. Having formed their citizens with one national language to worship the petty earthly city, the Allied and Central powers set to work psychologically manipulating their citizens to now see the enemy nations as sub-human. Every excess of war gave the newspapers a fresh opportunity for the department of War propaganda, especially the atrocities committed by the Germans.[1]

Pope Benedict XV, calling the conflict "the Suicide of Europe," had urged a ceasefire for Christmas. Almost alone among the nations, the heir to imperial throne and later Holy Roman Emperor, Bl. Charles of Austria, strove to promote Benedict's exhortations and bring peace.

Whether or not the soldiers heard of what the pontiff had said, the power of Christian culture compelled the men to hold widespread truces for Christmas. German, French and English soldiers agreed to lay down their weapons and feast together for Christmas. These truces were truly a movement of "the people" who, Veuillot would have said, "when given the opportunity, had always spoken out against the revolution, while the bourgeoisie had continuously encouraged it."[2]

But since 1776 when the Americans wanted to increase the bloodshed on Christmas, the regime of the anti-culture was rooting out the *cultus* from

---

[1] Von Hildebrand called Germany's invasion of Belgium in August as "an atrocious crime" (Alice von Hildebrand, *Soul of a Lion*, 221). The German soldiers then committed unspeakable acts against civilians in Belgium, leading to their enemies exploding these things into effective war propaganda.
[2] Rao's words citing Louis Veuillot, *Mélanges* (Oeuvres complete, iii series, 1933), ix, 384; Also, xiv, 298-302 in Rao "Louis Veuillot and the Catholic 'Intransigence': a Re-evaluation."

every heart. The European nations would not be funding statues and paintings of the Christmas truces of 1914. Instead they increased the propaganda.

Thus the war raged on with the express purpose of destroying Christian sentiment among the armies and the general populace and erecting the god of nation above all. The British Crown paid writers such as Chesterton and Belloc to invent lies to support the war effort. Belloc lamented to Chesterton in 1917 that he found it necessary to "lie damnably in the interests of the nation."[3] Meanwhile, a young Bavarian officer named Adolf Hitler was bitterly opposed to having Christmas with the enemy.[4] In Russia, the Czar forced Bl. Leonid to abandon his parish of nearly eight hundred Russian Catholics and go into exile to Siberia. The Czar could allow freedom, but not for Russian rite Catholics, who threatened the ideology of *Roma*. In Siberia, the saintly Feodorov offered more suffering for the conversion of Russia.[5]

Back in Germany Dietrich von Hildebrand, in his mid-twenties, was working to help the wounded. His German comrades were infuriated when he helped the enemy and spoke to them in French.[6] English Catholic Christopher Dawson, also then in his mid-twenties, would later write that the nations had "ignored the existence of a European culture" and "attempted to build a new world on different foundations."[7]

The French Jesuit Teilhard de Chardin was on the front lines in Morocco as a stretcher-bearer. He was having a spiritual experience on the front lines where blood was shed and families destroyed, which he would soon describe as "nostalgia for the Front," "a plenitude of being and of something more than human... carrying the world of man towards its new destiny."[8] The Ottoman Empire sided with the Central Powers and Muhammadans were able to use the opportunity to massacre 1,500,000 Armenian Christians, 700,000 Greek Christians and 275,000 Syriac

---

[3] This appears to be at a time before Belloc was very pious. Letter to G. K. Chesterton (Dec. 12, 1917) in Robert Speaight, *Life of Hilaire Belloc* (New York: Farrar, Straus & Cudahy, 1957), 355-356.

[4] Thomas Vinciguerra, "The Truce of Christmas, 1914," *The New York Times* (Dec 25, 2005).

[5] Mailleux, *op. cit.*, 103, 108.

[6] Alice von Hildebrand, *Soul of a Lion*, 151-196.

[7] Christopher Dawson, *The Judgement of the Nations* (Washington, DC: Catholic University of America Press, 2011), 49.

[8] Letters dated September 23rd and 25th, 1917. Teilhard de Chardin, *The Making of a Mind: Letters from a Soldier-Priest 1914–1919* (London: Collins, 1965).

Christians.[9] Armenian Catholic Blessed Archbishop Ignatius Maloyan and 447 Companions and Chaldean Catholic Bishop Servant of God Flavianus Michael Malke won the crown of martyrdom.[10]

By 1916, the Angel of Portugal was appearing to three children, showing them "the Body and Blood of Jesus Christ, horribly insulted by ungrateful men," teaching them to pray and offer sufferings for the "reparation for the sinners."[11]

But by Christmas of 1916, there were no more truces. The calls for peace from Pope Benedict XV and Emperor Charles were drowned by the false crusade of earthly cities and their psychological warfare. Whole monuments to culture centuries old were being razed in the name of petty earthly cities. The bloodshed continued.

While this was happening, government leaders in Mexico were continuing their futile struggle against Our Lady of Guadalupe begun in 1810. Germany maintained a delicate peace with the United States after American citizens were killed in a German attack.[12] Meanwhile, Lenin and Trotsky were plotting.

The Year of Our Lord, 1917

In February, the Mexican leaders resorted to desperate measures and imposed a Communist constitution on the Mexican people. A few weeks later the peasants revolted in Russia, leading to the abdication of Czar Nicholas, and Lenin and Trotsky saw their moment. But so did Ven. Andrey Sheptytsky, a Ukrainian Catholic bishop, who restored Bl. Leonid from exile and consecrated him as bishop.[13] While the Bolsheviks were seeking yet another earthly city, Sheptytsky was planting the mustard seed for the conversion of Russia.

But while the Marxist conspiracy was forming in the east, a Masonic conspiracy was forming in the west. In that same month in Rome, Masons were celebrating their bicentennial by marching up to St. Peter's Basilica with banners saying "Satan must reign in the Vatican. The Pope will be his

---

[9] Robert Spencer, *History of Jihad*, 291.
[10] Bieszad, *Lions of the Faith*, 268-270.
[11] William Thomas Walsh, *Our Lady of Fatima* (New York: Image Books, 1990), 36-42.
[12] This was the infamous sinking of the Lusitania in 1915. The British were using ships of civilians to carry military weapons.
[13] Mailleux, *op. cit.*, 117-132.

slave."[14] The young Pole named St. Maximilian burned with the true crusading spirit to see his Holy Father mocked and the usurper exalted. It was "Freemasonry," he said, who was the demonic enemy, for "their deceits have been spread throughout the world, in different disguises. But with the same goal—religious indifference and weakening of moral forces, according to their basic principle—'We will conquer the Catholic Church not by argumentation, but rather with moral corruption.'"[15]

The man of God understood the crusade that was necessary. "In the face of such attacks of the enemies of the Church of God, are we to remain inactive? Is that all we can do—complain and cry? No! Every one of us has a holy obligation to personally hurl back the assaults of the foe."[16] When he heard the story of how Our Lady converted the Jew Alphonse Ratisbonne, he burned with holy zeal. It is said he chose to celebrate his first Mass in the same Church where she appeared to Ratisbonne. But in 1917, Our Lady was about to appear again.

On the third of March, the newspapers reported that the Germans were plotting with the Mexicans against the United States, which became the opportunity for the United States to increase the bloodshed.[17] On Good Friday, 1917, the pope led the faithful: "Let us pray, dearly beloved, for the holy Church of God: that our God and Lord may be pleased to give it peace, keep its unity and preserve it throughout the world: subjecting to it principalities and powers."[18] But a few hours later, the American Empire declared war on Germany and entered the Great War.

That very week, Bishop Leonid was boldly leading Russian Catholic Easter processions, together with Latin Bishop Edward Ropp.[19] While the whole world was soaked in blood, the joyous song rang out through the streets of St. Petersburg: *Christ is risen from the dead, trampling down death by death, and upon those in the tombs bestowing life!*

The United States hired Edward Bernays, the Jewish nephew of Sigmund Freud for their propaganda. He faced a difficult task: convincing German-Americans, who were at that time very numerous and influential, to support a war against Germany. But he used the scientism psychology

---

[14] Bro. Francis M. Kalvelage, ed., *Kolbe: Saint of the Immaculata* (Franciscans of the Immaculate, 2001), 31.
[15] Ibid.
[16] Ibid., 32.
[17] Coulombe, *Puritan's Empire*, 338.
[18] Good Friday, Solemn Prayers, Traditional Holy Week.
[19] According to Mailleux, the Russian Catholics celebrated Easter on the prior Sunday of that same week, or April second, 1917. This was due to the Julian Calendar. Mailleux, *op. cit.*, 119.

of his uncle to conduct what he termed "Psychological Warfare" to manipulate the populace.[20]

Pope Benedict condemned the "carnage solely for economic reasons" and called for peace without revenge (falsely called "reparations").[21] President Wilson rejected his plan and, drawing on the propaganda, preached that Americans were fighting to deliver Germany from their "ruthless masters," making the world "safe for democracy."[22] At this point the United States had trampled for generations on the African and Native American cultures and the second Christendom with the regime of anti-culture, and still the pride of the American ideology could not be stronger. Wilson advocated the "removal of economic barriers" meaning the freedom for American business in Germany, which would have a devastating effect after the war.[23] The pope and president were preaching their gospels. The war would decide which one would master the world.

And then the Queen herself appeared. On May 13, she came to ask the children if they were willing "to endure all the suffering that He may please to send you, as an act of reparation for the sins by which He is offended, and to ask for the conversion of sinners?"[24] The pious children consented to the cross, and she said to them, "You will have much to suffer. But the grace of God will be your comfort," and that they must pray the Rosary every day for the end of the war.

On May 31, the Russian Catholic Synod of St. Petersburg commenced which organized the Russian Catholic Church under Bl. Leonid and, in its canons, formally submitted:

> To the patronage of the Most Holy Queen, our Mother of God who has not shared in Original Sin, all the territory of Great Russia...we beseech the all high to make those

---

[20] "During the war years, Bernays joined the army of publicists rallied under the banner of the CPI and concentrated on propaganda efforts aimed at Latin American business interests. Within this vast campaign of 'psychological warfare,' as he described it, Bernays—like others of his generation—began to develop an expanded sense of publicity and its practical uses." Stuart Ewen, *PR! A Social History of Spin* (New York: Basic Books, 1996), 162-163. See also Alan Axelrod, *Selling the Great War: The Making of American Propaganda* (Palgrave Macmillan, 2009).
[21] Pope Benedict XV, Peace Plan.
[22] Dos Passos, 282 in Coulombe, *Puritan's Empire*, 339.
[23] Wilson's "Fourteen Points."
[24] Walsh, 50-2

> dioceses obedient to the Church of Ancient Rome, the Mother of all Orthodox Churches.
>
> Mindful of the words of our Saviour and Lord Jesus Christ: "Pray therefore the Lord of the Harvest to send forth laborers into his harvest" (Matt. 9:38) we beseech Him to grant our Church as great a number as possible of great saints, apostles, martyrs, and confessors for the achievement of the union of all Christian in our Country with the Holy Catholic Church.
>
> Upon all priests is imposed the obligation to beg each day for the favor of this grace.[25]

In the opinion of the author, the Bolshevik revolution was the response to this mustard seed. Nothing but the greatest evil could challenge this consecration of Holy Russia for the sake of her conversion and the liberation of the Russian people from the regime of *Roma*.

In July Our Lady gave the children a vision of the fires of hell "where the souls of the poor sinners go," telling them that God is establishing devotion to the Immaculate Heart of Mary "to save them" from eternal damnation. She said the Great War will end but "if they do not stop offending God, another worse one will begin in the reign of Pius XI" prophesying "a night illuminated by an unknown light" as the sign that God is "going to punish the world for its crimes by means of war." To avert the wrath of God, she called for the consecration of Russia and the Communion of Reparation on the Five First Saturdays.

> If they listen to my requests, Russia will be converted and there will be peace. If not, she will scatter her errors through the world, provoking wars and persecutions of the Church... In the end my Immaculate Heart will triumph. The Holy Father will consecrate Russia to me, and it will be converted and a certain period of peace will be granted to the world... In Portugal the dogma of the Faith will always be preserved.[26]

---

[25] "The Synod of Petrograd" (1917), Canons, 9-11, published with permission from archivist Rev. Ussas in *The Ark* (Aug-September, 1953), vol. 8, no. 8-9.
[26] Walsh, *op. cit.*, 80-2.

The Apparitions culminated with a great public miracle on October thirteenth, witnessed by thousands and bishop Eugenio Pacelli, the future Pope Pius XII. Within months, Russia was convulsing in the Bolshevik revolution as Marxists and liberal Jews united to impose a new and more terrible *Roma:* Communist anti-culture on the Russian people.

The Death of Fatherhood

God sent a plague to humble man, the Spanish Flu, which infected millions, hindering the ability of the earthly city to exalt itself. At last, on St. Martin's Day 1918, November 11th, the armistice was signed, but the war was not over. The Allies quickly moved to enforce a strict blockade to cut off food supply. Hundreds of thousands of German families starved to death or died of disease.[27] The German leaders had blood on their own hands, but they had no choice but to come to terms. The French were able to make the peace conference on January 18th, 1919, seeking revenge against their humiliation by the Germans in 1871. The press reported that Bernays was sent to keep up "a worldwide propaganda to disseminate American accomplishments and ideals."[28]

This inaugurates the third phase of the American Empire, from 1918-present. The Americans had decimated the second Christendom of the Americas and imposed anti-culture on the ancient peoples of Africa and countless native tribes because of the superstition of Manifest Destiny. Continuing the same advance, the United States would now pressure countries across the world by bloodshed, economic coercion and propaganda to accept their message of *Libertas* and its political and economic system of anti-culture.[29] Using much the same means with the Communist form of anti-culture, the Soviet Union would do the same until 1990, while the Chinese Communist empire will rise to join them 1949-present.

Since the United States rejected the pope's peace plan of no war revenge, and with the Allied starvation of Germany families, the Germans were forced to sign the Treaty of Versailles in 1919, which punished them

---

[27] The numbers are still disputed but estimates range from 100,000-700,000. S.L. Bane, *The Blockade of Germany after the Armistice* 1918–1919 (Stanford University Press, 1942); C. Paul Vincent, *The politics of hunger: The Allied Blockade of Germany, 1915–1919* (Athens, OH: Ohio University Press, 1985).
[28] Bernays was seen at this time as an agent of propaganda. He disputed this phrasing by the press in *Biography of an Idea* (Open Road Media, 2015), ch. 11.
[29] As always, for the history of this period the reader is recommended to Charles Coulombe, *Puritan's Empire*.

for a war for which all sides were to blame. This treaty had a "disastrous effect on the German economy" and "created a situation ripe for the emergence of the National Socialist movement."[30] Blessed Charles of Austria was forced out and died a holy death in exile. The president of the United States, according to Coulombe, had pushed the monarchs from their thrones in the name of "freedom," which paved the way for Stalin and Hitler.[31]

---

[30] Alice von Hildebrand, *Soul of a Lion*, 197.

[31] This according to Charles Coulombe, citing Winston Churchill, in an interview with Taylor Marshall, *The Taylor Marshall Show* (Oct 20, 2020) <https://taylormarshall.com/2020/10/542-blessed-charles-austria-emperor-father-saint-charles-coulombe-podcast.html>, accessed March 28, 2021. Charles Coulombe, *Blessed Charles of Austria* (TAN, 2020).

XVIII

THE FIRST SEXUAL REVOLUTION

"The reaction was reminiscent of a life-saving maneuver on a choking body."[1] Europe had indeed committed suicide, but while she lay dying, she was jolted back to life. The Catholic culture of New Orleans suddenly burst onto the scene but was twisted by one thing—money.

It is difficult for us to understand the explosion that occurred in 1919 in Euro-American society, but the change was evident in the largest cities without "economic barriers" like America wanted: Berlin, London, Paris, New York City. Suddenly everywhere the music, alcohol and Dionysian spirit were flowing. The slang term for "fornication" came to be used for the new sounds—"Jass," later known as Jazz. "Harlem's famous image spread until it swarmed nightly with white people from all over the world," says Malcolm X, producing an economy of sin which "catered to white people's money."[2] Rich whites were funding Blacks to, in the words of Langston Hughes, "be primitive."[3] But these Americans had a vision of "Africa" that came from the Curse of Ham ideology, not reality. They wanted to use and abuse Blacks and African culture for sexual revolution and rationalize it as a moral crusade against Black oppression.[4]

---

[1] Juliet Nicolson, *The Great Silence: Britain from the Shadow of the First World War to the Dawn of the Jazz Age* (Grove Press, 2011), ch. 10.
[2] Malcolm X, *The Autobiography of Malcolm X as Told to Alex Haley* (Ballatine Books: 1964), 85.
[3] Langston Hughes, *The Big Sea: An Autobiography* (Hill and Wang: 1940), 325 in E. Michael Jones, *Dionysius Rising: The Birth of Cultural Revolution out of the Spirit of Music* (South Bend, IN: Fidelity Press, 2012), 77.
[4] Pieterse discusses how the sexualization of African men and women, both practiced in America and Europe differently, "began to reconverge" with the Jazz era in Britain, France, America and elsewhere, showing that the "correlation exists between sexual politics and racial politics... To the extent that 'black' denotes libido, in the subliminal code of western culture, if libido is allowed freer

The greatness of African music is seen in its climate of abundant wildlife and thus animal skins, and a culture of rhythm, dancing and singing. From the ancient Ethiopian civilization to the universities of the Mali empire, the rhythm of drums act as melody, which creates a unique cultural music. This is shown exquisitely in the rhythmic blend of traditional kora music, as heard today with Mamadou Diabate or the percussion orchestras of drum masters like Doudou N'Diaye Rose. These sounds blended the logos of *volk* music with high artistic beauty.[5]

But from the tribes of Celts and Huns in Europe, the bushmen of west Africa and the Korean civilization, there was a form of music that was used for the occult in most every culture. The shaman and his shamanic music was designed not to elevate the intellect and culture to logos, but induce an emotional state to allow demons to take control. The shamanic music focused on thrusting beats and moaning to produce an emotional intoxication from the music itself.

In the Catholic Caribbean, African styles blended with European to create the Afro-Cuban blend, the native Haitian and New Orleans sounds, among others. But with the public *cultus* providing the divine grace, these movements could organically develop and be cleansed of any shamanic content and help create Christian peoples.

But because the second Christendom was poisoned with slavery, the development of divine grace between African and European was slowed and tainted by the love of money. And as the United States gradually dismantled the second Christendom, the Catholic organic development was arrested when the public *cultus* was removed from New Orleans. Slavery promoted the lie that African culture was "hypersexualized."[6] Without the *cultus* and Sacramental Marriage, a long legacy of fornication between whites and blacks could be felt even in the most rural and traditional

---

rein, colour may not be such an issue either." This also included Feminism, so that Pieterse can conclude that there "may, then, be a nexus between sexual liberation, the emancipation of women and that of blacks and 'others' generally." This mixture of sinful passion with zealous crusading against actual injustice is the crucial point to understand the sexual revolutions even into our own day. Jan Nederveen Pieterse, *White on Black: Images of Africa and Blacks in Western Popular Culture* (Yale University Press, 1995), 187

[5] For an introduction to the aesthetics of music according to Von Hildebrand, see T. S. Flanders, "The Logos of Music," *The Meaning of Catholic* <https://www.meaningofcatholic.com/2021/10/01/the-logos-of-music/>.

[6] Whitford, *The Curse of Ham in the Early Modern Era* 122-133; Steven C. Tracy, *Hot Music, Ragmentation, and the Bluing of American Literature* (University of Alabama Press, 2015), 301ff.

THE FIRST SEXUAL REVOLUTION

villages in the United States.[7] Meanwhile, the revolutionaries in Europe were searching for musical styles to promote revolution, like the pagan Nietzsche who wanted something "African" and the Jew Schönberg who tried to alter the logos of music by creating the twelve tone system to impose sexualized voluntarism.[8]

At the moment when Europe was devastated and the United States was going global, the love of money accentuated any part of Jazz that was the most sexualized, most shamanic, and most profitable. This was the birth of *popular shamanism*, which was a massive industry that sold musically induced emotional addiction, sexualized as much as possible. "Harlem places crawled with white people. These whites were just mad for Negro 'Atmosphere,'" recalls Malcolm X, "I saw the white man's morals with my own eyes. I even made my living to guide him to the sick things he wanted."[9] Notwithstanding this perversion, Jazz continued to develop and created great beauty, and some Jazz musicians would dedicate their art to the glory of God. There was a very unique and powerful musicality to the music which became potent for connoisseurs of high art. But this beauty was not as profitable and was eventually marginalized from the mainstream, popular shamanism of the dance halls. This allowed popular shamanism to be a leading force of anti-culture.

The mark which shows this is that there was immediate generational disintegration. Jazz helped create a rebellious youth culture which then restlessly re-created a new rebellion in every generation. The "lindy-hop" sound was created by 1927, and by 1938 the thrusting rhythm was being isolated to create the "back beat," which helping to create the swing music of the 1940s.[10] Every new generation would have its own sexualized music which helped disconnect them from their parents in a moral rebellion to become enslaved to corruption. The Black family was being destroyed again for the sake of unclean lusts, but this was being created by Blacks and Whites both worshipping money. The legacy of popular shamanism dominates our world even today.

---

[7] Malcolm X, *op. cit.*, 92.
[8] Schönberg composed his opera *Moses und Aaron* (1932) in this twelve-tone system, which, according to its stage directions, included a ritual murder of "four naked virgins" whose blood is poured on the altar, and then an "erotic orgy" takes place on stage. Jones, *Dionysius Rising*, 47-90, 91-124. On beauty nevertheless present within Schönberg's work, see Roger Scruton, *The Aesthetics of Music* (Oxford, 1997), 53-54, 239-307.
[9] Malcolm X, 96, 94.
[10] Ibid., 86.

Masonic Anti-Culture and the Uglification of the World

As this began, women were being commoditized further in the new "moving pictures" of Hollywood. Studios immediately realized they could make enormous profits by producing pornographic movies. These shocked the consciences of the Protestant majority in the United States, but the innumerable sects were too divided to influence society, exactly as James Madison predicted. It was the coin free from logos that created and governed public morality, not *cultus* and not the family. The cultural momentum was rapidly shifting for the little children transforming everything in an instant.[11]

At the same time, woman's voting rights were being passed around the world. Women asserted that their dignity was based on power, and so voluntarism entered the marriage and a contest of power continued to increase in the home and in society. The family was breaking down ever more rapidly, but the Puritan spirit of America thought the answer was not the *cultus*, but to outlaw alcohol. This was a disaster as the young adults engaging in fornication in the Jazz scene now openly rebelled against the law of the land and their parents, urging on the generational disintegration that endures to this day. The National Reform Association had failed to enthrone Christ as King of the Nation, and the money interests now were defining society.

Meanwhile, in 1922 Walter Lippman published *Public Opinion*, explaining that it was the duty of the leaders in a democracy to manipulate the irrational masses to do the right thing. Edward Bernays was making a name for himself turning the techniques of wartime "psychological warfare" into peacetime "public relations." He would explain his 1923 book *Crystallizing Public Opinion* by praising the "temples, paintings and statues" of Ancient Roman propaganda to "build goodwill with the public."[12] In 1929, he was paid to use psychological manipulation on a massive scale against women, convincing them to buy cigarettes as "torches of freedom," playing on the ideology of dignity as power. They now had the technology to accomplish propaganda on a broad scale, to imprint their will onto the minds of young men and women and urge an economy of effeminacy, addicting everyone to instant pleasure of every kind. In the Jazz bars, female singers were paid to perform topless or naked, while the pornographic films were making enormous profits.

---

[11] Modris Eksteins, *Rites of Spring: The Great War and the Birth of the Modern Age* (Mariner Books, 2000).
[12] Edward L. Bernays, *Crystalizing Public Opinion*, New Ed. (New York: Lighthouse Publishing Corporation, 1961), xi-xii.

Thus women were used for money whether it meant "empowering" them or using them for lust. As a result, beauty was in decline throughout Euro-America. Even Church architecture was being transformed into the mechanized aesthetic that imitated machines. Cities were being built whose design had no beauty but only compartmentalization.[13] It was the uglification of the world.

The ideology of Providential Capitalism still promotes the idea that the first Sexual Revolution was a time of economic prosperity (the "Roaring Twenties"). The scientism of Freud spread the idea that it was part of mental health to unleash all emotions and impose your will, especially sexually. (Freud and the reform party of Jews in Psychology would overshadow the Jews doing psychology according to logos, like Viktor Frankl and Erik Erikson.) Sanger promoted the scientism of eugenics with her motto: "Birth Control: To Create a Race of Thoroughbreds."[14] This was tied closely with the scientism of overpopulation, as if God's command to "be fruitful and multiply" was too much for Him to handle. Sanger promoted forced mutilation by the government, which was then imposed by two dozen states in America and confirmed by the Supreme Court, inspiring a young Adolf Hitler.[15]

Marxist Anti-Culture

While business was promoting the Sexual Revolution in the west, the government was promoting the same thing in Soviet Russia.[16] The Soviets openly promoted "Sexual Revolution in Russia" by means of feminism, divorce, sodomy, and child murder. As anti-culture had already done for five generations, the bonds of the family were subordinated to voluntarism as the definition of justice. "A society based on these principles," wrote Dr. Grigory Batkis of the Soviet Social Hygiene Institute,

---

[13] E. Michael Jones, *Living Machines: Modern Architecture and the Rationalization of Sexual Misbehavior* (South Bend, IN: Fidelity Press, 2012), 29-36, *passim*.

[14] Marco and Wiker, *Architects of the Culture of Death*, 298.

[15] Timothy F. Murphy and Marc A. Lappé, eds., *Justice and the Human Genome Project* (University of California Press, 1994), 17-18; cf. Edwin Black, *War Against the Weak: Eugenics and America's Campaign to Create a Master Race* (Dialog Press, 2012); Alison Bashford and Philippa Levine, eds., *The Oxford Handbook of the History of Eugenics* (Oxford University Press, 2010).

[16] Igor S. Kon, *The Sexual Revolution in Russia*, trans. James Riordan (The Free Press, 1995), 51-66.

> Would be a society of harmony and love of life. Today, we have already seen the liberation of love from all political and economic constraints. Free love in Russia is not some kind of rampant and wild self-realisation but rather a relation between two free and independent human beings.[17]

What mattered was not logos, but whether two parties consented to something. Voluntarism was becoming the new principle of moral order just as it was in every economic contract.

Meanwhile, Lenin and Trotsky pioneered the labor camp to "liquidate" their enemies.[18] Nearly 200,000 Russian Catholics disappeared in Soviet Russia from 1917 to 1925, virtually eradicating the Church there in favor of the Communist state church.[19] Bishop Leonid was sent to the Gulag, and the prayer of the Synod of St. Petersburg was answered as untold thousands obtained the glorious crown. Meanwhile, Wall Street invested indiscriminately in the Masonic or Marxist Sexual Revolution.[20] Business was sin, and business was booming.

The family was now under attack in a new way, for men were now being presented with an entire economy to be addicted to pleasures. This was a revolutionary era which was driven by the love of money. The crucial difference was that generational disintegration had been introduced. The "teenagers" who had been separated from their parents and left idle were now the target of an advanced marketing campaign to sell them fornication and lust. From this moment the bond between generations is severed and historians will separate out the generations in the twentieth century between the "Lost Generation" of this era to the "GI Generation," "Silent Generation," "Baby Boomers," "Generation X," and on and on. This generational isolation was fueled by marketers trying to isolate the youth from their parents in order to use them for money. It will be a serious blow to the family in the modern era.

---

[17] Grigory Batkis, *The Sexual Revolution in Russia*, trans. by editors at *In Defense of* Marxism from the German translation by Stephanie Theilhaber, 1925; Published by Dr. Felix A. Theilhaber – Pamphlet IV, 1925 <https://www.marxist.com/the-sexual-revolution-in-russia.htm>, accessed March 20, 2021.
[18] The infamous gulag, memorialized by Solzhenitsyn.
[19] Robert Royal, *Catholic Martyrs of the Twentieth Century*, 51
[20] Antony C. Sutton, *Wall Street and the Bolshevik Revolution: The Remarkable True Story of the American Capitalists Who Financed the Russian Communists* (Clairview Books, 2012).

Dawson observed at this time that the Soviet and American empires were both promoting a gospel wherein "civilisation is being uprooted from its foundations in nature and tradition" because both empires practiced "the same cult of the machine and the same tendency to subordinate every other side of human life to economic activity."[21] And this, of course, was merely "the tail-end of the great Liberal assault on authority and social tradition which had its origins in the eighteenth century."[22] And thus, after the monarchy was finally destroyed, the spirit of anti-culture was coalescing into one voluntarism of power in the very heart of all peoples—the family. Feminism formed the one spirit of providential capitalism and Communism—both defined dignity as power, and the unborn holocaust would be the result in both systems. Their unity of negation was now clearly seen. It did not matter if the government was republican, oligarchic, or Communist, as long as dignity was power and the public *cultus* was suppressed. The new idols were being erected from the capital to the kitchen.

The Weakening Unity among Elders

In 1924, Pope Pius XI repeated what his predecessors had been saying for generations.

> These manifold evils in the world were due to the fact that the majority of men had thrust Jesus Christ and his holy law out of their lives; that these had no place either in private affairs or in politics: and we said further, that as long as individuals and states refused to submit to the rule of our Savior, there would be no really hopeful prospect of a lasting peace among nations.[23]

Our Lady and the angels wanted the Church to arise to this new crusade, which helped institute the Feast of Christ the King for His rule over souls and society. But the Vatican was strained over the *cultus* when the divisions

---

[21] Christopher Dawson, *Enquiries into Religion and Culture* (Washington, DC: Catholic University of America Press, 2009), 214-215.
[22] Ibid., 217.
[23] Pius XI, *Quas Primas* (1924).

in the liturgical movement continued to increase after the Great War, as the moderates and the strict debated over liturgical renewal.[24]

This was particularly a reflection of the deepening division among Catholics in political life. The moderates who supported some form of Christian democracy also sought to make changes to the rite itself. The strict supported the monarchy and were opposed to any changes.

As the United States grew in influence in the Church, the monarchical mindset was losing influence. The ideas of Americanism were spreading. In 1922 a prominent German American Catholic could complain that "[these ideas] are wide-spread and constitute a grave danger to Catholicity in a country where so many are inclined to put 'patriotism' above religion."[25] The superstition of unlimited progress was spreading in Europe with Teilhard de Chardin, while in France a new generational disintegration was forming a bitter rivalry between the traditional advocates of *Action Française* and the partisans of a new social order, which continued the division since 1801.[26]

The best of the moderates wanted the success of the fourth Greco-Roman renewal. They wanted to restore the Patristic sources and especially reverse the legacy of Latinizations against the Eastern Catholics who were then shedding their blood against Communists rather than forsake Rome. But other moderates wanted to mix these good efforts with the unlimited progress promoted by the United States and Teilhardianism. Now that the public *cultus* had been removed from across Euro-America, the situation was similar to Lord Baltimore and Fr. Andrew White centuries ago in the United States. The moderates were uniting with non-Catholics of the same political and social views, but they needed to unite with the strict to avoid falling into the extremes of anti-culture.

The strict, for their part, were attempting to defend the old Christian social order of king, coin, and kitchen. Veterans of the Great War were

---

[24] Reid, *Oranic Development of the Liturgy*, 73-144; Fr. Didier Bonneterre, *The Liturgical Movement: Roots, Radicals, Results* (Kansas City, MO: Angelus Press, 2002), 19-32; in particular the reader is recommended to read this crucial study: Carol Byrne, "Dialogue Mass: A Plea for Silent Participation in the Liturgy," *Tradition In Action* (Feb 26, 2014), <https://www.traditioninaction.org/HotTopics/f073_Dialogue_1.htm>, accessed March 29, 2021.

[25] Commenting on calls to democratize the church. Arthur Preuss, *The Fortnightly Review*, Vol. XXIX, No. 17 (Sep. 1, 1922), 324.

[26] Jon Kirwan, *An Avant-garde Theological Generation: The Nouvelle Théologie and the French Crisis of Modernity* (United Kingdom: Oxford University Press, 2018), 96-134.

arising to lead the people in defense against the Sexual Revolution. The greatest of these at this time was Benito Mussolini, who was gaining power over Italy by 1922.[27] Moderates still view him as a tyrant, while the strict favored him against the Sexual Revolution, notably Belloc.[28] This was the beginning of the movement known as fascism.

Dawson would observe by 1936 that "there seems no doubt" that the social teachings of Popes Leo XIII and Pius XI "have far more affinity with fascism than with those of either [America] Liberalism or Socialism."[29] Yet "there still seems a wide gap between the Catholic and fascist ideals of the State" because the Fascist state does not allow for "the individual, the family, the Church" to have their own "autonomous spheres of activity and their independent rights."[30]

The problem was that the good efforts of the fourth Greco-Roman renewal were mixed with the poison of anti-culture. Some who had the good intention to restore patristic sources also wanted to use this as a pretext to join the unlimited progress.

While the moderates were willing to unite with the superstition of unlimited progress of Masons and Marxists, the strict were willing to unite with Fascism even if it is was secular. These movements were pulling the Church apart at its very roots. The Catholic Church alone had the organization, leadership and moral tradition to confront the sexualization of the economy. But the existing divisions were exacerbated after the war as the generations were rapidly disintegrating.

Meanwhile, the third party, the heretics, wanted to change any and every doctrine of the theological or social order. Their allies were the liberal Jews and neo-pagans, with added force from new occult movements like Crowley's wicked *Thelema* cult. Men of God could see something ugly arising.

Leading the crusade for the whole Church, the pious Mexicans began a just war against their government to restore the order of Christ the King in their society. It perfectly combined the gentle love of the Indian for Our

---

[27] John Pollard, "Pius XI's Promotion of the Italian Model of Catholic Action in the World-Wide Church," *The Journal of Ecclesiastical History*, vol. 63, no. 4 (October 2012), 758 – 784; Albert C. O'Brien, "Italian Youth in Conflict: Catholic Action and Fascist Italy, 1929-1931," *Catholic Historical Review* (1982): 625-635.
[28] Hilaire Belloc, *The Cruise of the Nona* (United Kingdom: Constable & Company, 1925).
[29] Christopher Dawson, *Religion and the Modern State* (London: Sheed and Ward, 1936), 134.
[30] Ibid., 136.

Lady of Guadalupe with the fighting spirit of Santiago. This was the Cristero War with their war cry: *Viva Cristo Rey!* (Long Live Christ the King!) Here arose the great martyrs like Bl. Miguel Pro who died like a man of God forgiving his enemies. The Communists imprisoned and raped pious Mexican girls who offered their sufferings through Our Lady. The Communists tortured and murdered even the young like fourteen-year-old St. José Sánchez del Río, who trampled on the serpent and won the palm of victory.[31] The United States, continuing their legacy against the second Christendom, sought to secure their interests and supported the Mexican government fighting the faithful, even helping with a Vatican betrayal, which Pius XI committed unwittingly.[32] The American Catholics supported the Cristeros but naively trusted both the American and Mexican governments.

In 1925, Our Lady requested the First Saturday devotion from St. Lucia. This would strike at the very heart of the degradation of society and the commodization of woman. For enthroning Mary and making reparation for the offenses to her Immaculate Heart would turn men away from the wickedness of using and abusing woman for the lust of money. Mary as throne of Christ would restore order just as she has crushed the serpent from the beginning.

But the advisors in the Vatican misled Pope Pius XI about Fatima, the Cristero War, and even made him censure Padre Pio. Pope Pius XI also suppressed *Action Française* as being too secular, which divided French Catholics further as the war had already weakened the generational transmission.[33] The two leading supporters, Jacques Maritain and Garrigou-Lagrange, who had united on this effort would become divided on the question of secular democracy. Kirwan says this action definitively

---

[31] Coulombe, *Puritan's Empire*, 366-367.

[32] Ibid. "Drawing his inspiration from the system invented by Weyler in Cuba and applied by the British in South Africa, and following the advice of the American Military Attache to use the methods employed by the Americans in the Philippines, Amaro [specialised in the technique known as 'reconcentration']. This consisted of clearing the civilian population completely out of a given area, before ravaging that area systematically. In Jalisco, Michoacan, Colima, Durango, and parts of Guanajuato, Queretaro, Zacatecas, and Guerrero, reconcentration caused indescribable suffering to the population concerned (nearly one million people). It also produced the opposite effect to that which was sought; it spread the rebellion." Jean A. Meyer, *The Cristero Rebellion: The Mexican People Between Church and State 1926–1929* (United States: Cambridge University Press, 2008), ch. 9; Meyer, *La Cristiada*, vol. 1, 157 in Javier Olivera, *La Contrarrevolución cristera* (Buenos Aires: Katejon, 2017).

[33] Kirwan, *op. cit.*, 105.

shifted the balance of power in favor of the moderates and liberals with Maritain carrying the torch of the moderates promoting a new social order.[34] De Mallerais says this was the "turning point in the history of the Church; from then on the bishoprics were given to left-wing clerics whilst all opposition to liberalism was falsely tarred with the same brush as Action Française."[35] A new generation was emerging in French Catholicism that broke from their elders and the cultural transmission was arrested.[36] (The suppression of *Action Française* was such a controversial act that it was reversed by Pius XII in one of his first acts as pope.)

Meanwhile in Germany, with its economy destroyed by the Treaty of Versailles and now dominated by the American economy of sin, the society was ripe for revolution. Communists were assassinating other politicians and trying to overturn society. Enemies of the Church were promoting the scientism of Freud with men like the Jewish psychoanalyst Wilhelm Reich, who wrote *Orgastic Potency* in 1924, and later *The Sexual Revolution* in 1935, explaining in his works that "religious sentiments result from inhibited sexuality" and thus promoted self-abuse among children and the sexualization of Catholics to undermine their faith.[37] This scientism from Jews melded with the American economy and the legacy of German idealism to provide the fuel for the Dionysian lust in Germany.[38] Liberal Jews were involved in the problems in Germany, but they were just one factor in the Grand Coalition of the Status Quo. But soon all the blame would be placed on the Jews based on American eugenics. Orthodox Jews, of course, were totally against Sexual Revolution.

The strict in Germany reacted to the Sexual Revolution with a Jansenist spirit, seeking to reduce Holy Matrimony to a *use* of woman for procreation only. They also opposed the Jews, but were too imprecise with their critique, leading to a condemnation of all Jews instead of just the Liberals.

In his opening salvo as Doctor of the Church in the twentieth century, Dietrich Von Hildebrand wrote *In Defense of Purity* in 1927. This work placed marriage and virginity within one virtue of purity, placing the ends of marriage in procreation and fidelity with the Tridentine theology of

---

[34] Ibid., 97.
[35] De Mallerais, *The Biography of Marcel Lefebvre*, 49.
[36] Kirwan, 137.
[37] See his work *The Mass Psychology of Fascism*, which included the quoted text, cited by E. Michael Jones in *The Catholic Church and the Cultural Revolution* (South Bend, IN: Fidelity Press, 2016), 37.
[38] Adrian Daub, *Uncivil Unions: The Metaphysics of Marriage in German Idealism and Romanticism* (United Kingdom: University of Chicago Press, 2012).

sacramental holiness against the scientism of Freud.[39] Von Hildebrand, knowing that he was clarifying certain points of the Faith not yet explicated, was scrupulous to keep all of his writings in strict conformity with orthodoxy, and personally expounded them to Eugenio Pacelli (Pope Pius XII) who gave his full approval.[40] (Hildebrand would also see through the exaggerated critique of the Jews.) But the strict viewed this as "heresy" because they were rightly concerned about the loosening of sexual morals.[41] Indeed as we will see, this crucial renewal of Sacred Marriage would be quickly twisted. It was absolutely crucial that the moderates and the strict unite on this fundamental aspect of society because of the Sexual Revolution.

Under Mussolini's Italy there was a reaction against the sexualized economy of the United States, which helped protect the family from the assault of sexualization, but also imposed an excess of state power. The Polish crusader St. Maximilian Kolbe found it necessary to go to a deserted plot of land and start to build an entirely new city in order to restore the order of Christ the King. He always preached the Gospel to "Freemasons, Jews, heretics" with great charity and truth "looking with great compassion on the souls that had been misled."[42]

But by 1929, Stalin had gained power in the Soviet Empire. Realizing the chaos in society resulting from Lenin's Sexual Revolution, he attempted to check the spread of Dionysius, and then imitated the worst persecution of the Church seen in centuries.

In the same year, Pope Pius XI signed the Lateran Treaty with Mussolini. The treaty returned a tiny plot of land for the entire Papal States that had been seized and made small concessions to the Church. The treaty was a fraction of reparation that the Italian government owed the Holy Father.

At that time Our Lady of Fatima came to Lucia to ask for the consecration of Russia to the Immaculate Heart of Mary to avert another war, but this too was avoided, seemingly by bad advisors of Pius XI. In the same year, the economy of sin suffered a worldwide economic collapse.

---

[39] "Sigmund Freud's thesis, on which the so-called psychoanalytical method is based, in spite of the valuable psychotherapeutic discoveries it has produced, embodies a completely erroneous view of the structure of human personality, which betrays the influence of an exploded sensationalism." Von Hildebrand, *In Defense of Purity*, 6 n1.

[40] Alice Von Hildebrand, *Soul of a Lion*, 212.

[41] Ibid., 212 n16.

[42] Fr. Karl Stehlin, *The Immaculata: Our Ideal*, trans. Michael J. Miller (Kolbe Publications, 2016), 55.

Meanwhile in Africa, the Church was penetrating into South Chad with the Gospel and by 2000 there would be ninety-nine parishes in the country.[43] While Euro-America was disintegrating in death, Africa was coming to life. "Africa in the twentieth century went from a Catholic population of 1.9 million in 1900 to 130 million in 2000, a growth rate of 6,708 percent, the most rapid expansion of Catholicism in a single continent in two thousand years of church history."[44] Lefebvre labored among the Africans as a priest from 1932-1945, as bishop from 1947-1962 overseeing 46 dioceses, working to raise up the African clergy.

But by 1930, men did not repent of their Dionysian lust. The Anglican Church allowed contraception, breaking from all Protestant condemnations up to that point. Pope Pius XI responded in one of his greatest encyclicals, *Casti Connubii*, which condemned feminism, contraception, and placed Marriage on firm foundation. He predicted what feminism would do when the rights of women to their throne was violated by the false ideology of dignity as power. The American and Soviet ideologies both proclaimed that woman's dignity was based on power, and when she achieved more power, she was "emancipated."

> This, however, is not the true emancipation of woman, nor that rational and exalted liberty which belongs to the noble office of a Christian woman and wife; it is rather the debasing of the womanly character and the dignity of motherhood, and indeed of the whole family, as a result of which the husband suffers the loss of his wife, the children of their mother, and the home and the whole family of an ever watchful guardian.
>
> More than this, this false liberty and unnatural equality with the husband is to the detriment of the woman herself, for if the woman descends from her truly regal throne to which she has been raised within the walls of the home by means of the Gospel, she will soon be reduced to the old state of slavery (if not in appearance,

---

[43] "The Catholic Church in Chad," *New Catholic Encyclopedia* (2003), vol. 3, 359, 361.
[44] John Allen cited in Philip Jenkins, *The Next Christendom* (Oxford University Press: 2011), 72-73. Cf. John Allen, *The Future Church* (New York: Doubleday, 2009).

certainly in reality) and become as amongst the pagans the mere instrument of man.[45]

Indeed, the first Sexual Revolution had already been "booming" with an economy of sin that commoditized women into objects of lust for the love of money. And on the other hand, the reaction especially in Nazi Germany was seeking to *use* women as objects of the state for procreation only. Both were an objectification of woman based on a denial of Sacramental Marriage.

Meanwhile, the Jesuit Heinrich Pesch was penning his economic treatises that helped influence Pope Pius XI in *Quadragesimo Anno*, addressing the great economic crisis of the factory that was facing much of the world. It was fundamental that Catholics unite on kitchen and coin, but the politics were straining them.

By God's grace after 1930 in the United States, the Catholic Church was organizing. At this point there was enough of a minority that the organization of the Church could not be rivaled by any other Christian group. Increased immigration was also building up what Cardinal Gibbons had opposed—ethnic neighborhoods and parishes speaking the mother tongue and binding the faithful to the Church. As the uglification of the world destroyed woman and beauty, our fathers sacrificed and raised up exquisite monuments to God's glory in the United States. Beautiful Catholic churches were now in every major city.

Then they turned and faced the onslaught with the power of the Cross. They organized a nationwide boycott of all pornographic films. Orthodox Jews and Protestants joined in with the leadership of Catholics against the liberal Jews, Protestants and neo-pagans in Hollywood. This was known as the Legion of Decency that spread to Europe. It was the crusade to protect children from the influence of Dionysius. From this point American Catholicism, flowing from the nearly-public *cultus* in little ethnic communities, began to rise to the zenith of its influence in souls and society of the United States. The time had come for the Constantine moment. If the moderates and strict in America could unite, the idol of *Libertas* could be dethroned and Christ receive His rights as King in America. This could stop the generational disintegration in its tracks.

Meanwhile by then, St. Maximilian had traveled to bring the Gospel to Japanese pagans, laboring among the Catholic Church in Nagasaki which had existed for some four hundred years. But he moved to the pagan

---

[45] Pius XI, *Casti Connubii* (1930), 75.

area of Hongonchi and erected at the highest point, visible to the whole community, the throne of Christ—Mary, Immaculate.[46] This was what the United States and the world needed to avert the wrath of God.

But at this same time, Teilhard was spreading his superstition of unlimited progress, even though his superior suppressed him in 1926 for denying Original Sin. His ideas fit perfectly with the superstition of progress from Whig history, American Manifest Destiny and Darwinian evolution since it Christianized in a spiritualized scientism the claim that all of history was developing toward man in general and Christianity in particular.[47] What was worse, by attempting to reconcile scientific evolution with Christian faith, he imbedded evil within the very cosmos of unlimited progress, seeing evil itself as a necessary stage of a greater consciousness.[48] Further, since Teilhard was a committed evolutionist, he seemed to lend support for the American scientism of eugenics, saying things like Blacks "by biological necessity," may need a "special function" in society different than whites or that the Chinese may be "arrested primitives, victims of retarded development whose anthropological substance is inferior to ours [Europeans]."[49]

Maritain, who met him several times, insinuates that Teilhard wanted to conduct his research in isolation from criticism, which De Lubac interprets as exonerating him from the obligation of theological precision. But Maritain asserts Teilhard by this means "remained in perfect ignorance and forgetfulness of the *Doctor Communis* [St. Thomas]."[50] Nevertheless the evolution of dogma proclaimed by the Modernists seems to have been deeply imbedded in his thought, as Maritain would indict him with his own words:

> What is coming to dominate my interests and inner preoccupations... is the effort to establish within me, and spread around me, a new religion (let us call it, if you like, better Christianity) in which the personal God ceases to be the great Neolithic proprietor of old in order

---

[46] Kalvelage, *Kolbe: Saint of the Immaculata*, 62.
[47] See E. L. Boné's sympathetic treatment in "Pierre Teilhard de Chardin," *New Catholic Encyclopedia* (2003) vol. 13, 789.
[48] Henri de Lubac admits this in *Teilhard de Chardin* trans. Rene Hague, (New York: Hawthorne Books, 1965), 103
[49] Cited in Paul A. Wickens, *Christ Denied: Origin of The Present Day Problems in the Catholic Church* (TAN: 1982), 46.
[50] Jacques Maritain, *The Peasant of the Garonne: An Old Layman Questions Himself about the Present Time*. (Wipf and Stock Publishers, 2013), 117.

to become the soul of the World which our religious and cultural stage of development calls for."[51]

Even interpreting his thought as sympathetically as possible (as De Lubac would do in the 1960s), the significant omission of Original Sin and the evolutionary view of evil allowed men to see the world wars not as a punishment for sin, but a process of becoming something greater. With the immense mechanization and technology of this era, it was easy to forget what these machines had done in the Great War and marvel at the immense power that man had created, and believe in the unlimited progress of spiritual enlightenment that Teilhard preached. Teilhard's affirmation of the dogma of Original Sin was vague at best and constituted an outright denial at worst.[52] Following Tyrell, more and more priests were uncritically accepting and disseminating the teachings of Teilhard. This would have devastating effects. From 1932-33, the Soviets were imposing the Holodomor massacre of Ukrainians, starving some 3.5-12 million to death. Bishop Leonid Feodorov joined the chorus of angels in 1935 with untold thousands of others under the mass murderer Stalin.

In 1935 Yves Congar wrote his essay "The Deficiency of Theology," calling attention to the fact that the Thomism of the Strict was increasingly degenerating into what Sire admits as "treating St. Thomas's work not as a philosophical system but as a store from which infallible answers were to be extracted."[53] Congar's essay was the beginning of the movement of "*Nouvelle théologie*" which, according to its moderate party, sought merely to effect the fourth Greco-Roman renewal by applying the patristic texts to the Faith. But according to others, sought to use these texts to evolve dogma itself in the spirit of Teilhard. What was needed was a synthesis to integrate the Patristic revival into Thomism, but the moderates and the strict were becoming hardened in their positions, and the strict were urging the Magisterium to come down hard even on the moderates.

But with the ideologies of power and anti-culture, unity in the Roman Rite *cultus* was more deeply threatened. The *cultus* expressed a hierarchy

---

[51] *Lettres à Léontine Zanta* (Paris: Desclée De Brouwer, 1965). Maritain in *Peasant*, 118 quotes this in full as a negative criticism with no further comment other than that it is "something to the delight of ancient Stoics."
[52] His most ardent defender, Henri de Lubac, admits that "In dealing with Original Sin (*peccatum originans*) it may be true that, yielding to pressure from teachers who looked to him, in view of his knowledge of human origins, for the explanation they lacked, he occasionally offered explanations that were rightly judged unsatisfactory." Henri de Lubac, *The Religion of Teilhard de Chardin*, trans. René Hague (New York: Desclee Company, 1967), 119-120.
[53] Sire, *Phoenix from the Ashes*, 137.

from the priest down to the faithful. The pious customs of the faithful were being seen as "oppressive" and they must take a greater share of the "participation." The worldwide promotion of liberal democracy by America ended up questioning all forms of hierarchy.

In 1936, the enemies of the Church took action against Spain. The Communists and others used democratic means to begin imposing their regime. The spirit of Santiago was aroused once again as Catholics rose to fight. This would be yet another victory for Our Lady of Covadonga as the Spanish defeated yet another enemy of the faith. But the American and Soviet empires sided with the Spanish Communists.

By 1937, the British and American empires were switching their military fuel to oil and funding the rise of Saudi Arabia, which became the "light of the world" as a pilgrimage site, by a religious obligation on all Muhammadans.[54] Belloc then observed that since Europe had lost the faith and the Muhammadans still had religion, they may one day rise again.[55] In that year, Jorge Bergoglio was a one-year-old boy in Argentina. His parents were Italians who had fled Mussolini.

Spiral into Darkness

In Germany the Nazi party was taking the scientism of eugenics and drawing upon the shocked consciences of Germans to blame all the evils on the Jews. His neo-pagan racial ideology was condemned by the German bishops, who excommunicated any Catholic members of the Nazi party. Von Hildebrand immediately understood the intrinsic evil of their philosophy, and began to publicly denounce the movement, pointing out the logos inherent in the rational Jewish party.

Meanwhile he published his fundamental treatise, *Liturgy and Personality*, which integrated a liturgical vision into a spiritual philosophy of holiness. As the liturgical movement was gaining momentum, he wrote that the transforming power of the words and rites of the *cultus* were in the fact that they sought the glory of God above all else. As soon as the liturgy was turned toward man as an educational experience, it lost its cultural power. In this, he would prove to be prophetic.

But when the Nazis were able to take power in 1933 he had a choice: stay silent or speak and be assassinated. He had a wife and a son. He did

---

[54] Every Muhammadan is bound in his lifetime to go on pilgrimage to Mecca, and the Saudi Arabian terrorist state is its guardian. Spencer, *History of Jihad*, 293, 294.
[55] Belloc, *The Crusades*, 250.

not hesitate. Knowing he had a duty to speak against the evil, he left the country with his wife and child and fled to Florence.[56] He made an alliance with Catholic Fascist leader Engelbert Dolfuss of Austria to fund his anti-Nazi newspaper, *The Christian Corporate State*. Through this publication the Doctor of the Church became the Hammer of the Nazis and the Communists as two sides of the same anti-culture.[57]

Hitler acted quickly. In 1934, the Nazis shot Dolfuss. While he bled to death, he asked for a priest but the Nazis refused. Von Hildebrand refused to stop and continued to denounce the regime, knowing he could be next.

The Vatican broke off diplomatic relations with the regime. With Eugenio Pacelli's help the Church denounced Communism in *Divini Redemptoris*, which caused the Nazis to praise Catholicism. Then the only German encyclical ever produced, *Mit brennender Sorge* was smuggled into Germany and read from every Catholic pulpit. Every priest condemned the Nazi regime by order of the pope. The Nazis quickly moved to eliminate Catholicism.

Meanwhile, the great Jewish philosopher St. Teresa Benedicta of the Cross was completing her final vows. In 1929 she had already published a *dialogos* between St. Thomas and Husserl. In it she had St. Thomas name Brentano as a scholastic link between Thomism and Phenomenology. Then St. Thomas says to Husserl, the father of Phenomenology, "We are both convinced that a logos is the force behind all that is."[58] In her great work of 1931, *Potency and Act*, she began to synthesize the Phenomenological, Augustinian philosophy of Husserl with the Classical realism of St. Thomas.[59] Her writings were crucial to keep this Augustinian philosophy of Phenomenology from becoming a relativism and subjectivism. If the moderates could only adopt her insights of synthesis, the fourth renewal would conquer this new age for Christ.

But as Hitler's intentions became apparent, St. Teresa made a vow to accept this cross "placed upon the Jewish people...willingly in the name of all."[60] In her philosophical works and her holiness, she combined and embodied the Marian, Jewish soul—fierce loyalty to her people perfectly harmonized with eternal hospitality.

---

[56] On this period until the Nazi invasion of Austria, see Alice von Hildebrand, *Soul of a Lion*, 255-293.

[57] At the time, some were becoming Nazis to oppose the Communists.

[58] St. Teresa Benedicta, *Knowledge and Faith*, 1-64.

[59] Ibid., *Potency and Act*, trans. Walter Redmond (Washington, DC: ICS, 2009), viii.

[60] Fr. Paul Hamans, *Edith Stein and Companions on the Way to Auschwitz*, trans. Sr. M. Regina van den Berg (San Francisco, CA: Ignatius Press, 2010), 68 n17.

But men did not repent. In January, 1938 the great geomagnetic storm appeared and was seen across the world, as something like the Northern Lights. It was the great sign of Fatima that God's wrath was imminent.

Von Hildebrand kept writing against the Nazis, knowing he could be assassinated at any moment. The Nazi foreign minister in Austria, Franz von Papen confirmed to Hitler that Von Hildebrand was "the most dangerous enemy of National Socialism."[61] Hitler induced the compliant Austrian minister to allow the annexation of Austria. With this in place, Hitler could easily take Von Hildebrand. The Austrian minister would not allow it until he let all the Austrians vote on it. But Hitler did not take any chances. In March of 1938, he invaded. The war had begun under Pope Pius XI as prophesied by Fatima. Von Hildebrand knew they were coming for him. He took his wife and fled immediately. The Nazis went straight for his house. They fled Vienna on the last train leaving before the Nazis arrived.[62] But at the border the Nazi-controlled guards stopped the train and would not allow any Austrian citizen to leave the country.

---

[61] Franz von Papen to Adolf Hitler, April 30 1937. See also Rudolf Ebneth, *Die Österreichishe Wochenschrift*, 252ff in Alice von Hildebrand, *Soul of a Lion*, 291.
[62] Ibid., 297.

XXIX

A MASS MURDERER AND HIS ALLIES AGAINST A MASS MURDERER AND HIS AXIS

By God's Providence, the Von Hildebrand family eluded the Nazis as Dietrich had his Swiss passport which got the past the Nazi guards. Meanwhile, Hitler now had Austria. The Nazi empire had begun and the fires of the death camps were coming.

By the Feast of the Annunciation, 1939, Hitler had decreed that all young boys had to join the Hitler Youth. The education of children by the state found a new acuteness with Hitler who used force to impose the rigid engineering. Joseph Ratzinger turned fourteen and had to officially register, but he refused to appear. His seminary increased its discipline and rigor to counter-attack the increasing propaganda on the youth. The German bishops attempted to keep the Concordat, but Ratzinger recalled that "even then it dawned on me that they (the bishops) partly misjudged the situation."[1] As the prospects of armed conflict became apparent, Pope Pius XII was pleading for Germany, France, Poland, Italy, and Britain to meet in conference but they refused.[2]

Meanwhile, that fall, Stalin and Hitler signed "a simple aggression pact against Poland" which allowed the Soviets a "stronger position than at any time since the regime came to power."[3] Immediately the Communists, directed from Moscow worldwide, were praising the Nazis and funneling resources to them.

---

[1] Seewald, *Benedict XVI: A Life*, vol. 1, 73-88.
[2] Coulombe, *Vicars of Christ*, 321.
[3] Paul Johnson, *Modern Times*, rev. ed. (Harper Perennial, 1992), 360-361.

A MASS MURDERER AGAINST A MASS MURDERER

On September 1st, the Nazis invaded Poland from the west, and the on the 17th the Soviets invaded from the east. Hitler instructed the Nazi army to kill "without pity or mercy all men, women and children" to get "the living space we need."[4] During the occupation, the Nazis carried out 714 executions, killing 16,376 Poles.[5] The Soviets began their "cleansing" of Poland by deporting up to 1 million Poles and a mass execution of 25,700 Polish officers and civilians at Katyn, and moved to implement the agreed Soviet Empire in Eastern Europe.[6] A young Karol Wojtyła was in the underground seminary carrying on Polish Catholic resistance.[7] Pope Pius XII, meanwhile, was spending four million dollars smuggling Jews out of Europe.[8]

Britain and France declared war on Germany, but France, being internally divided, fell easily to the Nazis in May, 1940. The French people were then divided over the best course of action against the Nazis. At first, most followed the respected French veteran Philippe Pétain in a delicate armistice with the Nazis which allowed them self-rule in the South of France, creating the Vichy Regime.

Meanwhile, the French politician Charles de Gaulle fled to Britain and called on all Frenchmen to resist the Nazis under his leadership and side with the Allies. Garrigou-Lagrange, split with Maritain, who thoroughly believed in the American way as the best course of action. As they had formerly been united in *Action Française*, their split foreshadowed the fractioning of Catholic thought that was to come.

In September 1940, Japan and Italy allied with the Nazis and Soviets. Pope Pius XII never stopped calling for peace and like his predecessor he was ignored. The world powers continued the wicked tradition of exploiting Africans for economic gain. As with the Great War, the United States remained aloof, yet kept economic ties. In 1941 President Roosevelt declared that the gospel of America must be spread over the world.[9]

By the summer of 1941, the Nazis invaded the Soviet Empire and Britain chose to ally with Stalin against him. At the same time, Catholic

---

[4] Gumkowski and Leszczynski, *Poland Under Nazi Occupation*, 59 in Richard C. Lukas, *Forgotten Holocaust*, (New York: Hippocrene Books, 1997), 3.
[5] Lukas, *Forgotten Holocaust*, 3.
[6] Nicolas Werth, "A State against Its People: Violence, Repression, and Terror in the Soviet Union," Stéphane Courtois et al., eds., *The Black Book of Communism* (Cambridge, MA: Harvard University Press, 1999), 209-213.
[7] George Weigel, *Witness to Hope: The Biography of John Paul II* (Cliff Street Books, 2001), 44-75.
[8] Coulombe, *Vicars of Christ*, 321.
[9] Wemhoff, *John Courtney Murray*, 18.

Franco, Pétain, and Salazar sought to avoid both Hitler and Stalin, but were forced to favor Hitler as the Allies favored Stalin. It was a mass murderer and his Allies against a mass murderer and his Axis.

Rejecting the pride of Roosevelt's earthly city, Dawson proclaimed the war was "The Judgement of the Nations" in a book of the same title. "This is the greatness and misery of modern civilisation," he lamented, "that it has conquered the world by losing its own soul, and that when its soul is lost it must lose the world as well."[10] Yet as Von Hildebrand would write in 1953, "our epoch is above all great because it has given rise to many martyrs and many secret saints."[11]

As the Nazis and Soviet both persecuted Polish Catholics, they did the same to the Ukrainian Catholics. Venerable Andrey Sheptytsky fought Soviets and Nazis with the true crusading spirit. When the Soviets invaded, he sought to "evangelize the Soviets" and heal the schism with the Orthodox "to the benefit of both the Universal Church and the Ukrainian nationality."[12] When the Nazis invaded, while 250,000 Ukrainian Catholics were deported to camps, he fought for his people and sheltered the Jews from what he termed the Nazis' "diabolical" ideology.[13]

Meanwhile in the Netherlands, St. Teresa wrote her last testament and abandoned herself to Divine Providence:

> I joyfully accept in advance the death God has appointed for me, in perfect submission to his most holy will. May the Lord accept my life and death for the honor and glory of his name for the needs of his holy Church... for the Jewish people, that the Lord may be received by his own, and his kingdom come in glory, for the deliverance of Germany and peace throughout the world, and finally for all my relatives living and dead and all whom God has given me: may none of them be lost.[14]

After the Nazis took the Netherlands, the Dutch bishops resisted them and defended Jews and Jewish Catholics. But as the Gestapo were taking them from the convent, St. Teresa turned to her sister and said, "Rosa, come, we

---

[10] Dawsonn, *Judgement of the Nations*, 67.
[11] Von Hildebrand, *New Tower of Babel*, 5.
[12] Royal, *Catholic Martyrs of the Twentieth Century*, 75.
[13] Ibid.
[14] In Weigel, *Witness to Hope*, 539.

are going for our people."[15] Fulfilling her promise to God to accept this cross, she "wanted to offer her suffering for the conversion of unbelievers, for the Jews, for the blind persecutors, and for all who had lost God from their hearts."[16] Going to Auschwitz, witnesses reported her serene calm, spirit of prayer and resignation to their fate. When she arrived she was immediately executed and she won her glorious crown in the gas chamber. The great Jewish convert joined the chorus of angels.

Meanwhile St. Maximilian was risking his life to save starving Jews from the Nazis in Poland which made him a target of the SS. He received the call that they would come to take him he said, "Yes, Mary." When they boarded the train for Auschwitz, "someone intoned religious and national songs. It was Fr. Kolbe."[17] Perfecting the crusading spirit, Fr. Kolbe voluntarily offered to be starved to death so that a married man could live. In the starvation bunkers, the man of God led the others in "singing of hymns to Our Lady" and hearing confessions, and winning a glorious crown.[18]

Nagasaki Japan was the center of Japanese Catholicism where Kolbe had labored for the Gospel. In December of 1941, the Japanese attack on Pearl Harbor galvanized American public to support the war effort on the side of Stalin. In the United States, women began working far more for the war effort, while youth continued to engage in immorality with the newest form of music—Swing. The Legion of Decency would never see what hit them. Meanwhile, a young Malcolm X would soon find out the truth about the Jazz craze. The bloodshed of millions of civilians continued throughout the world.

In Christmas 1944, Pope Pius XII delivered a message acknowledging that the whole world wanted democracy as a means to avoid the totalitarian regimes which sought to destroy the personhood of man. In this address he set the fundamental distinctions necessary for the Church to navigate the new world of democracy. On the one hand, he gave the traditional definition of a "people" which we have maintained in this work, namely, a body of persons with a culture. In contrast to this, "the masses" are merely a mob which is spun about by the powerful who manipulate their emotions for their own ends:

> The people lives by the fullness of life in the men that compose it, each of whom—at his proper place and in

---

[15] Hamans, *Edith Stein and Companions on the Way to Auschwitz*, 81.
[16] Ibid., 85.
[17] Kalvelage, *Kolbe: Saint of the Immaculata*, 84.
[18] Ibid., 8.

his own way—is a person conscious of his own responsibility and of his own views. The masses, on the contrary, wait for the impulse from outside, an easy plaything in the hands of anyone who exploits their instincts and impressions; ready to follow in turn, today this flag, tomorrow another.[19]

Already we see during the war this contrast in the people of Poland compared to the people of the United States. In Poland, Wojtyła and other Catholic Poles were resisting Nazis and Soviets both by asserting their ethnic identity and heritage as Poles and Catholic. It was a cultural movement which sought a public *cultus* and truly democratic in the best sense of that word. By contrast, the people of the United States, having lost *cultus*, made their identity in the general slogans of *Libertas* and the rites and monuments dedicated to the earthly city. This sentiment was then manipulated by the powerful in whatever direction was necessary by men like Ed Bernays paid by government or business.

But at the same time, Dawson observed, "whatever the defects of their own social systems, Britain and America stand today as the bulwark of the freedom of the world."[20] Even more, the divine grace of the Catholic Mass celebrated throughout the United States was truly infusing the souls of Americans, leading toward the Constantine moment. "Everything depends," wrote Dawson "on whether it is possible to use the temporal struggle, not for destructive or purely material ends, but as a means of checking the demonic forces that have been let loose in the world."[21] Like the crusade of Herakleios, the United States needed only to renounce forever its hubris of *Roma*—Manifest Destiny and the idol of *Libertas*—surrender to the King, and Mary would be the throne of Christ.

Yet the economy of lust was like burning oil mixing with the waters of Baptism for American society. In 1944 it became apparent that the Sexual Revolution was flooding into the Church as some were promoting the error that the mutual love of spouses was equal or more important than procreation in marriage. Thus the Jansenist reaction of the strict was producing an overreaction among the moderates, leading to heresy. The Holy Office officially decreed that procreation is the first end of marriage, and mutual love is the second, which remains the authoritative clarification to this day.[22]

---

[19] Pius XII, "Christmas Message" (1944), 23-24.
[20] Dawson, *op. cit.*, 11.
[21] Ibid., 106.
[22] Holy Office, April 1, 1944 in Denzinger, 43rd ed., 3838.

A MASS MURDERER AGAINST A MASS MURDERER

Meanwhile the liturgical movement continued to deepen the existing divisions between the moderate and strict parties. Liturgical scholars like Parsch, Beauduin, and Casel began to work harder to spread their ideas. Some like Parsch and Hellriegel were making good efforts at traditional participation.[23] But during this period, again influenced by the politics, the moderates were coalescing into a "democratic party," seeking to advocate changes to the *cultus* in the name of "active participation."[24]

Annibale Bugnini, himself newly ordained, was assigned to the town of Borgata Prenestina where its 2,000 inhabitants were poor and had no parish of their own. He began experimenting with a vocalized liturgy so that the people could say the responses in Latin and Italian. He also composed paraphrases of the Holy Mass for the people to understand better.[25] Men like Bugnini believed so strongly in the righteousness of their cause they were willing to set aside obedience to law and custom to implement their ideas on the *cultus*.

In 1945, Hitler was surrounded and committed suicide. Later that year in August, Japanese Catholics were still regularly assisting at Mass at the Cathedral of the Immaculate Conception in Nagasaki built by the stalwart Japanese Catholics who endured for two hundred years, the greatest throne of Christ in Asia.[26] No doubt some of these Japanese Catholics had been converted or benefited from St. Maximilian's labors there. Mary as throne of Christ in Japan reached for the sky, pointing men to lift up their hearts to the Father in Heaven. But out of that sky came an object. Small at first, it quickly gained speed and then everything was flame.

The American forces detonated the Atomic bomb 500 meters away, destroying the Cathedral of the Immaculate Conception and killing any inside. Anyone who survived the blast was pierced by the sound of civilians burning alive. Japanese mothers suffered a "high percentage of neonatal and infantile deaths" and the radiation caused mental disorders for the unborn children exposed near the blast as they grew up over the next generation.[27] In all, the two bombs killed upwards of 200,000 Japanese

---

[23] Reid, *Organic Development of the Liturgy*, 110-115, 116-118.
[24] Bonneterre, *The Liturgical Movement*, 33-44.
[25] Yves Chiron, *Annibale Bugnini: Reformer of the Liturgy*, trans. John Pepino (Angelico Press, 2018), 23-25.
[26] Soichi Iijima, "The Effects of the Atomic Bombs – Hiroshima and Nagasaki," Joseph Rotblat and Michiji Konuma, eds., *Proceedings of the Forty-Fifth Pugwash Conference on Science and World Affairs* (Singapore: World Scientific, 1997), 199.
[27] Ibid., 208.

men, women and children. The voluntarist build up of militarism from Oliver Cromwell had finally reached the zenith of technological power.

But for Teilhard de Chardin, the "progress of humanity... in the invention of nuclear weapons matter[ed] more to him than the destruction of innumerable lives and the most terrible sufferings inflicted on individual persons."[28]

A New Birth of Freedom

As before, the Allies sought to punish the Germans and the United States gained more power. The Soviets held East Germany while the Americans held West Germany. The United States was helping the German people with food, but also pressing their ideological "gospel" of anti-culture, including pornography.[29] The Soviets imposed a state with Communist ideological propaganda.

The United States solidified an economic alliance with Saudi Arabia in order gain greater advantage over the Soviets in 1945. This economic alliance would indirectly fund the resurrection of Muhammadanism and the Saracens left Arabia inspired to begin a movement to massacre the rising Christian Church of Africa.[30]

As in the Middle East, the African continent was carved up by secular Euro-American empires who imposed anti-culture, leading to bloodshed of untold numbers. Between these empires and the Muhammadan states in Africa, innumerable executions happened "in the hundreds and thousands" and "millions" in Africa, as the soldiers of Christ won the victorious crown with blood.[31] The state of Israel, dominated by Liberal Jews, was imposed on Palestinian Christians, Jews, and Muhammadans, and led to a massive economy of pornography and sex slavery.[32] The alliance between the United States and Israel helped solidify the influence of Liberal Jews throughout the world.[33]

---

[28] Von Hildebrand, *Charitable Anathema*, 184.
[29] Seewald, *Benedict XVI: A Life*, vol. 1, 207; Jones, *Logos Rising*, 551-614.
[30] Spencer, *History of Jihad*, 293-296. The Wahhabi al-Hajj 'Abdullah Mahmud came from his pilgrimage to Saudi Arabia to found his center for Muhammadanism in 1949 in west Africa. Lapidus, *A History of Islamic Societies*, 755.
[31] Royal, *Catholic Martyrs of the Twentieth Century*, 378.
[32] Erella Shadmi and Esther Hertzog, eds., *Prostitution, Pornography and Trafficking in Women: Israel's Blood Money* (Routledge, 2019).
[33] For a Jewish source against the Liberal Jews and their influence in modern society, see the work of Charles Moscowitz. For a Jewish source, recipient of the

A MASS MURDERER AGAINST A MASS MURDERER

The United Nations was formed which allowed the Allied powers the greatest power over the post-war world. Using the most powerful technology yet, the American and Soviet Empires sought to manipulate the whole world into believing their ideologies in what the CIA termed "Doctrinal Warfare," and both targeted the Catholic Church.[34] Within a generation Dawson would observe that the "secular ideologies" of two empires had become "literally worldwide" so that "nationality has taken the place of religion as the ultimate principle of social organization, and ideology has taken the place of theology as the creator of social ideals and guide of public opinion."[35] The post-war propaganda was able to vilify anything mildly "fascist," discrediting the Catholic efforts of Dolfuss in Austria, Salazar in Portugal, Franco in Spain, Duplessis in Quebec, and Pétain in France.

During this time Franco was building a cemetery to bury all the dead of the Spanish Civil War to reconcile the Spanish people. In France, Pétain was sentenced to death as a traitor, but de Gaulle commuted his sentence to life imprisonment. De Gaulle removed the cross from the Free France flag and started the Fourth Republic in 1946 without the cross of Christ. The cross was also removed from the West German flag.[36] Thus the old ways were abandoned and the new way of *Libertas* adopted. The French left-wing gained the influence over society and Europe, paving the way for the anti-culture of the Second Sexual Revolution. The Allied propaganda was pushing for a new birth of democracy and freedom throughout the world. But unlike the first time that happened, America more than ever had been infused with grace. Therefore the Sexual Revolution did not commence in the few years after the war as it had done before. Unlike the Lost Generation, something was beginning after Hitler. But now everything depended on the Church.

National Jewish Book Award, supporting the modern world, see Yuri Slezkine, *The Jewish Century* (Princeton University Press, 2019). Cf. Jones, *The Jewish Revolutionary Spirit*, 917-922, 959-986.

[34] "PSB Planning Objectives" Top Secret [Declassified 1998] April 7, 1952, "Doctrinal Warfare" Memoranda, "Psychological Strategy Planning for Western Europe" and "Latin America," Jan-Feb, 1953, *Dwight D. Eisenhower Library* in Wemhoff, *John Courtney Murray*, 278-319.

[35] Dawson, *The Movement of World Revolution*, 84-85; Eliot says the same in "The Idea of a Christian Society," *Christianity and Culture* (New York: Harvest, 1976), 7.

[36] Seewald, *Benedict XVI: A Life*, vol. 1, 207.

The Church in France

In France, a new missionary effort of priests was born called worker-priests. The problem had arisen that the working class French had nearly abandoned the Catholic Faith and was susceptible to Communist ideology. The worker-priests were French priests who got jobs working in factories and manufacturing plants to try to reach out to the working class. This movement was vulnerable, however, to the French Communism which was gaining ascendency in society.

On the level of tradition, the momentum of theology was continuing to shift in favor of the younger French generation and Jesuits such as Henri de Lubac, Henri Boulliard, Jean Daniélou and German Hans Urs von Balthasar (Jesuit until 1950) were promoting the new theological method that emphasized the Church Fathers and Scripture.[37] According to Maritain, Teilhard was bitter against the Church authorities for censuring him, but his writings were being circulated anonymously in the seminaries.[38]

This Teilhardian optimism was mixed with good efforts at the fourth Greco-Roman renewal by publishing numerous editions of Church Fathers in new publication titled *Sources chrétiennes* ("Christian Sources") that began in 1942.[39] In publications from Boulliard, Daniélou and De Lubac from 1944 to 1946 these patristic sources were applied to a renewal movement that envisioned a positive method to engage the modern world.[40]

The Dominicans in Rome noticed that in the footnotes of these publications there was a bitter attack on the recent efforts of Thomistic thinkers to accomplish the Thomistic renewal. The Jesuits in France seemed to be trying to meld a true *resourcement* with an attack on neo-Scholasticism based on Teilhardian optimism and anti-Christian philosophy.

On this point, Maritain and Garrigou-Lagrange once again united, for Maritain would later write of his absolute disdain for Teilhardian superstition. In 1946 Garrigou-Lagrange wrote against the new movement in an article entitled "Where is the New Theology Taking Us?" singling out the phrase given by Boulliard that "a theology that is not current is a

---

[37] Kirwan, *op. cit.*, 204.
[38] Maritain, *The Peasant of the Garonne*, 117.
[39] See Matthew Minerd's lectures on this topic at *Reason and Theology* (Jan 16, 2021) <https://reasonandtheology.com/courses/the-nouvelle-theologie-with-dr-matthew-minerd/>, accessed March 28, 2021.
[40] Jürgen Mettepenningen, *Nouvelle Théologie, New Theology: Inheritor of Modernism, Precursor of Vatican II* (T&T Clark, 2010), 33-37.

false theology."⁴¹ He called upon the Magisterium to intervene because it would lead back to Modernism and was joined in his attack by Michel Labourdette. These were the strict party. At best, they were anchoring the Church in the solid tradition of Thomism in order to effectively bring about the renewal. At worst, they were falling into the rote manualism.

These were the days of the manuals, when many men were trained to simply memorize facts about theology and regurgitate it. Even Garrigou-Lagrange admitted that "great risk is run of being superficial in materially classifying things and in substituting an artificial mechanism for the profound dynamism of the life of grace."⁴² Dawson went further and asserted that the dominance of the strict party, with "no competition of rival schools, as in the medieval university," was making it so that "Catholic education becomes identified with an authoritarian ideology, like Marxism."⁴³ At the same time, with the upheavals of the past few generations, a simple, solid foundation was understandable and also helped to elucidate the basics with clarity. Certainly not all manuals of theology were bad, especially those with case studies of moral acts.

This was the opportunity to form Christendom that was still unmade since Vatican I. What was needed was Thomism to provide the anchor to complete the fourth renewal. The Patristic sources could truly integrate a powerful synthesis to help win over Protestants and Orthodox back to the church, and moreover, lost souls of Europe and Africa and other lands. But like the Greeks in the east before Muhammadanism, the *dialogos* was never completed.

It is unclear which side was at fault in this period. Mettepenningen, a partisan of the moderate side, implies Pope Pius XII forced an end when he halted the debate personally in 1946 and then with *Humani Generis* in 1950.⁴⁴ The younger generation was inspired by the anti-Nazi resisters, and it seems to have been easy to resent the authoritative reactions coming from

---

⁴¹ Reginald Garrigou-Lagrange, "La nouvelle théologie où va-t-elle?" *Angelicum* (1946). English translation "Where is the New Theology Leading Us?" trans. Suzanne M. Rini, *Catholic Family News* <https://archive.org/details/Garrigou-LagrangeEnglish/_Where%20is%20the%20New%20Theology%20Leading%20Us__%20-%20Garrigou-Lagrange%2C%20Reginald%2C%20O.P._/mode/2up?view=theater>, accessed March 29, 2021.
⁴² Reginald Garrigou-Lagrange, *Three Ages of the Interior Life*, trans. Sr. M. Timothea Doyle (B. Herder Book: 1947), v
⁴³ Christopher Dawson, "The Study of Christian Culture," *Thought*, vol. 35 (1960), 485-93 in Birzer, *Sanctifying the World*, 68.
⁴⁴ Mettepenningen, 35.

Rome.⁴⁵ The academics north of the alps held what Ratzinger would call "a slight anti-Roman resentment," to the point of saying "the Antichrist sits in Rome."⁴⁶ Moreover, it would be certainly naïve to assert that neo-scholasticism was without any room for development, and part of this frustration was justified on the basis of the need for patristic renewal. Pope Pius XII himself admitted this and expressed the important parameters: "Everyone is aware that the terminology employed in the [scholastic] schools and even that used by the Teaching Authority of the Church itself is capable of being perfected and polished."⁴⁷

On the other hand, Minerd, a translator of Garrigou-Lagrange, asserts the moderate side refused *dialogos* and resorted to petty attacks that damaged the overall efforts.⁴⁸ When the Roman Dominicans published against them, the French Jesuits simply refused to respond. Even a liberal historian Fouilloux concedes this.⁴⁹ The problem was that on the extreme side of the moderate party, there was a tendency in the post-war world to exult in a Teilhardian optimism and a desire to "overthrow" the work of the Magisterium in reacting to the modern movements.

But whoever was to blame, no alliance was formed. *Humani Generis* did not create a new synthesis of the Patristic texts, but set the parameters for a proper renewal, which was still not yet. Meanwhile, an Italian priest named Giovanni Montini (Pope Paul VI), being a lover of French thought (he translated Maritain), attempted to soften the "clear denunciation" in the encyclical by distancing it from the anti-Modernist condemnations of Pope Pius X.⁵⁰

As this was happening, the five years of post-war world had already seen the shadows of the second Sexual Revolution. In the summer of 1950, shortly before *Humani Generis* was issued, Pope Pius XII canonized the eleven year old virgin martyr for chastity, St. Maria Goretti, whom he called the "St. Agnes of the twentieth Century."⁵¹ By her crusading spirit

---

⁴⁵ Seewald, *Benedict XVI: A Life*, vol. 1, 159.
⁴⁶ Ibid., 209; Benedict XVI, *Last Testament: In His Own Words*, trans. Jacob Philips (Bloomsbury, 2016), 126.
⁴⁷ Pius XII, *Humani Generis* (1950), 16, 30.
⁴⁸ See Matthew Minerd's lectures on this topic at *Reason and Theology* (Jan 16, 2021) <https://reasonandtheology.com/courses/the-nouvelle-theologie-with-dr-matthew-minerd/>, accessed March 28, 2021.
⁴⁹ Ibid. Étienne Fouilloux, "Dialogue theologique? (1946-1948)," in S.-T. Bonino, O.P., ed., *Saint Thomas au XXe siecle: Actes du colloque Centenaire de la "Revue Thomiste; Toulouse, 25-28 mars 1993* (Paris: Éditions Saint-Paul, 1994), 153-195.
⁵⁰ Kirwan, *op. cit.*, 257.
⁵¹ Rev. Hugo, Hoever, ed. *Lives of the Saints, For Every Day of the Year* (New York: Catholic Book Publishing Co., 1955), 259-60.

she had won a glorious crown and converted her rapist and killer, Alessandro Serenelli who became a monk. At the age of seventy-four, having witnessed two world wars, the great Pope Pius XII called attention to the evils that were growing in society:

> During the past fifty years, coupled with what was often a weak reaction on the part of decent people, there has been a conspiracy of evil practices, propagating themselves in books and illustrations, in theatres and radio programs, in styles and clubs and on the beaches, trying to work their way into the family and society, and doing their worst damage among the youth, even among those of the tenderest years, in whom the possession of virtue is a natural inheritance.[52]

The enemies of Christ had taken full advantage of all the technology and popular shamanism to destroy the family. Christendom had not been renewed among the clergy. The only hope left, it seemed, was in the Legion of Decency of the Americans.

That fall, Pope Pius XII solemnly dogmatized the Assumption of Our Lady. By this act the Holy Spirit exalted yet further her who is the throne of Christ in the hearts of men. She was the key to renewing the Church and forming the Christian peoples. The third part of the Secret of Fatima, moreover, was to be opened in the next decade. It was November, 1950.

---

[52] Pius XII, "Homily at the canonization of Saint Maria Goretti," June 24th, 1950.

XXX

THE FALSE CRUSADE OF EARTHLY EMPIRES

In 1936, Cardinal Eugenio Pacelli visited the United States. He dined with President Roosevelt, and "became very impressed with America and its strength."[1] As pope (1939-1958), he put the Church in a strong pro-American stance by his advocacy for democracy in 1944, his suppression of the prayers for the emperor and titles of nobility in Rome and in the Church, and the reliance on American money, making the United States "the financial heartland of the Church Universal."[2]

In 1942, he created the Vatican Bank and, facing a Communist takeover of Italy, allowed American funds to pass through to fund the Christian democratic movement against the Communists.[3] The accusations of corruption with the CIA, mafia and freemasons date to this period.[4] Nevertheless in the 1950s the Catholic and American spirit seemed to be coming together. American bishop Ven. Fulton Sheen converted famous Communist infiltrator Bella Dodd, who alluded to how the Soviets were targeting and infiltrating the Church.[5] Repeated condemnations of

---

[1] Coulombe, *Vicars of Christ*, 321.
[2] Ibid.
[3] For an introduction to the history of the Vatican Bank, see T. S. Flanders, "Timeline of Vatican Finances," *Meaning of Catholic* <https://www.meaningofcatholic.com/2020/04/15/timeline-vatican-finances/>.
[4] Paul Williams, *The Vatican Exposed* (Prometheus: 2003); Rupert Cornwell, *God's Banker* (Dodd, Mead: 1984); Fr. Paul Kramer, *The Mystery of Iniquity* (Unmasking Iniquity: 2011).
[5] Dodd said that "she had dealt with no fewer than four cardinals within the Vatican 'who were working for us' [Communists]." Interview with Dr. Alice von Hildebrand, *Latin Mass Magazine*, Summer 2001 <http://www.latinmassmagazine.com/articles/articles_2001_su_hildebran.html>. Accessed May 28th, 2021. On Bella Dodd and the existing evidence, see the

Communism had made that threat obvious to the Church, and Pope Pius XII would condemn the Chinese Communist regime in 1958.

But in this period, all of the positive talk about the United States seemed to be proving true. "American propaganda and psychological operations were being felt around the world, and America increasingly appear[ed] as the last great hope for humanity to many people."[6] But it was more than just an invention of CIA psychological warfare. As Benedict XVI would remember this post-war period before the Council,

> People came to realize that the American Revolution was offering a model of a modern State that differed from the theoretical model with radical tendencies that had emerged during the second phase of the French Revolution... Catholic statesmen demonstrated that a modern secular State could exist that was not neutral regarding values but alive, drawing from the great ethical sources opened by Christianity.[7]

Chief among these thinkers was Maritain who lived in the United States and "sought to describe a relatively 'secular' regime that would nonetheless recognize the principles of redistribution and transcendence and conform itself to them."[8] As Dawson observed in 1959, although the ideology of the United States was secular, it was "tending more and more to regard itself as the ally and protector of religion."[9] Considering the time, it was understandable that the American Empire was filling the Church with optimism, especially the German and French after World War II. For western Europe after World War II, America was a savior, a beacon of light, and an example of post-war democracy that was positive toward religion in general and Catholicism in particular.

The United States had launched an ideological war against Communism, and was filled with a great enthusiasm for religion, while Hollywood was producing world class films about hero priests, Marian

---

forthcoming book by Mary Nicholas; Kevin Symonds, "Rethinking Bella Dodd and the Infiltration of the Catholic Priesthood," <https://kevinsymonds.com/2021/01/13/dodd-infiltration-priesthood/>, accessed May 29, 2021.

[6] Wemhoff, *John Courtney Murray*, 22.

[7] Benedict XVI, "Christmas Address to the Roman Curia," (Dec. 22, 2005).

[8] James Matthew Wilson, "In Defense of Jacques Maritain Against His Neo-Integralist Critics," *Church Life Journal* (University of Notre Dame: November 18, 2020) <https://churchlifejournal.nd.edu/articles/in-defense-of-jacques-maritain-against-his-neo-integralist-critics/>, accessed February 27, 2021.

[9] Dawson, *The Movement of World Revolution*, 86.

nuns and Fatima. Fulton Sheen became a primetime TV host, provoking massive conversions, and America's strong stance against Communism found ready allies in the Church like Pope Pius XII himself. "For several decades, [Maritain's] idea seemed likely to succeed, and Christian democracy, to become the postwar alternative to totalitarianism and secular liberalism."[10] Indeed, this was the Constantine moment for the United States. At this moment all that was truly great about the United States was being elevated above itself to a greater Kingdom. If it would only renounce its version of *Roma*.

The United States had promoted a strong anti-culture regime from its founding, and yet a quasi-public promotion of private religious culture had also been maintained.[11] Nevertheless even the Protestants understood after the Civil War that something crucial was missing: the proclamation of Christ the King. The Founders were divided on their attitude toward religion influencing society, but they were far more unanimous when considering a Catholic-style public *cultus*, like Quebec.

To their credit, they allowed the states to have their own public cultus. But none of these provided the divine grace of the Holy Spirit, and anti-culture gradually eroded the Protestant sects until the Protestantism that was dominant in the 1950s—Billy Graham's evangelicalism—had been emptied of almost all culture and custom. Not even the Protestantism of the 1920s was able to culturally withstand the first Sexual Revolution. The Catholic Church alone had the *cultus* to provide the grace of culture. Without this divine grace, the country would turn to idols. "Their land also is full of idols: they have adored the work of their own hands" (Is 2:8).

Division Grows within the Church

In order to renew the Sexual Revolution and Communism, the remaining threats to Dionysian bloodlust had to be disarmed—South America was folding under Soviet propaganda, Africa was wresting itself from secular control and still nascent as a Christian civilization struggling with tribalism. American Catholicism, exported via Hollywood around the world was a massive threat to the post-war "conspiracy of evil practices." If American Catholicism could convert America to acknowledge Christ, they could transform a crusade between earthly empires into a true crusade for the City of God.

Therefore the enemies of Christ took three crucial actions. First, they broke piety with the families of the 1950s. These families did not raise their children. From the latest scientism from Freudianism, "American homes overnight became child centered" viewing physical discipline as

---

[10] Wilson, *op. cit.*
[11] Russell Kirk, *The American Cause* (ISI Books, 2002), 35-46.

"psychologically unhealthy."[12] Thus in the heart of the family, fatherhood rapidly died as authoritative punishment was condemned by scientism. The economy was quickly losing the spiritual benefit of manual labor and reinforcing endless pleasures, making men effeminate and unwilling to suffer, and certainly not discipline their children or be the head of the household.

Catholic communities were then broken apart by the dismantling of their ethnic neighborhoods.[13] Like the Irish and others in the nineteenth century, when the German, Polish, Italian and other Catholics lost their language and their culture, they lost their faith in the malaise of American anti-culture. And thus the children coming of age in the 50s and 60s in Protestant and Catholic homes were not given Christ as King but succumbed to the cultural momentum toward idols.

This brings us to our second tactic: erecting the idol of money. In the 1950s a number of idols were set up which the youth began to worship. Ed Bernays helped created a massive consumer market of luxuries which all Americans and ultimately the world became attached to. Accelerating the breaking of piety, marketers "targeted babies and children as distinct consumer groups rather than viewing them as little adults"[14] Above all the crucial product was the television which was able to control minds far more effectively than the newspaper. The second was the automobile, which allowed the youth the "freedom" for immorality and break down the norms of customary courtship.

Another form of popular Shamanic music arose through these two products which enhanced the sexualized bewitching of the youth—"rock and roll" music, which could also be used as slang for fornication.[15] By this time swing music had helped to develop the back beat, so that henceforth all popular music would emphasize the rhythm over melody or harmony in order to induce emotional addiction and intoxication, which was the definition of shamanic music.

The sexualized dancing of Elvis Presley shocked the parents, but by that time big business marketing had already gained control over the youth. Everyone knew it was provoking fornication, but they were powerless to stop it. The freedom of the coin allowed the profits to roll in, and it soon became a runaway train.

---

[12] Schweikart and Allen, *Patriot's History of the United States*, 682-683.
[13] E. Michael Jones, *The slaughter of cities: urban renewal as ethnic cleansing* (South Bend, IN: Fidelity Press, 2004).
[14] Schweikart and Allen, 682.
[15] Jerry Gerber et al., *Lifetrends: The Future of Baby Boomers and Other Aging Americans* (New York: Macmillan Publishing Company, 1989), 251-253. Rock and roll does not mean exclusively fornication but also dancing as well as an amalgam of three styles of music.

This was undergirded by private funding and promotion of scientism like Alfred Kinsey, who used data from child molestation to justify Sexual Revolution in his books in 1948 and 1953, which was discussed by prominent magazines as if they were real science and not rationalized magic.[16] Especially in this period, an inferiority complex before the wonders of scientism was gripping Catholics who naively believed the TV and the newspaper.

Meanwhile, pornography was spreading with the founding of *Playboy* in 1953, and the economic system increasingly turned toward sexualization as the most effective means of profit. The Supreme Court also started to dismantle the democratic movement of the Legion of Decency by imposing "freedom" on the people.[17] This shows how much a tiny minority of businessmen were able to have a massive effect on manipulating public opinion and morals.

The legacy of slavery in the Jim Crow south created the environment for a moral crusade led by Martin Luther King Jr. in 1955 to galvanize the world against injustice. Since the abolition of slavery, the American South suffered under another one hundred years of hatred and segregation. This helped provide a moral cause to rationalize the rebellion to come.

Is Christ King over America?

The Jesuits and Dominicans of Europe were at a ceasefire since 1950, but in this decade, an important dispute arose in American Church. With the ascendency of Catholicism in the United States, the time was right to call for the public *cultus* to Christ the King. If Catholics could set up the public *cultus*, divine grace could then baptize the society and the Legion of Decency would be solidified against the sexual economy. Then the Cold War could truly be an actual crusade, not a petty battle between earthly glory.

The dispute arose when John Courtney Murray, SJ, began supporting the proposition that the covenant of the Christian people need not be bound according to the *cultus* of Jesus as the King, but merely "natural law."[18] But his understanding of natural law denied the *cultus*, and thus was an

---

[16] Jennifer Roback Morse, *The Sexual State: How Elite Ideologies are Destroying Lives and Why the Church was Right All Along* (TAN, 2018), 118-24; Mark Whitaker, *Smoketown: The Untold Story of the Other Great Black Renaissance* (Simon & Schuster, 2018), 289-290.

[17] *Roth v. U.S.* (1957) helps legalize pornography, *Engel v. Vitale* (1962) rules that school prayer is unconstitutional, *Jacobellis v. Ohio* (1964) further legalizes pornography, *Griswold v. Connecticut* (1965) protects contraception.

[18] Later published in John Courtney Murray, *We Hold These Truths: Catholic Reflections on the American Proposition* (Sheed and Ward, 1960).

THE FALSE CRUSADE OF EARTHLY EMPIRES

irrational denial of natural law itself. As Pope Leo XIII had said, "Reason itself forbids the state to be godless."[19]

Moreover, even his truncated form of natural law was insufficient to overcome the effects of Original Sin and influence of fallen angels in souls and societies. What he was advocating was imposing the American error of "separation of Church and state" (already condemned by numerous popes) on nineteen centuries of Catholic Tradition. Murray was joined by Gustave Weigel, SJ and other Jesuits at America Magazine.

The dispute against these ideas was led by Fr. Francis J. Connell, Msgr. Joseph Fenton, Msgr. George Shea, as well as Italian and Spanish Jesuits. They wrote of "the duty of all societies to Christ the King, regardless of the form of their government," and the establishing of the public *cultus* for any governments.[20] This was indisputably the Catholic teaching taught and practiced by all the saints and Fathers. There was no room for compromise on this.

Murray's errors, however, were quickly promoted by the CIA psychological warfare and news magazine propaganda under CD Jackson and Henry Luce that targeted the Catholic Church.[21] As a result, the power of the United States was brought to bear to support this error, including the *Pro Deo* University in Rome, which was later supported by Giovanni Montini, who would be consecrated bishop in 1954 (later Paul VI).[22]

Pope Pius XII in *Ci Riesce* (1953), articulated the traditional teaching that among rites that exist within a nation, "that which does not correspond to truth or to the norm of morality objectively has no right to exist, to be spread, or be activated."[23] At the same time, "failure to impede this with civil laws and coercive measures can nevertheless be justified in the interests of a higher and more general good."[24] The Church had given freedom to Jewish worship under the condition that the public order was subordinated to Christ the King. Therefore the concordats with given nations may approve a situation or merely tolerate it, but "the Concordats are for her an expression of the collaboration between the Church and State. In principle, that is, in theory, she cannot approve complete separation of the two powers."[25]

Rome itself was divided on the issue based on strong Jesuit support, division with the Holy Office, and the actions of Jesuit Robert Leiber, who

---

[19] Leo XIII, *Libertas* (1888), 21.
[20] Wemhoff, *op. cit.*, 24.
[21] Ibid., 320-327, 373-382, 422-430, 441-454, 456-464, 492-497, 505-510, 530-533, 557-617.
[22] Ibid., 27.
[23] Pius XII, *Ci Riesce*, (1953).
[24] Ibid.
[25] Ibid.

was a known CIA intelligence source.²⁶ Nevertheless, Murray was censured in 1955 from teaching on this topic. Despite this, he was able to gain further influence with the help of American interests.

Democracy and America

Once again the pope revised the liturgy, and promulgated the 1955 Holy Week reform. The intent of this reform was to promote the concept of active participation. Nevertheless, it also indirectly opposed the pious customs and devotions of the faithful for the holiest week of the year (as well as suppressing the whole Vigil of Pentecost) which led to many faithful being disoriented.²⁷ At best, it unlocked some of the riches of the Holy Week liturgy for the faithful by making them easier to celebrate and more accessible. At worst, it was the beginning of a new iconoclasm based on antiquarianism, the false theory of cleansing liturgical corruption by restoring an imagined pure past.

By 1960, Von Hildebrand was pleased with the increase of the use of Gregorian chant but observed that "although this growth of emphasis on the Liturgy is encouraging and gratifying, it cannot be said that there has been a concurrent growth or deepening in the understanding of the authentic spirit of the liturgy."²⁸ Since the moderate liturgists were now uniting against the strict based on an ideology of active participation, the "authentic spirit of the liturgy" was being lost. Men more and more believed that every soul must conform to *one method* of liturgical piety alone—vocal, audible, active participation. This obscured what real participation is—participation in the sacrifice of the cross by sacramental grace. It was a democratic idea permeating the Christian liturgy.

But in that year, Teilhard went to his eternal reward. His work *The Phenomenon of Man* was boldly published, ignoring the bans. Already in 1951, Von Hildebrand, now a German-American, had personally rebuked Teilhard about his "utter philosophical confusion." Teilhard responded by "violently" condemning St. Augustine as having "spoiled everything by introducing the supernatural."²⁹

---

[26] Wemhoff, 29.
[27] On the 1955 reform, see the Una Voce position papers, <http://www.unavoce.ru/pdf/FIUV_PP/FIUV_PP14_Part1_HolyWeekReformFinal.pdf> and <http://www.unavoce.ru/pdf/FIUV_PP/FIUV_PP14_Part2_HolyWeekLiturgiesFinal.pdf>.
[28] Von Hildebrand, *Liturgy and Personality* (Hildebrand Project, 2016), preface to the Second Edition, 1960, xxi.
[29] Von Hildebrand, *Charitable Anathema*, 179.

THE FALSE CRUSADE OF EARTHLY EMPIRES

It was in the 1950s that Von Hildebrand published his devastating critique of Modernity in *The New Tower of Babel*. In this text he praised the fact that many in the modern world were fighting Communism, but raised the alarm that despite this modern man was anti-Christian, anti-God, anti-natural law, anti-truth; he denied his creaturehood and misunderstood beauty; modern thought dethroned God and man, and classic paganism was nobler than the modern stance.[30] Having fought Nazism and Communism, he now condemned the voluntarism in American and European democracy:

> [Modern man's] concept of democracy means rather that the majority arbitrarily decides what is right and wrong, and that arbitrary will of the individual is the very source of right and wrong. In other words, the arbitrary will of the individual replaces the objective norm. Instead of believing that there is a chance that the majority of men will choose that which is objectively right, independently of their will, this modern man believes that their arbitrary decision makes a law right and legitimate.[31]

Without logos, there is only voluntarism, which seeks to impose its will on objective reality. Then there is a loss of beauty, as reverence is lost in a "heresy of efficiency."[32]

> The heresy of efficiency... makes man a mere means for the production of impersonal goods. It is revealed in every exploitation of men by a ruthless capitalism. Man is then considered to have no importance as a person, only as an instrument for the production of other goods. This heresy culminates in the Communist attitude toward man. As soon as man is no longer useful as an instrument, he is discarded as a worn-out tool.[33]

Von Hildebrand understood the principles of anti-culture in both capitalism and Communism subjecting the weak to the will of the powerful. He had seen America for about a decade and he was not impressed.

Jacques Maritain, on the other hand, had lived in America for several decades and was deeply impressed. His *Reflections on America* appeared

---

[30] Von Hildebrand, *The New Tower of Babel*, 7, 9-50.
[31] Ibid., 14.
[32] Ibid., 145-156, 157-176.
[33] Ibid., 177-178.

in 1956. McInerny thought this was a "prime example" of Maritain's "naivete."[34] In it he praised:

> The formidable adventure begun in this country with the Pilgrim Fathers and the pioneers, and continued in the great days of the Declaration of Independence and the Revolutionary War... It will be necessary for the European spirit and the American spirit to meet and cooperate in common good will... if we want civilization to survive, a world of free men penetrated in its secular substance by a real and vital Christianity, a world in which the inspiration of the Gospel will direct the common life of man toward an heroic humanism...
>
> What they expect from America is: Hope. And please God that this critical fact may never be forgotten here.
>
> It is possible to be more specific, and to say: what the world expects from America is that she keep alive, in human history, a fraternal recognition of the dignity of man – in other words, the terrestrial hope of men in the Gospel.[35]

Thus while Von Hildebrand found many modern errors after living in America, Maritain found great hope. It was true that in America one could find many good things of society that were at times lost in European life. In particular, as we have noted, basic economic opportunities could often be found in America that were unknown elsewhere, and in the 1950s America had the outward appearance of great religion and even Catholicism. But it was Maritain's hope in America, not Von Hildebrand's realism, that would soon shape the course of Church history. Maritain, as an orthodox moderate, would help turn the question of "mob bloodshed or modernity" to the latter side through the idea of America, which added momentum to the growing fad of Teilhardian optimism.

In 1958, Karol Wojtyła was consecrated bishop in Poland. He immediately turned to face the Marxists. He went to the Communist-built city of Nowa Huta—a city without a church—to confront the Communists and celebrate the Holy Sacrifice for the workers on Christmas Eve, doing so every year. Thus began a long struggle to build a church there—a public

---

[34] Florian Michel, *La pensée catholique en Amérique du Nord*, 516 in Jones, Logos Rising, 628.
[35] Jacques Maritain, *Reflections on America* (1956) <https://maritain.nd.edu/jmc/etext/reflect0.html>, accessed November 5, 2021.

THE FALSE CRUSADE OF EARTHLY EMPIRES

throne to the King of Kings—against the will of the Communist authorities. Wojtyła began to synthesize the moderates and strict eventually writing *Love and Responsibility*, showing how the Puritan spirit of the Jansenists and the Dionysian spirit of the Freudians both tended to the objectification of spouses.[36] But eleven days after Wojtyła's consecration, Pope Ven. Pius XII went to his eternal reward.

Murray's errors were now in the ascendency and with Pope Pius XII now dead, Catholic John F. Kennedy publicly endorsed the false notion of the separation of Church and state:

> I believe in an America where the separation of church and state is absolute—where no Catholic prelate would tell the President (should he be a Catholic) how to act ... where no church or church school is granted any public funds or political preference—and where no man is denied public office merely because his religion differs from the President who might appoint him or the people who might elect him.
>
> I believe in an America that is officially neither Catholic, Protestant nor Jewish—where no public official either requests or accepts instructions on public policy from the Pope ... where no religious body seeks to impose its will directly or indirectly upon the general populace or the public acts of its officials—and where religious liberty is so indivisible that an act against one church is treated as an act against all.[37]

This thinking was only possible if Original Sin was not a large problem to be overcome by the divine grace of the *cultus* celebrated as a public act of the state. When Kennedy accepted this error and promoted it, the crusade against Communism was henceforth nothing more than a petty, false crusade between earthly cities.

But even then, the third part of the Secret of Fatima could avert this Teilhardian vision. In 1959 or 1960, the pope opened the secret, which contained a vision of the martyrs being attacked by the errors of Russia and a massacre of the pope and bishops.[38] It was completely opposed to the

---

[36] Karol Wojtyła, *Love and Responsibility* (San Francisco, CA: Ignatius Press, 1981), 57-72.
[37] John F. Kennedy, "Speech to the Southern Baptist Leadership," *New York Times* (Sep. 13, 1960).
[38] "The history of an entire century can be seen represented in this image... In the vision we can recognize the last century as a century of martyrs, a century of

superstition of unlimited progress, and called once again for penance against the evil in the world as the angel in the vision cried "Penance! Penance! Penance!"

At the opening of the Second Vatican Council, the unity of moderate and strict that had been formalized at Vatican I was at its weakest point. All alike had taken the vow against Modernism, but the debate in the 1940s had shown that the new Greco-Roman synthesis faced immense difficulty. On the one hand, the moderate party sought to renew the Church with the Fathers. On the other hand, the strict party sought to restate the same doctrine with Thomism. It was a great opportunity to truly confront the modern world and call them to repentance. St. Teresa Benedicta and Dietrich von Hildebrand had provided the models for this renewal in helping to integrate new insights from philosophy to the tradition.

The problem is that Communism and Americanism were and are both different forms of anti-culture which remove *cultus*, tradition, elders or piety. Both begin from an assertion that Original Sin is not the problem, so therefore a new political or economic arrangement will improve human nature. Both relied on false "education" to program children. Both believe in the superstition of unlimited progress. Yet the Church could tolerate Americanism because Americanism tolerated Catholicism to a much greater degree than Communism. If the Church could adopt a critical view of Americanism, the good things in the system could be distinguished from the bad.

Yet by adopting Teilhardian optimism about the modern world, like Kennedy, Church leaders ended up being overcome by Americanism and Communism. This optimism lay at the root of the moderates switching sides and adopting a principle of negation against the strict. The "prophets of doom" were rejected.

---

suffering and persecution for the Church, a century of World Wars and the many local wars which filled the last fifty years and have inflicted unprecedented forms of cruelty. In the "mirror" of this vision we see passing before us the witnesses of the faith decade by decade. Here it would be appropriate to mention a phrase from the letter which Sister Lucia wrote to the Holy Father on 12 May 1982: "The third part of the 'secret' refers to Our Lady's words: 'If not, [Russia] will spread her errors throughout the world, causing wars and persecutions of the Church. The good will be martyred; the Holy Father will have much to suffer; various nations will be annihilated.'" Joseph Ratzinger, "Theological Commentary," *The Message of Fatima* (Congregation for the Doctrine of the Faith, 2000). Ratzinger elaborated in the 2000 press conference that in the third part of the secret "the history of the martyrs of a century" is shown and "the passion of the popes in this century, and not exclusively the attack of 13 May, '81," although this was a culminating event. See the translation given by Kevin Symonds, *On the Third Part of the Secret of Fatima* (St. Louis, MO: Enroute, 2017), 372.

XXXI

THE MEDICINE OF MERCY FOR THE ANTICHRIST

"The principle cause of the evil, we believe, is the tendency... to concentrate all the authority Christ granted to his church in the one person of the Sovereign Pontiff."[1] So spoke Bishop Maximos IV and the Eastern Catholic Bishops on the Greek Schism in 1959, identifying the false spirit of Vatican I as the central problem to be addressed by Vatican II. The condemnations of *Nouvelle théologie* had alienated the good efforts of the fourth renewal and the false spirit of Vatican I helped create the idea that the right pope could upset the power of the Curia. They had found him in Pope St. John XXIII.

At the opening of Vatican II the Roman Pontiff rejoiced that mankind had progressed toward a "new order" so much that "men of themselves are inclined to condemn [their own errors]."[2] It was a speech deeply influenced by the French optimism of Teilhard and others of the *Nouvelle théologie*.[3] He thought that "modern man" could be won over to the truth by a simple demonstration of the same, underestimating the enemies of Christ. Like Lateran V, Vatican II addressed the issue, but did not see the storm on the horizon. And like Lateran V, the strict continued to warn the council about this storm, but the warning fell on deaf ears. Just as fatherhood died in the family when scientism condemned authoritative punishment, many Church authorities believed that the charitable anathema was no longer an act of mercy and this part of fatherhood should be abandoned. This would cause popes and bishops to choose unity at the expense of truth.

---

[1] Quoted in O'Malley, *What Happened at Vatican II*, 125-126.
[2] *Novum rerum ordinem...Hodie homines per se ipsi ea damnare incipere videantur*. Pope St. John XXIII, Address *Gaudet Mater Ecclesia* (Oct. 11, 1962).
[3] Kirwan, *An Avant-garde Theological Generation*, 262.

The ideas of Teilhard de Chardin of an unlimited progress "dominated the council," and even Ratzinger would admit, "something of the Kennedy era pervaded the council, something of the naïve optimism of the great society."[4] It is important for us to sympathize with the ideas of the 1960s from a Christian perspective. In particular, the moral crusade of Martin Luther King against real injustice captured the imagination of the whole world. Above all, this struggle against an actual evil was what inspired Christians in those days. King was a great man, but no saint. Lamentably, King's vision was strongly mixed with a Masonic idea of what "freedom" meant, and moreover, King himself was morally compromised. Unfortunately his very life exemplified the poisonous mixture of true liberation with sexual liberation.[5] This mixture was tragically overlooked by churchmen of the day.

And so the Fathers of Vatican II failed to read the signs of the times. As Ratzinger admits, "we certainly did not correctly assess the political consequences and the actual repercussions... and did not reflect on how these things would come across."[6] Or as Nichols concedes: "The Conciliar fathers... underestimated the unsettling effect of disturbing the post-Tridentine religious culture in place in the Church."[7]

After generations of strain, and the alienation of the moderates by the strict since Vatican I and Pope Pius X, the moderates finally broke with the strict. With the break down in the *dialogos* in the 1940s and 1950s, there

---

[4] Joseph Ratzinger, *Principles of Catholic Theology* (Ignatius: 1987), 367.
[5] The contrast between King's public persona and legacy and his private life is one of the most well-kept secrets in the history of America in the twentieth century, yet even the DuVernay production of *Selma* (2014) could not conceal this. King was privately known to be a serial adulterer and was criticized for his "compulsive sexual athleticism" to which he reportedly replied, "I'm away from home 25 to 27 days month. F--king's a form of anxiety reduction." David J. Garrow, *Bearing the Cross: Martin Luther King, Jr., and the Southern Christian Leadership Conference* (Open Road Media, 2015), 375. Cf. E. Michael Jones, *Libido Dominandi*, 459-463. King's morals in forgiving his enemies after the Montgomery Bus Boycott were thoroughly Christian. His theology, lamentably, was not. His celebrated "I Have a Dream" speech envisions all religions "joining hands" and singing "free at last," which reinterprets the meaning of the Negro spiritual in terms of the earthly city only. King's ideas reinterpret Gandhi and Tolstoy into a Christianized message of Marxist liberation theology. Clayborne Carson, ed., *The Autobiography of Martin Luther King, Jr.* (Warner Books, 1998), 13-16, 17-29, 30-33, *passim*.
[6] Benedict XVI, *Last Testament*, 105.
[7] Aidan Nichols, *Catholic Thought Since the Enlightenment* (University of South Africa: 1998), 164.

was deep resentment between the moderates and strict, and the whole Church would suffer because of this fissure.

What happened at the council was that the strict of the curia presented to the council their draft documents. But the moderate party of the *Nouvelle théologie* refused to ally with the strict. Instead by the time of the Council's beginning they had made the "European Alliance" against the strict, as O'Malley and Wiltgen admit.[8] They immediately seized control of the council just as the strict had done at Vatican I.[9] Among their number was Bishop Karol Wojtyła and the peritus, Fr. Joseph Ratzinger. Just as at Vatican I Georg Ratzinger and Lord Acton had allied with Döllinger who later died a heretic, a similar alliance with heretics was forming at Vatican II. But this time that alliance had control of the council.

Christian culture was broken. The moderates were in alliance with the heretics against the strict. The strict party formed as the *Coetus Internationalis Patrum* led in part by Lefebvre. However, their position was not only numerically weak, but theologically on the defensive and unable to achieve the necessary synthesis with the Patristic renewal and dismissive of the Augustinian Phenomenology. It was necessary to form a strong alliance with the Eastern bishops, whose Greek thought was more in accord with Bonaventure than Thomas. Thus the Eastern bishops tended to find support with the European alliance, not the strict.[10]

The heretics were able to use this confusion to their own ends, and pushed for ambiguities in the documents so they could promote heresy after the Council.[11] Like most councils, the whole thing was chaos, yet God still brought good out of it — most of all, the full repudiation by an Ecumenical Council of the evil legacy of Latinizations, paving the way for the fourth renewal.[12] But lamentably, this fourth renewal was deeply wounded by the discord among the Latin theologians.

In terms of Christian culture, the most important aspects of the Council were its documents on liturgy, religious liberty, and teaching on marriage. The true fourth renewal progressed, but it quickly became a pretext for the

---

[8] O'Malley, *What Happened at Vatican II*, 113-122; Ralph Wiltgen, *The Rhine Flows Into the Tiber* (Devon: Augustine Publishing Company, 1979), 15-18.
[9] Wiltgen, 15-24.
[10] O'Malley, 124-126.
[11] For example, the inerrancy of Scripture was confirmed by the CDF as recently as 1998 as a *De Fide* proposition. At Vatican II, Franz Cardinal Konig of Vienna openly stated on the Council floor that the Word of God contains errors, basing his assertion on recent archaeological discoveries. This resulted in the original precision on this doctrine being dropped from the final document in *Dei Verbum*, 11. See T. S. Flanders, *Introduction to the Holy Bible*, 217-240.
[12] *Orientalium Ecclesiarum* (1964), 1-6.

heretics to impose their views, with the moderate party giving them power by their alliance with them against the strict while abandoning the anathema.

Sacrosanctum Concilium

The European Alliance was able to get the Council to throw out all the original documents except one: the document on the liturgy, drafted by Annibale Bugnini, who had intentionally left it vague. In order to change the *cultus*, "proposals," Bugnini had said, must be:

> Formulated in such a way that much is said without seeming to say anything: let many things be said in embryo (*in nuce*) and in this way let the door remain open to legitimate and possible postconciliar deductions and applications... We must proceed discreetly.[13]

Thus the Council document called for a modest reform of the liturgy for the sake of active participation. But the document seemed to suggest that our fathers who did not "actively participate" in the Holy Sacrifice "were deprived of the true Christian spirit."[14]

By focusing on active participation defined narrowly as vocal, audible participation, Bugnini's reform of the *cultus* gave the impression that pious devotions of the faithful should be discontinued during the liturgy. The message that was sent through the media was that a group of progressives was dealing with a group of stubborn reactionaries. Lefebvre and the strict supported certain reforms in the liturgy, so the document was able to be passed without serious issues. But Bugnini's plans were soon enacted with Pope Paul VI's approval.

---

[13] Bugnini's opening to schema preparation commission, Oct 11, 1961, in Angelo Lameri, *La "Pontificia Commisio de sacra liturgia praeparatoria Concilii Vaticani II,"Documenti, Testi, Verbali* (2013) in Chiron, 82.

[14] "In the restoration and promotion of the sacred liturgy, this full and active participation by all the people is the aim to be considered before all else; for it is the primary and indispensable source from which the faithful are to derive the true Christian spirit" (*Sacrosanctum Concilium*, 14). Whereas Von Hildebrand (and Pius XII, *Mediator Dei*, 108) had sought to bring the faithful to the liturgy yet acknowledged that the true, holy spirit of the liturgy was also present in the pious peasant with "scant knowledge of the liturgy," Bugnini's thought began to pervade the Church with the idea that vocal participation in the parts of the Mass were the *only* means of the "true Christian spirit."

Religious Liberty

The document on liberty was heavily influenced by John Courtney Murray. He was able to convince the Council Fathers to adopt language that was very easily interpreted in favor of American-style liberty, which removed the public *cultus* to Christ the King. Meanwhile, the *Coetus* was successful in convincing the council to add the provision of the duty of societies to the true faith in the beginning of the document. Lefebvre moreover emphasized that liberty must not be defined as freedom from all restraint or else it would undermine a father's authority over his children.[15] Moderates like Wojtyła and Ratzinger would agree, and Wojtyła also criticized one of the drafts on Religious Freedom as giving not enough emphasis to the intrinsic connection of freedom to the objective truth.[16] Yet many in society wanted freedom from all authority. The full breadth of Murray's ideas were technically not accepted in the actual decree.

The media propaganda of the United States, however, was able to make use of the ambiguities of the document to declare that the Catholic Church had reversed its stance regarding the United States and adopted their politics as the new model. This seems to be how even popes have understood the document since, none of them claiming that the public *cultus* should be restored. At the same time, the efforts to condemn Communism were silenced.[17]

Marriage

Some Council Fathers began to assert that the two ends of marriage should be revised. At best, this was an attempt to cleanse the lingering remainders of Jansenism and the Nazi-Totalitarian *objectification* of woman by the state for procreation only, but it was used by some for a wholesale adoption of the Protestant notions of marriage and even contraception.

---

[15] Intervention, October 1964, in Marcel Lefebvre, *They Have Uncrowned Him: From Liberalism to Apostasy, the Conciliar Tragedy* (Kansas City, MO: Angelus Press, 1988), 41.

[16] Karol Wojtyła, Archbishop of Krakow, intervention of September 25, 1964, in *Acta synodalia Concilii Vaticani II*, Period III, vol. 2, 530-32 at 531 in Avery Dulles, *Truth as the Ground of Freedom: A Theme from John Paul II* (Acton Institute, 1995), 1.

[17] Roberto de Mattei, *The Second Vatican Council: An Unwritten Story*, trans. Patrick T. Brannan, et al., (Loreto Publications, 2010), 397-400, 469-480.

Some Council Fathers seemed to have an inferiority complex about the scientism of population control, and others directly or indirectly called for the teaching on contraception to be changed.[18] Others were advocating that a marriage without love was not a marriage.[19] The strict protested against this, warning this would undermine marriage validity and lead to an annulment crisis, but they were defeated in their efforts to prevent this.[20] Meanwhile, the Rockefeller foundation and other business leaders were already funding the efforts to force contraception on the world in general and the Catholic Church in particular.[21]

In 1963, the United States had finally allowed the pornographic novel *Fanny Hill* to be published. The next year, Liberal Jews and their allies in Hollywood were able to break the League of Decency by using the Holocaust itself in the first pornography since the 1920s in the movie *The Pawnbroker*.[22] This "conspiracy of evil practices" was continuing like Pope Pius XII had said, while too many Council Fathers were caught up in the clouds of theological excitement.

In March of 1965, Pope Paul VI celebrated a new order of Mass in Italian, facing the people at a table altar, and said that "the Church has sacrificed its native tongue, Latin" so that the faithful would go from being "spectators to becoming active participants."[23] Communion was distributed to the faithful standing.[24] Paul VI was promulgating and implementing Vatican II as he understood it.

In his own celebrations it was clear that "Pope Paul VI by no means intended the new Mass to be celebrated in continuity with the preceding

---

[18] Some Fathers publicly asked the Council to surrender to modern fads of scientism, since they did not want another "Galileo case." O'Malley, *op. cit.*, 237-238; De Mattei, 454-456.
[19] De Mattei, 389-396.
[20] De Mallerais, *The Biography of Marcel Lefebvre*, 302-303.
[21] Morse, *The Sexual State*, 89-190; Jones, *Libido Dominandi*, 403-417.
[22] E. Michael Jones, *John Cardinal Krol and the Cultural Revolution* (South Bend, IN: Fidelity Press, 2018), 301-354.
[23] Paul VI, Angelus 7 March 1965, *L'Osservatore Romano*, 8-9 March 1965; English Translation, International Commission on English in the Liturgy, *Documents on the Liturgy*, 1963-1979 (Collegeville, MN: Liturgical Press, 1982), 26 in Chiron, 118.
[24] Augustinus, "The 50th Anniversary of Paul VI's First Italian Mass Some hard truths about the "1965 Missal" and the Liturgical Reform" *Rorate Caeli* (March 7, 1965) <https://rorate-caeli.blogspot.com/2015/03/the-50th-anniversary-of-paul-vis-first.html>, accessed October 27, 2021.

liturgical tradition."[25] Pope Paul VI disparaged his critics as having a "poor understanding" and "spiritual laziness" and highlighted the positive responses as "enthusiasm and praise."[26] Meanwhile, priests were abandoning their vocations "by the thousand" already in that year.[27] As a young professor, Fr. Joseph Ratzinger took great issue with Pope Paul VI's implementation and would criticize him publicly.[28] The division of implementing the revised Mass would illustrate the division between the moderate and strict parties.[29]

On the 7th of June, 1965, the American Supreme Court yielded to the pressure and imposed "freedom" for contraception against state laws in the United States.[30] This was the fruit of failing to enshrine Christ as King in the Constitution and His *cultus*. Because the Logos Incarnate was not the moral principle of society, the voluntarism of power, money and "freedom" was all that was left.

Just two weeks later, Von Hildebrand wrote a long document to Pope Paul VI in which he "humbly requested a clear condemnation of heretical statements."[31] Meanwhile Rockefeller was writing to Pope Paul VI about the scientism of "the population problem."[32]

Pope Paul VI accepted the scientism but told Von Hildebrand his proposed condemnation "was a bit harsh."[33] Meanwhile, while Pope Paul VI was promoting the new *cultus*, the faith in the Real Presence was being shattered, and he felt compelled to issue an encyclical defending the

---

[25] Peter Kwasniewski, *Reclaiming Our Roman Catholic Birthright: The Genius and Timeliness of the Traditional Catholic Mass* (Angelico Press, 2020), 99.
[26] Paul VI, General Audience, (March 17, 1965) <https://www.ccwatershed.org/2014/03/26/17-march-1965-pope-paul-vi-confusion-and-annoyance/>, accessed October 1, 2021.
[27] Romano Amerio, *Iota Unum: A Study of the Changes in the Catholic Church in the XXth Century*, trans. Fr. John P. Parsons (Sarto House, 1996), 181.
[28] Ratzinger nevertheless says that before Paul VI made him a bishop, the pope was "safe in the knowledge that he and I were fundamentally in alignment." Benedict XVI, *Last Testament*, 136.
[29] Note: Gregorian chant is still the preferred musical genre and Latin is still the official language of the revised liturgy, albeit, in actual practice, and very unfortunately, they are little used.
[30] Morse, *The Sexual State*, 89-190.
[31] Interview with Dr. Alice von Hildebrand, *Latin Mass Magazine*, Summer 2001 <http://www.latinmassmagazine.com/articles/articles_2001_su_hildebran.html>. Accessed November 23, 2019
[32] Rockefeller Archives, JDF III to Pope Paul VI, 7/16/65 in Jones, *Libido Dominandi*, 435.
[33] Interview with Dr. Alice von Hildebrand.

dogma.[34] The revolt was gaining speed when the Council closed on the Immaculate Conception, 1965, and "the fallout of Vatican II was obvious to everyone."[35] "Catholic elites, first in Europe, began to argue 'local Church rights' against Rome."[36] Bishops and priests of the European Alliance told the faithful they could touch the Sacred Body of Christ our God, so that the Most Holy Sacrament should be treated like common food. In many cases the faithful were confused by the changes to the liturgy and became disoriented as chaos erupted in their parish churches. Paul VI immediately opposed Communion in the hand, calling it an "abuse," and attempted to stop it.[37]

The next year, 1966, the United States government began funding contraception and since the coin was free from logos, the economy was about to be injected with a new dose of the spirit of fornication.[38] The United States could now export not Fatima movies, but the murder of life-creation in contraception.

That same year, Pope Paul VI yielded to his advisors and decreed that works of charity can replace the mortification of fasting during Lent and abstinence on Fridays.[39] Just as the world was falling into slavery to screens and popular shamanism, the concupiscible appetite was not checked by salutary fasting, leading to the second Sexual Revolution.[40]

Meanwhile, the European Alliance was attempting to impose their vision of endless progress with the journal *Concilium*, which included both moderates like Congar, De Lubac and Von Balthasar as well as those with extreme, heretical views like Küng, Rahner, and Schillebeeckx.

By 1967, the hero of Pope Paul VI was sounding the alarm. Jacques Maritain wrote that the Church was in a "crisis" in which it was "kneeling

---

[34] Paul VI, *Mysterium Fidei* (1965).
[35] Msgr. George A. Kelly, *The Battle for the American Church* (Garden City, NY: Doubleday & Co., 1979), 7.
[36] Ibid., *The Battle for the American Church Revisited* (San Francisco, CA: Ignatius Press, 1995), 43.
[37] Paul VI, handwritten memorandum to the Council for Public Affairs (March 27, 1969) in Annibale Bugnini, *The Reform of the Liturgy 1948-1975*, trans. Matthew J. O'Connell (Collegeville, MN: The Liturgical Press, 1990), 656. On the Holy See's opposition to Communion in the Hand, see Bp. Juan Rodolfo Laise, *Holy Communion*, 5th ed. (PCP Books, 2020), 28-75, 76-89.
[38] Morse, *The Sexual State*, 89-190.
[39] Paul VI (1966), *Paenitemini*.
[40] The concupiscible appetite is that part of a person which desires two goods— bodily food and the conjugal act. Fasting therefore moderates excessive attachments to these pleasures and is essential to overcome both gluttony and lust.

before the world" and he vehemently condemned Teilhardianism.⁴¹ He had already signed a petition in 1966 to save the Latin Mass while the international lay organization *Una Voce* had already formed to preserve the rite.⁴² And yet it was Maritain's promotion of a Christian democracy that was "enshrined in the documents of Vatican II"⁴³ But his warning caused a shockwave.

In the same year the English translation appeared of Henri de Lubac's second of four books defending and promoting Teilhard.⁴⁴ Yet even De Lubac could admit that year that "the Church is facing a grave crisis" wherein "a different Church from that of Jesus Christ is now trying to establish itself: an anthropocentric society threatened with immanentism apostasy.⁴⁵ Daniélou and De Lubac saw a crisis, whereas Congar and Chenu were still optimistic.⁴⁶ Ratzinger was among the former, saying in that year that the faith was now surrounded "with a fog of uncertainty" as had "hardly been seen before at any point in history."⁴⁷ This was the beginning of the moderate party breaking from the European Alliance.

Von Hildebrand railed against the Teilhardianism by saying the same year in a large book condemning the "Trojan Horse in the City of God" that the vision of a new age based on "modern man" was a grave error because "terms such as nineteenth century man or modern man are ambiguous."

> No such universals exist; there are only intellectual and cultural trends that have a transitory dominance. The idea of modern man as a norm to which we all should conform is either deceitful or meaningless. Even if

---

⁴¹ Maritain, *The Peasant of the Garonne*, 53-63, 116-126.
⁴² Joseph Shaw, "Other Petitions in Favour of the Ancient Mass," *Gregorius Magnus* (2021, no. 12) <https://issuu.com/gregoriusmagnus/docs/gads1591_gregorius_magnus_12_winter_web_2021_ame/s/13650010>, accessed November 3, 2021.
⁴³ Kirwan, *An Avant-garde Theological Generation*, 257.
⁴⁴ In English *Teilhard de Chardin: the man and his meaning,* trans. Rene Hague, (New York: Hawthorn Books, 1965). *The religion of Teilhard de Chardin*, trans. Rene Hague, (New York: Desclee Co., 1967). *Teilhard explained,* trans. Anthony Buono, (New York: Paulist Press, 1968). *The Eternal Feminine: a study on the poem by Teilhard de Chardin,* trans. René Hague, (New York: Harper & Row, 1971).
⁴⁵ Henri de Lubac, Témoinage Chrétien (Paris, 1967) in Dietrich von Hildebrand, *Trojan Horse in the City of God* (1967), 8.
⁴⁶ Kirwan, 271.
⁴⁷ Benedict XVI, *Last Testament*, 141.

> understood only as a bearer of a temporarily prevalent mentality, modern man can never be a norm for us...
>
> There is no closed, homogenous epoch in history; there is no "modern man." And most important of all, man always remains the same in his essential structure, in his destiny, in his potentialities, in his desires, and in his moral dangers; and this is true notwithstanding all the external changes that take place in the external conditions of his life. There is and has been but one essential historical change in the metaphysical and moral situation of man: the advent of Christ and the salvation of mankind and reconciliation with God through Christ's death on the Cross.[48]

The European Alliance was implicitly stating that "modern man" was not darkened with Original Sin as to need the salutary condemnations of his errors, but, like Pope St. John XXIII had claimed, he would realize and condemn his own errors.

Meanwhile, the business interests were engineering an internal revolt within the Church by funding efforts to remove Catholic academic institutions from Church control.[49] In 1967, the Land O'Lakes Statement declared Catholic universities to have independence from Church authority, which was signed by none other than Fr. Theodore McCarrick. The Dutch bishops had also published a catechism which contained theological errors.

The Augustinian Phenomenology of Husserl was not distinguished from relativistic phenomenology, and the synthesis of St. Teresa Benedicta of the Cross was implicitly rejected by the European Alliance. The moderates who believed in objective truth were willing to ally with those who did not. Meanwhile, the strict tended to alienate the moderates by rejecting every philosophy except Thomism, which implicitly disparaged St. Bonaventure as Seraphic Doctor alongside the Angelic Doctor.

In 1967 the revised Mass was celebrated for the synod of bishops, and received mixed reactions but was not approved by the bishops. Even the Secretary of State pleaded for an end to liturgical change "lest the faithful be confused."[50]

---

[48] Von Hildebrand, *Trojan Horse in the City of God*, 153, 157.
[49] Jones, *Logos Rising*, 644-651.
[50] Chiron, 130,

While this was happening, a new scientism in the Human Potential Movement was gaining popularity all around Euro-America, which applied the worst of scientism's psychology to the ascetic life of priests and religious. The false gospel of psychology taught that one should let one's emotions out and desires flow freely. This ended up emptying religious orders as monks and nuns abandoned asceticism for scientism.[51] Very quickly the scientism of psychology was penetrating religious education, creating a "battle for the Catholic child" which was "psychology vs. parents."[52] By 1968, the second Sexual Revolution was breaking down families throughout the world. The bishops and priests were dominated by an inferiority complex regarding scientism, and more and more let these practitioners of scientism govern their pastoral work.

But by then, Pope St. Paul VI had the humility to change course from Teilhardian optimism and the medicine of mercy. He listened to the urgings of Maritain to do something like what Von Hildebrand had already said to do three years prior. In June and July of 1968, just as the generation of the 1950s were revolting inside and outside the Church, Pope Paul VI issued his orthodox Creed and, "the most important act of his own pontificate," *Humanae Vitae*.[53] The American economy was beginning to "boom" with the new technology, with government support. But like his predecessor Pope Pius XI, Pope Paul VI predicted the further abjection of woman from this new economy of sin:

> A man who grows accustomed to the use of contraceptive methods may forget the reverence due to a woman, and, disregarding her physical and emotional equilibrium, reduce her to being a mere instrument for the satisfaction of his own desires, no longer considering her as his partner whom he should surround with care and affection.[54]

The Protestants had attacked the monuments of the Church to Mary Immaculate, and thus the "reverence due to a woman" had been eroding ever since. With the American and Soviet ideologies of dignity as power, they had convinced woman that she must descend from her regal throne of the household and pursue power in the mechanized ugliness of modernity. If she did not do everything that a man did, then she was not powerful, and

---

[51] Jones, *Libido Dominandi*, 464-506.
[52] Kelly, *op. cit.*, 235-252.
[53] Amerio, *op. cit.*, 136.
[54] Paul VI, *Humanae Vitae* (1968), 17.

had no dignity. This false ideology attacked the glory of feminine nature as intrinsically beautiful and exquisite, and attacked the rights of children to have their mother and be sheltered under the shadow of her wings. Paul VI's encyclical confirmed the intrinsic evil of contraception, even though it accepted the scientism of population control.

Not ten years prior, Pope John had thought that "men of themselves were inclined to condemn their own errors," and now Pope Paul VI had seen how in this case, says Amerio Romano, "papal foresight indisputably failed."[55] It was thought that the new formulations of Vatican II would bring about a renewal, but the opposite was happening. Now the pope felt compelled to simply restate Catholic doctrine, against which arose immediately a worldwide revolt of laity, academics, priests and even bishops.[56] It was nevertheless thought that the new *cultus* would produce a renewal, but so far the opposite was happening. Bugnini was hard at work, however, to produce the desired renewal.

---

[55] Ibid., 82.
[56] On the Catholic revolt against *Humanae Vitae*, see Kelly, *op. cit.*, 164-198.

Part IV

The Triumph of New Iconoclasm

AD 1965–Present

XXXII

THE ATTEMPT TO SUPPRESS THE CULTUS

Annibale Bugnini believed in implementing his reforms by any means necessary, including deception. When he was pushing his ideas on the committee and they opposed him, he told them that the pope wanted it this way. The false spirit of Vatican I, now exacerbated by the false spirit of Vatican II, made the committee consent. When the pope himself opposed Bugnini, Bugnini told the pope that the committee had unanimously chosen this reform. According to Louis Bouyer, this was how Bugnini implemented his aforementioned plan with the vague *Sacrosanctum Concilium*.[1]

On January 1st, 1969, the Church had endured more than five years of upheaval. The changes already made to the Mass by Paul VI had not produced a renewal, bishops were in revolt, and many priests were abandoning their vocations. The situation was very similar to January 1st, 1848, when Pope Pius IX had given the liberals great concessions in an attempt to win them over. Instead, they had revolted. Pope Pius IX had realized his mistake and corrected it, and he was willing to live with the consequences. The result was a Catholic revival against an onslaught of revolution.

The greatest men of the day from all sides—Maritain, De Lubac, Ratzinger, Von Hildebrand, Ottaviani—had sounded the alarm against this revolt, causing Pope Paul VI to finally act and pronounce a creed and defend marriage. The new *cultus*, moreover, had not received the approval of the bishops and was not producing a renewal. But the pope's faith in Bugnini was unshaken.

---

[1] Louis Bouyer, *The Memoirs of Louis Bouyer: From Youth and Conversion to Vatican II, the Liturgical Reform, and After* (Angelico Press, 2015), 224-225.

Pope Paul VI, it seems, was terrified of schism, but the revolt was able to come about. The accusations and rumors of him being homosexual can be dismissed as tabloid calumny, but they would not have gained massive attention—to the point of Paul VI publicly denying them—if a deep consciousness had not stunned Euro-America that *masculine fatherhood was no longer present* in the office of the pope. This is the most important aspect about his pontificate which must be understood.

It was as if the Holy Father did not want to discipline his children because he knew they would leave the family. So he did not stop the stronger children from overcoming the weaker children, who left in the thousands. What father would allow his stronger children to abuse his weaker children? Would not a good father act to protect his children from the wolves? Von Hildebrand would soon write, "The valuing of unity over truth plays a central role in the crisis of the Church."[2]

Paul VI seemed convinced that if he suppressed the *cultus* of the Roman Rite and replaced it with a revised Mass, it would cause the intended renewal. And so in 1969 he imposed the New Mass on the faithful worldwide, with the clear intention of suppressing the traditional Roman *cultus* and replacing it with the new.[3] Like his suppression of Latin, he also suppressed Gregorian chant. "We will lose a great part of that stupendous and incomparable artistic and spiritual thing, the Gregorian chant," he explained, but "Participation by the people is worth more—particularly participation by modern people, so fond of plain language which is easily understood and converted into everyday speech."[4] He seems to have hoped Gregorian chant would continue in the monasteries and vernacular chant would grow from his *Missa Iubilate Deo*, deemed to be "the minimum plain chant repertoire" for the universal Latin Church.[5]

Concerning the divine office, some reformers wanted to remove certain prayers from the Psalms they thought were offensive. The Holy

---

[2] Von Hildebrand, *The Charitable Anathema*, 1.

[3] Joseph Ratinzger, *Milestones*, trans. Erasmo Leiva-Merikakis (San Francisco, CA: Ignatius Press, 1998), 146-148.

[4] "Perdiamo la loquela dei secoli cristiani, diventiamo quasi intrusi e profani nel recinto letterario dell'espressione sacra, e così perderemo grande parte di quello stupendo e incomparabile fatto artistico e spirituale, ch'è il canto gregoriano." Paul VI, *General Audience of November 26, 1969*.

[5] Cf. *Musicam Sacram* (1967), 50-52; Congregation for Divine Worship, "Letter to the Bishops on the Minimum Repertoire of Plain Chant" (1974) in Austin Flannery, ed., *The Vatican Council II* (Northport, NY: Costello, 2004), vol I: 273-276; Paul VI, "Address to Benedictine Abbots," (1966) in *The Monastic Diurnal* (St. Michael's Abbey Press, 2015), Introduction.

Psalter, the Church's prayer book, used by the saints for centuries to do battle with the world, the flesh, and the devil, was now seen to be "too militaristic or violent."[6] Thus these reformers wanted to remove the weapons of the crusading spirit from the lips of priests and religious battling demons on the front lines.[7] Others protested, saying that they need militant prayers "against the devil" especially in Communist countries.[8] Paul VI sided against the crusading prayers and decided to remove these parts of the Psalter. Thus by abolishing the old rite and bowdlerizing the Missal and Church's own prayer book in the Psalter, Paul VI implemented a hermeneutic of rupture on the liturgical level, even though his doctrine was orthodox.

This liturgical rupture was immediately seen by Ratzinger as a serious issue. According to Seewald, Ratzinger as a priest "criticized him [Paul VI] heavily when he was pope" because Paul VI "not only suspended the use of the old Missal, but immediately forbade it."[9] Ratzinger would later explain in his memoirs in 1997:

> The publication of the Missal of Paul VI... was accompanied by the almost total prohibition... of using the missal we had had until then. I welcomed the fact that now we had a binding liturgical text after a period of experimentation that had often deformed the liturgy. But I was dismayed by the prohibition of the old missal, since nothing of the sort had ever happened in the entire history of the liturgy...
>
> The prohibition of the missal that was now decreed, a missal that had known continuous growth over the centuries, starting with the sacramentaries of the ancient Church, introduced a breach into the history of the liturgy whose consequences could only be tragic...

---

[6] Chiron, *Annibale Bugnini*, 154.
[7] See T. S. Flanders, *Introduction to the Holy Bible*, 39-78
[8] Ibid.
[9] Benedict XVI, *Last Testament*, 136. In this interview Benedict clarifies in saying that "heavily is too strong I think" but that Paul VI, when he made Ratzinger a bishop in 1977 in the context of condemning Lefebvre, "was safe in the knowledge that he and I were fundamentally in alignment." This seems to imply that Ratzinger and Paul VI both agreed on the need for liturgical reform, but disagreed on its implementation.

> There is no doubt that this new missal in many respects brought with it a real improvement and enrichment; but setting it as a new construction over against what had grown historically, forbidding the result of this historical growth, thereby makes the liturgy appear to be no longer a living development but the product of erudite work of juridical authority; this has caused us enormous harm.
>
> When liturgy is self-made, however, then it can no longer give us what its proper gift should be: the encounter with the mystery that is not our own product but rather our origin and the source of our life.[10]

The "real improvement and enrichment" of the Missal was no doubt the product of the Fourth Renewal in restoring old prayers and uses that had fallen away. There was nothing wrong *in theory*, with restoring the ancient rigor of the Fathers in certain liturgical customs and prayers.

Yet it was a liturgical rupture in the history of the Church. The reformers wanted to restore old customs only insofar as it helped an agenda of rupture. The most conspicuous of course was Communion in the Hand, which did not restore the old rigor once practiced in communion in the hand and venerating the Particles of Our Lord in the Host, but rather the Protestant corruption of this practice without veneration of the Particles.[11]

The fundamental principle of piety for the *cultus* was broken. As Ratzinger would also say decades later, implying that Paul VI betrayed Vatican II's own intention:

> It is good to recall here what Cardinal Newman observed, that the Church, throughout her history, has never abolished nor forbidden orthodox liturgical forms, which would be quite alien to the Spirit of the Church. An orthodox liturgy, that is to say, one which express the true faith, is never a compilation made according to the pragmatic criteria of different ceremonies, handled in a positivist and arbitrary way, one way today and another way tomorrow. The orthodox forms of a rite are living realities, born out of the dialogue of love between the Church and her Lord. They are expressions of the life of

---

[10] Joseph Ratinzger, *Milestones*, 146-148.
[11] On this, see Juan Rodolfo Laise's critical work *Holy Communion* (PCP Books, 2018).

> the Church, in which are distilled the faith, the prayer and the very life of whole generations, and which make incarnate in specific forms both the action of God and the response of man. Such rites can die, if those who have used them in a particular era should disappear, or if the life-situation of those same people should change.
>
> The authority of the Church has the power to define and limit the use of such rites in different historical situations, but she never just purely and simply forbids them! Thus the Council ordered a reform of the liturgical books, but it did not prohibit the former books.[12]

But Paul VI was the promulgator of Vatican II and had decreed *Inter Oecumenici*, *Tres Abhinc Nos*, and *Comme le prévoit* which suppressed genuflections, turned table altars around for Mass facing the people, and suppressed Catholic theological terms. He then discouraged those seeking an allowance for the rite of our forefathers.[13] Concerning those who were rebelling, he thought that the revised Mass would win them over to orthodoxy. Liturgical abuses multiplied, and bishops across the world did not stop them with fatherly discipline.

The reformers kept claiming that Catholic prayers were offensive to modern man, and therefore by watering down the Catholic liturgy, music and architecture, it would appeal more to modernity. But then a group of non-Catholics made an official appeal to save the traditional Roman rite *in the name of culture itself*. On July 6th, 1971, various non-Catholic intelligentsia published this appeal to Paul VI in the London Times:

> If some senseless decree were to order the total or partial destruction of basilicas or cathedrals, then obviously it would be the educated—whatever their personal beliefs—who would rise up in horror to oppose such a possibility.

---

[12] Joseph Ratzinger, "On the 10th anniversary of Ecclesia Dei adflicta" (Oct 24, 1998) <https://adoremus.org/2007/12/ten-years-of-the-motu-proprio-quotecclesia-deiquot/>, accessed July 28, 2021.

[13] He did this in three general audiences on March 17, 1965, November 19, 1969 and November 26, 1969. See Peter Kwasniewski, "A Half-Century of Novelty: Revisiting Paul VI's *Apologia* for the New Mass," *Rorate Caeli* (April 2nd, 2019) <https://rorate-caeli.blogspot.com/2019/04/a-half-century-of-novelty-revisiting.html>, accessed March 29, 2021.

CITY OF GOD VS. CITY OF MAN

Now the fact is that basilicas and cathedrals were built so as to celebrate a rite which, until a few months ago, constituted a living tradition. We are referring to the Roman Catholic Mass. Yet, according to the latest information in Rome, there is a plan to obliterate that Mass by the end of the current year.

One of the axioms of contemporary publicity, religious as well as secular, is that modern man in general, and intellectuals in particular, have become intolerant of all forms of tradition and are anxious to suppress them and put something else in their place.

But, like many other affirmations of our publicity machines, this axiom is false. Today, as in times gone by, educated people are in the vanguard where recognition of the value of tradition is concerned, and are the first to raise the alarm when it is threatened.

We are not at this moment considering the religious or spiritual experience of millions of individuals. The rite in question, in its magnificent Latin text, has also inspired a host of priceless achievements in the arts—not only mystical works, but works by poets, philosophers, musicians, architects, painters and sculptors in all countries and epochs. Thus, it belongs to universal culture as well as to churchmen and formal Christians.

In the materialistic and technocratic civilisation that is increasingly threatening the life of mind and spirit in its original creative expression—the word—it seems particularly inhuman to deprive man of word-forms in one of their most grandiose manifestations.

The signatories of this appeal, which is entirely ecumenical and nonpolitical, have been drawn from every branch of modern culture in Europe and elsewhere. They wish to call to the attention of the Holy See, the appalling responsibility it would incur in the history of the human spirit were it to refuse to allow the Traditional

Mass to survive, even though this survival took place side by side with other liturgical forms.[14]

This spontaneous appeal from non-Catholics made it clear what truly appeals to "modern man." This appeal finally convinced Paul VI to allow the traditional Roman Rite *by indult* (that is, an exceptional to the universal law), even though the New Mass was obligatory for all.

Yet lamentably, Paul VI, as he had done with Dietrich von Hildebrand in 1965, did not read the signs of the times. For the times were bringing forth nothing less than the new iconoclasm into the heart of the Church: a revolt of the younger generation to destroy the work of past generations. And so the abuses continued to proliferate in Catholic churches as the new iconoclasm destroyed beautiful architecture, music, and liturgy—the monuments our forefathers sacrificed to build for us. In their place were raised uglified, concrete structures of a grotesque nature, banal and profane music, and liturgical chaos in presence of the Holy of Holies.

Meanwhile, since 1958, a Jesuit novice had been in the seminary. He was finally ordained on December 13, 1969. His name was Jorge Bergoglio.

Examining the New Mass

Dietrich Von Hildebrand understood perfectly that the abuses were not approved by the Church, and that the revised Mass promulgated was perfectly orthodox and sacramentally valid. Like all good churchmen of the time like Ratzinger, he condemned the abuses. Yet Von Hildebrand turned and analyzed the texts and rubrics of the revised Mass itself and lamentably concluded that it was "The Great Disappointment."[15]

In 1973 he wrote of the "Devastated Vineyard" and declared that the new *cultus* did not manifest the beauty of Logos nor was formed by piety:

> The new liturgy is simply not formed by saints...but has been worked out by so-called experts... We live in a world without poetry, and this means that one should approach the treasures handed on from more fortunate times with twice as much reverence, and not with the illusion that we can do it better ourselves... The new

---

[14] *The London Times*, 6 July 1971.
[15] Dietrich Von Hildebrand, *The Devastated Vineyard*, trans. Crosby and Teichert (Roman Catholic Books: 1973), 66-78.

> liturgy is without splendor, flattened, and undifferentiated... truly, if one of the devils in C.S. Lewis' The Screwtape Letters had been entrusted with the ruin of the liturgy, he could not have done it better.[16]

Obviously this last bit was hyperbolic language—Von Hildebrand never questioned the validity of the new rites. However, it was true that in its texts and rubrics, it was a work of iconoclasm, which rejected the reverence due to what was handed down through tradition. And moreover, the revised liturgy alienated the East, who still held that the *cultus* was to be revered and preserved, not completely revised by a committee, imposed by papal mandate. It would have been more pastoral for Pope Paul VI to have allowed a wider indult for those desiring to celebrate Mass according to the previous rite.

From his study of the new Missal, Von Hildebrand asserted that "the rubrics of the new *Ordo* (as distinct from the text itself) are at variance with the definition of the essence and *raison d'etre* of Holy Mass as given by the Council of Trent."[17] The New Mass produced a Sacramentally valid Eucharist, but diminished the rubrics which were designed to reinforce belief in the Real Presence and the sacrificial nature of the Holy Mass. A simple example is the suppression of the first genuflection at the Consecration. The rubric said when the King arrives, his priest must immediately bow before him.

Deep in the consciousness of European man was the *cultus* in his bones, where he saw the King arrive, the priest bowed low before the King, and faithful lifted up to see Him, and exclaimed with great faith, hope and charity: *My Lord and My God!* Then every heart was in silence before the King, Who is Logos Incarnate.

The revised Mass suppressed the first genuflection and then told the people to sing to greet the King, instead of reverently keeping silence. This was disorienting to the cultural faith in the Real Presence.

Within the text of the revised Missal, however, we also see the subordination of the *cultus* to the spirit of the times. For the reformers systematically targeted all words that would be offensive, as the official document explained, as "contrary to modern ideas."[18] These included words like "sacrifice" "sin," "death," "hell," "wrath," "despise the world,"

---

[16] Ibid., 71.
[17] Ibid., *Charitable Anathema*, 32.
[18] The official translation document approved by Paul VI (*Comme Le Prévoit*, 1969) says this explicitly.

"the enemies of holy church," "sacrifice," "fasting,"[19] Throughout the New Mass these phrases were deemed offensive and removed. Current research concludes that only 13% of the Old Mass prayers were preserved intact in the New Mass.[20] After these Catholic terms were removed from the Latin, words like "merit," "soul," "beseech," were also removed from the vernacular translations, as stipulated by the document *Comme le prévoit*, approved in 1969. Thus what they were not able to remove from the official Latin *Novus Ordo* Missal, they successfully removed in the vernacular, obscuring further and further the pious words of our forefathers.

This new *cultus*, designed with the help of Protestants, sought to make the *cultus* more palatable for non-Catholics.[21] Unfortunately, the new *cultus* diminished the beauty of Logos Incarnate in order to appeal to Protestants, hoping that they would convert.[22] The revised Mass allowed voluntarism to define the *cultus* itself. The new *cultus* thus arose at the same time as a new Iconoclasm was forming inside the Church. Paul VI could have simply translated the previous Roman Missal into the vernacular, but Bugnini insisted on revising the entire rite.

---

[19] On the removal of words like "sin" "death" "hell" and "wrath" see Lauren Pristas, "The Orations of the Vatican II Missal: Policies for Revision," *Communio*, 30, Winter 2003, 622-653; Ibid., *Collects of the Roman Missals: A Comparative Study of the Sundays in Proper Seasons before and after the Second Vatican Council* (T&T Clark, 2013).

[20] See Matthew Hazell, "'All the Elements of the Roman Rite'? Mythbusting, Part II," *New Liturgical Movement* (October 1, 2021) <www.newliturgicalmovement.org/2021/10/all-elements-of-roman-rite-mythbusting.html>, accessed October 19, 2021.

[21] See T. S. Flanders, "Why the Term 'Extraordinary Form' is Wrong," <www.meaningofcatholic.com/2019/08/09/why-the-term-extraordinary-form-is-wrong/>.

[22] The full quote from Bugnini in which he justifies his censoring of the Roman Rite is this: "E tuttavia l'amore delle anime e il desiderio di agevolare in ogni modo il cammino dell'unione ai fratelli separati, rimovendo ogni pietra che possa constituire pur lontanamente un inciampo o motivo di disagio, hanno indoto la Chiesa anche a quiesti penosi sacrifice" ("And yet it is the love of souls and the desire to help in any way the road to union of the separated brethren, by removing every stone that could even remotely constitute an obstacle or difficulty, that has driven the Church to make even these painful sacrifices") (March 19, 1965 edition of L'Osservatore Romano). Thus, the New Mass is the method of evangelization which Leo XIII condemned in *Testem Benevolentiae* (1899). The torrent of souls leaving the Church since 1969 seem to prove this method as woefully ineffective at best.

Pope Paul VI believed that *Sacrosanctum Concilium* and *Dignitatus Humanae* meant that the *cultus* should no longer function as all cultures everywhere had used it, but rather be something of a private affair. Therefore, he did not insist like his predecessors on the *cultus* and the divine grace for the United Nations, but seemed to place his hope in the secular institution with a "solemn moral ratification of this lofty Institution" since, as he told them and the world, he was "convinced...that this Organization represents the obligatory path of modern civilization and world peace."[23] The revised Mass removed the petition to "subordinate to the Church principalities and powers" and relegated the Kingship of Christ to the end times, instead of calling the earthly kingdoms to obey Christ as King.[24]

As the revised Mass was being implemented, the greatest Catholic historian of the twentieth century went to his eternal reward in the month of Mary, 1970. His final book on the French Revolution was published after his death, reflecting on the machinations in the American and French revolts, with obvious implication to the decade he had just lived through. He proclaimed in the final words of the book that "it is to Christianity that western culture must look for leadership and help in restoring the moral and spiritual unity of our civilization."[25]

And the Holy Father reflecting on the council, said:

> By means of some fissure the smoke of Satan has entered the temple of God... It was believed that after the Council there would be a day of sunshine in the history of the Church... There came instead a day of clouds, storms and darkness, of search and uncertainty... through an adverse power; his name is the devil... Perhaps the Lord has called me not to govern and save the Church, but to suffer for her, and to make it clear that he and no one else, guides and saves her.[26]

Coulombe laments this as an "effective abdication. His Holiness would do nothing to stem the tide, would not attempt to be the Rock of the Church,

---

[23] Paul VI "Address to the United Nations," October 4, 1965.
[24] Good Friday petition for the Church.
[25] Dawson, *Gods of Revolution*, 166.
[26] Quotations gathered from "various well reported 1972 statements" of Paul VI and cited in Coulombe, *Puritan's Empire*, 499.

but would be terribly upset by it all."[27] Obviously Pope St. Paul VI did not do *absolutely* nothing, trying patiently to guide the faithful toward the truth and, especially after 1973, began to reverse the openness he originally permitted in the 1960s, like Communion in the Hand and the promotion of Gregorian Chant.[28] Yet he refused to use his fatherly discipline of the anathema that Von Hildebrand had pleaded from him since 1965.

The Fabric of Christian Culture Unraveling

To their credit, the leading moderates finally broke from the heretical tendencies of the *Concilium* after seven years and founded their own journal *Communio* in 1972. But by that time the destruction was immense and Von Hildebrand claimed:

> An unprejudiced look at the present devastation of the vineyard of the Lord cannot fail to notice the fact that a 'fifth column' has formed within the Church, a group which consciously aims at systematically destroying her... Their systematic and artful undermining of the holy Church testifies clearly enough to the fact that this is a conscious conspiracy, involving Freemasons and Communists who... are working together toward this goal.[29]

The Masonic United States and the Communist Soviet Union had both been used to undermine the Church. The Spanish crusaders had beat both in the Spanish Civil War, but now Vatican II had opened the door to both. They were two sides of the same anti-culture which injected anti-culture into the Church. They both defined dignity as power, and this error helped create the idea about active participation in the rite, that vocal and audible participation is the *only and* best means to participate in the divine grace of the Sacraments, so that *Sacrosanctum Concilium* implicitly yet emphatically enshrined this idea. In 1974, De Lubac called attention to the

---

[27] Ibid.
[28] Nicola Bux, "Communion in the Hand: Disobedience Permitted," <http://www.pcpbooks.net/buxeng.html>, accessed June 6th, 2021. See also Frederico Bortoli, *La distribuzione della Communione sulla mano* (2018).
[29] Von Hildebrand, *The Devastated Vineyard*, xi.

fact that the French translation included "deliberate mistranslations of the Latin" and even Congar was concerned in a letter to the pope.[30]

But fearing the excesses of the strict in the prior era, the Conciliar Magisterium (1958-Present) abandoned what the Von Hildebrand deemed the "act of the *greatest charity* toward all the faithful"—the charitable anathema.[31] The moderates were still reluctant to form with the strict, but kept alienating them as well.

To a great degree, this was due to the false spirit of Vatican I, which asserted that Christian culture flowed from the eldership first, not from the tradition and *cultus*, and then from eldership as guardian. With the revised Mass, Pope Paul VI was asserting what Pope Pius X had done—the pope is not the guardian of the *cultus*, but has authority *over* the rite.

Fortunately Ratzinger led the moderates in critiquing this, defending Klaus Gamber, the most controversial critic of the text and rubrics of the New Mass. In his critical treatise against the New Mass, Gamber asserted that:

> Obviously, the reformers wanted a completely new liturgy, a liturgy that differed from the traditional one in spirit as well as in form; and in no way a liturgy that represented what the Council Fathers had envisioned, i.e., a liturgy that would meet the pastoral needs of the faithful.[32]

In his defense of Gamber, Ratzinger wrote that the liturgical reformers "no longer wanted to continue the organic development and maturation of something that had been alive down through the centuries, and instead they replaced it—according to the model of technical production—with a fabrication, the banal product of the moment."[33] He published the *Ratzinger*

---

[30] Bouyer, 229.
[31] Von Hildebrand, *The Charitable Anathema*, 5. Emphasis his.
[32] Klaus Gamber, *The Reform of the Roman Liturgy: Its Problems and Background*, trans. Klaus D. Grimm (Roman Catholic Books, undated), 100.
[33] The original text is in *Theologisches* 20.2 (February 1990): 103–4, quoting Ratzinger's work in the book *Simandron—Der Wachklopfer. Gedenkschrift für Klaus Gamber (1919-1989)* <http://www.theologisches.net/files/20_Nr.2.pdf>. For a history of this quotation, see Sharon Kabel, "Catholic fact check: Cardinal Joseph Ratzinger and the fabricated liturgy," (June 19, 2021) <https://sharonkabel.com/post/ratzinger-fabricated-liturgy/>, accessed October 19, 2021. Although Ratzinger disagreed with some aspects of the revised Missal's production, promulgation, or implementation, it is important to note Ratzinger's attempt (especially later as pope) to harmonize the new and old Missals as valid liturgical developments.

Report, which was at that time taboo in many seminaries. He was consecrated Bishop Ratzinger in 1977, as Pope Paul VI was nearing his death. By consecrating as bishop his own critic, sacking Bugnini and reversing Communion in the Hand, Paul VI was trying to correct his failures. But by that time the new iconoclasm had destroyed innumerable monuments for which our fathers had sacrificed to build to the glory of God.

The strict bishops during this time were men such as Cardinal Gagnon and Cardinal Siri, but the most strict were bishops De Castro Mayer, and Marcel Lefebvre. Lefebvre went further than Ratzinger and refused to celebrate the revised Mass, asserting that he had a canonical right to celebrate the Old Mass.

But Pope Paul VI decreed the revised Missal "as a law," leading all critics to be accused of schism with some justification.[34] Nevertheless, even after the revised Mass was decreed, the local ordinary gave his blessing to Lefebvre's Society of St. Pius X. Lefebvre sounded the alarm against the abuses and heresies hurting the faith, yet his public rhetoric was inflammatory and a scandal for some faithful, even though it was a refuge for others.

His right to celebrate the traditional Roman rite, however, was suppressed by the local ordinary, reversing the prior decision, and Lefebvre was suspended from celebrating the Sacraments. He appealed to the ecclesiastical court, asserting that his suppression was uncanonical and demanded a fair trial. But Pope Paul VI listened to his advisor Villot and refused to give Lefebvre a trial. He demanded simply that he recant and cease to celebrate the Old Mass. Ratzinger would later admit as pope that the Old Mass was never technically, legally abrogated. Yet even the defenders of Lefebvre cannot fail to admit that the French missionary bishop used extreme language like asking "Do we really have a pope or an intruder on the chair of Peter?"[35] This rhetoric led his priests and the faithful by simple logic to sedevacantism—that error that Lefebvre himself condemned saying, "This spirit is schismatic."[36] Yet if we consider this language sympathetically, one can understand why such frustration would

---

[34] For an expert defense to the critics of the New Mass on this legal argument, see James Likoudis and Kenneth D. Whitehead, *The Pope, The Council, and the Mass*, rev. ed. (Emmaus Road Publishing, 2006), 43-52.
[35] Lefebvre's rhetorical question in *Cor Unum*, the Society's internal newspaper in 1979. De Mallerais, 505.
[36] Ibid.

be expressed, when heresy and abuse of the Sacraments was rampant, all attacking the *cultus* of our fathers and saints.

Michael Davies in the 1970s openly rebuked a bishop who was suppressing the Old Mass since the bishops were acting precisely the same as the Anglican heretics had acted when Cranmer was imposing his table altars on children. Von Hildebrand congratulated Davies on this action.[37]

But more than any other group during this period, it was the children who suffered. They saw their mothers agitating for power and initiating a contest of power with their fathers, while their fathers acted like boys and refused to lead. The children were deeply confused when they saw the men rip out the beautiful high altars and replace them with table altars which looked more industrial than sacred, following the instructions and example given by Paul VI.

The children no longer had a refuge from the noise of the upheaval in the 1960s and 1970s, and the signs and symbols which had formed generations of children to believe in the Real Presence were explicitly removed. Like the Protestant rites, the New Mass put far more emphasis on *adult features*—more listening to reading, more verbal singing and praying—and specifically suppressed numerous *features for children*.

As educator Maria Montessori had noted in 1933, the traditional Roman rite was deeply impactful to children who are "very receptive to the language of symbols" and "they learn more easily from watching people *do* at a solemn liturgy than from hearing a lot of words with little action."[38] Thus when these symbols were removed, the children were not given as many symbols and as much beauty as former generations. Moreover, their parents sought to conform themselves with the spirit of the times, and this spirit was so ugly that it could not be passed down to the next generation.

The adults unfortunately were lost in a haze of Teilhardian 1960s, which is still difficult for the present generation to understand. Yet, this was how they were raised by their own parents, without discipline, and feeling the inferiority complex of scientism. They did not see the horrors of World War II, only the "strength" of the American economic and religious dominance, and they were swept up in the exuberance of "the Kennedy Era." They were filled with zeal to liberate Blacks from the unjust oppression of Jim Crow and stop the invasion of Vietnam, while any justice

---

[37] Michael Davies, "Dietrich Von Hildebrand on Vatican II: a 'Great Misfortune,'" *The Remnant* (June 23, 2014) < https://remnantnewspaper.com/web/index.php/articles/item/751-dietrich-von-hildebrand-on-vatican-ii>, accessed March 29, 2021.

[38] Kwasniewski, *Birthright*, 17; See 1933 edition of *The Mass Explained to Children* (Kettering, OH: Angelico Press, 2015).

in these causes was often mixed with the unjust rebellion against hierarchy. Unfortunately by that time, the slavery to screens was taking hold and many uncritically believed the media, whose motivation was increasingly the love of money, not the love of truth.

The Unborn Holocaust

In 1970, the annulment crisis had gained momentum. The efforts of Von Hildebrand and Wojtyła to wrest the theology of Matrimony from its Jansenist and Nazi-state captivity had been twisted by the heretics into disobedience to Pope Pius XII's ruling in 1944. The definition of consent was no longer simply saying "I do" knowingly to a lifelong bond of conjugal fidelity—but rather "I do" needed to be an intense interpersonal communion.[39]

This allowed proponents of the new formula to create a system of quick "Catholic divorce" by rationalizing that the couple did not have an intense interpersonal gift of self at the time of their wedding rite. In 1968 there were 338 annulments in the United States. By 1970, there were 5,403, an increase of 1322 percent. By 1976, that had increased sixfold to 30,324.[40]

This destruction of marriage was fueled by the scientism of false psychology, sexualized movies and music, an economy of endless pleasures, the belief in unlimited progress, with other factors. Thus, while Catholics were told by Pope Paul VI that they need not have bodily fasting during Lent, the fallen concupiscible appetite could more easily to be enslaved to emotional pleasure, which, if possible, was quickly joined to unclean lust.

By tearing down divorce law and custom in Euro-America, people were urging for nothing less than *experimenting on children* to rationalize their adultery. The evidence shows definitively that the children suffered immense harm for this neglect of their parents.[41] In 1974 in the United States for the first time, more marriages ended in divorce than death and since 1976, reports of child neglect and abuse have not doubled or tripled,

---

[39] William Marshner, *Annulment or Divorce? A Critique of the Current Tribunal Practice and the Proposed Revision of Canon Law* (Christendom Educational Corporation, 1978) <https://marshner.christendom.edu/?p=859#more-859>.
[40] Kenneth C. Jones, *Index of Leading Catholic Indicators* (Roman Catholic Books, 2003), 71.
[41] Popenoe, *Families without Fathers*, 52-80.

but quintupled.⁴² From this point, the divorce and annulment crises would only get worse as the contest of power pervaded the family and society. Women rejected the external sign of beauty and femininity—the dress—and put on the external sign of power—pants.⁴³ But while they put on pants like men, men themselves put on T-shirts and shorts like boys. This immodest imitation of boys was a manifestation of the lack of manhood in morals and society.⁴⁴

As if things could not get worse, the Dionysian orgy finally reached its end—the unborn holocaust. The murder of children has always been Satan's greatest desire. He had promoted the cult of Moloch through the Canaanites, which Jesus ben Nun and Josiah had destroyed, the Roman infanticide which the Church had destroyed and the Aztec human sacrifice, which Santiago had destroyed. After the moderates refused to ally with the strict, the enemies of Christ triumphed. They could now kill children *en masse* without Baptism and send them out of this world for good.

As the 1970s continued, a worldwide economy based on instant emotional or immoral pleasure began to dominate Euro-America and stretch itself into Asia and Africa. The Africans who were receiving the gospel in droves reacted strongly to this, and the Asians as well as we will see. The love of money had created a new gospel. The plague of pornography spread as the business interests worked on every possible slavery to pleasure that would maximize profits.

In the United States a strong belief in Providential Capitalism allowed these things to cause cultural momentum. Meanwhile, the international pornography and slavery to pleasures and luxuries was being exported into other countries which allowed free trade. Free market was allowing businesses to help the poor, but at the same time, no distinction was being made with the trafficking in idols of money and pleasure. The United States

---

⁴² Ibid., 53. See also the data provided by Meeker in *Strong Fathers, Strong Daughters* (New York: Ballantine Books, 2007), *Boys Should Be Boys* (New York: Ballatine Books, 2008).

⁴³ Obviously women today who wear pants are not asserting an ideology of power, but are merely following the common custom, and it is not sinful. However, in the 1960s and 70s, women wearing pants was part of the widespread movement of competition with men for power. Cf. Cardinal Siri in 1960, "Notification Concerning
Men's Dress Worn By Women," <http://olrl.org/virtues/pants.shtml>, accessed March 29, 2021.

⁴⁴ Through the 1800s and 1900s, shorts were understood by custom as a garment for boys until they became men, which is when they would only wear pants. After World War II, and especially in the later 20th century, men increasingly began to wear shorts publicly as customs broke down with the generations.

was defending countries against the Communists, but at the same time imposing their anti-culture ideology as the gospel.

Prominent Catholics in the United States like Michael Novak, who had previously supported opposition to *Humanae Vitae* (for which he later publicly repented), were supporting the theology of providential capitalism. Thus as the American Empire continued to dominate and the Soviet Empire declined, the international billion dollar industry of pornography continued to take hold, which led to an increase in child sex trafficking, child murder, and the destruction of marriage to the harm of children, while woman was increasingly commoditized and psychologically manipulated to believe that her dignity was in power and sex appeal, destroying the feminine nature. Men were effeminate and very few were willing to oppose this and suffer for it. This was the United States gaining control through the worldwide Providential Capitalist regime of slavery to pleasures, lawful or not. This system firmly embedded in society the breaking of the Third Commandment and businesses were increasingly open for profit on Sunday.

Through advanced marketing techniques, business leaders were increasingly able to commoditize each generation, shattering the bonds of parent and child with psychological manipulation. Yet the United States from this point was increasingly eclipsed by globalist business regimes.

In 1975, Pope St. Paul VI began one of his most important acts as pope. Seeing how his gentle hand against the enemies of Christ had not been effective, he began the drastic measures needed to root out the evil. He commissioned Cardinal Gagnon to investigate the curia. According to his close personal assistant Fr. Charles Murr, Gagnon took three years and interviewed virtually every person in the Vatican.[45] What he found was that the Church was living through a third Pornocracy: the Vatican Bank was deeply corrupted with men who would be publicly imprisoned or murdered by the mafia, and an unknown number of bishops were corrupted by money and unclean lusts.

The opponents of Bugnini and his revised Missal finally prevailed upon Paul VI to sack Bugnini (just as he was attempting to change more of the liturgy) who was sent to Iran. Evidence has continued to emerge which strongly suggests that Bugnini was in fact a freemason.[46]

---

[45] Charles Murr, *The Godmother* (2017), 277-278.
[46] On the accusation of Freemasonry, see Chiron, 167-175. On the new evidence see Kevin Symonds, "Taylor Marshall's 'Infiltration' Book Review Part One," < https://kevinsymonds.com/2020/05/05/marshall-infiltration-review/>, accessed October 21, 2021; Ibid, "New Evidence on the Freemasonic Membership of

At the same time the CCEE, led by Cardinal Martini, had been at work since 1971 in St. Gallen (where Crowley performed his *Thelema* cult) to undermine papal authority concerning contraception and the family.[47] Bishop Baggio, who was notorious for pushing heresy, was in charge of appointing bishops around the world.[48] In 1977, Fr. Theodore McCarrick was consecrated a bishop.

In the same year, the great Doctor of the Church in the twentieth Century, the Hammer of the Nazis and Communists, Dietrich von Hildebrand died in New Rochelle, New York. Having lived through so much ugliness—two world wars and two sexual revolutions, and the revolt in the Church—he wrote his final work, an extensive treatise on beauty, returning to the unfathomable life-giving power of the *cultus* over the heart and soul of man. This was published as *Aesthetics* (2 vol.) after his death and has only recently been brought into English.

During all this time, Cardinal Karol Wojtyła was facing the Communists fearlessly as archbishop of Kraków and in the Soviet dystopian city of Nowa Huta. He finally succeeding in planting the throne of Christ the King against the hubris of the Soviets with the Ark of the Lord church, the first altar erected in that city. In 1977, the faithful finally put the last stone into place. It was the culmination of a ten year struggle since 1967 when:

> Cardinal Karol Wojtyła led a groundbreaking ceremony, swinging a pickaxe and helping dig the first section of the trench for the church's foundation, in which the stone from St. Peter's tomb donated by Pope Paul VI would be imbedded. Ten years of volunteer labor from all over Poland and throughout Europe went into completing the Ark Church. Its exterior was decorated by 2 million small polished stones from the riverbeds of Poland. The interior was dominated by a great steel figure of the

---

Annibale Bugnini," (May 7, 2020) <https://rorate-caeli.blogspot.com/2020/05/bombshell-new-historical-evidence.html>, accessed October 21, 2021.

[47] Julia Meloni, *The St. Gallen Mafia* (forthcoming), 26-28, 40, 44-47, 51-52; Sandro Magister, "Cardinal Martini's Jesus Would Never Have Written "Humanae Vitae"' November 3, 2008 <http://chiesa.espresso.repubblica.it/articolo/209045bdc4.html?eng=y>, accessed March 2, 2021.

[48] Murr discusses Baggio with Madre Pascalina and they both agree on this opinion of the prelate in *The Godmother* to which John Paul II would later finally agree.

> crucified Christ forged by the workers of Nowa Huta's Lenin Steelworks. The tabernacle was a gift from the diocese of Sankt Pölten in Austria, and was shaped like a model of the solar system; its decoration included a piece of moon rock, given to Paul VI by an American astronaut. The Dutch had donated the church's bells. The Ark Church was dedicated by Cardinal Wojtyła on May 16, 1977. His sermon at the dedication Mass, attended by pilgrims from Austria, Czechoslovakia, Hungary, Yugoslavia, Germany, Holland, Portugal, Italy, Canada, the United States, England, Finland, and France, put a new definition on the model worker's town. "This is not a city of people who belong to no one," the cardinal insisted, "of people to whom one may do whatever one wants, who may be manipulated according to the laws or rules of production and consumption. This is a city of the children of God... This temple was necessary so that this could be expressed, that it could be emphasized."[49]

The Ark of the Lord church was nothing less than the City of God built on enemy territory. It was a great victory against the hubris of the earthly city.

Lamentably, the uglification of the world was so powerful at that point that Wojtyła could not prevent an ugly church from being built. Even the Soviet architecture was more beautiful than that church. With the Serpentine *Paul VI Audience Hall*, this may have been the greatest architectural tragedy of the post-conciliar era, since succeeding generations cannot look to this monument and remember the courage of Wojtyła and that generation with the same admiration they hold for the great monuments of our fathers. The churches throughout the world became monuments to ugly, new iconoclasm, not the metaphysical beauty of Logos.

Meanwhile, Gagnon presented his dossier to Pope Paul VI, detailing the third Pornocracy.[50] But Pope Paul VI was too old to act on it, and decided to pass the job to his successor. Gagnon was furious and left Rome. On the Feast of the Transfiguration, 1978, St. Paul VI passed to his eternal reward. In the same month, Pope John Paul I was elected as his successor. Rumors spread that he would finally initiate the crackdown with Gagnon's dossier and the rampant abuse both liturgical, ecclesiastical and moral.

---

[49] Wiegel, *Witness to Hope*, 190.
[50] Murr, 277-281.

XXXIII

POPE ST. JOHN PAUL II THE GREAT

Pope John Paul I died suddenly in September, 1978, which quickly became a rumor of murder. The fallen angels certainly had motive, means, and ends. If John Paul I did indeed intend to crack down on the corruption, it would have been the beginning of the end for the Conspiracy's strangle hold on the Vatican. But to this day, the evidence is inconclusive.[1] When Karol Wojtyła became his successor as John Paul II in October 1978, he was given the dossier from Gagnon and the wholesale corruption was explained to him.[2] His papacy showed that he was a pious man of God and an orthodox moderate.

Fluent in over a dozen languages, Pope John Paul II decided to take the Gospel to the world. He immediately made arrangements to begin traveling and preaching to the people everywhere. In his mind it seemed that the world's greatest danger was not the Vatican corruption, but worldwide Communism. Just as he had done when he was consecrated bishop, he immediately went to confront the Communists in his fatherland, Poland, in 1979.

From this moment, the Soviet Union was in swift decline because Pope John Paul II had the true crusading spirit, which was able to enflame the zeal of millions for Christ as King. Famously the crowd of pious Poles, listening to John Paul II preach, began to chant against the Communist domination, "We want God! We want God!" This visit confronted the Communists with the Gospel in order to convert them, and this helped spark the Solidarity Movement led by the great Lech Wałęsa. The power of the Soviet Empire was doomed. A fearless man of God, a strong father,

---

[1] The best work arguing appears to be a tabloid author with no love for the church (David Yallop, *In God's Name*). Murr, who was personally close to the events, thinks that John Paul I was *not* murdered (private interview conducted by the author, April 24th, 2020).
[2] Murr, *The Godmother*, 279.

had finally been brought back to the office of the Holy Father, and the faithful responded in droves.

The Errors of Russia

His other immediate act as Pontiff was to begin to preach on the Theology of the Body. This was a series of philosophical reflections on the Holy Scriptures to continue the efforts of winning over the world by the beauty of truth. His theology continued the work to provide a synthesis between moderate and strict on the sacramental theology of Marriage, as he had already begun with *Person and Act*.[3]

Pope Paul VI had issued *Humanae Vitae* but had failed to stop the rebellious clerics and the annulment crisis. Pope John Paul II changed this approach to show the beauty of conjugal love and he won over thousands to the Church's teaching on Matrimony, inspiring countless others to become priests and religious. After the tumult of the 1960s, and the depressing dryness of the 1970s, the spirit of joy had returned to the Church. The rising generation of young orthodox priests, religious and laymen in our own era were all conceived under the pontificate of Pope John Paul II. This was the mustard seed of Catholic families that we are now witnessing.

But lamentably, certain cracks in this revival were already apparent when Pope John Paul II ascended the throne of St. Peter. It was in 1978 that William Marshner tried to sound the alarm about the annulment crisis and the reform of canon law that would codify the errors of Marriage validity.[4] Despite his best efforts, Pope John Paul II redefined marriage in the 1983 Code of Canon Law, but did not foresee the consequences. If the traditional moral theology was solidly in place, this new language could

---

[3] See *Person and Act and Related Essays* (trans. Gregorz Ignatik, CUA Press, 2021). The best introduction to the Theology of the Body is not contained in the popular imitations of St. John Paul II, but in the introduction given by his translator Michael Waldstein in John Paul II, *Man and Woman He Created Them: A Theology of the Body*, trans. Michael Waldstein (Boston: Pauline Books and Media, 2006), 1-130. Then compare Kwasniewski's remarks with Engel's critique. Peter Kwasniewski, "Is the human body part of the 'image of God'?" *LifeSiteNews* (Nov 19, 2019) <https://www.lifesitenews.com/blogs/is-the-human-body-part-of-the-image-of-god>. Randy Engel, *Theology of the Body: A Study in Modernism* (New Engel Publishing).

[4] William Marshner, *Annulment or Divorce? A Critique of the Current Tribunal Practice and the Proposed Revision of Canon Law* (Christendom Educational Corporation, 1978) <https://marshner.christendom.edu/?p=859#more-859>

simply be a refinement of the Church's teaching on marriage, not a redefinition. But because moral theology, according to Ratzinger, had "suffered a collapse," and the worldwide economic regime of pornography and pleasures now captivated the minds of youth and adults, men sought to subordinate the truth to their desires, not their desires to the truth.[5]

For the strict held to the moral theology of marriage according to the two ends decreed by Pope Pius XII, and warned at Vatican II that the ambiguous doctrines would lead to disaster. Even after the second Sexual Revolution and the spread of child murder, Pope John Paul II did not see the overaction against Jansenism. What was needed was a balance between the two.

The other tragic compromise came with the wicked daughter of anti-culture: Feminism. St. Teresa Benedicta had attempted to respond to the Nazi objectification of woman for procreation only with a defense of Church teaching on woman. But even in Von Hildebrand too, there was a lack of affirming the fundamental hierarchy pervasive in the Holy Scriptures concerning man and wife in Holy Matrimony.

Pope John Paul II discussed the mutual submission of spouses from Ephesians 5, but neglected to affirm as well that sacred order of spouses which was so fundamental to *ending* the contest of power, and so the problem at the heart of the annulment crisis was not cut down from its root.[6] The rights of the children to their mother were not affirmed, but rather the rights of women to work outside the home, which left the children more vulnerable than ever, since the "ever watchful guardian" was affirmed in her false search for power as dignity.[7] If economy is the law of the home,

---

[5] Benedict XVI, "The Church and the Scandal of Sexual Abuse," translated by *Anian Christoph Wimmer* (National Catholic Register: 2019) <https://www.ncregister.com/daily-news/the-church-and-the-scandal-of-sexual-abuse>, accessed November 23, 2019.

[6] St. John Paul II, *Familiaris Consortio* (1981), 25; John Paul II, *Man and Woman He Created Them: A Theology of the Body*, 472-475.

[7] *Familiaris Consortio* 23: "Women have the same right as men to perform various public functions." In a qualified sense this is true. Yet the children have rights as well, corresponding to duties in the mother and father. There is *nothing* that can replace a mother's care for her little children, because the feminine genius alone can provide this. Moreover, men do not even have rights to public functions for their own sake. Rather, the rights of women and men in "public functions" are subordinated *both* to the rights of the children to their parents in general and their mother in particular. Women have a right to be a mother to their children and stay with them full time, and a man has the duty and the burden to work and sacrifice so that she can have her right as a mother and the children their rights as little ones. This does not mean that the woman does not "work," since

each spouse is bound to the children. The rights and duties of husband and wife are primarily duties to their children, and this language was abandoned in favor of the beauty of poetic verse. Poetry is indeed necessary to express the beauty of conjugal life and avoid Jansenism, but the clarity of moral teaching is also necessary.

Upheaval

In 1953, the Anglo and American Empires had overthrown the Iranian government and installed the Shah Mohammad Reza Pahlavi as king to impose western economic policies (including pornography) and allow western powers to profit from oil deals. By 1979, the Shia, the most rational of the Muhammadans, revolted against the economic regime of western pornography and put forth their chosen leader to defend them against oppression.[8] The United States was greatly threatened by this and has tried ever since to make the Iranians seem evil through propaganda to justify their imposing of imperial rule in the Middle East. But the reality of the United States' provocation of terrorism has since been expertly hidden by American propaganda.

The power of the United States in the Middle East continued to destroy the lives of Arab Christians by destabilizing the region, promoting an economy of sin and allowing the Muhammadans to attack them, and above all by funding the states of Israel and Saudi Arabia which both persecuted Christians.[9] From this point to 2017, the United States funded Saudi

---

the law of the home includes an enormous amount of work for the woman managing the household and also making money for the home if necessary, but always subordinated to the needs and rights of the child. For more on this, see the best living moral theologian, Fr. Chad Ripperger, "Feminism: Women & the Natural Order," <https://www.youtube.com/watch?v=9e7slbAugBQ&t=121s>, or Prümmer, *Manuale Theologiae Moralis*, vol. II; n. 593.

[8] Jones, *Logos Rising*, 657-659.

[9] The modern state of Israel, like American Jewry, is dominated by the Liberal Jews, and some of the rational party of Jews opposes the rulers of Israel today. Moreover, viciousness of the conquest by Israelis of Arabs (some of them Christians) and even other Jews is difficult to deny by any objective reader of modern history. At the same time, as Schoeman discusses (*Salvation is from the Jews*), there is a greater significance to the modern state of Israel than merely secular politics, even from a religious stand point. We cannot deny either, the intensity of Muhammadan Jihad and the need for Jews of Israel to merely defend their wives and children from Jihadis. From a cultural point of view, having a homeland, too, allows a Jew to be *whole* in a sense in which he has not been for centuries, and thus it is not a coincidence, in the view of this author, that massive

Arabia, which spent seventy billion dollars erecting mosques and printing Wahhabi terrorist literature throughout the world.[10] The United States and the Saudis supported Osama bin Laden and his jihad in Afghanistan.[11] Supported by the Saudis, the Muhammadans turned to massacre the African Christians and form Muhammadan states.[12]

But Pope John Paul II was inspiring a mass movement back to Christ by restoring fatherhood. Therefore the enemies of Christ tried to kill him and failed, due to Our Lady's intervention. Like a man of God, he forgave his would-be assassin. According to Murr, this effected a conversion for him and he realized he had not dealt with Vatican corruption.[13] He called back Gagnon and tried to find a way to root out the evil in Vatican City, finally deposing Baggio from corrupting the worldwide episcopate. This was a fearless move, since there had already been an assassination attempt and he could be murdered at any time. But God protected him from harm.

In 1984 he consecrated the world to the Immaculate Heart of Mary. The mainstream of Catholics accept that this was the Fatima consecration of Russia, but a vocal minority casts doubt on this. At the time, there was already a movement growing against the Soviets spurred by Pope John Paul II. Moreover, their economic errors were causing their empire to be in swift decline. Meanwhile, the United States' superior economic philosophy allowed them to gain dominance by this point on the world stage.

But Pope John Paul II sought to overcome the Soviet Empire by any means necessary, including a close relationship, like Pope Pius XII, with the United States. Meanwhile the errors of Russia were alive and well in the growing Chinese Empire—with help from American money—which the Pontiff resisted. Moreover, as one of the last great Jesuits would say in 1998, "The United States of America is the most powerful Marxist country in the world."[14]

---

conversions to Christ have occurred because Jews can be whole in their identify in their ancestral homeland, and thus also accepted the King of the Jews. For an excellent introduction to this modern controversy, see Sandy Tolan, *The Lemon Tree: an Arab, a Jew, and the Heart of the Middle East* (Bloomsbury, 2006).

[10] Spencer, *History of Jihad*, 295.

[11] Operation Cyclone. The CIA attempts to say they were supporting the Afghan Jihadis, not Osama bin Laden, and this is convincing for those who do not know what Muhammadanism is. They are all one movement of Muhammadans who call themselves Jihadis.

[12] Lapidus, *A History of Islamic Societies*, 756-760.

[13] Fr. Charles Murr, Personal Interview (March 31st, 2021).

[14] John Hardon, "The Influence of Marxism in the United States," <https://hardonsj.org/influence-of-marxism-in-united-states-today/>, accessed March 29, 2021.

Pope John Paul II wrote a letter to artists and musicians, which inspired true beauty in sacred artists like Cameron Smith.[15] By the grace of God, a new seed was planted in families by the saintly pontiff, and while the heretics were rebelling against *Humanae Vitae*, a new generation was being conceived and born to pious Catholic parents who followed Papa Wojtyła. Planting this mustard seed was Pope John Paul II's greatest act as pope.

The Strict

In 1982, Pope John Paul II had elevated the greatest moderate to head of the Holy Office, then three years a bishop, Joseph Ratzinger. He was viewed as an arch-conservative by many in the Church. Ratzinger was tasked by Pope John Paul II with resolving the Lefebvre situation.

Meanwhile, however, Pope John Paul II became convinced that a united prayer meeting with other religions would help with world peace. Interpreting this event in light of Ratzinger's own understanding enunciated in *Dominus Iesus* in 2000, "dialogue" and inter-faith meetings were intended to promote civil co-existence and conversion of non-Catholics by winning them over with charity. This is why the great African Cardinal Arinze, himself a convert from paganism, defended the Assisi meetings as a means to this end.[16] Thankfully, Pope John Paul II brought a much greater African influence into the hierarchy.

But Lefebvre identified Assisi as the act of a blind visionary, not a father. With Brazilian Bishop Antônio de Castro Mayer he condemned the meeting as a scandal according to the principle of St. Thomas.[17] It was this event that convinced him he needed to consecrate bishops to preserve the *cultus* and the eldership of the priesthood.

Now that Gagnon was trusted and relied upon by Pope John Paul II, he sent him to investigate Lefebvre and his Society of St. Pius X. The SSPX asserts that Gagnon's report was favorable, but others assert the report was

---

[15] Learn about Smith's work here: <https://smithcatholicart.wordpress.com/artist-cameron-smith/>.

[16] Cardinal Francis Arinze, *God's Invisible Hand: The Life and Work of Francis Cardinal Arinze* (San Franciscio, CA: Ignatius Press, 2011), 202-209.

[17] See St. Thomas on the definition of scandal, which is an occasion of your neighbor's spiritual ruin. For example he says that "if [an act] only have the appearance of sin, it should always be left undone out of that love for our neighbor which binds each one to be solicitous for his
neighbor's spiritual welfare; so that if he persist in doing it he acts against charity" II-II q43 a2. On Lefebvre's reasoning see De Mallerais, *Biography of Marcel Lefebvre*, 529-537.

mixed.[18] Murr, Gagnon's personal assistant at the time, reports Gagnon believed Lefebvre to be a "holy and pious man of God" who was doing the right thing.[19] Lefebvre and Ratzinger were able to sign an agreement for consecration of four bishops with the minimal condition being that Lefebvre had to accept *Lumen Gentium* 25.[20]

This was the moment especially which could renew the alliance between the moderates and the strict. By reuniting, the partisans of Lefebvre and the orthodox moderates under John Paul II could truly proceed with the necessary *dialogos* to achieve the fourth renewal and unite against the enemies of holy Church. This would allow the Thomistic Phenomenology of John Paul II and Augustinianism of Ratzinger to be synthesized with the neo-Thomism of the strict, to cleanse theology from the errors of relativistic Phenomenology, as St. Teresa Benedicta had begun to do.

But Lefebvre became convinced that the Vatican was not acting in good faith. The Vatican was not allowing him to go forward with the agreement by setting a date for the consecrations. On the doctrinal questions, the Vatican changed the terms of the agreement, by asking Lefebvre to publicly renounce all his "errors" without defining what those errors were.[21] This was the end of *dialogos* that pushed Lefebvre and De Castro Mayer to consecrate four bishops on their own, holding to the original agreement and rejecting the new one. Yet Rome formally defined this act as schismatic, resulting in an automatic excommunication for all six bishops.[22]

From Ratzinger's point of view, Lefebvre's action made a critical error in the internal logic of the authority of the Magisterium:

> The explanation which Msgr. Lefebvre has given, for the retraction of his agreement, is revealing. He declared that he has finally understood that the agreement he signed

---

[18] Ibid., 544-566.

[19] Fr. Charles Murr, private interview conducted by T. S. Flanders (April 24th, 2020, March 31st, 2021).

[20] Holy Office, "The Protocol Agreement of the Vatican and Archbishop Lefebvre," (May 5, 1988), <https://www.ewtn.com/catholicism/library/protocol-agreement-of-the-vatican-and-archbishop-lefebvre-2096>, accessed March 29, 2021.

[21] Marcel Lefebvre, "1988 Episcopal Consecrations Sermon," (June 30, 1988) <https://sspx.org/en/1988-episcopal-consecrations-sermon-of-archbishop-lefebvre>, accessed March 29, 2021.

[22] John Paul II, *Ecclesia Dei* (1988), 3-4.

aimed only at integrating his foundation into the "Conciliar Church." The Catholic Church in union with the Pope is, according to him, the "Conciliar Church" which has broken with its own past. It seems indeed that he is no longer able to see that we are dealing with the Catholic Church in the totality of its Tradition, and that Vatican II belongs to that.[23]

It seems that because of Lefebvre's extreme rhetoric, Ratzinger came to the conclusion that Lefebvre was denying the fundamental authority of the Magisterium of the pope and bishops. This, if true, would indeed be a fundamentally schismatic "spirit," as Lefebvre had admitted regarding the sedevacantists. Perhaps Ratzinger was convinced Lefebvre and his bishops were *at least* sedeprivationist in faith and morals.[24]

In response, Rome set up the Fraternity of St. Peter, which allowed all SSPX members to leave and stay with Rome, yet the Fraternity was not given their own bishop, as had been promised in the first agreement. Yet by integrating the traditional Roman Rite back into the Church Ratzinger was beginning to heal the breach in liturgical history he had identified from the beginning.

Lefebvre and his bishops had been formally cut off from the Mystical Body of Christ, which no pious soul should take lightly. Outside the Church there is no salvation. Lefebvre died excommunicated, believing that what he had done was the only thing possible in the chaos of that time to preserve the sacred *cultus* and tradition passed down from our fathers.[25]

Defenders of Lefebvre believe he will be eventually exonerated and declared a saint as St. Joan of Arc was, who also died excommunicated. They assert Lefebvre was exhibiting true fatherhood in an age of fatherlessness among the episcopate, as Hall asserts, "What can a father do in a situation such as this? Certainly he cannot look his children in the eyes and tell them that the fight is over."[26] Yet as Madrid and critics argue,

---

[23] Joseph Ratzinger, "Address to Chilean Bishops," (13 July 1988), <https://www.ccwatershed.org/2019/11/07/13-july-1988-josef-cardinal-ratzinger/>, accessed July 30, 2021.

[24] Sedeprivationism is the theory that the Magisterium has retained its validity but not its authority.

[25] His feelings are expressed in his own words: "When I am before my Judge, I do not want Him to be able to say to me: 'You as well, you let the Church be destroyed.'" De Mallerais, 613.

[26] Kennedy Hall, "Lefebvre: A Man Who Reminded us that Bishops are Fathers," *Catholic Family News* (April, 2020).

Lefebvre was ultimately asserting, against his own formal condemnation, that he was "more Catholic than the pope."[27]

But decades later, one can reasonably and charitably ask: if Lefebvre and De Castro Mayer were excommunicated as schismatics, why were the many heretics in the Church not given the same treatment? Why was the medicine of mercy not given to the strict?

It would seem that the merciful thing to do for Lefebvre was to give him a canonical trial or at least keep the agreement that had been made, and not ask him to "condemn his errors" without any definition of what those errors were. If we evaluate Lefebvre sympathetically, we see a pious bishop and a father doing his best to preserve the faith. On the other hand, Lefebvre could have also refused to separate himself and his flock from the Church by consecrating bishops, but waited patiently for a new agreement. In some sense, both sides abandoned their agreement and *dialogos*. We will not know the full story of this tragic event until all archives and documents are eventually released. But because of this failure, the alliance between moderate and strict remained tenuous in theology and the *cultus* of the Roman Rite, while the enemies of Christ were like wolves taking over dioceses and universities across the world and destroying the faith of children. Cardinal Martini's "St. Gallen Mafia" grew and plotted against the Catholic faith in general and St. John Paul II in particular.[28]

Providential Capitalism?

In the 1990s, perhaps due to the Lefebvre debacle, Pope John Paul II again became more strict. He clamped down on the moral "theologians" with *Veritatis Splendor*, issuing the *Catechism of the Catholic Church* and a new Oath against Modernism in the Oath of Fidelity. He also attempted to crack down on the revolting "Catholic" universities.[29] But the one thing the strict wanted most of all—the charitable anathema—was still abandoned.

Meanwhile, God freed the Russian people from the yoke of Communist *Roma*, as the Soviet empire imploded. Some suggest this transition was planned, as the Communist leaders themselves retained power. In addition, the Chinese Communists were still in an economic

---

[27] Patrick Madrid and Peter Vere, *More Catholic Than the Pope: An Inside Look at Extreme Traditionalism* (Our Sunday Visitor, 2004).
[28] See Julia Meloni, *The St. Gallen Mafia, passim*.
[29] Msgr. George A. Kelly, *The Battle for the American Church Revisited*, 107-130.

alliance with the United States, imposing child murder on the Chinese people. Nevertheless the American Empire was able to use this event to solidify their "gospel" firmly into the hearts and minds of their people. This allowed them to invade the Middle East in defense of Saudi Arabia and their money, and convince the American people it was a moral crusade for freedom.[30] More than ever at that point, the United States and its *Libertas* idol in New York City preaching "Liberty enlightening the world" seemed to be true. Vatican II, moreover, seemed to have given approval of this "gospel" as a replacement for former teaching. The question then was, should all the former Soviet countries now adopt the American "gospel" of providential capitalism? Can the economy be run without divine grace, but merely "providence"?

In 1991, Pope John Paul II issued the *Centesimus Annus*, which asked this question. In his answer, he seemed to draw the distinction between free market economy and Providential Capitalism:

> Can it perhaps be said that, after the failure of Communism, capitalism is the victorious social system, and that capitalism should be the goal of the countries now making efforts to rebuild their economy and society? Is this the model which ought to be proposed to the countries of the Third World which are searching for the path to true economic and civil progress?
>
> ...If by "capitalism" is meant an economic system which recognizes the fundamental and positive role of business, the market, private property and the resulting responsibility for the means of production, as well as free human creativity in the economic sector, then the answer is certainly in the affirmative.
>
> ...But if by "capitalism" is meant a system in which freedom in the economic sector is *not circumscribed within a strong juridical framework* which places it at the service of human freedom in its totality, and which sees it as a particular aspect of that freedom, the core of which

---

[30] For a Catholic condemnation of the neoconservative unjust war, see J. Forrest Sharpe, *Neo-conned! Just War Principles: a Condemnation of War in Iraq* (Light in the Darkness Publications, 2005).

is *ethical and religious*, then the reply is certainly negative.[31]

This was firmly in line with his predecessors in affirming the need for free market business to help the poor, yet denying that the market could ever help the poor if it was free from the *cultus*.[32] The goal of countries should be to achieve a free market economy that allows the poor to create and own their businesses, not accept the theology of providential capitalism that says that the market has no need of sacramental grace. Not especially to accept all international business as good, due to the pornographic marketing used by American and other businesses.

At this time, countries like Spain, Italy and Ireland and parts of Africa had opened its borders to international trade, which let the plague of pornography and pleasures to flood their people, spreading the slavery to screens further and attacking children with psychological engineering. This broke the fighting spirit of Santiago and the sons of *Pádraig*.

Spain and Italy would eventually legalize debauchery, and the pious Irish people would be conquered by Google and manipulated into legalizing child murder and sodomite "marriage."[33] There were real economic benefits to international trade, but everything had to be subordinated under the law of the home, but instead the rights of the children were violated. The international economy taught values and morals as a way of making money, and widespread cultural destruction was the result.[34]

Meanwhile, the Catholic partisans of the theology of providential capitalism would assert that "analysis of economic consequences" is "very far from the Church's competence" and yet nevertheless they would say

---

[31] St. John Paul II, *Centesimus Annus* (1991), 42. Emphasis mine.

[32] Rupert J. Ederer, *Economics as If God Matters: More Than a Century of Papal Teaching* (Scarecrow Press, 2011), 163-165.

[33] E. Michael Jones, "Google's Conquest of Ireland," *Culture Wars* (Jan 2020), vol. 39, no. 2, 18-41; Wemhoff, 896-901.

[34] For example, the author spent weeks traveling through Cairo simply to purchase an icon or print of indigenous *Coptic* iconography. Instead, every church had been taken over by western marketing to the point where it was almost impossible to find and purchase Egyptian Christian art. Meanwhile, western marketing had attacked the Egyptian woman so that a bride believed that her beauty was dependent on buying a product to make herself look American and blonde. So the Egyptian bride forsook her own ethnic beauty and bought a western product which dyed her hair lighter and put powder on her face to look Caucasian. This attack on cultural custom and even ethnicity is spread throughout the world through an economy which ignores the law of the home.

elsewhere that "we need to understand the mystery of the market in terms of theological categories such as providence."[35] Is it not the Church's competence to judge the theological assertion of providential capitalism?

The empirical claim of this system, moreover, would continue to be disputed by the best Catholic economics, indicating that their ideas were indeed matters of faith—they had faith in providential capitalism as a theological proposition, yet denied the Church's authority over their moral theology. On the other hand, their emphasis on the role of business in alleviating poverty is crucial to the Church's corporal works of mercy.[36]

However, the Church has never approved the proposition that Original Sin is overcome in the coin without the divine grace of the *cultus*. Rather, the tradition of the Church and Pope John Paul II emphasized that the coin must have a strong juridical framework rooted in the *cultus*. In short, the coin cannot be governed by voluntarism but needs Logos Incarnate and the grace of the Holy Spirit.

The partisans of providential capitalism fight for small government because they are correct in saying with Acton that "power corrupts and absolute power corrupts absolutely." But they neglect to challenge the corrupting power of big business and more pervasively, money itself. Helping the poor means giving them the necessities, not making them rich and powerful, since money is the most common form of corrupting power. That is why the infallible Word of God says *the love of money is the root of all evil*.

Meanwhile, the industrialization was reaching poor countries, and the low cost of international goods was undercutting the prices of poor farmers in villages across the globe. A father could no longer feed his family because, when he tried to sell his crop, an international GMO crop could undersell him. As a result, a mass movement of urbanization came again, leading to the new slavery of sex trafficking and debt, exploiting millions around the world.[37] Once again, the law of the home was disrupted and culture dismantled in favor of a world-wide mechanization. The slavery increased on a massive scale, beginning to rival prior forms of slavery in the breadth of its evil.[38]

---

[35] Woods, *Church and the Market*, 3; Jay Richards, *Money, Greed and God*, 242.
[36] For an introduction to this, see Acton Institute, *Poverty Cure* <povertycure.org>.
[37] Scott Bessenecker, eds., "Quest for Hope in the Slum Community," (World Vision: Authentic, 2005), 3-12; Mark Krame, *Dispossessed: Life in Our World's Urban Slums* (Maryknoll, NY: Orbis Books, 2006), 1-10; Ederer, 164-165.
[38] Kevin Bales, *Disposable People: New Slavery in the Global Economy*, rev. ed. (University of California Press, 2004), 1-33.

The poor were brought to "sweat shops" where they indeed had luxuries like indoor plumbing and medical care, but they had to sacrifice their culture to get it—their rural way of life, their extended family—and be forced to become a cog in a vast global industrialized machine of opulent pleasures. They lost the spiritual help of manual labor and began to find the slavery to screens more appealing. They had to reduce the family to the nuclear family and forsake their own community in order to get ahead and have wealth, breaking down cultures across the world.[39]

The rich bought the lower priced good made by cheap labor, and the economy of pornographic domination continued. At the same time, innovation continued to increase greater help for the poor especially with medical attention. In this period of international growth the United States lost dominance in the world in favor of global business beginning to control governments themselves. This indeed made everyone richer and more powerful, with less infant mortality—but at the cost of their culture, their families and lamentably their souls.

As the cultural momentum of the United States has already been seen, this gave children over to the slavery to screens, making the passing down of the faith extremely difficult, and as the generations succeeded, more and more left the Faith, and the industrialized nations became richer in money, and destitute of true, spiritual wealth. Meanwhile, the worldwide Capitalism continued to produce the most extreme sexualized ugliness falsely called "art" in music, architecture, and literature. The film industry increasingly relied on bloodshed and lust as the modern equivalent to the gladiatorial games to make money, leading to a spiral downward to open witchcraft.

The United States' funding for Saudi Arabia continued to provide a society as a worldwide pilgrimage site for Muhammadan terrorists and fund *jihad* including in Africa.[40] In 1994, three nuns and a brother were executed by Muhammadans in Algeria, but religious in Angola, Uganda, Bosnia and Zaire chose to face death rather than flee.[41] In 1996, they cut the throats of Dom Christian de Chergé and his six monastic companions, who won the palm of victory. Shortly thereafter they killed Algerian Bishop Lucien Caverie who joined his flock in the chorus of angels. This was happening within the same few years with the millions of deaths

---

[39] Ruby K. Payne, *A Framework for Understanding Poverty: A Cognitive Approach* (Aha! Process, Incorporated, 2013).
[40] On the Muhammadans' new efforts to massacre and destroy Christianity especially in Africa, see Jenkins, *The Next Christendom*, 201-236.
[41] Royal, *Catholic Martyrs of the Twentieth Century*, 371.

including Catholics in Burundi and Rwanda amid tribal warfare.[42] Then the Muhammadans attacked the Church in Sudan, crucifying some, enslaving others, and forcing women into genital mutilation and sex slavery.[43] Catechist Agostino El Nur refused to deny Christ and was tortured for four months suffering nails through his head, genital mutilation and consummated his glorious crown united to the Passion of Christ in a 24-hour crucifixion.[44]

In 2000, the greatest document since Vatican II was released in *Dominus Iesus*, which expertly clarified the whole reasons for "dialogue" was to convert all non-Catholics and the workings of the Holy Spirit in other religions is intended to convert them. But this document failed to affirm the danger of eternal damnation for non-Catholics and the dogma of no salvation outside the Church. But more than this, this great document proved that issuing more documents will never solve this crisis. No one listens to documents. The charitable anathema is the only proven method.

In 2001 Muhammadan terrorists attacked New York City, killing thousands of civilians.[45] Saudi involvement was concealed and used as a pretext to launch operations in the Middle East to secure the economic interests of the United States.[46] The American public was deceived into supporting the invasion of Iraq in order depose Saddam Hussein and impose the economic interests of American business leaders in the name of "freedom."[47] Pope John Paul II led Catholic bishops around the world in opposing the unjust invasion of Iraq by the American Empire, but unfortunately many American Catholics supported this citing American ideology as justification. But increasingly as American business melded with Communist business in China, from this point the international

---

[42] Ibid., 308-386.
[43] Ibid.
[44] Ibid., 387.
[45] Spencer, *History of Jihad*, 333-337. We set aside further questions regarding the official government narrative of this event, since it is clear that it was used as a pretext.
[46] For a Catholic condemnation of another neoconservative unjust war, see J. Forrest Sharpe, *Neo-conned! Again: Hypocrisy, Lawlessness, and the Rape of Iraq: the Illegality and the Injustice of the Second Gulf War*. (Light in the Darkness Publications, 2005).
[47] The documentation for this assertion comes from various sources. The difficulty is that many voices which condemn the unjust invasion in American media are Marxists and thus their spin on the issue becomes polluted by their errors. See Sharpe, *op. cit.* for a Catholic point of view.

businesses gained control over nations more than America itself.[48] The worldwide regime of pornography continues apace, and is able to influence politics heavily across the globe, justified by American "freedom" ideology.[49] Meanwhile, a growing alliance was forming to shape society and politics in Euro-America between Marxists, Feminists, Liberal Jews, Protestants and Muhammadans on the negating principle of *not Christ*. The American money funding Saudi Arabia was now being funneled to Euro-American universities to promote Muhammadanism, *shari'a* and a Marxist-Muhammadan history in academia.[50]

Pope St. John Paul II beatified Pius IX and Emperor Charles of Austria and canonized Maximilian Kolbe and Teresa Benedicta. He went to join the chorus of angels on April 2nd, 2005. He did not restore the charitable anathema nor root out the Third Pornocracy. Yet he inspired a worldwide Catholic revival in which Catholics embraced and lived their faith, especially in the family. Only a saint could have reversed the terrible decline the Church was enduring in the 1970s, and he did it in the heart of the family. This was the mustard seed which is now found in the children of those Catholic parents who responded to the call of John Paul II: "Do not be afraid!"

---

[48] The Chinese Communists were imploding like the Soviets, due to their utopian economic system, until American Business formed relationships with their slave labor to prop up their wicked regime, creating a blended Communist Capitalist system, as it exists to this day. Like the Soviets and Hitler, Israel and Saudi Arabia, the love of money in Wall Street fuels the wicked regimes behind the scenes. For introduction to China, see Greg Autry and Peter Navarro, *Death by China: Confronting the Dragon - A Global Call to Action* (Pearson Education, 2011); Steven W. Mosher, *Bully of Asia: Why China's Dream is the New Threat to World Order* (Regnery Publishing, 2017).
[49] Jones, *Libido Dominandi*, 556-607; Heather Brunskell-Evans, ed., *The Sexualized Body and the Medical Authority of Pornography: Performing Sexual Liberation* (Cambridge Scholars Publishing, 2017).
[50] For a critical work attacking this bias in academia, see Dario Fernandez-Morera, *The Myth of the Andalusian Paradise: Muslims, Christians, and Jews under Islamic Rule in Medieval Spain* (Intercollegiate Studies Institute, 2016).

XXXIV

THE HERMENEUTIC OF BENEDICT XVI

The new Roman Pontiff seemed to suggest he was afraid in his first homily, "Pray for me, that I may not flee for fear of the wolves."[1] Yet like Pope John Paul II, there did not seem to be a moral compromise in his past that allowed any blackmail from nefarious forces. After decades in the Vatican, he had refused the lusts of filthy lucre and the temptations of the flesh that only God knows they threw at him. Now he had an opportunity to act.

But if the Sacrament of Matrimony was the focus of Pope John Paul II, Pope Benedict's focus was the Holy Scripture and the *cultus*. This was really the heart and soul of the whole doctrinal crisis, since so much heresy was built upon denying the dogma of the inerrancy of Holy Scripture.[2] He spent time during his pontificate perfecting his knowledge in *dialogos* with the secular Biblical scholars and attempting to win them over to the tradition of the Church. One of His greatest accomplishments was the sacramentalizing of the Holy Scripture in his encyclical *Verbum Domini*, which is deeply tied to his sensitivity to the Holy Liturgy. To his great credit, he confirmed the fundamental dogma of the inerrancy of Holy Scripture as head of the Holy Office and challenged the hubris of secular Biblical scholarship.[3] However, when asked by the Synod of Bishops to clarify and confirm this dogma again, he refused to do so in the aforementioned encyclical.

---

[1] Benedict XVI, Mass for the Beginning of the Petrine Ministry of the Bishop of Rome, "Homily," (April 24, 2005).
[2] Flanders, *Introduction to the Holy Bible for Traditional Catholics*, 201-247.
[3] Joseph Ratzinger, "Biblical Interpretation in Crisis" 1988 Erasmus Lecture <https://www.firstthings.com/web-exclusives/2008/04/biblical- interpretation-in-crisis>, accessed November 23, 2019; Congregation for the Doctrine of the Faith, "Commentary on the Concluding Formula of the 'Professio fidei,'" (1998) <https://www.catholicculture.org/culture/library/view.cfm?recnum=439> .

At the same time, again to his great credit, he was cracking down on the evil in the Church. He defrocked Marcial Maciel and Tomislav Vlašić and is said to have ousted hundreds of priests who were breaking their vows of chastity against nature. Then he moved for the real heart of the matter: the *cultus*.

In his 2005 Christmas address, Pope Benedict spoke of a hermeneutic of reform and rupture—insisting on certain changes in the way that papal Masses were celebrated. Benedict insisted on Holy Communion kneeling and on the tongue and a greater use of Latin and Gregorian chant. *Comme le prévoit* had been reversed under Pope John Paul II and replaced with *Liturgiam Authenticam* saying the vernacular text must be "free from all ideological influence."[4] The problem was that the ideological influences were imbedded in the Latin text of the New Mass itself, not just the translations.

Yet more in 2007, Pope Benedict issued *Summorum Pontificum*. Paul VI had imposed the New Mass as "a law," but Benedict clarified that the Apostolic Roman Rite was "never juridically abrogated, and consequently, in principle, was always permitted."[5] This was a *de facto* exoneration of Lefebvre's central assertion of a canonical and pious right for a Roman rite priest to say the traditional Roman rite. Nevertheless Benedict explicitly stated it was not to exonerate Lefebvre, but to reconcile with the Church's own past.[6] Thus he stated to the world's bishops: "What earlier generations held as sacred, remains sacred and great for us too, and it cannot be all of a sudden entirely forbidden or even considered harmful."[7] As he had maintained from the beginning, the old Mass could not be abrogated by the principle of the binding force of Tradition itself.[8] Thus this was the most conspicuous application of the Hermeneutic of continuity which began to restore Catholic culture. Benedict later explained this by saying:

> It was important that something which was previously the most sacred thing in the Church to people should not suddenly be completely forbidden. A society that considers now to be forbidden what it once perceived as the central core—that cannot be. The inner identity it has with the other must remain visible. ...[It was] about the inward reconciliation of the Church with itself...

---

[4] John Paul II, *Liturgiam Authenticam* (2001), 3.
[5] Benedict XVI, "Letter Accompanying *Summorum Pontificum*," (2007)
[6] Ibid., *Last Testament*, 202.
[7] Ibid., "Letter Accompanying *Summorum Pontificum*," (2007)
[8] Joseph Ratzinger, *Milestones*, 146-148.

> It was important for me that the Church is one with herself inwardly, with her own past; that what was previously holy to her is not somehow wrong now. The rite must develop. In that sense reform is appropriate. But the continuity must not be ruptured. The Society of St. Pius X is based on the fact that people felt the Church was renouncing itself. That must not be. ...[It was] about the substance of the matter itself.⁹

The framework that Benedict articulated was the correct one—hermeneutic of continuity. This is the ontological nature of any council. But Bugnini had no intention of interpreting *Sacrosanctum Concilium* in continuity, nor did the early Paul VI. Therefore the rupture on the level of *cultus* is imbedded into the texts and rubrics of the New Mass which, as Ratzinger said, broke from "the organic development and maturation of something that had been alive down through the centuries." In his wisdom Benedict reversed the false spirit of Vatican I by restoring this organic growth and allowing the two rites to grow together and "mutually enrich" one another.¹⁰ The New Mass could recapture the Tridentine dogmas contained better in the old rite, while the old rite could adopt certain good reforms, such as some use of the vernacular, as Lefebvre had also advocated.¹¹ But Benedict showed the example of restoring the office of the pope to be in service to Tradition and the *cultus*, not its master.

Pope Benedict further in 2009 lifted the excommunications of the SSPX bishops and initiated *dialogos*. This effort also stalled, but the public documentation is not sufficient to tell the whole story about why. At least in public, the problem was that the moderate and strict parties continued to use old animosities to justify renouncing the *dialogos* in favor of a voluntaristic sloganeering and a lack of charity. To this day, partisans on both sides seem to ignore the complexities of this issue in favor of group identity politics.

With *Anglicanorum Coetibus*, Benedict facilitated what might be the largest Anglican and Lutheran mass conversion to Catholicism since the Protestant revolt. Yet he seemed to promote American-style religious liberty and had another Assisi meeting. Meanwhile the spread of child murder continued and thrived under religious freedom and the pornography

---

[9] Benedict XVI, *Last Testament*, 201-202.
[10] Ibid., 202.
[11] De Mallerais, *The Biography of Marcel Lefebvre*, 330.

industry help to develop technology, leading in 2007 to the smart phone.[12] This device allowed the most intense slavery to screens hitherto known.

Now even poor families can purchase a screen to program the minds of their children for their whole lives. Adults too, became slaves to social media, which was consciously designed to create psychological slavery. Facebook co-founder Sean Parker admitted they were "exploiting a vulnerability in human psychology… we understood this consciously and we did this anyway."[13] Increasing numbers of Silicon Valley employees, the designers of the tech, would begin "sounding alarms in increasingly dire terms about what these gadgets do to the human brain."[14] One tech businessman would describe it like this: "On the scale between candy and crack cocaine, it's closer to crack cocaine."[15]

This has allowed the media conglomerates to gain the greatest control over the minds of men they have ever had. All of these gravitate to one thing—not Christ. Slavery has always been the most profitable thing. Therefore the media sensationalizes the news with emotional content and marketing uses psychological manipulations and wicked lust which addicts all viewers and creates slavery. Meanwhile, the believers in providential capitalism continue to assert that this system spiraling out of control is God's work of Providence, and not the work of fallen men in need of divine grace.

It was Pope Benedict (then Cardinal Ratzinger) who wrote that "I am personally convinced that, when, at some time in the future, the intellectual history of the Catholic Church in the twentieth century is written, the name of Dietrich von Hildebrand will be most prominent among the figures of our time."[16] Whether or not he agreed with Pope Pius XII in calling him the Doctor of the Church of the twentieth century is not clear. What seems

---

[12] On the influence of the porn industry on modern technology, see Ross Benes, "PORN: The Hidden Engine That Drives Innovation in Tech," <https://www.businessinsider.com/how-porn-drives-innovation-in-tech-2013-7>, accessed May 28, 2021; Patchen Barss, *The Erotic Engine: How Pornography has Powered Mass Communication from Gutenberg to Google*; Frederick Lane, *Obscene Profits: The Entrepreneurs of Pornography in the Cyber Age*.

[13] Interview on *Good Morning America* (Nov 10, 2017); T. S. Flanders, "Don't Let Social Media Send you to Hell," *Catholic Family News* (Dec 19, 2020), < https://catholicfamilynews.com/blog/2020/12/19/dont-let-social-media-send-you-to-hell/>.

[14] Nellie Bowles, "A Dark Consensus about Screens and Kids," *New York Times* (Oct 26, 2018).

[15] Ibid.

[16] Alice von Hildebrand, *The Soul of a Lion*, 12.

to be clear is that Pope Benedict, like his predecessors since Pope John XXIII did not believe that the charitable anathema was the solution.

In 2012 it is known that another investigation was completed of the Curia similar to Gagnon's.[17] This dossier seems to have presented the same information that Gagnon's did—the third Pornocracy was in power spiritually, financially, and morally. In January 2013 the finances of Vatican City were struck dead for an unknown reason.

Let us assume for the best that Benedict did not resign because he was afraid. He had already provoked the enemies of Christ more than any pope had done since Pius XII. They could have killed him, but they did not. Then, for whatever reason unknown to us, Pope Benedict XVI believed that resigning was the only way to serve the Church in that moment with what he knew to be true. Perhaps in one hundred years we will finally know what he knew when he resigned.

---

[17] The dossier's contents, ultimately are unknown.

EPILOGUE

UNITING CATHOLICS AGAINST THE ENEMIES OF HOLY CHURCH

Since the election of Pope Francis, the strain between moderates and strict has begun to relax as recent events have caused Catholics to reconsider everything. As Meloni and others have shown, the current Roman Pontiff seems to serve the interests of the heretical Cardinal Martini party and has stopped the effort by Benedict to root out Church corruption.[1] He has welcomed the global leaders of the unborn holocaust who have profaned the Blessed Sacrament in his diocese.[2] For Christian culture, he has restored the hermeneutic of rupture in regards to the *cultus*.

As we have seen, by 1975 Paul VI had begun to reverse his own decisions regarding the liturgy, and this continued under John Paul II as Ratzinger began to heal the "breach in liturgical tradition" by integrating the traditional Roman rite back into the Church in 1988. He promoted the New Liturgical Movement and the "reform of the reform," and reversed Paul VI's *Comme le prévoit*, with *Liturgiam Authenticam* in 2001. The full healing of the breach, at least canonically, came with *Summorum Pontificum*. He then appointed the saintly Cardinal Sarah to implement the reform of the reform.[3]

---

[1] Julia Meloni, *The St. Gallen Mafia* (TAN: 2021); Edward Pentin, *The Rigging of a Vatican Synod? An Investigation into Alleged Manipulation at the Extraordinary Synod on the Family* (Ignatius Press, 2015).

[2] We refer to American President Joe Biden and Nancy Pelosi, welcomed in the Vatican by Pope Francis in the fall of 2021. President Biden, a vociferous advocate for the unborn holocaust, received Holy Communion in Rome.

[3] Cardinal Robert Sarah, "Reform of the Reform," (July 5th, 2016) <https://www.ccwatershed.org/2016/07/07/robert-cardinal-sarah-address-2015-july/>, accessed July 28, 2021.

But Ratzinger's vision to heal the liturgical rupture was controversial to the liberal wing of bishops who wanted to conform to the desires of the Grand Coalition of the Status Quo. They wanted to concede that Luther was right in rejecting the Mass as a sacrifice. These heretics in the Church never wanted the traditional Roman rite because it safeguarded the dogmas of Trent. They did not believe in the Real Presence or the Sacrifice. As Ratzinger observed:

> Only against this background of the effective denial of the authority of Trent can one understand the bitterness of the struggle against allowing the celebration of Mass according to the 1962 Missal after the liturgical reform. The possibility of so celebrating constitutes the strongest and thus (for them) the most intolerable contradiction of the opinion of those who believe that the faith in the Eucharist formulated by Trent has lost its validity.[4]

And so when John Paul II promulgated *Liturgiam Authenticam*, some bishops conferences, like Italy and Germany, refused to obey and re-translate their vernacular liturgy. Pope Francis confirmed this disobedience by issuing *Magnum Principium* in 2017, which reversed the reversal of Paul VI. He then stopped all efforts of Cardinal Sarah to heal the liturgical breach as Ratzinger had envisioned.[5] Finally, Francis abrogated *Summorum Pontificum* with *Traditionis Custodes* in 2021 and attempted again, as Paul VI had done, to suppress the traditional Roman *cultus* which had built western (and especially Baroque) civilization. Thus Francis has reversed the liturgical work of Paul VI in the 1970s, John Paul II and Benedict XVI, and brought the Church back to the liturgical vision of 1965-1969 Bugnini.

All of these things and more have brought the moderate and strict parties closer together under Francis, as more and more efforts are raised to oppose the Roman Pontiff himself.[6] The best effort in this regard seems

---

[4] Joseph Ratzinger, *Complete Works: Theology of the Liturgy* (Ignatius, 2008), 544.

[5] Gerard O'Connell, "Pope Francis: There will be no 'reform of the reform' of the liturgy," *America* (Dec. 6, 2016) <https://www.americamagazine.org/faith/2016/12/06/pope-francis-there-will-be-no-reform-reform-liturgy>, accessed July 28, 2021.

[6] For example, *First Things*, "An Appeal to the Cardinals of the Catholic Church," <https://www.firstthings.com/web-exclusives/2018/08/an-appeal-to-the-cardinals-of-the-catholic-church>, accessed July 28, 2021; Bishop Schneider et al.,

to be the *Declaration of Truths*, which is a confession of faith against modern errors, implementing the hermeneutic of continuity in doctrine.[7]

At the same time, innumerable Catholics are suffering in despair after years of liturgical and other abuse and are beginning to seriously question their faith in the Roman Catholic Church. The wounds of pious souls run deep, and the darkness of our time seems to have no hope of resurrection.

Yet our King has told us there is only one way out of this. There is only one path to the resurrection:

> If any man come to me, and hate not his father and mother and wife and children and brethren and sisters, yea and his own life also, he cannot be my disciple. And whosoever doth not carry his cross and come after me cannot be my disciple (Lk. xiv. 26-27)

In this saying the saints understand that Our Lord is telling us to mortify and detach ourselves from every earthly affection and adhere to Christ Crucified and His sufferings—to die with him, in order to be His disciple. This is the cross, and it is the only way through this crisis. We must embrace suffering. The cross is not only the remedy for sin, but the Passion of Our Lord is the way to conquer every enemy as St. Thomas says:

> It is a remedy, for, in the face of all the evils which we incur on account of our sins, we have found relief through the passion of Christ. Yet, it is no less an example, for the passion of Christ completely suffices to fashion our lives. Whoever wishes to live perfectly should do nothing but disdain what Christ disdained on the cross and desire what he desired, for the cross exemplifies every virtue.
>
> If you seek the example of love: *Greater love than this no man has, than to lay down his life for his friend*s. Such

---

"Profession of the Immutable Truths about Sacramental Marriage," <https://www.reginamag.com/profession-of-the-immutable-truths-about-sacramental-marriage/>, accessed July 28, 2021; Cardinal Müller, "Manifesto of Faith," <https://www.ncregister.com/blog/cardinal-mueller-issues-manifesto-of-faith>, accessed July 28, 2021.

[7] Cardinal Burke, et al., *The Declaration of Truths* (May 31, 2019), <https://onepeterfive.com/wp-content/uploads/2019/06/Declaration_Truths_Errors_final_version_clean.pdf>, accessed July 28, 2021.

a man was Christ on the cross. And if he gave his life for us, then it should not be difficult to bear whatever hardships arise for his sake.

If you seek patience, you will find no better example than the cross. Great patience occurs in two ways: either when one patiently suffers much, or when one suffers things which one is able to avoid and yet does not avoid. Christ endured much on the cross, and did so patiently, because when he suffered he did not threaten; he was led like a sheep to the slaughter and he did not open his mouth. Therefore Christ's patience on the cross was great. In patience let us run for the prize set before us, *looking upon Jesus, the author and perfecter of our faith who, for the joy set before him, bore his cross and despised the shame.*

If you seek an example of humility, look upon the crucified one, for God wished to be judged by Pontius Pilate and to die.

If you seek an example of obedience, follow him who became obedient to the Father even unto death. For just as by the disobedience of one man, namely, Adam, many were made sinners, so by the obedience of one man, many were made righteous.

If you seek an example of despising earthly things, follow him who is the King of kings and the Lord of lords, in whom are hidden all the treasures of wisdom and knowledge. Upon the cross he was stripped, mocked, spat upon, struck, crowned with thorns, and given only vinegar and gall to drink.

Do not be attached, therefore, to clothing and riches, because *they divided my garments among themselves.* Nor to honours, for He experienced harsh words and scourgings. Nor to greatness of rank, for *weaving a crown of thorns they placed it on my head.* Nor to anything delightful, for *in my thirst they gave me vinegar to drink*.[8]

This is the Passion of Jesus Christ, and it is only the path to resurrection. Every Christian must take up this cross.

How is this possible? *What is impossible for man is possible for God* (Lk. xviii. 27). It is the unfathomable life-giving power of grace. All that is needed is contained in the Body, Blood, Soul and Divinity of Our Lord Jesus Christ.

When Blessed Pope Urban preached the first eastern crusade, it was also a dark time, as the Church was just barely recovering from the first pornocracy. Yet when the Roman Pontiff asked our fathers to leave their families and homes, travel to a distant land to suffer and die for their brethren, they spontaneously started crying out "God wills it! God wills it!" They marched east, suffered and died and miraculously liberated Jerusalem by the power of grace. They were worthy of the name Christian.

Many men today are soft and effeminate. We have become addicted to the pleasures of likes, retweets and shares, and are unwilling to suffer and die for our brother as men of God. We are attached to every earthly pleasure imaginable because of an economy of endless self-gratification. It is an economy fueled by effeminacy—the addiction to the pleasure and comfort causing an reluctance to suffer.

As our fathers and bishops have continued to flee for fear of the wolves, we are tempted to blame everything on the popes or bishops. Yet we will also have our own particular judgement:

> To many the saying, "Deny thyself, take up thy cross and follow Me," seems hard, but it will be much harder to hear that final word: "Depart from Me, ye cursed, into everlasting fire."[9]

When you die and face judgement, Our Lord will say: I punished the world and called you to take up your cross. Did you offer penance, love suffering and convert souls with truth and charity? Did you take up the cross to die for your neighbor, as I did, and all of my saints have done? Or did you hate your brother and blame him and fail to convert him?

---

[8] St. Thomas, *Collatio 6 super Credo in Deum*, trans. *Liturgy of the Hours* (New York: Catholic Book Publishing Co., 1975), vol. III, 1335-1336.
[9] *Imitation of Christ*, bk. II, ch. 12.

Men have been deceived into fighting the false crusade against flesh and blood for the earthly city, and this is because we are attached to pleasures. Men must practice bodily fasting to become men of God. Only bodily fasting attacks our concupiscible attachments to pleasures and makes us love suffering like Christian men.[10]

Men of God must restore the crusade against the principalities and powers by overcoming our own sin, converting our brethren and liberating them from Satan. *He that loveth not, knoweth not God: for God is charity* (I Jn. iv. 8) and again, *If any man say, I love God, and hateth his brother; he is a liar* (I Jn. iv. 20).

In that day the King will question you: did you lead your wife as I have shown you by dying for the Church? For who among you has an ordered home according to the infallible Word of God:

> Let women be subject to their husbands, as to the Lord: Because the husband is the head of the wife, as Christ is the head of the church. He is the saviour of his body. Therefore as the church is subject to Christ: so also let the wives be to their husbands in all things. Husbands, love your wives, as Christ also loved the church and delivered himself up for it (Eph. v. 22-25).

Some men are effeminate because they would rather not upset their wives than be the man of the house. But by doing this, their wives do not respect them. And the children suffer a disordered contest of power between their parents.

Or, on the other hand, a man demands that his wife submit but he himself lives like a tyrant over his wife and children, lording it over them. He too is effeminate. The man of God sacrifices everything—even his own life—for his wife and children and seeks to do God's will even if he suffers for it. This is the love of the Cross. And this is the Catholic masculinity that women want and the children need.

Once the order of your home is restored, lead your family in praying one third of the Rosary every day (five decades). Then lead them in making the First Saturday devotions. Enthrone the Sacred Heart as King over your family.[11]

---

[10] A positive development in this regard is the program Exodus 90 <exodus90.com>.

[11] Matthew Karmel, "Enthronement of the Sacred Heart: The Spiritual Anchor of the Domestic Church" *OnePeterFive* (June 28, 2019)

Then you must restore your economy to be the law of the home. Make sacrifices so your wife can stay home and be queen and your children can have a mother full time. Remove screens or at least severely curtail their use in the home. Educate your children with the true faith and teach them the Holy Mass. Then you can discern your secondary vocation in terms of evangelization and political or social action. In all things, remember the poor.

After this, you can then begin to restore the family. This means refusing to reduce the family to the nuclear family, invented by the industrial revolution. Let your children live in your home. Live in the same neighborhood. Then your children can marry and have children early with your support. This is what all our fathers did. This community of kin is what is natural. This is the mustard seed.

If you do not have an ordered soul and an ordered home, you have no business going online, talking to other Catholics about what you think should happen in the crisis of the Church. Restore the true crusade now, and become the Terror of Demons. This crisis began when men were effeminate. It will end when the men of God arise.[12]

Everything starts with the mustard seed of the family. This is stronger than the strongest demonic Conspiracy. Because of disordered souls and homes, men have turned the Mystical Body of Christ into petty politics. Some say they are "traditionalists," some say they follow John Paul II, but who is worthy of the name "Catholic"?

As we have endeavored to show in this work, the complexities of this and every crisis have many layers and factors, and it is only when men form a new alliance of Christendom that the full synthesis and renewal has come about against the enemies of holy Church. Read the spiritual works and restore the order of your soul and your home.[13] Read the ancient wisdom

---

<https://onepeterfive.com/enthronement-of-the-sacred-heart-the-spiritual-anchor-of-the-domestic-church/>. Find the full traditional ceremony here: <www.catholictradition.org/Two-Hearts/enthronement-3.htm>.

[12] T. S. Flanders, "Conquer Effeminacy and Be a Man – Five Things," *Meaning of Catholic* <https://www.meaningofcatholic.com/2019/08/02/conquer-effeminacy-and-be-a-man-five-things/>; K. Hall, *Terror of Demons: Reclaiming Traditional Catholics Masculinity* (TAN, 2021).

[13] The most necessary masculine spiritual books are *The Imitation of Christ*, *Spiritual Combat* (Scupoli), *True Devotion to Mary* (Montfort), *Humility of Heart* (Bergamo), *Institutes* (Cassian, Paulist Press), and *Conferences* (Cassian, Paulist Press). A more recent text which is fundamental is *The School of Jesus Crucified* (Ignatius of the Side of Jesus) which will help a man love suffering. Finally, Fr. Calloway's *Consecration to St. Joseph* will help all men restore fatherhood in themselves.

of our faith and the basic texts on doctrine.[14] Once you are grounded, then proceed to address the crisis.

If you are a "strict" Catholic (many use the term "traditionalist"), read Dietrich von Hildebrand and St. Teresa Benedicta of the Cross and Jacques Maritain, or the living saint, Cardinal Robert Sarah.[15] If you are a "moderate" Catholic (some call themselves "conservative") read Reginald Garrigou-Lagrange and Fr. Chad Ripperger.[16] Then both must read St. Augustine's *City of God* and Christopher Dawson, the two greatest historians that have formed the synthesis attempted in the present book. After this, the moderates must read Marcel Lefebvre and the strict must read Joseph Ratzinger and Karol Wojtyła.[17] Then an honest appraisal of Vatican II can happen.[18]

---

[14] The *Roman Catechism*, and *Catechism of Pius X*, Ludwig Ott, *Fundamental of Catholic Dogma*, Heinrich Denzinger, *Enchiridion Symbolorum* (Ignatius Press, 2013) and the *Catechism of the Catholic Church* (1992). See meaningofcatholic.com/resources for most of these texts online for free.

[15] Von Hildebrand: Life (*Soul of a Lion*), *Charitable Anathema*, *Trojan Horse in the City of God*, *The Devastated Vineyard*, *The New Tower of Babel*, *In Defense of Purity*, *Liturgy and Personality*, *Ethics*, *Aesthetics*; St. Teresa Benedicta a Cruce (Edith Stein): Life (Teresia Renata Posselt, *Edith Stein: the Life of a Philosopher and Carmelite*; Waltraud Herbstrith, *Edith Stein: A Biography*), *The Science of the Cross*, *Knowledge and Faith*, *Potency and Act*, *Finite and Eternal Being*; Jacques Maritain, *The Peasant of the Garonne*, *Art and Scholasticism*, *Introduction to Philosophy*, *The Primacy of the Spiritual: On the Things that are Not Caesar's*. Sarah, *God or Nothing*, *The Power of Silence*.

[16] Ripperger, *The Binding Force of Tradition*, *Magisterial Authority*, *Topics on Tradition*, *Introduction to the Science of Mental Health*. Garrigou-Lagrange, *Three Ages of the Interior Life*, *Thomistic Common Sense* (trans. Minerd), *The Sense of Mystery* (trans. Minerd), *The Order of Things* (trans. Minerd).

[17] *A Biography of Marcel Lefebvre* (De Mallerais), Davies, *Apologia Pro Marcel Lefebvre*; Marcel Lefebvre, *They Have Uncrowned Him*, *Letter to Confused Catholics*. John Paul II Life (*Witness to Hope* by Weigel), *Love and Responsibility*, *Person and Act and Related Essays* (trans. Gregorz Ignatik, CUA Press, 2021), *Man and Woman He Created Them: A Theology of the Body* (trans. Michael Waldstein, Pauline Books and Media), *Veritatis Splendor*. Ratinzger Life (vol. I and II by Seewald), *Dominus Iesus* (CDF, 2000), *Introduction to Christianity*, *Jesus of Nazareth*, *Verbum Domini*, *The Spirit of the Liturgy*, *Complete Works: Theology of the Liturgy* (Ignatius, 2008) as well as Ratzinger's own recommended liturgical books, Klaus Gamber, *The Reform of the Roman Liturgy: Its Problems and Background*, Alcuin Reid, *The Organic Development of the Liturgy*.

[18] The best texts which interpret Vatican II with Tradition seem to be Aidan Nichols, *Conciliar Octet*, *The Council in Question*; Wicks, *Investigating Vatican II*; Lamb and Levering, eds., *Vatican II: Renewal within Tradition*. The best texts which discuss the deficiencies of the Council are de Mattei, *Vatican II: An*

Then, the charitable anathema is the only way out. All bishops must confess the Declaration of Truths and excommunicate all who oppose it.[19] The precise nature and theology of Vatican II is not as urgent as the charitable anathema. This is the most important act of the spiritual sword. The restoration of the *cultus* of our fathers must then form the uniting principle of continuity which serves as the liturgical basis for the synthesis. There can be no continuity if the old Mass is abolished, as Ratzinger has articulated.[20]

Once this is in place, the Vatican and the SSPX, with others, must set up a theological journal together to debate all the issues *publicly*. The Vatican publishes official dialogues with Protestants and non-Christians, why not the SSPX and the strict? This is the spiritual sword. This debate will help resolve the remaining issues. This is the true *dialogos* which has been breaking down rapidly since the First Vatican Council. Then the elders of Christian culture can relieve the laity of the burden of the spiritual order, and create the necessary synthesis which St. Teresa Benedicta began, and John Paul II and Benedict continued

Meanwhile, ordered families must build cities.[21] "It is Christian civilization, it is the Catholic City. It has only to be set up and restored continually against the unremitting attacks of insane dreamers, rebels and miscreants." At the heart of the restoration must be green martyrdom— those monastic communities that renounce the earthly city and witness to the world to come.[22] The year 2020 has shown us that the American Empire has lost control of the world. International business interests are now attempting to use the COVID-19 crisis to seize more power. The tech giants are innovating faster than legislators can legislate, tightening their grip on the minds of men, women, and children. The regime of scientism rules the world. We must make a refuge so that our children can have their rights to a Christian family and then rise to conquer the world for Christ. At the

---

Unwritten Story; Ferrera and Woods, *The Great Façade*; Sire, *Phoenix from the Ashes* as well as Romano Amerio, *Iota Unum*.

[19] T. S. Flanders, "Every Bishop must Confess the Declaration and Excommunicate those who Oppose it," *Meaning of Catholic* <https://www.meaningofcatholic.com/2019/07/19/every-bishop-must-confess-the-declaration-and-excommunicate-those-who-oppose-it/>.

[20] Joseph Ratzinger, *Complete Works: Theology of the Liturgy* (Ignatius, 2008), 544. Cf. Ibid., *Milestones*, 146-148; *Complete Works: Theology of the Liturgy*, 536-538, 539-557, 558-568, 574-588, 589-594.

[21] Positive developments here seem to be happening in St. Mary's, Kansas, Hulbert, OK, and Tyler, TX with the Veritatis Splendor community <splendorhq.com>.

[22] Some great examples here are the Monasteries of Norcia, Our Lady of Clear Creek and Our Lady of Ephesus.

same time, other Catholics must continue to be salt in the midst of secular communities and politics. The public square must be sanctified by the Holy Name of Jesus at the same time as the Catholic cities are built.

We must restore the public *cultus*. This starts in the home, and flows to the public order. Find land and build a city like St. Maximilian. It may be one family at first, but set up Mary as the throne of Christ in the public order, and the graces will flow from there.

We must restore the monuments of our fathers. The new iconoclasm is at an end—it was so ugly that the children could not stomach to pass it down. We must celebrate the liturgy and create beautiful monuments for the greater glory of God alone. "The Liturgy is not primarily intended as a means of sanctification or an ascetic exercise. Its primary intention is to praise and glorify God, to respond fittingly to Him."[23]

The whole fabric of society must be restored from its very foundations. "Everything must crumble that is not grounded on the one corner stone which is Christ Jesus."[24] A new *dialogos* must be established by priests and laity: debating the foundation of secular republics, economics, and the crusade of the temporal order.[25] But this is ultimately a question of the temporal sword. The clergy must provide the theological foundation, and the laity must wield that sword against the evildoer. It is the laity who must make the final judgement on the particular matters of governance which are not faith and morals. The Two Swords must once again work together within one Church.

> *In the same city, and under the same King, there are two people and two authorities. The city is the Church, the King is Christ, the two peoples are the clergy and the laity.*

Stop fighting against flesh and blood. Restore the crusading spirit against the world, the flesh and the devil. Plant the mustard seed and the Kingdom of God will rise and triumph.

---

[23] Von Hildebrand, *Liturgy and Personality*, 2.
[24] Pius XI, *Divini Redemptoris* (1937), 38.
[25] Excellent contributions in this regard are being made at places like *Sword and Spade* magazine, *Newpolity.com*, and *TheJosias.com*.

GLOSSARY

Anti-Culture: a force of voluntarism which destroys the unity between generations by undermining one or more of the four elements of culture. Forms of anti-culture include Liberalism, Communism, and Feminism.

Beauty: in the supernatural order—God. In the natural order—what God makes; the logos of what man makes. The highest degree of beauty is present when man is conformed to truth and goodness. However, since every man has logos as a rational creature, all cultures can make beauty. The mark of a true culture is beauty passed down. The *cultus* is meant to manifest the metaphysical beauty of Logos by means of audible and visual beauty.

Christendom: the City of God among the Church militant built in Catholic peoples as divine grace slowly converts king, coin and kitchen, always seeking the world to come. The moderate and strict parties create a synthesis of the Greco-Roman renewals which is at the heart of Christendom.

City of God: men and angels, with all creation, in union with and worshipping God in time and eternity. The Kingdom of God. The Church Triumphant, Suffering and Militant. The New Jerusalem of Revelation 21. The harmony of hierarchy. The logos of creation united with the Logos of God.

City of Man: men and angels seeking to impose their will against God's Logos and hierarchy, for the sake of their own glory and power. Mob bloodshed. The ugliness of monotone and noise of chaos.

Coin: the economic exchange between families.

Crusading Spirit: the fight against the world, the flesh and the fallen angels directly by means of the cross, seeking to convert the members of the city of man to Baptism.

Cultural momentum: the social inclination directing all persons, especially children, toward what a culture values and away from what it shuns. This takes place by means of one's own family, other families, public monuments and festivals, the economic values and especially the public *cultus*.

Culture: the growth of truth, goodness, and beauty over generations by means of the four elements of culture: *cultus*, tradition, elders and piety. The soul of a people which seeks the supernatural end of persons.

***Cultus*:** a religious rite seeking the divine. The public *cultus* is an official act of the ruling government to seek the divine. The first element of culture.

Curse of Ham: the theological error that Ham was cursed, not Canaan, and therefore all sons of Ham (Africans) must be enslaved as cursed and sub-human. This also includes various false ideas about Africans and African culture designed to economically exploit the Black African family, leading to the rise of popular shamanism.

Dialogos: an act of humility whereby two or more parties penetrate and subordinate themselves to the truth. The Socratic dialogue or the Summa is an example in literature. The Council of Jerusalem and of Alexandria 362 is an example in Church history.

Dionysius, Dionysian: the Greek god also called *Liber* who is the personification of voluntarism. "Dionysian" is used as a synonym for voluntaristic.

Economy: the law of the home. The logos of exchange between families to provide for their natural needs. In Christendom, an interdependent hierarchy guided by Sacramental grace and the *cultus* which alleviates all forms of poverty in a gradual manner subordinate to the needs of the family. Man, woman and child work from and for the home.

Elders: an office tasked with guarding and passing down the tradition. Parents, priests, sages. One of the four elements of culture.

Empire: a ruling government which expands its borders by means of voluntarism and bloodshed.

Free Market Economy: an economy free from undue pressure from big business and big government so that subsidiarity can prevail and family businesses can be created to sustain peoples.

Goodness: in the supernatural order—God; in the natural order—what God does; the Logos of what man does; act of the will in conformity with the truth of God's Logos as apprehended by the intellect.

Greco-Roman Renewal: a movement within Christian Culture brought about by the League of Christendom and some recovery of Greek and Latin and other ancient traditions, in which a true development of doctrine takes place. This clarifies the faith against heresy and penetrates the truth. These movements restore the Greek philosophical mind and the Roman legal mind in a given era to create a new synthesis of Christendom in all peoples and all languages. There are four great Greco-Roman renewals in history.

Heretic: a Christian who persistently holds false doctrines about Christ for the sake of voluntarism. Unlike moderates and strict among the elders, the heretic seeks to change something substantial in tradition in order to limit the rights of Christ the King in society.

Hierarchy: the sacred order of angels and men and all creation. Interdependence whereby the higher serves the lower and the lower serves the higher by rights and duties. The subjects must serve their king, but the king must fight and die if necessary on the battlefield for his people. A wife must submit to her husband, but a man must lay down his life for his bride.

Iconoclasm: a movement of rejecting piety and tradition manifested by destroying art, architecture and other monuments passed down by our fathers. Condemned and anathematized at the Seventh Ecumenical Council. There have been three major movements of Iconoclasm in Church history.

King: the ruling government of a people whether monarchy, aristocracy or republic.

Kingdom of God: the instantiation of the sovereignty of God in heaven and earth, from the soul of man to society, to the chorus of angels and the whole universe. The Holy Spirit incarnates the reign of Christ everywhere, and Mary is His throne on earth. This removes the usurping demonic thrones and restores the order of God's reign.

Kitchen: the family, the most basic unit of a society and a people. A community of persons.

***Liber*:** lust for power causing disorder *without any rationalization*; named after the drunk orgy rites of *Liber Dionysius*. Its most obvious note is a *direct* attack on Christ as King over souls and society.

***Libertas*:** lust for power causing disorder *with rationalization*. The rationalization is a philosophical assertion which disguises the principles of voluntarism; named after the goddess *Libertas* who worshipped after Tarquin the Proud was overthrown and the Roman Republic was founded. Its most obvious note is its *indirect* attack on Christ as King over souls and society—*by means of attacking the Virgin Mary*.

Liberty: freedom from the dominion of the world, the flesh and the devil to unite to God in charity by divine grace.

Logos: the order of the universe as apprehended by natural reason (logos) and the Second Person of the Trinity as supernaturally revealed and known by faith (Logos); in morals, the subordination of the will to Logos in the intellect.

Martyr: he who bears witness to the Kingdom of God. A red martyr gives his life for Christ, a green martyr forsakes the world as a monk or nun, and a white martyr is the ordinary witness by all Christians who keep themselves unpolluted by this world.

Moderates: a party of elders within Christian Culture which advocate for moderate changes within the tradition in order to safeguard the rights of Christ the King in society against the Conspiracy.

Pagan: someone who is not a member of one of the major monotheistic religions, and, in particular, to those who believe in polytheism or worship nature itself.

People: a community of families formed by a body and soul. The soul is culture, which transmits Logos to the society, which is the body of the people.

Person: a man or woman consisting of body and soul, called to eternal life.

Piety: the reverence due to the elders of a people. The younger generation must have piety for the older generation in order to receive the *cultus* and tradition and pass it down themselves. One of the four elements of culture.

***Pontifex Maximus*:** the sacred priest-emperor of the Roman Empire. The sacralization of the ruling government to claim the priesthood for themselves.

Pornocracy: a period in which the Vatican is deeply corrupted morally, spiritually, and sometimes theologically. There have been three major pornocracies.

Private order: society which is private: the family as well as the soul, known only to God and the individual. Here the rights of man are seen because no one can be forced to be baptized. God still has the right of dominion over the private order, but error can be tolerated here for the sake of the public order.

Providential Capitalism: the belief that God's Providence orders the economy apart from Sacramental grace to the degree that the love of money is changed from the root of all evil to the mainspring of social good.

Public order: society which is public to all: the king and coin. The rights of God must be respected here by the public *cultus* governing king and coin. The thrones of demons must be torn down.

Roma: the goddess personification of the Roman Empire. The divinization of a ruling government. This serves as an ideological justification for the voluntarism of empire.

Science: an act of the intellect whereby the logos in the physical order is understood; an act of the will whereby the physical order is observed or arranged by man for the sake of logos.

Scientism: the use of physical and empirical science to achieve a metaphysical, philosophical, or some other end.
Ex: *the ball bounces up and down, therefore this ball is morally good.*
Ex: *this is a homo sapiens before and after birth, therefore the former is not a person and the other is.*
Ex: *we have mutilated this human being, therefore he is now a she.*

Shamanism: a demonic corruption of *cultus* which involves the use of emotional intoxication through music in order to surrender to the power of evil spirits and/or fallen nature. Shamans use shamanic music to induces trances for this purpose. This practice is passed down in many peoples through history and the world.

Society: the king, coin and kitchen seeking the natural end of persons. The body of a people.

Spiritual Order: the culture. The spiritual sword is wielded by the clergy and religious who fight directly against the fallen angels by means of the Holy Mass and the Sacraments, and their life of prayer, poverty and penance. By their chastity, they also testify to the supernatural world by renouncing earthly marriage.

Strict: a party of elders within Christian Culture which advocate strictly that no change must be made to the tradition in order to safeguard the rights of Christ the King in society against the Conspiracy.

Temporal Order: the society. The temporal sword is governed by the physical "sword" of the government, whose sword is meant to keep order and defend the common good, directing the people to its final end in Christ.

Tradition: everything passed down by the elders to the next generation. All things from the Logos contained in the *cultus* and the wisdom of the fathers to the cuisine, customs of courtship, fashion, dancing, music, aesthetics, monuments and more. One of the four elements of culture.

Truth: in the supernatural order—God; in the natural order—what God is; the Logos of what man knows; reality as apprehended by the intellect.

Two Swords Doctrine: the organic unity of the temporal and spiritual order in Christendom.

Usury: taking unjust interest on a loan. Interest can only be taken if it is for other reasons than the loan itself (an "extrinsic title").

Voluntarism: the subordination of the intellect to the desires of the will metaphysically and morally. Lust for power. Might makes right. Truth is the opinion of the powerful. Pure power, stripped of meaning.

BIBLIOGRAPHY

Aberth, John. *From the Brink of the Apocalypse*. Routledge, 2009.

Acton, Lord. "Ultramontanism." *Essays on Church and State*. Thomas Y. Cromwell Company: 1968.

Agathangelos, *History of St. Gregory and the Conversion of Armenia*, bk. III, trans. anonymous <https://www.livius.org/sources/content/agathangelos/agathangelos-history-3/>, accessed March 23, 2021.

Amerio, Romano. *Iota Unum: A Study of the Changes in the Catholic Church in the XXth Century*. Translated by Fr. John P. Parsons. Sarto House, 1996.

Anderson, Bonnie S. and Judith P. Zinsser. *A History of the their Own*. New York: Harper and Row, 1988.

Andringa, William Van. "Rhetoric and Divine Honours: On the 'Imperial Cult' in the Reigns of Augustus and Constantine." Maijastina Kahlos, ed. *Studies across Disciplines in the Humanities and Social Sciences 20*. Helsinki: Helsinki Collegium for Advanced Studies, undated.

Anonymous. *Life of St. John Vianney*. New York: Joseph Schaefer, 1911.

Arinze, Francis. *God's Invisible Hand: The Life and Work of Francis Cardinal Arinze*. San Francisco, CA: Ignatius Press, 2011.

Arnold Eberhard, ed. *The Early Christians In their Own Words*. Farmington, PA: The Plough Publishing House, 1997.

Ascoli, Albert Russell, ed. *The Cambridge Companion to Petrarch*. Cambridge University Press, 2015.

Augustine. City of God. Translated by Marcus Dods. *Nicene and Post-Nicene Fathers, First Series*. Edited by Philip Schaff. Buffalo, NY: Christian Literature Publishing Co., 1887.

Augustus, Caesar. *Res Gestae*. Trans. Thomas Bushnell (1998) <http://classics.mit.edu/Augustus/deeds.html>. Accessed January 10, 2021.

Baikley, Nels ed. *Readings in Ancient History*. Cengage Learning, 2011.

Bales, Kevin. *Disposable People: New Slavery in the Global Economy*. Revised Edition. University of California Press, 2004.

Baraga, Frederic. *Diary*. Translated by Joseph Gregorich and Paul Prud'homme. Detroit: Wayne State University Press, 1990.

Barber, Malcolm. *The Cathars, Dualist Heretics in Languedoc in the High Middle Ages*. Routledge, 2000.

Batiffol, Pierre. *History of the Roman Breviary*. Translated by Atwell M. Y. Baylay. London: Longmans, 1898.

Baum, Wilhelm and Dietmar W. Winkler. *The Church of the East: A Concise History*. Translated by Miranda G. Henry. London: Routledge, 2003.

Beard, Mary. *The Roman Triumph*. Belknap of Harvard: 2007.

Bede. *Ecclesiastical History of the English People*. Translated by L. C. Jane. 1903.

Belloc, Hilaire. *The Crusades*. TAN: 1937.

———. *The Servile State*. London: T. N. Foulis, 1912.

Benedict XVI. *Last Testament: In His Own Words*. Translated by Jacob Philips. Bloomsbury, 2016.

Bernays, Edward L. *Crystalizing Public Opinion*. New Edition. New York: Lighthouse Publishing Corporation, 1961.

Bessenecker, Scott, ed. *Quest for Hope in the Slum Community*. World Vision: Authentic, 2005.

Bieszad, Andrew. *Lions of the Faith*. Lux Orbis Press, 2013.

Binns, John. *An Introduction to the Christian Orthodox Churches*. Cambridge University Press, 2002.

Birzer, Bradley J. *Sanctifying the World: The Augustinian Life and Mind of Christopher Dawson*. The University of Virginia: Christendom Press, 2007.

Blanchard, Shaun. *The Synod of Pistoia and Vatican II: Jansenism and the Struggle for Catholic Reform*. Oxford University Press, 2020.

Bonneterre, Fr. Didier. *The Liturgical Movement: Roots, Radicals, Results*. Kansas City, MO: Angelus Press, 2002.

Bosworth, A. B. *From Arrian to Alexander: Studies in Historical Interpretation*. Clarendon Press: 1988.

Bougaud, Msgr. *Life of Margaret Mary Alacoque*. Translated by anonymous. New York: Benzinger Brothers, 1890.

Bouyer, Louis. *The Memoirs of Louis Bouyer: From Youth and Conversion to Vatican II, the Liturgical Reform, and After*. United States: Angelico Press, 2015.

Bowersock, G.W. and Peter Brown, eds. *Late Antiquity*. Second Edition. Cambridge, MA: Belknap Press of Harvard University Press, 1999.

Bowley, Mary. *Universal History on Scriptural Principles*. Samuel Bagster and Sons: 1850.

Brown, Peter. *The Rise of Western Christendom*, Second edition. Malden, MA: Blackwell, 2003.

Browning, Robert. *Justinian and Theodora*. Revised edition. London, Thames and Hudson: 1987.

Bunson, Matthew. "The Pope Who Outlasted a Tyrant." *This Rock*. Catholic Answers, Inc., El Cajon, CA, April 2008.

Burke, Edmund. *Reflections on the Revolution in France*. 1790.

Butler, Cuthbert. *Benedictine Monasticism*. Speculum Historiale, 1924.

Byrne, Carol. "Dialogue Mass: A Plea for Silent Participation in the Liturgy." *Tradition In Action*. <https://www.traditioninaction.org/HotTopics/f073_Dialogue_1.htm>. Accessed June 9, 2021.

Cahill, E. *The Framework of a Christian State*. Fort Collins, CO: Roman Catholic Books. Reprint of 1932 Imprimatur.

Cameron, Alan. "The Imperial Pontifex." *Harvard Studies in Classical Philology* 103 (2007): 341-84.

Cantor, Norman F. ed. *The Medieval Reader*. HarperCollins, 1994.

_____. *In the Wake of the Plague*. Reissue edition. Simon and Schuster, 2015.

Caponnetto, Antonio. *The Black Legends and Catholic Hispanic Culture*. Central Bureau of the Catholic Central Verein of America, 1991.

Carlyle, R. W. *A History of Mediaeval Political Theory*. New York: Barnes and Noble, 1915.

Cave, Herbert H. and Roy C. Coulson. *Source book of Medieval Economic History*. New York: Biblio and Tannen, 1965.
Chadwick, Henry. *East and West: The Making of a Rift in the Church*. Oxford University Press, 2005.
Chadwick, Owen. *A History of the Popes 1830-1914*. Oxford University Press, 1999.
_____. *The Popes and the European Revolution*. Oxford University Press, 1981.
_____. *The Secularization of the European Mind in the 19th Century*. Cambridge University Press: 1975.
Chesterton, G. K. *Orthodoxy*. London: John Lane, 1909.
Chiron, Yves. *Annibale Bugnini: Reformer of the Liturgy*. Translate by John Pepino. Angelico Press, 2018.
Cleenewerck, Laurent A. *His Broken Body*. Euclid University Press, 2013.
Codex Theodosianus, <https://sourcebooks.fordham.edu/source/codex-theod1.asp>. Accessed June 9, 2021.
Colby, Charles W. ed. *Selections from the Sources of English History*. New York: Longmans, 1913.
Coulombe, Charles. "The Politics of the Sacred Heart." *Catholicism.org*. Jun 21, 2013. <https://catholicism.org/the-politics-of-the-sacred-heart.html>. Accessed March 27, 2021.
_____. *Blessed Charles of Austria*. TAN, 2020.
_____. *Puritan's Empire: a Catholic Perspective on American History*. Arcadia: Tumblar House, 2008.
_____. *Vicars of Christ*. Arcadia: Tumblar House, 2014.
Counsell, Michael. *The Canterbury Preacher's Companion*. Hymns Ancient and Modern, 2011.
Courtois, Stéphane, et al., eds. *The Black Book of Communism*. Cambridge, MA: Harvard University Press, 1999.
Cousins, Ewert. "Introduction" in *Bonaventure*. Mahwah, NJ: Paulist Press, 1978.
Cowper, B. H. ed. *Syriac Miscellanies*. Williams and Norgate: 1861.
Crétineau-Joly, Jacques. *L'Eglise romaine en face de la Révolution*. Paris: Henri Plon, 1859.
Cross, Richard. *Duns Scotus*. Oxford University Press, 1999.
Da Bergamo, Cajetan Mary. *Humility of Heart*. Translated by Herbert Cardinal Vaughan. TAN:2006.
Dagron, Gilbert and Jean Birrell. *Emperor and priest: The Imperial Office in Byzantium*. Cambridge University Press, 2003.
Dante, *Paradiso*. Translated by Allen Mandelbaum. Bantam: 1984.
Daub, Adrian. *Uncivil Unions: The Metaphysics of Marriage in German Idealism and Romanticism*. United Kingdom: University of Chicago Press, 2012.
Davies, Michael. *Liturgical Revolution*. Revised edition. Kansas City, MO: Angelus Press, 2015. 3 vols.
Dawson, Christopher. *Progress and Religion*. Washington, DC: Catholic University of America Press, 2001.
_____. *Christianity and the New Age*. Angelico Press, 2021.
_____. *Dynamics of World History*. La Salle, IL: Sherwood Sugden, 1978.
_____. *Enquiries into Religion and Culture*. Washington, DC: Catholic University of America Press, 2009.
_____. *Gods of Revolution*. New York University Press, 1972.
_____. *Medieval Essays*. Image Books, 1959.

———. *Mission to Asia*. University of Toronto Press, 1980.
———. *Religion and Culture*. New York: Meridian Books, 1960.
———. *Religion and the Modern State*. London: Sheed and Ward, 1936.
———. *Religion and the Rise of Western Culture*. Garden City, NY: Image Books, 1958.
———. *The Crisis in Western Education*. Steubenville, OH: Franciscan University Press, 1989.
———. *The Dividing of Christendom*. San Francisco, CA: Ignatius Press, 2008.
———. *The Formation of Christendom*. San Francisco, CA: Ignatius Press, 2008.
———. *The Historic Reality of Christian Culture*. Routledge and Kegan Paul, 1960.
———. *The Judgement of the Nations*. Washington, DC: Catholic University of America Press, 2011.
———. *The Making of Europe*. New York: Meridian Books, 1956.
———. *The Movement of World Revolution*. New York: Sheed and Ward, 1959.
De Chardin, Teilhard. *The Making of a Mind: Letters from a Soldier-Priest 1914–1919*. London: Collins, 1965.
De Lubac, Henri. *Teilhard de Chardin*. Translated by René Hague. New York: Hawthorne Books, 1965.
———. *The Faith of Teilhard de Chardin*. Translated by René Hague. London: Burns and Oates, 1965.
———. *The Religion of Teilhard de Chardin*, Translated by René Hague. New York: Desclee Company, 1967.
De Mallerais, Bernard Tissier. *The Biography of Marcel Lefebvre*. Kansas City, MO: The Angelus Press, 2004.
De Mattei, Roberto. "The 'Ninth Crusade' of the Papal Zouaves." *The Remnant*. April 1, 2020.
———. "The Angelus: A Militant Christian Prayer." Translated by Giuseppe Pellegrino. *The Remnant*. March 6 2020.
———. *Blessed Pius IX*. Translated by John Laughland. Herefordshire: Gracewing, 2004.

———. *Plinio Corrêa de Oliveira: Prophet of the Reign of Mary*. Preserving Christian Publications, 2019.
———. *The Second Vatican Council: An Unwritten Story*. Translated by Patrick T. Brannan, et al. Loreto Publications, 2010.
Denzinger, Heinrich. *Compendium of Creeds, Definitions, and Declarations on Matters of Faith and Morals*. Edited by Robert Fastiggi. 43rd edition. San Francisco, CA: Ignatius Press, 2010.
De Oliveira, Plinio Corrêa. "Vocations of the European Peoples." <https://www.traditioninaction.org/OrganicSociety/A_006_Vocations_PCO.htm>. Accessed March 17, 2021.
De Varagine, Jacobus. *The Golden Legend*. Translated by William Granger Ryan. Princeton: Princeton University Press, 2012.
De Vocht, Jozef. *Eternal Memory! Father Achiel Delaere*. Gravelbooks, 2005.
Debrohun, Jeri Blair. *Roman Propertius and the Reinvention of Elegy*. University of Michigan Press: 2003.
Deneen, Patrick J. *Why Liberalism Failed*. New Haven: Yale University Press, 2018.

Denny, Frederick Mathewson. *An Introduction to Islam*. Third Edition. Upper Saaddle River, NJ: Pearson, 2006.
Denzinger, Heinrich, ed. *Compendium of Creeds, Definitions, and Declarations on Matters of Faith and Morals*. Peter Hünermann, ed. Forty-third edition. San Francisco, CA: Ignatius Press, 2012.
Dhalla, Maneckji Nusservanji. *Zoroastrian Civilization*. Oxford: 1922.
Dickens, A. G. *The Counter Reformation*. Norton & Company: 1979.
Din, Gilbert C. and John E. Harkins. *The New Orleans Cabildo*. Louisiana State University Press, 1996.
Doctrina Iacobi. Gilbert Dagron and Vincent Déroche. *Travaux et mémoires / Juifs et Chrétiens dans l'Orient du VIIe siècle*. Volume 11 (1991), 17-273.
Doherty, Catherine De Hueck. *Donkey Bells: Advent and Christmas*. Madonna House: 1994.
Duchesne, Monsignor L. *The Churches Separated from Rome*. Kegan Paul, 1907.
Dvornik, Francis. *Byzantium and the Roman Primacy*. Fordham University Press, 1966.
Ederer, Rupert J. *Economics as If God Matters: More Than a Century of Papal Teaching*. Scarecrow Press, 2011.
Ekonomou, Andrew. *Byzantine Rome and the Greek Popes*. Lexington Books, 2007.
Eksteins, Modris. *Rites of Spring: The Great War and the Birth of the Modern Age*. Mariner Books, 2000.
Eliot, T. S. *Christianity and Culture*. New York: Harvest, 1976.
_____. *What is Classic?* London: Faber & Faber, 1944.
Emmel, Stephen. "Coptic Literature in the Byzantine and early Muhammadan World." *Egypt in the Byzantine World, 300-700*. Cambridge, 2007.
Engel, Randy. *The Rite of Sodomy*. New Engel Publishing, 2012.
Erasmus. *In Praise of Folly*. Translated by Anonymous. London: 1876.
Eusebius, *The History of the Church*. Translated by G. A. Williamson. Penguin, 1989.
Evagrius. *Church History*. Translated by Walford. 1846. <http://www.tertullian.org/fathers/evagrius_4_book4.htm>. Accessed March 25, 2021.
Evans, Craig A. "Mark's Incipit and the Priene Calendar Inscription: From Jewish Gospel to Greco-Roman Gospel." *Journal of Greco-Roman Christianity and Judaism*. 1: 67–81 (2000).
Evans, J. A. S. *The Age of Justinian*. Routledge, 2000.
Farrar, F. W. *Early Days of Christianity*. Funk and Wagnalls, 1888.
Ferrara, Christopher. *Liberty: the God that Failed*. Angelico Press, 2012.
Finocchiaro, Maurice A., ed. *The Galileo Affair: a Documentary History*. Berkeley: University of California Press, 1989.
Fitzgerald, Thomas. "Toward the Reestablishment of Full Communion." *The Greek Orthodox Theological Review*, vol. 36, no. 2, 1991.
Flanders, T. S. *Introduction to the Holy Bible for Traditional Catholics*. Our Lady of Victory Press, 2019.
Fleiner, Fred S. *A History of Roman Art*. Cengage Learning: 2016.
Flood, Anthony. *Christ, Capital and Liberty*. Self-published, 2019.
Foreman, Amanda. "The Heartbreaking History of Divorce," *Smithsonian Magazine*. February, 2014.

Fortescue, Adrian. *The Early Papacy*. San Francisco, CA: Ignatius Press, 2008.
Franzelin, John Baptist Cardinal. *On Divine Tradition*. Translated by Ryan Grant. Sensus Traditionis, 2016.
Frend, W. H. C. *The Rise of Christianity*. Fortress Press, 1984.
Fuentes, Antonio. *A Guide to the Bible*. Dublin: Four Courts Press, 1999.
Gamber, Klaus. *La Réforme liturgique en question*. Translated by Simone Wallon. Monastere Ste Madeleine, 1992.
Garrigou-Lagrange, Reginald. *Three Ages of the Interior Life*. Translated by Sr. M. Timothea Doyle. B. Herder Book: 1947.
Garton, Stephen. *Histories of Sexuality*. New York: Routledge, 2004.
Gautier, Leon. *Chivalry: The Everyday Life of a Medieval Knight*. Tumblar House, 2015.
Gerber, Jerry et al. *Lifetrends: The Future of Baby Boomers and Other Aging Americans*. New York: Macmillan Publishing Company, 1989.
Gibbons, James. *Faith of Our Fathers*. Ninety-third edition. Baltimore, MD: John Murphy Co., 1917.
Goody, Jack. *Islam in Europe*. John Wiley and Sons, 2013.
Gordon, Timothy. *Catholic Republic*. Sophia Institute Press, 2019.
Granfield, Patrick. *The Limits of the Papacy*. Crossroad, 1987.
Gray, David L. *The Catholic Catechism on Freemasonry*. Belleville, IL: Saint Dominic's Media, 2020.
Gregg, Samuel, ed., *Lord Acton: Historian and Moralist*. Grand Rapids, MI: Acton Institute, 2017.
_____. *For God and Profit*. Crossroad, 2016.
_____. *Tea Party Catholic*. New York: Crossroad, 2013.
Gress, Carrie. "The Fascinating Link Between Lepanto and Our Lady of Guadalupe." *National Catholic Register*. October 7, 2016. <https://www.ncregister.com/blog/the-fascinating-link-between-lepanto-and-our-lady-of-guadalupe>. Accessed March 26, 2021.
_____. *The Anti-Mary Exposed: Rescuing the Culture from Toxic Femininity*. TAN: 2019.
Hahn, Scott and Brandon McGinley. *It is Right and Just*. Steubenville, OH: Emmaus Road, 2020.
Hahn, Scott and Curtis Mitch, eds. *The Ignatius Catholic Study Bible: New Testament*. San Francisco, CA: Ignatius, 2010.
Hall, Kennedy. *Terror of Demons: Reclaiming Traditional Catholic Masculinity*. Our Lady of Victory Press, 2020.
Hamans, Fr. Paul. *Edith Stein and Companions on the Way to Auschwitz*. Translated by Sr. M. Regina van den Berg. San Francisco, CA: Ignatius Press, 2010.
Harris, William V. "The Late Republic," Scheidel et. al., eds. *The Cambridge Economic History of the Greco-Roman World*. Cambridge, 2007.
Hendrix, Eugene Russell. *If I had not Come; Things Taught by Christ Alone*. 1916.
Herman, Arthur. *How the Scots Invented the Modern World*. New York: Three Rivers Press, 2001.
Hildebrand, Alice von. *Soul of a Lion: Biography of Dietrich von Hildebrand*. San Francisco, CA: Ignatius Press, 2000.
Hildebrand, Dietrich von. *Aesthetics*. 2 Volumes. The Hildebrand Project: 2018.
_____. *Liturgy and Personality*. Hildebrand Project, 2016.

_____. *Ethics*. Hildebrand Project, 2020.
_____. *In Defense of Purity*. The Hildebrand Project: 2007.
_____. *The Charitable Anathema*. Harrison, NY: Roman Catholic Books, 1993.
_____. *The Devastated Vineyard*. Translated by John Crosby and Fred Teichert. Harrison, NY: Roman Catholic Books: 1973.
_____. *The New Tower of Babel*. Manchester, NH: Sophia Institute Press, 1994.
_____. *Trojan Horse in the City of God*. Franciscan Herald Press, 1967.
_____. *What is Philosophy?* Hildebrand Project, 2021.
Himmelfarb, Gertrude. *Roads to Modernity*. New York: Alfred A. Knopf, 2004.
Hitches, Dan. "Becket and His Critics." *First Things*. January 2021. <https://www.firstthings.com/article/2021/01/becket-and-his-critics>. Accessed March 26, 2021.
Hölscher, Tonio. "The Transformation of Victory into Power: From Event to Structure." Dillon and Welch, eds. *Representation of War in Ancient Rome*. Cambridge University Press: 2006.
Holum, Kenneth G. "Pulcheria's Crusade AD 421-422." *Greek Roman, and Byzantine Studies*, 1977, no. 18.
_____. *Theodosian Empresses*. University of California Press, 1989.
Holzner, Joseph. *Paul of Tarsus*. Scepter Publishing, 2002.
Hopko, Thomas. *Orthodox Church History*, < https://www.oca.org/orthodoxy/the-orthodox-faith/church-history/>. Accessed June 14, 2021.
Hoyland, Robert. *Seeing Islam How Others Saw It*. Gorgias Press, 2019.
Ibn Hishaam. *Sirat*. Edited by Brünnow and Fischer. *Arabische Chrestomathie*. Leipzig: Veb Verlag Enyzklopädie, 1966.
Inascu, Carla. "The Enduring Goddess: Artemis and Mary, Mother of Jesus." PhD dissertation. York University, 2016.
Ionescu, Carla. "The Last Goddess: How Artemis Ephesia Lost Her Crown." *Bishops University Lecture*. February 26, 2018. <https://www.youtube.com/watch?v=9o_Y3yS-Ks4>. Accessed March 23, 2021.
Jackson, W. T. H. ed. *The Essential Works of Erasmus*. Bantam, 1965.
Jaki, Stanley L. *To Rebuild or Not to Try?* Royal Oak, MI: Real View Books, 1999.
Jefford, Clayton N. *Reading the Apostolic Fathers*. Peabody, MA: Hendrickson Publishers, 1996.
Jenkins, Philip. *The Lost History of Christianity*. HarperOne, 2008.
_____. *The Next Christendom*. Oxford: 2011.
Jewish Encyclopedia. 1906 edition.
Johnson, Paul. *Modern Times*. Revised edition. Harper Perennial, 1992.
Jones, Andrew Willard. *Before Church and State: A Study of Social Order in the Sacramental Kingdom of St. Louis IX*. Emmaus Academic: 2017.
Jones, E. Michael. *Barren Metal*. South Bend, IN: Fidelity Press, 2014.
_____. *The slaughter of cities: urban renewal as ethnic cleansing*. St. Augustine's Press, 2004.
_____. *Degenerate Moderns: Modernity as the Rationalization of Sexual Misbehavior*. Fidelity: 2012.
_____. *Dionysios Rising: The Birth of Cultural Revolution out of the Spirit of Music*. South Bend, IN: Fidelity Press, 2012.
_____. *John Cardinal Krol and the Cultural Revolution*. South Bend, IN: Fidelity Press, 2018.

_____. *Libido Dominandi: Sexual Liberation and Political Control.* South Bend, IN: Fidelity Press, 2000.
_____. *Living Machines: Modern Architecture and the Rationalization of Sexual Misbehavior.* South Bend, IN: Fidelity Press, 2012.
_____. *Logos Rising.* South Bend, IN: Fidelity Press, 2020.
_____. *The Catholic Church and the Cultural Revolution.* South Bend, IN: Fidelity Press: 2016.
_____. *The Jewish Revolutionary Spirit.* South Bend, IN: Fidelity Press, 2019.
Jones, Tom Devonshire, ed. *The Oxford Dictionary of Christian Art and Architecture.* Oxford University Press, 2014.
Joseph Rotblat and Michiji Konuma, eds. *Proceedings of the Forty-Fifth Pugwash Conference on Science and World Affairs.* Singapore: World Scientific, 1997.
Jowett, Garth and Victoria O'Donnell. *Propaganda and Persuasion.* Fourth Edition. Thousand Oaks, CA: Sage Publications, 2006.
Jütte, Daniel. *The Age of Secrecy: Jews, Christians, and the Economy of Secrets, 1400–1800.* Yale University Press, 2015.
Kaegi, Walter E. *Byzantium and the Early Muhammadan Conquests.* Cambridge University Press, 1995.
Kagan, Donald et al. *The Western Heritage.* Tenth edition. London: Prentice Hall, 2009.
Kalvelage, Francis M. ed. *Kolbe: Saint of the Immaculata.* Franciscans of the Immaculate, 2001.
Kamen, Henry. *The Spanish Inquisition: A Historical Revision.* Yale University Press, 2014.
Kappes, Christiaan. "A Latin Defense of Mark of Ephesus at the Council of Ferrara-Florence (1438-1439)." *Greek Orthodox Theological Review* 59. 2014.
Kappes, Fr. Christiaan and William Albrecht. *The Definitive Guide to Solving Biblical Questions about Mary: Mary among the Evangelists.* Eagle Pass, TX: Patristic Pilllars Press, 2020.
Katchen, Aaron L. *Christian Hebraists and Dutch Rabbis.* Harvard University Center for Jewish Studies, 1984.
Keevak, Michael. *The Story of a Stele: China's Nestorian Monument and Its Reception in the West 1625-1916.* Hong Kong University Press: 2008.
Kelley, Francis Clement. *Blood-Drenched Altars: A Catholic Commentary on the History of Mexico.* Milwaukee, WI: Bruce Publishing Company, 1935.
Kelly, Msgr. George A. *The Battle for the American Church.* Garden City, NY: Doubleday & Co., 1979.
_____. *The Battle for the American Church Revisited.* San Francisco, CA: Ignatius Press, 1995.
Kengor, Paul. *The Devil and Karl Marx.* TAN, 2020.
Kesich, Veselin. *The Birth of the Church.* SVS Press: 2007.
Kirk, Russell. *The American Cause.* ISI Books, 2002.
_____. *The Conservative Mind.* Chicago: H. Regnery Co, 1953.
Kirwan, Jon. *An Avant-garde Theological Generation: The Nouvelle Théologie and the French Crisis of Modernity.* Oxford University Press, 2018.
Kleiner, Fred S. *The Arch of Nero in Rome.* Giorgio Bretschneider Editore: 1985.

Klijn, Albertus Frederik Johannes. *Seth: In Jewish, Christian and Gnostic Literature*. Brill, 1977.
Klinghoffer, David. *Why the Jews Rejected Jesus*. Random House, 2005.
Kolbaba, Tia M. *The Byzantine Lists: Errors of the Latins*. Illinois Medieval Studies, 2000.
_____. *Inventing Latin Heretics: Byzantines and the Filioque in the Ninth Century*. Medieval Institute Publications, 2008.
Krame, Mark. *Dispossessed: Life in Our World's Urban Slums*. Maryknoll, NY: Orbis Books, 2006.
Kwasniewski, Peter. *Reclaiming Our Roman Catholic Birthright: The Genius and Timeliness of the Traditional Catholic Mass*. Angelico Press, 2020.
La Civiltà Cattolica, *The Jewish Question in Europe*, 1890. Translated by anonymous. South Bend, IN: Fidelity Press, 2020.
Laiou, Angeliki E. and Cécile Morrisson. *The Byzantine Economy*. Cambridge University Press: 2007.
Lamson, Alvan. *The Church of the First Three Centuries*. London: British and Foreign Unitarian Association, 1875.
Lancaster, H. O. *Expectation of Life*. New York: Springer Science, 1990.
Landau, Brent and Tony Burke, eds. *New Testament Apocrypha*. Eerdmans: 2016.
Langer, Ruth. *Cursing Christians? A History of the Birkat HaMinim*. Oxford: 2012.
Lapidus, Ira M. *A History of Islamic Societies*. Second edition. Cambridge University Press, 2002.
Lasance, F. X. *The Young Man's Guide*. Benziger Brothers, 1910.
Latham, Andrew. "Medieval Geopolitics: What were the Northern Crusades?" *Medievalists.net*. Undated. < https://www.medievalists.net/2019/02/what-were-the-northern-crusades/>. Accessed March 16, 2021.
Lefebvre, Marcel. *They Have Uncrowned Him: From Liberalism to Apostasy, the Conciliar Tragedy*. Kansas City, MO: Angelus Press, 1988.
Greer Margaret R. et al., eds. *Rereading the Black Legend: The Discourses of Religious and Racial Difference in the Renaissance Empires*. University of Chicago Press, 2008.
Lehner, Ulrich L. *The Catholic Enlightenment*. Oxford University Press, 2018.
Lethaby, William Richard. *Architecture, Mysticism and Myth*. New York: MacMillan, 1892.
Lewis, C. S. *The Abolition of Man*. MacMillan: 1947.
Liguori, Alphonsus. *History of Heresies*. Translated by John T. Mullock. Dublin: James Duffy, 1847.
_____. *Moral Theology*. Translated by Ryan Grant. Mediatrix Press, 2018.
Likoudis, James and Kenneth D. Whitehead. *The Pope, The Council, and the Mass*. Revised edition. Emmaus Road Publishing, 2006.
Limeris, Vasiliki. *Divine Heiress: The Virgin Mary and the Creation of Christian Constantinople*. London: Routledge, 1994.
Linberg, Carter. *The European Reformation*. Blackwell, 1996.
Louth, Andrew. *Greek East and Latin West*. St. Valdimir's Seminary Press, 2007.
Lukas, Richard C. *Forgotten Holocaust*. New York: Hippocrene Books, 1997.
Maas, Michael, ed. *Cambridge Companion to the Age of Justinian*. Cambridge, 2005.

Mackey, Albert. *Mackey's Revised Encyclopedia of Freemasonry*. Masonic History Company, 1929.
Mailleux, Paul. *Blessed Leonid Feodorov*. Fitzwilliam, NH: Loreto Publications, 2017.
Mamalakis, Philip. *Parenting Toward the Kingdom: Orthodox Principles of Child-Rearing*. Cesterton, IN: Ancient Faith Publishing, 2016.
Marco, Donald de and Benjamin Wiker. *Architects of the Culture of Death*. San Francisco, CA: Ignatius Press, 2004.
Maritain, Jacques. *The Peasant of the Garonne: An Old Layman Questions Himself about the Present Time*. Wipf and Stock Publishers, 2013.
Marshall, Taylor R. *The Eternal City*. St. John Press, 2012.
Marshner, William. *Annulment or Divorce? A Critique of the Current Tribunal Practice and the Proposed Revision of Canon Law*. Christendom Educational Corporation, 1978.
Marx, Karl. *The Civil War in France*. English Edition. Zodiac & Brian Baggins, 1871.
McCall, Brian. *The Church and the Usurers: Unprofitable Lending for the Modern Economy*. Ave Maria University, Sapientia Press, 2013.
Médaille, John C. *Toward a Truly Free Market*. Intercollegiate Studies Institute, 2011.
Meeker, Meg. *Boys Should Be Boys*. New York: Ballatine Books, 2008.
_____. *Strong Fathers, Strong Daughters*. New York: Ballantine Books, 2007.
Meloni, Julia. *The St. Gallen Mafia*. TAN: 2021.
Metcalf, William E, ed. *Oxford Companion to Greek and Roman Coinage*. Oxford: 2012.
Mettepenningen, Jürgen. *Nouvelle Théologie, New Theology: Inheritor of Modernism, Precursor of Vatican II*. T&T Clark, 2010.
Meyendorff, John. *Imperial Unity and Christian Division*. St. Vladimir's Seminary Press, 2011.
_____. *Living Tradition*. St. Vladimir's Seminary Press, 2011.
Meyer, Jean A.. *The Cristero Rebellion: The Mexican People Between Church and State 1926–1929*. United States: Cambridge University Press, 2008.
Mitchell, Samuel Augustus. *Ancient Geography, Classical and Sacred*. Nabu Press, 2011.
Montessori, Maria. *The Mass Explained to Children*. Kettering, OH: Angelico Press, 2015.
Morris, James. *Spain*. London: Faber & Faber, 1964.
Morse, Jennifer Roback. *The Sexual State: How Elite Ideologies are Destroying Lives and Why the Church was Right All Along*. TAN, 2018.
Mueller, John D. *Redeeming Economics*. Intercollegiate Studies Institute, 2014.
Muirchú, *Life of Holy Patrick the Confessor*. Translated by L. Bieler. <https://www.confessio.ie/more/muirchu_english#>. Accessed March 23, 2021.
Murphy, Timothy F. and Marc A. Lappé, eds. *Justice and the Human Genome Project*. University of California Press, 1994.
Murr, Fr. Charles. *The Godmother*. Self-Published, 2017.
Murray, John Courtney. *We Hold These Truths: Catholic Reflections on the American Proposition*. United Kingdom: Rowan & Littlefield Publishers, 2005.
N'Diaye, Tidiane. *Le genocide voilé*. Continents Noirs: 2008.

Nehme, Lina Murr. *1453: Muhammad II Imposes the Orthodox Schism*. Translated by Alfred Murr and Michel Nehme. Beirut: Aleph et Taw, 2001.

Neill, Thomas P. *They Lived the Faith*. Mediatrix Press, 2020.

Nestle-Aland, ed. *Novum Testamentum Graece et Latine*. Deutsche Bibelgesellschaft, 1986.

Neusner, Jacob. *A Life of Rabban Yohanan ben Zakkai*. Brill: 1970.

_____. *First-Century Judaism in Crisis: Yohanan ben Zakkai and the Renaissance of Torah*. Ktav Publishing House: 2006.

_____. *Introduction to Rabbinic Literature*. New York: Doubleday, 1994.

New Catholic Encyclopedia. Second edition. Catholic University of America: 2003.

Newman, Barbara. *God and the Goddesses*. University of Pennsylvania Press, 2005.

Newman, John Henry. "Discourse 17: The Glories of Mary for the Sake of Her Son." *Newman Reader*. National Institute for Newman Studies, 2007. <http://newmanreader.org/works/discourses/discourse17.html>. Accessed March 25, 2021.

_____. *An Essay on the Development of Doctrine*. Park Ridge: Word on Fire, 2017.

_____. *Arians of the Fourth Century*. Longmans, Green and Co., 1908.

Nichols, Aidan. *Catholic Thought Since the Enlightenment*. University of South Africa: 1998.

_____. *Rome and the Eastern Churches*, 2nd ed. San Francisco, CA: Ignatius Press, 2010.

_____. *Sophiology Man: The Work of Vladimir Solov'ev*. Herefordshire, UK: Gracewing, 2020.

Nicolson, Juliet. *The Great Silence: Britain from the Shadow of the First World War to the Dawn of the Jazz Age*. Grove Press, 2011.

Notker the Stammerer. *The Deeds of Charlemagne*. Translated by David Ganz. *Two Lives of Charlemagne*. Penguin: 2008.

Numbers, Ronald L. *Galileo Goes to Jail And Other Myths About Science and Religion*. Harvard University Press, 2010.

O'Malley, John. *The Jesuits: A History from Ignatius to the Present*. Lanham: Sheed and Ward, 2014.

_____. *Vatican I: the Council and the Making of the Ultramontane Church*. Belknap Harvard University Press, 2018.

_____. *What Happened at Vatican II*. Belknap Harvard University Press, 2008.

Olson, Roger E. *The Story of Christian Theology*. InterVarsity: 2009.

Oort, Johannes Van. *Gnostica, Judaica, Catholica: Collected Essays of Gilles Quispel*. Brill, 1990.

Ott, Ludwig. *Fundamentals of Catholic Dogma*. Baronius: 2005.

Ovid, *Erotic Poems*. Translated by P. Green. Penguin Classics, 1982.

Papdakis, Aristeides. *The Christian East and the Rise of the Papacy 1071-1453 AD*. St. Validimir's Seminary Press: 1994.

Patrick. *Confessions*. Translated by McCarthy. <https://www.confessio.ie/etexts/confessio_english#>. Accessed March 23, 2021.

_____. *Letter to the Soldier of Coroticus*. Translated by McCarthy. <https://www.confessio.ie/etexts/epistola_english#01>. Accessed March 23, 2021.

Payne, Ruby K. *A Framework for Understanding Poverty: A Cognitive Approach*.

Pelikan, Jaroslav. *The Christian Tradition: A History of the Development of Doctrine*. Chicago: University of Chicago Press, 1971.

Pesch, Heinrich. *Ethics and the National Economy*. Translated by Rupert Ederer. Norfolk, VA: IHS Press, 2004.

_____. *Liberalism, Socialism and Christian Social Order*. Translated by Rupert J. Ederer. Lewiston: The Edwin Mellen Press, 2000.

_____. *Teaching Guide to Economics*. Translated by Rupert J. Ederer. Lewiston: The Edwin Mellen Press, 2004.

Pieterse, Jan Nederveen. *White on Black: Images of Africa and Blacks in Western Popular Culture*. Yale University Press, 1995.

Pitkin, Timothy. *A Political and Civil History of the United States of America*. New Haven, CT: Hezekiah House, 1828.

Pliny the Elder. *The Natural History*. Translated by John Bostock. London: George Bell, 1893.

Popenoe, David. *Families without Fathers*. New edition. New Brunswick: Transaction Publishers, 2009.

Popkin, Maggie L. *The Architecture of the Roman Triumph*. Cambridge: 2016.

Posnov, Mikhail Emmanuelovich. *The History of the Christian Church Until the Great Schism of 1054*. Translated by Thomas E. Herman. Bloomington, IN: Authorhouse, 2004.

Powell, Philip Wayne. *Tree of Hate: Propaganda and Prejudices Affecting United States Relations with the Hispanic World*. University of New Mexico Press, 2008.

Pristas, Lauren. "The Orations of the Vatican II Missal: Policies for Revision." *Communio*, 30, Winter 2003.

Procopius, *Wars*. Translated by H. B. Dewing. London: William Heinemann, 1914.

Prümmer, Dominic. *Handbook of Moral Theology*. Harrison, NY: Roman Catholic Books, 1957.

Quispel, Gilles. "Valentinus and the Gnostikoi." *Vigiliae Christianae* 50, no. 1. 1996.

Rao, John. "Interview: The Catholic Revival of the 19th Century Confronts the Revolution." *Vendée Radio*. Sep 20, 2018.

_____. "Louis Veuillot and the Catholic 'Intransigence': a Re-evaluation." *Faith and Reason*. Winter, 1983.

_____. *Black Legends and the Light of the World: The War of Words with the Incarnate Word*. Forest Lake, MN: Remnant Press, 2011.

_____. *Removing the Blindfold: 19th-Century Catholics and the Myth of Modern Freedom*. Kansas City, MO: Angelus Press, 2014.

Rath, R. John. "The Carbonari: Their Origins, Initiation Rites, and Aims." *The American Historical Review* 69, no. 2. 1964.

Ratzinger, Joseph. *Principles of Catholic Theology*. San Francisco, CA: Ignatius, 1987.

Ratinzger, Joseph. *Milestones*. Translated by Erasmo Leiva-Merikakis. San Francisco, CA: Ignatius Press, 1998.

Reid, Alcuin. *The Organic Development of the Liturgy*. San Francisco, CA: Ignatius Press, 2005.
Rex, Richard. *Henry VIII and the English Reformation*. Macmillan International Higher Education: 2006.
Richards, Jay. *Money Greed and God*. Revised edition. HarperOne, 2019.
Riddle, John M. *Contraception and Child murder from the Ancient World to the Renaissance*. Harvard University Press, 1994.
Rietveld, James D. *Artemis of The Ephesians*. New York: Nicea Press, 2014.
_____. Interview. *The Magician and the Fool*. Jul 15, 2019. <https://www.youtube.com/watch?v=YTJ-HR_gEwc >. Accessed March 23, 2021.
Ripperger, Fr. Chad. "Moral Virtues." *Sensus Traditonis*. 2016. <http://www.sensustraditionis.org/Virtues.pdf>. Accessed March 23, 2021.
_____. *Introduction to the Science of Mental Health*. *Sensus Traditionis*, 2013.
Roberson, Fr. Ronald. *The Eastern Christian Churches: A Brief Survey*. Seventh Edition. Edizioni Orientalia Christiana: 2008.
Robinson, James Harvey. *Readings in European History*. Ginn and Co., 1904.
Rodríguez, Pedro Insua. *1492: España contra sus fantasmas*. Ariel, 2018.
Roper, William. *The Life of Thomas More*. 1626.
Rosenwein, Barbara H., ed. *Reading the Middle Ages*. University of Toronto Press: 2018.
Ross, James Bruce and Mary Martin McLaughlin, eds. *The Portable Medieval Reader*. New York: Viking, 1961.
_____. *The Portable Renaissance Reader*. New York: Viking, 1969.
Rousseau, Philip. "Procopius's 'Buildings' and Justinian's Pride." *Byzantion* 68, no. 1 (1998): 121-30.
Rowland, Kate Mason. *The Life of Charles Carroll of Carrollton 1737-1832*. The University of Virginia, 1898.
Royal, Robert. *The Catholic Martyrs of the Twentieth Century*. New York: Crossroad Publishing, 2000.
Ryan, Allen. *On Politics*. New York: Liveright, 2012.
Salvany, Don Felix Sarda y. *Liberalism is a Sin*. Translatedd by Condé B. Pallen. TAN, 2012.
Salza, John and Robert Siscoe. "St. Vincent Ferrer was never a Sedevacantist: The True Story of St. Vincent and Benedict XIII." *True or False Pope: Refuting Sedevacantism and Other Modern Errors*. Undated. <http://www.trueorfalsepope.com/p/st-vincent-ferrer-sedevacantist.html>. Accessed March 16, 2021.
Sayles, W.G. *Roman Provincial Coins*. Krause Publications, 1998.
Schafer, Peter. *Jesus in the Talmud*. Princeton University Press, 2007.
Schneider, Floyd. *Mark Challenges the Aeneid*. Wipf & Stock Publishers, 2019.
Schneir, Miriam ed. *Feminism: The Essential Historical Writings*. New York: Vintage Books, 1972.
Schoeman, Roy H. *Salvation is from the Jews*. San Francisco, CA: Ignatius Press, 2003.
Schutten, C.M. "Een episode uit de Tachtig jarige Oorlog. *Army Museum of the Netherlands*, undated.
Schweikart, Larry and Michael Allen. *Patriot's History of the United States*. Revised edition. Sentinel, 2014.

Schwickerath, Robert. *Jesuit Education: its history and principles viewed in the light of modern educational problems*. St. Louis, Mo., B. Herder, 1903.
Scruton, Roger. *Beauty: A Very Short Introduction*. Oxford University Press, 2011.
Secher, Reynald. *The Vendée: A French Genocide*. University of Notre Dame Press, 2013.
Seewald, Peter. *Benedict XVI: A Life*. Translated by Dinah Livingstone. Bloomsbury, 2020.
Shepard, Jonathan, ed. *The Cambridge History of the Byzantine Empire C.500-1492*. Revised edition. India: Cambridge University Press, 2019.
Siebler, Michael. *Roman Art*. Taschen, 2007.
Sire, H. J. A. *Phoenix from the Ashes*. Angelico Press, 2015.
Sirico, Robert. *Defending the Free Market*. Regnery Publishing, 2012.
Smith, Jeffrey. *Themistocles*. Pen and Sword Military, 288.
Soloviev, Vladimir. *Russia and the Universal Church*. Translated by Herbert Rees. London: The Centenary Press, 1948.
_____. "The Universal Meaning of Art." Translated by Vladimir Wozniuk. *The Heart of Reality*. University of Notre Dame, 2003.
Solzhenitsyn, Aleksandr I. *The Gulag Archipelago*. Translated by Thomas P. Whitney and Harry Willets. Abbreviated edition. New York: Harper Perennial, 1985.
Somerset, Anne. *The Affair of the Poisons: Murder, Infanticide, and Satanism at the Court of Louis XIV*. St. Martin's Press, 2004.
Soro, Mar Bawai. *The Church of East: Apostolic and Orthodox*. San Jose, CA: Adiabene Publications, 2007.
Speaight, Robert. *Life of Hilaire Belloc*. New York: Farrar, Straus & Cudahy, 1957.
Spencer, Robert. *The History of Jihad: From Muhammad to ISIS*. New York: Bombardier, 2019.
Spickard, Paul R. and Kevin M. Cragg. *A Global History of Christians*. Grand Rapids: Baker Academic, 1994.
Stearns, Peter N., ed. *The Encyclopedia of World History*. Sixth edition. Boston: Houghton Mifflin Co., 2001.
Stehlin, Fr. Karl. *The Immaculata: Our Ideal*. Translated by Michael J. Miller. Kolbe Publications, 2016.
Stein, Edith. *Knowledge and Faith*. Translated by Walter Redmond. Washington DC: ICS, 2000.
_____. *Potency and Act*. Translated by Walter Redmond. Washington, DC: ICS, 2009.
Strong, Roy. *Coronation*. Harper Perennial: 2005.
Sungenis, Robert A. and Robert J. Bennett. *Galileo was Wrong and the Church was Right*. Second edition. Catholic Apologetics International Publishing, 2008.
Taft, Robert. *The Byzantine Rite: A Short History*. Collegeville, MN: The Liturgical Press, 1992.
Tang, Li. *East Syriac Christianity in Mongol-Yuan China*. Harrassowitz Verlag, 2011.
Tannahill, Reay. *Sex in History*. New York: Stein and Day, 1980.
Teetgen, Ada B. *The Life and Times of Empress Pulcheria*. London: Swan Sonnenschein, 1907.

Teodosio, Rex. "The Marvelous Miracle of Empel Shows the Power of the Immaculate Conception." *The American TFP*, December 15, 2020. <https://www.tfp.org/the-marvelous-miracle-of-empel-shows-the-power-of-the-immaculate-conception/>. Accessed March 27, 2021.

The Epoch Times, ed. *How the Specter of Communism is Ruling Our World*. Epoch Times, 2020.

Theophanes. *Chronicle*. Translated by Henry Turtledove. University of Pennsylvania Press, 1982.

Thomas of Marga. *The Book of the Governors*. Translated by E. A. Wallis Budge. London, 1893.

Thomson, Robert. "The Formation of the Armenian Literary Tradition." Garsoian, Matthews, and Thomson, eds. *East of Byzantium: Syria and Armenia in the Formative Period*. Dumbarton Oaks: 1982.

Touati, Anne-Marie Leander. *The Great Trajanic Frieze*. Stockholm: 1987.

Tracy, Steven C. *Hot Music, Ragmentation, and the Bluing of American Literature*. University of Alabama Press, 2015.

Tutino, Stefania. *Empire of Souls*. Oxford: 2010.

Vaughn, Dom Jerome. *The Life and Labours of Saint Thomas of Aquin*. Abridged 2nd Edition. London: Burns and Oates, 1980.

Vélez, Iván. *Sobre la leyenda Negra*. Ediciones Encuentro, S.A, 2014.

Versnel, H S. *Triumphus: An Inquiry into the Origin, Development and Meaning of the Roman Triumph*. Leiden, 1970.

Veyne, Paul ed. *A History of Private Life*. Cambridge: Harvard University Press, 1987.

Vine, Aubrey R. *The Nestorian Churches*. London: Independent Press, 1937.

Virebeau, Georges. *Prelats et Franc-Maçons*. Paris 1978.

Virgil. *Aeneid*. Translated by Stanley Lombardo. Indianapolis: Hackett, 2005.

Voth, Harold M. *Real Men Don't Abandon Their Responsibilities*. Huntington House, 1993.

Walker, Donald Lee. *Alexander Hamilton's American empire*. University of Nebraska Lincoln, 2005. <https://digitalcommons.unl.edu/dissertations/AAI3186887>. Accessed March 27, 2021.

Walsh, William Thomas. *Our Lady of Fatima*. New York: Image Books, 1990.

Ware, Kallistos. *The Orthodox Church*. Penguin, 1993.

Warner, Bill. "The Doctrine of Deceit," *Center for the Study of Political Islam* (2008) < https://www.politicalislam.com/the-doctrine-of-deceit/>, accessed March 26, 2021

_____. *The Doctrine of Slavery: An Islamic Institution*. Center for the Study of Political Islam, 2010.

_____. *The Life of Muhammad*. Center for the Study of Political Islam, 2010.

Warrior, Valerie M., ed. *Roman Religion: A Sourcebook*. Newburyport, MA: Focus Publishing, 2002.

Weidenkopf, Steve. *The Glory of the Crusades*. Catholic Answers Press, 2014.

_____. *The Real Story of Catholic History: Answering Twenty Centuries of Anti-Catholic Myths*. Catholic Answers Press, 2017.

_____. *Timeless: A History of the Catholic Church*. Huntington, IN: Our Sunday Visitor, 2018.

Weigel, George. *Witness to Hope: The Biography of John Paul II*. Cliff Street Books, 2001.

Wemhoff, David A. *John Courtney Murray, Time/Life, and the American Proposition: How the CIA's Doctrinal Warfare Program Changed the Catholic Church*. South Bend, IN: Fidelity Press, 2015.

Whitaker, Mark. *Smoketown: The Untold Story of the Other Great Black Renaissance*. Simon & Schuster, 2018.

Whitford, David M. *The Curse of Ham in the Early Modern Era*. AshGate, 2009.

Wiesehöfer, Josef. "The Achaeminid Empire." *The Dynamics of Ancient Empires*. Edited by Morris and Scheidel. Oxford University Press, 2009.

Wigram, W. A. *An Introduction to the History of the Assyrian Church*. London: Society for Promoting Christian Knowledge, 1911.

Wild, John. *Introduction to Realistic Philosophy*. New York: Harper and Row, 1948.

Will, Allen Sinclair. *Life of Cardinal Gibbons*. New York: E. P. Dutton and Co., 1922.

Wilson, James Matthew. "In Defense of Jacques Maritain Against His Neo-Integralist Critics." *Church Life Journal*. University of Notre Dame, November 18, 2020.

Wiltgen, Ralph. *The Rhine Flows Into the Tiber*. Devon: Augustine Publishing Company, 1979.

Winkler, Dietmar W. and Li Tang, eds. *From the Oxus River to the Chinese shores: Studies on East Syriac Christianity in China and Central Asia*. Zurich: Lit, 2013.

Wojtyła, Karol. *Love and Responsibility*. San Francisco, CA: Ignatius Press, 1981.

Woods, Thomas. *The Church and the Market*. Revised edition. Lexington Books, 2015.

_____. *The Politically Incorrect Guide to American History*. Regnery Publishing, 2004.

Worth, Roland H. *The Seven Cities of the Apocalypse*. New York: Paulist Press, 1999.

Worthington, Ian. *Alexander the Great*. Taylor & Francis: 2014.

Wybrew, Hugh. *The Orthodox Liturgy*. Crestwood, NY: St. Vladimir's Seminary Press, 2003.

X, Malcolm. *The Autobiography of Malcolm X as Told to Alex Haley*. Ballatine Books: 1964.

Yossa, Kenneth. *Common Heritage, Divided Communion: The Decline and Advances of Inter-Orthodox Relations from Chalcedon to Chambésy*. Georgia Press: 2009.

Zanker, Paul and Alan Shapiro. *The Power of Imagers in the Age of Augustus*. University of Michigan Press, 1988.

Zetzel, James E. G. "Rome and its Traditions." *The Cambridge Companion to Virgil*. Edited by Martindale et al. Cambridge University Press: 1997.

Zizilouas, John D. *Eucharist, Bishop, Church: The Unity of the Church in the Divine Eucharist and the Bishop During the First Three Centuries*. Holy Cross Orthodox Press, 2007.

_____. *Being as Communion*. St. Vladimir's Seminary Press, 1997.

INDEX

A

Action Française, 365, 384, 397
Acton, Lord 189, 337, 338, 341, 343, 345, 346, 347, 421, 423, 463, 487, 492
Adams, Abigail 305, 306
Adams, John 305, 306, 316
Africa, 146, 150, 167, 169, 315, 323, 326, 351, 375, 377, 378, 386, 389, 402, 405, 410, 420, 448, 462, 464, 497, 498
African, 146, 170, 228, 234, 235, 236, 307, 317, 318, 326, 341, 351, 373, 377, 378, 389, 402, 456, 457, 482
Alexandrian, 128, 129, 131, 132, 134, 144, 146, 151, 152, 352
Alphonsus, St. 261, 280, 478, 495
Alta Vendita, 322, 332
angel, 49, 52, 57, 60, 63, 70, 74, 80, 162, 166, 175, 181, 418
annulment crisis, 424, 447, 453, 454
Antichrist, 12, 13, 67, 68, 69, 74, 109, 137, 164, 165, 267, 276, 368, 406
anti-culture, 104, 256, 269, 270, 271, 272, 273, 276, 281, 282, 284, 297, 298, 299, 300, 301, 304, 305, 306, 307, 308, 309, 311, 314, 320, 324, 326, 329, 332, 335, 336, 337, 339, 341, 342, 343, 352, 353, 362, 363, 365, 369, 373, 375, 379, 381, 383, 384, 385, 392, 394, 402, 403, 410, 411, 415, 418, 443, 449, 454, 482
Antiochian, 111, 129, 132, 134, 144, 145, 146, 151, 352

arch, 27, 28, 29, 30, 32, 33, 35, 36, 57, 71, 100, 101, 125, 130, 135, 151, 194, 197, 284, 457
Ariminum, 27, 28, 29, 35, 125, 130
Armenia, 39, 88, 100, 113, 115, 116, 119, 144, 148, 167, 182, 487, 501
Artemis, 11, 36, 37, 38, 39, 40, 41, 42, 44, 45, 46, 47, 55, 96, 97, 98, 99, 133, 134, 137, 205, 212, 221, 493, 499
Auctorem Fidei, 362
Augustine, St. 2, 14, 15, 33, 34, 35, 43, 44, 52, 54, 55, 57, 60, 67, 68, 69, 77, 88, 91, 94, 95, 102, 121, 126, 133, 135, 142, 155, 176, 187, 256, 342, 352, 414, 421, 478, 479, 487, 493, 502
Augustus, Caesar 27, 28, 29, 30, 32, 33, 35, 36, 38, 39, 48, 49, 56, 58, 62, 72, 125, 128, 130, 151, 173, 487, 496, 502

B

Bacon, Francis 246, 255, 262
Baltimore, Lord 291, 292, 293, 294, 295, 349, 384
Baroque, 223, 225, 226, 242, 243, 262, 282, 473
beauty, 28, 31, 34, 35, 42, 43, 47, 48, 50, 51, 52, 55, 56, 57, 58, 63, 77, 82, 83, 84, 126, 136, 138, 154, 166, 169, 178, 190, 191, 192, 193, 195, 200, 205, 206, 215, 216, 220, 224, 225, 226, 227, 228, 233, 239, 242, 243, 244, 246, 247, 249, 258, 262, 273, 325, 362, 378, 379, 381, 390, 415, 439, 441, 446, 448,

450, 451, 453, 455, 457, 462, 482
Beethoven, 262, 325
Bellarmine, St. Robert 179, 227, 233, 245, 248, 250, 251, 287
Belloc, Hilaire 40, 110, 192, 370, 385, 393, 487, 500
Benedict XV, 361, 369, 371, 373
Benedict XVI, 13, 34, 343, 396, 402, 403, 406, 409, 420, 425, 427, 435, 454, 467, 468, 469, 471, 473, 488, 500
Bernadette, St. 339, 342
Bernays, Edward 372, 373, 375, 380, 400, 411, 488
Bill of Rights, 186, 290, 294, 299
Boniface, St. 169, 171, 348
Brahe, Tycho 248
Brentano, Franz 355, 359, 394
Britain, 117, 240, 275, 277, 282, 285, 286, 290, 299, 303, 310, 317, 331, 366, 368, 377, 396, 397, 400, 497
Bugnini, Annibali 401, 422, 426, 430, 433, 435, 441, 445, 449, 450, 469, 473, 489
Burke, Edmund 45, 98, 304, 305, 474, 488, 495

C

Caesar, 28, 29, 30, 33, 36, 39, 48, 51, 52, 58, 63, 68, 72, 77, 79, 99, 100, 101, 131, 150, 151, 202, 203, 217, 229, 323, 479, 487
Capitalism, 278, 279, 312, 331, 381, 448, 460, 461, 464, 485
Carroll, Charles 294, 296, 308, 350, 499
Carroll, John 284, 296, 304
Cathars, 107, 179, 184, 487
chant, 160, 183, 191, 226, 233, 338, 362, 414, 425, 434, 452, 468
charitable anathema, 223, 224, 346, 366, 419, 444, 460, 465, 471, 480

Chesterton, G. K. 3, 50, 51, 250, 305, 370, 489
children, 11, 16, 29, 43, 46, 51, 53, 55, 58, 67, 81, 82, 83, 84, 85, 86, 87, 88, 112, 115, 138, 140, 142, 165, 166, 167, 172, 174, 176, 181, 184, 188, 192, 193, 195, 197, 204, 216, 219, 220, 224, 225, 227, 234, 239, 242, 250, 256, 268, 271, 273, 277, 281, 282, 291, 293, 297, 303, 304, 306, 307, 309, 310, 311, 313, 318, 326, 328, 334, 336, 338, 340, 341, 350, 351, 354, 357, 359, 360, 361, 362, 363, 371, 373, 374, 380, 387, 389, 390, 396, 397, 401, 410, 411, 418, 423, 429, 434, 446, 447, 448, 449, 451, 454, 455, 459, 460, 462, 464, 466, 470, 474, 477, 478, 480, 481, 482
China, 144, 169, 185, 196, 228, 231, 237, 238, 356, 465, 466, 494, 500, 502
Chinese, 28, 144, 169, 238, 375, 391, 409, 456, 460, 466, 502
Christendom, 3, 5, 12, 13, 15, 28, 30, 64, 66, 74, 77, 78, 79, 108, 110, 111, 123, 127, 136, 137, 141, 153, 157, 158, 160, 161, 163, 164, 167, 169, 172, 173, 176, 178, 180, 181, 184, 185, 187, 188, 189, 190, 192, 193, 194, 195, 197, 198, 199, 202, 203, 204, 205, 206, 208, 210, 213, 215, 217, 220, 221, 222, 226, 228, 229, 230, 236, 237, 238, 241, 242, 243, 244, 246, 250, 252, 253, 258, 259, 260, 261, 263, 265, 268, 273, 278, 279, 281, 282, 283, 285, 286, 289, 291, 295, 296, 297, 303, 305, 307, 309, 316, 318, 319, 321, 322, 324, 325, 327, 331, 332, 336, 339, 342, 343, 348, 350, 351, 352, 357, 361, 363,

373, 375, 378, 386, 389, 405, 407, 447, 453, 464, 478, 482, 483, 486, 488, 490, 493, 496
Cicero, 41, 200, 252
City of God, 2, 3, 4, 5, 7, 12, 13, 14, 15, 33, 43, 44, 52, 54, 55, 57, 60, 73, 77, 91, 95, 102, 121, 126, 129, 133, 135, 142, 143, 148, 155, 160, 168, 176, 177, 187, 197, 229, 262, 286, 342, 364, 410, 427, 428, 451, 479, 482, 487, 493
city of man, 73, 91, 147, 205, 482
Communism, 269, 314, 329, 335, 383, 394, 397, 404, 409, 410, 415, 417, 418, 423, 452, 461, 482, 489, 501
Communist, 332, 334, 346, 371, 375, 382, 383, 402, 404, 408, 415, 416, 435, 443, 452, 460, 465, 466
Congar, Yves 347, 392, 426, 427, 444
Constantinople, 127, 130, 132, 135, 136, 141, 143, 144, 146, 150, 152, 153, 155, 158, 163, 171, 176, 195, 197, 199, 202, 495
Crowley, Aleister 107, 361, 385, 450
Crusade, 12, 13, 135, 136, 138, 145, 148, 149, 158, 174, 180, 182, 184, 195, 196, 200, 201, 332, 333, 336, 342, 478, 490, 493
crusading spirit, 12, 13, 91, 92, 97, 98, 108, 114, 116, 130, 152, 158, 164, 168, 170, 213, 222, 227, 241, 249, 251, 259, 332, 372, 398, 399, 406, 435, 452, 481, 482
cultural momentum, 85, 86, 87, 88, 96, 112, 114, 115, 119, 157, 166, 167, 176, 181, 191, 192, 216, 242, 271, 273, 277, 293, 294, 300, 354, 380, 411, 448, 464, 482

curse of Ham, 234, 235, 236, 377, 378, 482, 502
Cyril, St. 131, 132, 137, 144, 145, 146, 177, 178, 342

D

Darwin, Charles 334, 335, 340, 366
Dawson, Christopher 2, 14, 15, 28, 29, 30, 47, 50, 51, 64, 92, 110, 111, 130, 133, 142, 143, 149, 154, 164, 166, 172, 175, 176, 177, 180, 185, 186, 187, 188, 193, 194, 195, 196, 197, 198, 199, 200, 202, 210, 211, 213, 217, 242, 254, 268, 269, 271, 276, 280, 285, 289, 291, 302, 307, 314, 326, 335, 337, 370, 383, 385, 398, 400, 403, 405, 409, 442, 479, 488, 489
de Chardin, Pierre Teilhard, 367, 370, 384, 391, 392, 402, 404, 414, 419, 420, 427, 490
de Gaulle, Charles 397, 403
de Lubac, Henri 367, 391, 392, 404, 427, 433, 443, 490
de Montfort, St. Louis 198, 261, 325, 355
de Toqueville, Alexis 300
democracy, 51, 268, 305, 320, 373, 380, 384, 386, 393, 399, 403, 408, 410, 415, 427
Descartes, René 246
dialogos, 31, 132, 142, 145, 147, 151, 153, 160, 177, 201, 209, 231, 248, 336, 394, 405, 406, 420, 458, 460, 467, 469, 480, 481, 483
Diego, St. Juan 221, 342
Dignitatus Humanae, 442
Dionysian, 32, 36, 39, 40, 79, 138, 140, 166, 179, 204, 220, 259, 282, 302, 377, 387, 389, 410, 417, 448, 483
Dionysius, 32, 34, 36, 38, 42, 43, 44, 45, 47, 49, 92, 167, 219, 377, 379, 388, 390, 483, 484

Dodd, Bella 408
Dolfuss, Engelbert 394, 403
Döllinger, Ignaz von 337, 343, 346, 421
Dominus Iesus, 457, 465, 479
Drexel, St. Katherine 355
Dutch, 239, 240, 242, 243, 246, 254, 256, 277, 285, 291, 300, 325, 398, 428, 451, 494

E

earthly city, 35, 50, 54, 55, 56, 63, 64, 67, 68, 69, 78, 81, 90, 91, 96, 97, 99, 101, 102, 105, 106, 109, 112, 114, 129, 136, 137, 141, 142, 143, 144, 145, 146, 147, 151, 153, 154, 157, 159, 163, 164, 171, 174, 178, 181, 183, 195, 197, 210, 212, 220, 222, 229, 252, 258, 259, 262, 269, 273, 283, 314, 321, 351, 364, 367, 369, 371, 375, 398, 400, 420, 451, 476, 480
Economy, 40, 57, 137, 200, 256, 279, 306, 463, 483, 487, 494, 495, 496, 498
education, 40, 244, 270, 273, 277, 282, 291, 306, 307, 329, 330, 335, 342, 357, 396, 405, 418, 429
effeminacy, 44, 84, 140, 159, 186, 270, 380, 476, 478
effeminate, 44, 70, 98, 134, 204, 252, 306, 313, 334, 411, 449, 476, 477, 478
empire of death, 34, 35, 36, 39, 42, 47, 48, 54, 56, 67, 72, 74, 77, 210, 216, 319
Empire of Freedom, 12, 263, 341
England, 4, 6, 33, 155, 156, 173, 186, 191, 197, 198, 211, 213, 214, 216, 217, 238, 241, 245, 246, 249, 250, 253, 262, 267, 276, 277, 280, 285, 288, 290, 291, 292, 293, 296, 298, 305, 322, 323, 324, 330, 342, 366, 451
Ephesus, 11, 38, 44, 45, 71, 96, 97, 98, 99, 102, 110, 134, 135, 137, 145, 152, 201, 202, 212, 221, 228, 480, 494
evolution, 144, 334, 343, 366, 391

F

fallen angels, 4, 35, 39, 50, 52, 53, 54, 55, 56, 58, 67, 70, 72, 87, 90, 92, 107, 126, 130, 140, 147, 178, 192, 193, 206, 212, 267, 277, 361, 413, 452, 482, 485
fascism, 385
Fascist, 385, 394
Fatima, 11, 229, 232, 371, 386, 388, 395, 407, 410, 417, 418, 426, 501
Feminism, 269, 306, 334, 341, 378, 383, 455, 482, 499
Feodorov, Bl. Leonid 353, 365, 370, 392, 496
France, 6, 148, 171, 179, 184, 197, 198, 211, 221, 222, 239, 241, 244, 251, 252, 261, 280, 281, 282, 285, 286, 298, 302, 304, 308, 309, 316, 320, 321, 327, 328, 333, 337, 346, 353, 360, 366, 367, 368, 377, 384, 396, 397, 403, 404, 451, 488, 496
Francis I, 361, 393, 439, 472, 473
Franco, Francisco 59, 348, 398, 403
Franklin, Benjamin 296, 304
free market, 40, 278, 279, 314, 461, 462
Freemasonry, 3, 107, 216, 276, 323, 372, 449, 492, 496
Freud, Sigmund 326, 355, 372, 381, 387, 388

G

Gagnon, Cardinal Édouard 445, 449, 451, 452, 456, 457, 471

Galileo, 247, 248, 257, 340, 424, 491, 497, 500
Garrigou-Lagrange, Reginald 365, 386, 397, 404, 405, 406, 479, 492
Gibbons, James 318, 330, 331, 349, 350, 354, 355, 390, 492, 502
Grand Coalition of the Status Quo, 15, 69, 70, 107, 112, 147, 274, 387, 472
Greco-Roman, 15, 28, 29, 30, 31, 32, 33, 34, 40, 41, 42, 43, 44, 45, 63, 64, 65, 67, 82, 84, 87, 88, 94, 96, 111, 132, 136, 138, 153, 154, 156, 157, 160, 169, 173, 174, 178, 192, 193, 195, 196, 200, 201, 219, 222, 223, 261, 281, 309, 322, 336, 352, 353, 367, 384, 385, 392, 404, 418, 482, 483, 491, 492
Greece, 31, 32, 38, 43, 45, 61, 65
Greek, 28, 30, 31, 32, 34, 37, 38, 39, 40, 44, 45, 51, 53, 62, 64, 65, 72, 73, 76, 79, 82, 96, 101, 111, 116, 125, 128, 132, 134, 136, 138, 141, 142, 144, 145, 147, 153, 154, 155, 157, 160, 166, 167, 168, 170, 171, 172, 174, 177, 178, 181, 193, 194, 195, 196, 201, 202, 203, 205, 210, 223, 228, 231, 232, 233, 247, 256, 258, 259, 269, 336, 370, 419, 421, 483, 491, 493, 494, 495, 496
Gregg, Samuel 40, 57, 279, 314, 337, 345, 492
Guadalupe, 11, 199, 221, 222, 227, 228, 230, 316, 319, 371, 386, 492
Guéranger, Dom 338, 362

H

Hagia Sophia, 130, 133, 135, 136, 141, 143, 150, 152, 153, 202
Hamilton, Alexander 310, 312, 501
Henry VIII, King 212, 214, 216, 263, 288, 305, 313, 349, 499
Herakleios, Emperor 158, 159, 160, 165, 168, 169, 400
heretics, 69, 99, 101, 104, 107, 112, 120, 129, 132, 172, 177, 209, 216, 239, 258, 261, 280, 288, 294, 342, 343, 362, 385, 388, 421, 422, 446, 447, 460, 472
Herod, 50, 62, 63, 66, 73, 74, 90, 99
Hierarchy, 52, 273, 483
Hitler, Adolf 370, 376, 381, 394, 395, 396, 397, 398, 401, 403, 466
Holy Alliance, 322, 323, 324
Humani Generis, 405, 406
Husserl, Edmund 355, 356, 394, 428

I

iconoclasm, 239, 273, 439, 445, 451, 481
idols, 39, 40, 41, 45, 59, 62, 65, 66, 87, 98, 112, 114, 116, 117, 133, 137, 142, 155, 181, 193, 200, 206, 209, 214, 231, 255, 273, 276, 290, 383, 410, 411, 448
Immaculate Conception, 63, 82, 87, 97, 137, 158, 196, 201, 208, 228, 241, 259, 284, 304, 325, 339, 342, 355, 356, 401, 426, 501
Indian, 221, 237, 281, 288, 292, 297, 298, 299, 307, 316, 317, 318, 319, 325, 332, 385
Industrial Revolution, 277, 312, 325, 351
Inquisition, 108, 184, 199, 237, 494
Iraq, 253, 461, 465

J

James I, King 245, 292
Jansenist, 308, 362, 387, 400, 447
Jansenists, 211, 261, 280, 281, 302, 308, 417

Japan, 237, 238, 397, 399, 401
Jazz, 377, 379, 380, 399, 497
Jefferson, Thomas 286, 290, 291, 298, 299, 301, 302, 303, 307, 316, 317, 324, 350, 357
Jesuits, 222, 223, 224, 227, 237, 238, 261, 275, 280, 281, 282, 283, 292, 296, 308, 318, 322, 329, 356, 367, 404, 406, 412, 413, 456, 497
Jews, 2, 46, 50, 61, 62, 63, 67, 69, 71, 78, 91, 94, 96, 99, 101, 102, 103, 104, 105, 106, 107, 108, 111, 112, 120, 129, 147, 156, 157, 158, 163, 170, 181, 184, 198, 199, 200, 212, 233, 235, 241, 259, 269, 326, 327, 349, 355, 356, 366, 375, 381, 385, 387, 388,390, 393, 397, 398, 399, 402, 424, 455, 466, 494, 495, 499
John Paul II, St. 13, 220, 225, 356, 397, 423, 450, 452, 453, 454, 456, 457, 458, 460, 461, 462, 463, 465, 466, 467, 468, 472, 473, 478, 479, 480, 501
John XXIII, St. 361, 419, 428, 471

K

Kabbalah, 184, 195, 200, 233, 259, 276
Kinsey, Alfred 412
Kirk, Russell 304, 337, 338, 345, 410, 494
Kolbe, St. Maximilian, 372, 388, 390, 399, 401, 481

L

Labouré, St. Catherine 325
Latin, 31, 51, 72, 82, 86, 110, 111, 119, 128, 132, 133, 136, 142, 144, 145, 150, 153, 154, 155, 157, 168, 172, 174, 175, 177, 178, 179, 195, 201, 202, 211, 216, 225, 238, 243, 252, 256, 274, 334, 336, 372, 373, 401, 403, 408, 421, 424, 425, 434, 438, 441, 444,468, 483, 494, 495
Lefebvre, Marcel 236, 387, 389, 421, 422, 423, 424, 435, 445, 457, 458, 459, 460, 468, 469, 479, 490, 495
Legion of Decency, 390, 399, 407, 412
Lenin, Vladimir 334, 366, 371, 382, 388, 451
Leo XIII, 43, 81, 271, 276, 298, 352, 353, 354, 355, 356, 357, 360, 361, 364, 365, 385, 413, 441
Liber, 32, 43, 48, 178, 219, 220, 255, 280, 282, 302, 483, 484
Liberalism, 39, 41, 129, 139, 175, 192, 246, 269, 275, 279, 284, 385, 423, 482, 490, 495, 498, 499
Libertas, 39, 43, 48, 219, 220, 238, 239, 240, 241, 242, 244, 245, 246, 249, 251, 254, 255, 256, 262, 263, 268, 271, 276, 277, 280, 284, 286, 300, 303, 308, 309, 319, 325, 326, 329, 332, 354, 358, 360, 361, 375, 390, 400, 403, 413, 461, 484
Lincoln, Abraham 310, 340, 350, 501
Locke, John 254, 255, 256, 257, 268, 270, 273, 276, 282, 286, 290, 306, 335
Loisy, Alfred 353, 366, 367
Lord's Day, 87, 138, 154, 314
Luther, Martin 163, 208, 209, 210, 212, 215, 217, 218, 220, 305, 412, 420, 472

M

Madison, James 300, 380
Magna Carta, 186, 212, 213, 217, 236, 238, 245, 253, 272, 287, 288, 289, 290, 295, 349

Maimonides (Rambam), 105, 106, 184, 195, 233, 259
Manifest Destiny, 286, 293, 294, 300, 316, 317, 332, 350, 357, 375, 391, 400
Maritain, Jacques 386, 391, 392, 397, 404, 406, 409, 410, 415, 416, 426, 427, 429, 433, 479, 496, 502
Marriage, 186, 220, 227, 277, 307, 316, 318, 341, 351, 378, 387, 388, 389, 390, 423, 453, 473, 489
Martini, Carlo Maria 450, 460, 472
Marx, Karl 326, 329, 335, 346, 494, 496
Mary, 11, 29, 32, 49, 63, 76, 77, 81, 82, 83, 84, 87, 88, 96, 97, 100, 102, 105, 115, 117, 135, 136, 137, 138, 140, 145, 150, 154, 176, 184, 186, 191, 196, 201, 203, 208, 216, 217, 218, 219, 221, 222, 227, 229, 239, 251, 253, 256, 260, 261, 267, 268, 273, 282, 293, 305, 306, 318, 325, 334, 339, 347, 350, 374, 386, 388, 391, 399, 400, 401, 409, 429, 442, 456, 478, 480, 481, 484, 487, 488, 489, 490, 492, 493, 494, 495, 497, 499
Maryland, 292, 293, 294, 295
Masonry, 263, 269, 275, 276, 277, 284, 308, 320, 330
Maximos IV, 419
mestizo, 221, 307, 319, 332
Métis, 316, 318
Mexico, 210, 216, 221, 228, 236, 281, 285, 316, 319, 324, 331, 332, 371, 494, 498
Meyendorff, John 117, 145, 147, 149, 151, 153, 154, 158, 177, 496
Milton, John 220, 236, 251, 351
moderate, 13, 15, 94, 111, 121, 131, 132, 145, 172, 193, 223, 225, 226, 238, 293, 294, 295, 303, 314, 320, 321, 328, 337, 338, 344, 346, 349, 352, 356, 361, 362, 392, 401, 405, 406, 414, 418, 421, 422, 425, 427, 452, 453, 457, 460, 469, 473, 479, 482, 484
Modernism, 343, 353, 366, 367, 404, 405, 418, 453, 460, 496
Mosaic, 12, 50, 56, 57, 58, 60, 62, 63, 64, 66, 71, 76, 77, 78, 79, 84, 93, 96, 103, 104, 105, 106, 111, 138, 139, 141, 215
Moscow, 203, 229, 259, 356, 396
Muhammad, 12, 162, 163, 165, 166, 167, 171, 202, 232, 233, 234, 235, 315, 341, 497, 500, 501
Muhammadanism, 163, 165, 166, 167, 194, 196, 203, 229, 231, 232, 233, 235, 402, 405, 456, 466
Murr, Charles 202, 351, 449, 450, 451, 452, 456, 458, 496, 497
Murray, John Courtney 5, 354, 397, 403, 409, 412, 423, 502
music, 29, 45, 51, 52, 56, 87, 117, 127, 166, 191, 225, 226, 243, 262, 325, 338, 362, 377, 378, 379, 399, 411, 437, 439, 447, 464, 485, 486
Mussolini, Benito 385, 388, 393
mustard seed, 72, 80, 81, 88, 99, 102, 112, 170, 171, 175, 178, 180, 371, 374, 453, 457, 466, 478, 481

N

Nagasaki, 237, 339, 356, 357, 390, 399, 401
Napoléon, Emperor 309, 315, 316, 320, 321, 322, 323, 324, 325, 326, 342
Nazi, 390, 393, 394, 395, 396, 397, 405, 423, 447, 454

Netherlands, 5, 199, 211, 239, 240, 241, 242, 253, 255, 366, 398, 499
Newman, John Henry 2, 93, 112, 129, 130, 131, 137, 146, 147, 176, 218, 267, 330, 338, 343, 344, 345, 347, 436, 497
Newton, Isaac 257, 262, 278, 286, 313, 334, 366
Northmen, 172, 173, 176, 185, 191
Nouvelle théologie, 392, 419, 421
Nowa Huta, 416, 450, 451

O

Ó Conaill, Dónall (Daniel O'Connell) 276, 330, 349
occult, 107, 131, 178, 184, 200, 246, 257, 268, 322, 361, 378, 385
oral Tradition, 80
Original Sin, 54, 55, 77, 86, 87, 107, 110, 115, 120, 192, 196, 201, 255, 257, 268, 269, 270, 272, 278, 279, 313, 325, 337, 367, 373, 391, 392, 413, 417, 418, 428, 463

P

Pádraig (St. Patrick), 88, 117, 118, 119, 138, 139, 173, 214, 246, 249, 250, 263, 314, 330, 331, 333, 347, 350, 423, 460, 462, 490, 492, 496, 497
pagans, 71, 99, 107, 118, 120, 140, 147, 201, 237, 294, 385, 390
Paine, Thomas 59, 287, 297, 298, 305
Patriot, 285, 287, 288, 290, 295, 296, 297, 298, 300, 301, 308, 316, 317, 331, 411, 499
Paul VI, St. 406, 413, 422, 424, 425, 426, 429, 430, 433, 434, 435, 436, 437, 439, 440, 441, 442, 443, 444, 445, 446, 447, 449, 450, 451, 453, 468, 469, 472, 473
Persian, 30, 31, 33, 35, 38, 39, 47, 49, 77, 93, 96, 97, 102, 110, 111, 112, 113, 120, 129, 136, 142, 144, 145, 150, 158, 159, 163
Pesch, Heinrich 39, 41, 139, 175, 192, 256, 279, 390, 498
Petrine primacy, 128, 131, 132, 146, 149, 151, 154, 161, 179, 180, 336
Phenomenology, 355, 394, 421, 428, 458
Pistoia, 281, 308, 309, 320, 336, 362, 488
Pius IX, Bl. 325, 328, 332, 333, 339, 341, 342, 344, 345, 347, 351, 353, 361, 433, 466, 490
Pius VI, 304, 307, 308, 309, 320, 321, 362
Pius VII, 309, 320, 321, 322, 323
Pius X, St. 13, 361, 362, 363, 364, 365, 366, 367, 368, 406, 420, 444, 445, 457, 469, 479
Pius XI, 76, 83, 84, 160, 306, 374, 383, 385, 386, 388, 389, 390, 395, 429, 481
Pius XII, 90, 361, 375, 387, 388, 396, 397, 399, 400, 405, 406, 407, 409, 410, 413, 417, 422, 424, 447, 454, 456, 470, 471
Plato, 31, 37, 41, 42, 44, 82, 126, 247
Poland, 211, 259, 260, 333, 342, 396, 397, 399, 400, 450, 452
polyphony, 191, 226, 258, 362
pontifex maximus, 29, 125, 133, 143, 145, 146, 148, 149, 151, 152, 157, 160, 161, 164, 165, 169, 172, 173, 174, 176, 177, 178, 180, 186, 192, 194, 203, 214, 217, 229, 258, 335
Pornocracy, 12, 178, 179, 180, 204, 205, 206, 221, 235, 248, 449, 451, 471, 485

pornography, 44, 145, 303, 402, 412, 424, 448, 449, 454, 455, 462, 466, 469
private order, 85, 86, 87, 114, 120, 140, 156, 157, 240, 276, 315, 485
providential capitalism, 279, 286, 313, 383, 449, 461, 462, 463, 470
public order, 87, 112, 114, 115, 116, 117, 119, 120, 140, 156, 157, 165, 169, 181, 188, 241, 252, 269, 271, 272, 273, 276, 285, 293, 294, 295, 299, 315, 350, 354, 413, 481, 485

Q

Quebec, 289, 290, 291, 295, 296, 299, 316, 319, 403, 410
Qur'an, 163, 165, 167, 232, 233, 234

R

Rampolla, Mariano 360, 361
Ratisbonne, Marie-Alphonse 327, 355, 372
Ratzinger, Joseph 343, 346, 396, 406, 418, 420, 421, 423, 425, 427, 433, 435, 436, 437, 439, 444, 445, 454, 457, 458, 459, 467, 468, 469, 472, 473, 479, 480, 498
Real Presence, 193, 209, 215, 216, 225, 226, 227, 267, 425, 440, 446, 473
Rockefeller, J. D. 424, 425
Roma, 35, 112, 125, 127, 129, 133, 141, 142, 144, 145, 153, 155, 157, 160, 161, 165, 168, 174, 176, 178, 181, 188, 192, 194, 202, 214, 228, 229, 258, 269, 353, 370, 374, 375, 400, 410, 460, 485
Rothbard, Murray 298

Rousseau, Jean-Jacques 141, 151, 268, 270, 273, 281, 306, 335, 347, 499
Russia, 127, 140, 143, 165, 258, 259, 260, 261, 286, 304, 322, 334, 348, 353, 356, 365, 366, 368, 370, 371, 373, 374, 375, 381, 382, 388, 417, 418, 453, 456, 500

S

Sacred Heart, 225, 238, 261, 280, 308, 368, 477, 489
Sacrosanctum Concilium, 422, 433, 442, 443, 469
Sanger, Margaret 358, 381
Sangnier, Marc 355, 364, 365, 367
Santiago, 4, 12, 175, 182, 190, 199, 210, 315, 386, 393, 448, 462
Satan, 3, 35, 49, 50, 52, 53, 54, 56, 58, 61, 64, 67, 69, 70, 71, 72, 73, 74, 75, 80, 85, 87, 91, 92, 95, 98, 99, 100, 101, 114, 116, 117, 129, 132, 133, 137, 214, 243, 267, 270, 271, 272, 297, 326, 329, 371, 442, 448, 477
Saudi Arabia, 315, 393, 402, 455, 461, 464, 466
scientism, 246, 247, 248, 255, 257, 269, 275, 276, 278, 286, 313, 325, 334, 335, 340, 355, 366, 372, 381, 387, 388, 391, 393, 410, 412, 419, 424, 425, 428, 430, 446, 447, 480
Scotus, Bl. Duns 196, 209, 489
Seleucia-Ctesiphon, 144, 145, 158, 159, 231
Seneca, 41, 46
Sexual Revolution, 13, 381, 382, 385, 387, 388, 390, 400, 403, 406, 410, 412, 426, 429, 454
shaman, 118, 378
shamanic, 45, 378, 379, 411, 485
shamanism, 56, 127, 318, 326, 379, 407, 426, 482
Sheen, Fulton 408, 410

Sheptytsky, Andrey 371, 398
Shia, 231, 233, 455
Sicut Judaeis, 156, 184, 186, 198, 252, 293, 326, 349, 356
Sidney, Algernon 250, 251
slave, 1, 41, 42, 46, 54, 75, 83, 102, 109, 110, 117, 138, 139, 140, 163, 170, 172, 173, 175, 185, 201, 222, 234, 235, 236, 237, 271, 277, 281, 282, 290, 308, 313, 326, 339, 341, 372, 466, 478
Slavery, 59, 139, 140, 163, 170, 233, 235, 378, 463, 470, 487, 501
Smith, Adam 286, 312, 313
social media, 470, 478
Soloviev, Vladimir 127, 128, 140, 143, 146, 165, 178, 191, 258, 304, 322, 353, 356, 365, 500
Soviet, 375, 381, 382, 383, 388, 389, 393, 397, 398, 403, 410, 429, 443, 449, 450, 451, 452, 456, 460
Spain, 33, 131, 170, 171, 173, 175, 182, 194, 203, 208, 222, 228, 239, 242, 243, 244, 252, 281, 282, 285, 286, 315, 317, 318, 324, 357, 393, 403, 462, 466, 496
spirit of Vatican I, 346, 352, 353, 364, 419, 433, 444, 469
Stalin, Joseph 376, 388, 392, 396, 397, 399
Stanton, Elizabeth Cady 334
strict, 13, 15, 58, 94, 95, 111, 121, 126, 128, 131, 132, 145, 150, 172, 193, 208, 216, 223, 225, 226, 238, 270, 293, 294, 295, 303, 314, 320, 322, 332, 337, 338, 339, 342, 343, 344, 349, 350, 352, 362, 364, 367, 375, 384, 385, 387, 388, 390, 392, 400, 401, 405, 414, 417, 418, 419, 420, 421, 422, 424, 425, 428, 444, 445, 448, 453, 454, 458, 460, 469, 472, 473, 479, 480, 482, 483
Syriac, 55, 82, 110, 128, 130, 136, 142, 144, 145, 146, 150, 153, 155, 158, 159, 160, 161, 164, 166, 167, 169, 173, 174, 178, 185, 192, 196, 228, 231, 253, 336, 352, 370, 489, 500, 502

T

Talmud, 104, 105, 106, 131, 234, 499
Teilhardian, 404, 406, 416, 417, 418, 429, 446
Temple, 59, 60, 61, 62, 63, 64, 65, 66, 103, 104, 106, 108, 114, 131
Teresa Benedicta, St. 356, 394, 418, 428, 454, 458, 466, 479, 480
Thirty Years War, 259, 298
Thomas, St. 28, 31, 34, 59, 83, 93, 97, 107, 119, 138, 147, 152, 166, 169, 181, 186, 193, 198, 199, 203, 209, 213, 214, 223, 228, 233, 247, 284, 286, 287, 295, 296, 297, 298, 303, 304, 305, 311, 324, 330, 337, 345, 349, 352, 367, 370, 371, 391, 392, 394, 406, 421, 457, 474, 475, 487, 491, 493, 497, 498, 499, 500, 501, 502
Trotsky, Leon 366, 371, 382
Turk, 202, 230, 245, 259, 260, 262, 269
Two Swords, 115, 148, 149, 155, 157, 169, 171, 173, 180, 181, 186, 187, 213, 245, 353, 364, 481, 486
Tyrell, George 354, 366, 367, 392

U

Ugly Revolution, 253, 254, 290, 294
Ultramontanism, 336, 337, 345, 487
Urban VIII, 248, 251, 252, 364

usury, 40, 57, 65, 139, 157, 197, 198, 236, 262, 277, 286, 356, 360

V

Vatican, 13, 166, 202, 204, 205, 235, 248, 281, 308, 315, 338, 342, 343, 344, 345, 346, 347, 349, 352, 353, 361, 363, 364, 366, 367, 371, 383, 386, 394, 404, 405, 408, 418, 419, 420, 421, 423, 426, 427, 430, 433, 434, 436, 437, 441, 444, 446, 449, 452, 454, 456, 458, 459, 461, 465, 467, 469, 471, 472, 479, 480, 485, 488, 490, 496, 497, 498

Vatican II, 281, 308, 352, 361, 367, 404, 419, 420, 421, 426, 427, 430, 433, 436, 437, 441, 446, 454, 459, 461, 465, 479, 480, 488, 496, 497, 498

Vendée, 303, 498, 500

Versailles, 375, 387

Veuillot, Louis 326, 335, 338, 369, 498

Vianney, St. John 331, 487

Virgil, 30, 31, 32, 49, 150, 501, 502

volk (music), 191, 378

Voltaire, 281

Von Hildebrand, Dietrich 2, 34, 50, 132, 191, 224, 226, 269, 270, 356, 365, 368, 369, 378, 387, 388, 393, 394, 395, 396, 398, 402, 414, 415, 416, 422, 425, 427, 428, 429, 433, 434, 439, 440, 443, 444, 446, 447, 454, 479, 481

W

Wahhab, 315, 326, 341

Washington, George 47, 193, 275, 284, 286, 288, 289, 290, 297, 299, 300, 302, 304, 315, 324, 337, 354, 356, 370, 383, 394, 489, 490, 500

Webster, Noah 270, 273, 306, 335

Whig history, 262, 263, 268, 278, 286, 291, 337, 391

Wojtyła, Karol 79, 356, 397, 400, 416, 417, 421, 423, 447, 450, 451, 479, 502

Wollstonecraft, Mary 306

women, 4, 38, 42, 43, 45, 46, 57, 58, 69, 77, 88, 97, 135, 137, 140, 162, 172, 174, 181, 195, 197, 202, 204, 220, 250, 251, 297, 303, 306, 309, 310, 311, 318, 320, 326, 333, 334, 341, 350, 351, 377, 380, 381, 389, 390, 397, 399, 402, 448, 454, 465, 477, 480

Woods, Thomas 296, 311, 312, 313, 463, 480, 502

Z

Zoroastrianism, 47

Made in the USA
Las Vegas, NV
03 December 2021

35984721R00282